SCOTTSBORO

A Tragedy of the American South

SCOTTSBORO

A Tragedy of the American South

DAN T. CARTER

REVISED EDITION

LOUISIANA STATE UNIVERSITY PRESS
Baton Rouge and London

The excerpt from A COMMUNICATION TO NANCY CUNARD (copyright 1937
by Kay Boyle) is reproduced by permission of Miss Boyle.

07 06 05 04 03 02 01 00 99   14 13 12 11

LIBRARY OF CONGRESS CATALOGING IN PUBLICATION DATA

Carter, Dan T
  Scottsboro: a tragedy of the American South.

  Includes index.
  1. Scottsboro case. 2. Trials (Rape)—Alabama—Scottsboro. I. Title.
KF224.S34C3 1979   345'.73'0253   79-1090
ISBN 0-8071-0568-6
ISBN 0-8071-0498-1 pbk.

The paper in this book meets the guidelines for permanence and durability of
the Committee on Production Guidelines for Book Longevity of the Council
on Library Resources. ∞

To Jane

*Hear how it goes, the wheels of it traveling fast on the
    rails*
*The box-cars, the gondolas running drunk through the
    night.*
*Hear the long high wail as it flashes through stations unlit
    Past signals ungiven, running wild through a country*
*A time when sleepers rouse in their beds and listen
    And cannot sleep again.*
Hear it passing in no direction, to no destination
*Carrying people caught in the box-cars, trapped on the
    coupled chert-cars*
*(Hear the rattle of gravel as it rides whistling through the
    day and night.)*
*Not the old or the young on it, nor people with any differ-
    ence in their color or shape,*
*Not girls or men, Negroes or white, but people with this in
    common:*
*People that no one had use for, had nothing to give to, no
    place to offer*
*But the cars of a freight-train careening through Paint
    Rock, through Memphis,*
    Through town after town without halting.

—Kay Boyle, from A COMMUNICATION TO NANCY CUNARD

CONTENTS

skim

skim

ILLUSTRATIONS

PREFACE

ROM the beginning, the Scottsboro Case seemed destined to become a *cause célèbre* of the 1930's. For most white Southerners it raised the specter of Communist subversion and racial insubordination; for Negroes it was a mirror which reflected the three hundred years of mistreatment they had suffered at the hands of white America; Communists and other radicals saw Scottsboro as the inevitable offspring of an economic system based upon racism and class exploitation; and for American liberals it became a tragic symbol of the sickness which pervaded the South's regional culture. *Scottsboro* is a narrative account which describes the case and deals with the major issues raised: radicalism, racism, and the operation of the Southern court system. Hopefully it also tells something of what it meant to the nine Negro youths whose lives were changed forever by one morning's ride on an Alabama freight train.

It was my adviser, George Brown Tindall, who first suggested this topic, and to him I am especially indebted. His suggestions, his encouragement, and his wry wit eased the task of research and writing. Others who read the manuscript and offered their suggestions were James W. Patton, John Semonche, Harold Bierck, and Charles Morgan. The History Department of the University of North Carolina financially supported this project by granting me a Waddell Fellowship during my last year of graduate study.

At every stage I received the complete cooperation of librarians from Alabama to Massachusetts. Specifically, I would like to xii Scottsboro

acknowledge the assistance of Milo Howard of the Alabama Department of Archives and History, Howard Gottlieb of the Boston University Library, David C. Mearns of the Library of Congress Manuscript Division, Miles M. Jackson, Jr., and Annette H. Phinazee of the Trevor Arnett Library of Atlanta University, Nancy Jessen of the Schomburg Collection in New York, Adele Cohn of the Birmingham Public Library, William E. Lind of the National Archives, Harry Bitner of the Cornell University Law Library, Elizabeth Drewry of the Franklin Delano Roosevelt Library, Richard Neal of the Alabama Supreme Court, Beulah Bullard of the United States Supreme Court Library, and the staff of the Southern Historical Collection at Chapel Hill.

I have also benefited from conversations and correspondence with several persons directly involved in the case. Judge Samuel Leibowitz directed me to important documentary trial material; William L. Patterson, former head of the International Labor Defense, referred me to that organization's papers, and the Reverend Allan Knight Chalmers assisted and encouraged me throughout my research. Former Judge James E. Horton, Jr., not only submitted to a lengthy interview, but he also carefully read pertinent sections of my manuscript for accuracy. It would have been easy for him to dismiss the case as a painful memory. The fact that he did not is another example of the courage which marked his career in the 1930's.

At every stage of the preparation of this book, I have had the help of my wife, Jane. She not only assisted in the research and gave me moral support through periods of discouragement, but also improved immeasurably the grammar, syntax, and style of the final draft. By rights her name should appear as coauthor, and I owe a debt to her I can never repay.

College Park, Maryland, 1968   D.T.C.

SCOTTSBORO
A Tragedy of the American South

I

INTERRUPTED
JOURNEYS

THE Chattanooga to Memphis freight was a half hour late. Conductor Robert Turner hurried up and down the tracks checking his gold pocket watch, but no amount of complaining could make the yard men hurry. It was 10:20 A.M., almost an hour behind schedule, before the engine turned westward out of Chattanooga's Southern Railroad yards. Turner ignored a score of hoboes who scrambled on board as the train picked up speed. According to regulations every railroad employee had to report trespassing on the trains, but few observed the directive. It was March 25, 1931, and across a stricken nation 200,000 boys, girls, men, and women made the rails their home.[1]

The slow-moving freight followed a winding route from Chattanooga to Memphis, dipping down into Alabama, westward through the upper part of the state, across the northeastern tip of Mississippi and back into Tennessee. With the temperature in the upper fifties, a brisk wind blew across the freight cars, but the sides of the half-empty gondolas gave shelter and the midday sun

---

[1] "State of Alabama, Plaintiff, vs. Haywood Patterson, Defendant, Morgan Circuit Court, April 3–9, 1933. Transcript of Testimony" (typewritten), p. 152, Cornell Law Library, Ithaca, N.Y., hereinafter cited as "Alabama vs. Patterson"; U.S. Congress, Senate, Subcommittee of the Committee on Manufacturers, Hearings, Relief for Unemployed Transients, 72nd Cong., 2nd Sess., pp. 35–38.

warmed the floors of the dusty cars.[2] Just across the Alabama line in Jackson County, the train crossed and then ran parallel to the Tennessee River through the heart of the Tennessee Valley.[3] Those who lived there proudly boasted it was the most beautiful valley of America. Although the evergreens—pines and cedars —gave the hillsides most of their foliage, the winter had been mild and green buds were scattered over the bare branches of the oak, hickory, poplar, and sweet gum trees. Across the mountainside were the soft colors of mountain laurel, rhododendron, and crab apple trees. In the valley, the timber had been cut away a generation before, but a blanket of grass covered the reddish brown soil.[4]

Still running almost an hour behind schedule, the Memphis-bound freight pulled into Stevenson and hurriedly added one box car before continuing southwestward. Within twenty minutes the train was on its way to Paint Rock, forty-two miles away. During the brief pause, a number of riders left their exposed positions and moved to niches protected from the wind. Thirty minutes after the train left Stevenson, a startled station master looked up from his desk to see a ragged crew of hoboes, one holding his bleeding head. Through short, gasping breaths, one of the boys explained that there had been a fight and a "bunch of Negroes" threw him and his companions from the train. The Negroes had started the fight, he said, and he wanted to "press charges against 'em." A hurried telephone call to Scottsboro, the next town down the line, revealed that the train had passed through minutes before. The next stop was Paint Rock.[5]

Deputy Sheriff Charlie Latham lived in Trenton, a small rural

[2] Birmingham *Age-Herald*, March 26, 1931. Gondolas were cars with sides extending upward about five feet from the floor. In this train, they were half-filled with ballast, a coarse gravel called "chert."

[3] Called Brown's Valley in this area.

[4] Thomas McAdory Owen, *History of Alabama and Dictionary of Alabama Biography* (Chicago: S. J. Clarke Publishing Company, 1921), II, 798–99; Alabama Department of Agriculture and Industries, *Alabama* (Montgomery: Brown Printing Company, 1907), 138.

[5] Scottsboro *Jackson County Sentinel*, March 26, 1931; Huntsville (Ala.) *Daily Times*, March 26, 1931.

community five miles north of Paint Rock, but on the day of the twenty-sixth he had gone into town to meet several friends. Shortly after 1:30 P.M. Jackson County Sheriff M. L. Wann telephoned Latham at the town's general store and ordered him to "capture every negro on the train and bring them to Scottsboro." He added, "I'm giving you authority to deputize every man you can find." Within twenty minutes Latham had informally deputized every man in Paint Rock who owned a gun and lined the men up beside the railroad tracks running past the depot. They stood in the warm sun handling their shotguns, rifles, and pistols nervously, talking in excited tones while Latham walked up and down the tracks urging them to remain calm and not to shoot unless it was absolutely necessary. They did not wait long. Just before two o'clock the slow freight came around the curve a half mile east of the station and pulled to a stop at the water tower. Members of the posse scrambled on board before the train had stopped moving. There were forty-two cars on the freight: gondolas, boxcars, and a few flat cars and oil tankers. It took the men less than ten minutes to make a complete search. They found nine Negro boys, one white youth, and—to everyone's surprise—two young white girls wearing men's caps and dressed in overalls. When one of the posse members first saw the girls, the older girl leaned heavily on the arm of her friend and seemed on the verge of fainting. Latham named two men to take the women over to Scottsboro in case they should need medical attention, but he was too busy rounding up the Negroes to be concerned about the girls.[6]

The nine Negro youths who stood before him were a ragged lot. Although the day had warmed up to sixty degrees, they were dressed for the cool mountain nights. At twenty, Charlie Weems was the only one who was not in his teens. To Latham, Weems looked "mean" with his soot-black complexion, shaded eyelids, and long, narrow face. Ozie Powell and Clarence Norris were ro-

---

[6] Scottsboro *Jackson County Sentinel,* March 26, 1931; Huntsville (Ala.) *Daily Times,* March 26, 1931; Scottsboro *Progressive Age,* March 26, 1931; J. Glenn Jordan, *The Unpublished Inside Story of the Infamous Scottsboro Case* (Huntsville, Alabama: White Printing Co., 1932) , 1, 3.

bust boys in their late teens, both somewhat slender, but muscular and healthy with white teeth set off against dark skins. Olen Montgomery was blind in his left eye and saw only poorly with his right one. His drooping eyelids gave him a "sleepy-eyed" appearance as he stood quietly beside the station platform. Willie Roberson had contracted syphilis and gonorrhea the year before and without medical attention his health had deteriorated. He walked with a cane. Weems, Powell, Norris, Montgomery, and Roberson were all from Georgia, but they said they did not know each other.[7]

The remaining four told Latham they were from Chattanooga and on their way to Memphis looking for work. Haywood Patterson, nineteen, spokesman for the four, reacted sullenly to Latham's question. Eugene Williams was only thirteen and looked it. Short and slender, with a chocolate brown complexion, he was the most handsome of the nine. Andrew and Leroy Wright were brothers, and they tried to stay close together. Andy was nineteen and he reassured his thirteen-year-old brother, but Roy (as he was called) was frightened and could not hide it.[8] While Latham tied the nine together with a length of plow line, the two girls sat under a sweet gum and talked with several women who had gathered at the station. About twenty minutes after the train stopped, the younger girl, identifying herself as Ruby Bates of Huntsville, asked to see the deputy. When Latham finished loading the Negro youths onto the back of an open truck he went over to where the women stood. Ruby told Latham that she and her girl friend, Victoria Price, had been raped by the nine boys. "It would have taken just a little leading for a wholesale lynching," reported a salesman traveling through the little community, but officials counseled calm and the crowd dispersed. Both Ruby Bates and her companion were in "such a nervous condition" they volunteered little information concerning the assault.[9]

[7] Arrest Report, in Drawer 108, Alabama Executive Files, Alabama Department of Archives and History, Montgomery.

[8] Ibid.; Haywood Patterson and Earl Conrad, Scottsboro Boy (Garden City: Doubleday and Company, 1950), 5–6.

[9] There was later to be a great deal of dispute over whether Victoria Price or Ruby Bates made the charge of assault. State witnesses in 1933 insisted that Ruby

When the Negro boys and the two girls arrived in Scottsboro, the Jackson County seat, an hour later, Sheriff M. L. Wann sent the two women downtown for an examination by two local physicians; but he made no effort to keep the charge confidential, and news of the alleged attacks spread throughout and beyond Scottsboro within the hour. Each person retelling the story added new embellishments. By late afternoon, townspeople solemnly asserted that the "black brutes" had "chewed off one of the breasts" of Ruby Bates.[10]

In Jackson County—as over all the South—a substantial number of persons agreed with the character in the Irvin Cobb story who thought a Negro rapist hanged and burned by a mob "got off awful light." [11] Farmers from the nearby hills began gathering, and by dusk a crowd of several hundred stood in front of the two-story jail. Sheriff Wann pleaded with the men to leave and "let the law take its due course," but the crowd had become a mob and was in no mood to listen to pleas for law and order.[12] The sheriff tried to strengthen the crumbling jail by hastily deputizing twelve citizens and, with his nine regular deputies, barricading the door of the jailhouse from the inside. He warned the crowd that his men would shoot to kill if necessary, but his threats made little impression. The men stood outside in their baggy, faded overalls, the uniform of the poor-white farmer, chewing tobacco and staring up at the jail's checkerboard windows. Many had brought wives who waited toward the back of the crowd with babies on

Bates first indicated they had been attacked. See *"Alabama* vs. *Patterson,* April 3–9, Transcript of Testimony," p. 202. Most of the newspaper accounts fail to throw any light on the question, but the Huntsville (Ala.) *Daily Times* interviewed a traveling salesman who was in Paint Rock that day and his account indicates that it was Miss Bates who first told of the alleged attack. Huntsville (Ala.) *Daily Times,* March 26, 1931. Apparently the boys did not learn that they had been charged with rape until they arrived at Scottsboro. Scottsboro *Progressive Age,* March 26, 1931; Birmingham *News,* June 8, 1931; Haywood Patterson to Jane Patterson, April 7, 1931, in International Labor Defense Papers, Schomburg Collection, New York Public Library, 135th Street Branch.

[10] Hollace Ransdell, "Report on the Scottsboro, Alabama Case" (American Civil Liberties Union of New York City, May 27, 1931), 13 (Mimeographed).

[11] Scottsboro *Progressive Age,* April 9, 1931.

[12] Chattanooga *Daily Times,* March 27, 1931; Birmingham *News,* June 8, 1931.

their hips and larger children clutching their dresses. When Glenn Jordan, the top reporter for the Huntsville *Daily Times*, arrived at the town square it seemed to him "the entire population of the little county seat, augmented by hundreds of visitors, surrounded the two-story dilapidated jail." It took him almost five minutes to work his way through the crowd and into the jailhouse. Inside, Sheriff Wann assured him the crowd was just "curious." [13]

After dark the crowd diminished in size, but it became more and more threatening. Members shouted up at the jail: "Give 'em to us." "Let those niggers out." And the ultimate threat, "If you don't we're coming in after them." Inside, the nine boys sat hot and sweating even though it was a cool March night and the jail had little heat. Eugene Williams and Olen Montgomery began to weep in their fear and, in spite of the tension, Haywood Patterson could not keep from laughing at the way that Olen twisted his face when he cried. Mayor James David Snodgrass climbed the steps of the jail and begged the crowd to go home. He asked them to "protect the good name of the city," and a few moved away, but most remained. Some spoke up and insisted they simply wanted to spare the county the expenses of trials for the nine.[14]

By 8:30 P.M. Sheriff Wann was convinced that the mob might rush the jail at any moment, and he decided to make a run to a sturdier lockup in nearby Etowah. Three deputies brought their cars to the back door of the jail and then manacled the boys together in groups of three. The nine feebly protested, certain that this was only preparatory to a lynching. "You could see the look in those deputies' faces," said Haywood, "already taking some kind of credit for turning us over." As the boys waited inside the door, one of the deputies started his car and pulled the headlamp switch. The narrow alley ahead remained black, for members of the crowd had cut the wires of all three cars. That was enough for the sheriff

[13] Jordan, *Unpublished Inside Story*, 5.

[14] Birmingham *News*, June 8, 1931; Huntsville (Ala.) *Daily Times*, March 26, 1931; Patterson and Conrad, *Scottsboro Boy*, 7; Files Crenshaw, Jr., and Kenneth A. Miller, *Scottsboro: The Firebrand of Communism* (Montgomery: Brown Publishing Co., 1936), 15.

of Jackson County. He hurried to his telephone and placed a long distance call to the governor in Montgomery.[15]

One acquaintance of Governor Benjamin Meeks Miller described him as a "rural man with a staid Presbyterian background, somewhat provincial in his outlook, and . . . very set in his ideas of his duty as Governor." [16] Miller's round, gold-rimmed glasses, his old-fashioned celluloid collar, and his thin, humorless lips gave him the appearance of a portly, Southern-style Calvin Coolidge. He had been elected governor of Alabama in 1930 on a platform attacking the "Klan domination" of the previous Bibb Graves administration. He argued that he was for a government which was neither pro-Klan nor anti-Klan, and he assailed the hooded order throughout the campaign on the grounds that Klansmen were wasteful and extravagant. With a slogan, "Save Millions with Miller," he promised the people of Alabama he would return financial integrity to the state. Since taking office early in the year he had spent most of his time slashing the budget in a fruitless attempt to keep the state operating in the black.[17]

On the evening of March 25, Miller had retired as usual at 8:30, and Sheriff Wann's call awakened him. The governor did not hesitate when Wann explained the situation; he had taken a firm stand against lynching throughout his political career. He requested the state's adjutant general to call Major Joseph Starnes of Guntersville, site of the National Guard Armory nearest Scottsboro. By 11 P.M. Starnes was leading a caravan of cars with twenty-five armed men over the twenty-mile road.[18]

[15] Birmingham *News*, June 8, 1931; Patterson and Conrad, *Scottsboro Boy*, 8.

[16] Will W. Alexander to George Fort Milton, January 26, 1932, in Commission on Interracial Cooperation Papers, Trevor Arnett Library, Atlanta University, Atlanta, Ga.

[17] Budget cutting came naturally to the white-haired former judge. When bulbs in the governor's mansion burned out, rather than replace them out of his salary (there was no maintenance budget), he began using a kerosene lamp. Marie Bankhead Owen, *The Story of Alabama: A History of the State* (New York: Lewis Historical Publishing Company, 1949), I, 306–307.

[18] Birmingham *News*, June 8, 1931. Dr. Henry M. Edmonds, chairman of the Alabama Commission on Interracial Cooperation, also called Miller when he heard of the threats of mob violence, but troops were already on the way. James D. Burton, Report Number 1 on the Scottsboro, Alabama Case, April 14, 1931, in Interracial Commission Papers.

Even as Starnes mobilized his men, the mob subsided. In part this was because of the threats of the sheriff; in part, because of the fact that neither of the girls was from Jackson County. As a Birmingham *News* reporter melodramatically put it: "The homes of Jackson County people were not being desecrated. There were no relatives of the girls to feel surging within them the demand for blood vengeance. The question was one of race unheated by personal relationships." What was perhaps more important, not one person volunteered to lead a charge on the jail, and as the night wore on, a cold wind began to blow in from the mountains. The men stomped around the jail, their breath making white puffs in the brisk night air. After 10:30 they began to drift away and when Major Starnes and his men arrived at midnight, there were only twenty or thirty men sitting quietly in their automobiles out in front of the county jail. Just before dawn the nine boys finally dropped off to restless sleep. It was a night they would never forget.[19]

[19] Birmingham *News*, June 8, 1931.

II

IN AN ALABAMA
COURTROOM

I N the spring of 1931 a visitor described Scottsboro as a "charming Southern village . . . situated in the midst of pleasant, rolling hills." The neat, well-tended farms of the Tennessee Valley lay around the town; the red clay of their freshly turned soil contrasted sharply with the dark green foliage of the hills. The legislature had selected the town as the seat of Jackson County in 1859, but it grew little until it became a stop on the Memphis and Charleston Railroad in 1870. By 1931 there were 3,500 people living within the town limits. Mayor James Snodgrass had served almost continuously since he was first elected in 1884, and under his leadership the town built a central water works system and sewage plant (for the white section), paved five miles of asphalt streets, and purchased a fire truck and the latest firefighting equipment. When the Depression came in 1929, Snodgrass cut the municipal budget and held fast to his campaign slogan: "Economy in business and in the affairs of the town." Despite unsettled economic conditions, the town operated in the black.[1]

Within Scottsboro itself, large oaks and Southern sweet gums shaded wide streets. The one-family houses that made up the residential areas usually had spacious front lawns and backyards, no

[1] Ransdell, "Report on the Scottsboro Case," 18; Chattanooga *Daily Times*, May 17, 1931; Owens, *History of Alabama*, II, 1229. The Memphis and Charleston later became a part of the Southern Railroad.

matter how modest the structures. Even the Negro section seemed, if not prosperous, at least warm and pleasant. On the streets there was the easy, first-name cordiality of all small, Deep South towns. The courthouse and surrounding square served as the social and political center of the community and as the March days grew warmer, the townspeople and local farmers stood in the shade of giant water oaks that framed the classical-revival structure or sat in the gazebo on the courthouse lawn.[2]

In 1931 gossip and the weather still formed the mainstay of conversation, but somehow the talk always drifted around to the Depression. Scottsboro was a merchandising center for the surrounding farms. There were two hosiery mills in the town, but they employed less than 850 persons. Jackson County was overwhelmingly composed of farmers. Out of a population of 37,000, only 1,600 persons worked in nonagricultural pursuits. The agriculture of the region had been hit hard by the 1929 crash. In the winter of 1930 Jackson County farmers purchased 108 freight cars of commercial fertilizer. During the same period in 1931 they used 52 cars of fertilizer, a certain sign of hard times in any farm community. In addition to the problems caused by the nationwide depression, the lower Tennessee Valley suffered two consecutive years of drought in 1930 and 1931. In the face of falling cotton prices and low production, local farmers cut their cotton acreage both years and shifted to subsistence crops. As a result, they had less cash to spend in Scottsboro.[3]

In the days that followed the arrest of the nine boys, however, only one subject occupied the conversation of Jackson County citizens—the "nigger rape case." There was much to talk about, for the county's two weekly newspapers had been filled with ac-

---

[2] Ransdell, "Report on the Scottsboro Case," 18.

[3] Chattanooga *Daily Times*, May 11, 1931. Fertilizer production declined throughout the state, but at a much slower rate. See *Alabama Economic Review*, I (July, 1931), 18. Editors of the *Review* had earlier noted a strong correlation between fertilizer consumption and cotton receipts during the preceding year. Cotton receipts and over-all income had declined steadily after 1927. *Alabama Economic Review*, I (December, 1930), 10. The reduction in cotton acreage went on throughout Alabama, though at a slower rate. *Alabama Economic Review*, I (December, 1930), 7.

counts of the alleged assault. The incident could not have occurred at a more advantageous time for the *Jackson County Sentinel* and the Scottsboro *Progressive Age*. The two papers had gone
to press on the evening of the arrest and though neither included
an account of the attempted lynching, both gave full coverage to
the events on the freight car. The *Progressive Age* noted modestly
that the "details of the crime coming from the lips of the two girls,
Victoria Price and Ruby Bates, are too revolting to be printed
and they are being treated by local physicians for injuries sustained when attacked and assaulted by these negroes." The *Jackson County Sentinel*, not so reticent, ran a banner headline: "All
Negroes Positively Identified by Girls and One White Boy Who
Was Held Prisoner with Pistol and Knives While Nine Black
Fiends Committed Revolting Crime." Editor P. W. Campbell told
his avid readers that "some of the negroes held the two white girls
[while] others of the fiends raped them, holding knives at their
throats and beating them when they struggled." The two were
"found in the [freight] car in a terrible condition mentally and
physically after their unspeakable experience at the hands of the
black brutes." [4]

Outside the state, the New York *Times* story credited National
Guardsmen with averting a mass lynching, and the Chattanooga
Daily Times and the Huntsville *Daily Times* sent special corre-
spondents to Scottsboro to get the full story. Under the glow of
such attention, the hitherto reticent Victoria Price began to ex-
pound at length on her plight. Victoria, slender and "pert"—a
handsome woman who spoke vigorously in the accents of up-
country mill workers—told newsmen how she had "grown up
hard" in Huntsville cotton mill villages. She recalled that she had
quit school at ten and gone to work in the mills and since 1927
had been the only support of her widowed mother. The work was
regular and the pay adequate until the Depression, but after 1929
cutbacks grew longer and salaries lower. She desperately looked for
work, but she emphasized to reporters that she did not think of

[4] Scottsboro *Progressive Age*, March 26, 1931; Scottsboro *Jackson County Sentinel*,
March 26, 1931.

"doing like a lot of other girls do." [5] Instead, she said, she had joined her friend Ruby and together they had gone to Chattanooga to look for honest work in some of the cotton plants there. All the time Victoria talked, the retiring Ruby sat quietly, "merely nodding her head once in a while."

Victoria told how she and Ruby found a job at the Standard-Coosa-Thatcher Mill in Chattanooga and then decided to hitch a ride back to Huntsville in order to collect their belongings. "We rode on the tank car until we got to Stevenson [Alabama]." The wind was "howling around us and it was awfully cold." At Stevenson they had climbed into a gondola half-filled with chert. Seven white boys were already in the car, she said, and by a remarkable coincidence, one of them was Victoria's half brother whom she had not seen for a number of years. Odell Gladwell had been on the road for some time and Victoria had much to tell him. As the train started out from Stevenson, they began singing. Then it happened: "A whole bunch of Negroes suddenly jumped into the gondola, two of them shooting pistols and the others showing knives." Within minutes, said Victoria, the gang had thrown all the white boys but one from the moving train. "I started to jump, but a negro grabbed my leg and threw me down into the car. Another punched me in the mouth." With a knife at her throat, she desperately looked to Ruby for help, but "a negro had a knife at her throat, too, and another was holding her down." She lowered her eyes modestly. "I guess you heard the rest. Mister, I never had a 'break' in my life." The Negroes had ruined her and Ruby forever. "The only thing I ask is that they give them all the law allows." Victoria's story so touched a group of Scottsboro citizens that the next day they brought her and Ruby new clothing to replace the overalls and threadbare dresses they had been wearing. [6]

Orville Gilley, the only witness besides the girls, gave newsmen

---

[5] New York *Times*, March 26, 1931, p. 21; Chattanooga *Daily Times*, March 27, 1931. Apparently Victoria was referring to the occasional custom in the mill villages of practicing prostitution to supplement the meager salaries paid by the mills. See Ransdell, "Report on the Scottsboro Case," 14.

[6] Huntsville *Daily Times*, March 26, 1931; Chattanooga *Daily Times*, March 27, March 29, 1931.

further details of the "outrage." Gilley had led a colorful life, having once been "buried for dead" by his mother, when she identified the body of a slain bank robber as that of her son. The nineteen-year-old hobo fancied himself something of a poet and made his living by reciting his works outside public buildings in the cities through which he passed. He had never willingly worked a day in his life and he was proud of it. Although he "built a few stretches of road" for the state, he would not have a job in a pie factory, he said. "I get by all right, don't I? I may postpone a few meals sometimes and I ain't dressed up for church at all hours, but I got no strings on me." When newsmen first talked with Gilley he seemed shy, but gradually he warmed to the subject. One of the Negroes had held a pistol on him, he said, while another kept a knife against his ribs. "I counted the Negroes and there were nine of them." He said that he would "know every one of them, if I saw them at midnight in a mine—that's how close I looked them over." [7]

John Ferguson had left the train when the fight started and did not claim to have witnessed the later attack, but he vividly described the fight. The Negroes had come over the top of a boxcar from a flat car, he said, while all of the white passengers sat in a gondola. "Weems waved a pistol and shouted: 'You white——— clear out of here, get over the sides, all of you all.' " All had jumped except Gilley, said Ferguson. "When I jumped I couldn't see because the blood was gushing from my head into my eyes." As he went over the side, Ferguson said he heard Weems fire "five times." And he was absolutely certain that all nine had taken part in the fight. "I'd know every one of those 'coons' even if they stripped naked." [8]

Ruby Bates remained silent throughout the interviews. Although she was a good-looking girl and a fluent talker when encouraged, she seemed dominated by Victoria Price when the two were together. Occasionally Ruby leaned forward and, carefully

[7] Chattanooga *Daily Times*, March 27, 1931. His account differed from Victoria's. She insisted there were twelve men.
[8] Chattanooga *Daily Times*, March 27, 1931.

holding one finger over half her mouth, sent a stream of snuff into the spittoon. But afterward she simply wiped her mouth with her arm and leaned back in her chair, her soft brown eyes almost expressionless.[9]

The nine boys did not fare so well with the press. Some of the first reports declared that all but one had admitted the assault. In fact, what had happened was that Roy Wright—when accused by Orville Gilley in the presence of newsmen—began insisting that he and his three friends were innocent; the other five had assaulted the girls. All the boys other than Wright remained silent, except to deny any part in raping the girls. The impression which the news media gave, however, was that several of the group had admitted taking part in attacking the girls.[10]

All day Thursday tension continued to mount in the town as rumors inflamed public opinion to the boiling point. National Guardsmen kept the crowd of onlookers at least a block away from the jail, but there were murmured threats of what would happen when night came. Late in the afternoon Judge Alfred E. Hawkins met with the circuit solicitor, H. G. Bailey. After a conference Hawkins announced to waiting newsmen that he would reconvene the grand jury which had adjourned only a week before. The grand jury would meet again on Monday, he said, and its sole purpose would be to consider an indictment against the nine boys. Solicitor Bailey declared that he would demand the death penalty for all nine. He hoped that they could all be tried at the same time, he said, but if they demanded separate trials, "the request

[9] *Ibid.;* Ransdell, "Report on the Scottsboro Case," 14.

[10] Birmingham *Age-Herald,* March 26, 1931. The *Progressive Age* on March 26, 1931, said that "several of the negroes have admitted their guilt." The *Jackson County Sentinel* declared that "one of the younger negroes was taken out by himself and he confessed to the whole affair, but said 'the others did it.' He was taken back to point out the guilty ones and the negroes immediately began accusing each other of the crime." Scottsboro *Jackson County Sentinel,* March 26, 1931. The Chattanooga *Times* also said the four defendants from that city were known to local police as the "worst young Negroes in Chattanooga." Chattanooga *Daily Times,* March 26, March 27, 1931. Police records, however, showed that they had never been convicted of any criminal offense. The boys had been accused of stealing a small amount of money from a Negro librarian earlier in the year. James D. Burton to Arthur Raper, August 1, 1931, in Interracial Commission Papers.

would have to be granted." Although a few citizens expressed resentment over what they considered an unnecessary delay, particularly in view of the fact that it might be several days after the indictment before the trial started, the *Jackson County Sentinel* noted that it was "necessary to allow certain time to elapse for legal procedure . . . in a case of this grave nature." While it was true that many citizens had "hoped to get a speedier trial . . . we feel sure that Jackson County people will accept this verdict and be a part in keeping peace in this time when it is hard to be law-abiding." [11]

As the *Progressive Age* put it, "The general temper of the public seems to be that the negroes will be given a fair and lawful trial in the courts and that the ends of justice can be met best in this manner, although the case charged against the negroes appears to be the most revolting in the criminal records of our state, and certainly of our county." Citizens of the county were convinced, in the words of the *Sentinel,* that "the evidence against the negroes was so conclusive as to be almost perfect." They had also decided "that the ends of justice could best be served by a legal process." Within hours after Judge Hawkins' announcement, the tension had perceptibly diminished. Nevertheless, as an added precaution, National Guardsmen transferred the nine late in the afternoon to a stronger jail in nearby Etowah.[12]

Judge Hawkins told reporters he intended to see that the proceedings were more than a legal sham. He was well aware that in cases involving capital punishment, it was the obligation of the court to see that the accused were represented by counsel. Hawkins, therefore, assigned all seven members of the Scottsboro bar to represent the boys. But one by one the town's lawyers found excuses to withdraw from the case. Local citizens retained three of

[11] Birmingham *Age-Herald,* March 27, 1931; Chattanooga *Daily Times,* March 27, 1931; Scottsboro *Jackson County Sentinel,* April 2, 1931. The *Progressive Age's* editor, James Stockton Benson, was satisfied with the speed of the trial, and he praised the judge and solicitor for their conduct. "It is best for the county that these things be disposed of in a speedy manner as it gives no excuse for people taking the law into their own hands. . . ." Scottsboro *Progressive Age,* April 2, 1931.

[12] Scottsboro *Progressive Age,* March 26, April 2, 1931; Birmingham *Age-Herald,* March 27, 1931.

the seven, John Franklin Proctor, James Moody Proctor, and John Milton Snodgrass, to assist Solicitor Bailey. D. P. Wimberly requested and received permission to withdraw.[13] Finally only one man remained who seemed at all interested in taking the case, Milo C. Moody.

Milo Moody was only two months short of his seventieth birthday and he was, as someone put it charitably, getting a bit forgetful. One person who met him at the time described him as a "doddering, extremely unreliable, senile individual who is losing whatever ability he once had." [14] His early career had seemed promising enough. He attended the University of Alabama and though he did not obtain a degree, he studied law and was admitted to the bar at Scottsboro in 1889. In 1891 he married Mrs. Fannie Aldrich Snodgrass, whose late husband was from one of the best families in Scottsboro. In the 1890's he moved up the political ladder steadily, serving as constable in 1896–97, as tax commissioner in 1897, and as the Jackson County delegate to the Alabama General Assembly in 1898. His constituents also elected him as a delegate to the important constitutional convention in 1901. But this was to be the peak of his political career. Thereafter he confined himself to the kind of minor court cases which were the lot of most small-town Southern lawyers. He did have something of a reputation as a man who would defend unpopular ideas, but the main reason for his interest in the present case was that it carried a fee, no matter how small.[15]

[13] Snodgrass was the mayor's son. Owen, *Story of Alabama*, IV, 432. Wimberly later said facetiously that he had a conflict of interests. As attorney for the Alabama Power Company, he stood to gain if the boys were electrocuted. Edmund Wilson, "The Freight Car Case," *New Republic*, LXVIII (1931), 39. Chattanooga *Daily Times*, April 6, 1931.

[14] Memorandum of Walter White on Conversation with Hollace Ransdell, May 2, 1931, Legal Series, Scottsboro Case, File Box 1, National Association for the Advancement of Colored People Collection, Library of Congress, Washington, D.C.

[15] Owen, *History of Alabama*, IV, 1220; Wilson, "The Freight Car Case," 39. One of the prosecution's special assistants reported that Moody's brother had been killed by a Negro in the early 1920's. "I do not know whether this has any influence in Mr. Moody's thinking or not," he told James Burton. James D. Burton, Report Number 3 on the Scottsboro, Alabama Case, May 7, 1931, in Interracial Commission Papers.

Sixty miles away one of Chattanooga's leading Negro citizens read with increasing concern of the charges against the nine boys. Dr. P. A. Stephens, the city's outstanding Negro doctor, also served as president of the Laymen's Association of the East Tennessee Conference of the [Northern] Methodist Episcopal Church. When he read of the serious nature of the charges and learned that four of the boys were from Chattanooga, he called a meeting of the Interdenominational Colored Ministers' Alliance of the city. After the group learned that Mrs. Ada Wright, mother of two of the boys, attended one of the churches in the Alliance, they were convinced that they should take some action. By nightfall of the day after the arrest, they had raised $50.08.[16]

It was a small retainer with which to approach any attorney, but Dr. Stephens knew one lawyer who might be willing to take the case. Stephen R. Roddy, a Chattanooga attorney, spent most of his time checking real estate titles or doing minor police court work, but he had taken cases for local Negroes on a number of occasions. Roddy's modest legal abilities were further limited by his inability to remain sober. Local police officials tried to overlook his periodic bouts of drinking, but he had been jailed in June of 1930 on a charge of public drunkenness.[17] The chairman of the Chattanooga Commission on Interracial Cooperation told James D. Burton that Roddy seemed adequate enough when sober, but even though he had been in the hospital several times in an effort to stop his drinking, those who knew him doubted the success of the treatments.[18] Although Roddy was initially reluctant when Dr. Stephens called him, he agreed to take the case and see what could be done for a total fee of $120. On Monday morning, March 30, Roddy drove down to Scottsboro for the hearing by the Jackson County Grand Jury. Before he left, he promised Chattanooga

[16] Dr. P. A. Stephens to Walter White, April 2 1931, in Scottsboro Legal File 1, NAACP Papers; New York *Daily Worker*, May 19, 1931; Wilson, "The Freight Car Case," 40.

[17] Affidavit of Luther Carter, October 27, 1931, in ILD Papers. Carter had served as constable and deputy sheriff in Hamilton County for seventeen years.

[18] James D. Burton to Will Alexander, April 14, 1931, May 23, 1931, in Interracial Commission Papers.

Negroes that he would defy any move to "railroad" the nine to the electric chair. "It is my intention to see that the Negroes get a fair trial." [19]

A fair trial under the circumstances was impossible. The nine Negro boys had already been tried, found guilty, and sentenced to death by the news media. "How much farther apart than night and day are the nine men who perpetrated those frightful deeds and a normal kind-hearted man who guards his little family and toils through the day . . ." melodramatically declared the Chattanooga *News*. The *News* urged the Jackson County grand jury to return speedy indictments. "We still have savages abroad in the land, it seems. Let us have the solace of knowing that at least we have risen above the justice of savages." The girls' hometown newspaper, the Huntsville *Daily Times*, described the rape as "the most atrocious ever recorded in this part of the country, a wholesale debauching of society . . . so horrible in its details that all of the facts can never be printed." It "savored of the jungle" and the "meanest African corruption." The white men of the South, the newspaper said, "will not stand for such acts. . . ." The "nine brutes" had been protected by the law since their arrest, but as soon as they could be convicted, "this newspaper joins with the public and the duly constituted authorities in seeing that the law is carried out to the letter." Swift, legal justice was the only answer to such a "heinous and unspeakable crime." [20]

When Roddy arrived in Scottsboro shortly after 9 A.M. he found a courtroom tense with excitement and guarded by three National Guard officers and thirty enlisted men. Major Joe Starnes allowed spectators into the courtroom, but he made them check

---

[19] Memorandum of Stephen Roddy, April 11, 1931, in Scottsboro Legal File 1, NAACP Papers; Chattanooga *Daily Times*, March 31, 1931.

[20] Chattanooga *News*, March 27, 1931; Huntsville (Ala.) *Daily Times*, March 27, 1931. In a news story on March 26, J. Glenn Jordan, the *Daily Times* staff writer, referred to the nine boys as "beasts unfit to be called human." *News* editor George Fort Milton later defended his newspaper's editorial response. "Until the details were contradicted, the circumstances were such as to arouse editorial indignation and I feel that my editorial writer was well within the rights of the situation in writing as he did." George Fort Milton to Bruce Bliven, August 25, 1931, in Interracial Commission Papers.

their weapons outside. There was not much to see, for after the nine pleaded not guilty, the grand jury voted to go into closed door hearings. The only testimony was from Victoria Price and Orville Gilley, and within an hour the jury returned to the courtroom. There was a twenty-four-hour delay caused by a mix-up over legal identification, but from the outset the grand jury was intent on prosecution. Roddy returned to Chattanooga without participating in the proceedings. The next day, the grand jury returned formal indictments and Judge Hawkins set trial for the following Monday, April 6.[21]

During the week officers of the National Guard met with the sheriff and town constable to discuss plans for handling traffic for the trial. They told newsmen that they expected the "largest crowd ever assembled at one place in the county. . . ." The fact that the trial opened on the first Monday of the month guaranteed a big turnout. Around the turn of the century, farmers in the hills had begun to bring their families to town to attend the county court trials on the first Monday of the month. Gradually, the occasion became known as "Fair Day," an excuse to engage in selling produce, bartering goods, buying, or simply exchanging gossip. By 1931, people came from as far away as forty or fifty miles.[22] As the sun came over the hills around Scottsboro, the crowd began gathering. From all the neighboring counties and even from Tennessee, the visitors poured into the courthouse square in autos and wagons, on horseback and on foot. By 7 A.M. there were several thousand people clamoring for admission through the National Guard picket lines. On orders from Judge Hawkins, however, the guardsmen kept the crowd pushed back one hundred feet from the building. The throng became so packed that many moved to the roofs of surrounding buildings in order to get a better view. The early morning crowd seemed somber and even sullen as they

---

[21] Photographs had been taken of the defendants, but the sheriff failed to list the names of the nine under their pictures. Chattanooga *Daily Times*, March 31, 1931. Memorandum of Stephen Roddy, April 11, 1931, in Scottsboro Legal File 1, NAACP Papers; Chattanooga *Daily Times*, April 1, 1931.

[22] Chattanooga *Daily Times*, April 6, 1931; New York *Times*, July 26, 1964, X, 19.

stood quietly around the courthouse. Four machine guns guarded the doors of the building and gave the scene the appearance of a fort under siege. As the day wore on, however, the mood brightened. The crowd realized the impossibility of but a few gaining admission to the trials and it was soon in the "best of humor," reported the editor of the *Progressive Age*. Farmers began to wander through the streets finding old friends they had not seen for months, and the merchants of Scottsboro did a "land-office business." [23]

Stephen Roddy had the misfortune to arrive at the courthouse when the crowd was most unfriendly. The firm resolve which he had expressed in Chattanooga faded when several onlookers openly cursed him as he walked into the courtroom. One of the special assistants to the prosecution noted that Roddy had liberally fortified himself with strong spirits against such a contingency. He was so "stewed," said J. K. Thompson, "he could scarcely walk straight." The Chattanooga attorney nervously took a seat at the front of the courtroom and just before 9 A.M., Judge Hawkins called the courtroom to order for Alabama's most famous criminal trials of the decade.[24]

Hawkins told the defense counsel to step down to the front inside the railing. Roddy replied he was not there as employed counsel, but at the request of "people who are interested in them [the Scottsboro boys]." Judge Hawkins told Roddy: "If you appear for these defendants, then I will not appoint counsel; if local counsel are willing to appear and assist you under the curcumstances [*sic*], all right, but I will not appoint them." Scottsboro attorney Ernest Parks, originally appointed as defense counsel, agreed. If the nine boys had counsel, he said, "I don't see the necessity of the Court

[23] Estimates of the crowd ranged from a minimum of five thousand to more than ten thousand. Scottsboro *Progressive Age*, April 9, 1931; Chattanooga *Daily Times*, April 7, 1931; Birmingham *Age-Herald*, April 7, 1931; Birmingham *Post*, April 6, 1931.

[24] Wilson, "The Freight Car Case," 39; P. A. Stephens to Walter White, April 12, 1931, in Scottsboro Legal File 1, NAACP Papers; James D. Burton, Report Number 3 on the Scottsboro Case, May 7, 1931, in Interracial Commission Papers.

appointing anybody, if they haven't counsel of course, I think it is up to the Court to appoint counsel to represent them." [25]

Despite requests from the bench, Roddy would neither clarify his position nor say that he was counsel. "If I was paid down here and employed it would be a different thing," he said, "but I have not prepared this case for trial. . . ." Moreover, he pointed out that he was unfamiliar with Alabama law. Under the circumstances, he told the court, if he had to take the case alone, "the boys would be better off if I step entirely out of the case. . . ." The trial seemed hopelessly stalled until Milo Moody stepped inside the rail and told Judge Hawkins: "I am willing to go ahead and help Mr. Roddy in anything I can do about it under the circumstances." This was satisfactory to Judge Hawkins, who told the rest of the Jackson County bar that they no longer had to appear on behalf of the defendants.[26] Thus, with no preparation, with less than a half-hour interview with their lawyers, nine Negro youths went on trial for their lives.[27]

Roddy opened the defense with a half-hearted petition for a change of venue. He relied in his petition on the inflammatory news stories in the *Jackson County Sentinel* and the Scottsboro *Progressive Age,* and on the fact that Sheriff Wann had asked for National Guardsmen.[28] The state easily disposed of the news items by pointing out that Roddy had not introduced any witnesses to show that these stories affected public opinion. Roddy did call to the stand Sheriff M. L. Wann to support his contention that Jackson County citizens were so enraged they almost lynched the nine. A week before, the sheriff had told newsmen of the dire threat of mob violence and modestly described his own role in

---

[25] *Weems* v. *Alabama,* 287 U.S. 45, Tr. pp. 57–59.

[26] *Ibid.,* 60.

[27] Memorandum of Stephen Roddy, April 11, 1931, in Scottsboro Legal File 1, NAACP Papers.

[28] The *Jackson County Sentinel* dismissed the claim of prejudicial publicity as "without foundation at all." In fact, said editor P. W. Campbell, "we tried very hard to temper the story down to keep from inciting people. . . ." Scottsboro *Jackson County Sentinel,* April 2, 1931.

safeguarding the lives of the nine defendants.[29] Apparently he had changed his mind during the week. The prosecutor asked if he could recall "threats or anything in the way of the population taking charge of the trial?" Wann replied firmly, "None whatever." In response to other questions he agreed with the prosecutor that the defendants would receive a fair and impartial trial in Jackson County, and likewise that there was no more sentiment against the nine "than naturally arises" on the charge of rape.[30]

Major Starnes proved even less helpful than Sheriff Wann. He readily admitted that he had thought it necessary to have over one hundred enlisted men and officers on duty for the trial, and that at least thirty men had been with the defendants at every stage of the proceedings. But he told the court he had heard no threats against any of the defendants and he attributed the presence of the huge crowd to "curiosity," not hostility. It came as no surprise to anyone in the court when Judge Hawkins over-ruled the petition for a change of venue.[31]

Circuit Solicitor Bailey had expected the defense lawyers to request a severance for all nine of the defendants, but Roddy told the court he was willing to have all nine tried at the same time. Bailey, however, for reasons which later became clear, moved to try Clarence Norris, Charley Weems, and Roy Wright. Roddy objected to including Wright in this group because he was a juvenile; rather than argue the motion, Bailey decided to try Norris and Weems and to discuss the question of Wright's age later. The noon recess interrupted proceedings; but the selection of the jury went smoothly, and shortly after 2:30 in the afternoon Victoria Price took the stand for the prosecution. Eight of the jurors were farmers, three were merchants, and one was a mechanic.[32]

---

[29] See Chattanooga *Daily Times,* March 27, 1931; Birmingham *Age-Herald,*
[30] *Weems* v. *Alabama,* 287 U.S. 45, Tr. p. 64.

[31] Birmingham *Age-Herald,* April 7, 1931; *Weems* v. *Alabama,* 287 U.S. 45, Tr. p. 68. The calumnies of outsiders annoyed Starnes, who declared that the nation would be a "goodlier land than Canaan" if the "harping critics of the South would . . . eradicate their own evils of bribery, corruption, sabotage and gang warfare. . . ." Letter of Joseph Starnes in Scottsboro *Jackson County Sentinel,* April 23, 1931.

[32] Chattanooga *Daily Times,* March 27, April 7, 1931; *Weems* v. *Alabama,* 287 U.S. 45, Tr. p. 69.

Victoria, wearing a new dress for the trial and minus her usual
dip of snuff, neither blushed nor lowered her voice even when relating the most sordid parts of her story. She punctuated her colorful account of the attack with vigorous gestures. Victoria said that
on Tuesday, March 24, she left Huntsville, along with her friend
Ruby, searching for work in one of Chattanooga's cotton mills.
They arrived about 7:30 P.M. and went directly to see Mrs. Callie
Brochie, the proprietor of a boardinghouse five blocks from the
railroad yards. The next morning Mrs. Brochie accompanied them
as they visited "every one of the mills in Chattanooga" in a futile
effort to find a job. Discouraged by their failure, they decided to
return to Huntsville, and Mrs. Brochie saw them off on the Chattanooga to Memphis freight train.[33]

The first part of the ride went smoothly, said Victoria. She and
Ruby boarded a tank car, but they soon shivered in the cool spring
air as they sat crouched on the open ledge of the car. When the
train stopped in Stevenson, they climbed into a gondola. Seven
white boys were already in one end of the gondola and one of them
helped the two girls into the open car. They exchanged remarks—
although Victoria emphasized that "it wasn't in no loving conversation"—and then settled down on the rough, warm chert of
the open freight car. Less than five minutes out of Stevenson, Victoria looked up to see twelve Negroes leaping over the top of the
adjacent boxcar and into the gondola; two of them brandished
pistols and "every one" had his knife open. One of the twelve—
she was not sure which—shouted, "All you sons of bitches unload." Then he knocked one of the white boys in the head and
threw him over the side. One by one the rest of the white boys
jumped. Roy Thurman fought desperately, she said, but when one
of the attackers hit him on the head with a pistol and shouted,
"Get off, you son-of-a-bitch," he got off. By this time, the train had
picked up considerable speed and the Negroes decided not to eject
Gilley, who sat helplessly in one corner of the gondola.[34]

According to Mrs. Price, Clarence Norris came straight to the

[33] *Weems* v. *Alabama,* 287 U.S. 45, Tr. pp. 25–26.
[34] *Ibid.,* 28.

point: "Are you going to put out?" he shouted above the roar of the train. She explained that she knew the meaning of this term and told him politely: "No, sir, I am not." At this point, six of the defendants overpowered her. "It took two of them to take my clothes off and took three of them to ravish me . . ." she said. And even then, "they wouldn't have if they hadn't had knives and guns." She gave an explicit description to the jury and all-male spectators of how one of the nine had held her legs and another a knife to her throat while a third removed her overalls and tore off her "step-ins." One by one, she pointed out the six she said raped her: Charley Weems, Clarence Norris, Roy and Andy Wright, Haywood Patterson, and Olen Montgomery. Roddy suggested that she might be mistaken about Patterson, but she was adamant. "I know his old mug," she snapped. The attack was horrible and seemed to last for hours, she said. And to make matters worse, "They would not let me up between times, not even let me up to spit [snuff]." As one finished and the next stepped up, she "begged them to quit," she said; but their only response was to tell her that they would take her and Ruby north and "make us their women." She told the jury how she was "beaten up" and "bruised up" by the repeated rapes, but she never stopped fighting. Finally it was over and as the train pulled into Paint Rock, she got up, pulled on her clothes and fastened them. As she turned to step off the stirrup, she said she slipped and "lost consciousness." The next thing she knew she was on her way to Scottsboro and the county jail.[35] Throughout her testimony, the courtroom was completely quiet.

Roddy's strategy was to show that Victoria Price was a woman of less than exemplary character, but the court quickly indicated that it would not tolerate this line of questioning. Victoria admitted that she had been married twice and was separated from her second husband, and that she had always gone by her maiden name, even when she was married; but when Roddy asked her how long she had "known" her husband before she married him, Bailey ob-

[35] *Ibid.*, 27, 29–31.

jected and Judge Hawkins sustained the objection. Roddy asked if she had ever been in jail. Again the court sustained an objection by the prosecution. The defense attorney said he thought that was all and shortly after 3 P.M. Victoria stepped down from the witness chair. She had been on the stand less than fifty minutes.[36]

The state did not plan to rest its case on the testimony of Victoria Price alone. Solicitor Bailey called to the stand Dr. R. R. Bridges, one of the two doctors who examined the girls within an hour and thirty minutes after the alleged rape. Bridges was from one of the old families in Jackson County. His father, William P. Bridges, had been Probate Judge for six years and later organized and served as president of the Bank of Paint Rock. Bridges took his medical degree at Vanderbilt University in 1911 and returned to Scottsboro three years later. By the end of the First World War he had developed a large practice and his residence on East Laurel Street—built in the grand style of the 1890's—was the showplace of Scottsboro's small, upper-class residential area.[37]

Dr. Bridges testified tersely on the results of his examination. The most important thing he revealed at the outset: Victoria Price had participated in sexual intercourse at some time previous to his examination. Even more damaging was his remark that he found "a great amount" of semen in the vagina of Ruby Bates. But beyond this his testimony did not bear out Victoria's assertion that she had been violently manhandled. She had small bruises about the top of her hips and a few "short scratches" on the left arm, but he emphasized that these were minor. When he examined her genital organs he found neither bruises nor tears. "She was not lacerated at all. She was not bloody, neither was the other girl." He added that the semen found was "non-motile." And he told the jury that "Victoria Price was not hysterical at all at that time. . . ." She had chattered away somewhat nervously as he examined her. Nevertheless, he said in reply to Solicitor Bailey's direct question,

---

[36] Chattanooga *Daily Times,* April 7, 1931; *Weems* v. *Alabama,* 287 U.S. 45, Tr. pp. 24–25, 31–33.

[37] Albert Burton Moore, *History of Alabama and Her People* (Chicago and New York: The American Historical Society, Inc., 1927), II, 190–91.

it was "possible" that six men, one right after the other, could have had intercourse with her without lacerations.[38]

Roddy and Milo Moody made no effort to ask the doctor about the medical evidence. To support their earlier questioning, they tried to get Dr. Bridges to say that the girls admitted they customarily had intercourse indiscriminately. The court, however, sustained repeated objections from the solicitor on this point, although Roddy managed to get across to the jury the purpose of his questioning. Judge Hawkins likewise would not allow the defense attorneys to inquire as to whether either of the girls had gonorrhea or syphilis.[39]

Dr. Marvin Lynch was a younger man than Bridges. He had received his medical degree from the Medical College of South Carolina in 1928. Although he served as part-time county health officer, he had been in practice less than three years.[40] His testimony was more equivocal. He recalled that they had found a good amount of semen in the vagina of Ruby Bates, but they had had to use a cotton swab in order to obtain a sample from Victoria Price. "We only got enough semen out of the vagina to make a smear." The two girls were not hysterical and both had talked quite calmly to him. He did note the presence of several slight bruises and scratches, but he said under cross-examination that "one man could have brought about bruises on the back having intercourse." He emphasized that the "vagina was in good condition on both of the girls. There was nothing to indicate any violence about the vagina." [41]

By the time Dr. Lynch completed his testimony, dusk had begun to fall outside and Judge Hawkins announced that court was adjourned until the next morning at 8:30. Many of the thousands who had poured into the town early in the day had several hours of riding before they reached home and had begun leaving earlier

[38] *Weems* v. *Alabama,* 287 U.S. 45, Tr. pp. 30, 33–34.

[39] *Ibid.,* 34.

[40] American Medical Association, *1965 American Medical Directory, 23rd Edition,* Part II (New York: American Medical Association 1965), 1028.

[41] *Weems* v. *Alabama,* 287 U.S. 45, Tr. p. 38.

when it became apparent that the case would not go to the jury before the next day.[42]

Tuesday, like the first day of the trial, was clear and warm, but it was apparent by 8 A.M. that the crowd would number fewer than three thousand. Nevertheless, the guardsmen kept machine guns at each entrance and carefully searched all who entered the courtroom.[43] The state did not charge that either of the two defendants on trial had raped Ruby Bates, but they called her to the stand as the first witness of the day in order to dispel any doubts about the premeditated nature of the attack. Ruby was young and fresh, with a sunny complexion, a pretty face, and an attractive figure. Her eyes, dark brown and very large, were her most appealing feature. But she lacked her companion's verve and self-confidence. Where Victoria had snapped her answers back firmly and without hesitation, Ruby appeared hesitant and unsure. She often paused for long periods in her account of the events, and the solicitor had to prod to elicit the details Mrs. Price had spontaneously offered. Ruby repeated her companion's account of how they traveled to Chattanooga on March 24, stayed overnight with Mrs. Brochie, and went to one of Chattanooga's cotton mills the next day looking for work. Victoria had told the court that one of the seven white boys on the train had helped them board the gondola where the rape took place, and she also testified that they had talked with the boys for some time before the fight began. Ruby, however, insisted that "I did not talk with them, didn't say a word. . . . Nothing had been said between either me or my companion to the white boys." The seven, she said, "were in one end of the car and we were in the other, sitting perfectly quiet, no sort of conversation, just sat there looking at each other." [44]

Ruby's account of the fight also differed from that of her friend. Victoria gave a colorful description of a desperate struggle with guns blazing, a pistol-whipping, and ending with the white boys leaving in an effort to save their lives. According to Ruby, two

---

[42] Chattanooga *Daily Times,* April 8, 1931; Birmingham *News,* June 10, 1931.
[43] Chattanooga *Daily Times,* April 8, 1931; Birmingham *News,* April 8, 1931.
[44] *Weems* v. *Alabama,* 287 U.S. 45, Tr. pp. 27–28, 44.

Negroes stepped down into the gondola and began arguing with several of the white youths. When several other Negroes came into the car a few minutes later, they told the white boys to unload. Only three put up any struggle; the other four simply jumped. She tersely described the rape that followed. One had held a knife on her, another a gun, while the third attacked her. In his cross-examination, Roddy brought out that she had first said nothing to the posse which stopped the train except "I told those men there had been a fight between the colored boys and the white boys and they had thrown some off the car. . . ." He asked her if her concern was because of the fact that she was traveling with some of the boys. She denied it. "There was nobody along with Victoria Price and myself when we went to Chattanooga; just we two girls." [45] Roddy did not press her on the ways that her account differed from Victoria's.

The state introduced five other witnesses to buttress the charges against Weems and Norris. Tom Taylor Rousseau and James Broadway both helped remove the nine boys from the train at Paint Rock. Rousseau, a clerk in his father's general store, said he had seen one of the girls rise up in the gondola shortly after it stopped and then drop down again. He was so busy rounding up the defendants that he did not see the girls again until two men brought Victoria from the depot into town. James Broadway was passing through Paint Rock on his way to Huntsville when he saw a crowd gathering at the depot. He stopped and, at the request of Deputy Sheriff Latham, joined the posse. Although he was around when Victoria Price "came to," he told the court: "I did not hear Victoria Price make any complaint, either to me, or anybody else there, about the treatment she had received at the hands of these defendants over there." [46] Broadway did not testify for the state in later trials.

Luther Morris was a better witness for the state. On the day of the incident, he had been standing in the loft of his barn, on his farm about one and a half miles south of Stevenson. The barn was

[45] *Ibid.,* 46–48.
[46] *Ibid.,* 41.

about thirty yards from the tracks. Shortly after noon he looked up at the passing freight just in time to see several Negroes "put off five white men and take charge of two girls." Morris said he could plainly hear the noise of the fight as the train passed. He climbed down from the loft and went outside to see if the boys were injured. Two were "hurt bad," he said, but when he tried to help, they "ran off and left me," running toward Stevenson. Roddy suggested that Morris might be mistaken about what he saw, but the old man replied with fervor that he had watched it all from his loft, and "I think I saw a plenty." [47] T. L. Dobbins and Lee Allen, the other two witnesses for the state, testified only that they saw some kind of scuffle from the right-of-way and later saw the white boys walking up the side of the tracks back toward Stevenson.

The state rested. Solicitor Bailey and his assistants had constructed a solid case against the defendants, and now it was up to the defense to disprove the evidence introduced by the state's witnesses. The only witnesses the defense had to offer were the defendants themselves; the only evidence, their unsupported testimony. Roddy called Charley Weems to the stand. Weems was one of two surviving from a family of ten. His mother, father, four sisters, and two brothers had died by the time he was a teenager. One brother still lived somewhere in Georgia, but Weems had not seen him for years and the only relative with whom he maintained sporadic contact was an aunt in Riverdale, Georgia. The lanky youth, over six feet tall and still growing, had stopped school in the fifth grade, and hit the road for the first of many trips. Like most of the other boys on trial he could barely read and write. Outwardly neat, composed, and somewhat apathetic, he brooded inside. And, as his fellow prisoners would discover, he was quick tempered and easily angered. [48]

[47] *Ibid.*, 48–50. According to the reporter for the Chattanooga *Daily Times*, this was "the most damaging evidence against the Negroes" in the entire trial. This was doubly true because he (and presumably some of the jurors) understood Morris to say: "I saw 'em do a plenty." Chattanooga *Daily Times*, April 8, 1931.

[48] Neuropsychiatric Examination of Charles Weems by Dr. G. C. Branche, January 10, 1937, Allan Knight Chalmers Collection, Boston University Library,

Weems answered Roddy's questions clearly and without hesitation. He readily admitted that there was a fight. He had been riding on an oil tanker, he said, when Haywood Patterson came along with a pistol in his hand and urged him to help throw several white boys off the train. Patterson told him, said Weems, that some of the boys had tried to knock him off the tanker where he sat. According to Weems, it wasn't much of a fight. Haywood hit one of the boys and without protesting too much, they began jumping off the train. By the time Orville Gilley was ready to leap, the train had reached forty miles per hour and they helped pull him back in the car.[49]

Solicitor Bailey was a kindly looking man, tall and rather distinguished in appearance, with gray hair and blue eyes. In his cross-examination of Weems, however, he showed only grim determination. In rapid succession he fired question after question in an effort to confuse the young Negro. But Weems held his ground. He denied vehemently that there were even any girls in the gondola where the fight took place. "I don't know where the girls were," he declared. "There wasn't a soul in that car with me and Patterson except those Negroes and one white boy." Several of the Negroes on the train jumped off and he did not see them again, he said, suggesting that they might have molested the girls. At the end of the cross-examination, he still asserted his innocence. "I never saw no girls in this gondola which we were in at all. . . . I had nothing to do with the raping of the girls. I never saw anything done to the girls." [50]

Although Weems had contributed no proof other than his unsupported word, Roddy and Moody had no other evidence to offer and they decided to put Norris on the stand. Born on a tenant farm near Molina, Georgia, Clarence attended school sporadically for three or four years, but he never learned to read and write. At

Boston, Massachusetts; Memorandum on Status of Boys' Parents, July 3, 1931, in Scottsboro Legal File 2, NAACP Papers; Arrest Report, Drawer 108, Alabama Executive Files.

[49] *Weems* v. *Alabama,* 287 U.S. 45, Tr. p. 53.

[50] *Ibid.,* 52–53; Crenshaw and Miller, *Scottsboro: The Firebrand of Communism,* 97.

age thirteen he went to work on the farm full-time with his father. He was a shy child who had never liked to play with boys " 'cause I was always afraid I would get hurt; I didn't like rough games." [51] It was a miserable existence on the farm after he left school. On a constant diet of fatback and corn meal he suffered from rickets and, worse to him, he worked from sunup to sundown with nothing to show for it. At fifteen, he wandered away from home to the nearest railroad siding and joined a gang of itinerants. He briefly returned to the farm in 1929, but his father died, and when his mother moved in with relatives in nearby Molina, there was no longer any home. He took to the rails once more. By 1931, he had spent close to five years wandering across the Southeast, taking odd jobs along the way. When officials stopped the train at Paint Rock, Clarence was on his way to Sheffield, Alabama, to stay with an aunt and look for work. Only the week before, he had been laid off from his job with the Capital Stone Company in Atlanta.[52]

On the witness stand, he confirmed Weems's account of the fight. Haywood and several other boys, he said, passed him going toward the front of the train as he sat on a lumber car. Although he refused to join them he clambered to the top of a box car next to the gondola where the fight took place and watched the Negro youths throw the white boys from the train.[53] Solicitor Bailey sat for a moment and then walked in front of the witness chair where Norris sat fidgeting. It took only three questions to unnerve Norris completely. Within five minutes Bailey elicited from him the admission that "every one of them have [had] something to do with those girls after they put the white boys off the train." Norris described the scene, with Roy Wright holding a knife on one victim

[51] Neuropsychiatric Examination of Clarence Norris by Dr. G. C. Branche, January 10, 1937, in Chalmers Collection.

[52] *Ibid.*; Arrest Report, in Drawer 108, Alabama Executive Files; Memorandum on Status of Boys' Parents, July 3, 1931, in Scottsboro Legal File 2, NAACP Papers; Affidavit of Clarence Norris, June 10, 1931, in Scottsboro Legal File 2, NAACP Papers.

[53] *Weems* v. *Alabama*, 287 U.S. 45, Tr. p. 56. He later insisted that he had actually seen nothing and that his testimony about the fight was based entirely on listening to the other accounts in court. Affidavit of Clarence Norris, June 10, 1931, in Scottsboro Legal File 2, NAACP Papers.

while the other seven took turns raping the girls. "They all raped her, everyone of them," he shouted. He insisted that he alone was innocent.[54]

Roddy watched in disbelief while Norris shattered the flimsy defense he had tried to construct. When Roddy's objections failed to halt Norris in his head-long accusations, the defense attorney requested and received a brief recess. During the break, Roddy pleaded with Bailey to accept a guilty plea with a guarantee of life imprisonment instead of death for the two boys. Solicitor Bailey, confident of a conviction, spurned any compromise.[55]

When court reconvened, Roddy desperately tried to repair the damage. Under questioning, Norris was extremely weak on the details of the rape he allegedly witnessed. Although he earlier told Bailey he had seen the girls plainly during the assault, he could not say whether they were nude or whether they wore dresses or overalls. The girls told of twelve attackers; he insisted there were only eight. Roddy looked at Norris sternly and asked if he had not sworn just before he went on the stand that he had not seen a fight, let alone a rape? Norris admitted he had, but said, "I am positive and I am swearing now. I hold up my right hand to tell the truth, and I am telling the truth. That negro Weems that was on the witness stand did ravish that girl. He was on her." Every one of the other eight had "something to do with those girls . . . but I did not." Roddy sighed, shook his head in disbelief, and returned to his chair. "The defense rests," he told the court.[56]

If Norris had hoped to save himself, he got little cooperation from the prosecution. As soon as he stepped down from the witness chair, Bailey called Arthur Woodall for rebuttal testimony. Woodall told the court he "searched all of these darkies" and removed a knife from Norris. Back on the stand again, Victoria Price examined it carefully, looked up, and said: "That is my knife. I had it on my person at the time of this trouble on the train." Norris, she charged, had taken it from her along with $1.50 in coins and a

[54] *Weems* v. *Alabama*, 287 U.S. 45, Tr. pp. 55–56.
[55] Birmingham *News*, April 7, 1931; Chattanooga *Daily Times*, April 8, 1931.
[56] *Weems* v. *Alabama*, 287 U.S. 45, Tr. pp. 57–58; Chattanooga *Daily Times*, April 8, 1931.

pocket handkerchief. The state rested. It had the direct testimony of Norris stating that he had seen Weems rape the girls, and it had the knife to link Norris to the rape. To Roddy and Moody the case seemed hopeless. They told Judge Hawkins they did not care to argue the case before the jury.[57]

The prosecution saw a solid victory within its grasp. Speaking for the state, Attorney Snodgrass urged the jury to bring in the death penalty for both defendants. After Snodgrass had completed his summation, Roddy said that he and Moody objected to any further statements by the state, on the grounds that since the defense had declined to make a summation, "any further argument on behalf of the counsel for the State to the jury would be contrary to the law . . . and would be harmful and prejudicial to the interest of the defendants." The court over-ruled him, and Solicitor Bailey spoke to the jury for another thirty minutes.[58]

It was still early in the afternoon when Judge Hawkins began instructing the jury. His charge was eminently fair. He outlined the law to the twelve men: that the burden of proof was on the state to satisfy them that the defendants had forcibly and against the victim's consent actually "penetrated her private parts"; or that they had aided and abetted in the attack. He reemphasized that it was up to the state to prove beyond reasonable doubt— "Not beyond every doubt, but beyond all reasonable doubt . . ." —the guilt of the two defendants. He pointed out that even though they were on trial together, the guilt of each had to be proved individually. He concluded by outlining the possible penalties—from ten years to death for rape, or from a fine to a sentence not exceeding twenty years if they decided on a lesser offense such as assault and battery or assault with intent to rape.[59]

Before the jury had cleared the room, the selection of a venire to try the next case began, and within less than an hour, Haywood Patterson went on trial alone. Once again, Victoria Price testified for the state, and her memory seemed to have improved. In the

[57] *Weems* v. *Alabama*, 287 U.S. 45, Tr. pp. 58–59.

[58] *Ibid.*, 59.

[59] *Powell* v. *Alabama*, 287 U.S. 45, Tr. pp. 48–49, 51.

face of the conflict between her initial testimony that she and
Ruby had gone to all the cotton mills in Chattanooga and Ruby's
assertion that they had gone to only one, Victoria decided that
they had gone to two mills. And she recalled precisely that it was
Haywood Patterson who had one of the guns, a .38 caliber pistol,
and Weems who had the other, a .45. She also remembered that
the two had fired once, possibly twice, over the gondola where she
sat. While she was no longer positive that every one of the twelve
held knives, she was sure that it "looked like all of them had
knives; I never saw the like in my life." Most of all she was certain
that Patterson was one of the defendants whose "private parts
penetrated my private parts." [60]

Roddy doggedly continued his efforts to attack Mrs. Price's
reputation and though the state successfully interposed objections,
Victoria insisted on answering Roddy's insinuations concerning
her reputation. When Roddy asked her if she had ever practiced
prostitution, she replied angrily: "I don't know what you are talking about. I do not know what prostitution means. I have not
made it a practice to have intercourse with other men." She added,
"I have not had intercourse with any white man but my husband;
I want you to distinctly understand that." [61]

Bailey called Ruby to the stand to confirm Victoria's charge of
rape by Patterson, but Miss Bates was indecisive on this point.
Initially she said she thought Patterson was the first person to assault her friend, but under cross-examination, she said that she
"would not undertake to say who was the first and second and
third and fourth and fifth and sixth of the boys that had intercourse with Victoria Price; I could not say that." Ultimately, she
concluded, she "could not be sure about the boys that had intercourse with Victoria Price." [62] If Haywood was to be convicted it
would have to be on the testimony of Victoria and not on that of
Ruby.

Just after Ruby stepped down from the witness chair, the bailiff

[60] *Patterson* v. *Alabama*, 287 U.S. 45, Tr. pp. 19, 22, 24.
[61] *Ibid.*, 23.
[62] *Ibid.*, 25, 29.

stepped up to the bench and whispered to Judge Hawkins that the jury for the case of Norris and Weems had reached a verdict. Hawkins ordered Patterson's jury taken into the jury room. The two juries passed each other, but none of the first jurors indicated in any way the results of their verdict. As the twelve men took their seats, absolute silence descended on the courtroom, and only the sound of the crowd outside could be heard. The foreman handed a folded piece of paper to the circuit court clerk who read the verdict firmly and loudly: "We find the defendants guilty of rape and fix their sentence at death in. . . ." A roar of applause drowned his last words as the spectators leaped to their feet, many of them rushing through the doors to tell those who could not get into the courtroom. The waiting crowd, fifteen hundred strong, burst into shouts and cheers. Hawkins futilely pounded the bench for order, but the noise of the crowd drowned the sound of the banging gavel. Finally he ordered the guardsmen to remove those who could not restrain their enthusiasm, and the soldiers ejected eight spectators before a measure of calm returned to the courtroom. Throughout the demonstration, Norris and Weems stared straight ahead without expression. It was the first break of the trials for the defendants, and Roddy capitalized on it. He called to the stand Major Starnes, who had been in the adjacent room with Patterson's jury. On cross-examination, Starnes admitted that the jury which would decide Patterson's fate had distinctly heard the frenzied reaction of the crowd to the guilty verdict of Norris and Weems.[63]

This was a crucial point. In the 1919 Arkansas riot cases twelve Negroes had been sentenced to death and sixty-seven to long prison terms in a courtroom dominated by a shouting mob outside. Justice Oliver Wendell Holmes, speaking for the United States Supreme Court, had declared:

If the case is such that the whole proceeding is a mask; that counsel, jury and judge were swept to a fatal end by an irresistible wave of

[63] Chattanooga *Daily Times*, April 8, 1931; Birmingham *Age-Herald*, April 8, 1931; *Powell* v. *Alabama*, 287 U.S. 45, Tr. p. 51.

public passion . . . neither perfection in the machinery for correction nor the possibility that the trial court and counsel saw no other way of avoiding an immediate outbreak of the mob can prevent this court from securing to the petitioners their constitutional rights.

The sentences of the seventy-nine were overturned.[64] In that case, the Supreme Court had gone behind the legal externals of the case and asked itself the question: were the proceedings a trial in fact as well as appearance? To Roddy, this seemed clear precedent for the Patterson case, but Hawkins denied his motion for a mistrial.

Dr. Bridges gave essentially the same testimony as in the Weems and Norris trial. The state dropped Dr. Lynch. Apparently they felt that his testimony gave undue emphasis to the physical and emotional well-being of the two girls; and they had a new witness, Ory Dobbins. Dobbins' father had been standing on the porch of his rural home when the train passed. He testified in the Weems-Norris trial that he saw a fight, but all he saw "was just some scuffling between some men there." Ory was there and had a much more vivid recollection of the event. As the train passed, he said, "I saw two girls and these colored people, and as it got by, one of the colored men grabbed a woman and threw her down, and the train then got by the barn. . . ." [65] Roddy did not cross-examine him.

As in the earlier trial, the defense opened with the testimony of

[64] *Moore* v. *Dempsey* (1923), 261 U.S. 86. These cases began when a group of whites in Elaine, Arkansas, fired on a group of Negro sharecroppers who had met to organize a union. The Negroes returned the fire and when several whites were killed, seventy-nine Negroes were arrested and tried for murder. At first it appeared there would be a mass lynching, but a local vigilante committee promised the mob that if they would refrain from lynching the defendants they would "execute those found guilty in the form of the law." Witnesses for the defense were beaten and forced to testify against the defendants; the court-appointed counsel failed to ask for a change of venue and called no witnesses. The trial of the entire seventy-nine men lasted less than an hour. The jury returned a verdict of guilty in less than five minutes. Although the Arkansas Supreme Court could find nothing wrong with these proceedings, the National Association for the Advancement of Colored People won a reversal in the Supreme Court. Raymond Pace Alexander, "The Upgrading of the Negro's Status by Supreme Court Decisions," *Journal of Negro History*, XXX (1945), 117–29. For a legal view of the importance of the case, see David Fellman, *The Defendant's Rights* (New York: Rinehart and Company, 1958), 60–61.

[65] *Patterson* v. *Alabama*, 287 U.S. 45, Tr. p. 30.

the defendant, Haywood Patterson. Most of the officials who had come in contact with Patterson immediately disliked him. Although he could be obsequious when the occasion suited him, he usually exhibited an insolent hostility that enraged white Southerners. Never involved in any major crime, by 1931 he had brushed with the Chattanooga police on several occasions. His father, Claude Patterson, was a Georgia sharecropper who sneaked away from a Georgia plantation late one night in 1923, leaving his employer with ten acres of cotton to pick and a debt which exceeded any possible return on the crop. He settled in Chattanooga, and by 1929 he was making up to $28 a week in a brake-lining factory. This amount did not go far when there were ten children to feed, and no one complained when Haywood dropped out of school at thirteen and began making longer and longer trips away from home. When arrested he was a seasoned rider of the rails and a functional illiterate. [66]

Contradictions and inconsistencies marked Patterson's testimony. He told a straightforward story of how he met three of his friends—Roy Wright, Gene Williams, and Andy Wright—and with them decided to go to Memphis to look for work. But he denied that he had taken part in a fight on the train, something which almost every other witness, including his three friends, had affirmed. He insisted that he had seen a fight from the top of the box car adjacent to the gondola where it took place, a fight between white boys and twelve Negroes other than himself, Andy, Roy, and Gene. In a confusing cross-examination, Patterson first said he had seen Weems and four of the other defendants "ravish that girl [Victoria]," although he and his three friends had not touched her. Within five minutes he denied that he had even seen the girls, let alone raped them. "I did not see the girls in there; I did not tell you a while ago I saw them . . ." he said. "I did not see any girls in there until we got to Paint Rock." [67] Patterson's testi-

[66] New York *Daily Worker*, April 16, 1931; Arrest Report, Drawer 108, Alabama Executive Files; Neuropsychiatric Examination of Haywood Patterson, January 10, 1937, in Chalmers Collection; Memorandum on Status of Boys' Parents, July 3, 1931, in Scottsboro Legal File 2, NAACP Papers.

[67] *Patterson* v. *Alabama*, 287 U.S. 45, Tr. pp. 32–34.

mony was so contradictory that the jury could only conclude he was hopelessly bewildered or consciously lying.

In an effort to buttress Patterson's shaky story, Roddy called his three friends to the stand. According to Roy Wright, the fight began fifteen minutes out of Chattanooga when several white boys passed him and his friends sitting on an oil car. One of them almost knocked Patterson off the train and "a few little words" resulted.[68] After the train left Stevenson, Roy said that fourteen Negroes scattered over the train gathered on a cross-tie car and decided to throw the white boys from the train. One of them had a gun, he said, but it was a "long, tall, black fellow" wearing duck overalls who later jumped off. As soon as they pulled out of Stevenson, the entire group crossed over the box cars and into the gondola where several white boys sat. The fight was brief, he said, and most of the boys bailed out without a struggle. By the time the last of them, Orville Gilley, had started to jump, the train was moving at more than forty miles per hour. Roy said that he and one of his companions "took pity on him and told him we would let him alone. . . ." Wright described how he and Eugene Williams pulled the youth back into the gondola. Calm returned to the car, said Roy, and the group scattered over the train. He and Haywood crawled up on the box car next to the gondola, and Eugene and Andy moved to the adjacent box car. But at another point in his testimony he declared that he had seen nine Negroes (excluding himself, Andy, Eugene, and Haywood) "down there with the girls and all had intercourse with them. I saw all of them have intercourse with them. . . . I saw that with my own eyes." [69] With the conclusion of Roy Wright's testimony, the second day of the trial came to an end.

As a squad of National Guardsmen returned the nine Negroes to their cells, the rest of the militia unit gathered on the courthouse lawn and to the music of the Scottsboro Hosiery Mill Band

----

[68] *Ibid.* As Patterson later recalled it, the white boy said: Nigger bastard, this is a white man's train. . . . All you black bastards better get off." And he had replied: "You white sonsofbitches, we got as much right here as you!" Patterson and Conrad, *Scottsboro Boy*, 1–2.

[69] Transcript of Record, pp. 34, 41, *Patterson* v. *Alabama*, 287 U.S. 45.

performed the formal guard mount. Afterward, the band played two military marches for the cheering onlookers and concluded with the national anthem.[70] The crowd gradually broke up.

On Wednesday the machine guns that had been mounted at the two entrances to the courthouse square were removed, for the crowd was now relatively small, numbering about two thousand. But the guardsmen kept their weapons out and held the throng away from the courthouse. For those who could not get into the building, there was much to talk about, notably Norris and Weems' convictions the day before. And even though the band did not put in another appearance, there was other entertainment. John B. Benson, the local Ford dealer, led a motor caravan of twenty-eight new A-Model Ford trucks in and around Scottsboro with a phonograph and amplifier blaring music to the crowd. The sound was clearly audible inside the courtroom, as Patterson's trial continued.[71]

Roy Wright's older brother, Andy, and Eugene Williams testified briefly. They told of a fight, but said they saw no one with a gun, and, unlike Haywood and Roy, they insisted they had not seen anyone raped. "I did not see any girls on the train," said Andy. He told the court that the first time he saw the girls was at Paint Rock. When Solicitor Bailey tried to shake his story in cross-examination, Williams admitted they all had gotten down in the gondola, "but I did not see any girls in there. . . . I swear to the jury that the girls were not in that gondola." [72]

Testifying in Patterson's behalf, Ozie Powell told the jury that he had followed a group of Negroes who said they planned to throw the white boys from the train, but by the time he got to the gondola, most of the white boys had already jumped. He said that he had not seen any knives or pistols, nor had he heard any shooting. He added that he walked from "one end to the other" of the gondola after the fight took place and he never saw any girls. Olen

[70] Birmingham *News*, June 10, 1931. Scottsboro citizens were proud of their thirty-piece band, one of the best in the state. Scottsboro *Progressive Age*, May 14, 1931.
[71] Birmingham *Age-Herald*, April 9, 1931; Birmingham *News*, June 10, 1931.
[72] *Patterson* v. *Alabama*, 287 U.S. 45, Tr. pp. 37–38, 40.

Montgomery also testified, but he told the jury that he had boarded the seventh car from the end of the train and had remained
there until arrested at Paint Rock. He swore that he did not know
how many Negroes or whites were on the train, did not know
there had been a fight, did not know anything. As he put it: "I
was by my lonesome." [73]

As in the first trial, Roddy and Moody declined to make a sum-
mation, and after brief statements by Bailey and Snodgrass and a
restatement by Judge Hawkins of his charge in the earlier case, the
Patterson case went to the jury at 11 A.M. The trial of Ozie
Powell, Willie Roberson, Andy Wright, Eugene Williams, and
Olen Montgomery was underway within fifteen minutes.

It was easy to see why the solicitor had postponed these cases
until last, as they presented a number of problems. In the first
place, each defendant so far had told a relatively plausible story
and had held to it through cross-examination. Norris, Weems, and
Patterson had all been positively identified by Victoria Price, the
state's star witness. In this trial, however, it was up to Ruby Bates
to point out at least three of the defendants.

This was Mrs. Price's last performance at Scottsboro and she
lived up to the state's expectations, testifying vividly and dramatically of the savage rape. The first one to "put his hands on me,"
said Victoria, was the one "with the sleepy eyes, Olen Montgomery." He was also the first to rape her, she said. While he ravished her, Eugene Williams held a knife open as he stood above
her and told her to keep her legs open. Willie Roberson, she said,
held her legs and kept saying "jerk her legs this way," while the
others ran up and down the box car shouting: "Pour it to her,
pour it to her," as they waved their open knives. Of the five defendants on trial, she swore that Olen Montgomery, Andy Wright,
and Eugene Williams had raped her. Ozie Powell and Willie
Roberson had raped Ruby, she said. She was sure that she "absolutely saw them have intercourse with the other girl." [74]

[73] *Ibid.*, 40–41, 44.
[74] *Powell* v. *Alabama*, 287 U.S. 45, Tr. pp. 22–23, 25.

Roddy shifted tactics in this trial and for the first time tried to shake Victoria's testimony instead of making futile assaults on her reputation. She was an unyielding witness, however, and failed to retract a single statement. Victoria did admit that she could not name, in sequence, the six who raped her "because they began to get down so fast I could not keep account of it." But she said she had "plenty of sense and I remember the faces of the six that had intercourse with me." Moreover, she recalled new details for the third trial. "It took three of them to get off my overalls." There were "so many hands you could not tell which three of them took off my overalls," but Weems was the leader. She distinctly remembered, she said, that there were "seven shots fired in all, from the time the racket started until it ended; five over the gondola where the boys were." [75]

As Judge Hawkins prepared to adjourn the court for lunch, word came that the Patterson jury—out less than twenty-five minutes—had already reached a decision. When the jury for the trial in process had filed out of the room and Patterson's jury had been seated, Hawkins spoke to the crowd. He warned that "if a single person makes a demonstration whatever I want the officers to bring them around, I am going to send them to jail." The courtroom, he declared, "is not like vaudeville or anything else—you cannot make any demonstration." He added: "To do that is liable to make the case have to be tried over. . . ." He backed up his warning by stationing twenty-five guardsmen throughout the courtroom. The circuit court clerk read the verdict and to the surprise of no one, the jury found Patterson guilty and sentenced him to death. The crowd remained completely silent.[76]

When the trial resumed shortly after 1 P.M., Ruby Bates took the stand for the state. As Bailey had feared, she was evasive and hesitant in her answers. She swore that the Negroes on trial had come into the gondola with guns and knives. Under cross-examina-

---

[75] *Ibid.,* 25–26. Earlier in the Patterson trial she swore there was only one shot and "possibly" two.

[76] New York *Daily News,* April 10, 1933; Birmingham *News,* June 10, 1931; Chattanooga *Daily Times,* April 9, 1931; Birmingham *Age-Herald,* April 9, 1931.

tion she said she had been raped six times and she thought "every one of the colored boys . . . had intercourse with me or with Victoria." But she could not point out any of the defendants specifically as having raped her. "I don't know which one of them ravished me. I just know an intercourse was held with me." [77] If Powell and Roberson were to be convicted, it would have to be on the testimony of Mrs. Price alone.

Dr. Bridges repeated his testimony for the third time, but now the state called on him to pass on new medical evidence. The defense (as Bailey knew) planned to insist that Roberson could not have raped either of the girls because of his syphilitic condition. Bridges said he had examined Roberson and found him "diseased with syphilis and gonorrhea, a bad case of it." Without a doubt he was "very sore" and any intercourse would be "attended with some pain." But under cross-examination he said he thought it "possible" for Roberson to have taken part in an assault. "I have seen them that had it worse than he has." [78]

Ozie Powell testified first for the defense, stating that he boarded the freight along with Willie Roberson, whom he had met in Chattanooga.[79] Once the two got on the train, Ozie lost track of his friend. At first Ozie sat on a cross-tie car, but because the wind was blowing he had crossed from the cross-tie car to a nearby gondola and crouched under the back edge to keep the wind from striking him. He made the change just after passing through the underground tunnel near Chattanooga. Shortly after leaving Stevenson, Ozie said he saw a group of Negroes—he did not know how many—cross over the gondola where he sat. "I heard them cursing. I heard fighting. I heard some boy say, 'Get off,' . . . ." Someone replied that "he was not going to get off unless they threwed [sic] him off." He denied he heard a woman scream. Powell told the jury he did not look up into the gondola while the fight went on, "and I don't know who was in there. I don't

---

[77] *Powell* v. *Alabama*, 287 U.S. 45, Tr. pp. 26–28.

[78] *Ibid.*, 29.

[79] Rousseau, Latham, T. L. Dobbins, and See Adams repeated their earlier testimony for the state. Bailey did not recall Ory Dobbins to the stand. *Ibid.*, 33–35.

know whether any girls were in there or not then." [80] A stiff cross-examination by Solicitor Bailey failed to shake his story.

Willie Roberson then took the stand. His head of bushy hair and his difficulty in speaking made him the butt of the spectators' humor, and he was known as "that ape nigger." [81] Less than a month after he was born in 1915, Willie's father had walked out on his mother. At her death in 1917, he went to live with his grandmother, who reared him until he was fourteen. When she died in 1930, he tried to live with his aunt in Columbus, Georgia, but she soon told him to "seek work for his living as we were not able to take sufficient care of him." At age fifteen, he began hoboing. Early in 1930, he contracted syphilis and gonorrhea and went to Atlanta's Grady Hospital in an effort to receive treatment. Hospital officials, however, told him they could not accept him because he was not a resident. Since he had lived for several months in Memphis the year before, he boarded the train to go there for help. [82]

Willie told the jury that he met Ozie Powell in Chattanooga, but they separated after they got on the train. He first boarded a log car, but it was so windy that when the train stopped at Stevenson he walked to the rear of the freight and crawled in an empty box car, the third from the caboose. Roberson said he felt awful and had tried to lie still because "there was something the matter with my privates down there; it was sore and swelled up." He stayed there until the train stopped in Paint Rock and a man jumped in the car and held a pistol on him, he said. [83]

Andy Wright testified he boarded an oil tank car at Chatta-

[80] *Powell* v. *Alabama*, 287 U.S. 45, Tr. p. 35.

[81] Willie had an intelligence quotient of less than 65. Although he went to the seventh grade, he could neither read nor write and he had always had difficulty in speaking clearly. See Neuropsychiatric Examination of Willie Robinson [*sic*] by Dr. G. C. Branche, January 10, 1937, in Chalmers Collection; Hamilton Basso, "Five Days in Decatur," *New Republic*, LXXVII (1933), 162–63.

[82] Neuropsychiatric Examination of Willie Robinson [*sic*] by Dr. G. C. Branche, January 10, 1937, in Chalmers Collection; Memorandum on Status of Boys' Parents, July 3, 1931, in Scottsboro Legal File 2, NAACP Papers; Lula B. Jackson to Walter White, May 18, 1931, in Scottsboro Legal File 1, NAACP Papers.

[83] *Powell* v. *Alabama*, 287 U.S. 45, Tr. pp. 36–37.

nooga and changed to a flat car in Stevenson. Shortly after that a fight broke out with some white boys on the train, but Wright insisted he did not actively take part except to help Gilley back on the train. He testified that several of the Negroes who took part were not on the train when it stopped at Paint Rock. Bailey's cross-examination was brief and fiery. Standing directly in front of the young Negro he demanded to know if he had said: " 'God Damn you, if you hadn't been so damn smart and tough and fought like you did, we wouldn't have bothered you.' " Andy insisted he had not. "And did you not tell her after the rape, 'Yes, you will have a baby after this?' " shouted the solicitor. In a torrent of words Andy fervently denied it: "I did not have any such talk as that; I swear that I was not in that car where the women were; I never saw this woman; I never had any talk like you stated, none at all. I will stand on a stack of Bibles and say it." [84]

Olen Montgomery told a story much like Roberson's. He boarded an oil tanker back toward the rear of the train, the seventh car from the end, he said, and he stayed on the same car all the way to Paint Rock. He denied that he had seen anything. As he put it: "If I had seen them, I would not have known whether they were men or women; I cannot see good." [85] Olen was blind in his left eye and had only 10 per cent vision in his right. When arrested he had been hoboing to Memphis, looking for work in order to buy a pair of glasses. On the train, as throughout his life, he was a "loner," sticking to himself and avoiding contact with others. In part this may have stemmed from his unhappy childhood, his mother and father having constantly quarreled and finally separated when he was a small boy. Under cross-examination, he refused to change his story. He insisted to the last that he knew nothing of any fight or rape and that he had been at the back of the train during the entire ride.[86]

[84] *Ibid.*, 38–39.

[85] *Ibid.*, 39–40.

[86] Arrest Report, in Drawer 108, Alabama Executive Files; Neuropsychiatric Examination of Olen Montgomery by Dr. G. C. Branche, January 10, 1937, in Chalmers Collection; Memorandum on Status of Boys' Parents, July 3, 1931, in Scottsboro Legal File 2, NAACP Papers; *Powell* v. *Alabama*, 287 U.S. 45, Tr. p. 40.

Eugene Williams had testified in Patterson's trial, and he repeated his testimony without change. He still insisted that "I did
not see the girls at all until we got to Paint Rock." They were not
in the car at all, he said. In cross-examination, Bailey stepped up
to Williams and showed him a knife. Was it his? he asked. Williams said he recognized the knife. "The man in Paint Rock took
it off me." He added, however, that he had "kept it all the time in
my pocket." He denied Bailey's assertion that he held the knife at
Victoria Price's throat while the other Negroes raped her. As soon
as the defense had rested, however, the solicitor recalled Victoria
Price to the stand. She testified that she had seen the knife in the
hands of both Williams and Weems and that they had held it at
her throat while she was raped.[87]

Bailey closed the remaining loopholes in the prosecution's case.
Roberson had testified that he crawled into a box car at Stevenson,
left the door partially open, and stayed there until he was arrested
at Paint Rock. Deputy Sheriff Latham and Tom Rousseau, when
brought back for the state, testified they arrested Roberson at the
front of the train with the other eight boys. W. E. Brannon said
that he was standing on the west side of the train as it came into
Paint Rock and he had clearly seen that there were no open box
car doors on his side. Another member of the posse said that all
the doors were closed on the other side of the train. To clinch the
case, Orville Gilley went to the witness stand for the first time.
Attorney Snodgrass, assisting the state, asked him if he had seen
the five men on trial in the gondola where the girls were. "I saw
those five in the car. I saw every one of those five in the gondola."
Snodgrass continued: "Were the girls in there?" And over the objections of the defense, he replied: "Yes, sir, I saw all five of them
in that gondola." The prosecution rested and Gilley stepped down
from the witness chair. Roddy made no attempt to cross-examine
him.[88]

As in the earlier trials, the defense lawyers declined to make a
summation and the case went to the third jury at 4:20 P.M. Roy

[87] *Powell* v. *Alabama*, 287 U.S. 45, Tr. pp. 42–43.
[88] *Ibid.*, 44–45, 47–49.

Wright, the last of the nine, presented a problem in that he was only thirteen years old. Under Alabama law he could be tried only in a juvenile court unless the state brought waiver proceedings, but Solicitor Bailey was anxious to wrap up the entire matter and he proposed a deal to Stephen Roddy. If Roy would plead guilty, said Bailey, the state would agree to a compromise: life imprisonment instead of the death sentence. Roddy refused to agree to this, for he knew that any plea of guilty would forfeit Wright's right to an appeal under Alabama law and he agreed only to make the defense brief. This was satisfactory to the solicitor and within an hour, Wright's case went to the fourth jury of Jackson County citizens to sit in as many days. In his summation, Bailey asked for life imprisonment in view of Wright's youth.[89]

At 9 P.M. the two juries still had not reached verdicts, although newsmen learned that the jury for the five was near a decision. Within an hour after deliberations resumed on Thursday, the jury for the five reported in with the verdict everyone expected: guilty. At noon, however, the case of Roy Wright was still undecided and Judge Hawkins ordered the jury polled in open court. In spite of the fact that the state had asked only for life imprisonment, seven of the jurors insisted on the death penalty for the thirteen-year-old boy. The foreman told the court that agreement was hopeless and Hawkins reluctantly ordered a mistrial. Late in the afternoon, the eight convicted men filed before the bench and the judge, his eyes wet with tears, pronounced the death sentence on each. These were the first capital sentences he had administered in his five years on the bench. The defendants stood before him, stocially calm throughout his remarks.[90]

In what he intended as a postscript to his story, the correspondent for the Birmingham *Age-Herald* remarked that the sentencing of eight persons to death on the same day for the same crime was "without parallel in the history of the nation, and certainly in

[89] Memorandum of Stephen Roddy, April 11, 1931, in Scottsboro Legal File 1, NAACP Papers; Chattanooga *Daily Times*, April 9, 1931; Birmingham *Age-Herald*, April 9, 1931.

[90] Chattanooga *Daily Times*, April 10, 1931; Birmingham *Age-Herald*, April 10, 1931.

Alabama." The case was far from over, however. Two days before, Judge Hawkins had received a telegram from Huntsville, Alabama, charging that the nine boys were being tried on "trumped up charges." The telegram, signed by the "International Labor Defense, New York City," demanded a change of venue and declared that Judge Hawkins would be held "personally responsible." The judge labeled the charges "absurd," adding that he would "personally . . . welcome any investigation." Solicitor Bailey laughingly dismissed the telegram as a prank.[91]

But on the day of the sentencing, the Central Committee of the Communist Party of the United States issued a lengthy statement. The incident at Scottsboro was a significant break with the past, said the Committee. In the past, the "Southern ruling class" had used the stake and the rope to protect its position, but in the case of the nine Negro "workers" they had sought to attain the same results by using legal procedures which differed only in form from the most "cold blooded 'illegal' lynching." The "parasite landlords and capitalist classes of the South" concocted the trial and sentence, said the Central Committee, because they saw a movement among the Negroes and whites in backward Southern communities which threatened their "super-exploitation." By enlisting the white workers in their "beastly lynching crimes" Southern capitalists could effectively split the working classes of the region. The Scottsboro Case was destined to be the decade's equivalent of Sacco and Vanzetti, a test of the growing strength of the masses against the capitalist bosses of the South and their cohorts throughout the United States.[92]

That night, the Party faithful assembled in Cleveland and New York and dutifully drafted telegrams protesting the "legal lynching" of the nine black "victims of 'capitalist justice.' " Across the nation, dozens of "workers' organizations"—the Trade Union Unity League, the League of Struggle for Negro Rights, the Anti-

[91] Birmingham *Age-Herald,* April 9, 1931; New York *Times,* April 9, 1931, p. 26; Birmingham *Post,* April 10, 1931; Birmingham *News,* April 8, 1931. The editor of the *Jackson County Sentinel* dismissed the group as a "socialistic disturbance raiser." Scottsboro *Jackson County Sentinel,* April 9, 1931.

[92] New York *Daily Worker,* April 10, April 11, 1931.

Imperialist League of the United States, the Young Communists League, and the Communist Party, U.S.A.—sent messages of protest to Governor Miller and court officials.[93]

Unexpectedly, however, spontaneous protests also poured into the governor's office. In New York City, a 61-year-old Negro maid begged Governor Miller to "let those pore boys get free." An Atlanta lawyer wrote to Governor Miller and made it clear that he was "not a 'nigger-lover,' or a Communist or anything other than a Georgia cracker who enjoys being a neighbor of Alabama." Nevertheless, he termed the sentence a "barbarous penalty . . . to be applied to these children, for children in years and mental development is exactly what they were." To execute the defendants after a trial under such conditions would be "nothing short of a massacre." He concluded: "I can understand how such savagery can exist in a state like Mississippi . . . but I refuse to believe that a civilized community like that of your state will be guilty of such an atrocity." [94] And the Alabama Interracial Commission convened in Birmingham to pass a resolution calling for a "careful review of these cases in the courts, that all lingering doubts may be cleared up. . . ." Each of the accused had to be dealt with on an individual basis, said the Commission. "God keep us from any false step that may cause terror and madness to flame among us." [95]

There had been many cases similar to that in Scottsboro and most of them had gone unnoticed. But the number of participants, their youth, the stunning rapidity of their trials, and, most of all, the harsh sentences they received, roused a wave of protest from millions of Americans. It was a concern which the radical left would channel and direct until the name "Scottsboro" became synonomous with Southern racism, repression, and injustice.

[93] *Ibid.*, April 17, April 18, 1931.

[94] Mrs. Claudia Mae Randall to Governor Benjamin Meeks Miller, April 11, 1933; William Sims to Governor Benjamin Meeks Miller, April 11, 1931, in Alabama Scottsboro Files, Alabama Department of Archives, Montgomery.

[95] James D. Burton, "Scottsboro and White Justice," *Christian Century*, L (1933), 716.

III

THE CLASH OF
DOGMAS

THE Communist Party's official organ, the New York *Daily Worker,* dutifully reported the events at Scottsboro as the latest "capitalist atrocity," but the remarkable appeal of the case initially surprised Party leaders. Accordingly, from the arrest through the trials, the *Worker* gave only token coverage and focused instead on such labor conflicts as the Paterson, New Jersey, strike.[1] Charles Dirba, the International Labor Defense's assistant secretary and a member of the Communist Party's Central Committee, first recognized the value the case might have in dramatizing the plight of Southern Negroes. Shortly after he learned of the arrest and attempted lynching from the New York *Times,* Dirba telegraphed Lowell Wakefield in Birmingham, and urged him to make a careful investigation. Wakefield, one of the few representatives of the Communist Party in the South during this period, worked for the Party, the ILD, and whatever short-lived front organization was currently most active. Accompanied by Douglas McKenzie, an itinerant Negro organizer for the League of Struggle for Negro Rights, Wakefield attended the trials in Scottsboro.[2]

---

[1] Max Urban, owner of a Paterson, New Jersey, silk mill, was shot and killed in an altercation on the picket lines. Paterson police charged two strikers with the murder, and the *Daily Worker* believed it had the makings of a "new Sacco-Vanzetti Case." New York *Daily Worker,* April 4, 1931.

[2] The LSNR was known derisively as the Jim-Crow section of the Communist Party. It never had more than a few hundred members and existed on paper for

After watching the first day's proceedings he enthusiastically cabled Dirba that it was another Sacco-Vanzetti case. Without a doubt, he said, Alabama authorities planned a "neck-tie party" for the Negro youths.[3] With this telegram, Dirba persuaded the Central Committee of the Party to issue its lengthy statement analyzing the "significance" of the Scottsboro Case and hinting at a more active role for the Communist Party.[4]

Walter White, executive secretary of the National Association for the Advancement of Colored People (NAACP), followed the case in the newspapers, but his organization remained aloof. Throughout its history, the NAACP depended primarily upon its branches for information and advice regarding such cases.[5] The nearest chapter in Chattanooga had collapsed in 1930, and the only facts which White received came from Southern newspapers which asserted incorrectly that able counsel represented the boys.[6] Two days before the first trial opened in Scottsboro, Dr. P. A. Stephens in Chattanooga described to White the steps the Ministers' Alliance had taken and asked if the NAACP planned to assist in any way. On the day that Judge Hawkins sentenced the boys to death, White's special assistant, William T. Andrews, replied to Stephens and noted that the case might be similar to the Elaine Riot Trials. Stephens asked for a statement of the facts, but his reply was circumspect and cautious. Officers of the NAACP were jealous of their organization's reputation. The last thing they wanted was to identify the Association with a gang of mass rapists

---

the most part. It eventually merged with the ILD. William A. Nolan, *Communism Versus the Negro* (Chicago: Henry Regnery Company, 1951), 76; Wilson Record, *The Negro and the Communist Party* (Chapel Hill: University of North Carolina Press, 1951), 34–35.

[3] Lowell Wakefield to Charles Dirba, April 7, 1931, in ILD Papers.

[4] New York *Daily Worker,* April 10, 1931.

[5] Gunnar Myrdal, *An American Dilemma: The Negro Problem and Modern Democracy* (New York: Harper and Brothers, 1944), 822–24.

[6] There were wire-service reports in many non-Southern dailies, but these were written by local reporters. At least one of these reporters, J. Glenn Jordan of the Huntsville *Daily Times,* was a violent Negro-phobe who wrote a pamphlet which was banned from distribution during later trials because of its strong prejudice. See J. Glenn Jordan to Governor Benjamin Meeks Miller, April 21, 1932, in Alabama Scottsboro Files.

unless they were reasonably certain the boys were innocent or that their constitutional rights had been abridged.[7]

The next day, however, the NAACP received inquiries from eight individuals, six branches, four other organizations, and the editor of *The Nation*. And the telephone in the New York office rang incessantly. Late in the afternoon, White received a call from Clarence Darrow, the nation's outstanding criminal lawyer and a member of the NAACP's Board of Directors. Darrow explained that he had been reached by the International Labor Defense's chief lawyer, Joseph Brodsky. They wanted him to serve as chief counsel in an appeal to the Supreme Court. White warned Darrow to steer clear of the Communists. "I have no objection to the ILD because it is a Communist organization," he said. "On the other hand, it has been our experience that it is impossible to cooperate with them in any legal case." Their main goal always remained propaganda instead of results. He assured Darrow that the NAACP had things under control.[8]

White's assurances to Darrow committed the NAACP to the case. With the activities of the ILD already underway, White knew he must act quickly. Through Andrews he telegraphed Stephens, urging him to airmail the transcripts as soon as these were complete. When they had not arrived four days later, Dr. Stephens reported that the court stenographer had not completed preparations on the transcripts. On April 22, White finally learned that they had never been ordered because the Ministers' Alliance had no funds and Roddy refused to guarantee costs to the court stenographer. White immediately sent a check for twenty-four dollars, but much time had been wasted.[9] It was standard NAACP administrative procedure to rely upon local contacts, but in this case the reliance on Stephens and the Chattanooga Ministers' Al-

[7] P. A. Stephens to Walter White, April 2, 1931, and William T. Andrews to P. A. Stephens, April 9, 1931, in Scottsboro Legal File 1, NAACP Papers.

[8] Walter White to Clarence Darrow, April 10, 1931, in Scottsboro Legal File 1, NAACP Papers. Rumors of these negotiations between Darrow and the ILD were picked up and printed in the Birmingham *Post*, April 10, 1931.

[9] William T. Andrews to P. A. Stephens, April 10, 1931, April 14, 1931; P. A. Stephens to Walter White, April 20, 1931, April 22, 1931; Walter White to P. A Stephens, April 22, 1931, in Scottsboro Legal File 1, NAACP Papers.

liance led to the loss of valuable time. This was the first of a number of costly hesitations and miscalculations by White.

The International Labor Defense, like the NAACP, normally depended on its field men. But when the ILD Executive Committee voted to defend the boys, George Maurer dispatched Allan Taub, one of his top attorneys, to Chattanooga to coordinate the organization's activities. Taub's first and most immediate goal was to gain complete control of the defense. Although the *Daily Worker* had branded Roddy a "tool of the reformist traitors," Wakefield suggested that the ILD try to work through him, at least during the initial phases. As Edmond Wilson later described it, "They went through all the gestures of taking him [Roddy] up into a high place and showing him the kingdoms of the earth." Taub told Roddy that he would become a national figure, the successor of Clarence Darrow. But when Taub explained that the money for his salary would be raised by holding mass meetings among Negroes, Roddy found this distasteful and declined the offer.[10]

Undismayed by this temporary setback, the two ILD representatives requested permission to speak to the April 18 meeting of the Chattanooga Negro Ministers' Alliance. Joined by Joseph Brodsky, they promised the organization they would take over the entire financial burden of the case. All three men impressed the ministers with their eloquence and lack of racial prejudice. Although they did not reach a written agreement, Wakefield triumphantly wired Maurer in New York that things were under control. The Alliance wanted to keep Roddy, he said, "but we will eliminate [him] somehow. . . ."[11]

The ILD's nominee for Roddy's successor was a courtly Southern gentleman who had once served as attorney general of Hamilton County (Chattanooga), Tennessee. George W. Chamlee, Sr., was the grandson of a decorated Confederate veteran and a member of one of the most prominent Tennessee families. He was an unusual, if somewhat erratic, figure in Southern politics. In 1926,

[10] New York *Daily Worker,* April 11, 1931; Wilson, "The Freight Car Case," 40–41.
[11] Lowell Wakefield to George Maurer, April 18, 1931, in ILD Papers.

he had written a magazine article for *Forum,* defending lynching under certain circumstances. Despite this defense of one of the South's most unsavory traditions, a coalition of trade unionists and Negroes had helped elect him county solicitor. And he was one of the few Chattanooga lawyers willing to defend Communists and other radicals. Less than three weeks before he was approached by the ILD, he defended three leaflet-distributing Communists arrested on vagrancy charges by Chattanooga police. When the prosecution charged that the Communists favored overthrowing the government, Chamlee quietly reminded the court that all their grandfathers had repudiated the federal government and had sworn allegiance to the Confederate States of America. For the relatively modest fee of $1,000 he agreed to serve as attorney for the boys.[12] As Will Alexander of the Commission on Jnterracial Cooperation readily acknowledged a month later, for "once, our Communist friends seem to have been more successful in their selection of an attorney." Without a doubt, he said, Chamlee was one of the best lawyers in southern Tennessee and far superior to Roddy.[13]

Spurred on by their success in hiring Chamlee, the team of ILD representatives moved quickly. The same day, Sunday, April 19, Wakefield and Taub spoke at two Negro churches in Chattanooga and collected a "love offering" for the ILD defense fund. The two ministers, who knew nothing of the Communist connections of the ILD, agreed to back Chamlee and to back Roddy's dismissal. While the two men courted the support of Chattanooga's Negroes, Brodsky boarded the train for Birmingham. The next day, he interviewed the nine boys who were being held in the Birmingham jail. The Scottsboro boys knew nothing about the strange, somewhat disheveled little man who spoke to them, but they liked what they heard. He promised no such halfhearted defense as they had

[12] George W. Chamlee, "Is Lynching Ever Defensible? The Motives of Judge Lynch," *Forum,* LXXVI (1926), 811–17; Wilson, "The Freight Car Case," 40–41; Chattanooga *Daily Times,* April 1, April 2, 1931; Lowell Wakefield to George Maurer, April 19, 1931, in ILD Papers.

[13] Will Alexander to Walter White, May 14, 1931, in Interracial Commission Papers.

received in Scottsboro, but the best lawyers in the country. What was more important, he said, they would have the support of "thousands of black and white workers across the nation." He proffered an affidavit turning the case over to the ILD. Andy Wright readily signed and the other boys placed their marks on the agreement.[14]

In Chattanooga, the three men congratulated each other on their success. By prompt and forceful action they had gained almost complete control over the case. On Tuesday, April 22, George W. Chamlee issued a statement from his office announcing that he had accepted a retainer from the ILD. He was proud to be associated with this organization, he said, which was "interested in defending workers, opposing fee-grabbing, and assisting the poor, regardless of color, nationality or creed." [15] Roddy still occupied a shadowy position in the case, but he lacked the support of the boys and the Ministers' Alliance which had originally hired him.

The swift and decisive activities of the ILD presented a *fait accompli* to the NAACP. White did not even know that Taub and Wakefield were in Chattanooga until he read of their speeches in the New York *Times* on April 20. In a belated letter to Stephens he urged him to "communicate with the eight boys . . . [and] urge them that they sign no agreement as to their defense or commit themselves in any way, pending opportunity by us to examine the transcript of the testimony and to determine what action we shall be able to take in this matter." White also supplied Stephens with information on the ILD, emphasizing that it was not just another civil rights group, or even a radical organization, but the legal arm of the Communist Party. For the first time, Stephens acted with dispatch. He convened a meeting of the Ministers' Alliance and told them of the ILD's "Communist leanings." And at Stephens' request, Roddy drove to Birmingham and talked with the boys. It took little persuasion to convince the boys—by now completely confused—that the ILD radicals were a millstone around their

[14] James D. Burton, Partial Report, Scottsboro, Alabama Case, April 23, 1931, in Interracial Commission Papers; Affidavit of Clarence Norris, Andy Wright, etc., April 20, 1931, in ILD Papers.
[15] Chattanooga *Daily Times,* April 23, 1931

necks. They readily signed a statement prepared by Roddy asking the Communists to "lay off." [16]

The Rev. L. P. Whitten, a prominent Negro minister of Chattanooga, released the statement to the press and assured newsmen that "Negro preachers of the South and Negroes in general, are not in sympathy with intervention in the case by the International Labor Defense." The New York radicals wanted only to help their organization, he said, and had no "sincere interest in helping these condemned Negroes." One week later the Ministers' Alliance formally censured the ILD and accused it of being "communistic in its doctrine and the principles which it advocates. . . ." According to the resolution, the Alliance concurred in the ILD's belief in "justice and fair play to all mankind, regardless of race or previous condition," but it believed that this could not be obtained "without a due regard for the principles which are fundamental to the common good of all mankind as embodied in the Constitution of the United States." [17] A relieved Walter White assured NAACP supporters that his organization had things under control.

He could not have been more mistaken, for the attacks by the Chattanooga ministers only goaded the ILD to a more determined effort to wrest the case from "the bosses and the NAACP." Working as a cohesive team, the ILD men in New York and the South developed a two-fold strategy: first, to gain the backing of the defendants, and second, to discredit publicly the NAACP and its supporters. As an attorney, Taub realized that the boys were minors; in the final analysis it was up to their parents to select legal representation. He and Brodsky rounded up as many parents as they could find in Chattanooga and explained what they planned to do if they were able to defend the boys. For Claude and Janie Patterson, Ada Wright, and Mamie Williams Wilcox it was an exhilarating experience. For the first time in their lives, white men were not telling them what to do, but asking their support, on the basis of complete equality. The contrast with the

[16] Walter White to P. A. Stephens, April 20, 1931, in Scottsboro Legal File 1, NAACP Papers; New York *Times*, April 24, 1931, p. 4.
[17] Chattanooga *Daily Times*, April 24, May 1, 1931.

Ministers' Alliance was all the more striking, since neither Roddy nor Stephens had bothered to talk with them about the cases. They readily supported the ILD and signed a statement which read in part: "We are the parents of Haywood Patterson, Andy Wright, Roy Wright and Eugene Williams. . . . Although our sons are minors, we were never consulted as to the retainer of Steve Roddy. . . ." They agreed to place all arrangements in the hands of the ILD. The next day, Mrs. Patterson sent her son, Haywood, a letter which told him that the parents had the International Labor Defense working for all the boys. "I don't want Roddy to have nothing to do with you," she said. All he wanted was money. She added: "Don't let nobody turn you around from what Mama says. . . ." Haywood's father was more explicit: "You will burn sure if you don't let them preachers alone and trust in the International Labor Defense to handle the case." [18]

Brodsky and Taub feared the boys might not heed the letters from home. On the morning of April 24 a special car pulled up in front of Birmingham Jail with Mrs. Williams, Mrs. Wright, and Mr. Patterson.[19] Accompanied by Wakefield and Chamlee, the three parents saw their sons for the first time since the arrests at Paint Rock. In a tearful reunion the boys "enthusiastically endorsed" the ILD once again, apparently as enthusiastically as they had repudiated it the day before. They said they did not "understand" the affidavit they had signed for Roddy April 23. "This statement was obtained without the consent or advice of our parents and we had no way of knowing what to do," the boys said in an affidavit they signed for Wakefield. "We completely repudiate that statement and brand those who obtained it as betrayers of our case." As they turned to leave, Patterson warned Haywood, "Listen son, this is our bunch. You stay by them." [20]

[18] Affidavit of Claude and Janie Patterson, Ada Wright and Mamie Williams, April 23, 1931, in ILD Collection; Chattanooga *Daily Times,* April 24, 1931; New York *Daily Worker,* April 25, 1931.

[19] Mrs. Williams sometimes used the name of her common-law husband, Wilcox. All of the boys but Roy were transferred on April 27 to the death house at Kilby Prison near Montgomery. Montgomery *Advertiser,* April 28, 1931.

[20] Chattanooga *Daily Times,* April 25, 1931; New York *Daily Worker,* April 27, 1931.

The second phase of the ILD struggle was to discredit the NAACP and firmly to fix their organization in the public eye as the only group competent and militant enough to handle the defense. With a flair for the dramatic, the ILD quickly succeeded in capturing public attention in the case by bringing Mrs. Janie Patterson to New York to speak to a "mass rally" in the heart of Harlem. On Saturday afternoon, April 25, Mrs. Patterson spoke to a small but enthusiastic crowd at the corner of Lenox Avenue and 140th Street. She received strong applause when she told them how the "Alabama boss-lynchers" framed her boy and eight others for a crime they did not commit. She urged her listeners to flood Alabama with telegrams to state officials demanding a new trial. New York police stood by and made no attempt to interrupt Mrs. Patterson. When ILD speaker Frank Alexander got on the platform, however, he began shouting that the sentence was a "railroading" unheard of in the history of the country and engineered "by capitalists against children of the working class." Within minutes he had whipped the crowd of two hundred to cheering enthusiasm. Finally, with a shout of defiance at the nervous policemen, he led the crowd in a fast march down Lenox Avenue through the center of Harlem, waving banners and placards: "Death to Lynch Law." "Smash the Scottsboro Frame-up." "Legal Lynching." Between 139th and 138th Streets the parade met a phalanx of policemen, but without hesitation they surged forward. New York's finest met them with flailing nightsticks, directing their blows primarily against those who held the banners and placards. The paraders fought back, screaming and clawing. At first, the police spared women in the mob, but when an enthusiastic female marcher drove her heel into the face of a prone policeman, necessity overcame gentility. After four arrests and numerous head-crackings, the crowd dispersed down the side streets. The next day the *Times* headlined: "Police Clubs Rout 200 Defiant Reds Who Attacked 'Lynch Law' in Alabama." Without a doubt, the ILD had established itself in the public's eye as a participant in the case.[21]

[21] Chicago *Defender*, May 2, 1931; New York *Times*, April 26, 1931, p. 2.

The *Daily Worker* scored a greater coup on April 24 when it reprinted on its front page a photostatic copy of a letter from William Pickens, the NAACP's field secretary in Kansas City. Pickens, a former academic dean at Morgan College in Baltimore, had resigned in 1920 to become director of branches for the NAACP. Egocentric, emotionally volatile and unpredictable, he often lost control of his temper. But he was a great orator in the old style and had a large following. In his letter to the *Daily Worker*, Pickens endorsed the activities of the ILD. Along with the *Daily Worker*, the International Labor Defense had moved "more speedily and effectively than all other agencies put together." He closed with a plea that "every Negro who has intelligence enough to read, to send aid to you [the *Worker*] and to the I.L.D." [22] During this period, the NAACP had assured interested persons that it had things under control. On April 22, for example, White told a member of the Wisconsin legislature that immediately "upon receiving word of the arrest of the men we engaged counsel through representatives of ours in the vicinity. . . . Our attorney made all the necessary motions . . . in order to have the court record in perfect shape for an appeal." [23] Now, after all these assurances, the news was out that the NAACP's field secretary was not even aware of his organization's activity in the case. It was a stunning setback for the Association.

The committee on administration, headed by Mary White Ovington, unanimously reprimanded Pickens for the "unwisdom —and what might be construed as the disloyalty—of your action." Pickens apologized roundly for his mistake and explained that he knew nothing of the national office's activities and had no idea his letter would be used by the *Daily Worker*. Miss Ovington noted acidly that the damage was accomplished and no apology could repair it. In the first crucial weeks of the struggle between the two

[22] G. James Fleming and Christian E. Buckels (eds.), *Who's Who in Colored America, 1950* (Yonkers on Hudson, N.Y.: Christian E. Buckels and Associates, 1950), 416; New York *Daily Worker*, April 24, 1931.

[23] William T. Andrews to G. H. Thornhill, April 15, 1931; Walter White to Benjamin Rubin, April 22, 1931, in Scottsboro Legal File 1, NAACP Papers.

organizations, the ILD used this document effectively to sway un-committed individuals.[24]

There was a certain Machiavellian touch to the Communists' use of the Pickens letter, but their campaign to discredit the NAACP lacked craft or duplicity. It had, as one Negro columnist observed, all the finesse and subtlety of an enraged rhinoceros. As early as April 7, the *Daily Worker* hinted that Roddy and Moody were double-crossing the boys. On April 15 the *Worker* attacked the NAACP by name for the first time. By failing to assert publicly the innocence of the boys, the "Negro reformists of the NAACP" had once again "expose[d] themselves as traitors to the Negro masses and betrayers of the Negro liberation struggle" And with the attack on the ILD by the Ministers' Alliance (which the Communists regarded as a tool of Walter White), the *Daily Worker* began an all out assault on the NAACP "obstructionists" and "pliant Negro preachers" who were helping "lead the boys to the electric chair." [25]

For the Communist Party in the 1930's, May Day was the focus of all public mass demonstrations. Under directives from the Central Committee, demands for the release of the Scottsboro boys became the key slogan of the celebrations throughout the country. At rallies from San Francisco to Boston, "the speakers all dwelt on the Scottsboro Case, exposing its vicious frame-up nature and calling upon the workers to join the fight to save the boys . . ." declared the *Daily Worker*. Huge banners screamed denunciations of the "NAACP Bourgeois Reformists" and "Murderers of Negro and White Workers." In Detroit some of the more zealous Party members suggested that they hang Judge Lynch in effigy, but cooler heads prevailed, noting that this might be misinterpreted by non-Party members. In an interminable editorial which set the pattern for the offensive against the NAACP, the *Daily Worker* accused Walter White and his compatriots of every crime short of

[24] Mary White Ovington to William Pickens, April 30, 1931, in Scottsboro Legal File 1, NAACP Papers. For an example of how the Communists used the letter see the Chicago *Defender*, May 9, 1931.

[25] Pittsburgh *Courier*, May 30, 1931; New York *Daily Worker*, April 25, 1931.

mayhem. The Association, said the *Worker,* considered the " 're-spectability' of this organization in the eyes of the liberal white millionaire and upper class people" more important than "saving the lives of nine children being murdered in Alabama." Above all, the NAACP wished to refrain from offending the " 'dignity' of the Southern white ruling class court which has just heartlessly railroaded these children to death." [26]

The verbal abuse of the ILD and the *Daily Worker,* however, was not half so painful as the barbed questions they asked. Why did the NAACP wait until April 24 to acknowledge any role in the case if they had hired Roddy in late March as they claimed? And, if this were true, why had they retained such an incompetent attorney? The *Worker* noted that, in Scottsboro, Roddy had re-fused to acknowledge that he had received a retainer; that his de-fense was so inadequate he had declined to make a final summa-tion; and that, according to Southern newspapers, he tried to get the boys life imprisonment as a "compromise." There could be only one explanation for such conduct: "treacherous men and women" who were "secret allies of the lynchers" and "ardent ser-vants of the system of capitalist and landlord slavery" controlled the national office of the NAACP.[27]

The sporadic sniping of the Communist Party and its affiliated fronts during the late 1920's had not prepared White and his fel-low officers for the stream of vituperation they received. Against the background of American communism in the spring of 1931, however, the vendetta against the NAACP had an unassailable logic and inevitability about it. The Southern sociologist, Guy Johnson, aptly summarized the philosophical approach of the NAACP and related groups. Theirs was a "bread-and-butter phi-losophy of gradualism, good will, and conciliation," said Johnson. It accepted the status quo for the most part and concentrated on limited goals. The moderates expected nothing sudden and saw no short cuts.[28] The only thing "radical" about the Association

[26] New York *Daily Worker,* May 2, May 5, 1931; Chicago *Defender,* May 9, 1931.
[27] New York *Daily Worker,* May 2, May 5, 1931; Chicago *Defender,* May 9, 1931.
[28] Guy B. Johnson, "Negro Racial Movements and Leadership in the United States," *American Journal of Sociology,* XLIII (1937), 71.

was its opposition to racial proscription, and often this was soft-pedaled in order to work for short-term goals. There was, for example, little or no opposition to American capitalism on the part of NAACP leaders. William Edward Burghardt DuBois, editor of the *Crisis*, readily accepted the Communists' contention that *ideally* there should be a coalition of white and Negro workers. But as DuBois observed, it "is intelligent white labor that today keeps Negroes out of the trades, refuses them decent homes to live in and helps nullify their vote." He expressed the general view of the Association: that Negroes should work with white capitalists who were "willing to curb this blood lust when it interferes with their profits." [29]

The Communist Party, with its revolutionary mystique, spurned the doctrines of gradualism. The Party's official position on the race question was far more complex, however, than the word "radical" implies. In 1922, the Fourth Comintern Congress, meeting in Moscow, discussed America's race problem for the first time, but the final report emphasized the Negro's role in the liberation of Africans from their colonial masters. Party leaders made no effort to formulate a broad and popular program which would capture the allegiance of America's black masses, but for the most part, simply adopted the old Socialist Party's position on race. The Socialists believed that the misfortunes of the Negro were only another phase of the capitalist economy's class exploitation, a problem which would be solved with the destruction of the existing economic order.[30] The Communist-created American Negro Labor Congress convened in Chicago in October of 1925, and Party leaders hailed it as the basis for an "unprecedented mass organization." In fact it was little more than a paper organization which maintained a shadowy existence until it was laid to rest in 1930.[31]

[29] William Edward Burghardt DuBois, "Postscript," *Crisis*, XXVIII (1931), 315.

[30] Theodore Draper, *The Roots of American Communism* (New York: Viking Press, 1957), 192, 387. In his first person account of American communism written in 1927, James O'Neal mentioned the race question only once. O'Neal and G. A. Werner, *American Communism: A Critical Analysis of its Origins, Development and Programs* (New York: The Rands Book Store, 1927), 238.

[31] Robert Minor, "The First Negro Workers Congress," *Workers Monthly*, V (December, 1925), 73; James W. Ford, *The Negro and the Democratic Front* (New

The Sixth Comintern Congress meeting in Moscow in 1928, and the Tenth Plenum of the Executive Committee a year later, signaled a new direction for the American Communist Party and outlined the theoretical structure for all efforts at Negro recruitment during the next seven years. At the Congress, a thirty-two-member "Negro Commission" (containing only seven Americans) concluded that American Negroes constituted an oppressed nation dwelling within the heart of the Deep South. Consequently, the Commission decided that the only solution to the American "race problem" was the secession of all black people from the United States. "The Communist party must stand . . . for the establishment of a Negro republic in the Black Belt." The architect of this resolution was Otto Kuusinen, a Finnish-born theoretician of Stalin, who had never met more than a handful of Negroes in his entire life. Privately, many of the American delegates regarded the program as so much nonsense. The American Communist Party was divided into a number of factions, however, each anxious to gain the important support of the Comintern (and Stalin). In the context of that struggle, accepting a fanciful scheme such as the Southern "black republic" was a small price to pay.[32]

The impetus for the revolutionary histrionics of 1931 had come in 1929 when the Comintern Executive Committee, completely dominated by Joseph Stalin, announced the "Third Period," or ultra-left shift of world communism. According to this new Stalinist theory, international capitalism's precarious postwar stabilization had ended, and its final contradictions would lead soon to worldwide depression and mass unemployment. Within this context, the duty of the Communist parties was to take the offensive in demonstrations, strikes, and—ultimately—revolution. The main tactic should be to smash the Social Democrats and other

York: International Publishers, 1938) , 81–83. That year it became the League of Struggle for Negro Rights.
    [32] Theodore Draper, *American Communism and Soviet Russia: The Formative Period* (New York: Viking Press, 1960) , 345–51; Irving Howe and Lewis Coser, *The American Communist Party: A Critical History* (Boston: Beacon Press, 1957) , 206–207; Jay Lovestone, "The Sixth World Congress of the Communist International," *Communist*, VII (1928) , 659–75.

leftist parties by creating a "united front from below" [33] while charging them with "social fascism." Such blatantly Fascist parties as the National Socialists of Germany were a secondary threat and could be crushed once the "pseudo-leftists" had been destroyed. In the United States, the Communist Party dutifully echoed the new line: American capitalism had entered its death throes and the masses were becoming increasingly militant and radical. Only the siphoning of the worker's strength into pseudo-radical groups from the NAACP leftward to the Socialist Party could postpone the inevitable collapse of the capitalist economy. These "social fascists" represented the greatest threat to the revolution. Irving Howe has noted that the result was high tragedy in Germany when the Party allowed Hitler to seize power. In the United States it bordered on low comedy.[34] Between 1929 and 1931 Party publications accused Norman Thomas of every sin from strike-breaking to collusion with Southern lynchers.[35] Robert Minor observed a curious similarity between the NAACP and the Socialist Party. He pointed out that Norman Thomas had increasingly cooperated with the Association. This was to be expected. "Social-Fascism tends to concentration in the effort to head off the rising movement of the Negro masses under the lash of the economic crisis and the race persecution that goes with it." [36]

The revolutionary offensive had seemed almost ludicrous when promulgated shortly after the election of Herbert Hoover, but the deepening depression of 1930 and 1931 seemed to justify the wildest predictions of the Comintern. The voice of American communism became shrill with the tone of the true believer. Party leaders easily convinced themselves that the Negro, as the most dis-

[33] In other words, by repudiating the Social Democratic leadership and drawing its membership into the Communist parties.

[34] Germany's Communist Party spurned all Social Democratic efforts to form a united front of anti-Fascist groups. Party chief Ernst Thaelmann explained this strategy in the slogan of 1933: "After Hitler—Our Turn!" Howe, *The American Communist Party*, 186–87. See also, Hugh Seton-Watson's *From Lenin to Khrushchev: The History of World Communism* (2nd ed.; New York: Frederick A. Praeger, Inc., 1960), 107–10.

[35] See the New York *Daily Worker*, August 27, 1930, for a particularly scurrilous attack.

[36] Robert Minor, "The Negro and His Judases," *Communist*, X (1931), 639.

advantaged and impoverished group in the country (and with the least stake in the capitalist system), should flock to the red banner. When the slogan of "self-determinism" failed to rally the black masses, the Central Committee soft-pedaled this ultimate demand and concentrated on short-term concrete issues. Particularly, the Party publicly purged itself of all "petty bourgeois" anti-Negro prejudice. The highlight of this housecleaning came with the public trial of August Yokinen, a Finnish immigrant who insulted a group of Negro comrades at a Communist dance in New York City. On March 1, 1931, before an audience of more than fifteen hundred, a "worker's jury" of fourteen voted to expel Yokinen from the Party. The flood of favorable publicity which the Communists received from the Negro press and community both surprised and heartened Party leaders. In large part, it was the Yokinen trial which laid the groundwork for the Scottsboro Case.[37]

The organization selected to lead the defense of the Scottsboro boys and the attack against the NAACP was the International Labor Defense. The Communist Party had organized the ILD in 1925 to counteract the activities of such extra-legal organizations as the Ku Klux Klan. From 1925 to 1931, the ILD waged campaigns to save Nicola Sacco and Bartolomeo Vanzetti and to force the release of convicted trade-unionists Tom Mooney and Warren Billings. It also supported about one hundred "class war prisoners" during the late 1920's by sending them a small monthly allowance. The International Labor Defense had never handled a prominent case in the South, but it periodically expressed concern over the legal disabilities of American Negroes.[38] ILD officers professed

[37]Howe, *The American Communist Party*, 209-11. For a Party account of the episode, see *Race Hatred on Trial* (New York: Workers' Library Publishers, 1931), *passim*. Earl Browder declared: "I think that we can say that without the prelude of the Yokinen case the Scottsboro Case would never have been heard of." The public trial of Yokinen "can be taken as marking the sharp turn which the Party began toward the struggle on specific concrete issues." Earl Browder, "To the Masses," *Communist*, X (1931), 800.

[38]Draper, *American Communism and Soviet Russia*, 181–82; Ralph Johnson Bunche, "Extended Memorandum on the Programs, Ideologies, Tactics, and Achievements of Negro Betterment and Interracial Organizations," 1940, p. 708, in Myrdal Collection, New York Public Library, 135th Street Branch. Wilson Record

independence from the Communist Party, but this was only a convenient fiction which aided in the recruitment of prominent non-Communists to the national committee.[39] From the time of its creation the ILD maintained close ties with the International Red Aid, a Comintern front established in Moscow in 1922. And no non-Communist ever attained a position of leadership within the organization.[40]

The ILD, as a supposedly independent organization, was ideally suited for the task of leadership in the case. Even as Taub and Brodsky struggled to wrest the case from the NAACP, in a posture of reasonableness, Labor Defense leaders called for "the broadest united front struggle" which would bring together "every person willing to fight in the defense of the boys." There were, to be sure, a few restrictions in the fine print. All who entered the coalition had to understand clearly that the Communist Party was more than an equal member. As the vanguard of the revolutionary proletariat, it would inevitably lead in the struggle to free the nine boys. Secondly, all who joined had to "throw off their blind faith in the ruling class courts of law. . . ." With pointed reference to the NAACP, the *Daily Worker* noted: "So deeply ingrained is the superstitious respect for the paraphernalia of capitalist class government that . . . they will kiss the rope that hangs their brothers, if only the rope is blessed by a ruling class judge." Appeals to the ruling class could not save the boys; "only the actions of hundreds of thousands in a mass movement of protest" would suffice.[41]

The Communist leadership knew (as did Walter White) that such preconditions completely excluded the NAACP and other non-Communist organizations. In keeping with the dogma of the

---

asserts that the ILD displayed a special interest in cases involving Negroes from 1925, but he does not cite any cases earlier than Scottsboro. Record, *The Negro and the Communist Party*, 34.

[39] Such respected non-Communists as Eugene V. Debs and California churchman Robert Whitaker sat on the first national committee. Draper, *American Communism and Soviet Russia*, 180–81.

[40] New York *Daily Worker*, August 29, October 11, 1931. William L. Patterson, executive secretary of the ILD from 1932 to 1936, was the Communist Party candidate for mayor of New York City in 1932. New York *Times*, September 8, 1932, p. 2.

[41] New York *Daily Worker*, April 25, April 29, 1931.

"ultra-left period" this was to be a "united front from below" under the unquestioned leadership of the Communist Party. No
revolutionary movement could hope to succeed by collaborating
with bourgeois and petty bourgeois elements like the NAACP. In
fact, at the same time that the Labor Defense called for a broad
united front, the *Daily Worker's* accounts of the case repeatedly
charged that the NAACP collaborated with the Southern lynchers.[42]
To White and his associates, therefore, the talk of a coalition was
unprincipled hypocrisy. As Herbert J. Seligmann, the Association's publicity director, asked, how was it possible "to work with
people who ignore a twenty-one-year record of pioneering, who
seek to discredit work done, who accuse the NAACP . . . of
'treason,' alliance with the Ku Klux Klan, 'lyncher boss' tactics
and anything else they see fit?" The Communists had a ready answer for this argument. Joseph Pass, an ILD spokesman, insisted
that it was the NAACP which had instituted attacks on his organization. "We did not even reply to the NAACP attacks," asserted
Pass, "until it became a matter of supreme importance, and the
Negro press demanded material." [43]

Many Negroes were inclined to agree. When the Pittsburgh
Courier, the Association's strongest supporter, defended the
NAACP's refusal to cooperate with the ILD and remarked that
Secretary White would announce his plans in "due time," the
Courier's readers showed a noticeable lack of both confidence and
patience. The Chicago *Defender,* America's largest Negro weekly,
charged that the NAACP had unnecessarily dragged its feet in the
boys' defense and urged Negroes everywhere to "put aside division
and bickering and join the effort" for a new trial under the leadership of the ILD, "an organization distinguished for its love of
justice, though unpopular among the wealth and power of the
land. . . ." The Florida *Sentinel,* another Negro weekly, admitted

[42] William W. Weinstone, "The XI Plenum of the Executive Committee of the
Comintern. Extracts from Report to the 13th Plenum of the C.C.C.P. U.S.A.,"
Communist, X (1931), 771-96; New York *Daily Worker,* April 15, April 25, April 29,
1931.

[43] Letter by Herbert J. Seligmann, in *New Republic,* LXVII (1931), 155; letter
by Joseph Pass, in *New Republic,* LXVII (1931), 75.

that occasionally the Communists' words were "ill-timed and carelessly hurled," but thought that "the men seem to be sincere and wholehearted" in their efforts to aid the Scottsboro boys and "all workers without regard to color." The influential Baltimore *Afro-American*, though it refused outright endorsement of the ILD, chided the NAACP for attacking friends of the Negro.[44]

Roy Wilkins, editor of the Kansas City *Call*, was a staunch supporter of the NAACP, but he finally wrote White in exasperation, not over the Association's refusal to coalesce with the Communists, but its failure to defend itself and present to the nation the reasons for this decision. In the month since the ILD had become involved, said Wilkins, the Communist organization had flooded the Negro newspapers of the country with reports attacking the NAACP's activity in the case and espousing its own role and ideology. "In all this time, mind you, not a word, confidential or otherwise from the national office reached the Negro press as to the association's activity in the case." Wilkins noted that it was not good policy to try cases in the newspapers, but felt that "where the organization is directly dependent upon public opinion for its prestige and its funds, it is not a bad idea to let that public have an inkling of what is going on." As a result of its inaction, the NAACP stood a good chance of losing the support of the Negro press, Wilkins argued. He reviewed the situation by pointing out that Roscoe Dunjee, editor of the *Black Dispatch* of Oklahoma City, had given full support to the Labor Defense along with the Chicago *Defender;* the Atlanta *World,* the New York *Amsterdam News,* and the Baltimore *Afro-American* had all cooled appreciably toward the NAACP; and the organization's strongest supporters, the Pittsburgh *Courier,* the St. Louis *Liberator,* and his own weekly, were completely confused.[45]

Following Wilkins' letter, White moved to correct some of the

[44] Pittsburgh *Courier,* April 14, April 19, 1931; Chicago *Defender,* May 9, 1931; Florida *Sentinel,* quoted in Minor, "The Negro and His Judases," 633; Baltimore *Afro-American,* May 16, 1931.

[45] Roy Wilkins to Walter White, May 15, 1931, in Scottsboro Legal File 2, NAACP Papers. Wilkins resigned later in the year to become assistant secretary of the NAACP. Fleming, *Who's Who in Colored America, 1950,* 554.

Association's errors by issuing periodic reports to the press on the case, but he was convinced that the NAACP's most important objectives should be to gain undisputed control of the case and to mobilize the support of prominent white Southerners. With these goals uppermost in his mind, he decided that his first action should be to hire a first-rate attorney for the boys. In keeping with his strategy, this would have to be a white Alabamian, preferably a moderate on the race issue, but not necessarily a radical. Roddy was out. Although the Association had to defend him because it claimed to have hired him in the first place, White and other officers had grave doubts about the Chattanooga attorney from the outset.[46] The initial choice was Congressman George Huddleston. Alabamians regarded Huddleston as a "fiery left-winger," but this was primarily because of his efforts to obtain direct federal relief. White had his doubts. As he noted to a Negro friend in Alabama, "A great many people are liberal on topics affecting the white people, but . . . are far from liberal when our problem enters in." [47] Further investigation confirmed his fears. When a representative of the American Civil Liberties Union (ACLU) interviewed Huddleston in his office and suggested a retainer, the congressman went into a tirade. He shouted that he did not care "whether they [the defendants] are innocent or guilty." The fact that the nine were found riding on the same freight car with two white women was enough for him. "You can't understand how we southern gentlemen feel about this question of relationship between negro men and white women," he explained.[48]

[46] As early as April 20, William T. Andrews concluded that Roddy was hopelessly incompetent. Memorandum by William T. Andrews to Walter White, April 20, 1931, in Scottsboro Legal File 1, NAACP Papers.

[47] Thomas Lunsford Stokes, *Chip Off My Shoulder* (Princeton: Princeton University Press, 1940) , 280; Walter White to Charles A. J. McPherson, April 29, 1931, in Scottsboro Legal File 1, NAACP Papers. Huddleston was extremely sympathetic to those who were suffering from the effects of the Depression, both black and white. See his testimony in U.S. Congress, Senate, Subcommittee of the Committee on Manufactures, *Hearings, Federal Aid for Unemployment Relief*, 72nd Cong., 1st Sess., pp. 244–45. But basically he was neither a racial nor an economic radical as he clearly indicated in a speech in 1933, Birmingham *Post*, July 13, 1933.

[48] Confidential Memorandum of Hollace Ransdell, May 7, 1931, in Scottsboro Legal File 1, NAACP Papers.

Charles A. J. McPherson, the head of Birmingham's NAACP chapter, suggested to White that a more likely candidate would be Roderick Beddow, the junior member of Fort, Beddow, and Ray, the best criminal law firm in Birmingham. There were a number of things about Beddow's background that appealed to White. While the Birmingham attorney was not a racial equalitarian (at least publicly), he did not have any particularly strong prejudices against Negroes. On one occasion he had walked through a howling mob in order to defend a Negro charged with attacking a white man.[49] Moreover, no one doubted his abilities. A prominent member of the Alabama Commission on Interracial Cooperation described him as the "shrewdest and perhaps the most successful criminal lawyer in our city [Birmingham]." Some detractors charged that his success was based upon his ability to fix juries and intimidate witnesses, noted C. B. Glenn, Birmingham's public schools' superintendent. "Personally," said Glenn, "I only know that a number have remarked to me if ever they should be so unfortunate as to commit murder, they would want to employ him to defend them." [50]

Once the NAACP's executive committee had decided that Beddow would be the best attorney, White moved quickly. On Wednesday, May 13, he traveled to Birmingham. He found Beddow and the other members of the firm polite and friendly, but noncommittal. Beddow, for example, pointed out that there was still some question as to who controlled the case. They could not commit themselves unless they could be certain that the Communists were completely excluded. White was convinced that the boys would listen to reason once they clearly understood their situation. After a lengthy interview with several local Negro ministers, he visited the boys in Kilby Prison in Montgomery. He spoke briefly and warned them that the Communists were using the case

---

[49] Charles A. J. McPherson to Walter White, May 6, 1931, in Scottsboro Legal File 1, NAACP Papers; Owen, *Story of Alabama*, IV, 471–72. In 1933, Beddow was discussed as a possible candidate for governor of Alabama, Birmingham *Post*, August 18, 1933.

[50] C. B. Glenn to Will Alexander, May 7, 1931, in Interracial Commission Papers.

for propaganda purposes. Their best hope lay with the NAACP, White told them. He promised that his organization would hire the best attorney in Alabama and would argue their case to the United States Supreme Court if necessary. Willie Roberson, Ozie Powell, Clarence Norris, and Charley Weems readily signed the affidavit he proffered. Andy Wright and Haywood Patterson said they wished to write their parents before they made any decision. Olen Montgomery and Eugene Williams stuck with the International Labor Defense.[51] With this affidavit, White once more talked with Beddow, who promised him that he would give the matter careful consideration after he had a chance to read the trial transcripts.

Back in New York, White issued his first lengthy public statement on the case. He told newsmen that the NAACP had retained "one of the most eminent criminal lawyers in the state of Alabama." Roddy and Moody, he explained, remained in the case, but under the close supervision of a new chief attorney. White admitted that several of the boys' parents seemed to have thrown in with the ILD, but he explained: "It should be remembered that the boys and their parents are humble folk and have had few opportunities for knowledge. They have been confused by the conflicting statements made to them." This condescending statement would later return to haunt White in his efforts to gain the support of the parents. As for the International Labor Defense, White insisted that there was "no objection to Communists . . . aiding in the defense of the boys . . ." but they had been so abusive in several telegrams to the sheriff and governor that they had inflamed public opinion against the defendants. Besides, the Association could not "in any way cooperate with the Communists who have vilified the NAACP, [and] accused it in documents submitted for the signature of the boys' parents of being traitorous. . . ."[52]

Less than twenty-four hours after White issued his statement,

[51] White said that only after pleading with local ministers could he talk even one of them into going to the prison with him. They were all "scared to death," he noted with disgust. Walter White to National Headquarters, May 15, 1931, in Scottsboro Legal File 1, NAACP Papers.
[52] Pittsburgh *Courier*, May 16, 1931.

the ILD rushed a carload of relatives to Kilby Prison. Once again, they succeeded in swinging all the boys against the NAACP and supporting the International Labor Defense. The parents also attacked White and the NAACP for trying to "persuade our children to disregard our advice in this matter." As they left, they warned their children "against the methods of Walter White and his preacher and Ku Klux lawyer allies." Once again, the NAACP was cast in the role of defender with no one to defend.[53]

White was discouraged but not defeated by the action of the parents. More determined than ever, he sent William Pickens (by now returned to the good graces of the national office) on a trip south to both Chattanooga and Birmingham. There were three things that had to be done, he told Pickens. First, remove the parents from the influence of the ILD; second, cement the agreement with Beddow; and third (and this was necessary to insure the retention of Fort, Beddow, and Ray), gain the firm support of the boys. In Birmingham, the interview with Beddow went well. Although the attorney refused to say definitely that he would take the case, he volunteered to go with Pickens to talk with the boys. On Sunday, May 31, the two men made the familiar trip to the prison. Pickens spoke to them first and he spoke bluntly. If you are ever to gain your freedom, he said, it will be because of the actions of the courts and "entirely in spite of the methods and present activities of those who were here and made you sign up again the other day." The ILD had "bewildered and amazed your poor parents and relatives; they have paid their fares to New York and other parts of the country, have put them on platforms and in parades, all for purposes of their own, and not for the primary purpose of keeping you out of the electric chair." However much their inflammatory speeches might help the Communists, Pickens told them, it had a negative effect on their case in Alabama.[54]

[53] New York *Daily Worker*, May 16, May 19, 1931. Clarence Norris later claimed that he had not signed the ILD affidavit.

[54] William Pickens to Walter White, May 31, 1931, in Scottsboro Legal File 1, NAACP Papers.

Beddow stood quietly until Pickens had finished speaking. For the next twenty minutes he closely questioned the boys. The main thing that concerned him, he said, was the testimony of Clarence Norris and Roy Wright declaring that they saw the other boys rape the two girls. Norris and Wright explained that the solicitor had hinted they might get off with a prison sentence if they would implicate the other boys; otherwise they would "certainly be convicted and perhaps lynched." Beddow, familiar with the techniques of Alabama's state attorneys in such cases, was convinced by this explanation. He told them earnestly: "If I thought you were guilty I would not for anything take your cases." He explained that he violently opposed "black men attacking white women, or . . . white men attacking black women, or . . . any man attacking a woman." But having read the records carefully and talked with the boys, "I frankly believe you innocent," he said. Several of the boys volunteered to sign another affidavit, but Beddow told them, "We are not going to ask you to sign anything. . . ." What was the use of signing first one paper and then another, he declared. "I will appear in court for those who want me to defend them." [55]

Beddow told the boys that they would win a new trial and acquittal, but his assurances disguised many misgivings in his own mind. When he first read the transcripts, he told Dr. McPherson with disgust that it was one of the most poorly tried cases he had ever seen. "The lawyers, judge, and everybody else who had anything to do with [it] . . . seem to have been frighten[ed] to death." [56] Two days before he interviewed the boys, Beddow telegraphed White that Roddy's inept handling of the case would make a successful appeal extremely difficult if not impossible. The only hope he saw was to depend upon the Supreme Court's decision in the Arkansas riot cases and to argue that the defendants did not get a fair trial because of the community's hostility. If that

[55] Roderick Beddow to Walter White, June 3, 1931; William Pickens to Walter White, May 31, 1931, in Scottsboro Legal Files 1 and 2, NAACP Papers.

[56] Charles A. J. McPherson to Walter White, May 18, 1931, in Scottsboro Legal File 1, NAACP Papers.

failed, as a last resort they could appeal to Governor Miller for a commutation of the sentences to life imprisonment.[57]

Despite Beddow's misgivings, his decision to enter the case elated both White and Pickens. They both knew that their success in retaining eminent Alabama counsel would be a powerful weapon against the ILD. Unfortunately for the NAACP, however, the Birmingham law firm brought along with its prestige a number of disadvantages. From the outset, for example, Beddow made it clear, $5,000 fee or not, his firm would take the case only through the Alabama Supreme Court and then to the governor for clemency if this should fail. While he might be willing to raise the fair trial issue in a federal appeal, his firm could not foresee raising the touchy question of the exclusion of Negroes from Jackson County's jury rolls. An even greater handicap was the aversion of Fort, Beddow, and Ray to any publicity. White had hoped to combat ILD propaganda by publicizing the hiring of Beddow, but Judge William E. Fort, the senior member of the firm, vetoed this plan. Let the Communists "blow off and wear themselves out," he argued, "but give no ground for controversy with them." Only after a long and earnest plea from Dr. McPherson did the three men agree to approve a brief statement acknowledging that they had been retained by the NAACP.[58]

The greatest cross that Walter White had to bear in the late spring of 1931, however, was one he could not even publicly acknowledge: Stephen Roddy. James D. Burton, Alabama's field secretary for the Commission on Interracial Cooperation, observed dryly that it was difficult to tell which was a greater problem for Roddy: lying or drinking. In neither case did he seem to be able to stop once he had started. On April 22, the enterprising Chattanooga attorney told Burton that he had less than a week to file a petition of appeal in the Circuit Court, and unless he received another $100 immediately, he would withdraw the petition he had prepared for the boys. When this bit of intimidation failed

[57] Roderick Beddow to Walter White, May 29, 1931, in Scottsboro Legal File 2, NAACP Papers.

[58] Charles A. J. McPherson to Walter White, June 9, 1931, in Scottsboro Legal File 2, NAACP Papers; Pittsburgh *Courier*, June 20, 1931.

to move the cautious Burton, he began putting pressure on the NAACP.[59] The leverage that Roddy held over White and his organization was that he was the attorney of record, and the circuit judge and the Alabama Supreme Court might be inclined to accept his petition of appeal. As soon as he realized the power he held, he began to exploit it fully. Initially, White offered Roddy and Moody $300 each to handle the case until it was accepted by the Alabama Supreme Court. Roddy, who had more grandiose ideas, demanded $600 immediately. When White refused, he reluctantly acquiesced in the smaller fee. In the early stages of the case, White sent Roddy $24 to pay his secretary, Mrs. Betty Thompson, for copying the transcripts of the first trials. Roddy pocketed the check and then blandly insisted that this was for "expenses"; they still owed Mrs. Thompson.[60] Moody, only slightly less cantankerous, told White that he planned to withdraw. "I have done work worth [a] $1,000 fee." [61] Only the careful negotiations of Beddow in Birmingham and Stephens in Chattanooga averted the withdrawal of both men. As Beddow later observed, when he first met Roddy, the Chattanooga attorney "stated then that the utmost thing in his mind was to defend himself personally, as the Communists had made a personal attack on him. Subsequent to that he began to demand fees for everything he did." [62]

The lack of commitment of both Roddy and Moody was clearly shown when Judge Hawkins fixed May 7, 1931, as the day for arguments on the motions for a new trial.

Judge Hawkins fixed May 7 as the day for arguments on the motions for a new trial. Despite specific instructions by White on

---

[59] Roddy early decided that the Chattanooga Ministers' Alliance did not have the financial resources to support him.

[60] James Burton, Partial Report, Scottsboro, Alabama Case, April 25, 1931, in Interracial Commission Papers; Walter White to National NAACP Headquarters, May 3, 1931; Mrs. Betty Thompson to Walter White, February 23, 1932; Walter White to Stephen Roddy, February 26, 1932, in Scottsboro Legal Files 1 and 4, NAACP Papers.

[61] Milo Moody to Walter White, May 20, 1931, in Scottsboro Legal File 1, NAACP Papers. In fact, he had done next to nothing.

[62] Roderick Beddow to Walter White, January 29, 1932, in Scottsboro Legal File 4, NAACP Papers.

this point, Roddy did not go down to Scottsboro and Moody remained in his office all day. Deaths in the families of two courtroom officials forced two postponements, but had it not been for this, the ILD might have won control of the case by default.[63] With Fort, Beddow, and Ray in charge of the case, White hoped for more competent defense efforts, but he was soon disappointed. Even after the Birmingham firm accepted a retainer of $500, it preferred to remain as inconspicuous as possible, leaving the lower court proceedings to the exasperatingly unreliable Roddy and Moody.

The first direct confrontation between the ILD and the NAACP came on Friday, June 5, when Judge Hawkins opened court at Fort Payne, thirty miles southeast of Scottsboro, to hear the request for a new trial. As soon as the hearing opened shortly after 10 A.M., the two sets of attorneys asked Hawkins for a ruling as to which group of lawyers should take precedence in the case. Roddy spoke up and declared that he would work with any reputable attorney "in this territory," but—and he paused and looked balefully at Brodsky—he did not need any "assistance from New York." Judge Hawkins, who was not particularly enamored of any of the defense attorneys, dismissed Roddy's remarks as irrelevant. The matter of counsel was something the defendants would have to settle for themselves, he said. The court did not care whether the defense had one, or a dozen, or a hundred lawyers. The faces of Brodsky and Chamlee mirrored their relief, for they had feared that the court might exclude them because they had not taken part in the initial proceedings. James Burton, who observed the proceedings for the Interracial Commission, noted that Roddy looked "scrambled" when the judge made his decision.[64] Roddy was so unnerved that he failed to question any of the witnesses at the hearing. Chamlee interrogated all those who took the stand.

[63] Chattanooga *Daily Times,* May 21, 1931. The absence of Roddy and Moody prematurely elated ILD attorney Brodsky, as he believed this meant the NAACP had capitulated. "Chamlee only attorney appearing. No other lawyer or organization," he wired to his office in New York. Joseph Brodsky to George Maurer, May 7, 1931, in ILD Papers.

[64] James D. Burton, Report Number 4 on the Scottsboro, Alabama Case, June 8, 1931, in Interracial Commission Papers; Chattanooga *Daily Times,* June 5, 1931.

In the request for a new trial, both the ILD and NAACP attorneys contended that the trial, conducted with a mob outside, deprived the defendants of their rights under the due process clause of the Fourteenth Amendment to the Constitution. During the trials at Scottsboro, Roddy had managed to insert into the record proof that Patterson's jury had heard the victory celebration when the first jury brought in its guilty verdict. Chamlee questioned the third jury which had brought in convictions against five of the defendants in an effort to show that they had been influenced by the mob-like atmosphere. Members of the jury readily admitted hearing some "hollering" and "clapping of hands," but, to a man, they insisted that this had not affected their deliberations.[65] Judge Hawkins refused to allow Chamlee to ask the jurors if racial prejudice had entered into their decisions.

In addition to the questioning of witnesses, Chamlee and Brodsky submitted a sheaf of affidavits in support of their motion. Hawkins hurriedly glanced through the statements, but he did not read them aloud; their contents were known by almost everyone in the judicial district. They were statements dealing with the character of Ruby Bates and Victoria Price, signed by ten residents of Chattanooga's Negro community. Some of the signers were lower class Negroes who frequented the gin mills of Chattanooga's less exclusive neighborhoods; others were members of the city's black bourgeoisie. They were unanimous in their evaluation of the characters of the two girls. McKinley Pitts of Chattanooga said he had seen Victoria "embracing negro men in dances in negro houses" and heard her talk to negro men "in the most foul and vulgar language and ask colored men the size of his [sic] privates. . . ." On one occasion, he said, Ruby Bates bragged she could "take five negroes in one night and not hurt her. . . ." Oliver Love, who ran a Negro boardinghouse in Chattanooga, admitted that, because he needed the money, he had allowed Victoria Price to use a room in his house as a base of operation for prostitution. Asberry Clay, a friend of Love, said that a white man had ap-

[65] *Powell v. Alabama*, 287 U.S. 45, Tr. pp. 51, 132–40.

proached her at the boardinghouse about going out and she declined because it was "negro night." [66]

State attorneys had earlier learned the substance of the imputations against the two girls. On May 28, the *Jackson County Sentinel* reported that ILD defense lawyers were in Chattanooga collecting affidavits which slanderously attacked the two girls. According to Editor Campbell, "One negro buck whose name appeared on the affidavits backed completely up and admitted he was in the workhouse for selling liquor at the time it was alleged these girls 'entertained' negro men in Chattanooga." And he emphasized that "THIS WAS A NEGRO BOOTLEGGER testifying as to the character of two white girls who had been brutally raped by nine negroes. . . ." On the day before the hearing, the *Sentinel* published a front page editorial attacking the "filthy affidavits made by Chattanooga wenches and negro men. . . ." These had been gathered and presented by "one Chamlee, a white lawyer in Chattanooga employed by the Communist party. . . ." It was inconceivable that such a "filthy attack upon two white girls and supplied by negroes of the lowest class would be given credency by anyone. . . ." [67]

Assistant Solicitor Thompson also charged in a statement to the press that he and Detective Jack Neil of the Chattanooga Police Department visited two signers of the affidavits and asked them if they were absolutely certain they made the right identification. The Negroes, whom Thompson described as of an "ignorant class," retracted their earlier statements and said that Chamlee had paid them fifty cents for placing their marks on the affidavits.[68] At the hearing, Solicitor Bailey filed several counter-affidavits. Three officials of the Margaret Mill in Huntsville insisted that Victoria had been employed at their plant during part of the time she was alleged to have been in Chattanooga. And they insisted that Ruby "bore a splendid character." They were not so unequivocal about

[66] *Ibid.*, 58–61.

[67] Scottsboro *Jackson County Sentinel*, May 28, June 4, 1931.

[68] Chattanooga *Daily Times*, June 6, 1931, January 10, 1932. Chamlee readily acknowledged giving them fifty cents, but he insisted this was for carfare to make the trip to his office.

Mrs. Price. Her character seemed to be good, but she had "possibly had a fight or two." [69]

During the trials at Scottsboro the state's attorneys had pictured the two girls as representatives of the flower of Southern womanhood. As the vile imputations against Ruby and Victoria spread through the little town, anger grew against the "scalawag" Chamlee and his Jewish carpetbagger associate, Joseph Brodsky. When Judge Hawkins adjourned the hearings shortly after 11:30 A.M., Brodsky gathered up his documents and pushed them into his briefcase. As he turned to leave the courtroom, a spectator walked to within a foot of him, saying, "It's about time you left town, or it might not stay too healthy for you." "Tell it to the judge," snapped Brodsky. Outside, about fifty hard-eyed men quickly gathered around the two lawyers. From the edge of the crowd, a grizzled mountaineer reached out and touched Brodsky's shoulder. "The best thing you can do is to get up the road right away," he said softly. Within five minutes, Brodsky and Chamlee were beyond Fort Payne's city limits. Despite his satisfaction at the outcome of the hearing, Brodsky admitted a few hours later that he had never been more frightened in his life.[70]

Although the citizens of Fort Payne chivalrously expelled Chamlee and Brodsky for their base imputations, the hapless Mrs. Price and Miss Bates came under attack from two other sources: the American Civil Liberties Union (ACLU) and the Commission on Interracial Cooperation (CIC). Three weeks after the completion of the trials, the ACLU's Executive Director, Forrest Bailey, asked Miss Hollace Ransdell to check the background of the two young ladies. At this time, Miss Ransdell lived in Louisville, Kentucky. As a devotee of many liberal causes, she occasionally performed special assignments for the Civil Liberties Union while she supported herself as a free-lance writer. Bailey encour-

---

[69] *Powell* v. *Alabama*, 287 U.S. 45, Tr. p. 143; James D. Burton, Report Number 4 on the Scottsboro, Alabama Case, June 8, 1931, in Interracial Commission Papers; New York *Times*, June 6, 1931, p. 6.

[70] James D. Burton, Report Number 4 on the Scottsboro, Alabama Case, June 8, 1931, in Interracial Commission Papers; Birmingham *News*, June 5, June 15, 1931; Joseph Brodsky to George Maurer, June 5, 1931, in ILD Papers.

aged her to go to Scottsboro and Huntsville and "saturate" herself with the case. In view of her sympathies, he cautioned: "It is important that you should keep your mind open and not allow yourself to be swayed either way by anything else than an impartial survey of the facts.[71]

In 1931, Huntsville, Alabama, depended heavily on the seven cotton mills scattered around the city limits. The largest, Lincoln Mill, had four separate units, employing more than 1,000 workers, and—along with the Merrimac, the Lowe, and the Dallas—was owned by outside capitalists. Local entrepreneurs controlled and operated the three smallest plants, West Huntsville, Helen Knitting Mill, and Margaret Spinning Mill. Not surprisingly, they were the most antiquated and paid the lowest wages. It was in the Margaret Mill that Victoria and Ruby worked before the trial and afterwards. In a shabby, run-down section of Huntsville near the mill, Hollace Ransdell interviewed the two principals in the celebrated Scottsboro Case. The two girls had been questioned by numerous people and they hospitably welcomed the tall, taciturn Miss Ransdell.[72]

Victoria lived with her mother, Mrs. Ella Price, in a small unpainted shack down a rain-gutted alley. The older Mrs. Price had fallen down the back steps two years before, permanently injuring her arm, and she was dependent on her daughter. Victoria, who had been married twice, readily admitted having left her last husband. He "lay around on me drunk with canned heat," she explained. Mrs. Price was a "lively, talkative young woman, cocky in manner and not bad to look at," Miss Ransdell observed. Obviously delighted by the attention suddenly showered on her, she readily described the rape "with zest, slipping in many vivid and earthy phrases." Details which the local press had described as "unprintable" or "unspeakable" she gave "off-hand in her usual chatty manner, quite unabashed by their significance." She insisted that the boys should be electrocuted for abusing her. Between carefully

[71] Forrest Bailey to Hollace Ransdell, April 29, 1931, in Scottsboro Legal File 1, NAACP Papers.
[72] Ransdell, "Report on the Scottsboro Case," 12–14.

aimed spurts of snuff, she told how she had completed her first shift in the mills at thirteen. During the 1920's, working a full week, she made as much as twenty cents an hour on the twelve hour night shift. But in 1931, the Margaret Mill reduced wages to $1.20 per day for three days, every other week. "You know nobody can't live on wages like that," she told her noncommittal listener, denying, however, that she had ever supplemented these meager earnings by part-time prostitution.[73]

Miss Ransdell heard a different story as she drove to Ruby's house. Her unofficial guide in Huntsville, Deputy Sheriff Walter Sanders, explained confidentially that he didn't bother Victoria since she was a "quiet prostitute, and didn't go rarin' around cuttin' up in public and walkin' the streets solicitin', but just took men quiet-like." There had been one unpleasant incident, he said, when a Chattanooga housewife learned of her husband's visits to Victoria's shack. The woman threatened both with mayhem and it took a stern warning from law enforcement officers to settle the altercation.[74]

Ruby Bates lived with her mother and two brothers; their bare, unpainted shack was the only house occupied by whites on the entire street. Mrs. Bates, out of work for some time, had taken in a "boarder" to share living expenses, and presumably her bed, during the hard times. Neither she nor Ruby seemed humiliated by the fact that Ruby had supposedly been "ruined for life" by the attack. To Miss Ransdell, it appeared that both looked upon sexual intercourse with whites or Negroes as a part of their routine of life. In their insistence that the nine boys be executed, "they have just fallen in with 'respectable' opinion," the writer said, "because that seems to be what is expected of them, and they want to do the proper thing." Ruby was "a large, fresh, good-looking girl," said Miss Ransdell, but extremely shy unless encouraged. During the interview she sat languidly, leaning forward occasionally to spit through a knothole in the floor. Only one thing struck a spark with her: the mention of Victoria Price. Ruby's vivacious

[73] *Ibid.*, 17.
[74] *Ibid.*

and talkative friend had pushed her into the background and she hated Victoria for it.[75]

When the ACLU publicized Miss Ransdell's report in May of 1931, it shocked those who read it. But Southerners (and particularly Alabamians) dismissed the findings as the product of radical outsiders who knew nothing of the peculiar problems of the region. A series of reports by the Commission on Interracial Cooperation during May and June was somewhat more difficult to dismiss. The Commission, formed in 1920, consisted of some of the most conservative members of both races in the South. Probably the majority of the white members, for example, approved of segregation and its concomitant institutions, but they sought to ease the more inequitable aspects of discrimination. The Commission devoted much effort to its antilynching program. Will Winton Alexander, one of the chief architects of the Commission on Interracial Cooperation, had served as executive director since its founding. The events at Scottsboro and the growing controversy around the case disturbed the genial "Dr. Will," and he instructed James D. Burton, the Commission's Interstate Secretary for Alabama and Tennessee, to make an independent investigation. He particularly wanted a complete rundown on the backgrounds of the two girls, he told Burton.[76]

J. A. Hackworth of the Hackworth Detective Agency in Huntsville interviewed neighbors of the girls and talked with county and city authorities. He confirmed the allegations of Miss Ransdell regarding the girls' backgrounds. They were common prostitutes, he said, and he offered to compile an extensive dossier outlining details of some of their more colorful escapades.[77] The Commission could not afford a full-scale professional investigation, how-

---

[75] *Ibid.,* 14–16.

[76] Wilma Dykeman and James Stokely, *Seeds of Southern Change: The Life of Will Alexander* (Chicago: University of Chicago Press, 1962), 153–55; James D. Burton, Report Number 2 on the Scottsboro, Alabama Case, May, 1, 1931, in Interracial Commission Papers. For a history of the Commission, see Edward Flud Burrows' "The Commission on Interracial Cooperation, 1919–1944: A Case Study in the History of the Interracial Movement in the South" (Ph.D. dissertation, University of Wisconsin, 1955).

[77] Leo Thiel to James D. Burton, May 19, 1931, in Interracial Commission Papers.

ever, and Burton decided to go to Huntsville and talk first-hand with the two girls. On his trip into the back alleys of Huntsville's worst slums, he was accompanied by a local contractor who confided that Victoria was a well-known prostitute who went under the name of "Big Leg Price." [78] When he finally found Mrs. Price, she was bending over the wash tub on the back porch of her dilapidated shack. Burton, who found Mrs. Price even more distasteful than he had anticipated, described the meeting vividly. "She stepped down into the yard, emptied her mouth of snuff . . . and proceeded to talk." With a shrill voice she told him that each and every one of the boys was guilty of raping her. "I hope to see everyone of them burned to death," she emphasized, adding that the crime was all the worse since she had been a "virtuous woman" until the train incident. Burton tried to find Ruby, but she was not at her mother's home. After talking with Huntsville police, he slowly rode through the downtown area, pausing at Woolworth's Five-and-Ten where the young woman often loitered. Although he was unsuccessful in his efforts to find Ruby, he left Huntsville convinced beyond a doubt that both she and Victoria were unreliable witnesses.[79] In the next two months, he wrote four reports for the Atlanta office of the Interracial Commission. The Commission was not involved in the case, however, and Alexander did not seek to distribute the results beyond a handful to key leaders in the organization. The reports were soon buried away in Commission files.

As excerpts from the ACLU's Ransdell report appeared in the press, pressure grew on the NAACP to take a more militant stand against the white Southerners who would sanction death for eight boys on the testimony of two "cut-rate whores." [80] A frontal assault on the South would have jeopardized White's strategy, however, for he hoped to win the support of the moderate elements in the region. In order to succeed, the first step had to be complete dis-

[78] James D. Burton to Arthur Raper, July 11, 1931, in Interracial Commission Papers.
[79] James D. Burton to Will Alexander, April 14, 1931, in Interracial Commission Papers.
[80] New York *Daily Worker*, June 1, 1931; Washington *World*, June 6, 1931.

association from the ILD and its activities. From the outset of the conflict between the two organizations, the NAACP had criticized the rhetoric and tactics of the Communists; and on May 27, Herbert Seligmann announced that the NAACP would not in any way associate with the Communists in their defense of the boys. The differences between the two groups were irreconcilable, he declared, for the NAACP had learned "that such cases must be won not in newspapers, but in courts of law." He blamed the Communists for intensifying the difficulty of saving the condemned boys.[81]

On June 7, William Pickens delivered an even stronger attack on the ILD and its Communist compatriots. Pickens was in Chattanooga trying to gain the confidence of several of the boys' parents, and at the request of the Ministers' Alliance he addressed a large group of Negro citizens and a few "interracial leaders." He observed that there was "some doubt" in the minds of many people, North and South, about the guilt of the Scottsboro boys. "But there is almost no doubt anywhere that a fair and impartial trial and a trustworthy determination of the question of guilt or innocence could not have been had in the hysterical and mob atmosphere which attended the trial. . . ." He called on white Southerners to help in attaining a calm and deliberate retrial. He combined his appeal with a bitter attack on the "communistic activity and propaganda among colored people of the South, based on the pretext of defending these boys." He manfully acknowledged that the ILD initially misled him. "It has since developed that their chief aim is communistic propaganda, and that the plight of these youths is only a vehicle for that propaganda." Pickens went on: "I even suspect that it is their feeling that if justice should miscarry or if the boys should be lynched, it would further play into their hands and give them material for still more sensational propaganda among the more ignorant of the colored population." He warned the white people of the South that they had once before made the mistake of leaving the Negroes of the region to look to outsiders for help, "and the result was the worst phases

[81] Letter by Herbert Seligmann, in *New Republic,* LXVII (1931), 47.

of carpetbaggery and two long generations of radical misunderstanding, suspicion and ill-will." The best way to fight communism and radicalism in the South would be to give the boys a fair
trial, he argued. This would discredit the charge that the "better
class" of whites did not want the Negro to have justice and equal
citizenship.[82]

As both White and Pickens had expected, the Communist press
fiercely denounced the Chattanooga speech. "Of all the lickspittles
of the capitalist class who are in the leadership of the NAACP, the
worst has proven to be William Pickens," declared the noted Communist, Robert Minor. On April 24 the *Daily Worker* had hailed
Pickens for responding to the "will of the masses," but now it
found him the most contemptible betrayer of the Negro people
since a house-servant delivered Denmark Vesey to the slaveowners
and death. With a "new bandana handkerchief on his head," he
toured the South in order to ingratiate the NAACP with the Ku
Klux Klan. And in Chattanooga, he "grovelled before the white
master and in whining 'admissions' did all that he could to deliver
the nine innocent boys to the hangman of Alabama," said the
Worker. In the *New Masses* Eugene Gordon described Pickens'
address as the final capitulation of the Association to the white
lynchers of the South. "It is no longer the National Association for
the Advancement of Colored People, but the Nicest Association
for the Advantage of Certain Persons," he wrote sarcastically.
Walter White and his associates had "as much to do with the black
masses of workers and sharecroppers as any similar group of scent-
ed, spatted, caned and belly-filled white parasites have to do with
the white masses." The entire organization appeared to be "ultra-
nice, ultra-respectable, and ultra-fastidious" and so intent on
maintaining its support from white capitalists that it could not
afford to be seen in the company of "dirty reds or other radicals,
no matter what the common end is supposed to be." [83]

---

[82] Chattanooga *Daily Times*, June 8, 1931.

[83] Minor, "The Negro and His Judases," 638; New York *Daily Worker*, June 9,
1931; Eugene Gordon, "The Negro's New Leadership," *New Masses*, VII (July,
1931), 14–15.

White and Pickens had braced for Communist calumnies, but they were chagrined to find that they gained little in the standing of Southern whites by their attack on the Communists. The Chattanooga *Times* perfunctorily praised Pickens' warnings against Communist agitators among the "densely ignorant portion of the colored population," but it went on to deplore his assertion that the Scottsboro defendants did not receive a fair trial. "Public utterances of this kind by supposedly responsible Negro leaders no doubt have the effect of preparing some who hear them for the seeds which Communists sow." And the *Times* added that his remarks would add to the difficulties of restraining the more "unruly elements" among Southern whites. "It is regrettable that Dr. Pickens was not able to perform the service of warning against the Communist menace without adding his . . . ill-advised remarks about the Scottsboro case." [84]

No matter what position the NAACP took, most Southerners distrusted it. George Fort Milton, the chairman of the Southern Commission on the Study of Lynching, and an avowed liberal, took the attitude of most moderate Southerners. Only the "liberal white people of the South" should handle the case, he said, since the NAACP and the ILD seemed "engaged in a joint battle to secure the exploiting possibilities of the case rather than to defend the boys themselves." As the Birmingham *Age-Herald* put it: "It is now clear that these darkies do not mean a tinker's dam to the organizations which have supposedly been moving heaven and earth in their behalf." The entire episode was a "nauseating struggle between the Communist group and the negro society, not so much that justice may be done as that selfish interests may be advanced through the capitalization of the episode." [85]

[84] Chattanooga *Daily Times*, June 9, 1931.

[85] George Fort Milton to Bruce Bliven, August 25, 1931, in Interracial Commission Papers. (Bliven was editor of the *New Republic*.) Birmingham *Age-Herald*, January 22, 1932. Beddow reported that he was criticized for his association with the NAACP "almost as much as if . . . [he] were acting for the REDS. . . ." L. L. Chambless to E. T. Belsaw, July 31, 1931, in Interracial Commission Papers. See also, Roderick Beddow to Walter White, May 29, 1931, in Scottsboro Legal File 1, NAACP Papers.

White gained a few supporters for the Association. The *New Republic* called on the Communists to turn the case over to more conservative groups like the NAACP, in order to make an appeal to the United States Supreme Court. The *Christian Century* characterized the Communist role in the case as "pathetic and ominous," and warned that such activities could thwart the development of Southern support for a new trial. *The Nation* professed neutrality in the struggle, but it implied that the Communists, by focusing on the "class-struggle" aspects of the case, had obscured the real issue: whether or not eight Negro boys less than twenty-one years of age should be electrocuted after such a farcical trial.[86]

The most important source of support for the NAACP was not the white liberal press, however, but the Negro middle class, the talented tenth, as DuBois had called them. White and Pickens were surprised to find that their attacks on the ILD and the Communist Party were heavily criticized. Robert L. Vann, editor of the Pittsburgh *Courier,* was one of the few prominent and influential Negroes who supported the NAACP in its refusal to cooperate with the ILD. His readers, many of whom professed to be nonradicals, disagreed with his decision. "Surely the ILD can't possibly make things any worse than they are," said a young woman from Pittsburgh. "Perhaps there are people who would contribute to one organization and not the other. . . ." Joseph Sunday of New York City praised the activities of the Communists and professed amazement at the NAACP's refusal to associate with the Communists because of their radicalism. "The organization was not so squeamish in having Clarence Darrow, an avowed radical and disbeliever, handle the Sweet case. Why this ultra-respectability?" he asked.[87]

[86] *New Republic,* LXVI (1931), 343; *Christian Century,* XXXVIII (1931), 941; *The Nation,* CXXXIV (1932), 63.

[87] Pittsburgh *Courier,* May 16, 23, 30, 1931. In the Sweet Case, Darrow successfully defended a Detroit Negro doctor and his family from murder charges after they returned gunfire and killed one member of a mob which had attacked their home in a white middle-class suburb. See Wilson Record, *Race and Radicalism: The NAACP and the Communist Party in Conflict* (Ithaca: Cornell University Press, 1964), 47–48.

White had clearly misjudged the temper of the American Negro community. Even during the relatively prosperous twenties, there were few militant Negro "anti-Communists." And if America's black masses had not rallied to the red flag (as the Communists hoped) they nevertheless remained immune from many of the anti-Communist ideas held by the majority of white Americans.[88] With the exception of Robert Vann, not a single Negro editor described himself as "anti-Communist." Frank M. Davis of the Atlanta *World* believed that the violent opposition of whites to Negro Communists in the South might bring trouble to an "already over-burdened race," but Carl Murphy of the Baltimore *Afro-American* insisted that the Communists were "the only party going our way." Since the abolitionists had disappeared after the Civil War, he said, "no white group of national prominence has openly advocated the economic, political and social equality of black folks." [89]

Even the more cautious editors like P. B. Young of the Norfolk *Journal and Guide* argued that American Negroes should not view communism as a complete evil, but simply as another political group which could aid them in achieving greater economic benefits and legal equality. And why should the Negro not look favorably on communism? asked William H. (Kid) Kelley of Harlem's *Amsterdam News.* Capitalism had given him little or nothing. "Oppressed on every hand, denied equal educational facilities, discriminated against in public places and in employment, Jim-Crowed on street cars and railroad trains . . . even lynched, it would seem that any program—Communistic or Socialistic—. . . should readily find converts among American Negroes." How was it possible to "go to war with the Communist Party," agreed the Chicago *Defender,* when it was the one organi-

[88] Of course there were differences between class groups and regions (the South being generally more conservative). But the attitudes held by Southern Negro "leaders"—who were generally conservative—did not always accurately reflect the beliefs of their followers. See Lessie Ophelia Toler, "The Negro and Communism" (M.A. thesis, University of North Carolina, 1932), 62.

[89] "Negro Editors on Communism: A Symposium of the American Negro Press," *Crisis,* XXXIX (1932), 119.

zation in white America that practiced complete political, economic, and social equality? [90]

In spite of their inability to gain widespread support for the NAACP and opposition to the ILD, the officers of the Association continued their efforts to gain control of the case. Through attorneys in Atlanta and Chattanooga, White obtained support from the nearest relatives of Willie Roberson and Charley Weems. On May 1, Mrs. Mamie Williams Wilcox, mother of Eugene Williams, had signed for the Association; but the next morning, White reported that "she walked three miles (having not even carfare) to Dr. Stephens' house to withdraw from this agreement." She explained that her husband, the stepfather of Eugene, abused her for forsaking the Communists and she had decided to rejoin the ILD.[91]

On his trip South in early June, Pickens tried to win the Chattanooga parents away from the Communists, but he had little luck. He first presented his case to Claude and Janie Patterson, and he seemed to have won Mrs. Patterson, but her husband told him: "Give us your phone number and we will see you before you leave. Let us think it over." A half-hour later, Pickens stopped his car in front of Mrs. Williams' home. There he found "one of the reds, leading the Patterson [sic] couple like two dumb animals, jumping them into his car and racing off to some place where the Williams woman had already been concealed to prevent any intelligence from reaching her." Pickens attributed the parents' loyalty to the fact that the "shirt-sleeved Communist ignoramus" gave them a check each month. In an outburst of temper, he declared they were "the densest and dumbest animals it has yet been my privilege to meet." [92]

The condescending attitude of both Pickens and White, which they expressed publicly, was a grave tactical error. The ILD national office in New York carefully clipped their disparaging re-

[90] *Ibia.,* 117–18; Chicago *Defender,* January 14, 1933.

[91] A. T. Walden to Walter White, May 20, 1931, and Walter White to National Office, May 3, 1931, in Scottsboro Legal File 1, NAACP Papers.

[92] Williams Pickens to Walter White, June 6, 1931, in Scottsboro Legal File 2, NAACP Papers.

marks and sent them to the parents, thus alienating them and destroying the slim chances of the NAACP to gain their support.[93] At an International Labor Defense rally in Cleveland, Mrs. Williams noted that the NAACP had said she and the other mothers were too ignorant to know what they wanted. "Well, we are not too ignorant to know a bunch of liars and fakers when we meet up with them and [we] are not too ignorant to know that if we let the NAACP look after our boys, that they will die." [94] When Claude Patterson learned of White's attitude, he wrote the NAACP's executive director, "We learn you went down there, said we was misslead." He angrily told White that he was not too misled to know that "We don't need you and none of your crowd for nothing for all you all is no good." [95]

As Pickens had suspected, the ILD sent a small monthly check to the families of the boys (from three to five dollars), but their loyalty to the ILD was not based on this alone. When Mrs. Janie Patterson returned from New York in early May she apologized for the homesickness which cut short her trip. This did not mean she was unhappy with the ILD. "I can't be treated any better than the Reds has treated me," she wrote. "I tell the white and I tell the black . . . I am not getting back of nothing else. I mean to be with you all as long as I live." She could never make them understand how much she appreciated the kindnesses they had shown her, and she signed herself in closing: "From one of the Reds, Janie Patterson." [96] The kindness and respect of ILD officials contrasted sharply with the condescending approach of the NAACP.

The success of the Communists in gaining the support of the parents aided the Party in its struggle for the loyalty of the Scottsboro boys. During the summer of 1931, it appeared to those who followed the case in the press that the boys switched sides weekly. The conflicting claims of the competing organizations aggravated

[93] Memorandum by George Maurer, June 12, 1931, in ILD Papers. See the Pittsburgh *Courier,* May 16, 1931.
[94] New York *Daily Worker,* July 17, 1931.
[95] Claude Patterson to Walter White, August 13, 1931, in Scottsboro Legal File 3, NAACP Papers.
[96] New York *Daily Worker,* May 9, 1931.

the confusion, and it was true that the boys had vacillated during the first weeks after their conviction.[97] But, beginning with the May 21 visit of William Pickens, the nine defendants broke into two factions which remained relatively stable for several months. Haywood Patterson, Andy and Roy Wright, Eugene Williams, and Olen Montgomery followed the lead of their parents and supported the ILD, while Ozie Powell, Charlie Weems, and Clarence Norris backed the NAACP.[98] Willie Roberson wavered erratically from one side to the other. At first he backed the NAACP. Then, on July 3, he wrote that he appreciated what the Association had done, but "I much rather for you all to let my case a long [alone]." He had to listen to what his friends said. A month later, he decided that he preferred the Association again.[99] On "Tuesday, Thursday, Saturday and Sunday, Roberson is with us all the way," wrote Beddow in disgust. "Monday, Wednesday and Friday is reserved for the IDL [sic]." [100] Throughout the hot summer months of June and July, White pleaded with Charles A. J. McPherson and W. E. Grey of the Birmingham and Montgomery NAACP chapters to visit with the boys and encourage them to affiliate with the NAACP. Both Grey and McPherson talked with the defendants, but they were not able to develop any rapport and their halting efforts were ineffectual when compared with the cigarettes, clothes, and pocket money the ILD furnished. The ILD also sent the mothers to visit their sons and, as Mrs. Patterson put it, they tried with every visit to clear "any poison out of their brains" that had been left by the NAACP.[101]

[97] White claimed the defendants supported the NAACP one hundred per cent. At the same time, the Communists asserted unequivocally that they had the support of all the boys and their parents. New York *Daily Worker*, May, June, 1931, *passim;* Chattanooga *Daily Times,* May 21, 1931; Baltimore *Afro-American,* July 11, 1931; Pittsburgh *Courier,* May 23, June 20, 1931.

[98] Janie Patterson to ILD Headquarters, June 21, 1931, in ILD Papers; Pittsburgh *Courier,* May 23, June 20, 1931.

[99] Willie Roberson to Walter White, July 3, 1931; Willie Roberson to Walter White, August 3, 1931, in Scottsboro Legal Files 2 and 3, NAACP Papers.

[100] Roderick Beddow to Walter White, August 14, 1931, in Scottsboro Legal File 3, NAACP Papers.

[101] Walter White to W. E. Grey, July 3, 1931; Walter White to Charles A. J. McPherson, July 8, 1931, in Scottsboro Legal File 2, NAACP Papers; Janie Patterson to ILD Headquarters, June 21, 1931, in ILD Papers.

On August 4 the NAACP's relations with the boys showed a sudden deterioration when Roderick Beddow visited them to discuss the pending appeal. When Beddow asked a few questions, they refused to talk and Haywood snarled: "We don't want you. You are representing the capitalists and are just trying to get us electrocuted." Even Clarence, Ozie, and Charley, who had always stood firmly behind the NAACP, remained silent. Beddow hurriedly informed White of the boys' attitudes and warned that he would withdraw if the Association could not make further progress in gaining the support of the defendants.[102] White and Pickens had already made three trips to Birmingham, but after discussing the situation with other national officers, White knew that he had no alternative but to try once more. On August 16, accompanied by Will Alexander and Dr. G. Lake Imes of Tuskegee Institute, he made his last appeal to the Scottsboro defendants. White told them that, if he were on trial in Alabama, he would want an Alabama firm such as that of Fort, Beddow, and Ray instead of out-of-state lawyers who had no standing in the courts of Alabama. The ILD, in contrast to the NAACP, frankly worked to overthrow the government, said White. Its only object was propaganda. With a touch of sarcasm in his voice, White noted that it was a "working class mob of whites" which almost lynched them at Scottsboro. If the boys agreed to cooperate with his organization, he promised them the support of the wealthiest people in the state. When he had finished, Weems, Norris, Powell and Roberson once more promised they would back the Association. Andrew Wright seemed undecided, but he explained that he had promised his mother he would stand by the ILD. When White asked him if he thought the judgment of his mother was necessarily sound just because she was older, Andy said with a look of complete despair: "Mr. White, if you can't trust you mother, who can you trust?" [103]

[102] Memorandum of telephone conversation between Walter White and Roderick Beddow, August 5, 1931. Clarence and Ozie wrote two days later that they still backed the NAACP, but Weems had changed sides along with Roberson (once more). Clarence Norris to Walter White, August 7, 1931; Ozie Powell to Walter White, August 7, 1931, in Scottsboro Legal File 3, NAACP Papers.

[103] Pittsburgh *Courier*, August 22, 1931; Walter White to Robert Russa Moton, August 19, 1931, in Scottsboro Legal File 3, NAACP Papers.

His answer captured the anguish of indecision in the midst of conflicting advice and recommendations. To the ILD and the NAACP, the case had become a struggle for vindication; to the Scottsboro boys, it was a decision on which their lives hinged.

The inability of White to persuade all the boys confirmed a decision which Beddow and his firm had reached at the first of the month; they saw no alternative but to withdraw. White managed to persuade them to reconsider by emphasizing that this would give the Communists complete control of the case.[104] After a week's further deliberation, Beddow advised White that their decision was final. He explained the factors in their verdict. There had been a number of "Communist inspired" racial disturbances in Alabama during the summer of 1931, and the ILD and its followers had inflamed public opinion needlessly by flooding the governor and other officials with "senseless and contemptible" letters. Moreover, he said, Fort, Beddow, and Ray could not continue in a case in which they had such a flimsy foothold. "I am not, you understand, blaming the boys," said Beddow. "Their position is analogous to that of a man drowning. They are panicky. They are stupefied, stunned and . . . placed in a predicament where they cannot wisely decide for themselves." And even if two or three of the boys wanted the NAACP to defend them, this would be foolish. The entire case was "so intermingled and interwoven it can be likened unto a bolt of cloth," he wrote. "Positively there can be no separation of interest. To allow a separation would be to remove their cause from a foundation of rock to one of sand." [105] James Burton unsuccessfully pressured the firm to

[104] George Fort Milton to William E. Fort, August 12, 1931, in Interracial Commission Papers; Walter White to Robert Russa Moton, August 19, 1931, in Scottsboro Legal File 2, NAACP Papers.

[105] Roderick Beddow to Walter White, August 26, 1931, Scottsboro Legal File 3, NAACP Papers. James Burton reported another factor which Beddow did not disclose. Investigators for the ILD had been questioning friends, associates, and enemies in an effort to gain derogatory information about Beddow and his family. "The firm felt that they would not have anything to do with a case where such tactics are used." Memorandum of long distance telephone call from James D. Burton to Walter White, September 1, 1931, in Scottsboro Legal File 3, NAACP Papers.

reverse its decision. Bewildered and exasperated, he told Alexander: "This is the most perplexing case I have ever known." [106]

As the ILD tightened its hold on the boys and their parents, its agents hammered away at the NAACP, using every method at their disposal to publicize their charges: pamphlets, mass rallies, speeches at Negro churches and social organizations, and leaflets on the streets. The most effective attack, however, was to gain the floor at NAACP meetings and then to expose the "misleaders" to their deluded followers. Beginning with William Pickens' speech at Chattanooga on June 7, Party members disrupted every major NAACP meeting dealing with the Scottsboro Case. At Chattanooga the pattern was set: Joe Burton, a "militant" young Negro Communist, interrupted Pickens in the middle of his remarks and shouted that he and White were "traitors to the Negro masses," that the Association raised money only to vilify the ILD, the one organization that could free the boys. When six strategically placed Communists reduced a Chicago rally to chaos a week later with jeering and catcalls, Pickens issued a memorandum to all chapters, warning them to have police present at their Scottsboro meetings. It was "impossible to reason or to compromise" with the Communists, he said. If allowed to speak five minutes, they would talk for forty-five; if refused or asked to wait, they would shout down the speaker.[107]

Pickens' advice proved ineffectual, however, for the Communists were willing to go to jail in order to spread their gospel. In fact, White suspected that they believed arrest would only enhance their success. During the next month more than a dozen meetings were interrupted by the shouting intruders.[108] The high point of these ILD attacks came at the annual National Conference of the

[106] James D. Burton to Will Alexander, September 1, 1931, in Interracial Commission Papers.

[107] William Pickens to All NAACP Branches, June 17, 1931, in Scottsboro Legal File 2, NAACP Papers; New York *Daily Worker,* June 9, 1931; Chicago *Defender,* June 20, July 4, 1931.

[108] New York *Times,* June 20, 1931, p. 3; Pittsburgh *Courier,* July 4, 1931. The New York *Daily Worker* has accounts of these in the June and July issues. Even when the ILD did not interrupt NAACP meetings, it often arranged to stage rival demonstrations. See New York *Times,* June 29, 1931, p. 18.

NAACP, which was meeting in Pittsburgh from July 2 through 4. As the meeting opened ILD members distributed a leaflet to the delegates charging that the NAACP "not only refused to have anything to do with the case, but actually carried on activities which helped the southern lynchers in the murder of the nine Negro boys." The leaflet also alleged that the Association had deliberately hired an Alabama lawyer who was a well-known "Negro-hater." Instead of defending the boys, he had helped to send them to the electric chair. At the final Sunday meeting, Communists scattered in the audience heckled speakers and demanded that Haywood's mother, Mrs. Janie Patterson, be allowed to speak. As the ILD had hoped, the request to allow Mrs. Patterson to speak placed the Association's leaders in a shaky position. How could they profess to be agents for the Scottsboro boys and then refuse one of their mothers the right to address the convention? Despite strong pressure from many of the members, the leadership held firm and police officers escorted the hecklers from the meeting. At the same time, White dropped broad hints that the woman who claimed to be Mrs. Patterson was an impostor.[109]

White had hoped that the "offensive tactics" of the Communists would backfire, but the ILD seemed only to gain strength. In the wake of an attack by White on the ILD, the Washington *World* editorialized on the NAACP's loss of militancy. "It is a traitorous clique that . . . malign[s] an organization that is fighting in its way for the release of the Scottsboro boys and has actually done more for them." The NAACP, said Negro editor Eugene N. Davidson, had "outlived its usefulness if it now feels that fighting the spread of communism is more important than fighting white Southerners who will lynch, massacre, and slaughter and expect to get away with it." White exploded in anger at this attack. "The NAACP does not hesitate to strike and strike hard," he told Davidson in a bristling letter. "It does not believe, however, in a futile, childish mouthing of empty threats which can serve no purpose other than to make infinitely more difficult the defense of the nine defend-

[109] Baltimore *Afro-American*, July 11, 1931.

ants." White defended the position taken by his organization and declared that Communist tactics had inflamed feeling against the boys to the extent that a retrial would almost certainly result in conviction.[110]

Despite White's efforts, the Baltimore *Afro-American* voiced the conviction held by most Negroes by midsummer of 1931. "It may be treasonable to say it," declared editor Carl Murphy, but "as the Scottsboro Case stands today the Communists have the National Association for the Advancement of Colored People licked." The ILD had secured the backing of the parents and most of the boys, said Murphy. The NAACP was in court with no clients. "And finally the Reds have so maneuvered the situation that the mother of one of the condemned boys is refused permission to speak at a public mass meeting in the interest of her son at which meeting funds were being raised to save him from the electric chair." [111]

With the NAACP on the edge of complete defeat, White turned to Clarence Darrow. "We had hoped that it would not be necessary for us to call on you in the now famous Scottsboro cases," White said, "but we are frankly right up against what is probably the most delicate and difficult situation of our history." He asked the aging courtroom genius if he would be willing to argue the case as far as the Supreme Court.[112] For Darrow it was a difficult decision. At seventy-four, his health had been failing for several years (he had been in semi-retirement since 1926), but he felt deeply that the International Labor Defense was jeopardizing any chance for the release of the defendants. And financial reversals of the Depression made the $5,000 fee attractive. He told White that he would be willing to take on partial responsibility for the case. Because of his health, he explained, he did not have the physical strength to prepare the appeal record, "but I would be willing to make one of the oral arguments before the Supreme Court [of

[110] Washington *World*, July 24, 1931; Walter White to Eugene Davidson, July 27, 1931, in Scottsboro Legal File 2, NAACP Papers.

[111] Baltimore *Afro-American*, July 11, 1931.

[112] Walter White to Clarence Darrow, August 31, 1931, in Scottsboro Legal File 3, NAACP Papers.

Alabama]." [113] As White had hoped, when he dangled before Beddow the distinction which would inevitably come from being associated with Darrow, the Birmingham law firm agreed to stay in the case. On September 14 the NAACP announced to the nation that Clarence Darrow had been retained to aid in arguing the appeal before the Alabama Supreme Court. Arthur Garfield Hays, a prominent lawyer involved in a number of civil liberties cases, including the Gastonia strikes, volunteered to serve without pay as associate counsel. The Association accepted his offer.[114]

The ILD leaders astutely saw that the NAACP hoped to use Darrow in order to regain a foothold in the case. But they could hardly hope to win support among liberals and within the Negro community if they put themselves in the position of declining the services of the famous Clarence Darrow. After a week of silence, the ILD cautiously responded through the *Daily Worker* with a letter from General Chamlee. Chamlee declared that he welcomed the entrance of Darrow into the case, "particularly because of his high standing in the legal profession as a result of his defense of a long series of working class and civil liberties cases. . . ." The International Labor Defense had approached Darrow in the earliest stages of the defense, "but at that time he did not seem to realize the importance of the case," Chamlee noted with a hint of sarcasm. He added, "Still I must point out that his [Darrow's] connection with the case through the NAACP must be regarded as an attempt on the part of those in charge of the NAACP to keep up their own criminal sabotage of this case to date." The ILD welcomed him, concluded Chamlee, but it had no intention of allowing the "discredited elements of the NAACP" to hide behind the "name and prestige of Mr. Darrow." [115]

To make certain that it would retain the upper hand in any

[113] Clarence Darrow to Walter White, September 2, 1931, in Scottsboro Legal File 3, NAACP Papers.

[114] Walter White to Roderick Beddow, September 2, 1931; Roderick Beddow to Walter White, September 12, 1931, in Scottsboro Legal File 3, NAACP Papers; New York *Times*, September 15, 1931, p. 1; Chicago *Defender*, September 19, October 13, 1931.

[115] New York *Daily Worker*, September 22, 1931.

negotiations, the ILD tightened its control over the boys. Mrs. Josephine Powell, the mother of Ozie, originally had supported the NAACP, but the ILD succeeded in persuading her to change sides in August. On September 26, Ozie wrote White that he had received a letter from his mother "and she told me to write you and tell you to keep hands off me. . . ." She had selected the ILD, he said, and he had decided that he was going to follow her instructions since "she nows [*sic*] the best for me. . . ." [116] Two weeks later, Clarence Norris explained to White that he still preferred the NAACP, but his mother, Mrs. Ida Norris, had persuaded him to sign for the International Labor Defense. On December 5, the last of the nine, Charley Weems, wrote George Maurer: "I would like for you to stop Mr. White from butting in my case for I dont want him to have my case. . . . I want you all to take my case." [117] General Chamlee confidently assured Maurer that the boys were no longer undecided and were firmly behind the ILD.[118]

Although White knew that he no longer had the defendants' backing, he still hoped that Darrow's prestige would keep the Association in the case. The NAACP proceeded as though nothing were amiss and two days after Christmas Hays and Darrow arrived in Birmingham to discuss strategy for the appeal pending in the Alabama Supreme Court. That night the two attorneys received a telegram signed by the Scottsboro boys denouncing them unless they agreed to work with the ILD. Darrow decided that the time had come for a showdown and through Lowell Wakefield of the ILD's Birmingham office, he called for a conference. The meeting began shortly after 6 P.M. on December 28 with a team of three representatives from each side: Beddow, Darrow, and Hays representing the NAACP: and Chamlee, Brodsky, and Schwab speak for the ILD. For more than five hours the six men argued and dis-

[116] Pittsburgh *Courier*, May 23, 1931; Ozie Powell to Walter White, September 26, 1931, in Scottsboro Legal File 3, NAACP Papers.

[117] Clarence Norris to Walter White, November 10, 1931; Charley Weems to Walter White, November 22, 1931, in Scottsboro Legal File 4, NAACP Papers; Charley Weems to George Maurer, December 5, 1931, in ILD Papers.

[118] George W. Chamlee, Sr., to George Maurer, December 8, 1931, in ILD Papers.

cussed the case. "At times it bordered on bedlam," according to one of the participants. Beddow opened the negotiations by explaining his position. He was hopeful that an appeal might be successful, he said, but if the final result should rest in the hands of Governor Miller, he assured the ILD representatives that they could expect "very little in the nature of executive clemency" in view of their "rotten propaganda." Darrow backed Beddow in this contention and argued that the type of campaign carried on by the ILD jeopardized any chance for reversal: "It is idle to suppose that the state of Alabama can be awed by threats or that such demonstration can have any effect, unless it is to injure the defendants." [119]

Chamlee and Brodsky countered by declaring that they welcomed the cooperation of Darrow and Hays (they pointedly ignored Beddow) , but they, along with the boys and their parents, were "unalterably opposed to having the misleaders of the National Association for the Advancement of Colored People in the case." To invite Darrow and Hays in as attorneys for that organization would be to "break faith with my clients," said Chamlee.[120] The meeting dragged on; tempers flared and accusations flew back and forth across the table. Shortly before midnight, Darrow stopped for a conference with Hays and Beddow. When he returned to the table he told the ILD attorneys that he, Beddow, and Hays had agreed to sever all connections with the NAACP if Chamlee and Schwab would do the same with the ILD. The five of them could defend the boys as private attorneys, he said, with none of the bickering over backing organizations that had taken place earlier. He put the proposal in writing and pushed it across the table to Chamlee. Schwab interjected that he would have to clear the matter with ILD headquarters in New York. As the conference ended, Darrow turned to the three men and warned them that if they refused the proposal they would accept full responsibility for the fate of the boys. Should the defend-

[119] Clarence Darrow, "Scottsboro," *Crisis*, XXXIX (1932) , 81; Roderick Beddow to Walter White, January 2, 1932, in Scottsboro Legal File 3, NAACP Papers.
[120] New York *Daily Worker*, December 31, 1931.

ants be executed, he said, "it will rest forever on your consciences." Chamlee seemed visibly shaken by Darrow's warning, but Schwab snapped that they would reply to the offer within twenty-four hours.[121]

During the rest of the night, telegrams went back and forth between Chamlee and the New York office. Although he did not have an alternative which was satisfactory to the ILD, Chamlee was extremely reluctant to refuse Darrow's services. But George Maurer, viewing the situation from New York, had only one proposal. Demand, he said, that "Darrow [and] Hays withdraw as NAACP attorneys with [a] public statement [to] that effect." Once they had done this, he told Chamlee, he would consider inviting them to serve as cooperating attorneys if they would abide by all decisions of the ILD.[122] Chamlee and Schwab knew that neither Darrow nor the other two attorneys would consider such conditions, but they relayed the decision and explained there would be no negotiations on this point.

A discouraged Arthur Hays wired White that he saw nothing for the NAACP to do but to withdraw completely from the case. He had concluded that the Communists would be satisfied with nothing short of complete subservience to their leadership. He, for one, could never agree to this. And Darrow argued that any further haggling over counsel would jeopardize whatever chances the boys retained.[123] When newsmen interviewed Darrow and Hayes as they left Birmingham, the two lawyers explained that they had decided to withdraw not because they feared involvement with the Communists, but because the ILD had made two unreasonable demands: that they repudiate the NAACP and agree to abide by the decisions of the ILD. "I have no objection to any

[121] Roderick Beddow to Walter White, January 2, 1932; Clarence Darrow to Walter White, December 31, 1931, in Scottsboro Legal File 4, NAACP Papers; Darrow, "Scottsboro," 81.

[122] George Maurer to George W. Chamlee [telegram], December 28, 1931, George W. Chamlee to George Maurer, December 28, 1931; George Maurer to Irving Schwab, December 29, 1931, in ILD Papers.

[123] Arthur Garfield Hays to Walter White, December 29, 1931 [telegram]; Clarence Darrow to Walter White, December 31, 1931, in Scottsboro Legal File 4, NAACP Papers.

man's politics," explained Darrow, "but you can't mix politics with law." If the cases were to be won, they would have to be won in Alabama, "not in Russia or New York." On January 4 the NAACP National Board of Directors announced that the Association had decided to withdraw formally from the case. With their announcement they took one last shot at the ILD. "If the International Labor Defense had as its only interest in the case the saving of the lives of these youths, it would have welcomed the entrance of Clarence Darrow and Arthur Garfield Hays, no matter who employed them." [124] And White managed to release some of his frustrations when Weems wrote that he "did not no [sic]" what was in the "pact" that Chamlee asked him to sign. He had decided he wanted the NAACP to stay in the case. White told him, "You and the other boys have vacillated, changing your minds so frequently that it is impossible for any organization or individual to know just what you do want." He added coldly, "You have chosen your counsel and that settles the matter so far as the NAACP is concerned." [125]

The ILD blamed the NAACP for the Hays-Darrow withdrawal. General Chamlee asked the two men to "cooperate in the defense with the ILD," explained the *Daily Worker,* neglecting to add that Schwab had insisted the two attorneys repudiate the NAACP. Now Hays and Darrow had joined the Association in fighting the International Labor Defense, "no matter at what cost to the innocent prisoners in Kilby prison." [126] With this ingenuous explanation, the *Daily Worker* ended all discussion on the subject. Despite temporary embarrassment over the Darrow episode, there was a feeling of elation within the ranks of the International Labor Defense when word came that the NAACP had officially withdrawn from the case. George Maurer credited the ILD's vic-

[124] New York *Times,* December 30, 1931, p. 1, and January 3, 1932, p. 28, and January 5, 1932, p. 2; Chattanooga *Daily Times,* January 5, 1932.
[125] Charley Weems to Walter White, December 30, 1931; Walter White to Charley Weems, January 4, 1932, in Scottsboro Legal File 3, NAACP Papers.
[126] New York *Daily Worker,* January 1, 1932. The *Daily Worker* did not think it important to mention the offer of Darrow and Hays to withdraw from association with the NAACP if Schwab and Chamlee would sever their connections with the ILD.

tory to the bold and aggressive tactics it had used.[127] To some extent, however, the organization's successes stemmed from the weaknesses of its opponents. Walter White and his associates moved slowly and cautiously during the initial stages of the case, relying on the same tactics that brought them limited success in the 1920's.[128] What they failed to understand was that there had been dramatic changes during the first two years of the Depression, changes which demanded new tactics and a new strategy. For better or worse, the politics of the nation had shifted to the left; the National Association for the Advancement of Colored People had not.

[127] New York *Daily Worker*, January 6, 1932; George Maurer to Lowell Wakefield, January 9, 1932, in ILD Papers.

[128] Too late, the NAACP learned that George W. Chamlee had written the *Forum* article in 1926 which had implied a defense of lynching under certain circumstances. There was some debate within the Association over whether the information should be released, but White concluded that it would do nothing but injure the case for the boys. Walter White to I. B. Page, January 13, 1932; I. B. Page to Walter White, January 20, 1932, in Scottsboro Legal File 4, NAACP Papers. Page was editor of the *Forum* magazine.

IV

ALABAMA,
1931

WHETHER it was the pattern of violence described by Wilbur J. Cash or the "plague of poverty" which plunged one native son into despair, Alabama's eccentricities were those of the entire South, sometimes diminished, more often than not magnified.[1] The state's proud but often unlettered hillbillies of the lower Appalachians little resembled their economic counterparts, the poor white class of the Black Belt, let alone the plantation pseudo-aristocrats. One fixation, however, united these people. The Georgia-born historian Ulrich Bonnell Phillips had described it in 1928. Whether expressed with the "frenzy of a demagogue or maintained with a patrician's quietude," he observed, the common resolve of all white Southerners was that the region "shall be and remain a white man's country." [2]

Between 1865 and 1900, white Southerners created an elaborate system of prohibitions for the Negro. However thorough and degrading in their totality, most of these restraints were minor and involved only social conventions which symbolized the subservience of the subordinate caste.[3] There was one restriction far more

[1] Wilbur Joseph Cash, *The Mind of the South* (New York: Alfred A. Knopf, 1941), 44–45; Clarence Elmore Cason, *90° in the Shade* (Chapel Hill: University of North Carolina Press, 1935), xi.
[2] Ulrich Bonnell Phillips, "The Central Theme of Southern History," *American Historical Review*, XXXIV (1928), 31.
[3] A number of social scientists have studied the operation of the caste system. For a thorough, if not particularly insightful, description of its many forms, see

significant. In 1932 the Winston-Salem, North Carolina, *Journal* noted that "in the South it has been traditional . . . that its white womanhood shall be held inviolate by an 'inferior race.' " And it mattered not whether the woman was a "spotless virgin or a 'nymph de pavé.' " There could be no extenuating circumstances. If a white woman was willing to swear that a Negro either raped or attempted to rape her, "we see to it that the Negro is executed," declared Arkansas poet John Gould Fletcher.[4] For most violations of the color bar, a Southern Negro would be punished by a stern admonition, at most a whipping. For the rape of a white woman, however, there was only one punishment: death.

In 1900 the Scottsboro boys probably would have been removed from their jail cells and summarily hanged on the nearest tree, no matter how firmly the local sheriff protested. Because of their forbearance in allowing the defendants to have their day in court, the citizens of Jackson County "swelled with pride," reported the correspondent of the Chattanooga *Times*. They had "snubbed 'Judge Lynch' " and remained calm when confronted with "the most outrageous crime in the annals of the state." James Stockton Benson, editor of the Scottsboro *Progressive Age*, complimented his fellow citizens upon their "patience and chivalry." "If ever there was an excuse for taking the law into their own hands, surely this was one," he said. But "after having a little time to cool off, [the people] realize they have saved the good name of the county and the state by remaining calm and allowing the law to take its course." P. W. Campbell, editor of the *Jackson County Sentinel*, pointed out that "the negroes were given every protection and every right of the law for defense. . . ." Jackson County's citizens

Bertram Wilbur Doyle's *The Etiquette of Race Relations in the South: A Study in Social Control* (Chicago: University of Chicago Press, 1937). A more interpretive analysis can be found in John Dollard's *Caste and Class in a Southern Town* (New Haven: Yale University Press, 1937), 303, 343–46, 385–87, 433–39.

[4] Winston Salem (N.C.) *Journal*, October 15, 1932; Letter by John Gould Fletcher on the Scottsboro Case in *The Nation*, CXXXVII (1933), 734–35. Idus A. Newby, in a recent study of anti-Negro thought in America from 1900 to 1930, discovered that the question of "sex and social equality" was the one subject on which there was general agreement among white Southerners. Newby, *Jim Crow's Defense: Anti-Negro Thought in America, 1900–1930* (Baton Rouge: Louisiana State University Press, 1965), 136.

had "shown the world that they believe in justice, regardless of color." [5] And other Southerners added their encomiums. In the face of "one of the most atrocious crimes ever committed in this section," the town of Scottsboro "set the rest of the South an impressive example in self-restraint and in readiness to let justice be done in a legal and orderly manner," said the Chattanooga *Daily Times*. [6] James D. Burton of the Commission on Interracial Cooperation also commended Jackson County's citizens, although he noted wryly that the presence of sixty armed guardsmen and four well-placed machine guns might have reinforced their good intentions. [7]

To the consternation of Alabamians, "outsiders" did not praise their forebearance and calmness. More characteristic was the disgusted outcry of a New York college student. "What kind of a mindless savage are you?" he asked Judge A. E. Hawkins. "Is condemning eight teen-agers to death on the testimony of two white prostitutes your idea of 'enlightened' Alabama justice?" [8] State officials initially dismissed as cranks those who wrote the handful of letters protesting the guilty verdicts. But the amount of mail increased rather than diminished in the days after the trial until Governor Miller reported that he was receiving a half dozen protests a day. [9] As the ILD stepped up its activities in the case, word soon reached Alabama that a "New York radical organization" had charged the state of Alabama with "legal lynching." [10]

The first public protest that Alabamians read in their news-

---

[5] Chattanooga *Daily Times*, April 12, 1931; Scottsboro *Progressive Age*, April 2, April 9, 1931; Scottsboro *Jackson County Sentinel*, April 9, 1931.

[6] Chattanooga *Daily Times*, April 13, 1931. For other editorials praising the town of Scottsboro, see the Decatur *Daily*, April 13, 1931; Birmingham *News*, April 12, 1931; Birmingham *Age-Herald*, June 18, 1931; Memphis *Commercial Appeal*, quoted in Chattanooga *Daily Times*, April 17, 1931; Huntsville *Daily Times*, quoted in Birmingham *Post*, April 20, 1931; Chicago *Defender*, April 18, 1931.

[7] James D. Burton, Report Number 1 on the Scottsboro, Alabama Case, April 14, 1931, in Interracial Commission Papers.

[8] Lawrence He——— to Judge A. E. Hawkins, April 13, 1931, in Alabama Scottsboro Files.

[9] Chattanooga *Daily Times*, May 21, 1931.

[10] New York *Times*, April 11, 1931, p. 40; Birmingham *Post*, April 12, 1931. Many Alabamians did not learn of the Communist affiliation of the ILD until early May.

papers was George Maurer's April 8 telegram to Judge Hawkins and his later message to Governor Miller. It was difficult to tell whether the contents or the tone of the ILD communications most offended Alabamians. White Southerners prided themselves on the fact that they were "raised polite." Rudeness was an egregious social error not to be tolerated by a social equal, and certainly not by an inferior or "outsider." Maurer had written, "We demand that you release the Scottsboro defendants immediately. The masses of black and white workers will hold you personally responsible for the safety of the nine black workers you have ruthlessly railroaded to the electric chair." [11] White Alabamians responded with violent and undisguised threats, and the Dothan *Wiregrass Journal* succinctly expressed the collective attitude of the state. "To Hell with 'em we say," declared the *Journal*. "We've not asked for their advice. Don't need it and feel that we are entirely capable of handling our own affairs without outside interference." [12]

Even the Birmingham *News*, Alabama's self-styled advocate of "moderation" on racial issues, joined the resentful chorus. "It is difficult to speak with patience of the attitude of the International Labor Defense toward the trial at Scottsboro . . ." said the *News*. Northerners should be grateful that local officials thwarted mob violence and observed "all the legal forms." There was no doubt, the newspaper continued, that the authorities had captured the guilty parties. Moreover, since the proceedings were conducted under the rules of law, "the activity of the International Labor Defense in the case can only be regarded as meddling." Alabama, said the *News*, would not tolerate the "offensive tone" of George Maurer's demands.[13]

There were exceptions to this reaction. William Terry Couch

[11] George Maurer to Governor Benjamin Meeks Miller, April 10, 1931, in Alabama Scottsboro Files.

[12] Several Alabamians bluntly threatened Maurer's life in letters to the editor. See Birmingham *Post*, April 12, April 18, April 21, April 27, 1931. Dothan (Ala.) *Wiregrass Journal*, quoted in Birmingham *News*, July 31, 1931. In much the same vein, the Decatur *Daily* declared: "The good citizens of Alabama do not need the interference of eastern nit-wits." Decatur *Daily*, April 13, 1931.

[13] Birmingham *News*, April 12, 1931. The Birmingham *Age-Herald* expressed essentially the same attitude on June 18, 1931.

of the University of North Carolina noted acidly that "every gang of thieves and cut-throats regards the law-abiding citizen as an outsider." [14] But most Southerners, whether avowed liberals or racial demagogues, believed that outsiders could never understand, and therefore should not question, the racial policy of the South. A native of Ohio who had lived in Birmingham for twenty years argued that the "only way a Northerner can get a complete and fair understanding of the relations between the two races in the South is for him to come down here and stay at least two years." [15]

The main problem with Northerners, noted the dean of Mississippi's Blue Mountain College, was that they seemed unable to understand that the Negro race was an inferior one. No Southern white man, rich or poor, educated or ignorant, doubted this, "because the truth of it is incontestable." Even when the Negro was taught to read and write, he remained a "creature of the jungles." J. M. McCary of Anniston, Alabama, argued that no "native African of unmixed descent was ever educated." Had men like W. E. B. DuBois, Booker T. Washington, and George Washington Carver been white and made the same achievements, they would have remained obscure. But simply because they had "enough Caucasian brain transmitted to them from white parentage to grasp and maintain a little education they are held up and looked up to as representing their 'race.'" Nor was there any hope for the future. American Negroes had been in contact with European civilization for "hundreds of years and save through infusion of blood, they have not lost a single one of their ape-like characteristics nor developed the slightest shade of mentality." The *Jackson County Sentinel* was not on the fringe of Southern thinking when it declared that the Southern Negro was "a great big manchild. . . . His conception of law is a policeman's club and his idea of liberty

[14] Letter of William Terry Couch in *The Nation*, CXXXVIII (1934), 76. Of Alabama's newspapers, only the Selma *Times-Journal*, published in the Black Belt, defended the ILD's right to criticize the Scottsboro decision. Selma (Ala.) *Times-Journal*, quoted in the New York *Times*, July 27, 1931, p. 14.

[15] Letter of Harold Atkinson in Birmingham *News*, April 30, 1933. See also letter of John W. Wilson, in *The Nation*, CXXXVIII (1934), 75.

is license; basically he is a human negation. His idea of civilization is limited by something he can get into his mouth." [16]

Should Northerners challenge this interpretation of the Negro's place in Southern society, the region had a perfect historical justification for its attitude: the post-Civil War period. Reconstruction was the alpha and omega of Southerners' attempts to justify their treatment of the Negro. Even nonracists accepted the validity of the Reconstruction totem, and to men like P. W. Campbell of the *Sentinel,* no explication of Southern racial policy was complete without a summary of "the dark days when reconstruction was in full bloom." In came the carpetbaggers swarming in ant-like hordes over "the broken, mutilated and impoverished South." Unscrupulous outsiders used "the bayonets of negro troops" in an effort to "put the black foot upon the white neck." [17] According to Alabama historian Frank L. Owsley, Reconstruction in the South "probably had no counterpart in the history of the world." Radical leaders allowed, even encouraged, their black followers "to commit universal pillage, murder and rape." The result was "the most abominable phase barbarism had assumed since the dawn of civilization." [18]

Owsley also developed the argument that Southerners constantly repeated: any "outside interference" with the South's racial system would only "result in . . . organizations like the Ku Klux Klan and in violent retaliation against the Negroes—themselves often innocent." [19] Moderate Southerners couched their argument in a tone of regret. The intrusion of "Northern organizations" into the South's legal processes "can serve no purpose other than to make it more difficult to stop lynchings in the South," said the

---

[16] Letter of George T. Buckley, *The Nation,* CXXXVIII (1934), 75; Letter of J. M. McCary, in Birmingham *Age-Herald,* July 4, 1931; Scottsboro *Jackson County Sentinel,* April 27, 1933. See also letter of John W. Wilson in *The Nation,* CXXX VIII (1934), 75.

[17] Scottsboro *Jackson County Sentinel,* April 6, 1933. See also Birmingham *News,* June 28, 1933; Letter of Kenneth D. Coates in *The Nation,* CXXXVIII (1934), 74–75.

[18] Frank L. Owsley, "Scottsboro: Third Crusade; Sequel to Abolitionism and Reconstruction," *American Review,* I (1933), 267–68.

[19] *Ibid.,* p. 285.

Chattanooga *Daily Times.* "Nothing has done more to aggravate the race question in this section than just such meddling by outside agencies." Once a Negro had been found guilty by a jury, said the Statesboro, Georgia, *Times and News,* any continued resistance to legal punishment was a powerful incentive for the summary punishment of all suspects.[20] Other Southerners seemed less regretful. The *Jackson County Sentinel* noted the demands and threats from "outsiders" that Alabama reverse its decision and the "filthy insinuations" that the verdicts at Scottsboro were unfair. All this, said editor Campbell, "allows room for the growth of the thought that maybe after all 'the shortest way out' in cases like these would have been the best method of disposing of them." [21]

The white Southerner almost invariably declared that he believed the Negro should receive fair and impartial justice in the courts. The South's legal system was "not instituted for the purpose of keeping any racial element 'in their place,' " argued the Norfolk *Virginian Pilot.* Nor was it designed "to preserve castes in their fancied prerogatives." And yet this is essentially what the courts became in many instances. The South's legal system refused to regard "nigger killings" as serious matters for the most part.[22] But when the crime involved a conflict between the two races, then the entire judicial apparatus became, as a civil rights lawyer later put it, "a sham used not to grapple with tenacious questions of fact and law, guilt or innocence, but solely to maintain class and race power." [23]

[20] Chattanooga *Daily Times,* April 13, 1931; Statesboro (Ga.) *Times and News,* June 4, 1931. The Memphis *Commercial Appeal* editorialized that the intrusion of Northern troublemakers would result in the restoration of mob violence. Quoted in Chattanooga *Daily Times,* April 17, 1931. See also a special article by Alabama columnist John Temple Graves, II, in New York *Times,* June 21, 1931, III, 5.

[21] Scottsboro *Jackson County Sentinel,* April 16, 1931. Rather than "permit our own peculiar conceptions of justice to be questioned," said John G. Fletcher, "we will take the law into our own hands, by a resort to violence." Letter of John Gould Fletcher, in *The Nation,* CXXXVII (1933), 734–35.

[22] Norfolk *Virginian Pilot,* June 24, 1933; Letter of Jonathan Daniels, *The Nation,* CXXXVIII (1934), 75.

[23] Michael Meltsner, "Southern Appellate Courts: A Dead End," in Leon Friedman (ed.), *Southern Justice* (New York: Pantheon Books, 1965), 154. "No person who has lived in the South for many years and has seen the misuse of the Negro can deny that he suffers from inequality before the state-operated . . . judicial

In the weeks following the convictions at Scottsboro, Alabamians had ample opportunity to learn the details of the trials. James Burton's report, distributed to a number of "interracial leaders," concluded that the inflamed emotions in the little town had made a calm consideration of the evidence impossible. The defendants' case was inadequately prepared, their lawyers were incompetent, and the "judge, the lawyers, the jury knew that these people [the mob outside] were demanding the death penalty and that failure to impose it might well precipitate a very dangerous situation." Could such an atmosphere possibly have failed to affect the verdicts? he asked.[24] While Burton's reports reached only a limited audience, J. F. Rothermel, the top reporter for the Birmingham *News,* did a lengthy series on the arrest, trial, and conviction of the boys. He found that shortly after the arrest the mob was "quieted in large part by the assurance of officials that a speedy trial would be held." Throughout his articles, Rothermel defended the beleaguered town, and he quoted approvingly the statement of a county official that a speedy trial was better than no trial at all. The Alabama-born reporter did admit there was "some justification" to the charge of the ILD that the boys had inadequate counsel. Neither Roddy nor Moody talked with the defendants until a few minutes before the trial began. "Moreover, working without assurance of pay, as these state-appointed attorneys were, there was naturally a reluctance to go to any great expense in preparing the defense case." And there was no question, concluded Rothermel, but that the second jury and some members of the third and fourth juries, heard the roar of applause which greeted the first conviction. They assured him, however, that this had no effect on their deliberations.[25] In addition to the Burton and Rothermel reports, the mob-like atmosphere during the trials had been headlined in Southern newspapers. The Alabama and

---

tribunals," admitted a columnist for the Auburn, Alabama, *Plainsman.* Claims that the Negro received fair treatment in the "white man's court" were completely mythical, he sadly concluded. Quoted in the Montgomery *Advertiser,* May 2, 1933.

[24] James D. Burton, Report Number 1 on the Scottsboro, Alabama Case, April 14, 1931, in Interracial Commission Papers.

[25] Birmingham *News,* June 9, June 10, June 11, 1931.

Tennessee press also reprinted several of the most inflammatory articles by the two Scottsboro weeklies.

But Alabamians and their neighbors saw nothing wrong with the Scottsboro deliberations. Even as the trials ended, P. W. Campbell of the *Jackson County Sentinel* predicted that "over the country there will be many people who . . . will cry that prejudice ruled." He adamantly denied this. The boys were given "every protection and every right of the law for defense. . . ." In fact, said Campbell, they received "as fair a trial as they could have gotten in any court in the world. . . ." Editor Benson of the *Progressive Age* welcomed a full and rigid investigation. "We believe they [the investigators] will find that no man or set of men were ever given a fairer trial. Every safeguard our Constitution gives to any defendant was given these negroes." The editor of the Huntsville *Daily Times* expressed his personal opinion that "each of the Negroes was given a fair and impartial trial, that each had been given his day in court and was given every protection afforded any defendant." And when these assurances failed to allay doubt, the editors of the Birmingham *Age-Herald* announced that they had taken it upon themselves "to assure the people of the entire United States that no reasonable fault can be found with the fairness or the legality of the trials at Scottsboro." [26]

Far from being concerned about the precipitous rapidity of the indictment and conviction, the press singled this aspect out for special praise. "Alabama is to be commended upon the dispatch with which this matter was disposed of," said the Chattanooga *Times* at the conclusion of the trials. "If justice were uniformly as swift as it was at Scottsboro, hotheads would take the law into their hands much less frequently." The *Progressive Age* noted that it was "delayed justice that causes mob violence." It was best for all concerned "that these things be disposed of in a speedy manner.

[26] Scottsboro *Jackson County Sentinel,* April 9, April 16, 1931; James Stockton Benson, quoted in "Alabama's Race War," *Literary Digest,* CX (August 1, 1931), 8; Huntsville *Daily Times,* June 13, 1931; Birmingham *Age-Herald,* June 18, 1931. In an editorial on April 12, the Birmingham *News* also sought to assure non-Alabamians that the trial at Scottsboro was completely fair.

. . . There is little reason for long drawn out trials and delay. . . ." [27]

Only one Alabama newspaper had doubts. "Whether the eight Negroes are guilty of the crime alleged, God only knows," declared the Selma *Times-Journal*, "but we do know that the environment in which they were subjected to the ordeal of life or death left much to be desired." The *Times-Journal* reviewed the circumstances: proceedings conducted under the shadow of fixed bayonets and in a courtroom "surcharged with racial hatred," while a crowd of ten thousand milled about the courthouse, and then thunderous applause as the guilty verdict was returned. "Any fair minded person knows that a court proceeding under such circumstances is a travesty on the constitutional guarantee of 'a fair and impartial trial,' that it is a mockery of justice. . . ." The Black Belt daily expressed hope that the Alabama Supreme Court would reverse the verdict and order a new trial. And across the border in Tennessee the Chattanooga *World* added that the "impression grows that the Scottsboro trial was a hasty affair, that psychology decreed the verdict in advance. . . ." [28]

The response to such skepticism was an outcry of anger from a resident of northern Alabama. Such a "meddling fling at the judiciary and criminal court machinery" was "right along in line with the ravings of the International Labor Defense organization." When good Southern newspapers failed to take a vigorous stand against such talk, the result was "communism and anarchy." Fortunately, he noted, "as yet, communism is not running the courts of Alabama, the mutterings and ravings of foreign 'reds,' Bolsheviks, revolutionists, busy-bodies, meddlers . . . and other undesirables to the contrary. . . ." [29]

Part of the difficulty was that the Scottsboro trials, whatever their imperfections, were a genuine step forward. A substantial number of white Southerners believed that the rope was necessary to check the Negro. "The system is a harsh one," observed the

[27] Chattanooga *Daily Times*, April 13, 1931; Scottsboro *Progressive Age*, April 2, April 16, 1931.

[28] Selma *Times-Journal*, quoted in the New York *Times*, July 27, 1931, p. 14; Chattanooga *World*, quoted in the Chattanooga *Daily Times*, January 9, 1932.

[29] Letter of W. D. B. Chambers in Chattanooga *Daily Times*, January 9, 1932.

Winston-Salem *Journal,* but it was the only way to prevent "racial amalgamation among the lower strata of society." And if Southerners condoned racial degeneration among the lower classes "it may creep upward." A University of Florida professor interviewed ten male students in his classes on their attitudes toward lynching. Nine of them condoned extra-legal execution in the case of Negroes accused of raping white women.[30] At Alabama State College for Women a female instructor proudly reported that after having had a chance to be "liberalized" only 15 per cent of her third-year students approved lynching.[31]

White Southern moderates usually came from the South's upper or upper middle class, and they had a ready explanation for racial injustice. As Clarence Cason argued, "social station" determined the Southerner's attitude toward the Negro. "A warm and personal connection with black retainers is a part of the family tradition of those Southerners who are linked with the ante-bellum squirearchy." Admittedly this did not help the Negro in his more "radical social aims," but it guarded him from "actual cruelty and flagrant injustice." [32] The primary offender was the "poor white." Generations of battling for marginal existence had narrowed his outlook and made him illogically prejudiced. A New York executive and former Tennessee newsman explained sympathetically that the poor white "cannot be blamed if he is bigoted in his few beliefs, if resentment at things he doesn't understand has cankered so long within him that he acts savagely and violently when an opportunity for expressing this resentment presents itself." [33]

This explanation conveniently absolved white Southern moderates from ultimate responsibility. In contrast they prided them-

---

[30] Winston-Salem *Journal,* October 15, 1932; Letter of Thomas B. Stroup, in *The Nation,* CXXXVIII (1934), 75–76.

[31] Mrs. Lee M. Brooks to Mrs. Jessie Daniel Ames, March 26, 1936, in Association of Southern Women for the Prevention of Lynching Papers, Atlanta University, Atlanta, Georgia. As the observant Alabamian, Clarence Cason, noted, the most tragic thing about lynchings was that the community usually endorsed them or gave tacit support by its silence. Cason, *90° in the Shade,* 119–20.

[32] Clarence Cason, "Black Straws in the Wind," *North American Review,* CCXXXVI (July, 1933), 84–86.

[33] Ben Cothran, "South of Scottsboro," *The Forum and Century,* XCIII (1935), 325.

selves on their efforts on behalf of the Negro. They protested lynching and, to a lesser extent, such inequities as economic persecution and educational inequalities. Occasionally, a particularly courageous Southerner even objected to the political disfranchisement of the Negro. From 1900 to 1930, the number of lynchings gradually decreased from more than a hundred to less than a dozen annually. Beginning in 1930, however, the number rose to an average of almost twenty per year.[34] Even when officials rescued the accused from the mob's vengeance, he seldom obtained impartial justice in the courts. Southerners had earlier discovered that lynchings were untidy and created a bad press. The possibility of a federal antilynching law also acted as a mild restraint. As a result, lynchings were increasingly replaced by situations in which the Southern legal system prostituted itself to the mob's demand. Responsible officials begged would-be lynchers to "let the law take its course," thus tacitly promising that there would be a quick trial and the death penalty. As Arthur F. Raper, author of several works on lynching, observed, such proceedings "retained the essence of mob murder, shedding only its outward forms." [35]

By placing their emphasis on thwarting lynchings and maintaining the legal formalities, Southern leaders created a dilemma. "In the beginning of our [interracial] work, patience and forbearance was urged," declared Mrs. J. F. Hooper, a member of the Alabama Interracial Commission. This had been rewarded by the absence of a lynching in Scottsboro. Now the outcry over the

[34] Southern Commission on the Study of Lynching, *Lynchings and What They Mean* (Atlanta: Southern Commission on the Study of Lynching, 1931), 76; Arthur F. Raper and Walter Chivers, *The Mob Still Rides: A Review of the Lynching Record, 1931–1935* (Atlanta: Commission on Interracial Cooperation, 1936), 7.

[35] Arthur F. Raper, "Race and Class Pressures," 277–78, in Myrdal Collection. See also by Raper, *The Tragedy of Lynching* (Chapel Hill: University of North Carolina Press, 1933), 46. Mrs. Jessie Daniel Ames discusses this aspect of lynching in her seventy-page pamphlet for the Interracial Commission, *The Changing Character of Lynching, 1931–1941* (Atlanta: Commission on Interracial Cooperation, 1942), *passim*. Officials of the Interracial Commission realized the Negro did not receive justice in Southern courts, but they concentrated their efforts on eradicating lynching, in part because they had greater support in Southern communities for such a program. For example, see T. J. Woofter, Jr., and Isaac Fisher, *Cooperation in Southern Communities: Suggested Activities for County and City Interracial Committees* (Atlanta: Commission on Interracial Cooperation, 1921), 45–48.

results of the legal trial presented a new challenge. "It is a problem that never confronted us before and it is hard to get the proper perspective," she noted. "Just as we adjust our thinking and act on one line of cooperation and justice, something new comes up to confront us." [36]

The Scottsboro Case involved more than the usual question of legal formalities: it went to the heart of the race question in the South and demanded of the white Southern liberal that he take a stand on more fundamental questions than whether the letter of the law had been observed. In the context of Southern social thought in the 1930's, it required a measure of radicalism. And radicalism was the last thing Southern interracial leaders wanted. The "enlightened Southern white man," said an Alabama newspaper columnist, had adopted a position "necessarily and mathematically in the middle ground of moderation where the only proper solution or adequate survey of passion provoking problems is to be found." [37] Surrounding the entire interracial movement in the South was an atmosphere which bordered on intellectual escapism. In despair, a Texas-born sociologist active in Southern race relations during the thirties indicted the movement. "We are always in danger of becoming silly romanticists," he said, "mistaking gestures for action, our programs for achievements, our dreams for realities." More than reformers anywhere else in America, Southerners placed undue reliance on "fine phrases, ideals, gestures and resolutions," instead of recognizing that these were impotent in the face of deepseated traditions and embedded vested interests.[38]

Gunnar Myrdal overstated his case when he argued in 1941 that the South was "exceptional in Western nonfascist civilization since the Enlightenment in that *it lacks nearly every trace of radical*

[36] Mrs. J. F. (Nellie G.) Hooper to Mrs. Jessie Daniel Ames, April 28, 1931, in Association of Southern Women for the Prevention of Lynching Papers.

[37] The writer was John Temple Graves, II. Birmingham *Age-Herald,* July 29, 1931.

[38] William O. Brown, "Interracial Cooperation: Some of Its Problems," *Opportunity,* XI (1933) , 272–73.

thought." His thesis, however, was essentially correct.[39] On the surface, it would appear that there were relatively large numbers of Southerners who were caustic critics of their region. In the 1920's, for example, three Southern newspaper editors won the Pulitzer Prize for attacks on the Ku Klux Klan. Editorial prizes went to the Charleston *News and Courier* for an editorial on the decline of Southern statesmanship and to the Norfolk *Virginian Pilot* for a campaign against lynching. But without exception, these critics attacked evils from a conservative stance, and none could by any stretch of the imagination be termed radical.[40] A handful of liberals, primarily located around academic institutions such as the University of North Carolina, were tolerated and occasionally respected because of their national prominence. But they remained such a minority that they became, in Myrdal's words, "inclined to stress the need for patience and to exalt the cautious approach, the slow change, the organic nature of social growth." Most remained aloof from direct involvement in Southern social problems. Those who did not saw so little hope for clearcut victories that they avoided a direct confrontation with controversial issues whenever possible. Their strategy focused around persuading their less advanced white neighbors to accept changes without really understanding what had taken place.[41]

Probably the majority of Southerners involved in interracial work fancied themselves as intellectual descendants of the "old aristocracy." They saw the South's racial problem as an essentially one-to-one (and servant to master) proposition. "If a Negro whose grandfather belonged to your grandfather gets in a jam, he comes to you, tells you about it and ceases to worry," said one Southerner.[42] When forced to grapple with the racial dilemma in its entirety, the Southern moderates differed little from South-

[39] Myrdal, *An American Dilemma*, 466. There was a strain of agrarian radicalism in the South, particularly during the late nineteenth century, but this was relatively unimportant during this period.

[40] George Brown Tindall, "The Benighted South: Origins of a Modern Image," *Virginia Quarterly Review*, XL (1964) , 289.

[41] Myrdal, *An American Dilemma*, 466–73.

[42] Cothran, "South of Scottsboro," 328.

erners in general. They refused to accept the view that the conditions they condemned—lynching, economic and educational discrimination—were inevitable results of the South's insistence on complete segregation. In 1933 a Nashville rabbi closed the annual conference of the Tennessee Interracial Commission with a plea for "peace and justice." In his last sentence, he declared that this could only be accomplished if both races remained within their "separate sphere." [43]

The artificial, elaborately polite and limited contacts between the two races perpetuated the illusion that Southern Negroes were happy with their lot. Southern Negroes (at least those who met occasionally with white leaders) found it expedient to acquiesce in the status quo. When the Alabama Interracial Commission issued a position paper on the Scottsboro case in the summer of 1931, it assured white Alabamians that Negroes "of wide contacts among their people" testified that they had never known more pleasant and harmonious relations between black and white.[44] Interracial leaders of the Deep South had two goals, segregation and justice, and it seldom occurred to most of them that the two might be incompatible. Ben Cothran, a descendant of the "old aristocracy," put it bluntly. The average white man, he said, is "superior to the black man because he is black. My quarrel is not with superiority, but with the method of asserting it at the expense of justice. . . ." [45]

The Interracial Commission remained aloof from the case after the controversy between the ILD and NAACP erupted, but the mere consideration of a future role was enough to bring angry responses from its membership. "I have always been the negro's friend," declared Jesse B. Hearin of Mobile. "But I believe there

[43] Chattanooga *Daily Times,* April 25, 1933.

[44] Report of the Alabama Commission on Interracial Cooperation, August 11, 1931, in Interracial Commission Papers.

[45] Cothran, "South of Scottsboro," 328. There were exceptions. Will Alexander stated frankly in the 1920's that segregation was morally indefensible. Others such as Howard W. Odom (after earlier accepting racist ideas) almost ostentatiously refused to endorse segregation. The majority of Southern moderates, on the other hand, went to great lengths to profess their opposition to "social equality" (*i.e.,* integration) . The charge of "nigger-lover" was the most deadly of blows.

is a line beyond which we cannot go." Should the Interracial Commission take any part in the defense of the Scottsboro boys, "I will thank you to tender my resignation as a member of the Commission." [46] Zebulon Judd, dean of the Auburn University School of Education, captured the mood of Alabama's "better class" when he expressed complete satisfaction with the trial and conviction. "The whole state seems satisfied not only that justice was meted out, but that it was done in an orderly legal fashion," he said. The only disturbance was caused by the "pestiferous interferences from the outside world that knows little or nothing about the case." As to the speed of the deliberations: "All sensible men will agree that the surest way to prevent heat and extralegal measures is to give speedy trials." Another member of the Commission, a prominent Methodist layman in Alabama, insisted that an appeal of the conviction would amount to approval of Negroes' raping white women. [47]

To the fears of race and sex was added the phobia of communism. Moderate Alabamians repeatedly insisted that most of the animosity aroused by the case was not against the defendants' color, but against their red backers. According to John Temple Graves II, the social and economic issues raised by the ILD unfortunately overshadowed the judicial question of whether or not the boys were guilty. [48] Judge Hawkins went so far as to tell Roddy that he did not "really think the boys should be put to death, but . . . the Communists are more of an issue than are the FACTS of the case." [49] And Governor Miller's secretary explained to Robert Russa Moton, superintendent of Tuskegee Institute, that the boys were a "white elephant" on the governor's hands as a result of Communist intervention. He might like to examine the case more

[46] Jesse B. Hearin to James D. Burton, September 12, 1931, in Interracial Commission Papers.

[47] John W. Radney to Mary Moore McCoy, September 7, 1933, in Interracial Commission Papers. Mrs. McCoy was head of the Alabama chapter of the Association of Southern Women for the Prevention of Lynching. Zebulon Judd to E. C. Branson, July 6, 1931, in E. C. Branson Papers, Southern Historical Collection, University of North Carolina, Chapel Hill.

[48] New York *Times,* January 10, 1932, III, 5.

[49] William Pickens to Walter White, Scottsboro Legal File 2, NAACP Papers.

closely, but the ILD had "tied his hands," making it impossible for him to do more than commute the sentences to life.[50]

It is difficult to judge how much of this resentment was real and how much was feigned. Alabamians had a penchant for using "anti-communism" as a weapon against undesirables. "Whomping the reds" was a more respectable national pastime than "nigger-baiting," noted one cynical observer.[51] Alabama industrial leaders, for example, had early seized upon the "red" issue in order to discredit all unionism just as they earlier had incited racial hostilities in an effort to split Negro and white labor unionists.[52] Even the Alabama AFL, a bitter enemy of the Communists, noted that the "reds" had become convenient scapegoats for all unrest in Alabama during the Depression. The large industrialists had raved about the Communists, declared the *Southern Labor Review,* so that the people of Alabama would overlook the real causes of their trouble.[53]

Alabamians were unanimous, however, in their firm conviction that the Communists had seized the Scottsboro Case for purely mercenary motives. If the reds think they can use the friends of any victim of public or private action, then they begin to "bellow and stink," said the Montgomery *Advertiser*'s Grover Cleveland Hall. "Otherwise, all children under ten in this hated capitalistic republic could be chloroformed like surplus kittens without exciting a murmur of protest from any Communist agitator. . . ." [54] The

[50] Robert Russa Moton to Walter White, June 1, 1931, in Scottsboro Legal File 2, NAACP Papers. "God, what a confessional," exclaimed Pickens when Moton told him the governor's attitude. William Pickens to Walter White, June 1, 1931, in Scottsboro Legal File 2, NAACP Papers. J. F. Rothermel, in his reports on the case for the Birmingham *News*, also attributed much of the resentment to the activity of the Communists. Birmingham *News,* June 15, 1931.

[51] Birmingham *Reporter,* undated clipping in ILD Papers.

[52] See Robert David Ward and William Warren Rogers, *Labor Revolt in Alabama: The Great Strike of 1894* (University, Ala.: University of Alabama Press, 1965), 71–74. Horace R. Cayton and George S. Mitchell discuss the practice from a longer historical perspective in their study, *Black Workers and the New Unions* (Chapel Hill: University of North Carolina Press, 1939), 316–20.

[53] Birmingham *Southern Labor Review,* May 9, 1934, quoted in Cayton and Mitchell, *Black Workers,* 341.

[54] Montgomery *Advertiser,* July 19, 1931.

Alabama Interracial Commission charged that there was "brilliant leadership, sleepless energy and apparently unlimited money behind the malevolent [Communist] activity." These "apostles of revolution" pretended friendship for Negroes, but this was only a means to reach their selfish ends. The Commission even attributed to one of the Scottsboro defense lawyers a statement that the eight defendants would be more valuable executed than alive.[55] Without a doubt, declared the Commission, "Race hatred, race discord, murder, rape [and] lynchings" were the Communists' "immediate object." [56] And Will Alexander charged the ILD with seizing the case only as "an opportunity to make propaganda. . . ." It began a "world-wide agitation under the assumption that it [the case] was part of the class struggle," when actually there was no element of class conflict "and the interference of the Communists . . . injects into the case elements which make it very difficult to get adequate defense for the boys." [57]

In the summer of 1931 a series of events confirmed the direst predictions of Alabamians who argued that the Scottsboro Case was a dangerous vehicle of Communist agitation. In late 1930, a young Communist, Donald Burke, had opened an office for the Communist Party, USA, in Birmingham. He organized a few meetings, distributed handbills and leaflets, and sporadically published a newspaper called the *Southern Worker*. Birmingham police periodically raided Burke's office and arrested him, but they were never able to hold him permanently on a vagrancy charge because he could show evidence of employment. Burke concentrated on the Negro district of the city which had been hardest hit by the Depression, but police continuously disrupted Party meetings and intimidated the few Negroes who attended. The Scottsboro Case renewed the Party's hopes that it could organize a significant number of Negroes in the area, and three new assistants joined Burke

[55] The ILD called this statement a "typical capitalist lie." ILD Publicity Release, August 14, 1931, in ILD Papers. Even had attorneys believed this, it is unlikely that they would have been so indiscreet as to make such a statement.

[56] Montgomery *Advertiser*, July 19, 1931.

[57] Will Alexander to Carter Taylor, August 5, 1931, in Interracial Commission Papers.

in his office.[58] Despite repeated threats, ILD representatives distributed leaflets in Scottsboro, Huntsville, Paint Rock, and other areas of Alabama, calling on white and Negro workers to "smash the Scottsboro lynch verdict." On April 29, 1931, the ILD and the League of Struggle for Negro Rights called an "all-Southern Scottsboro Defense Conference" to meet May 24 in Chattanooga, Tennessee. The conference, said the ILD, would use the Scottsboro Case as a symbol of the injustices of black workers in the South.

In spite of extensive preparations and widespread publicity, fewer than two hundred persons, mostly Negroes from the immediate vicinity, attended. The *Daily Worker* blamed the failure on "a carefully planned campaign to terrorize and prevent the delegates to the all-Southern Scottsboro Conference from being elected and allowed to assemble." There was a measure of truth in the charge. Chattanooga police harassed the group by arresting B. D. Amis, President of the League of Struggle for Negro Rights, Tom Johnson of the ILD, and Harry Heywood of the Communist Party. The three men had stepped outside during a recess in the meeting. Police charged them with "loitering on the sidewalk" and held them in jail until the conference had ended. The Birmingham delegation planned to leave at 4 A.M. in order to be at Chattanooga when the conference opened. When they met at Burke's office and began getting into the assembled cars, however, police picked up the entire group and charged them with a violation of Birmingham's curfew law. They were later released without fines, but too late to reach Chattanooga.[59] The basic reason the ILD's ambitious hopes largely remained unfulfilled was not police harassment, but the general hostility within the South dur-

[58] Report of Lt. Ralph E. Hurst, October 19, 1932, in Alabama Executive Files, Drawer 32. Hurst, a former member of Representative Hamilton Fish's staff, was attached to the Military Intelligence Reserve Corps of the 62nd Infantry Brigade of the Alabama National Guard. At the request of his commanding officer, Brigadier General J. C. Persons, he made a thorough investigation of Communist activity in the Birmingham area through late 1932 and submitted it to Governor Miller.

[59] New York *Daily Worker*, June 1, 1931; Chattanooga *Daily Times*, May 25, 1931; Birmingham *Reporter*, June 1, 1931; New York *Daily Worker*, June 3, 1931. Amis, Johnson and Haywood were ultimately fined ten dollars and released.

ing this period. And the Party's weak organizational structure did little to compensate for this disadvantage. There were few native Communists and it took a dedicated Party member to risk a sojourn in any Deep South city, let alone the rural areas. But the very fact that the Communists, for the first time on a substantial scale, had operated openly, even blatantly, in the old Confederacy, alarmed and disturbed conservative Southerners.[60]

In spite of the failure of the Chattanooga conference, a handful of Communist organizers moved quietly into the rural areas of a few of the Deep South states in the summer of 1931. They made one of their greatest efforts at organizing the "oppressed black peasantry" in Tallapoosa County, Alabama, an impoverished cotton-growing county in central Alabama. Here white and Negro tenants lived in separate but equal squalor. Annually, per capita education expenditures for whites were less than twenty-five dollars, while the budget for Negro education was negligible. Yet the deprivation was not so pronounced as in some of the Black Belt counties such as Dallas, Lowndes, and Greene. And by rural standards of the period, race relations were better than average. Despite the fact that one-third of the county's 31,000 residents were Negroes, there had not been a lynching during the twentieth century.[61]

In early June, 1931, four white men and one Negro from Chattanooga moved without announcement into the most predominantly Negro section of the county around Camp Hill. After two days, the white men drove away, leaving their Negro comrade the task of organizing the tenants of the region. More out of despair than conviction, the sharecroppers paid their five cent initiation fee and joined the "Society for the Advancement of Colored People," a name designed to conceal the fact that it was in reality a "sharecroppers union." The organizer concentrated on specific

[60] Chattanooga *Daily Times*, May 6, 1931.
[61] Charles Spurgeon Johnson, *Statistical Atlas of Southern Counties; Listing and Analysis of Socio-Economic Indices of 1104 Southern Counties* (Chapel Hill: University of North Carolina Press, 1941), p. 53. The value of the white schools was $24,515 as compared to $1,500 for the Negro schools.

economic issues and generally ignored any discussion of a "black republic." He promised his listeners that if they would organize in a tightly knit group they could force the plantation owners to increase the quantity of "furnishings" through the winter and double the wage for cotton picking.[62]

The young Negro organizer hoped to remain unnoticed by white Tallapoosa residents, but in mid-July, a cooperative Negro tenant informed Sheriff J. Kyle Young that "radical meetings" were being held in the county. On a tip from the same informer, Sheriff Young interrupted a meeting of the group's officers on Wednesday, July 15, in a sharecropper's shack near Camp Hill. Of the eight Negroes present, all were from Tallapoosa County, and they insisted they had just happened to meet that night. They denied membership in a radical group and insisted they knew nothing of any outsider. Early the next evening, however, the sheriff learned that two hundred Negroes were meeting in the Mary Church, also near Camp Hill. The purpose of the meeting, he discovered, was to draft a resolution of protest on the Scottsboro Case and send it to Governor Miller. Shortly after 8 P.M., accompanied by Camp Hill Chief of Police J. M. Wilson and two deputies, Young rode out to the church for an investigation. Down the winding road leading to the church, the sheriff hailed a young Negro sharecropper, Ralph Grey, who was walking along carrying a large bundle under one arm and a shotgun under the other. According to one Camp Hill resident, the sheriff asked Grey what he had in the bundle under his arm, and "the nigger said it was none of his damn business." When Sheriff Young reached back into the car for his gun, Grey fired both barrels of his shotgun. Several pellets struck Young and one of his deputies in the side and arm. Before Grey could reload, Chief Wilson and the other deputy emptied their shotguns and he dropped to the ground.[63]

---

[62] New York *Daily Worker,* July 20, 1931.

[63] Reports on the Camp Hill incident are voluminous and while they differ on several points, they are in general agreement on major details. This account is based on news stories in the Birmingham *News* and *Age-Herald,* July 17 through July 20, 1931, and the New York *Times* for the same period. In the New York *Daily Worker,* July 20, 1931, there is an account supposedly written by the Communist organizer

At the first sound of gunfire, the meeting at the church abruptly adjourned and the tenants fled into the night. While one of the deputies took Thompson and Young to a nearby doctor, Chief Wilson organized a posse which eventually numbered more than five hundred men. Alarm gave way to panic and by 11 P.M. the town had dissolved into chaos. Three hapless Negroes who happened to drive through Dadeville shortly before midnight were greeted by a volley of buckshot through one window. They escaped by convincing the armed men who surrounded them that they knew nothing of any uprising. Shortly after midnight Wilson learned that Grey, who was not dead as he had thought, had been taken by friends to his cabin near the church. Fifty "deputies" surrounded the two-room, unpainted shack. When the wounded Grey failed to respond to a call from the chief of police, the posse began firing through the closed shutters. In the space of ten minutes, they fired over a thousand rounds into the flimsy building. When they threw open the door they found Grey dead on the floor, his earlier wounds smeared with Mercurochrome. They also found three men and three women huddled behind a cast iron stove. By some freak accident, only two had been slightly wounded.[64]

By 2 A.M. all white men within twenty miles had armed themselves with sawed-off shotguns, rifles, pistols, and, according to one account, an ancient breech-loading shotgun. They patrolled the highways, riding on the running boards of cars in an effort to

---

in the area. Howard A. Kester, the Southern Field Secretary for the Fellowship of Reconciliation, made a ten-day visit to the Black Belt in August and summarized his findings in a letter to Walter White, August 15, 1931, Scottsboro Legal File 2, NAACP Papers. Henry Fuller went to Tallapoosa County for the *New Republic* and gave a colorful and occasionally unreliable description of the incident in "Sunday at Camp Hill," *New Republic*, XCIX (1931), 132-34. John Beecher has provided a thorough discussion of the causes of the uprising in his article, "The Share Cropper's Union in Alabama," *Social Forces*, XIII (1934), 124-32.

[64] After Wilson had several days to mull over the incident he gave a far more colorful description of Grey's arrest. When the posse reached the shack, said Wilson, "Grey shouted curses and dared the men to capture him. It was then that the real gun battle began." According to Wilson, the Negroes in the shack opened fire first; "the officers hugged the ground and shot back." Birmingham *Age-Herald*, July 20, 1931. While this account has a certain dramatic flair, it completely contradicts other descriptions given by both black and white participants.

round up every possible culprit. This proved extremely difficult, for most Negroes had left their houses and taken to the woods. Occasionally a Negro woman might be found, but there were virtually no men remaining within their homes in a five mile radius of the church. On Friday, instead of subsiding, the unreasoning fear increased as rumors of armed Negro mobs spread wildly. With the temperature sweltering in the nineties, perspiring deputies roamed through the county searching Negroes' homes and roughly questioning the occupants. They were particularly interested in finding the organizer who had fled at the first gunfire. Grey's body, recovered from his shack, was thrown on the piazza of the courthouse at Dadeville, and throughout the morning spectators came to view the riddled body. Shortly after noon, Wilson received news that automobiles filled with Negroes from nearby Alexander City were on their way to Dadeville to "spring" the handful of Negroes who had been arrested. Fifty men took up positions with shotguns and rifles around the jail, while another fifty formed a roadblock on the highway coming into town. They waited into the night for the nonexistent cars.

The inaccurate rumors were not challenged by the newspapers. On Saturday morning, the Birmingham *Age-Herald* headlined: "Negro Reds Reported Advancing." Supposedly eight carloads of Negro Communists had left Chattanooga and were on their way to aid their comrades. One hundred and fifty men, weary with chasing the phantom mobs, but determined to defend their homes, formed a blockade at the highway bridge north of Tallapoosa. Shortly after noon a lookout car roared across the bridge to report that at least two dozen cars filled with Negroes were on their way. The men tensely waited, but when they stopped the lead car and snatched the terrified driver from behind the wheel, they learned it was a Negro funeral procession driving from Sylacauga, Alabama, to a country graveyard north of Dadeville. None of the mourners was armed. Somewhat embarrassed, the men allowed the procession to go on and gradually began returning to their homes.

On Sunday a measure of sanity returned to the community.

Sixty Negroes had been arrested; five were immediately charged with assault with intent to commit murder, seven with carrying concealed weapons, and twenty with conspiring to commit a felony. Chief Wilson said an examination of minute books at the Mary Church revealed that 170 Negroes had joined the group. He also told newsmen he had uncovered literature urging members to "demand social equality with the white race, two dollars a day for work," and not to ask, but to "demand what you want and if you don't get it, take it." Solicitor Sanford Mullins' investigation differed somewhat. According to him, the group was primarily intent on freeing the Scottsboro boys and had threatened Governor Miller with violence unless he agreed to their release. By this action, said Mullins, they openly condoned the raping of white women.[65]

Despite the number of armed men roaming through the community, casualties were relatively light. The sheriff and his deputy were only slightly wounded, and the Negroes injured at Grey's house recovered. All, that is, with the exception of one who was alleged to be a "ringleader." He was taken from the jail by several possemen, according to Wilson, to "cut stovewood." When asked by reporters when he would be brought back, the chief replied: "He has lots to cut," and refused to comment further. Grey's was the only confirmed death, but Howard Kester of the Fellowship of Reconciliation reported after a ten-day investigation that several others died from wounds suffered in the shootings and were quietly buried. The church in which the sharecroppers met mysteriously burned to the ground on Friday and the nearby shack of a member also went up in flames.

White Alabamians reacted with a mixture of fear and horror. At the urgent request of the Alabama Interracial Commission, Superintendent Moton of Tuskegee sent several carloads of prominent Negroes to the area to prevent Tallapoosa Negroes from "going red." [66] The Birmingham *News* urged the white people of

[65] Sheriff Young, Chief Wilson, and Solicitor Mullins discussed in general terms the "inflammatory literature" they found at the church, but despite repeated requests from newsmen, they refused to release it for examination.

[66] Mrs. Zebulon Judd to E. C. Branson, August 8, 1931, in E. C. Branson Papers.

Tallapoosa County to "keep their outraged passions well-reined in this extremity." Unfortunately, said the *News*, the "simple minded Negroes" of the area had "hearkened to the wily words of these Negro Pied Pipers. . . ." But the most guilty persons were the "black Communist evangelists" who had demoralized the community. It was the responsibility of the Negro leaders and preachers in the entire state to "disarm any belief the rank and file [of Negroes] may entertain that these Red evangelists are their friends." There was no greater responsibility at this point than to "cooperate with Alabama law enforcement officials in weeding out these social enemies whenever they appear with incendiary talk." [67] The *News* blamed the ignorance of the Tallapoosa Negroes on their foolish belief that the Scottsboro boys were not guilty and called on Alabamians to be charitable in their judgment. The Chattanooga *Daily Times* attributed the "Camp Hill disaster" to the "so-called liberals" who had aided and abetted the Communists in their nefarious work of discrediting the South's legal system. As long as these liberal elements joined in criticizing the Scottsboro verdict, there would be further bloodshed.[68]

Not one Alabama newspaper pointed out that, far from being a bloody Negro race riot, it was the whites who formed mobs and terrorized the countryside. The only violence by a Negro was Grey's shooting of the sheriff and deputy, the act of a single individual. Instead, the press and local officials seemed intent on proving to the satisfaction of everyone that the local Negroes were bent on raping and killing the whites of the community. The real crime of the hapless Negroes was simply their effort to organize. Local whites correctly saw this as a threat to the status quo. Any effort to give the Negro tenant a voice in the renting and share-cropping contracts and a role in determining wages was essentially

[67] Birmingham *News*, July 18, 1931. Negro middle-class leaders in the Birmingham area dutifully responded with a joint statement pledging their efforts to stamp out the "baneful influence of Communism" among the ignorant Negro masses. Black Alabamians were "intensely loyal" to the white people of the state, according to the statement; and they would oppose without ceasing the doctrines "calculated not only to overthrow our form of government, but to uproot our very civilization." Birmingham *News*, July 20, 1931.

[68] Chattanooga *Daily Times*, July 18, 1931.

"revolutionary." At heart, Tallapoosa white citizens knew that the movement also threatened the existing biracial relationship. Thus they were unduly concerned about the sharecroppers' stepping "out of their place" in protesting the Scottsboro verdict. This was "white man's business" and of no concern to black tenants. But none of the major Alabama newspapers mentioned in any way the stark deprivation of Tallapoosa Negro tenants which had led them to join the sharecroppers' union in the first place.[69]

The Tallapoosa County furor had scarcely subsided before Alabamians received evidence of further consequences from the infamous Scottsboro Case. Late on the afternoon of August 4 two sisters and a friend from prominent Birmingham families were on their way home after an afternoon movie. As they slowed for a narrow bridge, an armed Negro leaped onto the running board of their car and forced them to follow a narrow winding road to a deserted wooded area just outside the city limits near Leeds, Alabama. The man first raped and then "harangued" the three girls concerning the way in which white people had mistreated his people. When Augusta Williams, one of his victims, distracted him for a moment, her sister, Nell, lunged for the pistol. The assailant began firing wildly and seriously wounded the two Williams girls and killed their young friend, Jennie Wood. Several hours after the shooting, Augusta died, but her pretty younger sister carefully described their attacker from the hospital bed where she lay. He was in his middle thirties, she said, soot black, short and stocky, with a "Charley Chaplin mustache." He appeared to be from "up North" and "very educated," she said, but he apparently knew his way around the area. She was vague about

[69] The hearings for the Negroes were postponed for a month. Then charges were dropped against all but seven of the defendants. Eventually, a number of prominent Alabamians, concerned about the publicity that a mass trial might bring on top of the Scottsboro trials, persuaded local officials to postpone the cases indefinitely. Birmingham *Age-Herald*, July 29, 1931; New York *Daily Worker*, August 6, 1931. James D. Burton to Lyman Ward, November 25, 1932; Lyman Ward to James D. Burton, November 30, 1932, in Interracial Commission Papers. Ward, principal of the Southern Industrial Institute in Camp Hill, was active in these negotiations, but he refused to disclose the names of the persons who had intervened.

what he had said during the two hours, but she repeatedly described his remarks as a "radical harangue." [70]

A Birmingham Negro welfare organization tried to temper the anger of white citizens with a statement deploring the "atrocious deed" and promising "to cooperate with the authorities and place ourselves at their disposal to do all in our power, under their instructions, to find the perpetrator of this heinous crime." They concluded: "We desire to say to our white friends of the city . . . [that the fact] that an awful crime has been committed against womanhood by one of our race causes us to hang our heads in shame." [71] One Birmingham newspaper called for "continuous offensive action" until the "negro madman, or fiend incarnate" was arrested and brought to justice. Birmingham citizens responded enthusiastically by bombing a Negro's barber shop and firing upon a group of Negroes as they stood quietly on a sidewalk. Self-styled "deputies" made house-to-house searches of the Negro homes in the area until the News had to call for a moratorium on the "sporadic outbreaks . . . against the persons and property of Negro citizens." [72]

The News believed the tragedy could be traced to the fact that the culprit had been corrupted by outside Communists. "If this is one of the outgrowths of Communism on these shores; if this is the aim of the propaganda of that doctrine, then Southerners and all Americans . . . who understand the inequalities of the races . . . must by every possible means lance out of the social body these infamous and unnatural teachings." [73] Authorities became doubly concerned when several of the unauthorized posses uncovered "radical literature" in the Negro homes they searched. Four days after the attack, Sheriff Hawkins arrested Harry Jackson of Birmingham's Communist Party office and held him on an open charge. Hawkins implied there was some connection between

[70] Birmingham News, August 5, 1931. It was never completely clear whether the attacker had actually raped all of the three girls. Miss Williams contradicted her story on this and medical evidence was never introduced at the later trials. The charge was murder, not rape.

[71] Birmingham News, August 9, 1931.

[72] Ibid., August 7, August 8, 1931; Birmingham Age-Herald, August 8, 1931.

[73] Birmingham News, August 8, 1931.

Jackson's propaganda efforts and the shooting and told reporters
he had formed a special "anti-red squad" composed of four new
deputies. They would spend all their time uncovering Communist
cell meetings and "breaking them up." [74] The Alabama department of the American Legion called the attention of the state to
the "horde of communists" who had descended upon Alabama
"spreading a flood of propaganda opposing our form of government and social conditions, our race relationships and all the bases
upon which our society rests, advocating race equality and destruction of law and authority by force and violence." The Legion said,
"Our system of race segregation" was being viciously attacked by
the Communists. The murder of the two girls and the uprising in
Tallapoosa County could both be traced to the influx of the reds
beginning with their defense of the Scottsboro "negro rapists."
The people of Alabama should stop at nothing until these communist inroads were halted.[75]

With public opinion in Alabama already stirred to "fever heat"
by the Scottsboro Case and the Camp Hill uprising, the Birmingham shooting produced a "maddening atmosphere," said Howard
Kester. In the *New Masses*, Norman MacLeod described white
Alabamians' fears of a Negro revolt. Northerners were arrested
and searched for literature whenever they passed through the
small towns of the state. Whites were tense, worried, almost hysterical. "The only stores that prosper in these hard times are those
which deal in firearms," MacLeod said. He exaggerated, but Alabama's liberals and conservatives alike were caught up in an atmosphere of foreboding. "If we can escape violence on a large
scale, or a break between white and colored people in the next
two or three years, we shall be very fortunate," said Will Alexander.[76] The Depression had settled over the state, particularly in

[74] *Ibid.*, August 10, 1931. When Lowell Wakefield, the ILD representative in
Chattanooga, went to Birmingham jail to post bond for Jackson, Sheriff Hawkins
arrested and threw him in jail on an open charge. Both Jackson and Wakefield were
finally released on bail and the charges later were dropped. Birmingham *News*,
August 12, 1931.
[75] Birmingham *News*, August 24, 1931; Birmingham *Age-Herald*, August 25, 1931.
[76] Howard Kester to Walter White, August 15, 1931, in Scottsboro Legal File 3,
NAACP Papers; Norman MacLeod, "Agitated Alabama," *New Masses*, VII (October,

the countryside and the mines. There had not yet been time enough for the deadening anesthesia of continually unfulfilled wants. From Camp Hill a middle-aged white woman wrote Governor Miller to beg him to commute the Scottsboro sentences. "I fully believe that something dreadful will take place if they are executed," she said. "Our county is almost sunk by the reign of poverty and fear. . . . Our people are at a breaking point now from poverty and trouble." The riots and rumors of further disorders had brought fear and suspense to the countryside. "Please, please, don't let us have to go through the like again." [77]

Other Alabamians were concerned, but their fears only strengthened their resolve to see the Scottsboro boys executed. "I see from the newspapers that you have received a number of threats to release the Scottsboro rapists 'or else,' " said one Alabamian. "I hope that this will not deter you from your duty in seeing that the sentences are carried through." As long as these "black fiends" remained alive, they would be "used by the reds to incite our colored people to riot, rape and kill." [78] A former native of Jackson County put it bluntly. "I'm sure you will not permit any pressure to weaken you," he said. "These burr-heads are fortunate that they were not burned. In fact they should have been skinned, as burning is too tame." [79]

The shooting of the two girls was a chilling dress rehearsal for the problems the Scottsboro boys faced. Approximately two months after the incident Miss Williams, fully recovered, was riding through downtown Birmingham when she excitedly pointed to a Negro man walking quietly down the sidewalk. He was the assailant, she declared. Her brother, Dent Williams, pulled a pistol from the glove compartment and took Willie Peterson into

1931), 18–19; Will Alexander to William G. McDowell, August 7, 1931, in Interracial Commission Papers.

[77] The writer was obviously well educated. She explained that she was from an old Alabama family, but she was writing anonymously because she feared publicity. [?] to Governor Benjamin Meeks Miller, May 2, 1932, in Drawer 49, Alabama Executive Files.

[78] Edward P. Smith to Governor Benjamin Meeks Miller, August 22, 1931, in Alabama Scottsboro Files.

[79] C. V. Henshaw to Governor Benjamin Meeks Miller, August 24, 1931, in Alabama Scottsboro Files.

custody. When authorities began a thorough investigation, however, a number of disturbing facts emerged. In the first place, Peterson did not in any way resemble the description of the assailant given by Miss Williams and her sister before she died. He was in his middle thirties, but, far from being short and stocky, he was gaunt and emaciated, his sallow face mirroring a four-year fight with tuberculosis. He had never worn a mustache and his skin color was light chocolate instead of black. Moreover, a half dozen neighbors were willing to swear that they had seen him on the opposite side of town at the time the shootings took place.[80]

In the face of this contradictory evidence, Jefferson County's Sheriff Hawkins tried to dissuade Miss Williams, but once she had decided she had the guilty party, she refused to retract her identification. When it became apparent that Miss Williams had made a mistake, her brother, Dent Williams, asked the sheriff to arrange one further meeting at which his sister might be sure she had the right man. As Williams and his sister entered the interrogation room, county officials searched him; but as soon as Peterson was brought into the room, Williams slipped his hand into his sister's purse, removed a pistol, and shot the thin Negro three times before the deputies could disarm him.[81]

Miraculously, Peterson recovered, but the aftermath of the shooting was a grotesque parody of Southern justice. State officials, knowing full well that Peterson was innocent, went ahead and indicted and tried him as soon as he was able to leave his hospital

[80] Mrs. Peterson told investigators that, because of his health, her husband was totally impotent and could not have had sexual relations with one person, certainly not with three. Peterson's physician noted that the ailing Negro could not walk rapidly because of his tubercular condition, let alone leap onto a moving automobile. And the idea that Peterson, who, as one observer kindly noted, was illiterate and "mentally limited," could have passed as an "educated Northerner" was ludicrous. See Robert Burns Eleazer's Confidential Memorandum re. *State* v. *Peterson,* September 2, 1933, in Interracial Commission Papers.

[81] Birmingham *Age-Herald,* October 7, October 9, 1931; New York *Times,* October 9, 1931, p. 19. Robert Eleazer, who investigated the case for the Interracial Commission, reported that it was common knowledge among officials that Williams had vowed to end questions about the identification of Peterson by killing him. Confidential Memorandum re. *State* v. *Peterson,* September 2, 1933, in Interracial Commission Papers.

bed. On the stand, Miss Williams' testimony was so filled with contradictions and inconsistencies that the first jury was unable to reach a verdict after forty-four hours.[82] The International Labor Defense offered to come to the aid of Peterson, but on the advice of white interracial leaders in Birmingham, he stuck with his local court-appointed attorney. The second time, the jury deliberated only twenty minutes before returning with a guilty verdict. Peterson was sentenced to die in the electric chair.[83] Will Alexander tried to persuade Alabamians to take the lead in fighting for Peterson's freedom. The indigent Negro had refused to cooperate with the ILD when it tried to step into the case and instead put his faith in the good people of Alabama. Was this to be his reward? Alexander received little support. "The young woman is a well balanced person of intelligence and belongs to a quiet and highly respected family," said Episcopal Bishop William G. McDowell of Birmingham. He could not believe she would send an innocent person to his death.[84]

No doubt McDowell was sincere in his belief that Peterson was guilty. But, as one Birmingham attorney said, "Miss Williams has very surely picked the wrong negro. The officials of the state of Alabama know this. The solicitor knows it. . . ." [85] And yet they had gone ahead. This far would Alabamians go in defense of the caste system. Rather than humiliate Miss Williams by contradicting her story, the state of Alabama was willing to convict an innocent man. The "honor" of one white woman was more important than the life's blood of a black man, said the Birmingham *Reporter*. A Negro accused of rape by a white woman had not the "chance of a sheep-killing dog to establish his innocence or to get the benefit of any doubt." [86] Ultimately, through the personal

[82] Birmingham *News*, December 8, 9, 10, 11, 12, 1931.

[83] Birmingham *Post*, January 25, 1932.

[84] Will Alexander to William G. McDowell, July 29, 1933; William G. McDowell to Will Alexander, August 3, 1933, in Interracial Commission Papers.

[85] Patrick Appelbaum to Lowell Wakefield, October 9, 1931, in ILD Papers. Peterson was "innocent beyond the shadow of a doubt," said Eleazer in his report. Confidential Memorandum re. *State* v. *Peterson*, September 2, 1933, in Interracial Commission Papers.

[86] Birmingham *Reporter*, April 1, 1933.

pleas of Alexander and a number of Alabamians (including Sheriff Hawkins) Governor Miller was persuaded to commute the sentence to life imprisonment in Kilby Prison where Peterson died several years later of tuberculosis. Dent Williams was never indicted for the shooting of Peterson.[87]

The Scottsboro boys had one advantage over Peterson. Their accusers were not from Alabama's finest families. Their liabilities, however, far outweighed this one asset. During the summer of 1931, for many Americans, the Scottsboro Case became almost a talisman, a symbol of the daily injustice Southern whites inflicted upon the Negroes of the region. In white Alabama, it also became a symbol of the horrors of communism and the accompanying dreaded "social equality." [88] Most of the concern was groundless. Communist activity in Alabama was ineffectual and extremely limited; the state's news media exaggerated the strength of the movement all out of proportion to its real significance. The Communist press also encouraged these inaccurate estimations because it gave them a facade of strength with which to appeal for further support.[89] Moreover, there was little proof of any connection between the shooting at Leeds and "Communist infiltration," let alone between the attack and the Scottsboro Case. But Carl Car-

[87] Were the sources not so scattered, a study of the entire subject of "black rapists" would make a significant contribution to an understanding of Southern racial attitudes. For example, earlier in 1931, a middle-aged woman and her seventeen-year-old daughter were attacked in their home just outside of Birmingham. Altogether the daughter "positively identified" four suspects successively, only to learn that each had an iron-clad alibi. (One was three hundred miles away; another was on a road gang at the time.) The fifth suspect was not able to explain his movement at the time of the crime. He was tried, convicted, and sentenced to a long term in the Alabama state prison. Birmingham *News*, April 5, April 6, April 16, April 20, April 28, April 29, May 4, 1931.

[88] Kester found genuine interest among Southerners in the economics of communism, "but at the mention of a classless society . . . they fly into a RED rage." Howard A. Kester to Walter White, August 15, 1931, in Scottsboro Legal File 3, NAACP Papers.

[89] "Local law enforcement officials and business interests in Southern communities reacted on a hysterical basis to even the slightest manifestation of mass discontent," declared Wilson Record. "The violent handling of Communist organizers and the publicity surrounding it, gave the impression that their program and influence were far more pervasive than they actually were." Record, *The Negro and Communism*, 74.

mer captured the attitude of many Alabamians when he talked with an old Harvard classmate from the northern part of the state. "I might have been for acquittin' them at the first trial," his friend declared, "but now after all this stink's been raised, we've got to hang 'em." The friend pointed to the Leeds incident and related how Peterson had talked to the girls "about how white folks oppress the niggers and about Communism." That would not have occurred, he said, "if it hadn't been for this God-damn Scottsboro business and I'm for seeing that it doesn't happen again." [90]

[90] Carl Carmer, *Stars Fell on Alabama* (New York: Farrar and Rinehart, Inc., 1934), 76–77. As one of Governor Miller's constituents put it, the "God fearing people of the South . . . truly hope no threat or demand from dirty yankees or damn communists from the North and throughout the world will sway you either way in the death sentence of the seven negroes for assaulting white girls." Whether "in box cars or asleep," white women should be protected. "Remember the three young girls in Birmingham who were out riding in their car." J. F. Smith to Governor Benjamin Meeks Miller, September 22, 1932, in Alabama Scottsboro File.

V

RED ON
BLACK

ONE overriding conviction dominated the thinking of American Communists as they began their defense of the Scottsboro defendants. "Precisely because the Scottsboro Case is an expression of the horrible national oppression of the Negro masses," said the *Daily Worker,* "any real fight . . . must necessarily take the character of a struggle against the whole brutal system of landlord robbery and imperialist national oppression of the Negro people." [1] The fight for the Scottsboro boys' freedom would be inextricably joined with the class struggle. The constant linking of Scottsboro with the Sacco-Vanzetti case by Party publicists often gave the impression that the nine defendants had been not only class conscious members of the proletariat, but also revolutionary activists. In general, however, Party leaders made more modest claims. "The issue of the oppression of Negroes is obviously an economic question," said one official of the International Labor Defense. The bourgeoisie, terrified at the growing solidarity of the Negro masses with their white co-workers, had decided to execute the nine defendants in order to crush this new black and white militancy. Rape was simply the charge most useful in separating the two races. In the face of such tactics, freedom for the nine could be gained only by successfully waging the class struggle. [2]

---

[1] New York *Daily Worker,* January 31, 1933.
[2] Letter by Anna Damon, in *The Nation,* CXXXIX (1934), 674. "Some say this is

The Communist Party, acting through the ILD, accepted the need for legal action, but Party leaders repeatedly stressed the futility of relying upon capitalistic justice. The courts were the "instruments of national and class oppression," and it was therefore the Party's duty to destroy "all democratic and legalist illusions among the masses." Any appeal to the high courts of Alabama and the United States had to be subordinated to the "development of revolutionary mass action outside of courts and bourgeois legislative bodies." [3] Mass action—the two words invoked a profound response from American communism in the 1930's. It was as though the Party's leadership and many of its members had been mesmerized by the jerky silent films of 1918, showing the workers, soldiers, and peasants racing across Red Square to storm the Duma and establish the first dictatorship of the proletariat. In the midst of the 1919 Palmer raids, arrests and deportations, Party leader Louis Fraina demonstrated this ideological passion. "Our comrades are languishing in prison," he said. "Amnesty cannot reach them and we don't want amnesty for them! *We want them released by the industrial might of the proletariat, by class conscious action.*" [4] The struggle to free the Scottsboro boys and other "political prisoners" went beyond the particular case at hand. It was an exercise in education for the masses and a catalyst for transforming them into a class-conscious proletariat. Critics assumed from this that the ILD was willing to sacrifice the boys for the revolution. But, if the Party's stated assumptions were intellectually honest (and this was a question violently debated), the mass appeals were indispensable for victory. Since the capitalist ruling class controlled the state and federal judiciary, the struggle for the complete freedom of the Scottsboro boys could succeed "only

---

not a labor case," noted Josephine Herbst in the *New Masses*, "but these boys were on the move because their families were poor and they had no work. The ignorance and poverty of the Southern Negro were not the result of mystical factors," she said. He was "ignorant and poor because it has seemed to be an economic advantage to keep him that way." Josephine Herbst, "Lynching in the Quiet Manner," *New Masses*, VII (July, 1931), 11.

[3] Harry Haywood, "The Scottsboro Decision: Victory of Revolutionary Struggle over Reformist Betrayal," *The Communist*, XI (1932), 1068.

[4] Howe, *The American Communist Party*, 59.

if linked up with the struggle against the whole system which breeds similar Scottsboros." [5]

The contention that the Scottsboro boys were victims of "class war" dismayed and disturbed American liberals. The *World Tomorrow*, a Protestant-Socialist publication, predicted sadly: "Communist doctrine makes it inevitable that the fate of the boys will be made subservient to the case of dramatizing the class struggle in America." Depiction of the condemned youths as "victims of capitalist injustice" was both pathetic and ominous, argued the *Christian Century*. In fact, it would be impossible to misinterpret more completely the entire case. Here were nine Negro youths, eight of them illiterate and all completely baffled by their predicament. To describe them as conscious participants in class conflict "is to ignore all the elements in the case which made it appeal to those with social conscience—their friendlessness, their ignorance, their bewilderment." The class struggle thesis aroused "unreasoning prejudice," said the *New Republic*. Along with *The Nation*, the *New Republic* called for nonradical control of the defense efforts. The alternative was to subordinate the main issue—the guilt or innocence of the boys—to the Communist Party's struggle for proletarian hegemony.[6]

The Communists retained a number of intellectual allies. The author of a letter to the *Christian Century* agreed that the boys were both unlettered and unsophisticated. Nor was their arrest incidental to any actual class or labor conflict, he said; but the manner in which they were imprisoned, tried, and sentenced was an obvious result of the Southern economic structure. The very "passion of the 'poor white trash' of the south toward the black

[5] Haywood, "The Scottsboro Decision," 1068.

[6] The *World Tomorrow*, quoted in Ralph Lord Roy, *Communism and the Churches* (New York: Harcourt, Brace and Company, 1960), 50; "This Misinformed World," *Christian Century*, XXXVIII (1931), 941; "The Communists and the Scottsboro Case," *New Republic*, LXVIII (1931), 343; "Scottsboro," *The Nation*, CXXXIV (1932), 941. Editors of the *New Republic* later accepted the contention of the Communist Party that the boys were convicted primarily because of class hatred, but declined to support the ILD. "Scottsboro Case Again," *New Republic*, LXXIV (1933), 147.

man derives undeniably from the economic exploitation of both." [7]
Roger N. Baldwin, the American Civil Liberties Union's executive director, stopped short of endorsing the revolutionary
methods of the Communists, but in other respects he gave the
Party complete support. He noted that while assistance from any
source was helpful, "middle class groups are without much force,
for their motives are not rooted in self-interest, and they therefore
tend to be intermittent and half-hearted." More reliable were al-
liances based on "economic self-interest—unions of workers, of
share-croppers, of the unemployed." Baldwin endorsed the "demonstrations, mass action by white and black workers together and
world-wide appeals and publicity." Only through these methods
could the workers "nakedly expose" the South's "white ruling
class." [8]

Despite the fact that there were a large number of Americans
who shared in part the intellectual outlook of the Communists,
the ILD failed to develop a broad coalition of these individuals
and groups. In keeping with the "popular front from below"
strategy, the Party courted the rank and file of such groups as the
NAACP, the National Urban League, and the Socialist Party. A
genuine united front was impossible, however, because the Communist Party refused to compromise with the "ideological corruption" of the " 'liberals' of the Civil Liberties Union, the 'Nation' and the 'New Republic,' and their associates of the Socialist
Party." [9] There were reasonable tactical reasons behind the
Party's violent attacks on the NAACP. It was necessary to discredit
the Association in order to gain complete control of the case, but
the excoriation of all non-Communist groups was something else
again. However much the Communists talked of a "popular

---

[7] Letter by Robert Whitaker, *Christian Century*, XXXVIII (1931), 941.

[8] Roger N. Baldwin, "Negro Rights and the Class Struggle," *Opportunity*, XII
(1934), 264–66. Baldwin went even further and argued that the Communists were
the "only group" with a sufficiently aggressive leadership. Alone, they had challenged the "Divide and Rule" policy of the "whole property-owning South, as of all
ruling classes." With this philosophy, it is easy to see why many Southerners (and
conservative Americans) professed an inability to distinguish between the ACLU
and the Communist Party.

[9] New York *Daily Worker*, May 25, 1931.

front," leaders of such groups as the ACLU and the Socialist Party
—potentially the Communists' intellectual allies—rapidly learned
that the slogans were a facade behind which the Party worked un-
scrupulously and unceasingly to "win the masses away from their
bourgeois and petty-bourgeois leaders." In the Scottsboro campaign, the ILD demanded complete subservience to the leadership
of the Communist Party, USA.[10]

On May 14, 1931, the Communist Party's Central Committee
issued its "Organizational Directives on the Scottsboro Case,"
which outlined in detail the tactics to be used. Freedom for the
Scottsboro boys required the recruitment of thousands of "hitherto politically inactive elements or of workers previously following
reformist leadership." Whenever possible, branches of the various
bourgeois-liberal groups should be won for permanent affiliation
with the ILD or LSNR. Whenever these organizations refused to
join, Party and non-Party sympathizers should "fight against the
leaders who block the entrance of the organization as a whole. . . ."
Ideally, the campaign would lead to LSNR and ILD "Neighbor-
hood Committees" on a block-by-block basis in urban areas. Eventually, those who joined the local fronts could be brought directly
into the Party.[11]

Initially, the Party concentrated on public protests to publicize
their presence in the case. The ILD, the LSNR, and the Anti-
Imperialist League of the United States kicked off the campaign

[10] Weinstone, "The XI Plenum of the Executive Committee of the Comintern,"
793. Branches of the Socialist Party at first opened their meetings to ILD speakers
soliciting funds and support for the boys. They were rewarded with abusive attacks
on the Socialist Party and a demand that (in effect) they submit to the discipline
of the Communist Party. In July, the National Office instructed all Socialist
branches to continue working for the boys but separately from the Communist
Party. Instructions from National Office, July 18, 1931, in Socialist Party Papers,
Duke University, Durham, N.C. The Communists and the Socialists had been at log-
gerheads for several years. Even Baldwin, of the ACLU, who worked hard at cooperating with the ILD, later had to admit that real collaboration with the Communists
was almost impossible. Forrest Bailey to Walter White, October 21, 1931, in Scottsboro Legal File 3, NAACP Papers.

[11] New York *Daily Worker*, May 14, 1931. It was an article of faith that only the
"leaders," never the membership, would block entrance into the "united front."

with several "mass meetings." [12] The April 26 riot touched off by Mrs. Patterson's appearance gained the first big headlines for the Party, and during the next four months the size of the demonstrations steadily increased. On May 16, a parade ran through Harlem and down to Frawley Circle at the upper end of Central Park. It began with two hundred Communists, mostly white, but by the time the marchers turned off Lenox Avenue, a predominantly Negro crowd of three thousand had fallen into step to listen to speeches protesting the "framing of nine Negro boys at Scottsville [sic]. . . ." [13] On June 27, Harlem demonstrators carried so many placards that two city dump trucks were required to remove them after a mixed crowd of fifteen hundred heard two hours of violent attacks on the state of Alabama.[14]

At times the enthusiasm of the demonstrators led to violence. Young Communists in Dresden, Germany, marched on the American consulate and when officials refused to accept their petition, they hurled bottles through several windows. Inside each was the note: "Down with American murder and Imperialism. For the brotherhood of black and white young proletarians. An end to the bloody lynching of our Negro co-workers." The Dresden incident, reported on page one of the New York Times, set off a rash of stonings and bottle throwings. Demonstrators smashed the windows of American consulates in Berlin, Leipzig, and Geneva during the summer of 1931. And in Havana, a mob of Communists, carrying red banners attacking "Yankee Imperialism" and the Scottsboro verdicts, attacked the Galiano Street Branch of the National City Bank of New York and shattered the plate glass window with stones.[15]

[12] New York Times, April 11, 1931, p. 40. The Times reported simply that the three organizations had wired protests to Governor Miller. Their telegrams referred to meetings of 375, 350, and 200 workers. Alabama Scottsboro Files. Like many other front groups, the Anti-Imperialist League, formed in 1925, amounted to little more than a few boxes of letterhead stationery. It was replaced by the American League Against War and Fascism in 1933. Draper, American Communism and Soviet Russia, 179.

[13] New York Times, May 17, 1931, p. 29.

[14] Ibid., June 28, 1931, p. 18.

[15] Ibid., June 10, 1931, p. 1; July 1, 1931, p. 9; July 12, 1931, p. 9; April 8, 1932, p. 11.

Often these demonstrations around the world were triggered by local issues; Scottsboro was a convenient and popular excuse for public rallies. Nevertheless, the incidents succeeded not only in establishing the ILD as the organization most active in the case, but also in bringing the Scottsboro boys to international prominence. Traditionally, the predominantly Negro National Bar Association had supported the NAACP. During the 1931 convention, an ILD attorney in the Association offered a resolution commending the International Labor Defense and requesting the NAACP to support the "United Front campaign." It failed by only five votes.[16]

Despite the whispers of "Moscow Gold," financing was always a problem for the Party and its front groups. The International Labor Defense was one of the most solvent of the fronts throughout its history—a circumstance resulting in part from the leadership's keen appreciation of fund-raising tours. The relatives of other "class-war prisoners" had earlier traveled across the country soliciting funds, but the ILD developed the technique most completely during the Scottsboro Case. At one time, there were so many "Scottsboro mothers" traveling through the country that Walter White charged fraud. "When the supply of 'mothers' was inadequate . . . substitutes were found," he declared. "All over the country 'mothers' were produced; in one instance the 'mother' presented had lived in that Northern city for upwards of twenty years." [17] There may have been a few examples of this, but there was little incentive for such deception. There were usually enough genuine mothers to go around, and most of them were more than willing to travel for the Party. Olen Montgomery's mother, like most of the others, enthusiastically embraced the Communist pro-

---

[16] Pittsburgh *Courier*, August 15, 1931; New York *Daily Worker*, August 18, 1931.

[17] Walter White, "The Negro and the Communists," *Harper's Magazine*, CLXIV (December, 1931) , 68. White specifically referred to the NAACP national convention the previous summer when Communists on the floor demanded that two women, allegedly Mrs. Wright and Mrs. Patterson, be allowed to speak. Following publication of the White article, both Mrs. Wright and Mrs. Patterson signed affidavits asserting they were present at the convention. There were no fake mothers, they insisted. New York *Daily Worker*, January 16, 1932.

gram as she understood it. The part she liked best was the promise
to "get rid of this so called goverment [sic] and the big boss. He
keeps us pressed to death," she said. "I want to be somebody but
I can't. . . ." She added: "This so called goverment [sic] has put a
many a good woman in the garbage can and put the lid on it, but I
tell the world I will fight like hell to stay out. . . ." [18]

And "fight like hell" they did, traveling through hundreds of
towns and cities, speaking to crowds which often consisted of a
handful of the Party faithful, but occasionally numbered more
than three thousand persons. In the six months after the arrest
and trials, Mrs. Wright and her ten-year-old daughter traveled
through the Northeast and upper Midwest; Mrs. Mamie Williams
—her one-year-old baby on her arm—through the South; Mrs.
Ida Norris down the West Coast; and Mrs. Viola Montgomery
across the Southwest. The pace was grueling. For one ten-day trip
through Minnesota in September of 1931, the ILD scheduled talks
for Mrs. Wright at Eveleth, Ely, Carson Lake, Chisholm, Hibbing,
Nashwaul, Bemidiji, Crosby, Minneapolis, and St. Paul.[19] Initially, many of the mothers were frightened by the crowds and spoke
haltingly and often incoherently. As they gained confidence from
the warmth of the crowds, however, they became more at ease on
the platform. Mrs. Patterson, in particular, became a fiery if somewhat ungrammatical orator. "They tried to tell me that the ILD
was low-down whites and Reds," she told a New Haven, Connecticut rally. "I haven't got no schooling, but I have five senses and
I know that Negroes can't win by themselves." The ILD had
saved her son, she said, "and I have faith that they will free him if
we all is united behind them." She added: "I don't care whether
they are Reds, Greens or Blues. They are the only ones who put
up a fight to save these boys and I am with them to the end." [20]

The enthusiasm for hearing the Scottsboro mothers waned in
1932. During one spring trip that year, collections barely netted

[18] Mrs. Viola Montgomery to Anna Damon, February 24, 1934, in ILD Papers.
[19] New York Daily Worker, September 7, 1931.
[20] Report on Fall, 1932 Tour of Mrs. Janie Patterson, by Richard Moore, undated, in ILD Papers.

enough money to pay the traveling expenses of the mother and her ILD chaperone.[21] Nevertheless, the tours succeeded in keeping the case in the public eye, even when there were no significant new developments. A stream of petitions, protests, and demands prompted by the mothers' trips poured into the office of Governor Miller in Alabama and President Hoover in Washington. The wording of the protests varied to suit the type of group and its degree of "class consciousness," but a typical form distributed by the Party read:

We the [number of workers or organization] assembled at [location] on [date] denounce the brutal slave drivers of Alabama acting through a Ku Klux Klan judge and jury inflamed by race hatred in order to send nine innocent children to the electric chair.

We brand this sentence of the white ruling classes as an attempt at willful, cold-blooded and deliberate murder. We recognize this as an attack against the Negro masses and the working class as a whole.

We demand the immediate and unconditional release of these boys through a new trial—a trial by a jury at least half of whom are Negro workers—with the right of an armed defense corps of Negro and white workers to defend the prisoners, jurors, and defense attorneys from the bosses' lynching mobs.[22]

No meeting protesting the Scottsboro verdict was complete without a plea for letters to Alabama officials. Through the summer of 1931, Governor Miller received several thousand communications from around the world, some rambling on incoherently for pages, others pleading eloquently for pardon. Most, however, were brief, abusive, and to the point. At one point, the attorney general of Alabama became so enraged at the torrent of insults and threats he refused to accept them and ordered the telegraph company to cease delivery.[23]

[21] The encouraging thing, however, was that large numbers of Negroes continued to attend despite poor preparation and publicity. Lowell Wakefield to William L. Patterson, March 31, 1932, in ILD Papers.

[22] Approximately 75 per cent of the communications to Governor Miller and later to Governor Bibb Graves were printed material similar to this. These letters are found in the Alabama Scottsboro Files.

[23] For a short time, the New York office of Western Union declined to accept the most strident wires, but it soon resumed sending all messages without comment.

The ILD and other Party organizations encouraged letters from all concerned persons, but as always the names of prominent Americans were preferred. Many of the famous petitioners were perennial protestors: Theodore Dreiser, Lincoln Steffens, Upton Sinclair, and John Dos Passos. Others, however, such as Clifton Fadiman, Hubert C. Herring, and the eminent Symphony conductor, Leopold Stokowski, also wrote to express their outrage.[24] In Germany, former Argentine Professor Alfonso Goldschmidt, a traveler and noted lawyer, formed a committee composed of Professor Albert Einstein, Thomas Mann, and three hundred other German intellectuals. They petitioned President Hoover and Governor Miller "in the name of humanity and justice" to pardon the boys. From England came a petition signed by H. G. Wells and thirty-three members of Parliament requesting a reversal of the "inhuman" death sentences. And on the strength of names such as Sherwood Anderson and John Dos Passos, the ILD solicited support through *The Nation* and other liberal magazines.[25]

The Communist Party and the various affiliated organizations which conducted the Scottsboro campaign talked continuously of building a Negro-white coalition of workers to free the defendants, but they concentrated their greatest efforts in the Negro community, particularly in the northern ghettos where the Party at least had a sketchy organizational framework. During the first month of the campaign, the *Daily Worker*'s editor noted a sharp increase in circulation in the heavily Negro districts of Northern and Western cities, and the Party's central committee optimistically predicted a sharp increase in Negro membership.[26] Unquestion-

---

New York *Daily Worker*, April 7, 1932. In one ten-day period from May 20 until May 30, 1932, Miller received six hundred messages by cable, telegraph, and mail. New York *Times*, March 31, 1932, p. 44.

[24] These letters, in the Alabama Scottsboro Files, were written between May, 1931, and March, 1933.

[25] New York *Times*, March 27, 1932, p. 25; September 6, 1931, III, p. 3; letter by Sherwood Anderson, *The Nation*, CXXXV (1932), 506; letter by John Dos Passos, *The Nation*, CXXXV (1932), 172. It does not follow from this that all prominent intellectuals who gave their support to the ILD campaign fully endorsed the programs of the Party. See Theodore Dreiser to Dallas McKown, June 9, 1932, in Robert Henry Elias, ed., *Letters of Theodore Dreiser: A Selection* (Philadelphia: University of Pennsylvania Press, 1959), II, 586–87.

[26] New York *Daily Worker*, April 29, May 14, 1931.

ably, the ILD captured the imagination of the nation's Negroes as Communist orators spoke in churches, conventions, union halls and on street corners, demanding defiance of the "Southern lynchers." The Reverend Asbury Smith, pastor of one of the largest Negro churches in Baltimore and a member of the Urban League's executive board, asserted that the rapid swing of Negroes away from their traditionally conservative position was due almost entirely to the Communist campaign for the Scottsboro boys.[27] In the three months following the trial, in Chicago alone, the Communists conducted fourteen meetings under the auspices of the LSNR, the ILD, the "Young Liberators of Chicago," and the "United Front Scottsboro Defense."[28] The case had little to do with the day-to-day problems of Northern big city Negroes, but it accurately reflected the sense of community they shared with their fellow Negroes in the South.

Encouraged by the response from the Scottsboro campaign, in April, 1932, the Party named four additional Negroes to the Central Committee and another to the Political Bureau. Even more significant was the Communist Party's 1932 nomination of James W. Ford for the Vice-Presidency. The ticket of Ford and William Z. Foster had no chance for success, but this detracted little from the fact that the Communists were the first national political party to nominate a black man for one of the highest offices in the nation. In September of the same year, in order to show the "unity of the Negro and white workers," the International Labor Defense unanimously selected as its national secretary William L. Patterson, a Negro attorney from Harlem.

Patterson, who replaced the ailing J. Louis Engdahl, had been a key figure in the ILD for over a year. Born in California, he lived three years in the Soviet Union during the 1920's, "studying conditions there, especially in relation to the question of national

[27] Asbury Smith, "What Can the Negro Expect from Communism," *Opportunity,* XI (1933), 211.

[28] Harold Foote Gosnell, *Negro Politicians: The Rise of Negro Politics in Chicago* (Chicago: University of Chicago Press, 1935), 328. See also Henry Lee Moon, *Balance of Power: The Negro Vote* (New York: Doubleday and Company, 1948), 124.

minorities." When he returned to the United States he declared: "The Soviet Union is the only country in the world where there is no discrimination, the only country where there is equality for all races and nationalities." During the late 1920's, he served as attorney for the Metal Workers Industrial Union and the National Miners Union, Communist competitors of the AFL. At the time of his selection, he was in Washington, acting as attorney for several Negro army veterans arrested following the expulsion of the Bonus Expeditionary Force from Anacostia Flats.[29] He stated his ideological position in 1931 when he declared: "I stand in the ranks of those revolutionary toilers who over the length and breadth of the world are rallying in revolutionary class solidarity under the banner and leadership of the world's Communist Parties and the Communist International. . . ." His consuming desire, he said, was the "destruction of that social order that thrives on the life blood of the exploited and oppressed masses." [30] The Party had recognized his fiery oratorical talents and unquestioned ability in 1932 when it named him the Party candidate for mayor of New York City.[31] With these talents Patterson also brought a fierce inflexibility to his new position. In 1933, Broadus Mitchell, professor of economics at Johns Hopkins University, tried to mediate an agreement between the ILD and other sympathetic groups. In an hour-long conversation, however, Mitchell found Patterson fanatical, unyielding, and suffering from acute egomania. The economist left the conference deeply shaken and pessimistic concerning the future of the case.[32]

While Patterson served on the executive committee of the ILD in late 1931 and early 1932, the organization faced a crucial decision. From Lenin's early antireligious writings to the *Daily Worker*'s 1930 dismissal of the clergy as "pie-in-the-sky bunk dis-

[29] New York *Daily Worker*, September 8, 1932. Engdahl had been in Europe since June of 1932 on a tour with Mrs. Ada Wright. He died in Moscow in late November after several weeks of illness. New York *Daily Worker*, November 22, 1932.

[30] New York *Daily Worker*, May 4, 1931.

[31] New York *Times*, September 8, 1932, p. 2.

[32] Will Alexander to William G. McDowell, August 7, 1933, in Interracial Commission Papers.

pensers," the Communist Party bitterly opposed all forms of religion.[33] The Scottsboro Case had forced a rethinking of this attitude, for many Negro churches had heartily welcomed Communist speakers who wished to talk about the case. "The Communist is the same . . . as a Holy Roller, Republican or Elk," declared Adam Clayton Powell, Jr. He was to be judged on one question: whether or not he backed full civil rights.[34] And on many occasions, conservative ministers were overruled by congregations unconcerned with the abstractions of dialectical materialism, but heartily in favor of the uncompromising stance of the ILD. Patterson and a handful of other Party leaders fought any change in the Party's attitude, but gradually the *Daily Worker* and Communist speakers began distinguishing between friendly clergy and the "lackeys of the bourgeoisie." Nevertheless, the Party publicly continued its antireligious campaign.[35]

The greatest challenge and the greatest opportunity for the Party lay not in the Northern black ghettos, however, but among the Negro masses of the deep South. "Gaining [Negro] adherents in the big cities is frosting on the cake," said Lowell Wakefield, "but we will win or lose in the black belt." [36] The garish headlines surrounding the abortive Camp Hill "uprising" gave the false impression that the Communist Party had penetrated the South in great numbers, but working through the LSNR and the ILD, Communists did little more than reconnoiter the defenses of

[33] See Ralph Lord Roy's chapter, "Religion, An Opium of the People," in *Communism and the Churches*, pp. 29–47.

[34] Adam Clayton Powell, Jr., *Marching Blacks: An Interpretative History of the Rise of the Black Common Man* (New York: Dial Press, 1945) , 69–70.

[35] Gosnell, *Negro Politicians*, 328. One Chicago church, hopelessly divided over whether to give its love offering to the NAACP or the ILD, compromised and gave half to each organization. Pittsburgh *Courier*, May 23, 1931. In Baltimore, a Negro minister joined the ILD and combined his preaching with organizing for the ILD during the week. Roy, *Communism and the Churches*, 51. The willingness of many Negro churches to sign any document proffered by the ILD is convincing evidence of the appeal of the Scottsboro Case. The files of the governor of Alabama and the Department of Justice are filled with letters and printed petitions from hundreds of churches expressing their opposition to the "fascist lynch attempts of the industrial overlords and landlords and their official puppets. . . ." See Alabama Scottsboro Files and Department of Justice Central Files No. 158260, Sub. 46, National Archives, Washington.

[36] Lowell Wakefield to William L. Patterson, November 22, 1932, in ILD Papers.

the enemy. Two organizers with experience in the region noted in the summer of 1932 that a substantial number of Southern Negroes were basically sympathetic, but their support was "inchoate and insignificantly organized." At the same time, Communist support among white Southerners was "unbelievably small." As usual, the two men, Harry Jackson and Nat Ross, attributed many of the failures to doctrinal impurities.[37] More concretely, the two men pointed to three specific failures. First there was the unnecessarily abstract approach to both white and Negro workers. The handful of Communist organizers aroused little fervor among Southern Negroes with their description of a "black republic," and they stimulated violent opposition from whites. The program of the Communist Party in the South had to be linked with the "immediate struggles of unemployment and starvation." Ultimate demands such as black separatism could wait for a more opportune moment. Secondly, the two men urged the Party to relax its insistence that white Southerners purge themselves of all race prejudice before they joined the Party. A joint fighting effort, concentrating on specific economic issues would, they argued, break the prejudices of whites. Finally, Jackson and Ross insisted that the Party had foolishly believed that simply because of the distribution of a few thousand leaflets, white workers would discard their prejudices and join the proletariat. There was no solution to the problem of recruitment except continuous, difficult, and sustained organizational work.[38] Jackson and Ross did not publicly admit what other organizers privately noted: the Scottsboro Case was a powerful organizing weapon among Negroes, but it had a completely opposite effect upon white Southerners. Ultimately, without ever acknowledging the change, the Communist Party concluded that the opportunities and potential rewards were greater among Southern Negroes than whites. Publicly the slogans and promises of "Negro-white solidarity in the black belt" continued unabated.

[37] In particular, "We failed to make a real fight against the treacherous Negro reformists and fakers." New York *Daily Worker*, July 2, 1932. Actually, it is unlikely that a "substantial" number of Southern Negroes had more than the vaguest idea who the Communists were, or what they backed.

[38] New York *Daily Worker*, July 2, 1932.

In reality, during the next four years when the Communist Party concentrated on the Scottsboro Case, the overwhelming emphasis in the South was upon Negro recruitment.[39]

In 1930, the Party had opened headquarters in Birmingham, signaling its arrival with the sporadic publication of the *Southern Worker,* the "communist paper for the South." In the summer of 1932, the ILD moved its Southern office from Chattanooga to Birmingham and (in effect) combined with the Communist Party by sharing office space and personnel. Together the two organizations added new staff members and increased their budget. Although Alabama officials reported an increasing number of Communist meetings around Birmingham and in the Camp Hill area, there were few public rallies.[40] On September 18, 1932, ILD Secretary Donald Burke announced that the International Labor Defense would sponsor an "All-Southern Scottsboro and Civil Rights Congress" to meet October 2, in Birmingham. While demands for the freedom of the Scottsboro boys would be the main purpose of the meeting, he said, the conference would also discuss a number of broader questions: freedom of speech, assembly, and press; repeal of the vagrancy laws; abolition of the chain gang; the right of all people to vote without payment of poll tax, ownership of property, or other qualifications; and an increase in welfare appropriations.[41]

The beginnings of overt Communist operations in the Deep South alarmed white Southerners. Earlier, the American Legion had called for an unceasing struggle against the reds, and Burke's announcement touched off a series of reprisals. The same evening the conference was announced, Birmingham police raided the

[39] Lowell Wakefield to William L. Patterson, November 22, 1932, in ILD Papers.

[40] George Brown Tindall, *The Emergence of the New South, 1913–1945* (Baton Rouge: Louisiana State University Press, 1967) , 377. In May of 1932 there was one brief demonstration when fifty Birmingham Negroes, addressing each other as comrade, staged a hunger march to City Hall. When the spokesman stepped forward to present a petition of grievances, a burly policeman felled him with a billy club and the marchers scattered. Donald Burke, local representative of the Party, insisted that the march was completely spontaneous and was not organized by him. New York *Times,* May 14, 1932, p. 3; Birmingham *Post,* May 16, 1932.

[41] New York *Daily Worker,* September 23, September 24, 1932.

ILD-Communist office in the Martin Building, arresting Burke along with a correspondent of the *Daily Worker* visiting in Birmingham, and Fred Keith, one of the few white natives of Birmingham active in the Party. After photographing and fingerprinting the three men, police held them incommunicado and questioned them for twenty-six hours. Only when ILD attorney Frank Irwin threatened to institute *habeas corpus* proceedings did the police release the men without charges. From the confiscated ILD files, authorities learned that Otto Hall, a Negro organizer for the ILD, was scheduled to arrive in Birmingham on September 21. When he stepped off the bus, police bundled him into a car, drove beyond the city limits, pushed him out, and suggested he "keep going." Hall returned to New York City.[42] At the same time, the dormant Ku Klux Klan revived with a midnight demonstration on October 1, complete with placards announcing that "The Klan Rides Again to Stamp Out Communism." Klansmen posted these throughout the Negro district of Birmingham and passed out handbills warning Negroes to stay away from the "Bolsheviks." [43]

Despite these obstacles, plans for the conference proceeded. William Z. Foster, Communist candidate for the Presidency, scheduled an appearance, and Burke leased the Negro Masonic Temple auditorium.[44] Foster became ill at the last minute and failed to appear, but a crowd of more than three hundred Negroes and fifty whites walked through a phalanx of eighty policemen to enter the auditorium. Once inside, city officials announced that the assembly would either have to segregate or meet outside. Even this failed to dampen the crowd's spirits; they gathered on an open lot, under the shadow of three machine guns mounted across the street, to hear a few remarks from Mrs. Viola Montgomery and the announcement by Keith that the group would meet again the

[42] *Ibid.,* September 23, September 29, 1932; Birmingham *Post,* September 21, September 23, 1932.

[43] Report of Lt. Ralph E. Hurst, October 19, 1932, in Alabama Executive Files, Drawer 32.

[44] The Klan sent Foster a telegram: "Your presence in Birmingham, Alabama, is not wanted. Send nigger Ford." New York *Daily Worker,* October 10, 1932.

following Sunday in a Negro theater.[45] In terms of numbers the next week's meeting was an even greater success. Altogether about nine hundred Negroes and three hundred whites attended. In other respects, it was a disaster. Clarence Hathaway, Foster's campaign manager, had been scheduled to appear, but New Orleans police had arrested him the night before. Mrs. Montgomery also failed to put in another appearance after receiving several threats. And Keith had scarcely called the meeting to order before hostile whites, strategically stationed in the balcony, began throwing "stink bombs" onto the floor below. The conference dissolved into chaos as the members fled into the streets for fresh air.[46]

Although the efforts to disrupt the meeting succeeded, the ability of the Party to assemble one thousand persons unnerved not only conservative white Alabamians, but moderates as well. During 1931 and 1932, the Interracial Commission declined any involvement in the case and watched with alarm the increase of Communist activity among Southern Negroes. Southern moderates took some solace from the fact that the "traditional" Negro leaders of the region exerted their influence against the Communists. Tuskegee Institute's principal, Robert Russa Moton, refused to take any public stand on the case. When questioned concerning the outcome of the Scottsboro trials, he declared that there "never was a time when there was a greater disposition among thinking men and women of the white race in this section to manifest an attitude of justice and fairness towards my people than obtains today." He warned Alabama Negroes "against permitting themselves to be stirred up by agitators from outside . . . who come with plausible arguments and fair promises creating suspicion and ill will between the races." Negroes in the South should practice "diligence and frugality" and "seize every opportunity for honest

---

[45] New York *Daily Worker,* October 4, 1932; Birmingham *Age-Herald,* October 3, 1933; Report of Lt. Ralph E. Hurst, October 19, 1932, in Drawer 32, Alabama Executive Files.

[46] Report of Lt. Ralph E. Hurst, October 19, 1932, in Alabama Executive Files, Drawer 32; Birmingham *Post,* October 10, 1931; Birmingham *Age-Herald,* October 10, 1931. Hurst, who was present, asserted that approximately sixty of the white persons in the theater were Klansmen.

employment, however meagre the pay. . . ." [47] Nor was Tuskegee an exception. Negro poet Langston Hughes was amazed and disgusted at the apathy of Negro students and educators. When a handful of students at Hampton Institute proposed a silent march of protest, the administration denied them permission, with the explanation, "That is not Hampton's way. We educate, not protest." [48]

As evidence of radical activity increased, a few Southerners reassessed their attitudes toward the NAACP. The Birmingham *News* still found the Association's activities distasteful, but it had to admit that it was "almost aristocratic as compared with the unruly chaotic and anarchistic International Labor Defense." [49] Most whites, however, simply turned to the "natural Negro leaders" and sought reassurance that there was no danger of radicalism among members of their race. And these leaders responded with assurances that all was well, that race relations had never been better, that "the South is our natural home and the Southern leading white people are our best friends." [50] The Rev. P. Colfax Rameau, director of the "Negro Welfare Educational Industrial Uplift Service," was singled out as a Southern Negro leader in the "best tradition of Booker T. Washington." Rameau assured white Southerners that the mass of Negro men and women knew "the pure Southern doctrine of race distinction. . . ." Only the maneuvers of "radical agitators" threatened the "traditional friendship which has existed between better thinking whites and better thinking blacks," declared a Negro bishop.[51] As the Birmingham

[47] Baltimore *Afro-American*, October 10, 1931.

[48] Langston Hughes, "Cowards from the Colleges," *Crisis*, XLI (1934), 227; Langston Hughes, *I Wonder as I Wander: An Autobiographical Journey* (New York: Rinehart and Company, 1956), 44, 61.

[49] Birmingham *News*, February 19, 1933. Paul Ernest Baker, in his study on interracial relations in the early 1930's, remarked with premature optimism that "under the impending danger from this Communist organization [the ILD], the South begins to look with favor upon the National Association." *Negro-White Adjustment* (New York: Association Press, 1934), 71.

[50] Birmingham *Post*, October 15, 1932.

[51] *Ibid.*, May 3, 1933; Statement of Bishop Cameron C. Alleyne at the 38th Annual Session of the Central Alabama Conference, A.M.E. Zion Church. Birmingham *Age-Herald*, November 25, 1932.

News asserted confidently: "In these troubled times, some [Negroes] may be tempted to follow after false prophets." Without a doubt, however, the teachings of Booker T. Washington and other race leaders would fortify them against "false lures." [52]

Even as Southern whites murmured their incantations of peace and harmony, they glanced nervously over their shoulders. Episcopal Bishop William G. McDowell reported after an interracial meeting in Birmingham that Negroes "seem to have lost all faith in the ability of the interracial forces to do any good." Hopeless and disorganized in the face of the ILD attacks upon the moderates, "some of them are wavering before the vigorous and widespread effort on behalf of the equal civil rights . . . the ILD is undoubtedly making on their behalf." They suspected the motives of the ILD, he said, "but many of them are inclined to do as the Chinese did: accept the proffered help of the Communists, and then hope to get rid of . . . [them] later." In contrast, "their former white friends in the South seem absolutely helpless and take it out in privately wringing their hands which is as unimpressive as it is futile." [53]

Despite the Party's fight against "legalist illusions," attention had centered in the spring of 1932 on the appeal to the Alabama Supreme Court. General Chamlee told George Maurer he was hopeful that the Alabama Court would grant a new trial. The demonstration that greeted the verdict in the Norris and Weems case, he said, seemed adequate grounds for a reversal. But Chamlee was also frank enough to admit that "officers at Scottsboro and court officials there think we have not got a ghost of a chance and that our case is just hopeless and impossible." [54] The *Daily*

[52] Birmingham *News*, April 11, 1933.

[53] Rt. Rev. William G. McDowell to Will Alexander, June 30, 1933, in Interracial Commission Papers. McDowell's suggestion of a solution was symptomatic of white Southern liberals. He called for a bold and unceasing public campaign by the Interracial Commission against the radicals. This would be better than to leave the fight to "Southern demagogues and negro haters." Will Alexander, however much he disagreed with the Communists, was unwilling to expend the limited resources of the Interracial Commission in a fruitless "anti-Communist campaign." The real solution to this problem, he believed, was for the moderates to take positive steps to ameliorate some of the hardships Negroes suffered.

[54] George W. Chamlee to George Maurer, December 8, 1931, in ILD Papers.

Worker was also pessimistic. The Alabama Supreme Court was a servant of the same ruling class which originally railroaded the boys to death. As an "instrument of the Wall Street Imperialists," its sole aim would be to "justify and carry through this legal mass murder. . . ." Make no mistake, said the *Worker,* the Alabama justices met "not to decide some fancy legal point that is supposed to concern their guilt or innocence—for everybody knows that these boys are innocent—but only to find the best means to give the legal murder of these children the appearance of punishment of [a] social crime. . . ." The only thing which could possibly stay the Alabama executioner was the aroused anger of the proletariat. In the face of the masses of white and Negro toilers, the court might decide it was "better policy to hold off this cold blooded butchery so as to avoid arousing the masses to further fury." [55]

As the first hearing on the case approached, the Birmingham *Post* assured the nation that the "high court [of Alabama] sits in an atmosphere of calm detachment." The court would abolish any "lingering doubt as to whether justice has been done. . . ." In fact, however, the members of the Alabama Supreme Court were seething with anger at an avalanche of protests, demands, and threats.[56] When court opened, January 21, 1932, Chief Justice John C. Anderson issued an unprecedented remonstrance concerning the mail he and his colleagues had received. "These messages are highly improper, inflammatory and revolutionary in their nature," he said. They were "sent with the evident intent to bulldoze this court." Chamlee assured the court that the ILD had nothing to do with the mail, but the icy attitude of the justices betrayed a lack of confidence in his assurances.[57]

Joseph Brodsky carried most of the argument for the defense, and even the hostile Montgomery *Advertiser* acknowledged his eloquence in the courtroom. He touched on a number of points,

[55] New York *Daily Worker,* December 28, 1931, January 19, 1932.

[56] Chief Justice John C. Anderson to Walter White, April 25, 1932, in Scottsboro Legal File 5, NAACP Papers.

[57] A sizeable number of the protests were sent by ILD chapters around the country and one of the most bombastic telegrams was signed by the national secretary of the ILD. New York *Times,* January 22, 1932, p. 17; Birmingham *Age-Herald,* January 22, 1932.

including the exclusion of Negroes from Alabama's juries, but his main argument revolved around the fair trial issue. All of the defendants had a right, argued Brodsky, to be tried by a jury "entirely free from bias or prejudice, and free from outside or extra-legal influences which might distract their minds from a dispassionate consideration of the merits of the case." This was not true of the Scottsboro trials. He described the huge throng which attended the proceedings, the demonstration that greeted the first guilty verdict, and the fact that officials had called in more than one hundred guardsmen. Roy Wright, twelve years of age and subject only to the jurisdiction of a juvenile court, was put on trial and almost convicted, said Brodsky. The fact that Judge Hawkins went ahead with Wright's trial despite his age "illustrated the speed and pressure of these trials and that the minds of the men were not normal." General Chamlee spent his allotted time on one issue: the inadequacy of the boys' defense counsel. He reviewed the record. Illiterate, bewildered, and friendless, the nine were indicted and brought to the day of the trial without once having consulted an attorney. From the transcripts, Chamlee read Roddy's denial that he had been hired to defend the boys, as well as the casual way in which Judge Hawkins had settled the entire issue of counsel.[58]

The next day, while six guards mingled with the courtroom audience in order to discourage a threatened demonstration, Attorney General Thomas G. Knight, the son of one of the court's associate justices, replied to the defense brief. He ignored the charge that the defendants had inadequate counsel and quickly dismissed the allegation that Negroes were systematically excluded from Alabama's juries. The charge that mob spirit dominated the trial most concerned Knight. "Why should we assume that the gathering of a curious mob would have influenced the jurors and judge of the trial court?" he argued. The preceding day Brodsky had quoted from Justice Oliver Wendell Holmes' dissent in the Leo Frank case. Holmes had argued that a trial conducted in the

[58] New York *Times*, January 23, 1932, p. 10; Montgomery *Advertiser*, January 23, 1932.

midst of mob pressure was invalid.[59] "I have the deepest reverence for Justice Holmes," declared Knight, "but I wonder if he had lived a little closer to the South whether he would have written these decisions, had he known how jealously we have striven to uphold our rights and protect our womanhood." [60]

Although the court took the case under advisement, given the defensiveness of Alabamians, the result was a foregone conclusion. Any observer could have predicted the results from the headlines that appeared in the Montgomery *Advertiser:* "Negro Partisans 'Dictate' Course to High Court." [61] On March 24, by a margin of six to one, the Alabama Supreme Court upheld the conviction of all but one of the eight defendants. They granted Eugene Williams a new trial on the grounds that he was allegedly a juvenile at the time of his conviction. In a decision written by Attorney General Knight's father, the court held that the affidavits supporting his age as thirteen "may be false, [but] there is nothing in this case to prove their falsity." [62] As for the other seven, however, Justice Knight and his colleagues saw nothing wrong with the newspaper accounts in the two Jackson County weeklies. And they insisted that the speed of the trials—far from being an indication of undue haste—was "highly desirable." If this were always the case, "life and property would be infinitely safer and greater respect would the criminally inclined have for the law." Knight pointed to the quick trial and execution of President William McKinley's assassin in 1901. It was true that this involved murder, but he was "of the opinion that something worse than death . . . happened to this defenseless woman, Victoria Price. . . ." As for the one hundred militiamen, their presence gave "notice to everybody that the strong arm of the State was there to assure the accused of a lawful trial." And Knight dismissed the argument that

---

[59] *Frank* v. *Mangum,* 237 U.S. 309 (1915). The majority later sustained Holmes's position in *Moore* v. *Dempsey,* 261 U.S. 86 (1923).

[60] Birmingham *Age-Herald,* January 23, 1932.

[61] Montgomery *Advertiser,* January 22, 1932.

[62] *Powell* v. *State,* 224 Ala. 553. Even Attorney General Knight admitted that he was no more than fifteen and thus subject to juvenile court jurisdiction. Chattanooga *Daily Times,* March 24, 1932.

the defendants had been deprived of their rights under the Fourteenth Amendment because of the systematic exclusion of Negroes from Jackson County's juries. "The State of Alabama," he said, "has the right, within constitutional limitations, to fix the qualification for jurors." [63]

Chief Justice Anderson dissented. He could find no single factor which would lead to a reversal of the verdict, "but when considered in connection with each other, they [the plantiffs' briefs] must collectively impress the judicial mind with the conclusion that they did not get a fair and impartial trial that is required and contemplated by our Constitution." [64]

The majority decision "should satisfy all reasonable persons" that the accused had received a fair trial, editorialized the Montgomery *Advertiser*. The justices knew more about the facts than anyone, said Editor Hall, and they had confirmed to the world that Alabama would go forward "with an orderly enforcement of the law against criminal assault in a particularly aggravated instance. . . ." In contrast to the *Advertiser's* stand, several Alabama dailies noted the decision with regret. None argued that the boys might be innocent, but as the Birmingham *Age-Herald* observed, "The fact remains that there was an element of mob feeling in the air and . . . a well-planned defense was not offered." Another trial would have done no harm, said the Birmingham *Post,* and a rehearing would have allayed any doubts that the boys were unfairly convicted.[65] Moderate Alabamians blamed the decision on "intimidating messages" from radicals. Members of the court had been so angered, said John Temple Graves, II, they "leaned unconsciously backward against what they considered attempts to push them to a decision favorable to the defendants." [66] Chief Justice Anderson confidentially admitted to Walter White that,

[63] *Powell* v. *State,* 224 Ala. 550, 551.

[64] Anderson avoided the question of the exclusion of Negroes from Alabama's juries. *Powell* v. *State,* 224 Ala. 554, 555.

[65] Montgomery *Advertiser,* March 26, 1932; Birmingham *Age-Herald,* March 25, 1932; Birmingham *Post,* March 25, 1932. The Selma *Times-Journal* took no stand as to the guilt or innocence of the defendants, but found the decision "regrettable." Quoted in Birmingham *Post,* March 30, 1932.

[66] New York *Times,* May 1, 1932, III, 6.

while men on the highest courts should be capable of standing above outside influence, the Communist propaganda had "possibly injured the defendants. . . ." [67]

No one was surprised when the *Daily Worker* attacked the majority decision, but the newspaper also assaulted Anderson's dissent and the court's decision to grant a new trial for Eugene Williams. These were "fake gestures" intended to conceal "the bestial oppression of the Negro masses. . . ." The *Worker* warned the nation's workers against placing any hope in the United States Supreme Court. It was simply an appeal from "one capitalist court to another capitalist court, and the same hatred toward the Negro masses and the working class will govern whatever actions are taken by the United States Supreme Court." A review of the case by the high court would be a "mere gesture aimed at facilitating the legal lynching of these children. . . ." The only hope was that the "toiling masses, white and black, [will] continue to build the united front fight to rescue these working-class children from the bloody claws of the murderous ruling class." [68]

Despite their outspoken disdain for the legal processes, ILD officials retained Walter Pollak, one of the nation's most eminent constitutional attorneys. After a preliminary hearing on May 27, 1932, the Supreme Court agreed to hear the case.[69] The *Worker* hailed the decision as a "tremendous partial victory for the revolutionary working class"; but it warned that, while the action was due entirely to mass pressure on the "bosses' courts," the bourgeois liberals would use it as an attempt to disrupt the "mass defense by fostering illusions as to the 'fairness' and 'justice' of the bosses' courts." [70]

The arguments, delivered almost five months later, were substantially the same as before the Alabama court with one exception. Pollak stressed the jury question, contending that there had not been any Negroes on Jackson County juries since Reconstruc-

[67] John C. Anderson to Walter White, April 25, 1932, in Scottsboro Legal File 5, NAACP Papers.

[68] New York *Daily Worker*, March 25, March 26, September 27, 1932.

[69] New York *Times*, May 28, 1932, p. 8; June 1, 1932, p. 8.

[70] New York *Daily Worker*, June 1, 1932.

tion. Knight seemed defensive in his reply and concluded somewhat plaintively that he had no apology to make for the verdict.[71] The Supreme Court did not indicate when it would decide the case, but during the first week of November, rumors spread that the justices would announce their decision Monday, November 7. On the seventh, at least seventy-five demonstrators gathered with pickets outside the Supreme Court building. They refused police requests to disperse, and arrests and angry fighting began. Inside the Supreme Court building, however, there were no disturbances. Shortly before 11 A.M., Chief Justice Charles Evans Hughes nodded to Justice George Sutherland, one of the most conservative members of the court. After briefly reciting the background of the case, Sutherland went to the main body of the decision. The court had restricted itself to one question, he said, "whether the defendants were in substance denied the right of counsel, and if so, whether such denial infringes the due process clause of the Fourteenth Amendment." After quoting at length from the transcript, Sutherland characterized the appointment of counsel as unacceptably casual. Judge Hawkins' earlier naming of all members of the Jackson County bar to defend the boys was an "expansive gesture" which completely diffused final responsibility for the defendants' case.[72]

At this point, it was clear that the court intended to reverse the lower verdict on the grounds of inadequate counsel. But there was a crucial question. What constitutional peg would support such a decision? The Sixth Amendment guaranteed the "right to counsel," but it clearly referred to the federal courts, not those of the states. The solution was the "due process" clause of the Fourteenth Amendment. In *Hurtado* v. *California* (1884) the Supreme Court had denied that the defendant's right to "due process" in a state court included the first eight amendments to the Constitution.[73] In the same decision, however, the court

[71] New York *Times,* October 11, 1932, p. 19.

[72] *Powell* v. *Alabama,* 287 U.S. 56, 57.

[73] The court adopted the legal maxim of *inclusio unius est exclusio alterius; i.e.,* "no portion of the Constitution is considered as including any other portion." In the federal Bill of Rights, the Fifth Amendment included the due process clause plus

described due process in extremely vague terms. It was "that law of the land in each state which derives its authority from the inherent and reserved powers of the state, exerted within the limits of those fundamental principles of liberty and justice which lie at the base of all our civil and political institutions. . . ." Due process required no particular form. The people could institute new methods or procedures so long as these were in "furtherance of the general public good. . . ." Of course it was up to the Supreme Court ultimately to decide what was in "furtherance of the general public good." [74]

And Sutherland quoted that part of the *Hurtado* decision which read: "The rule is an aid to construction and in some instances may be conclusive; but it must yield to more compelling considerations whenever such considerations exist." The Supreme Court had already used this escape hatch to extend the application of the First Amendment to the states in *Gitlow* v. *New York* (1925). [75] After reviewing legal precedents dating back to the Colonial period, Sutherland declared that the right to have counsel heard had been so accepted by the states that it was an integral part of due process. And in the most crucial part of the decision he concluded that the "right to have counsel appointed when necessary is a logical corollary from the constitutional right to be heard by counsel." [76] The cases were reversed and remanded to the lower court.

Justices Pierce Butler and James C. McReynolds, two of the most conservative members of the court, dissented on the grounds that the defendants had received a completely adequate and fair trial. Even if the boys had not, declared Butler, who wrote the minority opinion, this "is an extension of the Federal authority

---

the right of trial by jury and protection against self-incrimination and double-jeopardy. This meant that the makers of the Constitution regarded "due process" as something altogether different from such practices as trial by jury and the other eight amendments. And the assumption was that the "due process" clause of the Fourteenth Amendment, which affected the states, had the same meaning. *Hurtado* v. *California*, 110 U.S. 516.

[74] *Hurtado* v. *California*, 110 U.S. 516, 537.

[75] *Gitlow* v. *New York*, 268 U.S. 652, 666.

[76] *Powell* v. *Alabama*, 287 U.S. 72.

into a field hitherto occupied exclusively by the several states." [77] To a great extent, the force of their criticism had been deflected by Hughes' success in persuading the conservative Sutherland to write the majority opinion.[78]

The New York *Times* hailed *Powell* v. *Alabama* as a landmark in American jurisprudence. It "ought to abate the rancor of extreme radicals while confirming the faith of the American people in the soundness of their institutions and especially the integrity of the courts." The decision proved false the Communist charges that "a spirit of wicked class prejudice pervades the United States and that here no justice can be had for the poor and ignorant." The *New Republic, The Nation,* and *Christian Century* joined in praising the court's action. If the Supreme Court had confirmed the death sentences, a "pronounced swing toward economic and political radicalism [among Negroes] would have been the inevitable result," said the *Century*.[79]

The Communist Party's view was somewhat different. "A careful reading of the official decision shows that the Supreme Court has taken great care to instruct the Alabama authorities how 'properly' to carry through such lynch schemes and bolster their discredited 'judicial' institutions," said the *Daily Worker*.[80] Others, more moderate in outlook, were also disappointed in the outcome of the appeal. Three main points had been raised by defense counsel, noted a leading Socialist, Morris Ernst: the lack of a fair trial, the inadequacy of counsel, and the systematic exclusion of Negroes from Alabama juries. The court ignored the first and third issues, those with "deep social significance." Even worse,

[77] *Ibid.,* 75–77.

[78] Although Sutherland believed in laissez-faire economics, a strict construction of the Constitution, and states' rights, he had at least a mild concern for civil liberties. Joel Francis Paschal, *Mr. Justice Sutherland, A Man Against the State* (Princeton: Princeton University Press, 1951) , 79, 111, 212.

[79] New York *Times,* November 8, 1932, p. 8; "Scottsboro Negroes," *Christian Century,* XLIX (1932) , 1396; *New Republic,* LXXIII (1932) , 3; *The Nation,* CXXV (1932) , 545.

[80] New York *Daily Worker,* November 8, 1932. The contention that the court decision was a set of instructions on how to "legally lynch" the boys became the standard Party line. Letter of Louis Colman, *The Nation,* CXXXV (1932) , 467; Letter of Louis Colman, *New Republic,* LXXIII (1932) , 100–101.

said Ernst, dissenting Justice Butler had written in his opinion: "The court, putting aside—they are utterly without merit—all other claims that the constitutional rights of the petitioners were infringed, grounds its opinion and judgment v·)on a single assertion of fact." The inability of the majority to persuade Butler to delete these remarks meant that the "liberal justices were outtraded," declared Ernst, and the matter of counsel was "an empty and meaningless victory." [81] Moreover, the right to adequate counsel still was not guaranteed for all capital cases. Sutherland, in the majority opinion, had emphasized the defendants' illiteracy and poverty, and he had restricted the decision to this particular case by saying, "Whether this would be so in other criminal prosecutions or under other circumstances, we need not determine." [82]

Felix Frankfurter of the Harvard University law faculty put the issue in its proper perspective. For more than forty years the court had used the conveniently vague wording of the due process clause to protect property rights and to thwart legislation which extended the economic regulatory power of both the state and national governments. "Now, in the hands of the same Justices, they return to their more immediate purpose of protecting black men from oppressive and unequal treatment by whites." In *Moore* v. *Dempsey* (1925), the court accepted Justice Holmes' contention that the due process clause guaranteed an impartial court, free from hysteria and mob spirit. In *Powell* v. *Alabama,* the court broadened the defendant's rights to include adequate counsel in capital cases, at least—in Justice Sutherland's words—"where the defendant is unable to employ counsel and is incapable adequately of making his own defense because of ignorance, feeblemindedness, illiteracy or the like. . . ." In no sense, said Frankfurter, was the Supreme Court an appeal tribunal for the correction of all criminal errors. In a nation of 120 million this would be impossible. But even though the court would continue to act with hesitation, it would not, declared Frankfurter, condone "judicial mur-

---

[81] Morris Ernst, "Dissenting Opinion," *The Nation,* CXXXV (1932), 359.
[82] *Powell* v. *Alabama,* 287 U.S. 74.

der." "Here lies perhaps the deepest significance of the case." [83]

For the Communist Party, the case was positive proof that "mass organization and militant struggle outside the legal forms of capitalist 'democracy' is the most effective method for all oppressed." Elliot Cohen, Secretary of the National Committee for the Defense of Political Prisoners, hailed the ILD as the organization "with the wisdom to see the case . . . not as an isolated accidental 'miscarriage of justice,'" but as a typical example of the South's legal process. The decision, said the *Daily Worker*, irrefutably answered the "vicious slanders of the Socialist Party and the NAACP to the effect that the Communists were endangering the lives of the boys." [84] Had the Supreme Court affirmed the death sentences, the Party could have pointed to this as evidence that the courts were instruments of the ruling class. A reversal of the decision confirmed the correctness of the "mass struggle" tactics. The Communists could not lose.

Eleven hundred miles away, Olen Montgomery sat down and wrote the ILD for all the Scottsboro boys. "Since the Supreme Court have granted we boys a new trial I thank [*sic*] it is my rite to express thanks and appreciation to the whole party for their care. . . ." All of the boys were "so happy over it," he said. "I my self feels like I have been born again from the worrying . . . I have had. . . ." [85] The eighteen months since their conviction had been difficult for the nine youths. First there had been the agonizing decision over whether to accept the ILD or the NAACP. The decision made, there was a brief period of euphoria as the boys were flooded with visitors on weekends and every day with letters including small monetary gifts. Even on death row at Kilby, they were able to buy special food, candy, and cigarettes to make prison life more bearable. [86]

[83] Article by Felix Frankfurter, New York *Times*, November 13, 1932, III, 1, 2.

[84] New York *Daily Worker*, November 8, 1932; New York *Times*, November 9, 1932, p. 40.

[85] Olen Montgomery to George Maurer, November 8, 1932, in ILD Papers.

[86] Andy Wright to George Maurer, November 10, 1932, in ILD Papers. The bulk of this letter was also printed in the New York *Daily Worker*, November 16, 1932. Roy Wright to George Maurer, December 29, 1931, and Haywood Patterson to ILD

Satisfaction from these minor pleasures soon faded, however, as the boys faced the same unchanging schedule day after day. Several spent a few hours each day with a dictionary and Bible, learning to read and to write. For the most part, it was up at 5:30 A.M. for breakfast, try to make the time pass until lunch, the same until dinner, and finally to sleep again. They were not in solitary confinement. They could talk with each other and with the other condemned prisoners in the cell block, but after a few hours the conversation lagged; there was nothing new to say, nothing to do except wait. "At times I believe I am going insane," wrote the younger Wright youth. Every day it was harder to get himself together. It was worse, he said, because all he could think about was the girls' accusing him. "I wouldn't ever attempt to do such [rape], even if I had ever thought of such a thing in my whole life." And yet he was still in jail with little hope of freedom. His older brother, Andy, begged the ILD to have all the boys at Kilby moved back to Birmingham County Jail. At least there was an exercise yard there. At Kilby there was no room to walk around, no "exercise, no kind of joyment to keep your mind together." It would soon drive anybody crazy, he said.[87]

Late in January of 1932, Negro poet Langston Hughes was visiting at Tuskegee Institute when a local Negro minister suggested that a reading of some of his poems might cheer the boys. On Sunday afternoon, January 24, Hughes visited the death house of Kilby Prison. He found the boys dressed in their gray prison uniforms, at the end of a long corridor in their small grilled cells. To the left down another corridor was the steel door leading to the electric chair. The eight youths sat or lay listlessly in their bunks. They did not know Langston Hughes, and they did not seem to care. When the minister introduced him, only Andy came over to the bars and shook hands. Hughes read humorous poems to them without mentioning their case or the problems of the South. "I

Headquarters, October 22, 1931, in ILD Papers. Wright and Williams were lodged in the Birmingham jail since they were not under sentence of death.

[87] Roy Wright to William L. Patterson, reprinted in New York *Daily Worker*, September 14, 1931; Andy Wright to Jane Dillon, April 12, 1932, in ILD Papers.

said nothing of any seriousness," he said, "except my hope that their appeals would end well and they would soon be free." When he had finished, the minister prayed, but none of the boys changed expression. As the two men turned to leave, Andy thanked them and said good-bye. Hughes looked back and the rest of the boys were still sitting, unmoving, dozing or staring blankly at the walls.[88]

The boys could and did take solace from the fact that they were world celebrities. They never aroused the furor of Sacco and Vanzetti, but their names had become bywords in the households of world radicalism. Throughout the world, the Communist press devoted considerable space to the case. Even the Russian novelist Maxim Gorky commented on the boys' plight in *Pravda*.[89] Scottsboro had "roused hundreds of thousands of Negro and white workers in protest and struggle against Negro oppression," boasted Earl Browder.[90] It may have aroused them, but Party leader William Weinstone was closer to the truth when he concluded that "very few members have been brought into the Party as a result of the Scottsboro campaign. . . ." [91] During 1931, the year of the greatest efforts, only 1,300 Negroes actually joined the Communist Party. And more often than not, the new recruits attended a few meetings and then quietly drifted away. At no time during this period did Negro membership in the Party total more than one thousand. Negroes appreciated the Communists' efforts on their behalf. They supported common causes, joined willingly in united fronts, and fought side by side in crusades. With the excep-

[88] Hughes, *I Wonder as I Wander*, 61–62.

[89] New York *Daily Worker*, September 5, 1931. According to the U.S. Embassy in Riga, Latvia, stories on the case outpaced all other news from the United States, at least during 1931 and early 1932. The *Komsomolskaya Pravda*, organ of the Young Communists' Union, in particular devoted a tremendous amount of space to the case. Memorandum by Latvian Embassy, March 8, 1932, in Department of Justice Central Files 158260, Sub. 46.

[90] Browder, "To the Masses—To the Shops!" 800–801.

[91] Weinstone, "The XI Plenum of the Executive Council of the Comintern," 793. The inability to capitalize on Negro gratitude for defending the Scottsboro boys disturbed and frustrated the Party throughout the 1930's. See Earl Russell Browder, *Communism in the United States* (New York: International Publishers, 1935), 136–37.

tion of younger, urbanized, and often intellectual Negroes, however, few were willing to become completely involved in the work of the Party.[92]

Harry Haywood, a former Wobblie and an outspoken advocate of the "self-determination theory," blamed the Party's lack of success on a failure to carry through with the correct ideological line. Everywhere "the correct line was sacrificed in an attempt to establish a 'united front from the top'. . . ." Party organizers should have approached the Negro masses directly at the bottom instead of negotiating with their traitorous petty bourgeois leaders, said Haywood. Such opportunistic deviations had placed the Scottsboro campaign, for example, "at the mercy of the petty-bourgeois reformist and religious leaders" who were then able to strike "shattering blows against the united front at the most critical moment." The most inexcusable error, he continued, lay in giving Negro ministers a position at various meetings and conferences. The Party could never hope for victory in the Scottsboro campaign unless it brought forth and popularized the full Negro program of self-determination, equal rights, and the confiscation of land.[93]

The disagreement over immediate versus ultimate aims reflected a difference of opinion between the generals and the troops. In New York, Party leaders confidently manufactured slogans, outlined Party dogma, and then assembled paper legions of Negro and white workers marching side by side. Organizers in Detroit, Chicago, or, even more so, in Camp Hill, Alabama, soon learned from hard experience that it was practicable to use the Scottsboro Case to enlist Negroes emotionally into Party causes.

[92] Nathan Glazer, *The Social Basis of American Communism* (New York: Harcourt, Brace and Company, 1961), 174–76; Donald Ramsey Young, *American Minority Peoples: A Study in Racial and Cultural Conflict in the United States* (New York: Harper Brothers, 1932), 160–61; Nolan, *Communism Versus the Negro*, 100–101. As Wilson Record has noted, it is extremely difficult to ascertain either the Negro or the total Party membership. Record, *The Negro and the Communist Party*, 177.

[93] Harry Haywood, "The Scottsboro Decision," 1073–74; "The Scottsboro Struggle and the Next Steps: Resolution of the Political Bureau," *The Communist*, XII (1933), 564–76.

From there, it was often possible to shift the emphasis to their concrete economic problems, such as unemployment or low pay, discrimination, and poor housing. But ethereal plans for a "black republic," or slogans on the defense of the Soviet Union simply had no appeal.[94] *Revolutionary Age,* mouthpiece of the Party's outlawed Lovestone faction, was essentially correct when it noted that the doctrinaire and sectarian policies of the Scottsboro campaign had effectively isolated the Party from millions of potential followers. "Only those who accepted the ultimate slogans of the Communists and then subordinated themselves to the ILD were regarded as 'in the united front'—all others became 'staunch allies of the white masters.' " [95]

The Communist Party aroused admiration for its often courageous campaigns, declared a sympathetic leftist, but "disgust for its wholly unscrupulous misrepresentations." As one Communist research worker bitterly admitted, "It is utterly impossible to believe a word one reads in a Communist paper, even if one wants to." [96] The underlying causes of the widespread lack of confidence in the Party went beyond its clumsy prevarications in the *Daily Worker.* There was always the general suspicion—carefully nurtured by the Party's opponents—that the ILD was perfectly willing to sacrifice the boys for whatever were deemed to be the Party's best interests. There was, of course, no monolithic attitude among Communists, but a number of incidents supported these misgivings.

In the first place, the ILD needlessly antagonized supporters who might have been influential in helping the defendants. It is difficult to see what the International Labor Defense hoped to

[94] In 1930, when the handful of Communist organizers in the South would have found it difficult to stage an integrated, open-air meeting, one Party leader called for an attack on Southern laws prohibiting intermarriage between the races. Myra Page, "Inter-racial Relations among Southern Workers," *The Communist,* IX (1930), 164.

[95] *Revolutionary Age,* quoted in White, "The Negro and the Communists," 71. The Lovestone faction was a small splinter group which had been expelled from the CPUSA by Joseph Stalin at the 1929 International Congress in Moscow. Howe, *American Communist Party,* 172–74.

[96] Lillian Symes, "Blunder on the Left: The Revolution and the American Scene," *Harper's Magazine,* CLXVI (December, 1933), 100.

gain from its unrestrained attacks upon such liberal publications as *The Nation* and the *New Republic*. Perhaps like all zealots, they felt duty-bound to bludgeon sinners who strayed from the narrow way. When *The Nation,* for example, approved the Supreme Court's decision in *Powell* v. *Alabama,* the ILD's publicity director charged that the editors had given "objective aid to the legal lynchers. . . ." The *New Republic's* failure to emphasize sufficiently the role of mass protest brought the ILD accusation that the magazine's editorial was fiendishly designed to stifle worldwide protest. "At this stage of the case it can serve no other purpose," wrote Louis Colman the ILD publicity director.[97] As Lillian Symes observed, the result of such "stupid calumnies" against non-Party radicals was that "no intelligent person believes any of them." [98]

Behind the scenes, ILD maneuvers supported this negative appraisal. After the Alabama Supreme Court decision remanding Eugene Williams to juvenile court, the ILD moved to have Williams and Roy Wright freed on bond through a writ of *habeas corpus.* The Birmingham office of the Communist Party retained Crampton Harris, a prominent local attorney. The terms were clearly understood. For a $700 retainer he would investigate the case; for another $1,000, institute *habeas corpus* proceedings. An additional $1,300 would be paid upon successful completion of the

[97] Letter by Louis Colman, *The Nation,* CXXXV (1932), 467; Letter by Louis Colman, *New Republic,* LXXIII (1932), 100–101.

[98] Symes, "Blunder on the Left," 100. When Alabama Chief Justice Anderson dissented from the majority opinion upholding the verdict, he was rewarded with a telegram branding him a "traitor to the masses." His willingness to abide by the majority decision was an "objective aid to the landlord lynchers." Chicago ILD to Chief Justice John C. Anderson, April 4, 1932, in Alabama Scottsboro Files.

On the other hand, there is little evidence to support the constantly reiterated charge that the Communists raised as much as one million dollars from the case. (See Chalmers, *They Shall Be Free,* p. 199; Reynolds, *Courtroom,* p. 249; Murray Kempton, *Part of Our Time: Some Ruins and Monuments of the Thirties* (New York: Simon and Schuster, 1955), p. 253; Ralph McGill, *The South and the Southerner* (Boston: Atlantic-Little, Brown and Co., 1959), p. 198. The proletarian nonchalance with which the International Labor Defense kept its records makes definitive conclusions difficult, but the ILD's financial reports and other internal evidence indicate the Party and its affiliates raised less than $150,000 with the great majority of this amount going to unavoidable defense costs. See ILD Financial Reports for 1931, 1932, 1933, 1934, 1935 and 1936 in ILD Papers.

case. Harris became convinced that it would be best to wait until after the United States Supreme Court had reached its decision, but he asked for the additional $1,000 in order to begin preparing the brief.[99] In New York, acting ILD Secretary Carl Hacker exploded with anger at Harris' request. Lowell Wakefield begged him to handle the Birmingham attorney gently. "You must remember that overhasty actions can lead to a great deal of trouble for us in the case and especially down here." Harris was in a position to help or hurt the case a great deal, said Wakefield.[100]

Hacker's response was a bitter letter to Harris. "We demand that you immediately proceed with your work on the case." The ILD was a "class defense organization, defending the working classes against the terror and attacks of the ruling class . . . and we always adjust our legal activities to conform to our mass campaigns." Moreover, sending $1,000 was "out of the question." The ILD was supported by the "pennies, nickels and dimes that have been gathered by the workers." Hacker did not specify what reprisal he had in mind if Harris refused to go ahead with the case immediately.[101] General Chamlee also expressed misgivings over the timing of *habeas corpus* proceedings because of racial disturbances in the state. William L. Patterson overruled him, however, with the observation that there would be tremendous publicity from additional appeals. "The chances for raising it [the case] to a higher political level and of securing more sympathizers is greater." [102]

Nowhere was the subservience of the boys' interests to Party

[99] Charles Dirba to Irving Schwab, May 3, 1932; Crampton Harris to Carl Hacker, June 24, 1932, in ILD Papers. A favorable decision by the Supreme Court would give the defense a decided psychological boost, argued Harris. Therefore it was foolish to begin proceedings before the court had decided. Crampton Harris to Carl Hacker, June 24, 1932, in ILD Papers.

[100] Lowell Wakefield to Carl Hacker, September 18, 1932, in ILD Papers.

[101] Carl Hacker to Crampton Harris, September 22, 1932, in ILD Papers. Harris replied coldly that the terms of the agreement were clearly understood. He added that, in any case, he would not "be interested in making moves that would jeopardize the interests of my clients in order to get material for political propaganda." Crampton Harris to Carl Hacker, September 27, 1932, in ILD Papers.

[102] William L. Patterson to George W. Chamlee, December 12, 1932, December 24, 1932, in ILD Papers. Ultimately the plans for an additional appeal were dropped because Brodsky and Schwab thought it would accomplish little.

goals more evident than in the European tour of Mrs. Ada Wright. The mother of the two Wright brothers had been invited to make a six months' tour of the Continent by the International Red Aid. The purpose was supposedly to arouse a "world-wide mass campaign for the release of the Scottsboro boys." From the outset, however, attacks on the Social Democrats took precedence over the plight of the Scottsboro boys. Each "Scottsboro Rally" was simply another excuse to expose the perfidy of Europe's Socialists and Social Democrats. J. Louis Engdahl, Mrs. Wright's chaperone, customarily devoted his introduction of Mrs. Wright to a vilification of the "social fascists" who were "fawning at the feet of the lynchers and their spokesman." At each stop he explained that only the aroused anger of the masses had overawed Socialists and forced them to allow Mrs. Wright a speaking platform.[103] And when Mrs. Wright spoke, more often than not instead of discussing the plight of her sons, she haltingly read a speech prepared by Engdahl denouncing the "fascists and social fascists" and urging "mobilization of the masses against the imperialist war and for the defense of the Soviet Union." In Amsterdam, Mrs. Wright explained to a group of Communists that the fight for the freedom of her two sons was a "struggle against imperialist war, because the Scottsboro persecution grows out of the war preparations of the American boss class." [104] The American consul in Strasbourg, France, noted that the Communists had hoped to make Scottsboro another Sacco-Vanzetti case, but they had failed. There were a few broken consulate windows, but there was nothing approaching the uproar over the Massachusetts case.[105] There was considerable sympathy for the boys, said the *Journal D'Alsace et de Lorraine*, but the Communists dissipated much of the indignation by guile-

---

[103] New York *Daily Worker*, May 10, May 18, May 28, June 9, June 13, June 16, June 24, August 11, October 8, 1932. The "social fascists" were the same all over Europe, said Engdahl. They were all "on the side of the Alabama lynchers, against the workers, seeking to aid the capitalist reactionaries in maintaining a wide gulf of hatred and prejudice between the oppressed masses of different races and nationalities." New York *Daily Worker*, June 24, 1932.

[104] New York *Daily Worker*, September 27, 1932.

[105] Report of O. Gaylord Marsh, American Consul in Strasbourg, France, August 10, 1932, in Department of Justice Central Files, No. 158260, Sub. 46.

lessly manipulating the issue for their own political advantage.[106]

No amount of reservations or criticism, however, could alter one basic fact. The International Labor Defense had succeeded in winning eight of the Scottsboro boys another chance for life. The ILD had succeeded in the face of numerous predictions that a commutation to life imprisonment was the most that could be expected. But winning a new trial was only the first hurdle. The International Labor Defense could have blamed an unsuccessful appeal on the incompetence of Moody and Roddy, but the Supreme Court's decision placed responsibility for the lives of the nine boys squarely upon the ILD. "We are hopeful that you will all be free in a few months," William Patterson wrote the Scottsboro boys. The masses would demand and obtain their freedom, he promised.[107] The future of the nine defendants would be decided not by the militant masses, however, but by the unanimous decision of twelve Alabama jurors. There were Southern voices which warned against prejudging the Scottsboro boys simply because of their sponsors. The state's only hope should be to see that complete justice was done, said the Birmingham *News*.[108] But the Talladega *Daily Home* added its conviction that the boys were guilty. "Our goal now should be to obtain a decision —one way or the other—which will stand up in case of appeal." [109] The Communist Party initially had much to gain from the case; it now had much to lose.

[106] *Journal D'Alsace et de Lorraine,* August 10, 1932, in Department of Justice Central Files, No. 158260, Sub. 46.

[107] William L. Patterson to Scottsboro boys, November 10, 1932, in ILD Papers. The same letter was sent to all the seven whose cases had been appealed.

[108] Birmingham *News,* November 8, 1932.

[109] Talladega *Daily Home,* quoted in Birmingham *News,* November 10, 1932.

VI

ALABAMA,
1933

A S the ILD attorneys prepared for the new trials, an outbreak of racial violence in Tallapoosa County compounded their difficulties. County and state officials believed that they had destroyed the Sharecroppers' Union after the 1931 Camp Hill uprising. In the summer of 1932, however, two Negro Communists from Chattanooga quietly returned and began once more the difficult task of organizing the tenants. Initially the results were meager. Several Negro ministers warned their flocks against joining the union, and Tallapoosa County whites made it clear that they would not tolerate any further "agitation." But many of the county's Negroes were already on the verge of starvation, and there were few economic reprisals which could be levied against them. Late in the summer, the pastors of two small Negro churches covertly began supporting the movement.[1]

In November, Sheriff Kyle Young learned that Cliff James, the owner of a farm between Reeltown and Notasulga, had assumed leadership of the union. James, one of the few Negro landowners in the county, had borrowed money to buy his small farm in 1924, faithfully making payments until the Depression's five-cent cotton

---

[1] The Reverend M. N. Nunn, pastor of the Alexander City Bethel Baptist Church (Tallapoosa County), worked closely with county officials in discovering the names of local Negroes who joined the group. M. N. Nunn to Governor Benjamin Meeks Miller, January 9, 1933, in Alabama Executive Files, Drawer 32. Beecher, "The Share Croppers' Union in Alabama," 127.

forced him into arrears. In addition to his mortgaged farm he owned a large amount of livestock. At one time he had driven a dilapidated car around the county until, for reasons of economy, he had sold the car in 1930. Hopelessly in debt, he was nevertheless prosperous by the standards of the community. One night in early December, Sheriff Young came unannounced and searched James' home. He found a considerable amount of radical literature including membership blanks for the union. Young relayed the information to W. S. Parker, a Notasulga merchant who held the mortgage on James' farm. Parker agreed to issue a writ of attachment against both of James' mules and two of his cows. Parker knew that the loss of the two draft animals would make farming impossible for the young union leader.[2]

On the afternoon of December 19, Deputy Sheriff Witt Elder went to collect the livestock, but James stood his ground. According to Elder, he warned: "You nor Sheriff Young, nor all his deputies is gonna get them mules." When Elder returned with three other deputies an hour later, James was waiting with over two dozen union members, several of them armed. During a heated argument, one of the deputies suddenly whipped out his pistol and shot one sharecropper in the hip. The "Negro army," as the press later called it, scattered for cover. Two bullets struck James in the back as he ran. For twenty minutes the two sides exchanged gunfire until the deputies, running low on ammunition, retreated for reinforcements. The aftermath was a repeat of the previous year's rioting, but the casualties were heavier. The deputies killed one Negro as he attempted to escape to his house and accidentally wounded his five-year-old son. Elder and another of the deputies were wounded; and James and a close friend, Milo Bentley, later died from wounds incurred in the shooting.[3] What was worse for

[2] Birmingham *News,* December 24, 1932; Birmingham *Age-Herald,* December 20, 1932. James's farm was located in Tallapoosa County near the Macon County line, twelve miles north of Tuskegee Institute and approximately forty miles northwest of Montgomery. There is no question that the writ of attachment was a direct reprisal against James because of his union activities. See Birmingham *News,* December 24, 1932.

[3] The men were captured three days later and—though they were seriously wounded—placed in the Montgomery County jail with only minimal medical care.

the local Negroes, officials discovered the union's official membership roll in James' home. For three days a posse numbering over five hundred men under the leadership of the sheriffs of Tallapoosa, Elmore, Macon, and Montgomery counties hunted down the union members. Sheriff Young promised he would "get every Negro that runs." As at Camp Hill, Negroes fled their cabins and slept in backwoods houses or in the open. Deputies, taking no chances, shot one member of the "Negro army" as he sat at his kitchen table and then pistol-whipped his wife, who had been dressing his wounds. Several other Negroes were reportedly beaten and told to leave the county, while one white doctor treated nearly a dozen Negroes with gunshot wounds.[4]

The Birmingham *Post* alone refused to accept the widespread notion that the affair had been a "race war" deliberately fostered by the Communists. "The causes of the trouble are essentially economic rather than racial," said the *Post*. The resistance of the sharecroppers against officers "bears a close parallel to battles fought in Iowa and Wisconsin between farmers and sheriff's deputies seeking to serve eviction papers." The very fact that white farmers had reportedly expressed their sympathy for the Negroes was evidence of the "relentless economic pressure" which had prompted the Negroes to resistance. The *Post* counseled forbearance and moderation in the handling of the disturbance.[5]

Most Alabamians, however, reacted almost hysterically. The Birmingham *News* complained bitterly that the agitation and propaganda of the reds was "clearly the motivating influence behind such outbreaks as that in Tallapoosa County Monday." And yet the authorities were unable to halt these Communist inroads because of the hampering constitutional guarantee of free speech. Not only were the "principles of Sovietism . . . preached at the

---

Twenty-four hours after the arrest, James died lying on the floor of his cell. A physician called in reported Bentley's condition critical, and he was transferred to Kilby State Prison Hospital where he died two hours after arrival. Beecher, "The Share Croppers' Union," 131.

[4] Birmingham *Age-Herald*, December 20, 1932; Birmingham *News*, December 20, 1932; Birmingham *Post*, December 20, December 21, 1932; Beecher, "The Share Croppers' Union," 131.

[5] Birmingham *Post*, December 22, 1932.

meetings," confided the *News*, but elimination of "racial and social lines, and a banding together of the workers to take what they
want is advocated by the speakers. . . ." The Birmingham daily
carefully noted the location of the Communist office in the Martin
Building and re-emphasized that law enforcement officers were
"without legal power to stop Communist agitation and propaganda flow. . . ." The same night the *News'* editorial appeared, several
men showing badges took the keys of the Martin Building's night
watchman and raided the ILD Communist headquarters. They
ransacked the office and carried off all the files. The next day, city
and county officials explained that they knew nothing of the confiscation, and Birmingham's police chief made it clear that he
would not lose any sleep in an effort to find the guilty parties.[6]

Alabamians had been particularly alarmed at news that some
white sharecroppers had openly sympathized with the Negroes
(though not with their armed resistance). One local white
farmer even hid a wounded unionist for two days.[7] A representative from Tallapoosa County introduced a bill in the legislature
which made it a felony for "two or more persons to bind themselves together in order to resist the enforcement of any civil or
criminal law of the United States of America or of the State of
Alabama. . . ." The law could be violated by circulating any "papers, petitions, cartoons, pictures or other matter—written or
printed—that would have a tendency to create a disrespect for
law and order or to influence others to violate any law, state or
federal." [8] Birmingham and Bessemer city authorities, convinced
that their ordinances banning only "scurrilous or abusing materials" were insufficient, passed new measures penalizing the possession of more than one copy of any kind of literature "advocating the overthrow of organized government by force or any unlawful means." [9]

[6] Birmingham *News*, December 20, December 21, December 22, 1932.

[7] When officials discovered them, they threw the wounded Negro and his white
benefactor into jail. Birmingham *Age-Herald*, December 22, 1932.

[8] Despite the *News's* concern over the Communist agitation, it opposed the bill
as going "too far." Birmingham *News*, March 1, 1933.

[9] Cayton, *Black Workers and the New Unions*, 340. On the surface, the ordinances
were less far-reaching than a number of other proposals. Local officials, however,

Alabamians received a further jolt when the leaders of the union were tried for attempted murder. At the date first set for the trial, so many Negroes (and a few white sympathizers) attended that the proceedings were postponed. When they resumed on Monday, April 24, county officials blocked the main roads coming into town in order to discourage Negro attendance. Despite this, the number of Negro sharecroppers was so great that the presiding judge had to empty one side of the courtroom in order to allow some of them to be seated. Although the five selected by the solicitor for trial were all convicted by white juries and given sentences ranging from five to fifteen years, the harsh reprisals did not destroy the Sharecroppers' Union. It grew steadily, if unspectacularly, spreading into several counties south of Tallapoosa. By the fall of 1933 officials of the Sharecroppers' Union claimed more than five thousand members.[10]

Even before the Tallapoosa County violence, Jackson County residents had judged the Scottsboro defendants and found them guilty. Three weeks after the 1931 trial rumors of an appeal of the case spread through the northeastern county. The people of the area were fearful that the boys would succeed in getting a new trial, noted the Scottsboro *Progressive Age*. Editor James Stockton Benson assured his readers that the higher courts would never consider such an action, even should an appeal be made. All the "Christian leaders" of the community "agreed that the punishment fitted the crime since the assailants were *black*," reported an Alabama Women's Missionary Society leader. And they were determined that "justice must be meted out and quickly. . . ."[11]

used them to outlaw any material they considered "Communist stuff." Under this rubric came such magazines as *The Nation* and the *New Republic*. Thomas A. Krueger, *And Promises to Keep: The Southern Conference for Human Welfare, 1938–1948* (Nashville: Vanderbilt University Press, 1967), 5.

[10] Olive Matthews Stone, "Agrarian Conflict in Alabama," (Ph.D. dissertation, University of North Carolina, 1939), 524–26; New York *Daily Worker*, April 28, 1933; Stuart Marshall Jamieson, *Labor Unionism in American Agriculture* (Washington: United States Government Printing Office, 1945), 295–97. Despite its modest success in recruiting members, the union achieved only meager successes such as the right to cultivate gardens and a guarantee of credit in the slack seasons. Tindall, *The Emergence of the New South*, 380.

[11] Scottsboro *Progressive Age*, April 23, 1931; Mrs. Daisy F. Morris to Mrs. Jessie

When it became apparent that the boys' execution would be delayed by legal appeals, a cold hard fury settled over the little town. Scottsboro residents upbraided Milo Moody because of his minor role in the NAACP appeal efforts. Moody explained to Roderick Beddow that there had been no objection to his defending the boys in court. Once they had been fairly sentenced to death, however, it was wrong to continue the case.[12] After her visit to Scottsboro in May of 1931, Hollace Ransdell reported that most of the people were absolutely convinced the defendants were guilty. And they "all wanted the Negroes killed as quickly as possible in a way that would not bring disrepute upon the town." [13]

As the *Progressive Age* and *Sentinel* reported the ILD agitation across the nation, resentment among their readers rose. In vain, the editor of the *Jackson County Sentinel* defended the county. "In Scottsboro, there has never been racial trouble of any kind." There was nothing but "friendliness and understanding between the races," he said. Negroes had their own school, their own churches, their own organizations, and their own stores. There was "not a place anywhere a negro can have freer rein for the promotion of any honest effort than right here in this town now being attacked under false pretenses." The *Sentinel* explained that the people of the county had adopted the only policy which could

Daniel Ames, April 27, 1931, in Association of Southern Women for the Prevention of Lynching Papers. Mrs. Morris, a resident of Birmingham, interviewed a minister and three church women from Scottsboro at a WMS district meeting on April 24. The conversations deeply disturbed her.

[12] Roderick Beddow to Walter White, November 19, 1931, in Scottsboro Legal File 4, NAACP Papers.

[13] According to Miss Ransdell, the few people who had any doubts about the guilt of the defendants nevertheless favored execution. The common refrain, she said, was: "We white people just couldn't afford to let those Niggers get off because of the effect it would have on other Niggers." Ransdell, "Report on the Scottsboro, Alabama, Case," 18–19. Undoubtedly she was correct; the great majority of residents favored the Negroes' execution. A small and silent minority, however, opposed the execution on the grounds that the "New Testament, the code which Jesus Christ gave us to live by, positively forbids murder in any way or manner. . . ." Robert H. Oury to Governor Benjamin Meeks Miller, March 23, 1932, in Alabama Scottsboro Files. Oury, a native of Scottsboro, explained to Governor Miller that he was "born under southern skies, and I love the Southland." But he concluded, I "just don't want my people to be condemned at the Eternal Judgment of God, for something we can avoid here."

solve the race problem, "namely: THE WHITE RACE LET THE NEGROES ALONE AND THE NEGROES LET THE WHITES ALONE." Citizens of Scottsboro proudly pointed to the statement of a local Negro minister. The Reverend A. Edward Berry of the Scottsboro A.M.E. Church assured everyone that "harmony, peace and good will and understanding prevails among the races in Scottsboro." The "better class of negroes" believed the defendants received a fair trial, he said.[14] As much as anything, the pride of Jackson County citizens was hurt by the widespread newspaper accounts picturing them as ignorant, barefooted, mule-riding, tobacco-chewing illiterates.[15]

Once local citizens had convinced themselves of the boys' guilt, they seized upon the more outlandish ILD exaggerations of the case as proof that the news media were distorting the facts. Jackson County had given the boys as "fair a trial as they could have gotten in any court in the world," said the *Sentinel*. The demands and threats from outsiders that the verdict be reversed and the "filthy insinuations that our people were murderers" were incredible, said Editor Campbell. He was confident, he said, that "the matter is closed so far as a new trial might be concerned." [16]

General Chamlee had further concrete evidence that a fair trial would be impossible in the county. It was common knowledge that the ILD planned to raise the explosive issue of the exclusion of Negroes from the jury rolls. Two weeks after the first trials in Scottsboro one of the local newspapers branded this idea as "the

[14] Scottsboro *Jackson County Sentinel,* May 7, 1931. The Reverend Berry protested against the "unkind" accusations by fellow Negroes that he had backed the Scottsboro convictions in order to curry favor from whites. Scottsboro *Jackson County Sentinel,* May 21, 1931. Berry's account differed from that of another Negro minister, the Reverend G. W. Buckner, who said that since the trial Jackson County Negroes had constantly feared mob violence. New York *Times,* March 8, 1933, p. 14.

[15] One local farmer with a sense of humor assured a visitor to Scottsboro that very few people in his community, Big Sandy, had ever seen a mule. They "made their crops with electrically controlled tractors while listening to Einstein lectures from Germany and grand opera from Paris over the same machine." The last mule in the area, he solemnly assured his listener, "was with Haag's Mighty Circus several years ago when people paid 50 cents each to see the strange beast." Most people, however, did not think the outside ridicule was very humorous. Scottsboro *Jackson County Sentinel,* April 16, 1931.

[16] Scottsboro *Jackson County Sentinel,* April 16, 1931.

most dangerous movement launched in the South in many years. . . ." The *Jackson County Sentinel* had declared: "After we forget the 'rope' to pick up 'the code' for the safety and benefit of the negroes, we are told that we must have negro jurors on any jury trying the blacks if they are to get 'their rights.' " A Negro juror in the county would be a "curiosity," noted the *Sentinel,* "and some curiosities are embalmed, you know." [17] When the Supreme Court announced its decision in *Powell* v. *Alabama* and implicitly criticized the county for its conduct of the trial, the *Progressive Age* called for "calmness and composure," but Judge A. E. Hawkins acknowledged that the court's action exacerbated the already inflamed public opinion. "The presence of troops will be more imperative now than ever," he said.[18]

These conditions made it likely that a change of venue would be granted by Judge Hawkins. Even if the defense succeeded in moving the location of the trials, however, there was no guarantee that public opinion would be appreciably more favorable elsewhere. Chamlee warned the ILD national office that public opinion throughout the state of Alabama had crystallized against the defendants, in part because of the Tallapoosa County disturbance. As always, Chamlee remained hopeful, but he warned ILD officials that acquittal would require a superb defense. Establishing "reasonable doubt" would be insufficient; they would need to prove beyond question the innocence of the defendants.[19] Convinced that desperate measures were necessary, William L. Patterson turned to a New York lawyer, born in Rumania, the son of Jewish parents: Samuel Leibowitz. With the retirement of Clarence Darrow in the early 1930's, Leibowitz had become one of

[17] *Ibid.,* April 23, 1931. While Editor Benson of the *Progressive Age* was less flamboyant in his comments, he left no doubt as to his resentment over the interference of the "outsiders." Scottsboro *Progressive Age,* April 30, 1931, December 31, 1931.

[18] Scottsboro *Progressive Age,* November 10, 1932; Birmingham *Post,* November 7, 1932. Jackson County was already on the edge of bankruptcy; the projected costs of the trials made it certain that the schools would be opened for only a few months. "Scottsboro Schools," *Crisis,* XL (1933), 40.

[19] George W. Chamlee to William L. Patterson, December 22, 1932, in ILD Papers.

the leading American criminal lawyers. A graduate of the Cornell University Law School, he began his law practice in 1919 and within a decade had established his reputation as a superb, if somewhat flamboyant, criminal attorney in New York City. In that year he became nationally known when he won an acquittal for Harry L. Hoffman. Hoffman had been tried and convicted of the brutal murder of a mother of two, but when he gained a new trial, Leibowitz took his case and brilliantly demolished a mountain of circumstantial evidence to gain Hoffman his freedom.[20]

Patterson frankly told Leibowitz that the ILD would not be able to pay a fee. "We do have this to offer you," he said: "An opportunity to give your best in a cause which for its humanitarian appeal has never been equalled in the annals of American jurisprudence." He explained that the ILD did not ask him to relinquish his social, economic, and political views. Leibowitz responded by asserting his conviction that the case "touches no controversial theory of economy or government, but the basic rights of man." He was confident, he declared, that the people of Alabama would live up to their "great heritage of honor, and to those brave and chivalrous generations of the past, in whose blood the history of the State is written." If the ILD's views coincided with this, said Leibowitz, he would be willing to take the case without pay.[21]

Leibowitz knew full well that this was not the position of the ILD, but he was carefully sparring with Patterson. A complete identification with the ILD would not only diminish his chances of winning a conviction in Alabama but also compromise his professional future. He was willing to cooperate with the ILD, but

[20] There are two biographies of Leibowitz, neither of which is altogether satisfactory. Fred D. Pasley's *Not Guilty! The Story of Samuel S. Leibowitz* (New York: G. P. Putnam's Sons, 1933) covers the period through mid-1933. While it is extremely journalistic, Pasley has considerable information on Leibowitz's early career. Quentin Reynolds' *Courtroom* (New York: Farrar, Straus and Cudahy, 1950) was written with the cooperation of Leibowitz. Reynolds read many of the transcripts from Leibowitz's most important cases, and his analysis of the attorney's legal abilities is often keen. Like Pasley, however, Reynolds is generally uncritical of Leibowitz and his information is often unreliable.

[21] William L. Patterson to Samuel Leibowitz, January 28, 1933; Samuel S. Leibowitz to William L. Patterson, January 31, 1933, in ILD Papers. These letters are printed in Reynolds, *Courtroom*, 242–45.

only after staking out an independent position. The Leibowitz letter touched off a sharp debate within the Communist Party. Party leaders not connected directly with the ILD insisted that an acceptance of Leibowitz on his terms was a betrayal of the masses. The often inflexible Patterson and other ILD leaders were convinced, however, that they had to retain someone of Leibowitz's stature and ability if the ILD's defense efforts were not to be completely discredited. Leibowitz also demanded from Patterson a tacit agreement that political activities would be soft-pedaled until after the trial. Reluctantly, Patterson agreed, emphasizing that his organization remained convinced that mass defense was an "inseparable part of defense activity." Only the activities of the masses, he said, had saved the boys from the electric chair and only the masses could ultimately gain them their freedom. Despite this disagreement, said Patterson, the ILD had accepted Leibowitz on the basis of his "proven ability as a legal practitioner." [22] From the outset, however, the relationship between Leibowitz and the ILD was a marriage of convenience, never of preference.

Occupied with other cases, Leibowitz was unable to appear at the March 6 hearings to petition for a change of venue and Chamlee represented the ILD. In contrast to the trials two years before, both wire services, the Birmingham newspapers, and the New York *Times* sent reporters to Scottsboro. F. Raymond Daniell, the *Times* correspondent, found feelings bitter. Many on the streets "declare regretfully that the old way of the rope was better than the newer way of the law," he reported. The day before the hearings opened, Scottsboro police had discovered the representative of a Negro press service interviewing in the town's Negro section. They immediately suspected that he was "a Red from New York" and after overnight questioning they told him to leave town.[23] As everyone had expected, the defense opened with a request for

[22] "The Scottsboro Struggle and the Next Steps," 576; John Henry Hammond, Jr., "The South Speaks," *The Nation*, CXXXVI (1933), 465; William L. Patterson to Samuel Leibowitz, February 6, 1931, in ILD Papers.

[23] New York *Times*, March 8, 1933, p. 14. The reporter explained later that the sheriff apparently suspected that he had come to "help them 'niggers' [the Scottsboro defendants] in some way." New York *Daily Worker*, March 20, 1933.

a change of venue. As sites for the new trials, Chamlee specifically objected to neighboring Etowah, Blount, Cherokee, DeKalb, Madison, and Marshall counties. He explained to Judge Hawkins that the defense preferred Birmingham as the nearest site free from prejudice. During the weekend before the hearings, the Birmingham *News* reported it had learned from "reliable sources" that Judge Hawkins would name Birmingham. On Tuesday, March 7, before a packed courtroom, Hawkins announced that he had granted the defense request for a change of venue. The trials, however, would be held not in Birmingham, but in Decatur, Alabama, fifty miles west of Scottsboro. The first trial would open March 27, with Judge James Edwin Horton, Jr., presiding. After court adjourned, Attorney General Thomas Knight publicly commended Judge Hawkins and explained proudly that he had not opposed the motion because "I want the people of all these United States to know that these defendants will get a fair trial." [24]

Hawkins' decision bitterly disappointed the defense lawyers. "I had just about as soon try the cases here," said ILD attorney Irving Schwab. "They are the same class of people there." Chamlee remarked wearily, "The same need for military protection will exist there as existed here." Knight, who apparently misunderstood the central objection of the defense, heatedly replied that if it became necessary he would "call out every company of militia in the State of Alabama to give them a fair trial. . . ." Despite the general disappointment among ILD lawyers, Chamlee expressed their view when he observed that anything was an improvement over Scottsboro.[25]

On March 13, Leibowitz arrived in Birmingham and officially assumed command of the case. The New York attorney knew that the case could not be won unless public opinion on the "Com-

[24] New York *Times,* March 8, 1933, p. 14; Birmingham *Age-Herald,* March 8, 1933.

[25] Birmingham *Age-Herald,* March 8, 1933; Birmingham *News,* March 7, 1933; New York *Times,* March 8, 1933, p. 14. The Birmingham *Post* publicly regretted the decision of Hawkins. His transfer to Decatur "adhered more strictly to the letter of the law than he would have done had he ordered the cases tried in Birmingham." Birmingham *Post,* March 8, 1933.

munist issue" was mollified and at press conference he shrewdly released the exchange of letters between himself and the ILD. He also assured the people of Alabama that he had no intention of telling them how to administer their laws or run their affairs. "I am coming here simply as a lawyer to try a law case, fully mindful of the sincere desire of the good people of the great South to give every living thing on God's green earth a square deal." [26]

During the two weeks before the trial opened, Leibowitz conferred daily with Chamlee to map out strategy. On March 20, Chamlee disclosed that the defense would open by requesting Judge Horton to quash the original indictment against the Scottsboro boys. The Supreme Court had early held that the deliberate exclusion of Negroes from the jury lists was a violation of the equal protection clause of the Fourteenth Amendment.[27] Negroes comprised almost 10 per cent of Jackson County's population, but court officials admitted they could not recall a black juror in the period since Reconstruction. The defense had issued supoenas for the three Jackson County jury commissioners, said Chamlee. In addition, it planned to call a number of Negroes from the county to prove its contention that qualified jurors had been excluded purely because of skin color. Chamlee warned Leibowitz the jury question might completely prejudice the jury against the defendants, but there was no guarantee they could gain an acquittal under any circumstances. Proof of discrimination would at least give the boys another trial in case of conviction. For several days, reporters heard rumors that the state of Alabama would avoid the issue by placing the names of a few Negroes on the Morgan County (Decatur) venire. The state's peremptory challenges could then prevent the possibility of black jurors. Others noted that this would have no effect on the issue. The defense specifically objected to the indictments which were returned by the 1931

[26] New York *Times,* March 14, 1933, p. 10; Birmingham *Age-Herald,* March 14, 1933.

[27] *Strauder* v. *West Virginia* (1880), 100 U.S. 303. Shortly afterwards, however, the court effectively emasculated all attempts at federal enforcement in *Neal* v. *Delaware* (1881), 103 U.S. 370.

Jackson County grand jury, and placing a few Negroes in the
Morgan County venire would not nullify the motion. Knight decided to meet the issue squarely. The selection of jurors was left
entirely to the discretion of the jury commissioners, he said. To
take away their freedom of choice would attack the very principle
of states' rights.[28]

Knight was concerned about more than the jury issue. From
the Huntsville police he had received word that Ruby Bates was
missing from her home. She had left suddenly on the evening of
February 27, her mother reported, and had not been seen since.
Although Victoria was the star witness, Knight knew that the loss
of Ruby would cripple the prosecution. A conference with Sheriff
Ben Giles was even more alarming. Giles, who had been keeping
an eye on Ruby for the state, reported that she had told him she
had been offered a large sum of money if she would disappear
before the second trial.[29]

Ruby had caused trouble for the prosecution almost from the
first. Annoyed because the vivacious Victoria had pushed her out
of the limelight, she hinted as early as June, 1931, that she had
some "important" information for the defense.[30] On January 5,
1932, Huntsville police had arrested Miron Pearlman, alias Danny
Dundee, on a routine charge of drunkenness. When they searched
the ex-prize fighter, however, they found a letter which caused
consternation from Scottsboro to Montgomery. The letter, written
by Ruby to a boyfriend, declared in part:

> dearest Earl
>
> I want to make a statement to you Mary Sanders is a goddam lie
> about those negros jassing me those police man made me tell a lie.
> . . . those negros did not touch me . . . i hope you will belive me

[28] New York *Times*, March 21, 1933, p. 36; Montgomery *Advertiser*, March 21,
1933. As soon as it became apparent that Alabama's jury system would be challenged, Knight announced that he would take personal charge of the prosecution.
New York *Times*, March 11, 1933, p. 28.

[29] Huntsville *Daily Times*, March 7, March 10, 1933; New York *Times*, March 11,
1933, p. 28.

[30] Will Alexander to Walter White, July 3, 1931, in Interracial Commission
Papers. The original of this letter is not in the NAACP Papers.

the law don i love you beteor [better] than Mary does are any
Body else . . . i know it was wrong too let those negros die on account of me. . . . i was jaze But those white Boys jazed me i wish
those negroes are not burnt on account of me. . . .[31]

Pearlman, in serious trouble, swore to Huntsville police that he
had been paid by George W. Chamlee of Chattanooga to "get her
drunk and have her write a letter to one of her fellows stating that
the negroes did not attack or assault her. . . ." This was exactly
what he had done, he declared. Ruby was "drunk as she could be
when she wrote the letter." He told police he had agreed to Chamlee's plan solely because he was broke and badly in need of money
and not because he was "sweet-talked by the idea of saving eight
niggers' lives." After questioning by the police, Ruby signed an
affidavit agreeing with Pearlman's account: "I was so drunk that
I did not know what I was doing." According to the affidavit she
signed, the letter contained "all falsehoods, no truth being in
it. . . ." Chamlee branded the story an "absolute falsehood," although he admitted that he knew Pearlman. In the uproar that
followed Huntsville Chief of Police H. C. Blakemore disclosed
that he had monitored a telephone conversation between Chamlee
and the cooperative Pearlman on the evening of January 5; there
was absolutely no doubt that Chamlee had arranged the entire
thing. Two days later Stephen Roddy, who had never forgiven
Chamlee for pushing him out of the case, filed a report before the
Chattanooga Bar Association. Prepared by Scottsboro officials, it
called for the disbarring of Chamlee for "conspiracy" and interference with pending criminal proceedings.[32]

An investigation by the Bar Association disclosed that Chamlee
had been only peripherally involved in the incident. Miron Pearlman had approached Chamlee, and the Chattanooga lawyer referred him to George Proctor, a free-lance writer for the *New*

[31] Ruby Bates to Earl Streetman, January 5, 1932, in ILD Papers. A photostat of
the letter was furnished the ILD by Huntsville police only after Chamlee threatened a court order.

[32] Huntsville *Times*, January 6, January 10, 1932; Chattanooga *Daily Times*,
January 7, January 8, January 11, January 12, 1932.

Masses. It was Proctor who had made all the arrangements and he denied that he had ever told Pearlman to get Ruby intoxicated. "I believe Pearlman has been terrorized by the police of Huntsville into telling a false story reflecting on Mr. Chamlee," declared Proctor. The entire story had been concocted, he said, "for the express purpose of injuring Mr. Chamlee's reputation and through him to discredit the whole Scottsboro defense." In a supporting statement, Chamlee declared upon his "word of honor for truth and justice" he had nothing to do with any bribery attempts.[33] Although the charges against Chamlee had been dropped, Knight hoped that this unfortunate experience the previous year would deter the defense from trying to contact either of the two girls again, but he could not be sure. He alerted all state and local officials and told them to take the young Bates girl into custody.

Defense and prosecution attorneys spent the last few days before the trial haggling over whether the militia should guard the prisoners. Knight contended that Morgan County citizens held no strong prejudice against the defendants; a handful of guards would be quite sufficient. Sheriff A. W. (Bud) Davis settled the issue when he informed Judge Horton he needed at least thirty militiamen, not to protect the prisoners, but to prevent their escape. The jail, a crumbling, decaying brick building, was so insecure (and unsanitary) it had been declared "unfit for white prisoners" more than two years before. During 1931 and 1932, jail-breaks by the Negro inmates were so common that the Decatur *Daily* ceased to regard them as news unless the escapee was a dangerous felon.[34]

As the trial approached, newsman Raymond Daniell reported what Schwab and other ILD lawyers had feared—the success "in obtaining a change of venue from Jackson County seems a little

[33] Chattanooga *Daily Times,* January 13, January 14, January 15, 1932. Earlier, a Chattanooga newsboy told reporters that his friend, Miron Pearlman, needed no coaxing on the part of anyone else. He had approached Chamlee, not vice-versa. Chattanooga *Daily Times,* January 10, 1932. The full details of the incident will perhaps never be known.

[34] Confidentially, town officials admitted to reporters there was always the danger of sudden mob violence. New York *Times,* March 18, 1933, p. 30; Birmingham *News,* March 29, 1933.

like a pyrrhic victory. . . ." Decatur was situated in northern Alabama on the south bank of the Tennessee River. Created in 1820 in order to honor Stephen Decatur, it remained a part of the Cherokee Indian lands until President Andrew Jackson forcibly removed the aboriginal inhabitants. During the next one hundred years, the town had grown steadily to a population of more than 15,000. Although agriculture supported about half the residents of the county, a substantial number of Morgan County citizens worked in the town's textile mills, small factories, and the shops of the Louisville and Nashville railroad. The people prided themselves on their progressive outlook and reporters found their town attractive, with broad, well-paved streets. Even in the poorer sections the houses had open porches and wide lawns, and the trees which arched across many of the town's streets gave it all a cool appearance, in the midst of summer.[35]

The townspeople seemed sincerely intent on living up to their duty as they saw it, but Decatur was Southern to the core. Several of the town's buildings still contained shot fired during the Civil War. The town had been a center of Klan strength in both the Reconstruction period and during the 1920's, and the position of Negroes was much the same as in Scottsboro. Among the 3,000 residents of "black Decatur" were eight ministers, three doctors, a dentist, and numerous small businessmen. Only a handful voted. Moreover, many of the officials and residents were from Jackson County, the scene of the first trials, or Madison County, where Ruby Bates and Victoria Price lived. One county official told Raymond Daniell, "If this thing had happened twenty-five years ago, there would not have been any trial." [36] Probate Judge B. L. Malone, a former mayor of Decatur, admitted frankly that the overwhelming consensus among residents in Decatur was that the boys were guilty beyond question. He conceded that the girls, as ladies of "low character," might have persuaded the boys to do

[35] New York *Times,* March 18, 1933, p. 30; April 16, 1933, VIII, p. 2; New York *Post,* January 28, 1936.
[36] New York *Times,* March 18, 1933, p. 30.

what they did and then accused them when they got caught. But this, he argued, was a remote possibility.[37]

Resentment over the Supreme Court decision was another obstacle to obtaining an acquittal. Almost every Alabama newspaper commenting on the reversal urged that the state comply gracefully and willingly with the edict.[38] Columnist John Temple Graves, II, insisted that there was "little public tendency here to protest the new trial. . . ." [39] Privately, however, there was a widespread resentment over the way that the decision had damaged the "prestige" of the state supreme court.[40] The Birmingham *Post* had reported after the decision: "No more stinging rebuke has been administered to a state court in years than the . . . decision . . . ordering the state of Alabama to re-try the seven Negro boys. . . ." [41] Thus, even though it was "constantly . . . iterated that the Negroes will receive a fair trial . . . nowhere is there the slightest doubt that they will be convicted a second time. . . ." said Daniell.[42]

As the trial opened on March 27, however, there was little evidence of bad feeling. Decatur's only hotel, taxed to the utmost, had opened up a wing closed for some time. Western Union rented space across from the courthouse and brought in extra operators to handle the expected press reports. And on the streets, townspeople went out of their way to greet the strangers in their midst, as if to assure them that their fears were groundless.[43] The Decatur *Daily* noted that the selection of the town as site for the trials was a compliment to the people of the county. The *Daily* urged its readers to live up to this by being courteously hospitable to all who came to the trials. "Let the world see Decatur

[37] Norfolk *Journal and Guide*, April 1, 1932.

[38] Birmingham *News*, November 8, 1932; Montgomery *Advertiser*, November 8, 1932; Chattanooga *Daily Times*, November 9, 1932; Birmingham *Age-Herald*, November 8, 1932; Scottsboro *Progressive Age*, November 10, 1932.

[39] Birmingham *Age-Herald*, November 8, 1932.

[40] New York *Times*, March 12, 1933, p. 16; see letter by R. E. Crowder, Birmingham *Post*, April 12, 1933.

[41] Birmingham *Post*, November 8, 1932.

[42] New York *Times*, March 27, 1933, p. 11.

[43] *Ibid.*, March 24, 1933, p. 13; Birmingham *News*, March 29, 1933.

and Morgan County as they really are, a fine little city, a splendid county and a citizenship without peer." The Birmingham *News* promised the nation that the state would "exercise the most scrupulous care to see that the conduct of the trial proves to be entirely irreproachable in every detail." [44] During the first twenty-four hours of the trial only one dissonant voice was heard. The prisoners had been transferred first to Birmingham and then to Decatur, and Andy Wright complained vehemently about their home away from home. He and the other boys objected to the falling plaster and the rank smell, but "the bedbugs, they's the worst. They get in our clothes and we got no change, just this prison suit." Despite every remedy supplied by the boys' ingenuity, there was no getting rid of the bedbugs. "We got powder and tried to clean the mattresses," Andy said, "but they just eat the powder and come back for more." [45]

---

[44] Decatur *Daily*, March 27, 1933; Birmingham *News*, March 4, 1933.
[45] New York *Daily Worker*, April 4, 1933.

VII

"A HORRIBLE
MISTAKE"

MARCH 27, the opening day of the trials, was warm and spring-like. Before 7 A.M. a large but good-natured crowd had gathered outside the two-story yellow brick courthouse. Even the announcement that there would be a half-day's delay in the hearings did not seem to disturb the Morgan County residents. Throughout the morning, members of the crowd wandered in and out of the courthouse while Negroes and whites lolled around the building or sunned lazily on the wide lawn. And in groups of four and five they gathered around the two courthouse statues, one honoring justice and the other paying tribute to those Confederate soldiers "who gave their lives for a just cause—state's rights." Leibowitz, who mingled among the townspeople, told reporters, "The people here impress me as being honest, God fearing people who want to see justice done." They were, he said, genuinely cordial and friendly.[1]

Shortly after lunch, word came from court officials that the trial would soon get underway, and the crowd hurried to get good seats in the courtroom. Within minutes, a ragged line stretched through the corridors and past the brass spittoons resting on their tobacco-stained rubber pads. In less than a quarter hour, the 425 seats had been filled, with whites down three rows and Negroes in the

[1] Decatur *Daily*, March 27, 1933; New York *Daily Worker*, April 4, 1933; New York *Daily News*, April 6, 1933; Norfolk *Journal and Guide*, April 1, 1933.

fourth section. The front of the courtroom was dominated by the judge's elevated bench and chair. At a table on the left side of the room sat the ILD lawyers and the defendants; the state's attorneys were in the center and on the far right stood the empty jury box. Just inside the spectators rail, the courthouse officials hastily had constructed a long table for the major newsmen: T. M. Davenport of the Associated Press, Ralph E. Hurst of the Birmingham *News,* Raymond Daniell of the New York *Times,* Tom Cassiday of the New York *Daily News,* and Stanley Gibson of the New York *Daily Worker.* The two Negro newsmen, P. Bernard Young, Jr., managing editor of the Norfolk *Journal and Guide,* and William N. Jones of the Baltimore *Afro-American,* sat at a separate table. At 2 P.M. Judge Horton entered from a side door, settled into his chair, adjusted his tortoise shell spectacles, and nodded to the prosecutor to begin reading the indictment.[2]

It was the first time the defense lawyers had seen the man who would conduct the famous trials. Lank, raw-boned, and more than six feet tall, Horton often reminded those who first met him of Lincoln without his beard. The descendant of an old Alabama family originally from Virginia, Horton had attended Cumberland University in Lebanon, Tennessee, receiving his B.A. degree in 1897. Unlike many self-educated lawyers of his day, he had continued work at the University and had received a Bachelor of Laws in 1899. Although his district elected him a state senator shortly after he began practicing law, Horton was never politically ambitious. In 1915 he was selected to fill an unexpired term as Chancellor of the North Chancery Division of Alabama. When Alabama reorganized its court system in 1922, the constituents of the Eighth Judicial District elected him circuit judge over two well-known opponents. In 1929 he was re-elected without opposition.[3] In the courtroom, he was a newsman's favorite judge, easy-going and lenient, unbothered by the clatter of "silent" typewriters. During the two week trial he would be called upon to rule

[2] *Ibid.;* Birmingham *News,* March 27, 1933; New York *Times,* March 28, 1933, p. 6.
[3] Owen, *Story of Alabama,* V. 1147–48; Decatur *Daily,* February 12, 1966.

on questions of law he had spent most of his life accepting without question. But he always seemed unperturbed and seldom raised his voice above a soft conversational tone. Even before the trial had opened, he favorably impressed the two Negro reporters. Bernard Young of the Norfolk *Journal and Guide* sought him out the first morning to express his thanks for a special pass which Horton's office had mailed. When he introduced himself, Horton unhesitatingly offered a warm handshake, said Young, despite the fact that it obviously annoyed several local townspeople passing by.[4]

As soon as Morgan County Solicitor Wade Wright had completed reading the indictment, Leibowitz made a motion that Judge Horton quash the indictments. They were, he said, "null and void," because the grand jury which originally returned them in 1931 was illegally constituted. At the time the Jackson County commissioners drew up the jury roll in 1930, there were approximately 7,800 male citizens qualified by age to serve. Of this number, over 600 were Negroes, most of whom were "honest and intelligent men" fully meeting the requirements of the Alabama jury law. The authorities, however, had "arbitrarily refused, omitted and neglected to place [upon the rolls] the names of any of the aforesaid Negroes." This, noted Leibowitz, clearly violated the defendants' rights under the Fourteenth Amendment of the United States Constitution.[5]

As the first witness to support his motion, Leibowitz called to the stand James Stockton Benson, editor of the Scottsboro *Progressive Age.* Benson was one of Scottsboro's most distinguished citizens. He had moved to the little town in 1912 as a schoolteacher and over the next decade served as postmaster and county registrar. A devoted member of the local Civitan Club, he was also a

---

[4] New York *Times,* April 16, 1933, VIII, p. 3; Norfolk *Journal and Guide,* April 8, 1933.

[5] "Motion to Quash Indictments, Morgan Circuit Court, *The State of Alabama,* Plaintiff, vs. *Haywood Patterson, Ozie Powell, Willie Roberson, Olen Montgomery, Clarence Norris, Charley Weems, Andy Wright, Roy Wright and Eugene Williams,* Defendants, March 27, 1933," (Typewritten.) Cornell University Law Library, Ithaca, N. Y. Because this case was never appealed to a higher court, the motion was not printed; apparently this is the only extant copy.

Mason, an Odd Fellow, and a member of the Woodmen of the World. In 1928, his fellow Alabama newsmen had named him president of the Alabama Press Association. With his metal rimmed glasses and rotund face he was a kindly and gentle-looking man. Smiling apologetically at Attorney General Knight, he readily acknowledged that he had never seen a Negro serving on a Jackson County grand or petit jury, but he denied that this was due to a conscious policy of exclusion. Benson explained that there were some Negroes with a "good reputation," but none with sound judgment. Negroes (and women, he hastily added) had not been "trained for jury duty in our county . . . and I don't think their judgment—you could depend on it all together. . . ." They simply "haven't made a study of jury duty and law and equity and justice and so forth. . . ." [6]

Leibowitz noted gently that there were white men on the jury lists who were completely illiterate and had never gone to school. Was their judgment any more sound than that of a Negro pastor who had attended divinity college and studied the Scriptures? Reluctantly, Benson acknowledged that some of them "has got education enough," but he added hastily, "they will nearly all steal." A ripple of laughter swept through the courtroom, and the defendants who had been dozing at the table grinned while Horton lazily rapped for quiet.[7] Leibowitz, relaxed and smiling, continued gently to prod Benson. Do you mean, he said, that every Negro in Jackson County—ministers of the gospel, church and community leaders—would steal? Benson paused for a moment, perspiring profusely in the courtroom, which had suddenly become hot and stuffy. No, he finally admitted. Leibowitz focused on one Negro citizen whom Benson considered honest, of good character and "pretty intelligent." Yet Benson argued he would still "knock him out" if he were a jury commissioner. "Because he is a negro?"

[6] Owen, Story of Alabama, IV, 603; Chattanooga Daily Times, May 9, 1931; "Motion to Quash Indictments, March 27, 1933," 29, 32–33, 37; New York Times, March 28, 1933, p. 6.

[7] "Motion to Quash Indictments, March 27, 1933," 39; Birmingham Age-Herald, March 28, 1933.

asked Leibowitz. "No, not altogether," Benson paused for a moment; "that is partly it." [8] And that was what Leibowitz was trying to show.

In his questioning of Benson, Leibowitz had been diffident, and gently inquisitive, as though he were politely trying to fathom some strange new idea. With the next witness, the chief attorney for the defense was firm and sometimes brusque in his examination. J. E. Moody was "president" of the board of jury commissioners. He insisted to Leibowitz that he had never barred any colored citizens because of their race. When confronted with the names of about two dozen prominent Negroes, he explained that they did not comply with the law. Leibowitz looked at him for a moment and then asked almost absentmindedly for the legal requirements for jury service. Moody sat still in the witness chair, his eyes blinking as though deep in thought. He was not sure, he said; they had to be of "good character." Under the skillful cross-examination of Leibowitz, it was soon apparent that the unnerved Moody had not the vaguest notion what the law provided. The Jackson County official finally admitted that Negroes were not excluded for any particular reason because "negroes was never discussed." [9]

The jury commissioner's lack of knowledge of the state's jury statute, however embarrassing to the prosecution, was understandable. For Alabama's statute on the subject was deliberately vague and verbose. During the Constitutional Convention of 1901, the political leaders of Alabama had bluntly stated their goal: "to secure permanent white supremacy in this State. . . ." [10] Out of the convention and the legislative sessions that followed came a law which limited jury service to all male citizens between the

---

[8] "Motion to Quash Indictments, March 27, 1933," 49; New York *Times*, March 28, 1933, p. 6; Birmingham *Age-Herald*, March 28, 1933.

[9] "Motion to Quash Indictments, March 27, 1933," 59–68, 85.

[10] *Official Proceedings of the Constitutional Convention of the State of Alabama, May 21st, 1901 to September 3rd, 1901* (Wetumpka, Alabama: Wetumpka Printing Company, 1940), III, 3363. The convention had been most concerned over the suffrage issue, but the delegates also made it clear they planned to exclude all those from jury service who did "not belong to the white race." *Ibid.*, I, 274.

ages of twenty-one and sixty-five. Habitual drunkards, the physically disabled, and anyone "convicted of any offense involving moral turpitude" could not serve. One provision barred illiterates, but allowed their names if they were freeholders. The most crucial section in the law closed the jury box to all men except those "generally reputed to be honest and intelligent" and "esteemed in the community for their integrity, good character and sound judgment. . . ." [11] Had the law been fairly enforced, there would have been few objections, but as a native Alabamian and noted Southern lawyer admitted, these vague laws were nothing more than a mask for excluding the names of any and all Negroes.[12]

It was late in the afternoon when Leibowitz called to the stand his fourth witness: a fifty-year-old Negro plasterer from Scottsboro. John Sandford had not been subpoenaed; in the face of white opinion in the community, his decision to appear for the defense required genuine courage. Leibowitz's examination of Benson and the two jury commissioners had been traditional. Rather than simply prove that Negroes had never served on Jackson County's juries, however, he set out to show conclusively there were many Negroes who met the standards laid down by the law. With Sandford, Leibowitz summarized all the requirements and asked him if he were qualified. Sandford nodded yes and also volunteered the names of at least a dozen people in his church he believed met the legal conditions for jury duty. From a list compiled before the trial, Leibowitz called out the names of Jackson County's leading Negroes. Of those he knew, Sandford excluded two who were over sixty-five and one who had suffered a stroke. The rest, in his opinion, were qualified.[13]

It was the next day before Attorney General Knight had his chance to cross-examine Sandford, but he lost no time. He walked

[11] Alabama, *Revised Statutes* (1931), No. 47, Sec. 14.

[12] Elvy E. Callaway, *The Other Side of the South* (Chicago: D. Ryerson, 1936), 147–48. Although Southern officials used many methods to maintain all-white juries, several states relied on vague and highly subjective statutes similar to Alabama's. For a summary of these provisions, see Fred Minnis, "The Attitude of Federal Courts on the Exclusion of Negroes from Jury Service" (M.A. thesis, Howard University, 1934), 77–81.

[13] "Motion to Quash Indictments, March 27, 1933," 98–111.

to within a foot of the witness chair and asked: "Do you know all of these [Negro] people the defense asked you about yesterday? And know they possess all of the qualifications prescribed for a juror, do you?" Sandford, his eyes on the floor, replied almost inaudibly, "Yes sir, what he asked me I do." Well, "what did he ask you?" snapped Knight. Sandford, who was visibly shaking, explained that he couldn't remember all of the things that were asked. "That is one of the reasons you are not on the jury right now, you can't remember?" asked Knight sarcastically. He observed that Sandford had agreed with the characterization of one Negro as "esteemed." Could you, said Knight, "tell me what the word esteemed means?" "I don't know whether I could tell you that or not," replied Sandford. Knight, pointing his finger inches from the witness's face, shouted: "How do you know they possess the qualifications inquired about then?" [14] Leibowitz leaped to his feet. "You are not going to bully this witness or any other witness," he shouted. Turning to Judge Horton, he demanded that Knight be instructed to "stand back a little bit, and just lower his voice, and stop sticking his finger into people's eyes." Knight, clearly agitated, stepped back, composed himself, and then spoke in a confidential voice to the witness. "And you don't know what the word esteemed means, John?" "Call him Mr. Sandford please," interrupted Leibowitz. There was in the courtroom an audible gasp from the spectators. A shocked Knight told Leibowitz that he was "not in the habit of doing that." Once more it took the firm voice of Judge Horton to calm the two men. [15]

Altogether Leibowitz called nine Negroes from the community, including a Pullman porter, the owner and operator of a Scottsboro dry cleaning establishment, and a trustee of the Negro schools. Alternately cajoling good-naturedly and alternately threatening, Knight managed to show that they were not aware of the more intricate details of the jury selection system and they did not

[14] *Ibid.*, 117–19; Birmingham *News*, March 28, 1933; Decatur *Daily*, March 28, 1933.

[15] "Motion to Quash Indictments, March 27, 1933," 119; Birmingham *News*, March 28, 1933.

know the precise meaning of the term "moral turpitude." But he was not able to conceal what Leibowitz was trying to prove. The men were far more qualified for jury service than many whites; they testified that many of their friends were equally qualified, and yet none had ever heard of a Negro sitting on a jury in the county.[16]

Knight eventually ceased arguing that there were no qualified Negroes and asserted instead that there was no proof their names were not on the jury roll. There were many qualified whites, he insisted, who had never been called to duty. In exasperation, Leibowitz declared that "if the Attorney General is going to insist on proving it [the absence of Negroes on the roll] . . . I will have to ask the indulgence of the Court to get the jury roll, and we will bring every living man on that jury roll if it takes twenty-five years to do it, and we will prove that they are white." At first it appeared Horton might have the jury lists brought into court, but when the session resumed after lunch on Tuesday he abruptly announced that he had decided not to hear any more testimony. "The motion to quash is overruled," he said. "I respectfully except," replied Leibowitz, who took the decision in good humor. Judge Horton's action came so suddenly and unexpectedly that several reporters missed his announcement and had to inquire about it at the press table.[17] Leibowitz, however, had not really expected Horton to do otherwise; he was simply making certain he had his evidence in the transcript in case an appeal became necessary. At the conclusion of the brief session, Horton announced that the court would be adjourned all day Wednesday at the request of the defense.

During the one-day recess granted by Horton, Leibowitz and the other two ILD attorneys were seen in the Negro section of Decatur. Rumors quickly spread that they would attack the Morgan County petit jury system just as they had done in the case of the grand jury in Jackson County. When court reopened the next morning, the gossip proved correct. Almost apologetically Leib-

[16] "Motion to Quash Indictments, March 27, 1933," 152–222.
[17] *Ibid.*, 152, 231; Decatur *Daily*, March 28, 1933.

owitz told the court: "We are not launching a crusade, but we are doing everything we can to protect the rights of the boys who are defendants in the case." [18] Despite his assurances, observers in the court noted a perceptible rise in tension and hostility over the first three days of the trial.

The tension was reflected in the often acrimonious cross-examination. When Arthur J. Tidwell, one of the three Morgan County jury commissioners, took the stand Leibowitz peremptorily demanded the county's jury list. Tidwell sat without moving, darting puzzled looks at the prosecution table and then back at Judge Horton. Over the objections of Knight, Horton ordered the sheriff to bring in the huge, leather-bound book. In a hostile tone, Leibowitz asked Tidwell if it was not a fact that all the people whose names were written in the book were white. Like his counterparts in Jackson County, Tidwell replied, "I don't know." Leibowitz, who had heard the answer one too many times, snapped back: "Do you mean that for an honest answer?" Tidwell swung around in his chair, the color rushing to his face. "Do you mean to say that I would swear falsely?" he asked in a low, harsh voice. "I don't mean to say anything," Leibowitz retorted. "I'm asking you a question." Quickly Horton intervened to sustain an objection from Knight, but it was clear that Leibowitz had antagonized the white spectators.[19]

Knight was even more brusque and aggressive in his cross-examination of the Morgan County Negroes who appeared to testify on their competency for jury service. Leibowitz had succeeded in producing a blue book of Negro society in the county. With a non-white population of almost nine thousand, Morgan County had a much larger Negro middle class than Jackson County, and the most prominent were on hand. Altogether ten Negroes testified for the defense and, as the Birmingham *News*

[18] Decatur *Daily*, March 30, 1933. An abridged transcript of the motion to quash the Morgan County venire was later introduced and reprinted in the *Norris* v. *Alabama*, 294 U.S. 534, Transcript of Record.

[19] New York *Times*, March 31, 1933, p. 9; Decatur *Daily*, March 31, 1933; *Norris* v. *Alabama*, 294 U.S. 534, Tr. p. 427.

reporter observed, uniformly they were "unusually intelligent in appearance and employed good English."[20] Frank J. Sykes, a Negro dentist from Decatur, had graduated from Howard University in Washington and was one of the handful of registered Negro voters in the county. A handsome man with a brush mustache, he was polite but ostentatiously self-confident in his replies to Knight.[21] When he gave the court a list of over two hundred Negroes he personally knew and believed were eligible for jury duty Knight asked him if he was aware that one of the Negroes on the list had recently been in court charged with a felony. Sykes replied firmly he did not. "I do," snapped Knight, as he ended his questioning. He bluntly asked the Rev. W. J. Wilson, "Are you a member of the Communist Party?" "No, sir," replied Wilson, "I am a Republican." Knight fared even worse when he cross-examined Dr. N. E. Cashin, a Morgan County Negro physician, educated at Phillips-Exeter Academy and a graduate of the University of Illinois. "Do you know that this county has a jury commission?" he asked. Cashin looked Knight squarely in the eye and with a tone of unmistakable disgust replied, "I know it is supposed to have one."[22] As the columnist Mary Heaton Vorse observed, the defense witnesses were all men of importance—doctors, ministers, and businessmen. "Almost all have college degrees— some more than one." Of course none had ever been called to jury service, and all of Knight's fiery questions on minor points could not obscure that fact.[23]

When the testimony on the quashing motion resumed the following morning, the atmosphere was even more disturbing than the day before. There had been no open threats, but throughout the town there were angry comments over Leibowitz's attack on

[20] Birmingham *News*, March 30, 1933. It was the Birmingham *News* reporter who described Knight as brusque in his cross-examination.

[21] As warning for his "stepping out of line," the local Ku Klux Klan later burned a cross in Sykes's front yard. Norfolk *Journal and Guide*, May 6, 1933.

[22] Birmingham *News*, March 30, 1933; New York *Times*, March 31, 1933, p. 9; Birmingham *Age-Herald*, March 31, 1933. An abridged version of the testimony of Sykes, Wilson, and Cashin can be found in *Norris* v. *Alabama*, 294 U.S. 534, Tr. pp. 430–39, 456–59.

[23] New York *World Telegram*, April 6, 1933.

the jury system. Robert Burns Eleazer, attending the trial for the Interracial Commission, reported to Will Alexander that Leibowitz had "handled the case remarkably well" and generally, he said, "with fine courtesy." But Eleazer concluded he had "prejudiced unfavorably his chance for acquittal by his fight on the jury system. . . ." Raymond Daniell of the New York *Times* also observed a perceptible hardening of attitudes. Leibowitz's insistence on referring to Negro witnesses as "Mr." had only perplexed the spectators. But when he questioned the honesty of jury commissioner Tidwell, "row upon row of rough-faced unshaven countrymen in blue denim overalls" set their faces in "hard, unsympathetic lines." [24] Leibowitz concluded his case on the motion shortly before noon on Friday, and Horton, almost as abruptly as he had done in the case of the earlier motion, announced that the motion was denied. Significantly, however, he also ruled that the defense had established a *prima facie* case of exclusion. Leibowitz, inwardly confident that no conviction could now stand before a higher court, responded with "I respectfully except." [25]

After the noon recess, the venire of jurors assembled in the courtroom, ready at last to begin hearing the actual testimony. But before the arduous task of jury selection began, Horton announced that he had a few remarks he wanted to make. The judge, outwardly maintaining his customary calmness, was deeply disturbed. During the morning, several court officials had told him there was widespread talk in the streets of permanently ending the New York lawyer's attacks on Alabama's jury system. In his quiet, even voice, Horton addressed the assembled jurors, the spectators, and through them all the citizens of the county. "Now gentlemen under our law when it comes to the courts we know neither native nor alien, we know neither Jew nor Gentile, we know neither black nor white. . . ." To each, he said, "it is our duty to mete out even handed justice." Only by obeying all the laws of the land could a free people enjoy the benefits of liberty,

[24] Robert Burns Eleazer to Will W. Alexander, March 31, 1933, in Interracial Commission Papers; New York *Times*, April 16, 1933, VIII, 2.

[25] New York *Times*, April 1, 1933, p. 34; Birmingham *Age-Herald*, April 1, 1933.

Horton declared. "No other course is open to you . . ."—and for the first time his voice became stern and harsh—"and let no one think they can act otherwise than in this manner." Let us begin selection of the jury, he concluded.[26]

It took the rest of the afternoon to select the twelve men who would decide the fate of Haywood Patterson, first of the seven to be tried. Leibowitz was not altogether satisfied. The state had used its challenges to exclude younger men from Decatur who it feared might favor more "liberal" ideas, but, on the other hand, Leibowitz had managed to keep off most of the "redneck" types who had dominated the first juries in Scottsboro. On the jury were three farmers, two mill workers, two bookkeepers, a barber, salesman, bank cashier, storekeeper, and draftsman.[27]

During the weekend, the jurors whiled away their time in their hotel rooms, playing cards and amusing themselves with jigsaw puzzles. Judge Horton had specifically forbidden them to discuss the case in any way. On Sunday morning they attended the local Episcopal church and then returned to the hotel to wait for the opening of the trial the next day. Both the defense and the prosecution staffs spent their time in constant conferences, discussing strategy for the coming week. Leibowitz and Knight were staying at the Cornelian Court Apartments and despite the courtroom pyrotechnics, they often chatted amiably on the lawn outside their rooms. The cordiality did not extend beyond the apartments. Horton's warning ended the violent threats which had been heard on the streets, but Raymond Daniell of the New York *Times* found resentment smoldering beneath the surface. Townspeople were particularly angered by accounts of the trial published in the Negro press. The Chicago *Defender*'s report that the trial was being conducted in a holiday mood—"the kind of holiday Morgan County likes"—somehow became widely circulated.[28]

---

[26] "Alabama vs. Patterson, April 3-9, 1933, Transcript of Testimony," 3–5; New York *Times,* April 1, 1933, p. 34; Birmingham *Age-Herald,* April 1, 1933.

[27] New York *Times,* April 2, 1933, p. 5.

[28] *Ibid.,* April 3, 1933, p. 34; New York *Daily Worker,* April 4, 1933. Community tensions were further exacerbated over the tense weekend when Decatur police arrested three young New Yorkers who were attending the trials as representatives of

When the trial resumed on Monday morning, the seats were jammed for the first time since the opening day of the preliminary hearings. It was cool in the building when the courtroom doors opened at 8:30 A.M., but within an hour the spectators had begun to shed their coats. Before noon, courthouse officials turned on the overhead fans in an effort to dispel the gray haziness and stifling stuffiness caused by the constant smoking and closed space. Just after 9 A.M.., Victoria Price took the stand and for the fifth time told her story. Wearing a blue straw hat and a black dress with a fichu of white lace at the throat, she was in stylish contrast to her first appearances at Scottsboro. She seemed somewhat nervous in the witness chair, crossing and uncrossing her legs and fingering the string of glass beads around her neck. When Attorney General Knight began questioning her, however, she spoke in a clear, firm voice which carried to the back of the courtroom.[29]

The direct examination by Knight went smoothly. She began her story from the time she and Ruby boarded the train at Chattanooga to return to Huntsville. She told of seeing the Negro youths coming across the top of a box car and leaping from the top of it into the gondola where she and her friend sat. Thrusting her finger toward Patterson she identified him as one of the attackers. Knight asked her if Patterson's "private parts penetrated your private parts," and she agreed they had. Suddenly Knight pulled a torn cotton undergarment from a briefcase on the prosecution table and showed it to the witness. "I will ask you Miss Price to examine this garment please, are these the step-ins you had on that occasion?" Leibowitz leaped to his feet. "We object to them, this is the first time in two years any such step-ins have ever been shown in any court of justice." "Well," grinned Knight, "they are here now," and he whirled them through the air and into the lap

the National Students' League, a militantly left-wing student organization. The three, Muriel Rukeyser, Edward Sagarin, and Hank Fuller, were eventually released on condition that they leave town. Local officials implied there was some sinister motive behind their appearance in Decatur. New York *Times*, April 2, 1933, p. 5; Norfolk *Journal and Guide*, April 8, 1933; Interview with Muriel Rukeyser, June 5, 1966, New York City.

[29] New York *Times*, April 4, 1933, p. 10; Birmingham *Age-Herald*, April 4, 1933; New York *Daily Worker*, April 4, 1933.

of one of the bewildered jurors. The courtroom exploded into laughter and futilely Horton gaveled for quiet. The court would not permit any disorder, he sternly warned. "I will say this much now, the Court has the right to clear the courtroom, and if it is necessary to keep order, the Court will not hesitate to do it." For anyone who could not restrain his feelings, the proper place was on the outside, he concluded.[30] Over the objections of the defense, Mrs. Price's panties were placed on the table and marked "State Exhibit A." After another dozen brief questions, Knight abandoned his star witness to Samuel S. Leibowitz.

The slightly balding lawyer, much younger than most had expected, exuded confidence. He was convinced that Victoria Price was lying, and he had often reduced even honest witnesses to incoherent confusion during his long career. Leibowitz had all the attributes of a good trial lawyer: an actor's sense of timing, a flair for the dramatic, and a clear, forceful voice. But his main strength was his almost infallible memory for detail, and above all, for contradictions. "I am not a great lawyer," he said in response to a compliment. "I'm only thorough." He began his cross-examination gently, almost kindly: "Miss Price, shall I call you Miss Price or Mrs. Price?" "Mrs. Price," answered the witness sullenly. She looked at her interrogator as though he were a poisonous snake circling her chair.[31]

Leibowitz had planned to open with a discussion of the events on the freight, and for that purpose the Lionel Corporation had constructed an exact replica of the original train. He had a foretaste of his problems when Mrs. Price refused to agree that the model looked like the train she rode. What were the differences? he asked. "That is not the train I was on," she snapped. "It was bigger, lots bigger, that is a toy." No amount of cajoling from Leibowitz could force from her an admission that it was a suitable replica. To each question about how the train on which she rode differed from the model she sullenly replied: "I won't say," "I

[30] "Alabama vs. Patterson, April 3-9, 1933, Transcript of Testimony," 13–14; Patterson and Conrad, *Scottsboro Boy*, 39–40.

[31] Mary Heaton Vorse, "The Scottsboro Trial," *New Republic*, LXXIV (1933), 276-77; "Alabama vs. Patterson, April 3–9, 1933, Transcript of Testimony," 17.

can't say," and "I can't tell you that." [32] For more than three hours Leibowitz put her through a grueling cross-examination. He had three goals. First, he sought to discredit her testimony by introducing evidence to show that she was a common prostitute and thus unworthy of belief. Secondly, he hoped to confuse her in the cross-examination to such an extent that it would be apparent to the jury that her testimony, on its face, was so contradictory as to be unreliable. Most importantly, he planned to show what really happened during the day of the alleged attack and the preceding twenty-four hours. As Leibowitz later admitted, however, she was one of the toughest witnesses he had ever cross-examined. At times he was shouting at her, but whenever he managed to push her into contradictions, she would regain her poise with a terse "I can't remember."

As the first attack on her character and credibility, Leibowitz offered in evidence records from the Huntsville, Alabama, city court showing that Victoria Price had been found guilty of adultery and fornication on January 26, 1931. Along with her boyfriend, L. J. (Jack) Tiller, who was married, she had been fined and sentenced to a short term in the city jail. Knight interjected that the state did not care if she had been convicted of "forty offenses, the charge is rape." Besides, he noted, the Alabama Supreme Court had earlier ruled that conviction by a municipal court did not affect the credibility of the witness. Horton sustained Knight's objection and instructed the jury to disregard the conviction, but Leibowitz had managed to present all the information he wanted. The jurors could not ignore it if they tried.[33]

At the Scottsboro trials Mrs. Price had been colorful and inventive in her account of the attack, describing in vivid detail even the most insignificant events. At Decatur she stuck to a plain, unembroidered story, as lacking in details as possible. In an effort to draw her out, Leibowitz noted solicitously that it must have been gruesome with the heavy Negroes lying "like brutes" on her

[32] "Alabama vs. Patterson, April 3–9, 1933, Transcript of Testimony," 21–22.

[33] *Ibid.*, 74–78; New York *Times*, April 4, 1933, p. 10; Decatur *Daily*, April 3, 1933.

as she lay, semi-nude, on the jagged chert. "Was your back bleeding when you got to the doctor?" "I couldn't say," replied Victoria. "When you got to the jail did you find any blood on your back?" A little, she recalled, but she quickly added: "I ain't sure, that has been two years ago." Well, went on Leibowitz, "when you got to the doctor's office, were you not crying in any way?" "I had just hushed crying, the best I remember I was crying—I won't say, I ain't positive." The defense attorney finally managed to extract from her a statement that she was bleeding from her vagina, a statement which Leibowitz knew the doctor who examined her would contradict.[34]

Leibowitz noted that she had told of staying with Mrs. Callie Brochie at a Seventh Street boardinghouse the night before the incident on the train. And he pointed out that she had said the house was three or four blocks from the train yards. "Wouldn't you say it was two miles?" asked Leibowitz. "No sir, I wouldn't say two miles," she replied. "I won't say how far it is." Hadn't the earlier story been that it was a short distance from the railroad yards? "Well, yes, it must have been that far," she agreed. "Suppose I told you that Seventh Street in Chattanooga, the nearest point . . . to the railroad yards of the Southern Railroad is two miles and show you the map, would that refresh your recollection?" he asked sarcastically. "I don't know," retorted an equally sarcastic Victoria, "I haven't got a good enough education." At another point when he showed that her testimony was inaccurate, she broke into Leibowitz, shouting, "That's some of Ruby Bates' dope." She added, "I do know one thing, those negroes and this Haywood Patterson raped me." Leibowitz stood and stared at her for a minute. You are a "little bit of an actress," he said slowly. "You're a pretty good actor yourself," she quickly replied.[35]

Leibowitz quickly established Mrs. Price's unreliability as a witness, but he knew that a sympathetic jury might overlook this and ascribe her errors to forgetfulness or confusion. He had to give

[34] "Alabama vs. Patterson, April 3–9, 1933, Transcript of Testimony," 64–65.
[35] *Ibid.*, 102–104, 132–34; Decatur *Daily*, April 3, 1933.

an explanation for the spermatozoa which the Scottsboro doctors had discovered when they examined her. Leibowitz began casually asking her about her movement on the day before the incident. Suddenly the tone of his voice distinctly changed. Gravely, he asked her: "Do you know a man by the name of Lester Carter?" He was thrown off the train, she replied, but she had never known him before that in her entire life. He paused for a moment and then continued. "Mrs. Price, I . . . want to ask you that question again and give you an opportunity to change your answer if you want to. Did you know Lester Carter before that day, yes or no?" By his tone, both spectators and jurors knew the question was crucial, and they leaned forward to hear her answer. Mrs. Price, losing her composure for the first time, mumbled: "Before in Scottsboro—he—was on the train." "I didn't ask you that," said Leibowitz, "before this day on the train did you know Lester Carter?" "I never did know him," she said firmly. "I never did know him." He continued in the same low tone. "Did you ask a companion of yours to pose as your brother, since you didn't want the authorities to know you were traveling across the state line from Chattanooga . . . [with] somebody with you?" Mrs. Price looked to the table where Knight sat and then back at Leibowitz. "If I said that I must have been out of my mind." "Did you say it?" he repeated firmly. Shouting, she replied: "If I said it I must have been out of my mind." [36]

Knight interrupted with an objection. "What relevancy can that have?" he asked. "I want to show this," said Leibowitz, "I want to account for her condition, for her vaginal condition which Dr. Bridges is going to testify to. . . ." The courtroom waited. Horton wrinkled his brow for a moment and then said quietly, "Overrule the objection. I would permit you to show any intercourse approximately within twenty-four hours of this time." [37]

[36] "Alabama vs. Patterson, April 3–9, 1933, Transcript of Testimony," 67–69; Birmingham Post, April 3, 1933; Vorse, "Scottsboro Trial," 277; New York World Telegram, April 6, 1933.

[37] "Alabama vs. Patterson, April 3–9, 1933, Transcript of Testimony," 70–72; New York Daily News, April 4, 1933.

Inwardly, Leibowitz experienced a rush of relief, and he moved rapidly into the heart of his cross-examination. He questioned Mrs. Price concerning Jack Tiller, the man with whom she had been convicted of adultery. "Did you have intercourse with Tiller a short time before you left Huntsville [for Chattanooga]?" She shook her head emphatically. "In the railroad yards?" he asked, still in the same quiet voice. "I have told you three times, and I am not telling you any more—no sir I didn't." Leibowitz returned to Carter. He asked her once more if she had arranged with Carter or "whatever man that was with you, he wasn't supposed to know you on the train because you were afraid to cross the state line and [afraid of] being locked up for the Mann Act?" She turned angrily to Judge Horton: "I haven't heard no such stuff," she shouted, "that is some of Ruby's dope he has got." [38]

The jury and the audience were not able to understand the complete details from Leibowitz's questions, but it was clear he was implying some connection among Tiller, Carter, Ruby, and Victoria. He asked Mrs. Price once again about where she had spent the night before the alleged attack—perhaps a hobo jungle? Victoria stared at him, her eyes filled with hatred. Mary Heaton Vorse, one of the two women in the courtroom, found it impossible to describe her "appalling hardness." She was more than "tough," said Miss Vorse. She was "terrifying in her depravity." [39] Through clenched teeth Victoria repeated again the account of how she had stayed at the home of Mrs. Brochie. Leibowitz questioned her about the boardinghouse. What size was it? Four rooms? Five rooms? One story? Two stories? "I never did pay any attention to that," replied Victoria grimly. Leibowitz continued asking her about her activities during the evening. What did she have to eat with Mrs. Brochie, what sort of bed or room did she and Ruby sleep in? Victoria answered each question tersely or with an "I don't remember," or "I won't be positive." He asked her if she didn't want to change her story. She shook her head.

[38] "Alabama vs. Patterson, April 3–9, 1933, Transcript of Testimony," 83, 85–86.
[39] Vorse, "Scottsboro Trial," 276.

Timing his opening carefully, the attorney said with open disgust: "By the way, Mrs. Price, as a matter of fact the name of Mrs. Callie you apply to this boarding house lady is the name of a boarding house lady used by Octavus Roy Cohen in the *Saturday Evening Post* stories—Sis Callie, isn't that where you got the name?" Knight leaped to his feet in protest and Judge Horton sustained his objection. Leibowitz, however, had dramatically made his point and he was pleased with the results of his cross-examination.[40]

Other knowledgeable observers correctly surmised that his attacks on Mrs. Price had been costly.[41] "One possessed of that old Southern chivalry cannot read the trial now in progress in Decatur . . . and publish an opinion and keep within the law," fumed the Sylacauga *News*. The "brutal manner" in which Leibowitz cross-examined Mrs. Price "makes one feel like reaching for his gun while his blood boils to the nth degree." Leibowitz made the fatal mistake of regarding Victoria Price as a cut-rate prostitute. He was "not accustomed to addressing Southern juries," said Robert Eleazer. Too late the chief defense attorney realized that Mrs. Price had become a symbol of white Southern womanhood.[42]

Dr. Bridges was the next scheduled witness for the state, but Leibowitz requested permission to examine R. S. Turner, conductor of the train on which the alleged rape took place. He explained that Turner had to be back at work the following day. Knight readily agreed to hearing the testimony out of order and the Southern Railroad man took the stand. After describing the make-up of the train, he told the jury he had seen the two girls standing beside the fourth gondola from the engine. In the same car he found a half-empty snuff box, apparently Mrs. Price's, since she had testified she lost hers during the rape. Turner's testimony flatly contradicted the state's star witness, who had testified firmly

[40] "Alabama vs. Patterson, April 3–9, 1933, Transcript of Textimony," 97, 99–100; Birmingham *Post*, April 3, 1933; Birmingham *Age-Herald*, April 4, 1933.

[41] Robert Burns Eleazer to George Haynes, April 11, 1933, in Interracial Commission Papers.

[42] Sylacauga, Alabama *News*, April 7, 1933; Robert Burns Eleazer to Will W. Alexander, April 17, 1933, in Interracial Commission Papers.

DIAGRAM I
THE CHATTANOOGA TO MEMPHIS FREIGHT TRAIN
OF THE SOUTHERN RAILROAD
MARCH 26, 1931*

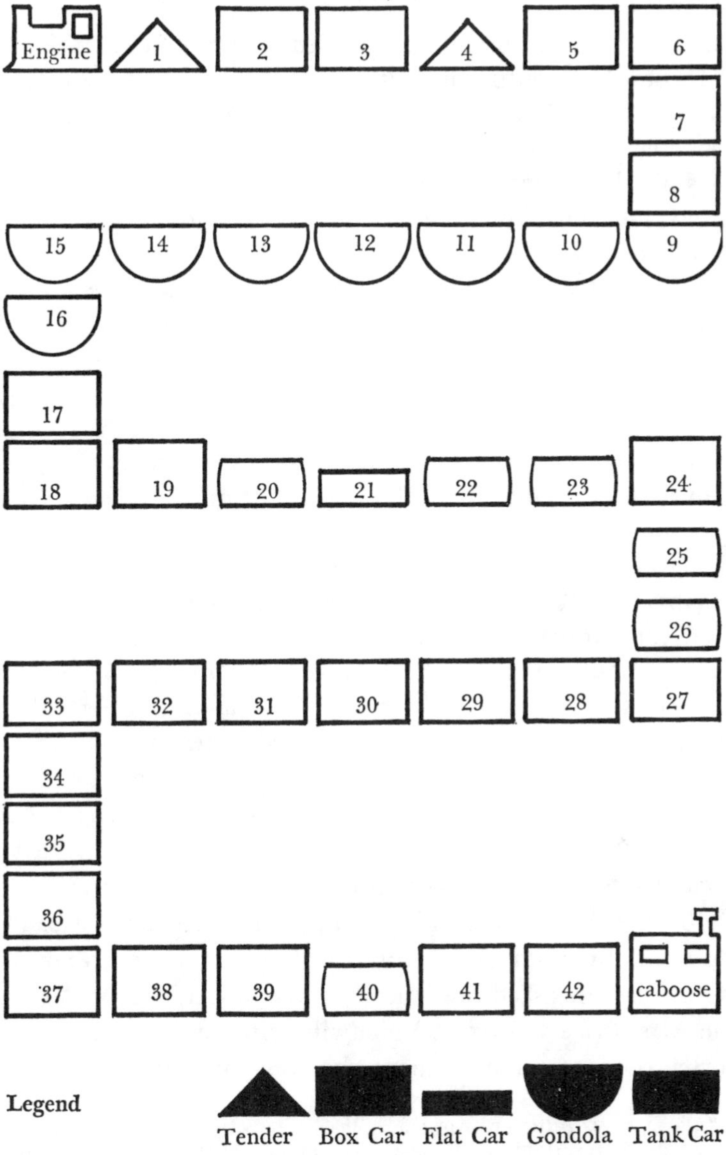

Engine 1 2 3 4 5 6

7

8

15 14 13 12 11 10 9

16

17

18 19 20 21 22 23 24

25

26

33 32 31 30 29 28 27

34

35

36

37 38 39 40 41 42 caboose

Legend   Tender   Box Car   Flat Car   Gondola   Tank Car

*Patterson v. Alabama, 294 U.S. 599, Transcript of Record, pp. 613–14.

that she and Ruby were in the gondola immediately adjacent to a box car.[43]

Inexplicably, the prosecution called Victoria Price back to the stand instead of continuing with its next witness. Jackson County Solicitor H. G. Bailey asked Mrs. Price what the Negroes said when they jumped into the gondola where she and the boys sat. "All you white Sons of Bitches unload," replied Victoria. In answer to questions from Bailey, Mrs. Price told the jury that the men had demanded to know if she was going to "put out." When she declined they threatened to throw her in the river. She also reported that "one of them pulled out his private parts and says, 'when I put this in you and pull it out you will have a negro baby.' " Leibowitz objected vehemently. The entire testimony, he said, was designed only to inflame the jury and push from their minds the damaging testimony of conductor Turner. Judge Horton over-ruled Leibowitz and Bailey continued: "I will ask you to refresh your recollection if anything was said about you hollering?" Mrs. Price recalled that they had "made fun of me for hollering. . . ." Bailey asked, "Do you recall anything else they said at that time and place when this defendant was present?" When she sat without answering, he went on: "I will ask you to refresh your recollection if one of them said, 'you haven't holler[ed] at all yet?' " Mrs. Price suddenly remembered. "Yes sir, one of them said, 'you haven't hollered none yet until I put this black thing in you and pull it out.' " She gave this testimony, reported Raymond Daniell, "without the flutter of an eyelash and in a voice that carried to the furthest corner of the court room." [44]

Leibowitz, his voice shaking with anger, stared at Mrs. Price. "You are not embarrassed before this huge crowd when you utter these words?" he asked sarcastically. "We object," shouted Knight, while Mrs. Price looked at Leibowitz with such venom that one reporter thought for a moment she was going to strike her tor-

[43] "Alabama vs. Patterson, April 3–9, 1933, Transcript of Testimony," 139. In other words, Turner testified the girls were in Car 12, while Mrs. Price insisted they were in Car 16. See Diagram I, p. 211.

[44] *Ibid.*, 157–58; New York *Times,* April 4, 1933, p. 10.

mentor. "You testified in four different trials at Scottsboro right after this alleged rape is supposed to have happened," continued Leibowitz. "Did you ever say anything like that?" She insisted she had. He turned to Horton and, offering the transcripts of the four Scottsboro trials in evidence, said: "I will ask your honor to take judicial notice of the fact that no such statement was made. . . ." He looked back at Victoria Price. He had one more question, he said. "I want to ask you if you have ever heard of any single white woman ever being locked up in jail when she is the complaining witness against negroes in the history of the State of Alabama?" Without even waiting for her answer or Knight's objection, Leibowitz angrily took his seat at the defense table.[45]

The last witness for the state on the first day of the trial was Dr. R. R. Bridges. Bridges' testimony, along with that of his colleague, Dr. Lynch, had been crucial for the state's case at Scottsboro. Under direct examination, he repeated almost word for word the same account he had given at Scottsboro two years before. Under cross-examination, however, Samuel Leibowitz made the doctor as much a witness for the defense as for the state. Less than one hour and thirty minutes after the alleged rape, the girls, acknowledged Dr. Bridges, were completely composed and calm. Their pupils were not dilated and their pulse and respiration were normal. In response to the defense lawyer's questions, Bridges noted that the semen was completely non-motile, and he readily acknowledged that this was unusual since the spermatozoa normally lived from twelve hours to two days in the vagina. "In other words," asked Leibowitz for emphasis, "you were not able to discover any single [living] spermatozoa [sic] from this woman who claimed she had been raped by six men. . . ." "Yes sir, that is right," replied Bridges. He acknowledged that although she had supposedly been raped six times, only with great difficulty did he and Dr. Lynch find enough semen to make a smear slide. Despite Mrs. Price's statement that she was bleeding from her vagina and had been cut "a little bit" on her forehead, the Scottsboro physician also testified he had seen no blood. And he volunteered the information that, even though Mrs. Price went through the examination calmly, she "seemed to be a bit cross with us and didn't want to co-operate. . . ." [46]

At the end of the first day of the trial, Robert Burns Eleazer of the Interracial Commission reported to Will Alexander that the day had been generally successful for the defense. In particular, he noted, the testimony of the doctor seemed to support the defendants about as much as it did Mrs. Price. Moreover, there had been "no injection of the Communist issue yet. . . ." Brodsky had been at the defense table, "but [he] hasn't said a word." [47] In the Southern press, however, the edge went to Attorney General Knight. The Birmingham *Age-Herald* reported that Mrs. Price was "unshaken," and neither it nor the Chattanooga *Daily Times* gave more than a hint of Dr. Bridges' testimony on the grounds that it was unprintable.[48]

Dr. Bridges returned to the witness chair on Tuesday morning and after a brief cross-examination, Leibowitz told the court he had no further questions. Dr. Marvin Lynch, the second Scottsboro physician who had examined the girls, was the next scheduled witness, but before he could take the stand, Attorney General Knight asked to confer privately with Judge Horton. During the brief recess, the Judge, Dr. Lynch, and the state's attorneys met in a smaller courthouse room. Knight explained that Lynch's statement would only be a repetition of Dr. Bridges' testimony and the state wished him excused. Judge Horton readily consented. When Knight and the other lawyers for the state returned to the courtroom, however, the doctor asked Horton if they could meet privately. The only room they could find was one of the courthouse

[46] "Alabama vs. Patterson, April 3–9, 1933, Transcript of Testimony," 161–67, 173–74, 176–77, 179, 188.

[47] Robert Burns Eleazer to Will Alexander, April 3, 1933, in Interracial Commission Papers.

[48] Birmingham *Age-Herald*, April 4, 1933; Chattanooga *Daily Times*, April 4, 1933. The Associated Press accounts also failed to give any of the doctor's testimony. Decatur *Daily*, April 4, 1933. Charles Edmundson of the Birmingham *Post* alluded briefly to the drift of Bridges' testimony. Birmingham *Post*, April 3, April 4, 1933.

restrooms and, with the bailiff standing outside the door, the two men talked. The young doctor, who appeared unnerved and agitated, went straight to the point. Contrary to Knight's statement, said Lynch, his testimony would not be a repetition of Dr. Bridge's, because he did not believe the girls had been raped. From the very beginning, said Lynch, he was convinced the girls were lying. Even Dr. Bridges had noted at the examination that the two women were "not even red." [49]

"My God, Doctor, is this whole thing a horrible mistake[?]" asked the stunned Horton. "Judge, I looked at both the women and told them they were lying, that they knew they had not been raped," replied the doctor, "and they just laughed at me." [50] Shaken by the news, Horton urged the doctor to testify for the state, but Lynch—with a look of anguish on his face—replied, "Judge, God knows I want to, but I can't." Emotions were running high in Scottsboro, he said. "If I testified for those boys I'd never be able to go back into Jackson County." He had graduated from medical school less than four years before and he did not want to start over again, he said.[51]

When Horton returned to the bench, he maintained his usual calm demeanor, but inwardly his thoughts were in turmoil. Before the trial opened Horton had believed that the Scottsboro boys were probably guilty. He had even instructed his court reporter to be exceptionally careful because he did not wish any technical errors to appear in the record.[52] The evasive and contradictory testimony of Mrs. Price and the statements of Dr. Bridges had caused him to reconsider his earlier opinion. Now came further evidence

[49] James Edwin Horton to Author, September 28, 1967.
[50] Ibid.
[51] Interview with former Judge James Edwin Horton, Jr., April 9, 1966, at Macedon Plantation, Greenbriar, Alabama. In late 1967, Dr. Lynch emphatically denied that he had made "such statements . . . to Judge James E. Horton or anyone else regarding the trial of Haywood Patterson versus Alabama." He added: "Of course it has been 35 years and better since this incident happened; and as far as I can recall, I was never put on the stand as a witness in this case." Dr. Marvin Lynch to author, October 16, 1967.
[52] John Temple Graves, II, "Fiat Justica, Ruat Coelum," New Republic, XCIV (1938), 218.

to refute the state's case. None of the alternative courses of action that Horton faced was appealing. He could force Dr. Lynch to take the stand or he could himself end the trial. In either case it would mean exposing and ruining an honest man who had taken a courageous step in even coming to see him. And it was only one man's opinion. In his mind, Horton went over the twelve jurors who sat on his left. However Leibowitz felt about them, Horton was convinced they were a good jury. He knew more than half of them personally and, although they were Southerners, he believed the evidence presented by the defense would convince them that Patterson was innocent. With many misgivings, he decided to allow the trial to continue.[53]

During the remainder of the day, the state called to the stand five additional witnesses: W. W. Hill, the Paint Rock railroad depot agent; Tom Rousseau, a mercantile clerk in the little town; Arthur H. Woodall, a deputy sheriff and Stevenson storekeeper; and two farmers who had observed the train as it traveled between Stevenson and Scottsboro. Hill told the court he had seen all of the defendants in the same gondola where the girls were. After the train stopped, the boys began "scrambling" trying to crawl out the side away from the station. On cross-examination, however, he acknowledged that he was not really sure which of the cars held the girls since he did not see the girls until they were on the ground. And Leibowitz threw doubt on Hill's description of the boys' scrambling across the top of the gondola when he pointed out that any of the defendants could have seen the posse of over seventy-five men from a quarter of a mile away. Why, asked Leibowitz, would they have waited until the train had stopped before trying to run? [54]

The next witness, Tom Rousseau, cast even more doubt on Hill's testimony when he told the court that the defendants, far from being in one gondola, were scattered across the entire front part of the train. And Lee Adams, a Jackson County farmer, was equally unhelpful to the state. He testified that he was hauling

[53] Interview with former Judge James Edwin Horton, Jr., April 9, 1966.
[54] "Alabama vs. Patterson, April 3–9, 1933, Transcript of Testimony," 197–99, 206.

wood one and one-half miles south of Stevenson when he saw what he thought was a fight in one gondola, but he was at least a quarter of a mile away. The defense, of course, had never denied there was a fight on the train.[55]

Adams' testimony failed to strengthen substantially the prosecution's case against the defendants, but Ora Dobbins could not have been more disastrous if he had been called by the defense. He told the packed courtroom how he had been on his way to catch a mule on his farm south of Stevenson when he saw the train passing by. He stopped and from the yard of his home saw several Negroes and one white girl in a gondola. The girl, he said, was "setting up on the end of the gon[dola] fixing to jump off—" but just as she started to leap, a Negro "grabbed her and threw her down in the car." He explained that he knew exactly where he was standing because he had taken a tape and measured the location when he learned he would be a witness.[56]

The chief attorney for the defense began his cross-examination by submitting a series of pictures taken in the Dobbins farmyard. Dobbins again carefully noted where he was standing, "next to the wood pile." With a second set of pictures, Leibowitz demonstrated to the jury and the attentive courtroom that the barn blocked the view to the railroad tracks on one side and the house on the other. At most Ora Dobbins had a field of vision of only fifty or sixty feet and the train was running at least twenty-five miles per hour. He could not have seen the car for more than one and one-half seconds. Secondly, Leibowitz introduced from the first Scottsboro trials testimony by Dobbins that he had seen two girls rather than one. With sarcastic rhetoric, Leibowitz asked him if he were even sure she was a girl. "I reckon so," replied Dobbins; "she had on woman's clothes." There was a shocked pause; Horton leaned forward over the bench and asked, "She had on woman's clothes?" Dobbins repeated his statement. "Are you sure it wasn't overalls, or perhaps a woman's coat?" asked Leibowitz. "No sir, dress," replied Dobbins emphatically. The jury knew that the girls were

[55] *Ibid.*, 241–42, 244–48; Decatur *Daily*, April 4, 1933.
[56] "Alabama vs. Patterson, April 3–9, 1933, Transcript of Testimony," 256–57.

wearing overalls with women's coats over them. And finally, Leibowitz drew from the witness an admission that he had an automobile in good operating condition, but he had done nothing. "That had no effect on you in any way," said Leibowitz with feigned incredulity, "seeing a white woman . . . being attacked by a negro and you didn't jump in your car and go over and inform the law about it, or make a complaint to somebody, you didn't do that at all?" "No sir," replied Dobbins.[57]

Of the witnesses called to support Mrs. Price, the most damaging to the defense was a middle-aged storekeeper from Stevenson. Arthur H. Woodall testified that the white youths thrown from the train came into his mercantile establishment shortly before noon on March 26, 1931. Since he was a part-time Jackson County deputy sheriff, he hurried down to Scottsboro, where he helped search the defendants when they were brought to the county jail. On one of them—he could not recall which—he found a small pen knife with a brad missing from one end. The knife had earlier been identified by Victoria Price as belonging to her. In response to Leibowitz's questions, Woodall could not recall which of the defendants had it, but he suddenly volunteered: "He said he took it off the white girl Victoria Price." Woodall's unexpected remark stunned the entire courtroom with the exception of the attorney general. The shocked look on Leibowitz's face so delighted Knight that he involuntarily laughed, slapped his hands on the table top, then ran outside the courtroom in order to contain himself. Furiously Leibowitz turned to Judge Horton. "I want that on the record and move for a mistrial," he shouted. "That is something I haven't seen in fifteen years' experience at the bar." Alabama officials had promised they would give the defendants a fair trial, declared Leibowitz, and yet everyone had seen the attorney general "jump up and clap his hands and dash out with a smile and a laugh." A nervous and chastened Knight returned and apologized profusely to the court and the jury. Horton

[57] *Ibid.*, 262–71, 277–78, 279–80; Birmingham *Post,* April 4, 1933; Decatur *Daily,* April 4, 1933.

refused to declare a mistrial, but he instructed the jury to disregard Knight's actions. Although the state had several other witnesses in the anteroom, Knight and his staff concluded that they had made their case. When Leibowitz completed his cross-examination, the state rested. It was shortly after 2:30 in the afternoon.[58]

After a brief recess the trial resumed. Much of the testimony for the defense would be aimed not only at disproving the state's contentions, but also at telling what had actually happened. During his legal career, Leibowitz had only been required to prove a reasonable doubt as to guilt; in Decatur he knew that he had to prove his clients' innocence beyond a reasonable doubt.

Dallas Ramsey, a middle-aged Chattanooga Negro, was the first witness for the defense. Ramsey lived in a small four-room shack near the Chattanooga railroad yards and immediately adjacent to a hobo jungle. Here, in a heavily wooded area, the men—and women—who rode the rails cooked their meals and made their temporary home. Just before 6 o'clock on the morning of the alleged attack, Ramsey said he had been walking with a friend through the edge of the jungle when he saw one woman sitting on a log and another squatting beside a tree. The older one stopped him and asked the departure time of the Huntsville train; Ramsey replied that it was sometime shortly after 9 A.M. The girl, who seemed in a talkative mood, said that she and her husband were in town looking for work. She added, "My old man has gone uptown to look for some food." Later in the morning, Ramsey said he had seen the woman and her quiet companion meet a "white gentleman" at the edge of the train yards and board the Huntsville freight. Over the violent objections of Knight, the bailiff brought Victoria Price into the courtroom. "Is this the girl you saw?" asked Leibowitz. "She seems like the same girl—it seems like she is a little heavier now than what she was then," he said; but he quickly added: "Yes sir, I recognize her." From an enlarged photograph,

---

[58] "Alabama vs. Patterson, April 3–9, 1933, Transcript of Testimony," 289–90, 292; New York *Times*, April 5, 1933, p. 10; Decatur *Daily*, April 4, 1933; Birmingham *Age-Herald*, April 5, 1933.

Ramsey also identified Ruby Bates as the quiet companion.[59]

When Leibowitz had completed his questioning, the court waited expectantly for the attorney general to begin his cross-examination. Thomas J. Knight, Jr., at thirty-four, was one of the youngest elected attorney generals in the history of Alabama. Short and slight, his behavior was that of a "small and enthusiastic child," observed one reporter. Although he lacked Leibowitz's skill and finesse in cross-examination, he often achieved the same results by simply overpowering witnesses with continuous, rapid questioning.[60] A fierce antagonist in the courtroom, Knight was affable and charming outside. Reporters always found him accessible and ready to discuss the case over a few drinks in his Decatur apartment. Even the correspondent for the *Daily Worker*—though repelled by Knight's social and political attitudes—described the Attorney General as appealing and likeable in a boyish way. Knight tried desperately to unsettle Ramsey, who was hesitant and ill at ease on the witness stand, but the Chattanooga Negro steadfastly affirmed his identification.[61]

General Chamlee took the stand to testify concerning the Brochie boarding house Mrs. Price had described. On direct examination by Leibowitz he told the court that since 1908 he had either lived or had his office on Seventh Street in Chattanooga, the alleged location of the rooming house. Only eight blocks long, Seventh was "perhaps the richest street for its length in Chatnooga . . ." said Chamlee. He described in detail every block from City Hall on one end to the residential district on the other. It was his opinion, based on a personal inspection of the street, the city's directories, and dozens of inquiries, that there never was a boarding house in Chattanooga owned by a woman named Callie Brochie. Nor, he added, did he believe any such woman had lived anywhere in the city from 1930 to 1933.[62]

[59] "Alabama vs. Patterson, April 3–9, 1933, Transcript of Testimony," 304–305, 310–14; Birmingham *Post*, April 5, 1933.

[60] John Henry Hammond, Jr., "The South Speaks," *The Nation*, CXXXVI (1933), 465–66.

[61] "Alabama vs. Patterson, April 3–9, 1933, Transcript of Testimony," 320–22; Birmingham *Post*, April 5, 1933; Decatur *Daily*, April 5, 1933.

[62] "Alabama vs. Patterson, April 3–9, 1933, Transcript of Testimony," 337–40.

When court reconvened on the third day of the trial Leibowitz announced his next witness: Willie Roberson. He had decided to put five of the Scottsboro boys on the stand. Leibowitz knew that it was a calculated risk, but it was one he felt he had to take for a number of reasons. He wanted to show that the fight had taken place in a different car from the one described by Victoria Price. He further wished to impeach her testimony by refuting her statement that she had seen all nine boys in the gondola where she and Ruby sat. And he hoped to dispel Knight's implication that the entire rape was a conspiracy among the nine Negro youths by showing that only four from Chattanooga even knew each other.

Roberson was the most pathetic of the nine boys. Short and stocky, with a shock of hair flying in all directions, he spent most of his time staring vacantly off into space. Four years later a psychiatric examination disclosed a mental age of nine and an intelligence quotient of sixty-four. He had been syphilitic since 1930.[63] Leibowitz gently asked Roberson about his physical condition at the time of the alleged rape. Roberson, who spoke with some difficulty, replied that he had open sores covering all of his "privates." The swelling and "chancres" had been so painful that he walked with a stick, he said. Victoria Price had testified that he was one of the defendants who had jumped off a box car into a gondola, fought and scuffled with several white boys, and then raped her, noted Leibowitz. "Were you capable of doing this?" he asked. "No sir," replied Roberson, who also told the court he was riding back towards the caboose. At Chattanooga he had crawled on the last tank car and rode outside until the train reached Stevenson.[64] He was in such pain, he said, he climbed into the nearest open box car toward the rear of the train and lay down.[65] When the train stopped at Paint Rock, a "white man came up and had a pistol and shotgun and told me to get out and

---

[63] Psychiatric Examination of Willie Roberson by Dr. G. C. Branche, January 10, 1937, in Chalmers Collection.

[64] This would be car number 40. See Diagram I, page 211.

[65] This was apparently somewhere between cars 27 and 39. See Diagram I, page 211.

I crawled out; I had my stick and he told me to throw my stick away, and we marched up to the store." [66]

Olen Montgomery, the next witness for the defense, was completely blind in his left eye; with his right he could "see good enough not to get hurt, that is all. . . ." The second of the Scottsboro boys to testify, he told the court he was traveling alone and had boarded the train on an oil tanker in front of a long line of box cars. [67] He had "stayed right there" for the entire ride. When the train stopped at Paint Rock a member of the posse "jerked me off" and carried him over to the little store. He denied he had participated in the fight or had even known a fight was taking place. [68] Knight failed to cross-examine either Montgomery or Roberson, perhaps because the stories they told were the same ones they had given at Scottsboro.

Ozie Powell told the court he had seen a fight on the train. He was crouching between a box car and an adjacent gondola, when several Negroes crossed over his head. [69] They had gone further up the train and in a few minutes, he saw several white boys jumping off onto the siding. Like Montgomery, he denied he had taken part in the fight. Powell, however, was not a good witness for the defense. Within minutes, Knight had him so confused he was first affirming and then denying the same statements. [70] Horton interceded and tried unsuccessfully to make Ozie understand what he was being asked. Pressing hard, Knight pushed excitedly closer to Powell, quoting question after question in rapid fire succession from the original Scottsboro transcripts to the hopelessly bewildered Powell. At the end of the half-hour cross-examination, Leibowitz tried to repair the damage inflicted on the defense's case. He stepped before the witness: "Ozie, tell us about how much schooling you have had in your life?" About three months, he mumbled. "Had three months schooling in your whole life?" Leibowitz gen-

---

[66] "Alabama vs. Patterson, April 3–9, 1933, Transcript of Testimony," 347–48, 352.

[67] This was either car 25 or 26. See Diagram I, page 211.

[68] "Alabama vs. Patterson, April 3–9, 1933, Transcript of Testimony," 361–64.

[69] According to Powell, he was between cars 16 and 17. See Diagram I, page 211.

[70] "Alabama vs. Patterson, April 3–9, 1933, Transcript of Testimony," 361–64, 368.

tly asked again. "Yes sir," replied Powell. Leibowitz stepped back to his chair.[71]

Observers in the courtroom during the second day of the trial had noticed an appreciable growth in hostility toward the defense counsel, most of it apparently triggered by Leibowitz's unrelenting cross-examination of Mrs. Price. The chief lawyer for the defense admitted that he had received a number of threatening letters, but he dismissed the writers as "cranks." [72] He had significantly underestimated the anger of the local citizens, however. During the second day of the trial, Mary Heaton Vorse overheard one spectator whisper to another, "It'll be a wonder if ever he leaves town alive." And a handsomely dressed and obviously well-educated young man told her frankly during a recess that he would be surprised if "they" let him finish the trial. "Do you mean there's a movement on foot to railroad him out of town?" she asked. They were not advertising or making speeches, he replied, "but they'll know what to do when the time comes." [73]

As the Wednesday afternoon session prepared to resume, a grim-faced Judge Horton ordered the jury taken from the courtroom. His voice quivering with emotion, he said, "The Court wishes to make an announcement." Word had reached him that some undescribed action was to be taken against the defendants or their counsel. The guilt or innocence of Haywood Patterson and his fellows was for the jury alone to decide, the judge said. "Any man on the outside who has not heard the testimony, and would try the case from rumor . . . has no right to say whether or not they are guilty or innocent." He wanted it known throughout the area, he declared, that the court intended to protect the prisoners and any other persons connected with the trial. "I say this much, that the man who would engage in anything that would cause the death of any of these prisoners is a murderer; he is not only a murderer, but a cowardly murderer. . . ." And anyone who attempted to take the lives of the prisoners "may expect that his own life be forfeited, or

[71] *Ibid.,* 397; Birmingham *Post,* April 5, 1933; Decatur *Daily,* April 5, 1933.
[72] Birmingham *Post,* April 5, 1933.
[73] New York *World Telegram,* April 6, 1933.

the guards that guard them must forfeit their lives." "I am speaking with feeling, and I know it, because I am feeling it," Judge Horton told the silent courtroom. For the first time in the trials he raised his voice almost to a shout. "I absolutely have no patience with mob spirit. . . . Your very civilization depends upon the carrying out of your laws in an orderly manner," he continued. "I believe I am as gentle as any man . . . ; I don't believe I would harm anyone wrongfully . . ." but, he added with emphasis, there would be no compromise with mob violence. Apparently a meeting had taken place on Tuesday night, he said, and the men who attended should be ashamed; "they are unworthy citizens of your town." He looked out over the courtroom. "Now gentlemen, I have spoken . . . harsh words, but every word I say is true, and I hope we will have no more of such conduct. Let the jury return." [74]

During a brief recess later in the afternoon, reporters hurried over to the jail to interview Captain Joseph Burleson, who commanded the National Guard unit. Somewhat reluctantly, Burleson admitted that an undercover man in the community had attended a meeting on Tuesday night at which two hundred people met to "protest against the manner in which Mr. Leibowitz had examined the state's witnesses." He also acknowledged that several people at the meeting openly advocated riding the New York lawyer out of town on a rail and then lynching the Scottsboro boys. On instructions from Judge Horton he had placed a fire engine on stand-by alert. If a mob assembled he would first try high-pressure water, then tear gas; as a last resort he would fire on the mob. Burleson said he had promised Horton that the prisoners would be protected "so long as we have a piece of ammunition or a man alive. . . ." Sheriff Bud Davis disparaged the reports, but the Jackson County solicitor acknowledged that emotions were even hotter around Scottsboro. He had heard nothing of any mob being formed over there, but he conceded: "There might be trouble though, if these Negroes are acquitted or if the trial lasts too

---

[74] "Alabama vs. Patterson, April 3–9, 1933, Transcript of Testimony," 398–401; New York *Daily News*, April 6, 1933; Birmingham *Age-Herald*, April 6, 1933; New York *Times*, April 6, 1933, p. 13.

long." The first trial cost the people of the county $3,000, he said, and the current one would cost much more than that.[75]

Judge Horton's stern lecture quashed any organized movement among local citizens to organize resistance to the trials. But during the next forty-eight hours rumors spread of mobs forming in Scottsboro, Huntsville, and on the outskirts of Decatur. The Communist Party and the International Labor Defense had remained quiescent during the early stages of the trial, content to allow Leibowitz a free hand in the defense. Once convinced that there was a real danger of mob violence, the Party machinery swung into action. "K.K.K. Gang of 200 Moves on Decatur Jail," headlined the *Daily Worker*. "Workers! Defend Lives of Scottsboro Boys." Within hours a steady stream of protesting telegrams began pouring into the courtroom, to the attorney general and his staff and even to Judge Horton, whom the *Worker* described as a "lyncher in sheep's clothing." The jury could plainly see the messenger boys hurrying in with dozens of telegrams during the next two days, and despite precautions by Judge Horton, they quickly learned the nature of their contents.[76]

Despite the distractions, Leibowitz continued doggedly through the case, calling to the stand during the rest of the afternoon Andy Wright, Eugene Williams, and the defendant, Haywood Patterson. The three boys told essentially the same story, that several white boys had begun throwing rocks and shouting "Black Sons of Bitches" on the train. The three boys, accompanied by Andy's younger brother Roy, gathered seven or eight Negroes from along the train and went up to "have it out" with the white boys. They found them in the middle of a string of gondolas.[77] One Negro youth, who later left the train, did have a gun, testified Andy; and he pistol-whipped one of the white boys, but most of them jumped before actually being hit. When the last, Orville Gilley, prepared

[75] New York *Times*, April 6, 1933, p. 13; Birmingham *Age-Herald*, April 6, April 7, 1933; Birmingham *Post*, April 5, 1933.

[76] New York *Daily Worker*, April 6, April 7, 1933; Birmingham *Age-Herald*, April 7, April 8, 1933; Decatur *Daily*, April 7, April 8, April 9, 1933; New York *Times*, April 9, 1933, p. 16.

[77] Eugene and Haywood thought the fight was in car thirteen; Andy said it could have been in car 14. See Diagram I, page 211.

to bail out, the train had picked up to full speed, and Haywood shouted: "Don't shove that boy off and make him hurt himself. ...." With Andy's help, he reached down, caught Gilley by the arms, and lifted him back into the gondola. After the fight, the group scattered across the train; the four Chattanooga friends returned to the nearest tank car, where they remained until they were arrested in Paint Rock.[78] They all vehemently insisted they had not even seen the two girls until the train stopped at Paint Rock.[79]

Knight had managed to unnerve Ozie Powell, but he had no luck with Wright, Williams, and Patterson. In particular, he bore down on Patterson, cross-examining him for more than an hour. After trying for several minutes to persuade Patterson he was incorrect in his testimony, he finally asked in desperation and with a note of sarcasm: "You were tried at Scottsboro?" Patterson corrected him. "I was framed at Scottsboro," he said. Knight flushed with anger. "Who told you to say you were framed?" he demanded. "I told myself to say it," retorted Haywood. Knight was able to quote from the Scottsboro record a statement by Patterson acknowledging that he had seen the girls raped. When Haywood vigorously denied it, Knight began running nervously back and forth in front of the witness chair, shouting and shaking his finger at the witness. Reading and rereading the record, he kept asking: "Didn't you make the statement?" Finally Leibowitz jumped to his feet. "I have treated his witnesses with much more courtesy and . . . decency than he is showing this negro on the stand," he complained to Horton. He asked the court to instruct Knight to stop "running at him and shouting and pointing his finger at him. . . ." Horton refused, however, and Knight angrily declared: "I will point anything I want to until the court tells me not to." [80] When Knight finally ended his cross-examination just before ad-

---

[78] This would have been car 20. See Diagram I, page 211.

[79] The direct testimony of the three boys is on pages 402–19, 422–38, and 441–48, of "Alabama vs. Patterson, April 3–9, 1933, Transcript of Testimony."

[80] "Alabama vs. Patterson, April 3–9, 1933, Transcript of Testimony," 450–52, 461–64, 468; Hammond, "The South Speaks," 465–66.

journment on Wednesday, the three boys remained unshaken in their testimony.

On Thursday morning Percy Ricks, the train's Negro fireman, told the court he was standing on top of the tender preparing to take water on as the train stopped at Paint Rock. From his vantage point he had a clear view of the entire train; the Negro youths arrested by the posse were taken from points all over the train. Some were in box cars toward the back; two were running along the top of the train near the center; and one came across a car toward the front of the train. What was more important, Ricks said, he had seen two women clamber out of a gondola and run crouching toward the engine. "They seen this crowd of men when they run down toward the engine and they saw they were meeting them. . . ." They reversed themselves again, he said, and "started back the other way, and the posse was coming that way and they stopped them there. . . ." From his testimony, the implication was clear that the two girls were trying to get away from the posse. Attorney General Knight took a break and Morgan County Solicitor Wade Wright cross-examined Ricks, but in twenty minutes of rigorous questioning failed to elicit a single contradiction from the young fireman.[81]

Leibowitz knew the jury would probably discount Ricks' testimony because he was a Negro. A more important witness for the defense was Dr. Edward A. Reisman, a forty-eight-year-old Chattanooga gynecologist. Reisman had been born in Alabama and spent all his adult life in Tennessee. To an attentive courtroom he gave a technical explanation of the female anatomy and then answered a series of hypothetical questions posed by Leibowitz. If six young, healthy men had raped a woman and she had then jounced around repeatedly—but not douched herself—would an examiner expect to find only a trace of semen ninety minutes later? "To my mind it would be quite inconceivable that six men would have intercourse with one woman and not leave telltale traces of their presence in considerable quantities in the vagina." Would it be likely, asked Leibowitz, that the doctor would find it

[81] "Alabama vs. Patterson, April 3–9, 1933, Transcript of Testimony," 484–505.

necessary to insert a swab all the way to the neck of the cervix in order to find enough semen for a slide smear? "To my mind that would be inconceivable," repeated Reisman firmly. In response to further questioning from Leibowitz he gave as his professional opinion that even under relatively unfavorable conditions, some sperm in a healthy vagina would remain motile for at least six to eight hours, and probably for as much as twenty to twenty-four hours. He added that as a physician he found it difficult to believe that respiration, pulse, and pupil dilation would be normal less than two hours after a savage rape by six men. Outward emotional manifestations were unpredictable, he said, but these three factors were difficult to control.[82] Reisman's testimony was a crucial key in Leibowitz's defense plans. This alone, he believed, should be enough to insure an acquittal. But a Decatur resident probably summed up the attitude of the jury as well as the spectators when he told Raymond Daniell: "When a nigger has expert witnesses, we have a right to ask who is paying for them." [83]

It was just before ten in the morning of the fourth day of the trials when Leibowitz called to the stand Lester Carter. The twenty-three-year-old hobo, wearing a new suit and a large flowered tie, filled in the last pieces of the story Leibowitz was presenting to the jury. In January, 1931, he had been convicted of vagrancy and sentenced to a term in the Huntsville County Jail. There he met Victoria Price and her boyfriend Jack Tiller; they were in for adultery. When he got out of jail, Tiller invited him to stay around Huntsville for a few days. The first night out of jail, March 22, Carter said he went with Tiller to call on Mrs. Price. Along with Victoria and her mother, he and Jack sat and chatted

[82] *Ibid.*, 514–20, 528. As in the case of Dr. Bridges, none of Dr. Reisman's testimony was reprinted in the newspapers.

[83] New York *Times,* April 16, 1933, VIII, p. 2. Dr. J. H. Hamil of Decatur was later called by the state to rebut Reisman. He disagreed on the question of whether or not the girls would have shown their emotional excitement, but he acknowledged that under favorable conditions the spermatozoa had been known to remain motile in the vagina for as long as twenty-five hours, and on the average about eight hours. The transcript quotes Dr. Hamil as saying spermatozoa would live up to twenty-five days, but this is clearly a misprint. "Alabama vs. Patterson, April 3–9, 1933, Transcript of Testimony," 762–63.

before the fireplace, recounted Carter. After about a half-hour, Victoria and Tiller got up and went into the back bedroom while he remained outside with the older Mrs. Price. When they returned, Victoria promised Lester she would get him a date with her friend Ruby Bates.

The next night, March 23, the four met outside the gates of the Margaret Mill and walked together to the hobo jungles of Huntsville. "What occurred in the jungles that night?" asked Leibowitz. "I had intercourse with Ruby Bates and Jack Tiller had intercourse with Victoria Price," he replied. Or, as he more vividly recounted later in his testimony, "I hung my hat on a little limb and went to having intercourse with the girl [Ruby]," while less than three feet away, Tiller and Victoria also were "having intercourse." When it began to rain gently, the four got up from the honeysuckle bushes where they had been lying and crawled into an empty box car pulled onto a sidetrack. During the night, between love-making, he said, "we talked and started planning this hobo trip. . . ." The girls complained they were sick of Huntsville and perhaps they could go to Chattanooga where they could "hustle" while the two men got temporary work. Tiller explained that he did not want to risk another conviction for adultery, but he promised vaguely to meet them in a few days. Just before daybreak the four separated while the girls went home to collect some clothes. They agreed to meet in the freight yards that same afternoon in time to catch the Chattanooga train.[84]

The young hobo raced through his account in a high-pitched voice, and he gesticulated frequently to illustrate his story. On the way to Chattanooga he had pretended he did not know the two girls, he said, and they rejoined each other only when they were away from the freight yards of the city. They arrived just before dark and "started walking around looking for some place to sleep, for we were all broke, no money." Just beyond the train yards they met a youth in his twenties who gave his name as "Carolina Slim." Later they learned his real name was Orville Gilley. Together the four of them hiked to the Chattanooga hobo jungles

[84] "Alabama vs. Patterson, April 3–9, 1933, Transcript of Testimony," 534–42, 544.

and built a small fire. Gilley, who had a few coins, went to a nearby chili parlor for some coffee and food. During that night, March
24, Carter said he once again had sexual relations with Ruby
Bates; he could not say for certain about Victoria and their new
friend.[85]

The next day, traveling together, they boarded the Huntsville-
bound freight first on a tank car, but because of the wind, they
moved to a gondola when the train stopped at Stevenson.[86] About
a half-dozen white hobos were in the next car toward the caboose.
Carter said he did not know what started the fight, but when he
and "Carolina Slim" saw the white and Negro boys fighting, the
two climbed into the gondola. After he saw the odds, however, his
courage evaporated and he admitted that he had "climbed down
where the couplings are, and got off," without ever striking a
blow. Shortly after he arrived in Scottsboro several hours later in
the back of a deputy's car, Victoria and Ruby rode up in another
vehicle. According to Carter, Victoria called several of the boys
who had been on the train over to the car and said, "One of you
boys has got to play like you are my brother, if you don't we will
be arrested for hoboing. . . ." Lester explained that he refused, but
one of the other boys, Odel Gladwell, readily agreed. Later in the
jailhouse that evening, Victoria and Orville Gilley engaged in a
"cuss fight" over her accusations against the Negroes. When she
asked him to back up the story, Carter recalled that "Gilley told
her to go to Hell. . . ." "What the Hell do we care about negroes,"
she replied. She personally didn't object if authorities "stuck all
the negroes up in jail in Alabama." Gilley still refused to back her
story, and, according to Carter, this was why he was not asked to
testify at length in the Scottsboro trials.[87]

Although Carter testified persuasively, both the jury and the
spectators listened with open skepticism. His eagerness to testify,

[85] *Ibid.*, 547–51; Decatur *Daily*, April 6, 1933.
[86] He was not certain whether the gondola was car 11 or 12. See Diagram I, page
211.
[87] "Alabama vs. Patterson, April 3–9, 1933, Transcript of Testimony," 558–60,
562–63, 566–67; Decatur *Daily*, April 6, 1933.

his frequent gestures, and his immaculate appearance all mitigated against him. He gave the impression, observed Eleazer, that he had been "carefully schooled" by the ILD lawyers. Perhaps the most damaging mannerism was Carter's insistence on saying "Negro," instead of the polite Southern pronunciation, "Nigra." [88] In cross-examination, Solicitor Wright first tried unsuccessfully to shake the young hobo's story. When he failed in this, he implied through questioning that Carter had changed his story because of financial rewards from the ILD. Wright drew from the witness an admission that Joseph Brodsky had paid his room and board for almost a month and had even bought him the new eleven-dollar suit he was wearing.[89]

Shortly after noon on Thursday, the defense rested "with reservations," but Leibowitz had scarcely taken his seat when a messenger brought him a note. Leibowitz approached the bench and whispered something to Judge Horton, who announced a brief recess. The courtroom remained quiet, but visibly excited. As always, Leibowitz had carefully planned his star witness for the most dramatic moment. Less than ten minutes after Horton had called the recess, guardsmen opened the back doors of the courtroom and a heavy-set, matronly woman in her forties came perspiring down the aisle; directly behind her slowly walked Ruby Bates, her eyes fixed on the floor. From the spectators there was first an audible gasp and then excited murmurs. Even though the prosecution staff had prepared for the worst, there was open consternation at the sight of the new defense witness. Miss Bates' chaperone was May Jones, a social worker from the Birmingham Church of the Advent. She testified that Dr. Charles Clingman, rector of the church, had requested her to bring the young woman to Decatur. She knew nothing concerning the case.[90]

[88] Robert Burns Eleazer to Will W. Alexander, April 17, 1933, in Interracial Commission Papers; New York *Times*, April 7, 1933, p. 3. The Associated Press reporter, T. M. Davenport, commented three times in the space of a half-column on Carter's "frequent gestures" and "high-pitched voice." Decatur *Daily*, April 6, 1933.

[89] "Alabama vs. Patterson, April 3–9, 1933, Transcript of Testimony," 573–624, 630.

[90] Birmingham *Post*, April 6, 1933; Decatur *Daily*, April 6, 1933; Birmingham *Age-Herald*, April 7, 1933; New York *Times*, April 7, 1933, p. 3.

Leibowitz's examination of his star witness was brief and pointed. On the night of March 23, 1933, "Did you have intercourse with Lester Carter. . . ." "I certainly did," Ruby replied softly. "Did Victoria Price have intercourse with Jack Tiller . . . in your presence?" he asked. "She certainly did," said Ruby. Judge Horton, who had sat behind the bench throughout the trials, got up and moved down to a seat in front of the spectators facing Miss Bates. Leibowitz asked that Victoria Price be brought in for identification. Charles Edmundson of the Birmingham *Post* observed that "Victoria's eyes fell and she flushed noticeably" when she first saw her old companion. She quickly recovered, however, and became so angry she was panting. Attorney General Knight stepped in front of her and whispered, "Keep your temper, you hear." Outside, after Ruby had completed her testimony, Mrs. Price declared loudly to all who would listen: "Can you imagine her a-lying so." [91]

Leibowitz continued his questioning. Did any rape take place on the Chattanooga to Huntsville freight train? Not that she knew of, Ruby replied, and she had been with Victoria Price for the entire time. While the jury and spectators leaned forward to hear her low voice, she related how she had left Huntsville with a boyfriend on February 27 and had gone to Montgomery. From there, she hitched a ride to New York along with an old girl friend. She worked for a "Jewish lady" for several weeks, but her conscience bothered her and one day she saw a news story concerning a famous New York minister, Dr. Harry Emerson Fosdick—or "Dr. Fostick" as she called him. She visited him in his study one evening late in March, and he urged her to return to Alabama and tell the truth. It was Fosdick who had arranged for her to go to Dr. Clingman's church. [92]

After less than a fifteen-minute direct examination, Leibowitz ended his questions. Knight stared at Ruby, who sat with her eyes downcast. "Where did you get that coat?" he asked. She bit her lip, hesitated for a moment, and then answered in a near-whisper

[91] Birmingham *Post*, April 6, April 7, 1933; New York *Times*, April 7, 1933, p. 3; New York *Daily News*, April 7, 1933.
[92] "Alabama vs. Patterson, April 3–9, 1933, Transcript of Testimony," 664–67.

without looking up. "I bought it." "Who gave you the money to buy it?" Knight asked her. Somewhat evasively, she replied, "Well, I don't know." "You don't know?" Knight repeated sarcastically. "Where did you get that hat?" he asked. "Who was the beneficent donor?" There was a long pause as Ruby sat biting her lip. From his seat inside the spectators' rail, Horton leaned forward and gently asked her, "Do you know?" Almost inaudibly she murmured, "Dr. Fostick of New York." [93]

Ruby was as evasive and contradictory on the witness stand as Victoria had been. When Knight questioned her about the letter she had written for Miron Pearlman, she first said it was true, then that she did not know what she had written. And whenever he queried her about her testimony at Scottsboro describing the rape, she repeated over and over: "I told it just like Victoria Price told it," or "I said it but Victoria told me to." [94] As in the cross-examination of Carter, the questioning seemed aimed at showing that Ruby had been bribed by the defense. Knight strongly suspected that her story of going to New York on her own was a prefabrication, and he surmised that she had instead been approached by the International Labor Defense.[95] Firing his questions rapidly at the subdued Ruby, Knight questioned her about her finances. How much money was she making when she left Huntsville? How had she paid for the trip between Montgomery and New York? Who gave her funds for the trip back to Alabama? She talked vaguely of loans from her employer in New York, but it was doubtful if anyone in the courtroom believed her. And he also drew from Ruby the damaging admission that she had suffered from syphilis shortly after the attack and had gone to a Huntsville

[93] *Ibid.*, p. 667; Birmingham *Age-Herald,* April 7, 1933.

[94] "Alabama vs. Patterson, April 3–9, 1933, Transcript of Testimony," 683–84, 703.

[95] He was correct in his guess. In early December of 1932 an ILD investigator had approached Ruby about coming over to the defense side. In late February, the sister of one of the ILD attorneys traveled to Alabama and brought Miss Bates back to New York over the bitter opposition of Leibowitz, who argued that she should remain in Alabama until the time of the trial. Roger Baldwin to Walter White, December 17, 1932; Walter White to Alfred Baker Lewis, March 11, 1933, Scottsboro Legal File 5; Memorandum of Interview between Samuel S. Leibowitz, James Marshall, and Walter White, October 1, 1934, Scottsboro Legal File 6, in NAACP Papers.

doctor complaining she contracted it from the Negroes who raped her.[96]

Ruby's lack of candor was so apparent at one point that several spectators began openly laughing. Leibowitz, already distressed at the performance of Ruby, was infuriated. Pointing at one of the loudest offenders, he declared, "Your honor I ask that you bring that man . . . before the Bar. It is discourteous to these men in the jury box for these people to be snickering and laughing, these rooters for the blood of this negro." Although Horton sternly reprimanded the spectators who had been laughing, the outburst made it clear that Ruby's testimony was not making a favorable impression on the jury. Perhaps the most damaging testimony that Knight introduced was an account by Ruby of a conference she had held with the attorney general and two other lawyers in December, 1932. "I will ask you if I didn't tell you then and there I did not want to burn any persons that wasn't [sic] guilty?" Ruby feebly protested that she had said nothing at the meeting. "Victoria told the whole story," she insisted. Knight persisted. "Did I not tell you the only thing I wanted was the truth?" "I guess so," replied the witness. "At the time I also told you I would punish anybody who made you swear falsely, did I not?" Ruby nodded silently.[97]

There were a few rebuttal witnesses by both sides, but the main testimony of the trial ended when Ruby Bates stepped down from the witness stand late Thursday morning. Her testimony caused an "immediate and bitter reaction among the residents of . . . [Morgan] and neighboring counties," said Raymond Daniell. The people of the area were convinced she had been bribed by the defense. Although Attorney General Knight was certain that the "mob spirit" would exhaust itself in talk, he admitted there was a real danger of violence. After consulting with Judge Horton, Knight had Ruby Bates taken from the courtroom and hidden by several

[96] "Alabama vs. Patterson, April 3–9, 1933, Transcript of Testimony," 685–91, 703. Dr. Carey Walker of Huntsville later confirmed that he had treated Miss Bates for both syphilis and gonorrhea in May, 1931, ibid., 750–71.
[97] Ibid., 742–43.

of the National Guardsmen, and nine soldiers were placed outside the Cornelian Court armed with riot guns.[98]

When Morgan County Solicitor Wade Wright began his summation the next afternoon he gave voice to all the fears and hatreds of the area residents.[99] He began calmly enough, but within a few minutes he was waving his arms and shouting at the top of his lungs. Wright was pre-eminent among local all-day singers, and he used his voice to good advantage as he bellowed his summation in the sing-song chant of a sawdust trail evangelist. At first he rambled on about the "fancy New York clothes" of the defense's chief witnesses, Lester Carter and Ruby Bates. But when he went over the testimony of Carter he shouted with exaggerated sarcasm: "What does Mr Carter tell you, Maybe it is Carterinsky now!" He continued: "If he had a-been with Brodsky another two weeks he would have been down here with a pack on his back a-trying to sell you goods. Are you going to countenance that sort of thing?" From a front-row seat among the spectators there came a "No," spoken, said Raymond Daniell, "with the fervor of an 'Amen' in church." Leibowitz sat at the table with a look of stunned disbelief on his face at Wright's performance, while across the way Attorney General Knight stared fixedly at a place in the floor, his face flushed with embarrassment. Leibowitz objected to the anti-Semitic slur and Horton reprimanded the solicitor, but Wright went tumbling on, lost in his own rhetoric. He turned and pointed a finger at the counsel table where Leibowitz and Brodsky sat. The meddlesome East had sold slaves at a profit and then taken them away, he said. "Show them," he paused for effect, "show them that Alabama justice cannot be bought and sold with Jew money from New York." Leibowitz leaped to his feet, slamming

[98] New York *Times,* April 7, 1933, p. 3. Nowhere was the resentment against Ruby more open than in her home town, Huntsville. There residents talked openly on the streets about riding her and her "red" guardians out of town on a rail.

[99] Jackson County Solicitor H. G. Bailey, who opened for the state, had made a brief and unemotional plea to the twelve jurors. The "state of Alabama wants you to send him [Patterson] to the electric chair. That is what . . . Alabama wants, and I believe you will be fair." Decatur *Daily,* April 7, 1933. The summations were not taken down by the court reporter, and this account is based on news reports from the trial.

his hand down hard on the defense table. "I move for mistrial," he shouted. "I submit a conviction in this case won't be worth a pinch of snuff in view of what this man just said." Horton sternly scolded Wright for his "improper" statements, but he refused to end the trial.[100] Several of the jurors sat stolidly without expression, but one reporter noted that a number of them were clearly excited by Wright's remarks.[101]

Leibowitz had the unenviable task of restoring calm to the feverish courtroom. He began his remarks late in the afternoon and spoke for another hour the following morning. His summation was a powerful blend of logic and emotion. "Let us assume that the prosecution is prejudiced," he began quietly. "Let us assume the defense is also prejudiced. Let us assume both sides are trying to prove their points." It was the sworn duty of each of them, he said, to convict only on the evidence. From memory he summarized the four days of testimony: Victoria Price's prevarications on the stand; the testimony of Dr. Bridges and Dr. Reisman which tended to throw doubt on her story of being raped by six men; and finally the testimony of Ruby and Lester which explained the presence of semen in her vagina on the day of the alleged assault. He noted that the so-called supporting witnesses such as Ora Dobbins and Tom Rousseau either were unreliable or tended to refute part of Mrs. Price's testimony. In the final analysis the state's case rested on the testimony of Victoria Price, he said; and her story was the "foul, contemptible outrageous lie . . . [of] an abandoned, brazen woman." [102]

By 10 o'clock the next morning he had been speaking for over three hours, but he continued on, his voice cracking with fatigue.

[100] New York *Times,* April 8, 1933, p. 30; April 16, 1933, VIII, p. 2; New York *Daily News,* April 8, 1933. Inexplicably, Davenport, whose account for the Associated Press reached most of the readers in the country, failed to mention any of the anti-Semitic remarks of Wright. Decatur *Daily,* April 8, 1933; Chattanooga *Daily Times,* April 8, 1933.

[101] Wright was completely bewildered by the uproar over his remarks. It was only his usual "prosecution speech" for rape cases. He plaintively told the court, "No one has even been harmed because of a speech I made." Chattanooga *Daily Times,* April 9, 1933.

[102] New York *Times,* April 8, 1933, p. 30; April 9, 1933, p. 1; New York *Daily News,* April 8, 1933; Decatur *Daily,* April 8, 1933; Birmingham *Post,* April 8, 1933.

Several times he paused as if to gather strength, drank a few sips of water, and then plunged on. He noted the "hangman's speech" of Wright. "What is it but an appeal to prejudice, to sectionalism, to bigotry?" Wright was simply saying, "Come on, boys! We can lick this Jew from New York!" declared Leibowitz. And he noted that several allusions had been made to "Jew money." "I'm not getting any fee in this case and I'm not getting a penny toward expenses . . ." he said. He emphasized he was not defending Ruby Bates; Ruby Bates was not on trial. The question was whether or not even this "poor scrap of colored humanity" would receive a "fair, square deal." [103]

It was late in the morning before Leibowitz wearily took his seat at the defense table and Attorney General Knight opened the final arguments for the state. Knight began by echoing sentiments that Solicitor Bailey had expressed the day before. Victoria Price might not be all that she should, but she deserved the full protection of the laws of the state. "I do not want a verdict based on racial prejudice or a religious creed," he shouted. "I want a verdict on the merits of this case." He emotionally appealed to the jurors on the basis of their patriotism and expressed his confidence that —like "six other men on the Alabama Supreme Court"—they were not cowards. Referring scornfully to the almost forgotten Patterson as "that thing," he told the jury in a tone of complete contempt: "If you acquit this Negro, put a garland of roses around his neck, give him a supper and send him to New York City." There, he said, "Dr. Harry Fosdick [will] dress him up in a high hat and morning coat, gray-striped trousers and spats." The defense had carefully "framed" its testimony to fit a false pattern, he charged. There was only one possible verdict: death in the electric chair.[104]

Even as the defense and prosecution completed their summations, messengers brought in scores of protesting telegrams,

[103] Reynolds, *Courtroom,* 265–66; New York *Daily News,* April 8, April 9, 1933; Decatur *Daily,* April 8, 1933.

[104] New York *Times,* April 9, 1933, p. 1; Decatur *Daily,* April 8, 1933; "Alabama vs. Patterson, April 3–9, 1933, Transcript of Testimony," 813–14.

many objecting to the intemperate remarks of Wright. Horton had silently noted the preoccupation of the jurors with the incoming messages, and when he delivered his charge to the jury he firmly instructed them to pay no attention to these protests; they were inconsequential "baubles." While the law was designed to protect all persons, regardless of their station, the law also had a "stern duty to perform when women of the underworld come before it. . . ." It was the solemn obligation of the jury to consider carefully this fact when weighing the testimony in a case of this kind. The testimony of the two girls was contradictory, he said. Ruby Bates had openly admitted on the stand that she perjured herself. On the other hand, evidence was introduced to show that Victoria made substantive false statements. And he pointedly noted that both Ruby Bates and Lester Carter had insisted that Victoria had consorted with Jack Tiller less than thirty-six hours before the alleged assault; the state had not contradicted this. "We are not trying lawyers. We are not trying state lines," he concluded. "We are not trying whether the defendant is white or black." The only duty of the jury was to ascertain whether there was a reasonable doubt as to the guilt of Haywood Patterson. Horton, his face drawn with exhaustion from the two-week trial, gave the case to the jury just before 1 P.M. on Saturday.[105]

Within a few moments, the courtroom was empty except for lawyers and newspapermen. Outside on the tree-shaded lawn, a few Negroes and whites sprawled in the sun; there was nothing to do but wait. The Scottsboro boys, almost forgotten in the proceedings, occupied themselves by singing gospel songs in their cells. For cigarettes (and a few smuggled drinks) Olen Montgomery and Ozie Powell, the best singers among the boys, answered requests from the guardsmen. Throughout the afternoon, the tension mounted as the jury remained locked in its room. At 11:30 P.M., the foreman announced they had not yet reached a final decision, and Horton ordered them locked up for the night.[106]

It was 10 A.M. on Sunday when word came to the Cornelian

[105] New York *Times,* April 9, 1933, p. 1; Decatur *Daily,* April 8, 1933.
[106] New York *Times,* April 9, 1933, p. 1.

Apartments that the jury had reached a verdict. Within minutes Leibowitz and Brodsky had walked to the courthouse. There they found Patterson, guarded by two militiamen, sprawled in a chair and smoking. Outwardly he appeared completely unconcerned in contrast to Leibowitz, who paced back and forth in the courtroom. Chamlee told Brodsky and Leibowitz he was encouraged by the sound of laughter drifting from the jury room. Across the room Knight sat at the prosecution table, the muscles of his face twitching nervously. When Judge Horton arrived at 11 A.M., the courtroom was about half full. He called for the jury and the court stenographer opened his notebook to take down the last words of the trial. As the jurors filed in they were still laughing from a joke someone had told, but they became solemn when they saw the tense courtroom. Tom Cassiday of the New York *Daily News* suddenly realized that Patterson was the only Negro in the room. "Have you agreed upon a verdict?" Horton asked the foreman. He replied, "We have, your honor," and handed a heavily creased slip of paper to the bailiff who laid it on the judge's bench. Patterson, completely overlooked, remained in his seat, still smoking his cigarette. Horton read from the large penciled letters: "We find the defendant guilty as charged and fix the punishment at death in the electric chair." There was not a sound in the courtroom; several spectators craned their necks to see Leibowitz. The chief defense attorney, white and drawn from lack of sleep, looked as though he had been struck and he leaned back slackly in his chair. Patterson's face did not change expression.[107]

After the last formal words had been spoken, Leibowitz walked to the bench and grasped Horton's hand. The judge warmly returned the handshake. "I am taking back to New York with me a picture of one of the finest jurists I have ever met," said Leibowitz, his voice trembling with emotion. "But I am sorry I cannot say as much for a jury which has decided this case against the evidence." Later Leibowitz learned that the jury had taken the first ballot less than five minutes after the judge gave it the case. The vote was: guilty—12; not guilty—0. On the next ballot, eleven jurors

[107] *Ibid.*, April 10, 1933, p. 1; New York *Daily News*, April 10, 1933.

voted to send Patterson to the electric chair; foreman Eugene D. Bailey, Jr., a draftsman, had held out for life imprisonment for twelve hours. One of the jurors frankly admitted that they had not even discussed, let alone considered, Ruby Bates' testimony.[108]

Those who attended the Decatur proceedings analyzed the factors leading to the guilty verdict. In the first place, anyone familiar with the "psychology of Southern juries" would have kept both Ruby and Lester in Alabama instead of bringing them directly from New York City, observed Robert Eleazer. Similarly, "it was a tactical error to dress Ruby so well." The jury as well as most people in the courtroom believed their clothes had been "bought with Jew money from New York," noted Mary Heaton Vorse. And their actions on the stand confirmed suspicions that they had been "contaminated" in their trip to New York.[109] A Childersburg, Alabama, native typified this suspicion when he charged that Ruby had been "tampered with and . . . dressed up in glad rags of questionable origin. . . ." The same was true for her companion, Lester Carter, who "suddenly found much prosperity in the midst of this history-making panic. . . ." [110] Another Alabamian charged that "Negro blood and tarnished white virtue in an awful mixup is being peddled as a great bargain day sale of slush over the world." [111]

The prosecution had also succeeded in arousing all of the latent fears of the local citizens. Reporters at the trial noted that Wade Wright's anti-Semitic summation was the most effective single statement by the counsel for the prosecution. Until he spoke most of the newspapermen felt there was an outside chance for a hung jury, but Wright "registered to perfection the repressed feelings and prejudices of the twelve good men," said John Hammond of *The Nation*. From then on the outlook was hopeless. State officials in Montgomery insisted that Wright's ravings were an aberration,

---

[108] New York *Times,* April 10, 1933, p. 2; New York *Daily News,* April 10, 1933.

[109] Robert Burns Eleazer to Will W. Alexander, April 17, 1933, in Interracial Commission Papers; Mary Heaton Vorse, "How Scottsboro Happened," *New Republic,* LXXIX (1933) , 356.

[110] Letter by B. H. Richardson in Birmingham *News,* April 19, 1933.

[111] Letter of R. E. Tyler in Birmingham *Post,* April 13, 1933.

and they reacted apologetically to the entire episode. But even though Southern Jews had "more freedom and suffer less prejudice than in the North," said Eleazer, the Shylock image was never far beneath the surface. The chant of "Jew money" at Decatur had "damaged the standing of Southern Jews" even more than the fulminations of the Ku Klux Klan during the 1920's.[112]

Somewhat defensively, several Southern newspapers attributed the jury's decision to the agitation of outsiders. "If there has been no fair trial, outside pressure on Alabama is chiefly responsible for it," said the Charleston, South Carolina, *News and Courier*. And the Charlotte *Observer* called the verdict a "natural reaction" to the flamboyant attempt on the part of outsiders to take a hand in an affair that the people of Alabama would . . . properly conceive to be for their own decision." [113] Talk about "outside agitation" was, however, an excuse, not an explanation, for the sentence of death against Haywood Patterson. In the final analysis Samuel Leibowitz had collided head-on with the same fears and the same antipathies which dominated the Scottsboro trials. As one old-timer said without heat after Victoria Price stepped down from the witness stand: "Anyone would have to [convict] after hearin' her say that nigger raped her." All the defense testimony "don't count a mite with the jury." [114] Throughout the trial, it was widely rumored that an acquittal would be used as a wedge toward achieving "social equality" for the Alabama Negro. No disclaimer

[112] Hammond, "The South Speaks," 466; New York *Times*, April 16, 1933, VIII, 2; Birmingham *Post*, April 11, 1933; Robert Burns Eleazer to Will W. Alexander, April 17, 1933; Robert Burns Eleazer to Will W. Alexander, April 17, 1933, in Inter-racial Commission Papers. And despite the state officials' insistence that this was an isolated outburst, someone in Governor Miller's office went through the ILD brochures and protests sent in, carefully circled all Jewish names, and noted in the margins, "Russian Jews." See brochures, letters and leaflets, May, June, 1931, in Alabama Scottsboro Files.

[113] Charleston *News and Courier*, quoted in Birmingham *Age-Herald*, April 16, 1933; Charlotte (N.C.) *Observer*, quoted in Birmingham *News-Age-Herald*, April 16, 1933. "It should be clear to all parties by this time that the significance of the case lies in the fact that it has been seized upon as a vehicle for propaganda," said the Chattanooga *Daily Times*. "Reds, cranks, and South haters" were using it for a rallying point; quite naturally, the people of Alabama had resented this. Chattanooga *Daily Times*, April 12, 1933.

[114] Quoted in Vorse, "Scottsboro Trial," 278.

from Leibowitz could counteract that belief, particularly after he attacked Alabama's all-white jury system. "Leibowitz in the Scottsboro Case has thrown down the challenge to the Democratic party to maintain white supremacy in the South," declared the Alabama *Wiregrass Journal.* Unless this "Russianized northern element" was defeated there could be no peace and tranquility in Alabama.[115] Conceivably, a local defense without the triple disadvantages of being radical, Jewish and "Northern" could have gained a compromise such as life imprisonment, but the jury's loyalty to its white caste could only be proved unequivocally by a guilty verdict. Whether Haywood Patterson was guilty or innocent was, at most, a peripheral question.

[115] Dothan, Alabama, *Wiregrass Journal,* quoted in Federal Council of the Churches of Christ in America, "The Scottsboro Case," *Information Service,* XII (June 17, 1933) , 1. See New York *Times,* April 10, 1933, p. 3.

Scottsboro Courthouse. The boys'
first trials were held here in April, 1931.

The Scottsboro boys
under guard in Decatur.

As they were being moved from the
jail to the courthouse in Decatur.

Samuel Leibowitz meets with his clients in a Decatur jail
cell. Seated next to Leibowitz is Haywood Patterson.
The other defendants, standing from left to right, are Olen
Montgomery, Clarence Norris, Willie Roberson (front),
Andrew Wright (partially obscured), Ozie Powell, Eugene
Williams, Charley Weems, and Roy Wright.

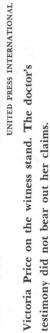

Victoria Price on the witness stand. The doctor's testimony did not bear out her claims.

Ruby Bates, one of the two alleged victims of rape. She later changed her story.

Judge James E. Horton, who presided over the first two trials which were held in Decatur.

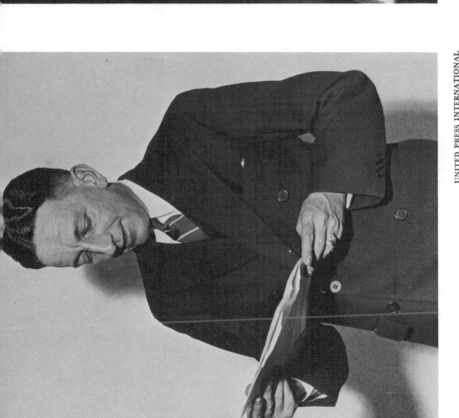

Thomas G. Knight, Jr., Alabama Attorney General, prosecuted the Decatur trials.

The twelve jurymen who found Haywood Patterson
guilty in the first trial at Decatur.

This courtroom scene at Decatur shows the model freight
train produced by defense attorneys to help prove
the Scottsboro boys' innocence.

Morgan County Courthouse in Decatur,
where all but the first trials were held.

Spectators in the Morgan County
courtrooms during the second trial.

Joseph R. Brodsky, the International Labor Defense's chief lawyer, wrested the case from the NAACP.

Three attorneys seen during the appeal hearing which won Haywood Patterson a new trial: W. N. Baskette, George W. Chamlee, and O. S. Fraenkel. Chamlee, grandson of a decorated Confederate soldier, had served as Attorney General of Hamilton County (Chattanooga), Tennessee.

Troops guard the side entrance of the Morgan County
Courthouse during one of the
trials of the Scottsboro boys.

Attorney Samuel Leibowitz with client
Haywood Patterson holding a horseshoe
and a rabbit foot for good luck.

Dr. R. R. Bridges testifying
before Judge Horton. He was the first
to examine Victoria Price and Ruby Bates.

Beatrice Maddox, sister of two
Scottsboro boys, Andrew
and Roy Wright, was a witness.

Dallas Ramsay testified that
he saw Victoria Price and Ruby Bates
in the hobo jungle at Chattanooga at
6 A.M., the day before the alleged attack.

Orey Dobbins said he saw a
Negro man and a white girl on the
freight train as it passed his farm.

Arthur H. Woodall "searched all
those darkies" and removed a knife
from Norris which Victoria
Price identified as hers.

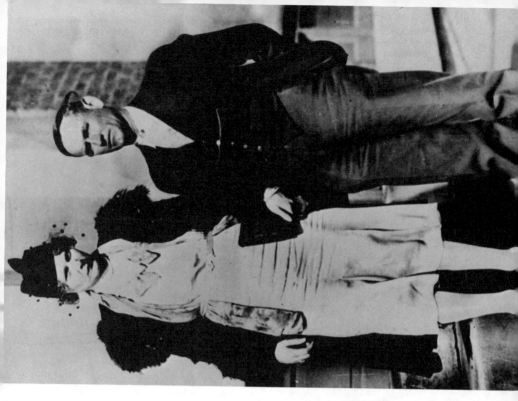

Orville Gilley, a witness
who mixed poetry with travel.

Victoria Price and Jack Tiller. Testimony
revealed they had been jailed in Huntsville
on a charge of adultery.

James V. Haring, New York handwriting expert, gave testimony that indicated jury rolls in Jackson County had been tampered with.

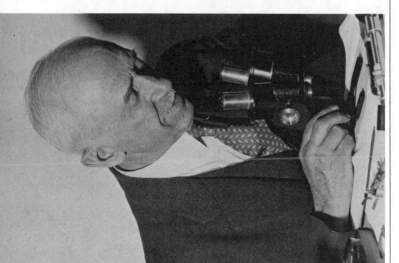

Governor Bibb Graves. He turned down a "Dear Bibb" invitation from President Franklin Roosevelt to come to the Warm Springs White House to discuss the release of the Scottsboro boys.

Wade Wright, Solicitor of Morgan County. "Alabama justice," Wright told the court, "cannot be bought and sold with Jew money from New York."

A communist-backed rally in support of the
Scottboro boys, Union Square, December, 1933.

May Day, 1934. Ruby Bates rode in a communist
parade in New York City with five mothers
of the Scottsboro boys.

Ruby Bates and the mothers of four of the Scottsboro boys
stand outside the White House after their unsuccessful attempt
to see President Roosevelt in 1934. From left to right, Mrs. Ada
Wright, Ruby Bates, Mrs. Janie Patterson, ILD spokesman Richard
Moore, Mrs. Mamie Williams Wilcox, and Mrs. Ida Norris.

Ruby Bates, who repudiated her testimony against the
Scottsboro boys, led a parade of 3,000 before the White
House in May, 1933, in an appeal for the boys' freedom.

Leibowitz and the four defendants whose release he won
arrive at Pennsylvania Station in New York in 1937.
From left to right, Roy Wright, Olen Montgomery,
unidentified assistant to Leibowitz, Leibowitz, unidentified
spectator, Willie Roberson, and Eugene Williams.

Andrew Wright, the last of the Scottsboro boys to
"go free" in 1950. His first release
in 1944 was revoked for parole violation.

VIII

"LET JUSTICE
BE DONE"

FIFTEEN hundred miles away, William H. (Kid) Davis, publisher of Harlem's *Amsterdam News,* posted the results of the Morgan County jury's decision. On the same bulletin board outside the *News'* office, he placed a statement calling on the people of Harlem to march to Washington to protest the outrageous verdict. By early evening, twenty thousand angry Negroes had signed a petition promising to take part in the Washington trek. Residents gathered in such numbers on the corner of Seventh Avenue and 135th Street that traffic came to a complete standstill. And throughout the throng the deep-seated bitterness was articulately expressed. The next day, when Leibowitz returned from Alabama, more than three thousand Negroes crowded the concourses of Pennsylvania Station. When Leibowitz stepped down from the car, the enthusiastic crowd nearly mauled its new hero, and only by lifting him over the heads of the crushing throng were friends able to get him out of the station and into a taxi. Police refused the crowd permission to parade outside the train station. When more than five hundred disobeyed the order and began walking up Broadway toward Harlem, mounted policemen and additional riot personnel managed to avert a dangerous riot and disperse the crowd.[1]

[1] New York *Times,* April 10, 1933, p. 2; April 11, 1933, p. 1; New York *Amsterdam News,* April 12, 1933

The roaring welcome seemed to revive Leibowitz's resentment. When a New York *Herald Tribune* reporter expressed incredulity over the jury's decision, the attorney was angry and bitter. "If you ever saw those creatures," Leibowitz declared, his face drawn with exhaustion, "those bigots whose mouths are slits in their faces, whose eyes pop out like a frog's, whose chins drip tobacco juice, bewhiskered and filthy, you would not ask how they could do it." The two weeks in Decatur made him feel he needed a "moral, mental and physical bath," he declared. The New York attorney's blunt remarks were a serious tactical error; there were eight additional defendants in Alabama who had to be tried before Morgan County juries. For the first time in his life, however, Samuel S. Leibowitz had allowed anger to overcome his better judgment. Friends had warned him that an acquittal under the circumstances would be impossible, but Leibowitz was egotistical enough to believe that he could overcome these prejudices. During his long career, he had gained acquittals on far flimsier evidence than he had presented at Decatur. The frustration and anger were greater because he thought for one brief moment he had succeeded. When he saw the twelve men emerge laughing from the jury room at Decatur he breathed an inward sigh of relief; then came the verdict. Apparently "condemning a man to death—'if he is a nigger'—is not a matter of very grave moment," Leibowitz later observed, and it was too much to take.[2]

Enthusiasm concerning the case remained high throughout the week. On Thursday night Leibowitz addressed four thousand Negroes in Harlem's Salem Methodist Episcopal Church. Leibowitz, hailed as a "new Moses," stirred the crowd to repeated applause with a promise to "sell his house and home" if that became necessary. "I promise you citizens of Harlem that I will fight with every drop of blood in my body, and with the help of God . . . these Scottsboro boys shall be free." The following night, ten thousand persons met in Union Square to hear Janie Patterson

---

[2] New York *Herald Tribune*, April 11, 1933; The sight of "twelve human beings sending an innocent creature to his death in such a spirit of joviality was more than anyone with a spark of human decency in his makeup could bear," he said. Letter by Samuel S. Leibowitz, New York *Herald Tribune*, April 30, 1933.

and ILD officials call for a continued fight against the oppression of the Southern Negro. Another meeting on Sunday, April 16, drew four thousand persons including New York Mayor John P. O'Brien and a number of other Democratic political leaders.[3]

The reaction was somewhat different in Alabama. Leibowitz's remarks might have gone unnoticed if someone had not called Knight's attention to them. While visiting in Decatur on April 15, the Attorney General issued a press release quoting the *Herald Tribune* story. "If this statement was made by Leibowitz it can be taken only as a wail of a contemptible loser. I, like every other Southerner, resent his despicable slurs." Whatever effect this "forensic discourse" had upon Harlem, declared Knight, it would not cause the good citizens of Morgan County to "deviate in the orderly and dignified course which was followed in the Patterson trial."[4]

The Decatur *Daily* maintained editorial silence, but the reaction throughout the state was understandably hostile. "The New York Jew says there is no such thing as a fair trial in Alabama," said the Athens *Alabama Courier*. "It seems to this paper . . . [that] this recent recruit from Russia is a poor sort of chap to try to blight the good name of Alabama." And the Sylacauga *News* proudly declared: "When these German communists . . . hear of the latest echo from their New York fog horn lawyer, they will doubtless learn true blue Americans have not yet grasped the meaning of the order to retreat." Even before the *Herald Tribune* story, the Montgomery *Advertiser* had branded Leibowitz as "arrogant, contemptuous and domineering." He was the "voice of bigotry." The Birmingham newspapers were more temperate in their criticism, but they also attacked Leibowitz for his statements.[5]

When Judge Horton visited Decatur the day after Knight issued his press release he found emotions more inflamed than at any

---

[3] New York *Times*, April 14, 1933, p. 5; April 15, 1933, p. 4; April 17, 1933, p. 4.

[4] Decatur *Daily*, April 15, 1933; Montgomery *Advertiser*, April 16, 1933.

[5] Athens *Alabama Courier* and Sylacauga *News*, quoted in Federal Council of Churches of Christ in America, "The Scottsboro Case," 1; Montgomery *Advertiser*, April 11, 1933; Birmingham *Post*, April 15, 1933; Birmingham *News*, April 18, 1933; Birmingham *Age-Herald*, April 18, 1933.

time during Patterson's trial. He had already considered post-poning the remainder of the trials, and the angry reactions to Leibowitz's statements made the decision inevitable.[6] On Monday morning, April 18, Haywood Patterson stood before Horton for the official pronouncement of the death sentence. The courtroom was so quiet that spectators in the back could hear the rustling of papers in Horton's hand. The judge asked Haywood if he had any-thing to say. Patterson, his eyes downcast and leaning on the bench, mumbled, "I ain't got a fair trial, I didn't see no girls on the train. I ain't got a fair trial." The jury had decided otherwise, said Horton; and it was the judgment of the court that he should die in the electric chair at Kilby Prison on June 16. As soon as he had set sentence, as he was required to do by law, Horton suspend-ed it on a motion for a new trial by Brodsky.[7]

The crowd waited impatiently for the beginning of the next trial, but instead of calling the venire, Horton read a prepared statement: "On account of certain influences, many of which to this court appear sinister . . . it has been difficult to try what are known as the Scottsboro cases upon the real facts." The statement of Leibowitz in the *Herald Tribune,* whether it was accurate or not, he said, made "impossible any just and impartial verdict. . . ." Exacerbating the tensions which already surrounded the proceed-ings such statements were a "millstone around the necks of the defendants." He announced he had decided to postpone the case of *Alabama* v. *Weems* and the trials of the other boys until the passions of local citizens had subsided. Brodsky, who was rep-resenting the ILD, denied Leibowitz had made any such state-ment. "Leibowitz's view," said Brodsky, "is that in Decatur and the South the white workers are imbued with the idea of white supremacy." Only in the "union of the white and negro workers warring against the ruling class can they gain their ends." Knight, his face livid, pounded on the table objecting "to such orations in a courtroom in Alabama." Social equality "cannot be advocated

* Interview with former Judge James Edwin Horton, Jr., April 9, 1966.
† New York *Times,* April 18, 1933, p. 3; Birmingham *Age-Herald,* April 18, 1933; Decatur *Daily,* April 17, 1933.

in my presence," he said. Only the sharp rapping of Horton's gavel ended the exchange. "So long as I sit on this bench, every defendant, white or black, shall have a fair trial," he sternly told Brodsky.[8] Despite Brodsky's disclaimer and Horton's reprimand, Leibowitz stood firmly behind his statement. The real problem was the attitude among many Alabamians that a "Negro is a chattel and that he can be referred to as 'my nigger' just as the master refers to 'my dog'. . . ." He respected Judge Horton and other fair-minded people of the state. But "as for the rest, the baying pack, the wolves of bigotry who raised the Hitler cry of 'Jew money from New York' because we dared to demand a square deal for a poor unfortunate whose skin was black, I stand pat. They are bigots." [9]

A mutual resentment over the Decatur verdict did not end the sniping between the NAACP and the ILD. The Association's Board of Directors could not refrain from rapping the International Labor Defense. The only remaining hope for the boys was to "remove from the already overwhelming prejudices which militate against them the additional burden of communism." In turn, the ILD accused its critics of "gloating" over Patterson's death sentence. The NAACP had made an "effort to do what the white lynch gangs have tried to do and failed—eliminate the one organization, the International Labor Defense, which has thus far prevented the murder of these innocent victims. . . ." [10] Even as the two groups exchanged denunciations, however, they were meeting with Leibowitz in an effort to work out some kind of agreement of cooperation. The Association eventually concluded that its differences with the ILD would have to be put aside. "Time will tell who has the best philosophy on the so-called race problem," said Walter White; "but the Scottsboro boys cannot wait." His organization offered to help pay the expenses of Patterson's appeal and any future trials.[11]

[8] *Ibid.*

[9] New York *Times,* April 18, 1933, p. 3; April 19, 1933, p. 8.

[10] *Ibid.,* April 11, 1937, p. 11; April 12, 1933, p. 12; New York *Daily Worker,* April 12, 1933.

[11] Walter White to William L. Patterson, April 13, 1933, in Scottsboro Legal File 5, NAACP Papers.

White's letter touched off another violent debate within the International Labor Defense and the Communist Party. As in the earlier disagreement concerning cooperation with the clergy, the Party officials took a harder line. Any cooperation with the NAACP now would be a repudiation of the Party's earlier position, argued Harry Haywood and George Maurer. But William Patterson pointed out there was little alternative if they were to gain the financial support they needed for Haywood Patterson's appeal and the future trials of the other boys. Despite the talk among Southerners of "Moscow gold," the ILD was deeply in debt, and Patterson and Brodsky foresaw additional expenses in the near future. Although there had been a steady stream of contributions since the conviction, there was little likelihood these would be sufficient. Reluctantly, Party leaders agreed to endorse cooperation with the NAACP.[12] "Our national committee welcomes the splendid offer of financial cooperation made by your organization," Patterson wrote White. "We believe that in this united front . . . tens of thousands more workers and their sympathizers can be drawn into a sincere, consistent and relentless struggle for the nine Scottsboro boys." Eventually under the terms of the agreement, the NAACP paid $11,854 for legal bills incurred by the International Labor Defense.[13]

While the NAACP and the ILD temporarily ironed out their differences, plans were underway for William Davis' "March on Washington." The ILD embraced the proposal so fervently that, too late, Davis learned that he was little more than a figurehead. When William L. Patterson took charge and called a news conference for April 16, he assured the *Amsterdam News* publisher it would be a true "united front." The Negro newsman soon learned that it was the usual "united front," however, with the Communists in the forefront and non-Party members tagging along in the rear. When the planning conference met it was dom-

[12] Memorandum of Conference re. the Scottsboro Case, April 15, 1933, in ILD Papers.
[13] William L. Patterson to Walter White, April 20, 1933, in ILD Papers; *Annual Report of the National Association for the Advancement of Colored People, 1934* (New York, 1935), 14.

inated by Communist Party and ILD members. Benjamin Davis, a strong Party member, became chairman; William L. Patterson one of the two vice-chairmen; and Miss Louise Thompson of the National Conference for the Defense of Political Prisoners, secretary. Heywood Broun of the Socialist Party was named vice-chairman, but he soon learned who controlled the group and quietly ceased active participation. William Davis also realized the entire plan had been sequestered by the Communists, and he considered withdrawing completely. But, as he explained to a friend, he had gone too far to end his commitment regardless of the outcome.[14]

Although the march began as a demand for the freedom of the Scottsboro boys, Patterson expanded the agenda to include current demands of the Communist Party in the area of civil rights: an end to discrimination in voting, jury service, schools, transportation, housing, public accommodations, labor unions, the army and navy, and stiff penalties against lynching. On May 2, the ILD secretary wired President Roosevelt's private secretary, Louis McHenry Howe, and asked that the President meet with Ruby Bates and the Scottsboro mothers. As he might have expected, this wire and three others were conveniently ignored.[15] Despite the lack of response on the part of the President, plans went ahead for the weekend of May 6 and 7.

A mass rally on Friday evening, May 5, kicked off the march to Washington. At St. Nicholas Arena in New York, Leibowitz and Chamlee spoke briefly to a crowd of over five thousand, but the highlight of the evening was an appearance by Lester Carter and Ruby Bates. Ruby told the crowd that she had told a false story at Scottsboro because "I was excited and frightened by the ruling class of white people of Scottsboro and other towns." If she had not told the story of rape, the ruling class of the Southern towns would have lynched her. After the trial she wanted to tell the

[14] New York *Times,* April 17, 1933, p. 4; Hector M. Lovell to President Franklin Delano Roosevelt, April 20, 1933, in FDR Library, Hyde Park, N.Y. Lovell, a Negro career serviceman, talked with Davis for two hours on April 19 in an effort to persuade him to drop the march.
[15] National Scottsboro Action Committee to President Roosevelt, May 2, 1933; William L. Patterson to Louis McHenry Howe, May 2, May 10, May 13, May 17, 1933, in FDR Library.

truth, she said, "but I was afraid of the Southern white ruling class people. . . ." Then she read in the newspapers how Louis J. Engdahl had given his life in the fight for the Scottsboro boys and she also read of the mass struggle of the ILD.[16] She had therefore decided to "go back to the Decatur Court house and tell the truth on the nine innocent Scottsboro boys." When she stepped down from the platform several hundred persons tried to shake hands with her.[17]

The New York caravan to Washington had planned to leave early the next morning, but the bus company hired to transport the group refused to accept post-dated checks. Throughout the day march leaders borrowed and begged enough cash to assemble a motley collection of trucks, buses, and private cars. Eight hours after the march was scheduled to begin, the last truck left Union Square. Altogether about five hundred of the two thousand had to stay behind because of the lack of transportation. That night the weary marchers slept in Baltimore's "Tom Mooney Hall" and in the homes of sympathizers.[18]

Shortly after noon on Sunday, marchers from New York, Philadelphia, Baltimore, and other Eastern cities began gathering outside the White House. When Patterson, accompanied by Ruby Bates and Mrs. Janie Patterson, asked to see the President, Louis Howe explained that he was busy conferring with Dr. Hjalmar Schact, a special German envoy. Thwarted in this attempt, they rejoined the crowd of three thousand and together marched down to the Capitol. Speaker of the House Henry T. Rainey and Vice-President John Nance Garner received representatives of the group, but they made it clear that they would do nothing except refer the civil rights petition to the proper committee. As for the Scottsboro Case, said Rainey, "that is a matter for the courts. Con-

---

[16] Engdahl accompanied Mrs. Wright on her trip through Europe and died in Moscow in the fall of 1931. The *Daily Worker* blamed his death on exhaustion caused by the strenuous efforts on behalf of the Scottsboro boys. New York *Daily Worker*, November 22, 1932.

[17] Speech by Ruby Bates at St. Nicholas Arena, May 5, 1933, in ILD Papers; New York *Daily Worker*, May 8, 1933; New York *Times*, May 6, 1933, p. 9.

[18] New York *Times*, May 7, 1933, p. 27; May 8, 1933, p. 4.

gress has no authority to direct the release of men charged with a crime." In a drizzling rain, the crowd somewhat dejectedly dispersed.[19]

The Washington demonstration was to have been the beginning of a nationwide "united front" campaign; instead it represented the high-water mark of national protests during the spring of 1933. Many Negroes felt—as they had in 1931—that once again the International Labor Defense was "polishing up the electric chair" for the Scottsboro boys by insisting on linking their case with the over-all program of the Communist Party.[20] The way in which the ILD and Communist Party members completely dominated the positions of leadership in the so-called "united front" aroused mistrust and suspicion. As usual, ILD officials accentuated this resentment by pillorying those who did not echo the current Party lines. Patterson called a rally on May 10 to discuss the results of the Washington pilgrimage. The audience of more than four thousand heard little about Washington. Instead, Richard Moore of the ILD and Larry Cohen of the Communist Party used the meeting to "expose" the NAACP, the Socialist Party, the *Amsterdam News*, the New York *Age,* the ministers of Harlem, and the "traitorous middle class." Moore and Cohen accused these groups of everything from "Hitlerism to petty larceny" during these speeches.[21]

Although the NAACP had agreed to assume part of the financial burdens of the case, Walter White had made it clear from the

[19] Washington *Post*, May 9, 1933; New York *Times*, May 9, 1933, p. 38. Ruby Bates and five of the Scottsboro mothers called at the White House again the following Saturday only to be told that the President was away on vacation for the weekend. And all of the White House secretaries were "off duty." New York *Times*, May 14, 1933.

[20] See letter by Joseph J. McClain in New York *Times*, May 13, 1933, p. 12. In fairness to the ILD, it should be noted that it did not include such ultimate goals as "black self-determination" in its agenda for the Washington march.

[21] New York *Amsterdam News*, May 17, 1933. Much of the ILD's resentment stemmed from the fact that William Davis and several other Negro newspapermen had gone to Washington, in advance of the march, to confer with sympathetic political leaders. New York *Times*, May 6, 1933, p. 9. ILD leaders regarded this advance trip as "treasonous." Speech by Richard Moore at Hartford, Conn., May 14, 1933, in ILD Papers.

outset that the organization would pay the ILD bills at its discretion. In June the Association declined to pay several ILD travel vouchers on the grounds that the purpose of the trips had been for propaganda as much as for legal business. Patterson demanded that the NAACP pay and accused White of "criminally squandering" more than $7,000 raised in the names of the Scottsboro boys. When the NAACP still refused, Patterson released a letter to the press which ruptured the fragile agreement hammered out in April. The NAACP had refused to recognize that the "courts of an oppressor class or nation are created to aid in preserving its existence," he charged. While the NAACP was not expected "to subscribe in toto to the philosophy and tactics of the ILD," the Association had to understand that the "mass pressure" campaign was an "inseparable part" of the defense. "We ask only that those who voluntarily agreed to cooperate with the ILD renounce any plan endorsed by the lynchers." Of course, the lynchers had "advocated and endorsed your policy in this case," he concluded.[22]

Patterson's inflexible attitude toward White resulted primarily from strong pressure by the Communist Party. In May the Party's Political Bureau had charged Patterson and the ILD with crass "right opportunism" in their relations with the NAACP. The ILD should have placed before the NAACP "straightforward and clear proposals of mass struggle and of mobilization of the masses against the capitalist frame-up courts. . . ." The bourgeois leaders would have refused such an offer, but this was irrelevant. What was important was: "if they had refused such an offer, this . . . would have cleared the issues before the eyes of the masses." [23] Whatever the rationale behind Patterson's decision to renew attacks on the "bourgeois misleaders," it effectively alienated much of the support which had mobilized behind the ILD after Haywood Patterson's conviction.

In the South there was a new development in the case. For the first time, many of the region's metropolitan newspapers outside

[22] Walter White to William L. Patterson, April 27, 1933; William L. Patterson to Walter White, July 11, 1933; William L. Patterson to Walter White, August 1, 1933, in ILD Papers.
[23] "Scottsboro Struggle and the Next Steps," 574–75.

Alabama unequivocally affirmed the innocence of the Scottsboro boys. "The men are being sentenced to death primarily because they are black," asserted the Richmond *News Leader*. Editor Douglas Southall Freeman noted that Alabamians had promised the nation that all doubts would be allayed by the Decatur proceedings. Instead, "the second trial confirmed all the suspicions aroused by the first hearing." Haywood Patterson had been convicted on the " 'unwritten law' that when a white woman accuses a white man she must prove his guilt, but . . . when she accuses a Negro he must prove his innocence." Josephus Daniels of the Raleigh *News and Observer* called the verdict "outrageous." The facts in the judge's charge alone should have been sufficient to establish a reasonable doubt. "Southerners have a deeper interest in the case than people elsewhere," said Daniels, "since all Southern justice in the eyes of the world will be discredited by the shocking verdict." And the Chattanooga *News,* while suggesting that the ILD lawyers withdraw from the case, concluded: "We cannot conceive of a civilized community taking human lives on the strength of this miserable affair." [24]

The only newspaper in Alabama which significantly changed its position was the Birmingham *Post,* one of the largest afternoon dailies in the state. Five days after the trial ended, the *Post* declared that the jury should never have convicted Haywood Patterson. It had polled the dozen leading reporters at the trial, including four representing Southern newspapers, said the *Post.* They were unanimous in their conviction that the defense had raised at least a reasonable doubt as to guilt. "We love justice enough to want it done regardless of the fact it may seem to play into the hands of unfair radicals." [25]

Even before the trial had begun at Decatur, a number of white Alabamians had assembled in Birmingham in an effort to form a

[24] Richmond *News Leader,* quoted in the Norfolk *Journal and Guide,* April 15, 1933; Raleigh *News and Observer,* April 10, 1933; Chattanooga *News,* quoted in "South Split Over the Scottsboro Verdict," *Literary Digest,* CXV (April 22, 1933), 4. The *Journal and Guide* and the *Literary Digest* reprinted editorials from more than a half dozen leading Southern newspapers.

[25] Birmingham *Post,* April 15, 1933.

coalition of local support for the Scottsboro boys. By Alabama's standards, the speakers at the May 26 rally were extreme liberals, and yet they were also prominent members of the community. In addition to Dr. Ernest W. Taggart, president of the Birmingham NAACP, there were four white speakers: Kenneth E. Barnhart, professor of sociology at Birmingham-Southern College; one of his students, David Hutto; Rabbi Benjamin Goldstein of Temple Beth Or in Montgomery; and Dr. Henry M. Edmonds, pastor of the Independent Presbyterian Church and chairman of the Alabama Interracial Commission. More than five hundred Negroes and about fifty whites jammed the Negro Congregational Church to hear the men. Goldstein, the presiding officer, told the audience that most of the speakers on the program appeared at the risk of losing their jobs, "but we are here in spite of it all." While the avowed purpose of the meeting was to petition for changing the site of future trials to Birmingham, Dr. Barnhart was closer to the truth when he declared that "our purpose in coming together today [is] to arouse public sentiment" which, he said, would support a "square deal" for the Scottsboro boys.[26]

Edmonds, the most conservative of the four, defended the role of the Alabama Interracial Commission, but he also pledged future cooperation with the ILD on legal matters. Several of the other speakers made what the Birmingham *News* called "inflammatory" remarks. Dr. Taggart, a Negro dentist, charged that the Alabama legal system proceeded on the presumption that "we [white folks] know the Negro; we know what is best for the Negro, and we know what the Negro can do." And white juries acted from these same assumptions of racial superiority. David Hutto, born and raised in the Black Belt, brought the strongest applause when he urged college students to "take the lead in breaking down racial barriers" and destroying the "shackles that bind the South to the past." Dr. Barnhart called on the state to enforce the Fourteenth and Fifteenth Amendments to the United States Constitution instead of pretending they did not exist. At the conclusion of

[26] Birmingham *Age-Herald*, March 27, 1933.

the meeting, Rabbi Goldstein asked the audience to contribute to the ILD defense fund.[27]

Despite the optimistic predictions of local ILD officials, the meeting had few concrete results. The great majority of Alabamians who considered themselves "moderates" on racial issues were completely unwilling to commit themselves in favor of the Scottsboro boys. Had they been willing, under no conditions would they have cooperated with the ILD. Although Dr. Edmonds attended the Birmingham rally, the angry reaction from members of the Alabama Interracial Commission later convinced him he had gone "too far." The Alabama interracial movement suffered from hesitancy and disunity. Edmonds represented the handful who believed it was necessary to cooperate with the ILD. Others would not consider such a move and insisted instead that the Interracial Commission take up cudgels against all Communists and their followers in the state.[28] The great majority thought that the Commission should only work to see that the boys received a "fair trial." Under no circumstances should the organization commit itself on the question of whether or not the Scottsboro boys were guilty.[29]

There was little likelihood that moderate Alabamians could work with other groups because they seemed as adamantly opposed to "outside interference" as the most reactionary racists. "There has been a vicious agitation against the people of Alabama since the first trial at Scottsboro," declared the Interracial Commission's field secretary in May of 1933. "Outsiders" had grossly misrepresented many elements in the state.[30] The criticism against Alabama "wearied the liberals of this State," said John Temple Graves. They had concluded it would "be better after all to con-

---

[27] *Ibid.;* New York *Times,* March 27, 1933, p. 2; Birmingham *News,* March 27, 1933; Lawrence Gellert, "Report on the Birmingham Scottsboro Rally," March 26, 1933, in ILD Papers.

[28] Henry M. Edmonds to Robert Burns Eleazer, May 11, 1933; William G. McDowell to Will W. Alexander, June 30, 1933, in Interracial Commission Papers.

[29] Jesse B. Hearin to James D. Burton, September 12, 1933, in Interracial Commission Papers.

[30] James D. Burton, "Scottsboro and White Justice," *Christian Century,* L (1933), 717.

fide their unpleasant truth-telling about their State to their home folks." The defensiveness of Southern liberals to the opinions of "outsiders" muted the Southerners' criticism and made them unwilling to admit openly what they all acknowledged among themselves.[31]

Moreover, the timid liberalism expressed by a handful of Alabamians was more than offset by a stiffened resolve on the part of the conservatives. "Each and every individual of high ideals and high morals in Alabama is depending on you to see that the penalty as set by the jury is carried out to the fullest extent," a Birmingham man wrote Governor Miller. The jury at Decatur had not been swayed by the "ravings of Mongrel races of people, negroes, Communists and all the outcast of different countries. . . ." He hoped the Governor would stand equally firm.[32]

The hardening of attitudes could be seen in the editorials of the Huntsville *Times*. The sight of Ruby, a home-town girl, "flanked by a Negro communist" traveling around the country was too much for the sensibilities of the Huntsville newspaper. "That sterling moral crusader and witness extraordinary" was on a platform in the East bringing news of "uplift and light and sweetness," reported the *Times* sarcastically. "Now that she has become Harlem's darling, set foot in the White House and addressed the speakers of Congress, there is but one wall Ruby has to scale to make her 'triumphs' complete." That would be to invade the social realms of Fifth Avenue's parlor pinks and "tell her story of oppression by the 'ruling classes' of the South." Then "on to a vaudeville engagement, where the emoluments should be more lucrative than working in a cotton mill, riding a boxcar as a hobo, or pursuing her avocation as a 'lady of leisure.' " Apparently, "being a 'martyr' to the 'cause' of the 'Scottsboro boys' is more profitable than plying the trade she once did in Huntsville." The *Times*

[31] New York *Times*, July 8, 1934, IV, 7. For a particularly pronounced example of gilding the lily for "outsiders," see Robert Burns Eleazer to George E. Haynes, April 11, 1933, in Interracial Commission Papers.

[32] Will M. Park to Governor Benjamin Meeks Miller, April 10, 1933. See also letters by Floyd Weldon, Thomas H. Henderson, and J. C. Porter to Governor Benjamin Meeks Miller, April 10, 1933, in Alabama Scottsboro Files.

called on Attorney General Thomas Knight to institute perjury proceedings against the "former Huntsville gutter snipe." [33]

There was nothing about the Decatur trial which changed attitudes at Scottsboro. A resident of the city insisted there was "no doubt" of the defendants' guilt among "those who are here and know the facts in the case." All of the Negroes were "vicious fellows," he said, who had "forfeited their rights to live under our law." He explained to Northerners that "we have in the South a situation that those outside cannot possibly understand." Southerners alone had to work out the race problem since "outside interference proves a great hindrance. It encourages insurrections and mob violence." [34]

Decatur's ministers—presumably representing the more moderate element in the town—adopted a unanimous resolution which attacked those who had unfairly "maligned, blackened and falsified" the reputation of the city and county. The pastors of the major Baptist, Methodist, and Presbyterian churches in the city declared that "during the trial, there was no disorder, or mob violence, that no mobs formed, or were disbanded by the National Guards." And they insisted that the jury so unfairly attacked by Leibowitz was composed of "respected and prominent citizens of the county with a high degree of intelligence; clean, moral, honest gentlemen . . . [who] would compare favorably with any jury selected in any section of the country." The Decatur ministers closed their resolution by insisting that there was "no racial strife in the county," nor was there any ill will toward the Negro. The white people of the area were "the friend of the colored race, and the negro recognizes the white man as his friend and helper." [35]

Alabamians reflected their resentment in more tangible ways than resolutions. The trial at Decatur had not ended before charges were openly circulated that Dr. Edmonds, Rabbi Goldstein, and Dr. Barnhart were in the pay of the ILD.[36] Barnhart had been under fire since he began teaching at Birmingham-

[33] Huntsville *Times*, April 19, May 7, May 9, 1933.
[34] Letter by I. J. Browder in *New Republic*, LXXVII (1934), 366–67.
[35] Decatur *Daily*, May 11, 1933.
[36] See letter by G. H. Lively in Birmingham *Post*, April 10, 1933.

Southern. During his first year, President Guy Snavely forced the professor to change textbooks in sociology because one of the ministerial students objected to a chapter on evolution.[37] The young professor of sociology was one of the few Birmingham-Southern faculty members who had published in his field, but college officials were appalled when he encouraged students to go into Birmingham's Negro districts and make firsthand observations concerning the general social conditions. Inevitably his writings on such subjects as prostitution, Negro housing, and general social welfare led to charges that he was a "nigger lover" and advocated "Communism and evolution." His open involvement in the Scottsboro case was more than the college would tolerate. In spite of the fact that his classes were among the most popular on campus, President Snavely announced that Barnhart would not be retained by Birmingham-Southern for the academic year, 1933–34. Although Snavely insisted that he had given Barnhart his notice on February 20, the decision was not made public until Barnhart defied the wishes of the school administration and appeared at the March 26 rally for the Scottsboro boys. Barnhart fought the dismissal before the Birmingham-Southern trustees and when they upheld Snavely's decision, he took his case to the American Association of University Professors. The AAUP refused to take his case. It acknowledged that his liberal views on social questions were a contributory cause, but it found the basic reason for his dismissal was the "financial stringency" caused by the Depression.[38]

Rabbi Benjamin Goldstein of Montgomery's Temple Beth Or also came under attack. In 1931 he had been convinced that the Scottsboro boys were victims of race prejudice, and he bluntly stated his views to Temple Beth Or and all who would listen. When his congregation learned that he planned to attend the Birmingham rally for the Scottsboro boys, it urged him to stay away. Although the Temple reluctantly acquiesced in his defiance,

[37] President Snavely acknowledged that he had asked Barnhart to drop the text, but he insisted that Barnhart voluntarily agreed to the change. Birmingham *News,* March 26, 1933.

[38] Birmingham *News,* March 26, 1933; Birmingham *Post,* March 27, May 27, 1933; Norfolk *Journal and Guide,* April 1, 1933.

Wade Wright's speech at Decatur forced the group to take sterner measures. The threatened revival of anti-Semitism shocked and dismayed Alabama's Jewish community, noted Charles N. Fiedelson, associate editorial writer for the Birmingham *Age-Herald*. Fiedelson, former secretary of the Young Men's Hebrew Association in Birmingham, was dismayed to learn that many people in the Decatur area "took for granted that a Jew was a Communist or at least in secret sympathy with the reds. . . ." As a result of these suspicions, Jews in Alabama leaned over backwards to show they were not sympathetic with the ILD, said Fiedelson.[39] On April 10, the day after Haywood Patterson's conviction, the president of Temple Beth Or presented Rabbi Goldstein with an ultimatum: sever all connection with the Scottsboro Case or resign. He agreed to resign.[40]

Goldstein had planned to stay in Alabama through the summer. In early May, however, he began receiving a steady stream of threatening telephone calls. And in a stormy conference, Montgomery Mayor William A. Gunter bluntly accused the young Rabbi of being a Southern agent for the ILD. Gunter referred Goldstein's attention to the city's new "criminal anarchy" ordinance. It had been designed to forestall the interference of such radical agitation, he noted pointedly. In late May, Goldstein moved to New York City with the bitter observation that anyone "who tries to take an impartial attitude towards the conduct of the Scottsboro case is immediately branded a communist and a nigger-lover." [41]

[39] New York *Daily Worker*, December 4, 1933. Novelist John Spivak interviewed Fiedelson for the *Daily Worker*.

[40] New York *Times*, April 10, 1933, p. 11. Several members of the congregation told a reporter for the *Montgomery Advertiser* that they privately agreed with Goldstein. But his outspoken statements created an "open threat to the welfare of the congregation." Montgomery *Advertiser*, May 28, 1933.

[41] Mayor Gunter tersely denied threatening Goldstein. Montgomery *Advertiser*, May 27, 1933; New York *World Telegram*, August 19, 1933. The Montgomery City Commission's criminal anarchy ordinance, adopted three days before the Gunter-Goldstein meeting, prohibited the dissemination of the "subversive doctrines" of criminal anarchy by "word, sign, or writing." It defined criminal anarchy as the "teaching of a doctrine advocating the overthrow of organized government," not the violent overthrow, but simply the overthrow of "organized government." Montgomery *Advertiser*, May 11, 1933.

Other Alabamians felt the wrath of hostile public opinion. During the trials at Decatur, a Negro teacher in a Hale County training school circulated a petition among his students asking the release of the Scottsboro boys. Trustees of the Black Belt school, the principal, and the white county superintendent of education reprimanded L. O. Harper and ordered him to stop all activities on behalf of the Scottsboro defendants. That fall he was not rehired.[42] The Reverend W. C. Crutcher, a Scottsboro Negro minister, had worked with ILD attorney George Chamlee in drawing up a list of Jackson County Negroes who qualified for jury duty. On April 6 he wrote the editor of the *Jackson County Sentinel* to explain a decision he had reached. He noted that he had received considerable criticism for his activities. "I am writing to assure you, and through you the people of Jackson County of both races, that I have not meddled in any way in these cases." He acknowledged that he had signed affidavits for Chamlee, but he retracted his naming of local Negroes as qualified jurors. He had decided, he said, that he did "not know what it takes to make a qualified juror." Crutcher promised he would take no part in such affairs in the future.[43]

Retribution was not limited to Alabama's Negroes or white newcomers. Mrs. Craik Speed was the granddaughter of the founder of Montgomery's First National Bank, a member of the Daughters of the American Revolution and the Colonial Dames. Her ancestors had included some of Alabama's most distinguished doctors, lawyers, jurists, and planters. As a follower of Norman Thomas, she had always been considered somewhat eccentric, but Mrs. Speed was a member of a distinguished Black Belt family, and citizens of Montgomery genially tolerated her intellectual aberrations. In 1931, however, she became interested in the Scottsboro Case, and—with the encouragement of her twenty-one-year-old daughter, Jane—she began reading all she could find on the case. At first she was confident that the "good people" of Alabama

---

[42] *Crisis*, XL (1933), 233.

[43] Letter of Reverend W. C. Crutcher in Scottsboro *Jackson County Sentinel*, April 6, 1933.

would come to the aid of the boys. Instead, she said, many of the city's best citizens readily acknowledged that the Scottsboro boys might be innocent, but insisted: "If we let Negroes get by with this case, no white woman will be safe in the South." In 1933 she and her daughter openly endorsed the activities of the International Labor Defense. When Jane addressed a May Day "united front" meeting in Birmingham, she was arrested, fined fifty dollars, and given a one-hundred-day sentence for disorderly conduct, speaking without a permit, blocking the sidewalks, and "addressing a meeting at which there were no physical barriers erected between white and Negro auditors." Rather than pay the fine, Miss Speed insisted on going to jail. In Montgomery, police placed Mrs. Speed's home under surveillance and friends completely ostracized her. When Jane was released after serving fifty-three days, she and her mother left the state and moved, as Mrs. Speed said, into exile.[44]

The fate of Rabbi Goldstein, Dr. Barnhart, and Mrs. Speed was ample evidence that there was a limit to the tolerance of Alabamians. Gradually the state's moderates settled into a position neither affirming nor denying the guilt of the Scottsboro boys. Instead, they talked vaguely about the mitigating circumstances of the case. Most Alabamians realized that Victoria Price and Ruby Bates were of "questionable character," said one Huntsville resident. They did not want to see the nine boys electrocuted; "the average Southerner is not bloodthirsty." [45] "Enlightened Alabamians . . . want with all their hearts to be fair," said John Temple Graves. While they believed the death penalty for rape was a "social necessity in the South," they were by no means "certain of guilt in this instance. . . ." The circumstances, he said, seemed to call for "executive modification of the sentence." [46]

[44] Montgomery *Advertiser,* May 5, May 19, May 20, May 26, 1933; New York *World Telegram,* August 19, 1933.

[45] Letter of Orville Fanning in New York *Times,* March 18, 1934, IV, 6. Alfred Truitt, President of Atlanta's Truitt Coal and Iron Company, suggested to Governor Miller that he commute the sentence to life imprisonment since that would be as good an object lesson for the "darkies" as electrocution. Alfred Truitt to Governor Benjamin Meeks Miller, April 12, 1933 in Alabama Scottsboro Files.

[46] Birmingham *Age-Herald,* April 14, 1933.

Thus life imprisonment became the goal of "moderate" and "enlightened" Alabamians; this was an acceptable compromise. As the Birmingham *News* observed on the eve of Haywood Patterson's second trial, "The matter is something about which . . . no one, perhaps, should venture to feel absolutely certain." Many persons had expressed doubts about the defendants' guilt. "Possibly the same persons could be helped to a better feeling about it if the governor should grant a commutation of the death sentence to life imprisonment." And after the trial had ended, the Birmingham *Age-Herald* declared: "Without being so cocksure about the matter, as observers at a greater distance have been, it appears to this paper that a more moderate finding would have been the just and rational conclusion in view of the contradictions in the testimony." When in doubt about a white man's guilt, the jury acquits or is deadlocked, said the Birmingham *Reporter*. But if it is " 'just a nigger' " life imprisonment is a safe middle ground.[47]

In defense against the attacks of outsiders, Alabama moderates hailed Judge Horton as "proof that our courts are not ravenous agencies of injustice to the Negro." The judge came out of the Patterson case with deserved admiration. Those interested in "lofty human achievement should see to it that Judge Horton's conduct is duly recognized as a sterling example of the heights to which a fine and sincere jurist can rise in the midst of extraordinarily trying circumstances," said the Birmingham *News*. The city's afternoon *Post* suggested his name for the next opening on the Alabama Supreme Court Bench. Praise also came from outside the state. The Presbytery of New York officially condemned the verdict, but it praised the fairness of the presiding judge. Judge Horton made "every effort to see that the accused was given a fair trial," said the New York *Herald Tribune*. He had emphatically repressed any hint of mob violence, his charge to the jury was "eminently fair in dealing with the evidence," and his appeal to

[47] Birmingham *News*, March 26, 1933; Birmingham *Age-Herald*, April 18, 1933; Birmingham *Reporter*, April 15, 1933.

put aside prejudice "reflected honor upon the standards of the Alabama bench." [48]

Others had misgivings. John Hammond, who covered the trials for *The Nation,* found Judge Horton "courteous, generous and scrupulous . . . an admirable presiding officer." But on the other hand, after admitting the ILD had proved systematic exclusion of Negroes from the jury, the judge had denied the motion to quash the indictment. And he failed to end the trial when Wright made his appeal to bigotry and fear.[49] Regardless of the warning to the mob and summation to the jury, said one Negro newspaper, "if Judge Horton is fair, then the definition of the term has been radically altered and changed." [50]

Plaudits for the Alabama jurist incensed the editors of the *Daily Worker.* "To exalt the 'fairness' of the judge is nothing more nor less than an insidious blow against the campaign of world protest. . . ." Those who approved Horton became, "unwittingly or not, part and parcel of the lynching machinery which gapes for the bodies of the nine Scottsboro boys." [51] The judge was the "official lyncher for the Scottsboro bourbons, dressed in sheep's clothing to hide the fangs of lynch justice." [52] As ILD attorney Joseph Brodsky explained: "Judge Horton . . . is fair according to his lights, but those lights are the lights of a 'Southern gentleman,' which means that he accepts and takes for granted the class position of the Negroes, [and] the necessity of white supremacy in the South. . . ."

[48] Birmingham *Age-Herald,* April 18, 1933; Birmingham *News,* April 9, 1933; Birmingham *Post,* April 10, 1933; New York *Herald Tribune,* April 11, 1933. The New York *Times* commended Horton as a judge who "bore himself with impartiality," and the Rochester *Times-Union* called his conduct "the sole consolation the white race can draw from this depressing drama." New York *Times,* April 11, 1933, p. 11; Rochester *Times-Union,* April 11, 1933.

[49] Hammond, "South Speaks," 466. Judge Horton was restricted in his actions in this area, however, since the Alabama Supreme Court has traditionally allowed the prosecution wide latitude in trial summations. The prejudice invoked must be so great as to be "ineradicable" by a statement from the bench. Thomas L. Smith, Jr., "Improper Arguments of Counsel—Appeals to Bias and Prejudice," *Alabama Law Review,* VI (1954), 309–11.

[50] Richmond *Planet,* April 22, 1933.

[51] New York *Daily Worker,* April 19, 1933.

[52] James S. Allen, "The Scottsboro Struggle," *The Communist,* XII (1933), 437.

The very gentleness and kindness of the man made him far more "objectively vicious" than the "blithering fool Wright." He was " 'democratic' and 'decent,' but he has a water-tight compartment in his brain and can't see that this is merely language that covers the worst and most vicious type of unfairness." Those who were aware of the nature of the class struggle should never be blinded by such democratic verbiage.[53]

Throughout the praise and criticism, Judge Horton remained silent at his Athens, Alabama, home. Although he had never publicly expressed any opinion, the decision of the jury was a keen disappointment. A verdict of not guilty would have had a tremendous effect on public opinion, he felt, much more so than reversal by any upper court. Throughout April and May he quietly communicated with state officials concerning the future of the case. Although he knew there was little likelihood the state would agree, he proposed to Attorney General Knight that the state *nol pros* the remainder of the proceedings and then pardon Haywood Patterson. Somewhat to his surprise, the attorney general agreed to consider the suggestion, but ultimately decided against it. "I think he knew it would be political suicide," Horton said later. It was no secret that Knight hoped to sit in the governor's chair in Montgomery.[54] The obvious reluctance of Horton to approve the jury's decision alarmed and disturbed Knight. Late in May an intermediary approached the judge with some suggestions from the attorney general's office. He explained to Horton that the state had committed itself to the prosecution of the defendants; any withdrawal at that late date would be a tacit admission that the Communists were right all along. And he noted pointedly that if Horton annulled the jury's verdict he would have little chance of gaining re-election in 1934. As Horton later recalled, he looked at his visitor with a half-smile and asked: "What does that have to do with the case?" The emissary laughed and replied, "I told 'em

[53] New York *Daily Worker*, April 15, 1933.

[54] Interview with former Judge James Edwin Horton, Jr., April 9, 1966; James Edwin Horton, Jr., to Author, September 28, 1967. According to political friends, Knight planned to run for the lieutenant-governorship in 1934 and the governorship in 1938. New York *Times*, January 14, 1934, IV, 1, 6.

you'd say that." That was the last communication the judge received from Montgomery.[55]

On June 22, 1933, Judge Horton convened court in his hometown, Athens, to hear a defense motion for a new trial. Although Chamlee and Osmund K. Fraenkel, a constitutional lawyer, were present for the ILD, they regarded the hearing as simply the first hurdle on the way to the United States Supreme Court. Instead of hearing arguments, however, Horton took his seat and, without any opening remarks, began reading. "Social order is based on law," he said, "and its perpetuity on its fair and impartial administration." The victim of deliberate injustice died quickly, and his suffering ceased, "but the teachings of Christianity and the uniform lessons of all history illustrate without exception that its perpetrators not only pay the penalty themselves, but their children through endless generations." In a style reminiscent of early nineteenth century jurists, Horton explained that the Court had "endeavored with the wisdom . . . [of] the most pure and enlightened judges who have ornamented the Courts of its own state as well as the distinguished jurists of this country and its Mother England." The law wisely recognized that "passions, prejudices, and sympathies" affected the decisions of juries in such cases. But as a judge, he had but one question to ask of himself: "Is there sufficient credible evidence upon which to base a verdict?" [56] The Associated Press reporter glanced at the counsel for the defense and for the state. Knight was listening tensely with mounting color, while Chamlee and Fraenkel had suddenly broken into hopeful smiles.[57]

In great detail, Horton reviewed Victoria's story of the assaults.

[55] Interview with former Judge James Edwin Horton, Jr., April 9, 1966.

[56] *The Scottsboro Case: Opinion of Judge James E. Horton* (New York: Scottsboro Defense Committee, 1936), 7–8. The official text of Horton's opinion may be found in "Alabama vs. Patterson, April 3–9, 1933, Transcript of Testimony." Although the reprint of the Scottsboro Defense Committee omits a few of the legal precedents Horton cited, it is accurate and far more readily accessible. For this reason, it has been cited rather than the original text. The Scottsboro Defense Committee pamphlet was also printed as appendix five in Patterson and Conrad, *Scottsboro Boy*, 260–78.

[57] New York *Times*, June 23, 1933, p. 11.

If her account were true, as the state contended, there were many possible areas of corroboration. He listed eight. Seven boys were on the gondola at the beginning of the fight and Orville Gilley saw the entire rape, according to Mrs. Price. She stated at the Scottsboro and Decatur trials that one of the defendants cut her head with the butt of a pistol. Third, her back was supposedly lacerated by jagged chert. Fourth, one would logically expect to find semen in the vagina in large quantities and its drying and starchy appearance in the pubic hair would be readily apparent to the trained observer. Further corroboration could be gained from the fact that Mrs. Price's vagina supposedly bled from the abuse of the six defendants. Sixth, the semen would surely have appeared with "increasing evidence on the pants of the rapists as each wallowed in its spreading ooze." Seventh, one would expect to find live spermatozoa in the vagina from the recent discharges. And finally, there would be two doctors to testify to the wretched mental condition of the two girls, and their dilated pupils, fast respiration, and rapid pulse.

One by one he analyzed these points. None of the boys took the stand, he noted, except for Lester Carter, who directly contradicted the state's chief witness. Although Mrs. Price insisted that she had been forced into submission by a blow on the head, Dr. Bridges had made a careful examination and found no cuts. Nor did Mrs. Price complain of any blow on the scalp at the time. The same thing could be said for her over-all physical condition. There were a few blue spots and one scratch. But this would be expected from a woman who had been riding cross-country on freight cars. Certainly "vastly greater physical signs would have been expected from the forcible intercourse of six men under such circumstances."

Judge Horton went into great detail concerning the condition of Mrs. Price's pubic area. She had testified that "as the Negroes had repeated intercourse with her she became wetter and wetter around her private parts; that they finished just as they entered Paint Rock, and that she was taken in an automobile to the doctor's office." Dr. Bridges testified that he had carefully looked for semen around her private parts, and he and Dr. Lynch found areas about her upper thighs which appeared to be semen. But these areas were infiltrated with the kind of dust one would gain from prolonged riding of a train and were completely dry. The emission of fresh semen would have had a tendency to wash off any dirty areas around the vagina, observed Horton. And it would have remained there for some considerable period of time before it became so heavily encrusted with dirt and coal dust. Moreover, Horton pointed out, the same doctor had testified that he had great difficulty finding enough semen to make a slide. And once the doctor examined it under the microscope he found that it was non-motile despite the fact that it supposedly had been deposited less than ninety minutes before. The judge concluded:

When we consider, as the facts hereafter detailed will show, that this woman had slept side by side with a man the night before in Chattanooga and had intercourse at Huntsville with [Jack] Tiller on the night before she went to Chattanooga; when we further take into consideration that the semen being emitted, if her testimony were true, was covering the area surrounding the private parts, the conclusion becomes clear and clearer that this woman was not forced into intercourse with all of these negroes upon that train, but that her condition was clearly due to the intercourse that she had had on the nights previous to this time.

Within the courtroom, there was no longer any question concerning the decision Horton had reached. Chamlee and Fraenkel relaxed and leaned back in their chairs, but Judge Horton continued, for he wanted his decision to be more than adequate for a reversal. He hoped that by proving Patterson's innocence as conclusively as possible with human logic, he would end the controversy over the cases which had brought shame and disrepute upon the state he loved. In the same low, steady voice, he continued commenting on the question of corroboration. Although the boys were arrested within minutes after the alleged acts, not one arresting official testified that their clothes were wet or damp. Ora Dobbins, Lee Adams, and W. W. Hill, who testified for the state, were either confused and contradictory or their testimony added little weight to the prosecution's case. Thus the testimony of most of the state's witnesses "corroborates Victoria Price slightly, if at all. . . ." And her account of her mental and physical condition varied so completely from that of the doctors "it has been impossible for the Court to reconcile their evidence with hers."

Since her story was not corroborated by the physical evidence or the affirmation of other witnesses, Judge Horton examined the state's case from the viewpoint of reasonableness and probability. Rape, he noted, was a crime usually committed in secrecy. But March 25, 1931, was bright and clear; the hour was noon and the gondola where the offense allegedly took place was filled to within eighteen inches of the top. If Victoria Price were to be believed, on top of this chert in plain sight, twelve Negroes attacked and undressed two white women, held them on the gravel and then successively had forcible intercourse with each. And this took place without interruption although the train traveled through the heart of Jackson County, through Fackler, Hollywood, Scottsboro, Larkinsville, Limn Rock, and Woodville. Finally, by a "fortuitous circumstance" just before the train pulled into Paint Rock, "the rapists cease and just in the nick of time the overalls are drawn up and fastened and the women appear clothed as the posse sight them." The natural inclination of any thinking person would be to doubt such a story, said Horton. And particularly when it was based entirely upon a witness who "refused to answer pertinent questions" or responded with contradictory and evasive replies. "The gravity of the offense and the importance of her testimony demanded candor and sincerity." Instead, she had "knowingly testified falsely in many material aspects of the case."

Horton noted that many observers had questioned Lester Carter's story. But, he declared, in many cases the facts and circumstances tended strongly to corroborate Carter rather than the state's chief witness. If the state really believed Victoria and Jack Tiller had not engaged in sexual intercourse on the night of May 23 and the morning of May 24, why was Tiller not summoned from the anteroom to testify for the state? And why, he asked rhetorically, had the so-called Mrs. Brochie never been summoned by the prosecution?

As to the credibility and reliability of Mrs. Price, Horton enumerated a number of points on which she was clearly and undeniably erroneous. Apart from the fact that Olen Montgomery had less than 10 per cent vision in one eye, there was ample evidence to suggest that he knew nothing about a fight, let alone a rape. He testified at Scottsboro and at Decatur that he was on an oil tank car seven cars from the caboose, and a trainman testified that one of the Negroes was taken from an oil-tank near the rear of the train. Willie Roberson was so diseased with syphilis that he walked with a cane. And yet Mrs. Price insisted that both of these defendants had leaped from a box car over her head and into a gondola where they fought several boys and then raped her. "The facts strongly contradict any such statement."

Judge Horton concluded his decision: "History, sacred and profane, and the common experience of mankind teach us that women of the character shown in this case are prone for selfish reasons to make false accusations both of rape and of insult upon the slightest provocation or even without provocation for ulterior purposes." There was ample evidence in the trial record alone, he said, to indicate that both of the women were "pre-disposed to make false accusations upon any occasion whereby their selfish ends may be gained." The court, he said, would pursue the evidence no further. The testimony of Victoria Price was not only uncorroborated, but it was also improbable and contradicted by evidence which "greatly preponderates in favor of the defendant." It was therefore ordered by the court that the motion of the defense be granted, the judgment of the jury set aside, and a new trial ordered.

Judge Horton had hoped his decision would effectively end the prosecution of the Scottsboro cases, but Attorney General Knight had no intention of quitting. As soon as court adjourned, he announced in a voice trembling with anger that the state would retry Patterson as soon as possible. Fortunately, he had a trump card which he had held back for just such a contingency. The next day he issued a press release from his Montgomery office in which he announced that Orville Gilley had returned to Alabama and voluntarily agreed to testify for the state. Gilley, he said, had submitted an affidavit corroborating in every detail the testimony of Victoria Price as to the rapes. Knight explained that the state had failed to call him at Decatur because he was hoboing somewhere through California and was unavailable.[58]

It was apparent that the fight to end the trials was far from over, and yet there were encouraging signs. The Birmingham *Post* praised Horton for showing that "political considerations mean nothing to him whatever." The *Post* also endorsed his opinion that the boys were innocent. Episcopal Bishop William G. McDowell was heartened by conversations he had with people following the decision. Public opinion, he said, had been "very definitely changed by the carefully pronounced judgment of Judge Horton. . . ." Unless the state could find "unimpeachable" evidence, "it is useless for juries to go on trying the boys on the old evidence, as verdicts would be successfully appealed." McDowell was pleasantly surprised to learn that Leo Oberdorfer, incoming president of the Alabama Bar Association, expressed a willingness to sign a statement with other prominent Alabamians supporting Horton's stand. In a burst of optimism, John Temple Graves declared the day after the decision that all "over the state his praises are being sung." [59]

Undoubtedly the opinion changed the minds of a handful of Alabamians such as Graves, who became fully convinced for the first time that the boys were innocent. The praise which Graves described was muted, however, and more than outweighed by criticism. The Huntsville *Builder* declared that the granting of a new trial did not come as a surprise to the citizens of the Tennessee Valley who had watched as Horton "wilted under fire." The defendant had been found guilty by twelve reputable citizens in

[58] *Ibid.*; Montgomery *Advertiser*, June 24, 1933.
[59] Birmingham *Post*, June 24, 1933; William G. McDowell to Will W. Alexander, July 27, 1933, in Interracial Commission Papers; Birmingham *Age-Herald*, June 23, 1933.

Scottsboro and again in Decatur. Such kowtowing to outside agitators was therefore inexcusable said the *Builder*. The Lafayette *Sun* attacked the decision as a "shocking surprise" which could easily have been avoided by excluding any of the testimony of Ruby Bates and Lester Carter.[60]

William Mosely of Decatur charged that Horton had turned the courtroom into a circus, "allowing that Jew lawyer who represented the defendants to say and do what he pleased." Mosely recalled that Leibowitz had ordered Knight to refer to a Negro witness as "Mr." Suppose, he said, that "you, Mr. Editor, had been in the place of the attorney general—would you then be willing to reiterate that Judge Horton is 'the brave and veteran judge whose behavior . . . won the praise of all thoughtful observers?' " It was obvious to those who lived in Decatur, Mosely continued, that Horton "was lacking in courage and that he was seeking notoriety. . . ." While his "political ability is well recognized, he had no more backbone than in an angle worm." George W. Read of Ensley, Alabama, described Horton's opinion as "worse than the action of the mob." Horton had set himself as a "judge superior to the Supreme Court of his own state, and again by implication accused all who had anything to do with the conviction of these negroes of being too ignorant to know what they were doing." And former Alabama Senator Thomas J. Heflin wired Attorney General Knight to share the "keen resentment that you feel over the strange and annoying action of Judge Horton. . . ." Heflin offered to assist Knight in any way necessary to remove Horton from the case. "This dallying about with the Scottsboro rapists is a humiliating insult to the white race in Alabama and the very worst thing that could happen to the law-abiding negroes of this state," said Heflin. It was "putting wicked thoughts in the minds

---

[60] Huntsville *Builder* and Lafayette *Sun*, quoted in Monroe N. Work (ed.), *Negro Year Book: An Annual Encyclopedia of the Negro, 1937–1938* (Tuskegee, Alabama: Negro Year Book Publishing Co., 1937), 115–16. In part the moderates' inability to gain support for Judge Horton could be attributed to the fact that his opinion was deemed "unprintable" by the Alabama press. Birmingham *Post*, June 23, 1933.

of lawless negro men and greatly increasing the danger to the white women of Alabama." [61]

The groundswell of opinion to back Horton never materialized. With the exception of the *Post*, the state's major newspapers were hostile or remained silent as state officials made it clear they planned to continue with the prosecution of the Scottsboro defendants.[62] In mid-October Will W. Alexander learned through confidential sources that Attorney General Knight had brought pressure on Chief Justice Anderson to have Horton removed from the case. Alexander hurried to Montgomery in an attempt to forestall replacement of Judge Horton and to bring about a postponement so that some sort of agreement might be worked out with the state.[63] When he arrived in Alabama, however, he found the situation worse than he had feared in his most pessimistic moments. Anderson, he discovered, had already been persuaded by Knight to write Judge Horton asking him to withdraw voluntarily from the case; reluctantly, Horton had acquiesced. State officials were intent on seeing that the "honor" of Alabama be upheld by conviction of the Scottsboro boys. In vain, Alexander tried to mobilize support for Horton, but the June "songs of praise" had evaporated under the heat of angry popular opinion. On the afternoon of October 20, the head of the Interracial Commission learned that the decision was final. The cases would be removed from under the jurisdiction of Horton and tried by Judge William Washington Callahan, the second judge of the district. The trials would begin in late November. Alexander had expected nothing from the political leaders with whom he talked. Their job was to gain re-election. But even though he would not waste his time in lambasting and criticizing the church, he told a friend, he was

[61] Letter of William Mosely in Birmingham *Age-Herald*, October 27, 1933; Letter of George W. Read in Birmingham *News*, October 12, 1933; Montgomery *Advertiser*, June 24, 1933.

[62] The Birmingham *Age-Herald* praised Horton for his courage, but it studiously avoided passing judgment on whether his decision was justified by the facts. Birmingham *Age-Herald*, June 23, 1933.

[63] It was no secret that Knight had insisted on having Horton removed. The attorney general began his efforts to have the judge removed as early as July 2, 1933. Montgomery *Advertiser*, July 3, 1933; Birmingham *Post*, October 21, 1933.

deeply hurt and angered by the refusal of most of Alabama's religious leaders to look "into the face of justice." That night he went to his room, he said, "with a deep sense of human helplessness and limitation." [64]

In the May, 1934, primary, James Edwin Horton, who had had no opposition in the 1928 election, ran second in a field of three candidates. In Morgan County his two opponents amassed 80 per cent of the votes.[65] A friend of Judge Horton reported that he traveled through much of Morgan County without finding anyone who would admit his support for the "Scottsboro Judge." [66] Although he campaigned vigorously over the district, Horton lost in the run-off, 9,416 to 6,856. While Judge Horton's constituents returned him to private life, the people of Alabama elected Thomas J. Knight as the state's lieutenant governor. As a candidate from the Black Belt, he was not expected to run well in the upper part of the state, but in Morgan County he handily defeated a strong opponent.[67]

Rejected by the district's electorate, Horton retired from active politics and devoted all his time to a busy law practice and to the Horton plantation. Thirty-two years after the trial he insisted he had no regrets. There was a hundred-year tradition in the Horton family, he said, a tradition best expressed in the Latin phrase he had learned as a child: *fiat justitia ruat coelum*—let justice be done though the heavens may fall.[68]

[64] Will W. Alexander to William G. McDowell, October 23, 1933, in Interracial Commission Papers.

[65] Decatur *Daily*, May 2, 1934.

[66] Interview with former Judge James Edwin Horton, Jr. April 9, 1966. Horton had decided to retire without even running because of the opposition to his decision. But on December 28, 1933, the bar of his home town, Athens, Alabama, released a statement commending him as a "judge of unimpeachable character and integrity" and urging him to place his name before the people. Birmingham *Age-Herald*, December 30, 1933.

[67] Decatur *Daily*, May 2, June 13, 1934. Knight's statewide margin over his opponent was 152,780 to 119,563. *Alabama Official and Statistical Register, 1935* (Wetumpka: Wetumpka Printing Company, 1936), 577.

[68] Interview with James Edwin Horton, Jr., April 9, 1966.

IX

A COLD HARD
VENGEANCE

JUDGE William Washington Callahan was born on a Lawrence County farm and, unlike Horton, had none of the advantages of college instruction. His early education came from reading books daily in his father's hayloft. Later, as a clerk in a local law office, he studied Coke and Blackstone and was admitted to the bar in 1886. Callahan enjoyed a reputation as a local humorist with his homely little sayings. And despite his lack of academic training, he was regarded by citizens of the district as a strong-willed character with plenty of "common sense." [1] Angered by the latitude which Horton allowed defense attorneys in April, the people of the area looked to Callahan to stand up for Alabama. "I venture the prediction that when the trial is had that it will be tried right . . . ," a friend of Callahan's declared. As long as this judge sat on the bench, "a circus will not be made of the courtroom, and . . . the people of Morgan County will not be humiliated by thinking that their Circuit Court has been made a political forum." [2] At seventy years of age, said one reporter, Callahan looked "the way a Hollywood producer thinks a Southern judge should look." Broad-shouldered and stocky, he had a habit of adjusting his silver-rimmed spectacles and then running his fingers

---

[1] *Alabama Official and Statistical Register, 1935*, pp. 109–10; New York *Herald Tribune*, November 27, 1933.

[2] Letter of William Mosely, in Birmingham *Age-Herald*, October 27, 1933.

through his thinning silver hair so that it stood up straight. Haywood Patterson, admittedly somewhat prejudiced, described him as the "toughest, most freckle-faced baldheaded man I was ever up against." [3]

Many Alabamians who dealt with Callahan found him stubborn, obstinate, and inordinately concerned with his own importance. More succinctly, a Birmingham newspaperman privately described him as a "perfect ass." His friends, however, insisted he was a jurist of unimpeachable integrity. Unquestionably, he had very fixed ideas about how the trials should be conducted. His primary goal was, as he put it, to "debunk the Scottsboro case." He told his friends that he felt that entirely too much had been made of the case. He hoped to dissipate the publicity surrounding the proceedings by barring all photographers and by making conditions as uncomfortable as possible for the newsmen. Horton's extreme precautions during the spring trial annoyed Callahan. "I do not believe now and have never believed that soldiers were necessary in the trial of these Scottsboro negroes . . . ," he told Governor Miller. While he acknowledged that a few persons had made loose statements about lynching the boys, he could not "believe that the sober minded people of this county have any such feeling as that. . . ." [4]

Others removed from the scene did not share Callahan's confidence in the people of Morgan County. As ILD Attorney Chamlee noted somewhat sarcastically, Callahan and Knight might think troops were unnecessary, "but mobs do not advise the trial Judge or the Attorney General of their intentions." "Our recollection of secret indignation meetings and of reports of incipient mobs at Decatur and Huntsville in the last trial . . . leads us to believe . . . that Judge Callahan underestimates the seriousness of the situation," declared the Birmingham *Post*. Mobs showed a

[3] Hamilton Basso, "Five Days in Decatur," *New Republic*, LXXVII (1933), 162; Patterson and Conrad, *Scottsboro Boy*, 49.

[4] Birmingham *Post*, November 18, 1933; Charles N. Fiedelson to Robert Burns Eleazer, November 26, 1933, in Interracial Commission Papers; New York *Times*, November 23, 1933, p. 6; Judge William Washington Callahan to Governor Benjamin Meeks Miller, November 14, 1933, in Drawer 39, Alabama Executive Files.

"serpentine ability" to rise suddenly; "a Judge cannot wait until mob violence is upon him to provide protection for defendants in his court." Callahan, however, was hardly in a mood to listen to criticism from Birmingham newspapers. In the wake of his appointment, the *Post* had bluntly voiced concern that Knight had been allowed "to shop around for a judge who combined some of the qualities of a prosecutor with those of a jurist." Indirectly, the Birmingham *Age-Herald* had also disapproved of the appointment.[5] Stung by these criticisms, Callahan was intent on proving to his critics that he had gauged the situation accurately. A delegation of Alabama newspapermen convinced Governor Miller that a National Guard company should at least be held in readiness. When Callahan heard of the conference he called the governor's legal adviser and successfully opposed the move.[6]

Callahan's assurances were cold comfort in the light of developments in Alabama during the summer and fall of 1933. In June, ILD attorneys had gone to Tuscaloosa, home of the University of Alabama, to defend three Negroes charged with raping and killing a twenty-one-year-old woman. When word spread through the normally peaceful town that the "Communists had come to town," an angry mob formed near the courthouse. It took a National Guard unit carrying fixed bayonets and firing tear gas grenades to get the three lawyers out of town alive. Faced with the prospect of another Scottsboro Case, Tuscaloosa deputies took the three men out into a deserted section of the county and turned them over to a hastily arranged firing squad.[7]

[5] George W. Chamlee, Sr., to Governor Benjamin Meeks Miller, November 18, 1933, in Drawer 39, Alabama Executive Files; Birmingham *Post*, October 21, November 18, 1933; Birmingham *Age-Herald*, October 24, 1933.

[6] Charles N. Fiedelson to Robert Burns Eleazer, November 26, 1933, in Interracial Commission Papers. Although Attorney General Knight stayed out of the controversy, on a trip to Montgomery Will W. Alexander overheard him say that he did not want the "damn military" around at the trial adding to the state's expenses. Alexander suspected that Knight had bolstered Callahan's determination to avoid a show of military force. Will Alexander to Henry Edmonds, November 27, 1933, in Interracial Commission Papers.

[7] Unfortunately for the deputies, one of the three left for dead survived the barrage of bullets though he was badly wounded. The next morning he crawled to a nearby farmhouse and told of the shooting. In 1934, Tuscaloosa County authorities

When another even more brutal mob murder occurred in September, the National Committee for the Defense of Political Prisoners launched a full-scale public investigation.[8] Tuscaloosa County citizens reacted to the interference of the "outsiders" with frenzied rage. A "Citizens' Protective League," originally organized to bring "law and order" back to Tuscaloosa, became a large-scale vigilante organization devoted to repelling the "dastardly insults of the I.L.D." During the months of September and October, the League terrorized the Negro community with masked parades and threatening handbills. Relying on an elaborate system of reporting and spying, by their own count the "Communist hunters" made thirty-two raids on Negro homes and Negro meetings in an effort to uncover suspected ILD activities. Two grand juries called to investigate the mob murders declined to return indictments against the "unknown" assailants.[9]

Birmingham's newspapers excoriated the Tuscaloosa authorities, but the local *News* blamed the "disturbances" on the "International Labor Defense, spreading their poisoned communistic propaganda among our contented Negro population. . . ." While the Negroes might have been killed by mobs, "they were 'LYNCHED' by the communistic . . . International Labor Defense. . . ." Even more chilling was the response of the influential Montgomery *Advertiser*. The Black Belt daily agreed with the Tuscaloosa *News*. The victims' "bodies were riddled with bullets by hotheads who . . . fear[ed] that outside interference would block the course of justice. . . . But the maggoty beaks of the belled buzzards of the International Labor Defense are stained with the

---

released him on the condition that he never return to the county again. Southern Commission on the Study of Lynching, *The Plight of Tuscaloosa: A Case Study of Conditions in Tuscaloosa County, Alabama, 1933* (Atlanta, n.p., 1933) , 13, 18; Birmingham *Post*, August 2, 1933; Tuscaloosa *News*, August 2, 1933; Will Alexander to George Fort Milton, August 19, 1933, in Interracial Commission Papers.

[8] Details of the third mob murder read like a burlesqued version of an Erskine Caldwell novel. A mentally retarded white woman accused an elderly syphillitic cripple of raping her. Police dismissed the claim but seven white men seized the elderly Negro at his home and riddled his body with bullets. Southern Commission, *The Plight of Tuscaloosa*, 27.

[9] Tuscaloosa *News*, September 27, October 8, 1933; Southern Commission, *The Plight of Tuscaloosa*, 34–35.

blood of the three Negroes. . . ." As Episcopal Bishop William G. McDowell observed, the ILD's decision to defend accused Negro rapists was widely construed as an assault on the South's entire social structure. "Apparently the war is on." While there was little evidence of such mass hysteria in Decatur, Alexander became more and more alarmed at the possibility of mob violence during the upcoming trials. If a community as cultured and genteel as Tuscaloosa could take such a flight from sanity, he reasoned, why should one hope for anything better from Decatur? [10]

On November 18, two days before the opening of the new trials under Judge Callahan, reporters discovered that a pamphlet attacking the ILD was on sale in Decatur. Woodford Mabry, a Grove Hill, Alabama, attorney, denied that he was an advocate of the mob, "but when a lot of outside negroes and white people send lawyers into our State who set themselves up insolently and lawlessly to defeat the law and cheat justice, I believe then that within certain limitations the people who authorize court executions retain the power themselves to put down crime." When the legal forms proved inadequate the community had no alternative but to band together extra-legally and "exercise its inherent right to defend itself." [11]

State officials insisted Mabry's pamphlet was representative not of public opinion, but Morgan County Sheriff James F. Hawkins confidentially told the governor that, even though he planned to guard the ILD lawyers twenty-four hours a day, he had nightmares that "a wild fanatic might attempt to pot-shot Leibowitz. . . ." Leibowitz's phrase about "lantern-jawed morons" was burned in-

---

[10] Tuscaloosa *News*, August 14, 1933; Montgomery *Advertiser*, quoted in Ames, *Changing Character of Lynching*, 51; William G. McDowell to Will Alexander, August 2, 1933, in Association of Southern Women for the Prevention of Lynching Papers; Will W. Alexander to George Fort Milton, November 19, 1933, in Interracial Commission Papers.

[11] New York *Times*, November 19, 1933, II, 1; Woodford Mabry, *A Reply to Southern Slanders in re. the Negro Question, Lynch Law, &c.; Being an Invitation to the International Labor Defense and all other Associations Advocating Political Equality to Get out of and to Remain away from the State of Alabama* (Grove Hill, Ala.: n.p., 1933), 41.

delibly into the consciousness of the people of Morgan County and the surrounding area.[12]

On the morning of November 20 seven of the Scottsboro boys took their seats in the Decatur courtroom.[13] The contrast from the hearings of Judge Horton was strikingly apparent. Instead of National Guardsmen, there were nineteen armed deputies in mufti recruited from the Birmingham area. In the spring, Negroes comprised one third of the audience, but this time Raymond Daniell reported that he could not find a black face within a block of the courthouse. As Judge Callahan had promised, he was going to "debunk" the Scottsboro cases. Newsmen were refused their previous privilege of reserved seats inside the railed enclosures.[14] Callahan also forbade typewriters and cameras, inside or outside the courtroom. When two photographers snapped a picture of the courthouse, the sheriff confiscated the cameras and brought the two men before the bench. "There ain't going to be no more picture snappin' around here," said Callahan as he held up the cameras. He warned that anyone who violated his instructions would be cited for contempt. Somewhat surprisingly, the courtroom was less than half full. Allen Raymond of the New York *Herald Tribune* inquired around and found that Knight had encouraged prominent people in the city and county to urge everyone to stay away.[15]

The first two days of the hearings before Judge Callahan were devoted to a motion for a new change of venue. Early in October, the ILD employed three men to sound public opinion on the case.

---

[12] Sheriff James F. Hawkins to Governor Bibb Graves, November 21, 1933; Hammond, "Due Process," 702. Even Callahan admitted that there had been some "feeling expressed against the lawyers in the case." William Washington Callahan to Benjamin Meeks Miller, November 14, 1933, in Drawer 39, Alabama Executive Files.

[13] Roy Wright and Eugene Williams had been transferred to Juvenile Court by Judge Horton in June.

[14] Reporters attributed this to the resentment of townspeople over accounts of the Horton trial. New York *Times*, November 21, 1933, p. 1.

[15] New York *Herald Tribune*, November 21, November 27, 1933; New York *Times*, November 21, 1933, p. 1; Decatur *Daily*, November 20, November 21, 1933. Eleazer reported that the state hoped by this to show that there was little or no interest remaining in the case. For that reason, "leading people had circulated requests that individuals not come to the courthouse. . . ." Robert Burns Eleazer to Will W. Alexander, November 22, 1933, in Interracial Commission Papers.

Posing as traveling salesmen, James Jones, a Birmingham Negro, and two white men, Victor Ellwood and John Williams, traveled through the area. Ellwood and Williams said they had interviewed storekeepers, barbers, farmers, and a half-dozen National Guardsmen and officers as well as many others. A few persons declined to express an opinion, but most were blunt and forthright. Several said they had fixed opinions, but would conceal these in order to get on the jury and send the Negroes to the electric chair. Most preferred sending the boys to the chair "legally," but they agreed that lynching should be used as a last resort. A National Guardsman declared that he and his friends would offer only sham resistance to an armed attack. And Jones said that the county's Negroes had told him they were terrified as a result of the way the "white folks" were feeling. The three men stated that, altogether, they had interviewed or talked with almost five hundred persons.[16]

Knight was ready for the defense motion. He called to the stand a number of Decatur residents quoted in the affidavits. They denied they had ever made the statements attributed to them and unanimously agreed that the accused would get a fair trial in Morgan County. Knight also produced affidavits from two undertakers in the area showing that four of the men quoted in the defense documents had been buried earlier in 1933. Brodsky protested that this in no way affected the validity of the affidavits. "A man dies, his household continues." The investigators had simply written down the name on the doorbell of several houses they visited, said Brodsky. "That is how the four names happen to be among the 500 we have presented." But, as everyone expected, Callahan denied the motion. The fact that the defense "quoted the language of the dead inevitably strikes at the very vitals of the probative force and credence to be given their affidavits," he said sarcastically. Moreover, the defense based its motion on the observations of strangers while the state's affidavits were made by "persons who had lived there for years and knew the temper of the people." [17]

[16] New York *Times,* November 10, 1933, p. 7; November 21, 1933, p. 14; Decatur *Daily,* November 20, November 21, 1933.

[17] New York *Times,* November 22, 1933, p. 42; New York *Daily Worker,* November 22, 1933.

After Callahan dismissed the motion for a change of venue, Leibowitz announced that he had further motions. The first was to quash the Morgan County venire on the grounds that Negroes had been systematically excluded by the jury commissioners. On this motion, Callahan agreed to accept the evidence offered in the trial before Judge Horton. The second motion offered by Leibowitz was to quash the Jackson County indictment on the same grounds. Callahan announced a one-day adjournment in order to study the evidence. When court resumed on Thursday, November 23, he told the defense lawyers he had carefully considered the evidence. He noted that the United States Supreme Court had concluded that if the officers in charge of jury selection "fairly and honestly endeavored to discharge their duty, then the Constitution of the United States has not been violated." Callahan was "not prepared to say that the officers of Morgan County, in selecting the jury list, have so administered the law as to violate the Constitution. . . ." He overruled the motion to quash the Morgan County venire.[18]

In order to prove or disprove a *prima facie* case against the Jackson County jury rolls, Callahan ordered the jury lists brought into the court. J. E. Moody, head of the jury commission, explained that he had been elected in 1931 and had taken office on March 20 of that year. The names of potential jurors were placed on the book and divided according to voting precincts. In order to distinguish the new from the old names, Moody had ordered the commission's secretary to draw a red line across the bottom of each page in the large leather-bound volumes. All names above the line were presumably placed there sometime between 1922 and 1931; those below the line were written after March 20, 1931. Leibowitz asked him to read from the lists and to identify the race of the persons he knew. Moody read for an hour without discovering any Negroes. When he became tired, C. A. Wann, clerk of the Circuit Court, took the stand and began going over the names. Like Moody, he failed to recognize any Negroes. During the boring

[18] New York *Times,* November 22, 1933, p. 42; November 24, 1933, p. 9; *Patterson* v. *Alabama,* 294 U.S. 599, Tr. pp. 496–97.

session, the spectators gradually began drifting out. Even Callahan eventually ignored the droning monotone of Wann's voice and stepped down near the spectator's rail to chat with some friends. Just after 4 P.M., while going over the list of jurors in precinct twenty-one, Wann read "Hugh Sanford,—who is colored." Among the newspapermen there was a scrambling for paper and pencil, and Callahan scurried back to his seat behind the bench.[19]

Wann's remark surprised Leibowitz as much as anyone in the courtroom, but the latter appeared completely undisturbed. He carefully examined Sanford's name and then asked that the record show that the name was written directly over or under a series of two red lines, "a portion of the writing being on both lines. . . ." Below the red lines were the figures, "3-20-31" and an additional list of names. Presumably these names had been added after that date. When recalled to the stand, Moody testified that he had ordered the lines drawn at the first meeting. Leibowitz asked him sternly, "Whatever you wrote, or your clerk wrote in this book was below the red lines?" Moody nodded his head and replied firmly, "Yes, sir." In several additional hours of testimony on Wednesday afternoon and the following day Leibowitz uncovered the names of at least ten Negroes. All their names were either written on the red lines or immediately above them. Kelly Morgan, clerk of the board from 1926 to 1931, testified that he was the only person who ever wrote any names in the jury lists during his tenure in office. At the instruction of Leibowitz, he wrote on a piece of paper the names of four of the Negroes on the jury lists.[20]

When court resumed on Saturday the defense was ready for the state. Catching the first train available to Birmingham, John Vreeland Haring had responded to a call from Leibowitz on Wednesday evening. Haring had spent most of his adult life as a handwriting expert. At sixty-five he was still vigorous and alert, with a poise on the witness stand which came from years of testifying in similar cases. On Saturday morning, in a well-lighted room on the

[19] *Patterson* v. *Alabama*, 294 U.S. 599, Tr. pp. 58–59, 62; New York *Times*, November 24, 1933, p. 9.

[20] *Patterson* v. *Alabama*, 294 U.S. 599, Tr. p. 67.

sunny side of the Decatur courthouse, he carefully placed pages of of the Jackson County jury ledgers under a high-powered microscope. Shortly after 10 A.M. he announced that he had completed his examination and was ready to testify.[21]

His testimony was detailed and involved as he described the technical manner in which he had examined the books. His conclusions, however, were simple and straightforward: the names of at least the majority of the Negroes—and probably all of them— had been fraudulently placed on the jury books. In some ways, the forgery had been adeptly accomplished. From the handwriting, Haring was able to tell that Kelly Morgan, the jury clerk from 1926 to 1931, had done the writing. He had even used green ink similar to that used earlier. The problem was that the commission had not foreseen this dilemma and red lines had been drawn at the bottom of each precinct list. Morgan tried to circumvent this by squeezing the names of the ten Negroes above the red lines, and in five cases he had succeeded. But the names of five others slipped down across the red lines. Under a twenty-power microscope it was apparent that they were on top of the red end lines. Perhaps the most conclusive proof was found in the examination of one Negro's name, Travis Mosely. Haring concluded that "it is demonstrated to me beyond a shadow of a doubt that the name referred to was written after the date 3/20/31 was entered in this volume because of the fact of the meeting of the ink of the name Mosely and the meeting of the ink of the date line 3/20/31. . . ." And there was absolutely no doubt that "the ink of the name crosses the [date] line and over it. . . ." [22]

Judge Callahan deliberated less than a half hour before passing on the motion. He noted that the red lines were superimposed over the notation of the date. The defense readily acknowledged this as did the chairman of the jury commission, who said they were written at about the same time, possibly moments apart. But

[21] Ibid., 149–51.

[22] Ibid., 151–59. According to Raymond Daniell, spectators completely discounted Haring's testimony when they learned he was being paid $50 a day. New York Times, November 26, 1933, p. 1.

Callahan insisted this cast "grave doubts" on the defense contention that the red lines were drawn at exactly the same time the date was noted. Admittedly, the chairman had acknowledged they were written at that time, but Callahan said, "Later, he qualified his testimony from my view point." [23] The judge concluded that he could not presume that fraud had been committed because members of the jury board were sworn officers of the law and it "would be a reflection on them." Moreover, the "books are kept by the probate judge. It would be a reflection on him." He denied the motion. Although disappointed, Leibowitz was undisturbed by the denial. He was confident, he later told reporters, that the Supreme Court would refuse to confirm any conviction under the circumstances. As far as an appeal was concerned, the record was in a "thousand per cent better shape than it was after the trial last spring or at any other time." [24]

The mounting costs of the lengthy proceedings annoyed Callahan. During a recess on November 24 he told Leibowitz, "We're going to make speed beginning Monday." Although it had taken a week to try Haywood Patterson before Judge Horton, he told the defense he planned to wrap it up in three days. He was as good as his word when the trial opened on Monday morning. Although Leibowitz kept trying to question the venire of one hundred men about their opinions on the case, the judge constantly exhorted him to "hurry it along" and several times cut him short with "that's enough on that." The jury which was completed just before 3 P.M. was a grave disappointment to the defense. Altogether there were nine farmers, one unemployed house-painter, a truck driver, and the operator of a small country store. It was a "proletarian" jury, but whatever the wishes of the ILD, that was the last thing Leibowitz wanted. Even after the jury was selected Callahan kept rushing the proceedings. Leibowitz, with the assistance of several grinning deputies, began assembling his toy train, and

---

[23] The only way he qualified it was to say that he did not actually sit and watch while the clerk drew each of the red lines.

[24] *Patterson* v. *Alabama*, 294 U.S. 599, Tr. pp. 166–67. New York *Herald Tribune*, November 27, 1933.

Callahan protested over the loss of time. "Everyone knows the difference between engines, box cars and cabooses," he complained. When Leibowitz continued assembling the model, Callahan fidgeted, looked at his watch, and sarcastically remarked: "I hope you'll get this done before Christmas because Santa Claus is going to get all that anyway." The spectators chuckled appreciatively at the judge's little joke; the ILD lawyers seemed to have lost their sense of humor.[25]

Late that afternoon, for the fifth time, Victoria Price told her story of the assault. Her account was about the same that she had given before Judge Horton, except that she needed no prodding from the solicitor to recall that the first thing the Negroes said was "All you white sons-of-bitches unload." When Leibowitz began his cross-examination, however, he discovered that Callahan's witticisms were the least of his problems. He asked Mrs. Price who had accompanied her on the train to and from Chattanooga. Without waiting for an objection from the state, Callahan leaned forward across the bench and told Leibowitz, "I can't allow the time of the court wasted on matters so immaterial. You mustn't ask that question again." Leibowitz had steeled himself for just such an eventuality, but he could not believe that Callahan would cut off all questioning along this line. "Had you had sexual intercourse with any man the night before you left Huntsville?" Once again, Callahan did not wait for Attorney General Knight to object and he sternly instructed Mrs. Price to remain silent on that question. "May I state the reason for it?" pleaded Leibowitz. "No sir," snapped Callahan, "I think I know." [26]

Callahan's refusal to allow the defense to investigate Victoria Price's movements over the thirty-six hours preceding the rape destroyed the heart of the defense plan. It meant that the testimony of Dr. Bridges, on which the defense hoped to rely heavily, would be useless. Doggedly, Leibowitz pressed on, hoping to insinuate the information before the jury despite the objections of

---

[25] New York *Herald Tribune,* November 28, 1933; New York *Times,* November 25, 1933, p. 4; November 28, 1933, p. 11; Decatur *Daily,* November 27, 1933.

[26] *Patterson* v. *Alabama,* 294 U.S. 599, Tr. pp. 509, 514.

Callahan. When he asked about the hoboes' jungle at Chatta-nooga, however, Judge Callahan slapped his hand on the bench and raised his voice: "That is far enough for me to know all I want to know, to know that the question is illegal." When Leibo-witz complained, Callahan replied, "The more I shut you off the better shape you're in." [27]

Although discouraged, Leibowitz fought back. For the rest of the afternoon and throughout much of the next morning he took Victoria Price through the most rigorous cross-examination she had faced. Her nondescript hair set in tight ringlets and her face heavily rouged, she was soon lost in a maze of contradictions. At Scottsboro and before Judge Horton she insisted Norris had tried to hurl her from the train; now she was first certain and then "pretty sure" it was Patterson. Although she had vividly testified of a ".45 caliber pistol" held by Patterson, she finally acknowl-edged under cross-examination that she did not know one gun from another. She recalled that it was Patterson who fired the gun, although she could not remember that at Scottsboro, less than two weeks after the incident. She became hopelessly confused about where she was struck, or how hard, or how seriously. Twice she appeared completely panicked, observed Raymond Daniell, and looked pleadingly at the table where Knight sat. At other times she turned to Callahan for support or simply made faces at Leibo-witz without replying. More often than not she simply replied that it had been "too long" and she couldn't be positive." [28]

During the cross-examination, it was difficult to tell who made more objections, the state or Judge Callahan. Whenever Mrs. Price seemed to be bogged down in contradictions, the judge would interrupt with: "Let's don't take up time on that; that is a waste of time." Or, "I think that's enough on that." When she be-came confused about the number of people who hit her, Callahan snapped, "That will do, she has gone over that enough to satisfy

[27] *Ibid.*, 517; New York *Times*, November 28, 1933, p. 11.

[28] *Patterson* v. *Alabama*, 294 U.S. 599, Tr. pp. 520–60; New York *Times*, Novem-ber 28, 1933, p. 11.

anybody, looks to me like." Once, when Leibowitz asked Mrs. Price, with a touch of sarcasm in his voice, if she had not removed the overalls she said were torn from her by the assailants, Callahan sternly warned him to "treat the lady with more respect." [29]

The state had other witnesses; W. W. Hill, Tom Taylor Rousseau, Lee Adams, and W. E. Brannum had testified in the early trials. When Sam Mitchell and Luther Morris took the stand for the first time, they once again proved Knight's unfortunate adeptness at picking witnesses who were about as helpful to the defense as to the state. Sam Mitchell, a middle-aged Negro tenant farmer, testified under direct examination that he saw a scuffle on the train (which the defense did not deny), but he also added under cross-examination that he saw Negroes scattered throughout the train. Luther Morris testified that he was working on the floor of his barn when the train passed. He looked up, he said, to see a fight "between seven or eight negroes, and five or six white boys. . . ." In the same car he spied the heads of two white girls. Leibowitz once again used the camera to show that even standing at full height (and Morris said he was bending over) the railroad bed was almost as high as the barn floor and it would therefore have been impossible to look into the gondola and see two girls. But Morris insisted vehemently that he had seen them; they were wearing "overalls with bibs," he declared. The girls, of course, were wearing women's coats over their overalls; it was the same trap into which several other witnesses had fallen before Judge Horton.[30]

When Leibowitz tried to point out the inaccuracy of the statement, however, Callahan interrupted. "Don't take up time asking that after he has described the whole surroundings," said the judge. Leibowitz explained with an edge in his voice that he was trying to show the unreliability of Morris, but Callahan insisted, that "is the very thing I told you we was through with." The stubborn Leibowitz, however, tried to bore in on Morris by asking

[29] New York *Times,* November 28, 1933, p. 11; *Patterson* v. *Alabama,* 294 U.S. 599, Tr. pp. 531–34.

[30] *Patterson* v. *Alabama,* 294 U.S. 599, Tr. pp. 570, 574–75, 586.

him how he knew they were women. "That's enough of that," Callahan interrupted again. "No, your honor, I want to—" began Leibowitz; but the hefty judge, his face red with anger, shouted: "You are mistaken, that is enough of that; go on to something else." From the back of the courtroom, one person said audibly, "Atta boy," while the rest of the spectators grinned appreciatively at Callahan's firm handling of Leibowitz.[31]

The state's new star witness was Orville Gilley, the traveling troubadour who had made only a brief appearance at Scottsboro and then wandered off to California for the next three years. Shortly after the first Scottsboro trials concluded, James D. Burton learned that Gilley had declined to corroborate the girls' story when he testified in closed door session before the grand jury. In the intervening two and a half years, he had apparently had a change of heart. The defense attributed this change of attitude to the fact that the attorney general had been sending his mother a "rations' check" each week and giving Gilley small amounts of cash for spending money.[32] The Jackson County solicitor insisted, however, that Gilley had volunteered of his own free will to return. The reason he had not testified in Scottsboro, said Bailey, was that his language was "too rough" for Judge Hawkins' court.[33]

Dressed in a new blue pin-stripe suit and shiny shoes, Gilley was an effective witness for the state. In his summation, Leibowitz charged that Gilley was a "dirty, filthy liar." A liar he may have been, but he was charming and entertaining on the stand. At the outset, Gilley made it clear that he was not an ordinary hobo. "I am an entertainer," he explained. "I recite poetry and take up a collection after I finish, in hotel lobbies, restaurants, out on the streets, any place." Gilley even volunteered to recite a few lines for

[31] *Ibid.*, 577–79; New York *Herald Tribune,* November 28, 1933.

[32] James D. Burton, Report Number 1 on the Scottsboro, Alabama Case, April 14, 1931, in Interracial Commission Papers; Hammond, "Due Process," 701. Gilley readily acknowledged that Knight had been feeding him and had "sent a little to my mother . . . while I was engaged in the case." *Patterson* v. *Alabama,* 294 U.S. 599, Tr. p. 604.

[33] New York *Times,* November 27, 1933, p. 3. In the spring Knight explained that Gilley was not called to testify at Scottsboro at length because he was not a resident of Jackson County. *Ibid.,* March 11, 1933.

the audience, but Callahan stepped in. "I don't like poetry anyhow," the judge said sourly. Gilley confirmed the story of rape, but his account differed from Victoria's in almost every substantive detail. He remarked offhandedly that Haywood Patterson "had intercourse with both girls," something that even Victoria in some of her more flamboyant testimony had never charged. Although he did say that Patterson initially threatened him with a pistol, Gilley denied that anyone had held a knife around his neck during the alleged assaults. He told of only one gun, and, in contrast to Mrs. Price, said that no shots were ever fired. He also counted nine rapists instead of the twelve described by Mrs. Price. But he did remember distinctly one line; that when the Negroes came into the gondola, "they said, 'All you white sons-of-bitches unload.' " [34]

Although Callahan had distinctly forbidden Leibowitz to go into the events preceding the alleged rape, the latter ignored the injunction and under skillful questioning made Gilley acknowledge he had been with Victoria Price in Chattanooga. But when Leibowitz tried to question Gilley about the events of the night before the alleged assault, Callahan cut him short. "But your honor, won't you excuse the jury and allow me to inform you of what I am trying to prove?" pleaded Leibowitz. "I can imagine," snapped Callahan as he ordered the chief defense counsel to move on to something else. Although prevented from further questions in this area, Leibowitz drew from Gilley a statement that he had been in the gondola at one end alone and yet he admitted that at "no time while this raping was going on did I ever make any attempt to notify any engineer, or any officials of that train what was going on in this gondola car." [35]

Leibowitz cross-examined Gilley closely concerning the car in which the rape allegedly took place. Victoria Price contended it was in the car next to a box car away from the engine. Other state witnesses had testified they saw the defendants unloading from

[34] *Patterson* v. *Alabama*, 294 U.S. 599, Tr. pp. 593–94, 599.
[35] *Ibid.*, 597, 609; New York *Times*, November 29, 1933, p. 4.

that gondola.[36] When Leibowitz asked Gilley to point out the car where the fight and the rape supposedly took place, he walked over to the model train and put his hand on the two gondola cars next to the box car nearest the engine. With difficulty, Leibowitz suppressed a smile of satisfaction. He asked Gilley if he were sure. The witness looked again and replied, "I am sure it was one or the other of these cars here. . . ." [37] This corroborated the defense's contentions and refuted Victoria's account.

When Gilley stepped down from the witness stand, Attorney General Knight and his assistants motioned him over to their table and conferred in low whispers for a moment. When they had finished, Knight explained that Gilley wished to "explain" some of his earlier statements. Callahan gave him permission to take the stand. Knight asked his witness if he knew "when you pointed out that car which end this engine was on?" At the time, said Gilley, "I figured that it was on that end," and he pointed toward the caboose. Leibowitz sat in his chair with a look of disbelief on his face. "Are you going to permit this, Judge Callahan?" he asked in a voice filled with incredulity. "I have permitted it," snapped Callahan. "I respectfully except, and I want the record to show—" began Leibowitz, but the judge cut him short. "The record will show," he said. Gilley stepped down from the stand, walked over to the model, and placed his hand on the gondolas away from the engine.[38] Leibowitz, his face colored with anger, asked Gilley if he could earlier see the engine without any difficulty. "Yes sir," replied the witness. "I asked you about the engine part and the caboose part, didn't I?" continued Leibowitz. "Yes sir," replied Gilley almost inaudibly. In other words, said Leibowitz, "you could see that engine when you made the first statement that it was the first or second car of the string nearest the engine?" Gilley

[36] Car No. 16, Diagram I, p. 211. On the other hand, the defense argued that the fight took place in car 12 or car 13, while the girls were closer to the engine, probably in car 10 or 11.

[37] In other words, car 9 or 10. *Patterson* v. *Alabama*, 294 U.S. 599, Tr. p. 605.

[38] Cars 15 and 16. See above, Diagram I, p. 211.

sat for a moment and than acknowledged, "Yes sir, I could see it." "You may step aside," concluded Leibowitz.[39]

Although it was unlikely that Ruby Bates' testimony would have had any effect, the defense had to dispense with it. Early in November, she had written William Patterson explaining that "since I was in Decatur almost every day now I get letters from the South calling me a 'nigger-lover' and saying that I should be lynched too." Ruby admitted frankly that she was afraid. "I am willing to tell the story here [in New York] again to any ministers or lawyers or anybody you want me to talk to, but I won't go back to Decatur. . . ." [40] The state agreed to allow interrogation in New York, but on the afternoon of November 28, defense lawyers learned that Ruby had become seriously ill and had been rushed to a Manhattan hospital. Brodsky explained that the defense would need a brief recess in order to allow her to recover enough to answer the questions submitted by both the defense and the state. But "Speedy" Callahan, as he had come to be known by reporters, was in no mood for delays. He told the defense they would have to go ahead without Miss Bates' deposition.[41]

For the third time in the trials, Haywood Patterson took the stand on his own behalf and told of the fight. One of the white boys called "me black son of bitches, and nigger son of bitches and such as that." Patterson readily acknowledged that he had "cussed him back. I called him mother-fuckers, son of bitches, and everything." But the young Negro insisted he saw no women on the train. "I seen some women at Paint Rock," he said. In his cross-examination, Knight wasted little time going over the facts of the case. "I will ask you, Haywood, if you, when you were tried at Scottsboro, didn't make the statement that you saw all of the negro boys who went into that gondola rape the women but three?" Haywood admitted that he had made some statement similar to that, but he claimed that one of the National Guardsmen and several officials "said they was going to kill us." He explained, "I didn't

[39] *Patterson* v. *Alabama.* 294 U.S. 599, Tr. p. 612; Decatur *Daily*, November 29, 1933.

[40] Quoted in New York *Daily Worker*, November 16, 1933.

[41] Decatur *Daily*, November 30, 1933.

have any friends and didn't know anyone." Despite this disclaimer, Knight introduced into the evidence incriminating questions and answers made at the Scottsboro trial. Leibowitz had expected Knight to insert this into the record and he planned under re-direct examination to show that Patterson had retracted the charge almost as soon as he made it. But once again, Leibowitz had not counted on Callahan. When the chief defense lawyer began reading Patterson's later statement, Callahan stopped him. The entire transcript was not offered in evidence, said the judge. While the defense could question Patterson further about the identical questions Knight had quoted, "You [Leibowitz] are not authorized to go through that record and pick out something else, what he said about something else." Leibowitz was dumbfounded. Such a ruling was completely contrary to the accepted rules of evidence and he protested that the defense had a right to introduce material which would point out the contradictions in Patterson's early statement. Callahan shrugged. "If the Attorney General wants to waive it, all right, but if it is put to me to pass on—." Knight interrupted firmly, "I am not waiving anything." [42]

In all of the trials since 1931, the state had called to the witness stand at least one of the Scottsboro doctors who examined Victoria Price and Ruby Bates. But Leibowitz's ability at turning the medical testimony in favor of the defendant caused a change of strategy on the part of Knight. When Dr. Bridges took the oath on Wednesday, November 28, it was as a witness for the defense. Bridges testified that he had ordered Mrs. Price to undress completely and he had examined her entire body. There was "no blood at all" coming out of the vagina. "I saw no blood on her face or on her forehead." There were a few very small scratches about the wrist, and there was one small blue mark on the small of the back. With difficulty, he had found enough semen in the va-

---

[42] *Patterson* v. *Alabama*, 294 U.S. 599, Tr. pp. 621, 623, 634, 640–41. Earlier, Judge Callahan had refused to allow the defense to question Victoria Price about her activities during the twenty-four hours preceding the alleged attack. But when Lester Carter took the stand for the defense, Callahan gave Knight complete freedom to question Carter about what he had been doing "up there in New York" during the months preceding the Horton trial. *Ibid.*, 682.

gina to make a smear. Under a glass slide he found spermatozoa, but they were all dead. It was substantially the same testimony he had given in the earlier trials.[43]

Callahan's refusal to allow the defense to go into the twenty-four hours preceding the alleged rape placed the defense in an untenable position. Leibowitz had introduced testimony from the doctor showing that semen was present in the vagina of Victoria Price, and yet the court would not let him give a logical explanation for its presence. When Lester Carter took the stand, Leibowitz desperately tried to get the facts before the jury. Question after question was interrupted with objections from the state. Finally, Leibowitz asked Carter point-blank if he and Ruby and Jack Tiller and Victoria Price "in the presence of each other, did not have sexual intercourse—." It was more than Callahan could take. Half rising out of his seat he angrily told Leibowitz, "I have ruled on that very legal point a half dozen times, and there can't be anything in it except a vicious attempt to get something before the jury that I have ruled is improper." Somewhat chastened, Leibowitz apologetically explained that he would not press this any further. But he added that in view of the court's charge that the defense had made a "vicious attempt" to force testimony into the record, "in justice to my client . . . I want to move for a mistrial." Callahan agreed to withdraw the word "vicious" but he overruled the motion.[44] As one reporter observed, Lester "left the witness stand without having contributed much more than some expert testimony about the proper way to board and alight from a moving freight train." [45]

Leibowitz had hoped to bring in several medical witnesses from Chattanooga, but he had thought the trial would extend at least until Friday, and he told the court he would need a recess until the next day. Callahan refused. Shortly after 4:30 on Wednesday afternoon, Thanksgiving eve, he ordered the defense and the

[43] *Ibid.*, 642–45.
[44] *Ibid.*, 662–63; Decatur *Daily,* November 29, 1933.
[45] New York *Times,* November 30, 1933, p. 40.

prosecution to begin their summations. He allowed two hours to each side.[46]

Wade Wright, the paunchy Morgan County solicitor who had led off the summations before Judge Horton with an anti-Semitic tirade, managed to be more moderate in tone, if not in volume. In a voice heard clearly outside on the courthouse lawn he demanded the death penalty. "Old brother Hill," the Paint Rock station agent, had corroborated Mrs. Price's story as well as those of the white farmers along the railroad who saw the girls "a-fixin' to get out and being drug back," he said. As for Lester Carter, he had "been breathing the atmosphere of that great metropolis [New York] too long." Over and over he repeated the words Victoria Price said were spoken by Patterson when he jumped in the car: "All you white sons-of-bitches unload." This, said Wright, proved that "the whole affair was a pre-meditated crime." [47]

Jackson County Solicitor H. G. Bailey was far more effective. There should be "no prejudice and no passion" in the deliberations, he told the jury. Admittedly, Victoria Price and Ruby Bates were not the prize of Southern womanhood, but they did better, he said, to travel to Chattanooga to find work than "to rouge up their faces and stand on the street corners of Huntsville." Bailey also repeated the line, "All you white sons-of-bitches unload," and concluded with a patriotic exhortation to uphold the good name of neighboring Jackson County. The defense had been yelling "frame-up" ever since the case began, he declared. "Who framed them? Did Tom Dobbins frame them? Did Brother Hill frame them?" He shook his head slowly in feigned disgust. "We did a lot of awful things over there in Scottsboro, didn't we? My, my, my." He concluded with a voice suddenly hard. "And now they come over here trying to convince you that sort of thing happened in your neighboring county!" It was the unanimous opinion of local people that his was the single most effective statement made during the trial.[48]

[46] *Ibid.*

[47] *Ibid.;* Basso, "Five Days in Decatur," 163.

[48] Basso, "Five Days In Decatur," 164; New York *Herald Tribune,* November 30, 1933.

Callahan briefly recessed the proceedings for dinner, but he drove on into the night, intent on finishing by the next day at the latest. Leibowitz had set three goals for his summation. First, to erase his earlier charges against Morgan County juries by flattering the twelve men who sat in the jury box. Second, he planned to emphasize the testimony of Dr. Bridges, and third, to supply a motive for Victoria Price. He praised the jury as men of "sound common sense" and appealed to them to acquit on the grounds of "reasonable doubt." Leibowitz said he would not be arguing the case if the charges had been brought by a "decent, respectable, Southern white woman." But they were made by a "lewd woman," a "girl tramp." [49]

Taking a seat by the toy train he pleaded with the jury. "What is this Scottsboro case—a battle of lawyers, a game or what?" He pointed out that Victoria's testimony had conflicted with that of Dr. Bridges. "Who's on the level in this case, this doctor or Victoria Price?" Leibowitz was certain, he said, that an Alabama jury would not convict its own doctor of perjury. Finally, the defense lawyer supplied a motive for Victoria Price by declaring that "with the vicious quick wit of a wanton," she realized she faced prosecution under the Mann Act when the train was stopped at Paint Rock. Thus she charged rape, "changing herself from a probable defendant into a complainant, assured of safety by Southern manhood." For the first time in the summation, Leibowitz raised his voice. Victoria Price was the guilty person in the case, he said. "Wasn't she ravishing the state of Alabama," he cried, "when she came in here and perjured herself before this honorable judge, before this jury and before her God . . . ?" Leibowitz, however, had miscalculated. The audience shifted in their seats and whispered angrily, their faces in hard, grim masks. As one spectator told a *Herald Tribune* reporter that night, Victoria Price "might be a fallen woman, but by God she is a white woman."

[49] New York *Herald Tribune*, November 30, 1933; New York *Times*, November 30, 1933, p. 40.

Shortly after 9:30 P.M., Leibowitz wearily concluded his summation for the defense.[50]

Knight made the final plea on Thursday morning, Thanksgiving Day. He passionately demanded the death penalty. "There is no middle ground in this case," he shouted. A death penalty would not avenge Victoria Price. "What has been done to her cannot be undone." But, he concluded, what "you can do is to see that it doesn't happen to some other woman." On his feet, Leibowitz protested. "That's an appeal to passion and prejudice." Knight, his voice trembling with emotion, whirled around and faced Leibowitz. "It certainly is. It's an appeal to passion!" Leibowitz demanded a mistrial, but Callahan refused and Knight continued. "We all have a passion, all the men in this courtroom and that is to protect the womanhood of the state of Alabama." Outside Victoria Price sat on a stool peering in through the partly opened door, occasionally stepping over to a nearby spittoon. Beside her stood Jack Tiller, her boyfriend, or, as she preferred to call him, her "bodyguard." Knight turned back to the jury. "And when you do protect the womanhood of the state of Alabama, it does not lie in the mouth of any man to tell you what's best for your commonwealth." It was the duty of all, he said, "to return such a verdict as you know, and I know, will be a deterrent to others." Like Wright and Bailey before him, he harped on the statement that Patterson had allegedly made, "All you white sons-of-bitches unload." Gradually, said Hamilton Basso of the *New Republic,* the jury began to understand. The defendants had not said mister. "They had not even said white folks. They had said white sons-of-bitches." When Knight had concluded his remarks, Callahan peered down at his pocket watch—it was 10:30 A.M.—and told the courtroom: "We shall now pause to go to our firesides in proper recognition and gratitude for the favors of the All-Wise Being Who has been with us through these trying years." [51]

At 1:30 P.M, Callahan was back at the bench, Haywood Patter-

[50] Decatur *Daily,* November 30, 1933; New York *Herald Tribune,* November 30, 1933; New York *Times,* November 30, 1933, p. 40; and Basso, "Five Days in Decatur," 164.
[51] *Ibid.*

son was in his chair, and the room was filled with spectators. At their table, Leibowitz, Brodsky, and Chamlee sat stiffly, their faces set and drawn. Opposite them, the state lawyers laughed and chatted confidently among themselves. As soon as the courtroom was quiet, Callahan began reading his charge to the jury. At first Patterson leaned forward, but soon he realized its meaning for the defense and gradually sank dejectedly into his chair. Step by step Judge Callahan destroyed the defense's case. Leibowitz had made much of the fact that Victoria Price showed no signs of resistance. Callahan, however, stressed that if she was frightened, even though the "prosecutrix . . . made no actual effort to resist," this was still rape within the law. In the same steady, even voice, he continued with a statement that stunned the defense lawyers:

Where the woman charged to have been raped, as in this case is a white woman there is a very strong presumption under the law that she would not and did not yield voluntarily to intercourse with the defendant, a Negro; and this is true, whatever the station in life the prosecutrix may occupy, whether she be the most despised, ignorant and abandoned woman of the community, or the spotless virgin and daughter of a prominent home of luxury and learning.[52]

It was not even important whether Patterson raped her, said Callahan. The "mere presence of a party at or while the crime is going on, and if his presence is for the purpose of aiding, encouraging, assisting or abetting in any way the commission of crime . . . he is as guilty as the one who committed the offense, although he never moved a muscle or said a word; provided his presence did encourage, aid or cause the other party to commit the offense." Judge Horton had made much of the lack of corroboration of Victoria Price's testimony, but Callahan insisted that the law "would authorize a conviction on the testimony of Vic-

[52] New York *Times,* December 1, 1933, p. 1. The defense, of course, never contended that she had submitted voluntarily. On the contrary, it argued that intercourse had never taken place on the train. But simply by Callahan's drawing the color line in this manner, Leibowitz and his fellow lawyers were convinced that the charge affected the thinking of the jurors. The following account is taken from the same source.

toria Price alone, if . . . that evidence, taken into consideration with all the other evidence in the case . . . convinces you beyond a reasonable doubt that she had been ravished." The law, he said, "does not require corroboration."

Leibowitz had tried desperately to insinuate information of the intercourse between Victoria and Jack Tiller by asking lengthy questions. But Callahan warned the jury not to take into consideration any of these questions. When the court ruled on them and said they should not be answered, "that ends it as far as you are concerned; and it makes no difference whether the court is right or wrong, fair or unfair. . . ." To do otherwise would allow "illegal and improper" information to drift into the jury box. He turned and glowered at Leibowitz. "If that is to be the law, then we have no law. And when we have no law the government fails." Leibowitz returned the stare without flinching. The defense attorneys had argued that there was something strange about the fact that the state refused to call the doctors who examined the girls and the defense had been forced to summon them. But Callahan declared firmly, "It doesn't make any difference who called the witness." The only important thing was his testimony.

In discussing the reliability of the witnesses, Callahan made his most damaging remarks against the defense. Referring indirectly to Mrs. Price, he declared that "because a witness has not been corroborated or even if [the witness] . . . has been contradicted or shown to be biased, that in and of itself doesn't warrant you in setting his evidence out of the case." But, he declared, "when it comes to the defendant, the law steps in and says that whenever a defendant takes the stand and testifies in his own behalf he is an interested witness." The defendant has to "suffer the penalties of the verdict against him or is to reap freedom from a favorable verdict." The fact that he was interested alone would not discredit him, but the law specified that his testimony should be carefully scrutinized. Drawing himself up straight in his chair, the judge noted that "something has been said through this case in argument about the defendant being a Negro." He would be "ashamed," he said, if this should enter into the considerations in the jury room. He outlined the forms for reaching a guilty verdict and then concluded: "Take the case, gentlemen, and give it your consideration." There was a moment of stunned silence at the defense table. Judge Callahan had not given the instructions for rendering acquittal.

Leibowitz raced to the bench and whispered fervently with the judge. When the attorney returned to his chair, Callahan continued. "Now gentlemen, I believe I overlooked one thing about the forms of the verdict." He had given the forms for conviction, he acknowledged a bit sheepishly, but he had not given the correct form for acquittal. If, he said, "you are not satisfied beyond all reasonable doubt that the defendant is guilty as charged then he ought to be acquitted. . . ." The form was " 'We the jury find the defendant not guilty.' " The jury filed into the room on the side.

As Allen Raymond of the New York *Herald Tribune* put it, it "was not alone the content of the judge's charges . . . which made it a more effective bludgeon against the defense than even the oratory of prosecuting attorneys," but with it also went "significant glares from the bench toward Mr. Leibowitz. . . ." Raymond Daniell added that the "cold stenographic report of the charge does not convey the full force of its blow to the defense." Time after time the judge changed the intonation of his voice significantly and "several times he glared in what seemed an unfriendly fashion at the defense counsel table while explaining to the jury that inference and innuendo were not evidence." Even though his omission of the forms for acquittal was probably unintentional, the *Christian Century* observed: "It is inconceivable that a jury would not interpret the judge's original oversight and this perfunctory footnote as indicating that he did not consider acquittal as a serious possibility." [53]

The jurors were not out of the room five minutes before the next venire had been brought in. Throughout the rest of the afternoon, the court continued the tedious business of selecting a jury

[53] New York *Herald Tribune*, December 1, 1933; New York *Times*, December 1, 1933, p. 1; "Passion Triumphs in Scottsboro Case," *Christian Century*, L (1933), 1563–64.

to try the next defendant, Clarence Norris. It was late the next afternoon before the state and the defense could agree upon twelve men. Norris' jury was much like Patterson's: nine farmers, a carpenter, an oil salesman, and a railroad employee. All were middle-aged, most of them dressed in the style of the community, overalls or unmatched coats and trousers. One wore a necktie. Just as Callahan began swearing them in, word came that a verdict had been reached in the Patterson case. Hurriedly, the bailiff removed the twelve men from the room, while deputies brought the man-acled Patterson from the nearby jail. The scene was like that of the spring, only this time Haywood Patterson stood beside Leib-owitz to face the jury while Court Clerk John Green read the verdict: "We find the defendant guilty as charged in the indict-ment and fix his punishment at death." Patterson had stood with a forced smile while the jury took their places, but as the verdict was read, he suddenly grimaced and his right arm came upward as if in protest. To one reporter, Patterson looked "like a caged animal about to lunge at a keeper who had mistreated him." After Callahan thanked the jurors they began to file out past the chair where Patterson sat. Eight walked past staring carefully straight ahead. Four started to leave, but when they saw the undisguised look of hatred on the face of the young Negro, they hastily turned and took the long way out.[54]

Inexorably the trial of Clarence Norris continued during the following week. Even though he knew there was little hope for acquittal, Leibowitz grimly forged ahead. In his cross-examination of Victoria Price, he trapped her in falsehood after falsehood and pointed out numerous contradictions from her early testimony.[55] When she testified that she was struck in the face with the butt end of a pistol, Leibowitz borrowed one of the deputy's pistols, handed it to her, and demanded to know which was the butt end and

---

[54] New York *Times,* December 2, 1933, p. 6; Decatur *Daily,* December 2, 1933.

[55] Two witnesses for the state marked in photographs where they saw Victoria Price "swoon." It was 520 feet from the spot where she said she fainted stepping from the gondola. And fireman Percy Ricks testified once more that he had seen her and Ruby Bates running frantically up toward the front of the train. *Norris* v. *Alabama,* 294 U.S. 587, Tr. p. 552; New York *Times,* December 3, 1933, p. 28.

which was the muzzle. She stared at it for a moment and then mumbled that she did not know; the only thing she knew about pistols was what she had "been told." As Leibowitz trapped her in a web of inconsistencies she turned desperately to Knight before answering until Leibowitz protested, asking if she was "looking for signals." [56]

As the trial continued and Judge Callahan continued to refuse Leibowitz permission to examine Victoria's background, the New York attorney became embittered over what he felt was a parody of courtroom procedure. His clashes with Callahan became more and more harsh. When one of the Jackson County deputy sheriffs began telling of how he had heard Norris accuse the other boys of rape in the jail on the night of March 26, 1931, Leibowitz objected, but Callahan overruled him. And when the New York lawyer tried to amplify his point, Callahan, his face flushed with anger, jumped to his feet and shouted: "That's enough, Mr. Leibowitz: Don't say another word; not one word." Leibowitz, biting his lips for control, whispered, "Except." "You're entitled to that," Callahan retorted, "but that's all you are entitled to." [57]

In spite of his clashes with Judge Callahan, Leibowitz dared to hope again. He noticed that two of the jurors returned his smiles and followed with close interest his explanations of photographs introduced to prove that Victoria Price could not have been in two places at once. When Judge Callahan prepared to give substantially the same charge he had given the Patterson jury, Leibowitz was ready, and he fought the judge every step of the way, objecting to almost every substantive point in the charge. On a few, the judge yielded. But for the most part, the jury went to its deliberations with the same instructions that had preceded the guilty verdict against Patterson.[58]

When court opened on Tuesday, December 5, the state pre-

[56] *Norris* v. *Alabama,* 294 U.S. 587, Tr. pp. 518, 527.

[57] *Ibid.,* 555; New York *Times,* December 3, 1933, p. 28.

[58] New York *Times,* December 3, 1933, p. 28; *Norris* v. *Alabama,* 294 U.S. 587, Tr. pp. 638–42. There was one difference. Callahan omitted the section arguing that no white woman, whatever her station, would submit voluntarily to sexual relations with a Negro.

pared to call the case of Charlie Weems. But Leibowitz argued for a postponement. "These trials may be only an empty gesture after the courts have reviewed them," he bluntly declared. Callahan, appalled at the high cost already, agreed to an indefinite postponement. The jury was out from 8:20 A.M. to 9:30 P.M. When the jurors came back into the courtroom, they were haggard, their collars open and soaked with perspiration. Reporters on hand learned that one person was holding out for life imprisonment. Callahan ordered the jury to return to its deliberations the next day. About halfway through the morning, the Norris jury returned with the verdict that everyone had expected: death in the electric chair. Just before noon, Judge Callahan recited the identical sentence over the two men, except he unintentionally neglected to ask the mercy of God upon Norris' soul.[59]

When Leibowitz and Brodsky left the courtroom they were heavily guarded by three special deputies and two personal bodyguards. Throughout the week there had been rumors that armed men planned to shoot Leibowitz when he came across the courthouse lawn and then to lynch the defendants. During the trials outbreaks of mob violence across the nation had fanned fears of a similar disorder at Scottsboro. For four consecutive days beginning November 27, the Decatur *Daily* headlined accounts of lynchings or near lynchings.[60] The madness that Will Alexander had feared seemed to have erupted nationwide. These disturbances, coupled with the openly expressed hatred of the townspeople for Leibowitz, led many observers to predict a mass assault on the lawyer and his clients. Robert Burns Eleazer was far closer to the truth,

[59] Decatur *Daily*, December 6, 1933; New York *Times*, December 7, 1933, p. 16.

[60] New York *Times*, December 7, 1933, p. 16. On the evening of November 26, a San Jose, California, mob broke into a local jail and lynched two men accused of kidnapping and slaying a small boy. The Decatur *Daily* headlined Governor Rolph's statement that he would pardon anyone accused of the lynchings. The following day the lead story told of efforts of a Salisbury, Maryland, mob to free accused lynchers from the county jail. On November 29 the *Daily* described in detail how a mob of St. Joseph, Missouri, whites took a nineteen-year-old Negro and burned him to death while women and children watched. The November 30 issue of the Decatur *Daily* told how Georgia officials had to call out the militia to protect a Negro convicted of attacking a white woman.

however, when he observed that the town of Decatur was "very quiet." In general, the people were not disturbed, he said, because they were absolutely certain that there would be no repetition of the spring's events leading to Horton's decision. Callahan had their complete confidence.[61]

The April, 1931, conviction of Patterson had ignited a massive wave of protests throughout Harlem and other Northern Negro ghettos. In December, 1933, there was only a kind of perfunctory regret, perhaps because the verdict was no surprise. On Saturday afternoon, December 2, the ILD held a parade. Fewer than 1,800 persons stood in the line of march, and most of them were white Party members.[62]

One of the strongest attacks on the trial and its verdict came from the Birmingham *Post*. The *Post* noted that it had "viewed with misgivings the appointment of Judge Callahan as the trial judge in the Scottsboro cases." The results had more than justified these fears. The *Post* assailed Callahan's refusal to wait for the Bates' deposition, his failure to describe the mode of acquittal, and his over-all prejudicial demeanor on the bench. "The record of this trial, when it comes to review by the United States Supreme Court, will not be a favorable commentary on Alabama judicial procedure." The ultimate blame for this disgraceful state of affairs, said the *Post*, lay upon Chief Justice John C. Anderson or his associates on the Alabama Supreme Court bench for removing Horton from trial of the cases.[63]

Leibowitz had said that he would do his talking before the United States Supreme Court, but he did not take into consideration the judge from Decatur. Using legal technicalities and an occasional sleight-of-hand, Callahan almost succeeded in depriving Haywood Patterson of his right of appeal. When Patterson was found guilty on December 1, Leibowitz and Chamlee understood that they had thirty days to make a motion before Callahan for a

[61] Robert Burns Eleazer to Will W. Alexander, November 22, 1933, in Interracial Commission Papers.

[62] New York *Amsterdam News*, December 6, 1933.

[63] Birmingham *Post*, December 2, 1933.

new trial. Leibowitz requested that the defense be given thirty days after the stenographer's minutes were typed, but Callahan refused. He told Leibowitz, as Allen Raymond of the New York *Herald Tribune* and Raymond Daniell of the New York *Times* reported at the time, that the defense had thirty days to file the motion, but if it was not then ready, it could apply for a continuance.[64] On December 26, Chamlee wired ILD headquarters that he would file a motion for a new trial on December 29 and then ask for a continuance. Judge Callahan accepted the motion and signed an order continuing the case until January 27. Because of a mix-up in obtaining the stenographer's record, the defense asked and received another continuance on January 25. Callahan set February 24 as the final date for a hearing on that motion.[65]

The defense received a jolt on the day of the hearing. Attorney General Knight cited an Alabama law which declared that the original motion for a new trial had to be filed by the last day of the court term, and the Circuit Court of Morgan and surrounding counties ended on December 23.[66] The defense protested. The noted constitutional attorney Osmund Fraenkel asked why Judge Callahan had given two continuances if he knew that the motion was already invalid. The attorney general had been present when the thirty-day time was noted, said Fraenkel, and he made no protest. He received copies of the motion papers and retained them without comment. Moreover, Knight had made no objection to the two adjournments Judge Callahan granted. "By all the rules of fair practice, he should have been precluded from making the motion to strike." [67] Judge Callahan, however, dismissed this argument and overruled the motion for a new trial. He acknowledged that he had granted two continuances, but he said these

[64] New York *Times,* December 2, 1933, p. 6; New York *Herald Tribune,* December 2, 1933.

[65] George W. Chamlee to William L. Patterson, December 26, 1933, in ILD Papers.

[66] Memorandum of Joseph Brodsky, October 26, 1933, in ILD Papers. The main part of this memorandum was reprinted in the *Daily Worker* on October 31, 1934.

[67] Letter of Osmund K. Fraenkel, in *The Nation,* CXXXIX (1934), 647.

were "null and void" since he had no power to grant an extension after December 23, the last day of court.[68]

The next step in the appeal was the filing of a bill of exceptions. Chastened by their oversight, Fraenkel, Chamlee, and other ILD attorneys carefully examined the Alabama law. They found that a bill of exceptions had to be filed *either* ninety days after the denial of the motion for a new trial *or* ninety days from the date "on which the judgement is entered. . . ." [69] Chamlee argued that Judge Callahan denied the motion on February 24; therefore they had ninety days from this date to prepare a bill of exceptions. But Fraenkel and Brodsky had become a bit wary of Alabama legal hairsplitting and they decided to assume the worst. The question then arose: when was the date of the entry of judgment? The jury reached its verdict in the Patterson trial on December 1, but Callahan did not sentence him until December 6 when Norris was convicted. Chamlee made a special trip to Decatur and carefully examined the Circuit Clerk's minutes of the trial. He saw in Callahan's handwriting the judgment and the date next to it, December 6.[70] Knight's motion on February 24 corroborated the ILD attorneys' belief that this was the date on which the judgment was entered. At that time, Knight declared that Callahan's court "no longer has jurisdiction, power or authority over the judgment rendered in this case on the 6th day of December, 1933." [71]

In order to avoid any question on the issue, ILD attorneys agreed to try to file the bill of exceptions in Montgomery by March 1, ninety days after Patterson was convicted, but not sentenced. When Brodsky and Fraenkel arrived back in New York on February 25, they had less than one week to prepare the voluminous record and to have it printed. Along with other ILD at-

---

[68] Decatur *Daily*, February 24, February 25, 1934; New York *Times*, February 25, 1934, II, p. 1. Judge Callahan was legally correct. See Alabama *Revised Code* (1923), Art. 6670. The judge later insisted that the defense charges were "entirely without merit." He added, "Even if I had been so despicable as to try to trick the defense by deceiving them, I still cannot disregard the law." New York *Times*, March 10, 1934, p. 30.

[69] Alabama, *Revised Code* (1923), Art. 6433.

[70] Memorandum of Joseph Brodsky, October 26, 1934, in ILD Papers.

[71] Decatur *Daily*, February 24, 1934.

torneys the two men worked far into the night, day after day, as they pored over the lengthy manuscript. When it became apparent that one printer could not get it ready on time they divided it up among three. On Wednesday afternoon, February 28, a motorcycle messenger waited outside the ILD office, accepted the bulky manuscript, and roared off to Newark Airport to place it on the last plane to Birmingham. The exhausted attorneys staggered off to bed and awoke the next morning to learn that the airplane carrying the bill of exceptions had crashed just north of Washington, D. C. A second copy of the documents did not arrive in Montgomery by mail until March 5. Despite their distrust of the Alabama courts, the ILD attorneys agreed there should be no question that they had met the deadline, since the three months' period was computed from the date of judgment.[72]

On May 25, Samuel Leibowitz, Osmund K. Fraenkel, and George W. Chamlee traveled to Montgomery to argue the case of their clients before the Alabama Supreme Court. Leibowitz argued the jury question. He asked that the convictions be set aside and the indictments quashed because Negroes had been systematically excluded from the Jackson County jury. The names of several Negroes were on the jury rolls, he said, but they were placed there by "brazen, frank and amateurish forgery." Fraenkel devoted most of his remarks to a discussion of Judge Callahan's conduct of the trial. He accused the judge of drawing the color line in the charge to Patterson's jury. Callahan had also condoned an "appeal to prejudice" by the attorney general, said Fraenkel. While he acknowledged that the failure to instruct the jury on the forms for acquittal was probably an oversight, it nevertheless had a "prejudicial effect" on the minds of the jurors. Among the other reversible errors Fraenkel cited were the court's refusal to allow the defense to offer evidence explaining the presence of semen in the vagina of Victoria Price, and its refusal to grant a brief delay for the defense, thus excluding material testimony by a Chatta-

[72] Letter of Osmund K. Fraenkel, in *The Nation*, CXXXIX (1934), 647; Washington *Post*, March 1, 1934.

nooga physician and a deposition by Ruby Bates contradicting
Mrs. Price.[73]

Attorney General Knight argued the case for the state. As the
defense had feared, he insisted that the high court should not even
consider Patterson's case since "the judgment was entered on December 1." [74] As for the Norris trial, he ignored the defense charges
against Callahan and focused on the jury issue. It was not for the
Supreme Court of Alabama to say whether or not the names were
forged on the jury rolls, contended Knight. The selection of jurors
on the basis of their moral fitness, character, ability, and reputation was entirely at the discretion of the jury commissioners. "If
this court, with no evidence showing that Negroes were excluded,
holds that systematic exclusion of Negroes took place, then the
court is constituting itself the jury commission of every court in
Alabama." He did make one reference to the contention of the
defense that it should have been allowed to examine witnesses concerning the events of the twenty-four hours preceding the alleged
assault on the train. The character and activities of Victoria Price
were irrelevant, said Knight. "The jury decided she was attacked
on that freight train and her past acts have no bearing on whether
Patterson and Norris committed that act." [75]

On Thursday, June 28, the Alabama Supreme Court unanimously denied the defense motion for new trials and set the execution date for August 31. In the case of *Patterson v. Alabama,* the
court upheld Knight's contention and struck the bill of exceptions
from the record on the grounds that it had not been filed within
ninety days after final judgment by the trial court. In the Norris
case, Justice Lucien D. Gardner, speaking for the court, rejected
the defense's contention that Negroes had been systematically excluded from the Jackson and Morgan County juries. There was
ample proof, said Gardner, that the absence of Negroes from the
jury rolls was due to "selection" rather than exclusion. Unques-

[73] New York *Times,* May 26, 1934, p. 10; Montgomery *Advertiser,* May 26, 1934.
[74] Fraenkel replied that Knight's "previous declaration about the date of the
judgment should in common decency preclude him from claiming otherwise."
Quoted in "Scottsboro to Date," *New Republic,* LXXXI (1934), 90.
[75] New York *Times,* May 26, 1934, p. 10.

tionably the commission "went about its duty with an honest and sincere purpose to select the best available men for this important service." Gardner admitted that Callahan "on one or two occasions manifested slight impatience," but the justice concluded that the trial was "conducted with proper regard to all administrative rules, as well as due regard for [the] defendant's rights. . . ." Gardner also dismissed the defense claim that it should have been allowed to show sexual relations by Victoria Price on the night before the assault. "All of this bore no relevancy to any issue in the case under the rule firmly established in this jurisdiction." [76]

After the Alabama court's decision disappointed Leibowitz and other ILD attorneys, they had not expected a reversal. The striking of Patterson's bill of exceptions from the record, however, was a grave and unexpected blow. This abolished Haywood Patterson's right to appeal the verdict to a federal court since technically his case had never been appealed to the state courts. Under federal law, the courts of the United States could not examine his case until he had exhausted all remedies on the state level. Defense lawyers could only hope that the federal courts would disregard the legal technicality. On July 9, Chamlee filed an application for a rehearing before the Alabama Supreme Court. Since the court was recessed until October, this operated as an indefinite stay of execution. [77]

During the brief lull in the appeals, Leibowitz and his wife took time off for a trip to Europe. He had been exhausted by the strenuous appeals (he had lost ten pounds during the trials before Callahan), and his wife insisted that he take a rest. In late June he boarded the French liner *Champlain* for a ten-week holiday on the Continent. [78] Shortly after he returned, he faced an entirely new development. Two ILD attorneys had been caught red-handed trying to bribe Victoria Price.

[76] *Patterson* v. *Alabama*, 229 Ala. 273. Gardner noted the charge of fraud in placing the names on the jury lists, but concluded it was "wholly immaterial, and we pass it by without any expression of opinion thereon." *Norris* v. *Alabama*, 229 Ala. 232, 234, 236, 238; New York *Times*, June 29, 1934, p. 9; Montgomery *Advertiser*, June 29, 1934.

[77] Montgomery *Advertiser*, July 10, 1934; New York *Times*, July 10, 1934, p. 23.

[78] Reynolds, *Courtroom*, 277.

As early as May, 1933, Victoria had chatted with George W. Chamlee and had implied that she would change her story for the right price.[79] Nothing came of this conversation. Then, in June of 1934, J. T. Pearson of Birmingham wrote the ILD officials and told them Victoria might be willing to change her story if she were properly rewarded. Brodsky selected Samuel Schriftman, a New York attorney associated with the ILD, to make the contact with Pearson.[80] Throughout the summer Schriftman, operating under the pseudonym of Daniel Swift, carried on the delicate negotiations. In late August, he reached a satisfactory agreement and Pearson made the offer to Mrs. Price. If she would be willing to sign an affidavit repudiating her earlier testimony, she would receive $500. Although the prosecution's chief witness did not report the offer to police, she remained noncommittal. On September 27, Pearson increased the amount to $1,000 and she readily agreed. What Pearson did not know was that Mrs. Price had decided to turn the tables on her tormentors. In mid-September she had gone to the Huntsville police and told them the entire story. They encouraged her to "play along" with the deal.[81]

On October 1, Schriftman and Sol Kone, a former associate of Brodsky, flew to Cincinnati and then chartered a private plane to Nashville, Tennessee. The briefcase they carried contained $1,500 in one dollar bills. The plan was to meet Pearson and Mrs. Price in the lobby of a downtown hotel. On schedule, Mrs. Price left Huntsville in a car driven by Pearson and headed north toward Nashville. Just outside the city limits, however, Madison County deputies forced Pearson to the side of the road and arrested him. Simultaneously Nashville police officials picked up the two New York lawyers as they waited nervously. They were carrying the $1,500.[82]

[79] George W. Chamlee to William L. Patterson, May 28, 1933, in ILD Papers.

[80] This is based on what Pearson said in early October. New York *Times,* October 2, 1934, p. 7.

[81] Remarks of Samuel S. Leibowitz to American Scottsboro Committee, October 17, 1934, in Scottsboro Legal File 6, NAACP Papers; New York *Times,* October 2, 1934, p. 7.

[82] Chattanooga *Daily Times,* October 2, 1934; New York *Times,* October 2, 1934, p. 7.

From the outset, relations between Leibowitz and the ILD had been strained. Trotskyite charges that the ILD had indulged in "rotten and dangerous opportunism" embarrassed Party officials. Somewhat defensively, William Patterson had insisted that Leibowitz was hired to take advantage of the "boss courts' legal technicalities." From that point of view he was a successful "courtroom technician." After the trial before Judge Horton, however, William Z. Foster labeled as "tragic" the statement by Leibowitz "endorsing the chief lyncher Horton and condemning the Southern masses indiscriminately as morons, lantern-jawed, etc., etc." [83] Patterson also reprimanded Leibowitz. In lumping together the workers and the exploiters, declared Patterson, "you have unwittingly played into the hands of the lynchers. . . ." Party writer James S. Allen attacked Leibowitz as a "representative of bourgeois democracy giving voice in the courtroom at Decatur and after, to many illusions about capitalist justice and democracy." Allen warned that as long as the New York attorney remained in the case, he constituted "a danger to proletarian hegemony . . . because of the opportunity he offers for the retrenchment of the Negro reformist organizations and the capitalist political parties among the Negro masses." [84]

For his part, Leibowitz found the alliance equally distasteful. As early as June, 1933, he met quietly with a number of Negro leaders to discuss the possibility of pushing the Communists aside. But he was not able to generate the kind of enthusiasm he had hoped.[85] As a result, relations remained outwardly pleasant. When Leibowitz returned from Decatur in April, 1933, he declared: "I am not a Communist, but had it not been for the Inter-

[83] New York *Daily Worker*, April 7, April 12, 1933.

[84] William L. Patterson to Samuel S. Leibowitz, April 22, 1933, in ILD Papers; Allen, "Scottsboro Struggle," 445–46. Party leaders were particularly incensed over the fact that Leibowitz continued to be active in the Democratic Party in New York City, the "party which, in the South, upheld slavery and now the exploitation of the Negro people and the white workers. . . ." New York *Daily Worker*, April 26, November 3, 1933.

[85] L. F. Coles to Walter White, June 29, 1933, in Scottsboro Legal File 5, NAACP Papers. Coles, a Negro author living in New York, kept in close contact with Leibowitz.

national Labor Defense, these nine Negro boys would be in their coffins now. . . ." In a letter to the New York *Herald Tribune,* Leibowitz praised the ILD for giving him a free hand in the conduct of the case. And the ILD responded by lauding Leibowitz for the "magnificent manner" in which he fought the case through the courts.[86]

The bribery attempt completely altered the public relationship. Shortly after noon, October 1, Leibowitz learned of the arrests in Huntsville and Nashville. Within minutes he reached Brodsky on the telephone and demanded to know the full details. Brodsky hurried over to Leibowitz's office and, for the first time, explained that the ILD had been negotiating with Victoria through Pearson since early June. If the plan had worked, said Brodsky, it would have been "good propaganda for the cause." Leibowitz flew into a towering rage. In violent language he told Brodsky that the ILD had "assassinated the Scottsboro boys with that sort of business." The ILD did not want the girl as a witness, but for "vaudeville," he shouted. Brodsky unsuccessfully tried to calm the excited Leibowitz.[87] When several NAACP officials met with Leibowitz later in the day he was still beside himself with anger. Pacing up and down his office he declared that he had "gotten a bellyful," and was "not going to take any more." The ILD had used the case to feed a lot of "parasites, chiselers, and hangers-on" around its headquarters, he said. The Ruby Bates episode was a perfect example of its idiocy. He had warned Patterson and Brodsky not to bring Ruby to New York because of the inevitable Southern reaction. After a two-hour conference they had agreed. "Next thing I knew Ruby Bates had been brought up by the wife of a lawyer . . . [on] their staff." And then "to top this off, they marched Ruby Bates

[86] New York *Herald Tribune,* March 20, 1933; Letter of Samuel Leibowitz in New York *Herald Tribune,* April 30, 1933; New York *Daily Worker,* April 26, 1933. When several impromptu Scottsboro "defense groups" tried to cash in on the indignation over Patterson's second conviction, Leibowitz pledged public support to the ILD alone. Statement by Samuel Leibowitz, May 23, 1933, in ILD Papers; New York *Times,* May 24, 1933, p. 23.

[87] Remarks of Samuel Leibowitz to American Scottsboro Committee, October 17, 1934, in Scottsboro Legal File 6, NAACP Papers.

into court at Decatur all dressed up in New York clothes and you can imagine what reaction that had on the farmer jury down there." Obliquely he hinted there was more to the retraction of Ruby Bates than most people knew. As Walter White later recalled, he declared "if he told the facts about the Ruby Bates reversal of testimony, it would be plenty. . . ." [88]

Two days later Leibowitz issued a statement announcing that he would withdraw as counsel for the defendants "unless all Communists are removed from the defense." The Scottsboro boys were innocent, he said. They needed no such help as that given by the two ILD men arrested in Nashville. He charged that the Communists had raised "huge sums of money by the exploitation of this case through paid admission mass meetings throughout the country and kindred forms of lucrative ballyhoo." The following day Patterson announced that Leibowitz had been dropped as chief attorney because of his inexperience in constitutional appeals. And on October 8, the *Daily Worker* charged that Leibowitz had joined the "Alabama lynch rulers" in spreading "lying stories of attempts to bribe Victoria Price and other slanders." [89]

Patterson and Brodsky had completely underestimated the resourceful Leibowitz, however, for he was convinced that he could do what the NAACP had unsuccessfully tried: oust the ILD completely from the case. At his request, several Harlem ministers headed South and obtained from Norris and Patterson an affidavit turning the case over to Leibowitz and dismissing the ILD. On the way back to New York they also convinced Mrs. Ada Wright and Mr. and Mrs. Patterson they should repudiate their former allies. The three Scottsboro parents signed a statement demanding that the ILD and all its "agents, servants, representatives, and employees" stop taking "any actions or steps with reference to these cases." With affidavits from the two boys and one of their parents,

---

[88] Memorandum of interview between Samuel S. Leibowitz and James Marshall, Roy Wilkins and Walter White, October 1, 1934, in Scottsboro Legal File 6, NAACP Papers. Marshall was a member of the NAACP's legal committee.

[89] New York *Times,* October 4, 1934, p. 8; New York *Daily Worker,* October 6, October 9, 1934.

Leibowitz publicly called upon Brodsky to relinquish all records in the case within forty-eight hours.[90]

The following day the *Daily Worker* admitted that "Leibowitz . . . aided by a certain group of bootlicking Harlem preachers and other reactionary white and Negro misleaders, had secured statements from two of the boys . . . giving him full power to carry on their further legal defense." [91] Reluctantly Brodsky agreed to turn over the documents in the case: "We will not do anything to jeopardize the defense. . . ." [92]

Even as Brodsky publicly capitulated to Leibowitz, the ILD gathered its strength to overcome the "bourgeois misleader" just as it had defeated the NAACP in 1931. Drawing on tactics developed three years before, William Patterson turned to the parents. In letters to Mrs. Wright and Mrs. Patterson he explained that Leibowitz had withdrawn because the ILD refused to allow him to argue the case before the Supreme Court. "He wanted the glory of being the big lawyer and put his glory above the defense of the boys." His attacks "only help the lynchers and hurt the boys' defense." [93]

On Saturday morning, October 13, Negro attorney Benjamin Davis and Mrs. Josephine Norris visited the boys in Kilby Prison. As confused and bewildered as they had been in 1931, they were convinced by Davis that an appeal led by Leibowitz would be a disaster. Davis, an ardent member of the ILD and the Communist Party, assured them that the charges of bribery were faked by the "Alabama lynchers" who had been joined by the turncoat, Leibowitz. Clarence and Haywood signed affidavits declaring: "I want my present appeal in the United States Supreme Court to be

[90] New York *Times,* October 11, 1934, p. 11.

[91] New York *Daily Worker,* October 12, 1934.

[92] New York *Times,* October 12, 1934, p. 26. Brodsky said he had "never been so disappointed in anyone as in Sam Leibowitz." He insisted that Leibowitz had become disenchanted when he learned that the ILD would again retain Walter Pollak to argue the case before the Supreme Court rather than himself. Leibowitz, Brodsky declared, was "more interested in personal aggrandizement than in the welfare of the defendants." New York *Herald Tribune,* October 11, 1934.

[93] William L. Patterson to Mrs. Ada Wright; William L. Patterson to Mrs. Janie Patterson, October 10, 1934, in ILD Papers.

handled exclusively by the International Labor Defense." Both agreed to accept "any lawyer they think proper. . . ." [94]

Shortly afterward, the ILD launched a vicious campaign against Leibowitz and his supporters. When Davis returned from Alabama he reported that Leibowitz had joined with Attorney General Knight. Together the two were "plotting with the lynch authorities against the boys and their connection with the ILD. . . ." Davis told a lurid tale of how Haywood Patterson had been "brutally tortured" in an effort to force him to support Leibowitz.[95]

A hurried visit by Leibowitz's chief aide the following week brought another reversal from the boys and an affidavit pledging undying support. They explained that their frequent change of counsel was because the "Communists have been sending their agents here and have our minds bewildered." [96] As Leibowitz painfully learned, gaining support from the Scottsboro boys was a game of musical chairs. On October 25 he found that all of the mothers had retracted their accusations against the ILD and returned to the fold. Mrs. Patterson explained that Leibowitz and his cohorts were "telling a lot of lies and frightened me, as any Mother would be frightened by lies about her boys' lives." Only her hand signed the affidavit for Leibowitz, she said; "my heart is with the I.L.D. . . ." Leibowitz knew the mothers would be a powerful weapon against him.[97]

In an effort to thwart the ILD he pleaded with Governor Miller to issue orders barring the Communists and their agents from seeing the two groups of boys in Kilby and Birmingham. Miller, however, replied icily that he "would not care to give any instructions or make any requests of the officials at either place. . . ." One of Leibowitz's supporters also asked Will Alexander to use his influence to isolate the boys from the "traducing reds." When Alex-

[94] New York *Daily Worker*, October 16, 1934.

[95] *Ibid.*, October 24, 1934.

[96] New York *Times*, October 21, 1934, p. 28.

[97] New York *Daily Worker*, October 25, 1934; George E. Haynes to Will W. Alexander, October 27, 1934, in Interracial Commission Papers.

ander declined, he was asked to urge local persons to counteract the pressure of the Communists who had virtually "camped on the outside of the jail. . . ." [98]

As the struggle for the boys' support continued, Leibowitz moved quickly to consolidate his forces. When news of the bribery attempt first broke, Leibowitz assured Walter White that the boys would do "anything I tell them," and he tentatively proposed that the NAACP sponsor the case. He, of course, would remain chief counsel. White and the other NAACP officials were reluctant to become involved again, particularly when the allegiance of the boys and their parents was so uncertain. Moreover, if the NAACP went into the case the Communists would inevitably yell " 'frame-up,' " said White, and charge that the arrest of the three men was a " 'conspiracy' " between Alabama, Tennessee and the NAACP. Charles H. Houston, special counsel for the NAACP, also argued that "if the Communists are put out and the boys are finally lost, you [White] have played right into the hands of the I.L.D." If the appeals failed, it would be due primarily to the disgusting actions of the reds, said Houston, but they would be able to say that "as long as the working classes had the case, mass pressure kept the bosses from the boys' throats, but that the N.A.A.C.P. as the bosses' minion formed a conspiracy to destroy the boys and betray the class struggle, etc., etc." If the case were to be scuttled because of the conflict between Leibowitz and the ILD, "at least keep the Association clear and free." White promised Leibowitz the NAACP would continue to take a deep interest in the case, but it could not become directly involved.[99]

[98] Samuel S. Leibowitz to Governor Benjamin Meeks Miller, October 22, 1934; Miller to Leibowitz, October 25, 1934, in Drawer 115, Alabama Executive Files; George E. Haynes to Will W. Alexander, October 20, 1934; Alexander to Haynes, October 25, 1934; Haynes to Alexander, October 27, 1934, in Interracial Commission Papers.

[99] Memorandum of Interview between Samuel S. Leibowitz and James Marshall, Roy Wilkins, and Walter White, October 1, 1934; Walter White to Will W. Alexander, October 11, 1934; Memorandum from Charles H. Houston to Walter White, October 12, 1934; Walter White to Samuel S. Leibowitz, October 2, 1934, in Scottsboro Legal File 6, NAACP Papers. Leibowitz insisted in his reply to White that he had not actually planned to turn the case over to the NAACP, he just wanted to

On October 11, Leibowitz had received public support from the New York Interdenominational Association of Preachers, representing the pastors of Harlem's twenty largest Negro churches. But Leibowitz needed broader cooperation. On October 17 a group of New Yorkers met in the attorney's office to form the "American Scottsboro Committee." Dr. George E. Haynes, executive secretary of the Federal Council of Churches' department of race relations, was named chairman. Among the other directors named were the famous Negro entertainer Bill "Bojangles" Robinson, William H. Davis, editor of the *Amsterdam News*, and J. Dalmus Steele, Harlem real estate operator.[100] Although ostensibly an independent, nonpartisan group, it was little more than a rubber stamp for Leibowitz. The meeting was called by him; it met in his office; it reached only one concrete conclusion: "Mr. Leibowitz is authorized to take any and all necessary steps to remain as counsel for Hayward [*sic*] Patterson and Clarence Norris in their appeals. . . ."[101]

The American Scottsboro Committee remained in existence for more than a year, but its successes were few. The arrest of Sol Kone and Sam Schriftman angered many in the American liberal community. *The Nation* accused the entire defense corps of inexcusable negligence in its conduct of the case. The *Christian Century* expressed confidence in the innocence of the boys, but it added: "We are equally certain that if there is not an immediate, root-and-branch clearing up of the entire situation with regard to the defense of these boys, they will be electrocuted." The *Christian Century* concluded, "We do not know what is going on behind the scenes, but we are convinced that something is rotten." The formation of the American Scottsboro Committee did little to dispel the suspicions concerning the defense efforts.[102]

---

keep them "informed" of developments. Samuel S. Leibowitz to Walter White, October 5, 1934, in Scottsboro Legal File 6, NAACP Papers.

[100] New York *Herald Tribune*, October 11, 1934; New York *Times*, November 16, 1934, p. 18.

[101] Minutes of Temporary American Scottsboro Committee, October 17, 1934, in Scottsboro Legal File 6, NAACP Papers.

[102] "The Scottsboro Case," *The Nation*, CXXXIX (1934), 607; "End the Scottsboro Scandal," *Christian Century*, LI (1934), 1401–1402. The *Christian Century*

Leibowitz had also hoped that by expelling the Communists he would alleviate some of the resentment against him in Alabama. This, however, was wishful thinking. Grover Cleveland Hall of the Montgomery *Advertiser* was unabashedly gleeful over the debacle. Leibowitz, "the New York police court lawyer who has saved many a guilty neck from the hangman's noose," has fallen out with his former associates, "the plate-passing, parading members of the International Labor Defense," reported Hall. Leibowitz became so angry that "he charged the ILD with doing the things Alabamians had been charging all along." And of course the ILD insisted Leibowitz was upset because they had retained another lawyer to argue the case before the Supreme Court. "Perhaps," said Hall slyly, "both are right." [103]

The continued presence of Leibowitz as chief counsel doomed any effort to build support for the ASC among Southern moderates. Haynes fervently insisted that the American Scottsboro Committee would refuse to join with any radical group. "The authorities of Alabama are no longer dealing with the Communists as representatives of the boys," he told Robert Eleazer. The ASC was "composed of American citizens, some of them residents of the South. . . ." But, as Will Alexander observed, even if the Communists could be expelled from the case, Leibowitz would continue to meet strong prejudice. This antipathy was because of his past connections with the ILD and the "violent attacks which he is reported to have made on the South generally after returning from the first trial. . . ." [104]

Leibowitz even agreed to associate himself with Southern lawyers, and Haynes sounded out John W. Davis, the 1924 Demo-

---

noted that one of the directors of the group was the publicity man of a Harlem department store conducting "Scottsboro Sales." An "honest defense of the boys should no more get mixed up with sordid commercialism of this sort than with the partisan tactics with which the I.L.D. has prejudiced the case." "The Scottsboro Scandal Continues to Grow," *Christian Century*, LI (1934), 1507.

[103] Montgomery *Advertiser*, October 13, 1934.

[104] George E. Haynes to Robert Burns Eleazer, November 18, 1935, in Interracial Commission Papers; Will W. Alexander to Walter White, October 18, 1934, in Scottsboro Legal File 6, NAACP Papers; Will W. Alexander to George E. Haynes, October 25, 1934, in Interracial Commission Papers.

cratic Presidential candidate. Davis, a conservative West Virginian and head of the American Bar Association, would be a welcome choice, acknowledged Alexander, but "even a strong name like that . . . would hardly be able to overcome the handicaps under which Mr. Leibowitz would work in trying this case." Bishop William G. McDowell told Robert Eleazer that as long as Leibowitz remained in the case, the ASC would be "playing the role of sucker." Bluntly, the Alabama interracial leader expressed his suspicion that Leibowitz's "public denunciation of the ILD was [a] stage play to save his face when they were caught trying to buy Victoria Price. . . ." McDowell said he would not be surprised to learn that Leibowitz "knew all along the ILD practices he denounced, and that he would like to recover his prestige by putting on another show at Decatur, no matter who pays the bills." [105]

While the ASC and the ILD each tried to consolidate public support, they continued their struggle to gain the allegiance of the boys. During the months of October and November, 1934, the boys changed sides five times. Haywood Patterson captured the spirit of confusion in a befuddled letter to Ben Davis on October 27. When he signed one of Leibowitz's affidavits he still hoped that everyone would work through the ILD, Patterson said. At least "thats what I thought I was signing." He concluded that he was "Daffy." "I mean I am half crazy . . . and I must admit that I dont know whether I signed such papers or not and if I did I didnt mean to do it intentionally." [106]

Despite the continuous switching of allegiance, Haywood leaned toward the ILD and Norris toward Leibowitz. In an unsolicited letter, Haywood told Brodsky, "I can truthfully say I havent been misrepresent[ed] by you and . . . I do not have the feeling that I will ever be misrepresent by you." Norris assured Brodsky, "I will always have the highest respect toward you." But he added, "I have sign up with Mr. Leibowitz and my intention

[105] George E. Haynes to Will Alexander, October 27, 1934; Alexander to Haynes, October 25, 1934; William G. McDowell to Robert Burns Eleazer, December 17, 1934, in Interracial Commission Papers.

[106] Haywood Patterson to Benjamin Davis, Jr., October 27, 1934, in ILD Papers. The *Daily Worker* reprinted the letter on October 31, 1934.

is to stick with him." Norris expressed the hope that his decision would not cause any "hard feeling between you and I," adding: "I do not think anyone could find any greater friend than what you have prove yourself to be toward me. . . ." [107] Leibowitz and the ILD lawyers realized that continued bickering would only jeopardize the chances of the boys. When the Supreme Court agreed to review the cases in early 1935, Leibowitz met with other ILD attorneys and worked out an agreement. Leibowitz and Chamlee (who had also disowned the ILD) would defend Norris, while Fraenkel and Pollak would represent Patterson.[108]

In mid-afternoon February 15, 1935, Samuel Leibowitz stood before the eight highest judges of the United States judicial system.[109] He had never argued a case before the Supreme Court, and he had paced nervously in the anteroom of the high court building. But now he calmly began by noting that the Alabama law did not specifically exclude Negroes from the state's juries, although there was a long and unbroken tradition of systematic exclusion in Jackson County and throughout the state. Leibowitz had been warned by experienced lawyers not to become emotional in his presentation, but when he began describing the alleged forgery of the Jackson County jury rolls he declared passionately that it was fraud, "not only against the defendants but against this very court itself." Chief Justice Hughes interrupted him. "Can you prove this forgery?" he asked. Leibowitz offered to exhibit the jury rolls which had been brought from Alabama. "Let's see them," declared Hughes. One by one, the eight justices examined the names in question under a magnifying glass while Leibowitz explained the mechanics of the forgery. Only after he finished his argument did he learn that it was the first time the high court had ever allowed such an exhibit brought into the court.[110]

---

[107] Haywood Patterson to Joseph Brodsky, October 27, 1934; Clarence Norris to Joseph Brodsky, October 29, 1934, in ILD Papers.

[108] *The Nation*, CXL (1935), 206.

[109] Justice James C. McReynolds, a Southerner, disqualified himself.

[110] As Leibowitz's biographer, Quentin Reynolds, observed, "The function of the court was to decide questions of law—not to decide whether or not names had been forged on a document." Reynolds, *Courtroom*, 283–84; New York *Times*, February 16, 1934, p. 2.

Thomas Knight, Jr., was a veteran of several appearances before the Supreme Court and he forcefully presented the state's case. In discussing the charge of forgery he frankly acknowledged that he could not "tell you whether or not those names were forged. I simply take the position that I do not know." Most of his remarks were an effort to refute the defense allegations of racial discrimination in jury selection. Relying heavily on the Alabama Supreme Court's decision, he argued that the small number of Negroes serving on the state's juries was due to careful selection.[111]

Knight's use of the term "selection" was nothing more than a mask for systematic exclusion as he well knew. As a native Alabamian and noted Southern lawyer admitted in 1934, "Negroes are excluded from jury duty in the South solely because they are negroes. . . ." Every Southern lawyer knew the truth of this.[112] In Alabama a handful of Negroes continued to serve on Mobile juries throughout the first three decades of the twentieth century.[113] Throughout the rest of the state, the end of Reconstruction also meant the end of Negro jurors. In 1910, Alabama officials frankly told an inquiring author that Negroes did not serve on the juries of the state. Occasionally, said one county registrar, a Negro's name was accidentally drawn. He always begged off. When one Negro insisted on his rights "he was taken out at night and severely beaten, and was then discharged on his own petition by the court," proudly reported one registrar.[114]

The readiness with which Southern officials admitted discrimination in 1910 was a measure of the change which had occurred

[111] Crenshaw and Miller, *Scottsboro*, 288; Reynolds, *Courtroom*, 284; New York *Times*, February 19, 1935, p. 42.

[112] Callaway, *The Other Side of the South*, 144.

[113] Judge Joel W. Goldsby of the Thirteenth Judicial Circuit in Mobile said that he was "satisfied that there are names of negro jurors in our jury box in Mobile County because I have personal recollection of having from time to time seen negro jurors report in my court for duty." He said that "one or two" had served in 1934. Judge Joel Goldsby to Governor Bibb Graves, April 8, 1934, in Drawer No. 108, Alabama Executive Files.

[114] As the registrar of one county with 5,000 whites and 27,000 Negroes said: "Negroes do not serve on juries in our courts. Such a state of affairs would be considered by the people of this county as farcical." Gilbert Thomas Stephenson, *Race Distinctions in American Law* (New York: Appleton Century, 1910), 253–54.

since Reconstruction. When the Fourteenth Amendment was initially framed and adopted, the national government pledged unequivocally to enforce the Negro's legal equality.[115] In 1880, the Supreme Court ruled in *Strauder* v. *West Virginia* that any systematic exclusion of Negroes amounted to a violation of the equal protection and due process clauses of the Fourteenth Amendment.[116] Almost immediately, however, the court effectively nullified the rule outlined in the *Strauder* case by *Virginia* v. *Rives,* which effectively emasculated the federal enforcement statutes.[117] The following year in *Neal* v. *Delaware* the court seemed to accept the idea that the exclusion of Negroes for a period of as much as ten years was *prima facie* evidence of discrimination.[118] Gradually, however, the court chipped away at this doctrine and favored the notion that there had to be specific proof of actual discrimination. And this was difficult so long as the jury officials were willing to lie.[119] By the turn of the century, the Fourteenth Amendment was a dead letter as far as Negro jurors were concerned. Only when the defendant was prevented from introducing evidence on his behalf or the jury-selecting officials openly admitted discrimination did the court intervene.[120]

In 1905, Edgar Gardner Murphy observed that the rest of the nation, with an "instinctive perception of the truth," had declined to enforce the Fourteenth Amendment as far as the Negro was

[115] For an analysis of early Southern attitudes, see Joseph B. James, "Southern Reaction to the Proposal of the Fourteenth Amendment," *Journal of Southern History,* XXII (1956) , 477–97.

[116] *Strauder* v. *West Virginia,* 100 U.S. 303.

[117] The federal statutes provided for a change of venue to a federal court when there was evidence of discrimination. The court ruled that the venue could be changed only when there was a specific state statute requiring discrimination. *Virginia* v. *Rives* (1880) , 100 U.S. 313.

[118] *Neal* v. *Delaware* (1881) , 103 U.S. 370.

[119] Bernard S. Jefferson discusses this increasing restrictiveness in a lengthy article, "Race Discrimination in Jury Service," *Boston University Law Review,* XIX (1939) , 424–29.

[120] *Carter* v. *Texas* (1900) , 177 U.S. 442; *Rogers* v. *Alabama* (1904) , 192 U.S. 226; *Kipper* v. *Texas* (1901) , 62 S.W. 420. Between 1882 and 1917 the Supreme Courts of Alabama, Arkansas, and Texas upheld convictions even when the jury commissioners stated their belief that all Negroes were incompetent. The federal courts failed to rule on the question. Jefferson, "Race Discrimination," 429.

concerned.[121] A noted Alabama lawyer observed during the same period, "Constitutional law cannot be superimposed upon a people accustomed to self-government." The Fourteenth Amendment was a product of "extra-legal methods" and was therefore ignored by the people of the South.[122] As non-Southern Americans increasingly grew more content to allow Southerners to handle the race question as they pleased, they also acquiesced in the annulment of the Fourteenth Amendment.[123] Despite this bleak background, there was some reason for the optimism which Leibowitz expressed. Ample legal precedents existed for a favorable decision. Moreover, despite the insistence of conservative Americans that the court operated on a plane above all but the most lofty considerations, the nine justices in 1935 were well aware of the general national indignation over the Scottsboro Case.

On April 1, Chief Justice Charles Evans Hughes delivered the Court's opinion in *Norris* v. *Alabama*. There was, he noted, "no controversy as to the principle involved." The exclusion of all Negroes from jury service deprived a Negro defendant of his right to the equal protection of the laws guaranteed by the Fourteenth Amendment. The question, therefore, was not the principle, but the facts. In a significant extension of judicial power, Hughes declared: "That the question is one of fact does not relieve us of the duty to determine whether in truth a federal right has been denied." [124]

As Leibowitz had hoped, Hughes and the court returned to the general principle laid down in *Neal* v. *Delaware*. The very fact that no Negroes had been known to serve as jurors for more than

---

[121] Murphy, a native of Arkansas and a leading Southern liberal of this period, was referring to the suffrage question, but the same could have been said for the jury issue. Edgar Gardner Murphy, "Shall the Fourteenth Amendment be Enforced?" *North American Review,* CLXXX (January, 1905), 131.

[122] Charles Wallace Collins, Jr., "The Failure of the Fourteenth Amendment as a Constitutional Idea," *South Atlantic Quarterly,* XI (April, 1912), 105–15.

[123] The retreat of the Supreme Court is traced by Alfred H. Kelly and Winfred A. Harbison in their study, *The American Constitution: Its Origins and Development* (New York: W. W. Norton and Co., 1948), 490–95.

[124] *Norris* v. *Alabama,* 294 U.S. 589–90.

twenty years alone created a *prima facie* case. "The case thus made was supplemented by direct testimony that specified negroes, thirty or more in number, were qualified for jury service." Hughes noted that the trial judge had rejected Leibowitz's charge of forgery. The members of the Supreme Court had examined the jury roll in question, said Hughes, and he bluntly concluded: "We think that the evidence did not justify that conclusion." There was ample proof that the defense charges were true. There had been long and systematic exclusion of Negroes and, to avoid judicial challenge, the local officials engaged in a fraudulent effort to forge the jury rolls.[125]

The evidence to justify a quashing of the Morgan County venire was even more substantial, declared Chief Justice Hughes. Although there were a large number of well-qualified Negroes in the county, a circuit court clerk with thirty years' experience testified that he could not recall "ever seeing any single person of the colored race serve on any jury in Morgan County." In the face of this, one of the county jury officials had asserted that he did not know of any Negroes in the county who met the state's qualifications for jury service. This, of course, was the traditional assertion of Southern officials when faced with the charge of discrimination. But in a strongly worded statement Hughes struck down this defense:

In the light of the testimony given by defendant's witnesses, we find it impossible to accept such a sweeping characterization of the lack of qualifications of negroes in Morgan County. It is so sweeping; and so contrary to the evidence . . . that it destroys the intended effect of the commissioner's testimony.[126]

The Chief Justice concluded by returning to the rule laid down in *Neal* v. *Delaware*. If a defendant were able to establish a *prima facie* case of exclusion of Negroes over a long period of time, the mere denials of local officials were not an adequate defense for the state. In view of the denial of Clarence Norris' rights under the

---

[125] *Norris* v. *Alabama*, 294 U.S. 593.
[126] *Norris* v. *Alabama*, 294 U.S. 598.

Constitution, "the Judgment must be reversed and the cause remanded for further proceedings not inconsistent with this opinion." [127]

Haywood Patterson's case presented something of a problem.
The high court almost never overturned decisions of the lower
courts based on valid technical points. And technically, Patterson's
bill of exceptions had been stricken. The court, however, was confronted with the awful fact that for a technical defect in procedure, one person would gain a new trial and the other go to the
electric chair on the same evidence. Hughes, in the Patterson decision, declared, "We cannot ignore the exceptional features of the
present case." If the Alabama Supreme Court had known what the
result would be in the Norris case, "we are not satisfied" that it
would have stricken Patterson's bill of exceptions. "At least the
state court should have an opportunity to examine its powers in
the light of the situation which has now developed." [128] Thus,
without actually ordering a new trial for Patterson, the Supreme
Court remanded his case back to the Alabama high court. Implicit
in the decision was the warning that it would review the case again
should the lower court refuse to overturn the verdict. As one of
Charles Evans Hughes' biographers observed, "With a little ingenuity in reasoning, the technical requirements of the law were
subordinated to the ends of justice." [129]

Earl Browder, General Secretary of the Communist Party,
hailed the decisions as "a smashing confirmation of the correctness
of the defense policy conducted . . . by the I.L.D. . . ." Anna Damon, who had replaced William Patterson as head of the ILD,
agreed. "The complete victory won from the United States Supreme Court . . . is another proof of the might of mass pressure
and mass protest." Leibowitz, however, interpreted the result from
a different perspective. The court's action was a "triumph for

[127] *Norris* v. *Alabama,* 294 U.S. 599.

[128] *Patterson* v. *Alabama,* 294 U.S. 601–608. For a discussion of this problem for
the court, see Mortimer B. Wolf's analysis, "Decisions," *Columbia Law Review,*
XXXV (1935), 941–42.

[129] Samuel Hendel, *Charles Evans Hughes and the Supreme Court* (New York:
Crown Press, 1951), 161.

American justice and . . . an answer to all those subversive elements who seek to engender hatred against our form of government." He was joined by the New York *Times,* which declared, "This judgment shows that the highest court in the land is anxious to secure and protect the rights of the humblest citizen." [130]

Governor Miller perhaps had a psychological stake in the original convictions since he was governor from 1931 to 1935. But the *Times* expressed the hope that his successor, Bibb Graves, might find sufficient reasons for issuing a pardon. "Wisdom—even the most shallow and opportunist kind of wisdom—would certainly dictate that the case be dropped now and forever," remarked the *New Republic.* The key figures in the case had been rewarded. Judge Callahan was re-elected without opposition. Thomas E. Knight, Jr., was the new Lieutenant Governor. "What more do they want?" Surely the state realized "that by continuing these useless and vengeful proceedings, it is dragging itself into disgrace and ill repute." [131]

Governor Graves' reaction to the decision gave some cause for hope. In a statement to the press he declared that decisions of the United States Supreme Court were the "supreme law of the land." Whether Alabamians like it or not, "it is the patriotic duty of every citizen and the sworn duty of every public officer to accept and uphold them in letter and in spirit." The action of the nation's highest court "means that we must put the names of Negroes in jury boxes in every county." On April 4 the governor mailed a copy of the opinion to all circuit judges in the state and told them: "Without in any matter assuming or intimating that the contents of your jury boxes in any way fail to conform to this Supreme Court opinion, I write to suggest . . . that you speedily take proper steps to remedy any such defects." He also suggested that all cases in which the question might be raised should be continued or *nol*

[130] New York *Daily Worker,* April 2, 1935; New York *Times,* April 2, 1935, pp. 15, 20.

[131] New York *Times,* April 2, 1935, p. 20; "Scottsboro—What Now?" *New Republic,* LXXXII (1935), 271.

pros-ed until a new and valid indictment could be presented.[132]

From outside the state an avalanche of praise descended upon Graves. His statement was "the sort of spirit that makes democracy workable," declared the Des Moines *Register*. Washington's *Post* said that Graves had "faced the larger issue involved. . . ." To "elevate law above prejudice is a mark of distinction that will bring him plaudits from far beyond the confines of his state." And the New York *Times* hailed Graves for his "prompt action in directing the circuit judges and solicitors throughout the state to accept and uphold the decision of the United States Supreme Court, 'in letter and spirit.' " He deserved the "approbation of the country at large. . . ." [133]

Within the South, the reaction was somewhat different. There was little breast-beating or fiery denunciation, but there was almost no praise for the court action. The Charleston *News and Courier* insisted bluntly that mixed juries were "out of the question." The Supreme Court decision "can and will be evaded. . . ." The *News and Courier* brushed aside the objection that this would violate the Fourteenth Amendment. That section of the Constitution was forced on the South and was "not binding upon its honor or morals." The Jackson, Mississippi, *Daily News* complained that it was a nuisance because Southern jurists and lawyers would have to take up their time designing methods to avoid the effects. And a survey of Southern press reaction by a national magazine revealed that many Southern newspapers urged their readers to remain calm; the jury decision would be circumvented by "lawful" means.[134]

Within Alabama, the Birmingham newspapers praised Graves for his action, but the court decision itself was greeted by silence

---

[132] New York *Times*, April 6, 1935, p. 1; Governor Bibb Graves to all Judges and Solicitors of Alabama, April 4, 1935, in File Drawer 108, Alabama Executive Files.

[133] Des Moines *Register*, April 12, 1935; Washington *Post*, April 7, 1935; New York *Times*, April 7, 1935, IV, p. 8.

[134] Charleston *News and Courier*, April 13, 1935; Jackson, Mississippi, *Daily News*, quoted in Pittsburgh *Courier*, April 13, 1935; "Scottsboro Decision," *Survey*, LXXI (May 1935), 144.

or, in the case of the Montgomery *Advertiser,* scathing ridicule.[135] For more than 140 years Negroes had been " 'systematically excluded' " from the United States Supreme Court, said Grover Hall. Did this mean, he asked, that the decisions involving Negroes were invalid? He went on to outline all the areas of the nation's legal system where Negroes were absent: the Supreme Courts of the states and almost all the lower state and federal courts. Why had the court not taken action in these matters? Sarcastically, Hall asked, "If negroes had served on Jackson County court juries every year for 29 years before the 'Scottsboro' infants came into the court in their diapers and shaking their baby rattlers, but for some reason—any reason—had not been drawn to serve on the jury that tried the infants aforesaid, would the . . . Supreme Court . . . have solemnly averred that justice had been outraged?" [136]

The Decatur *Daily* maintained silence except for reprinting Hall's remarks. But in mid-April, William Allen White, Jr., of the Emporia, Kansas, *Gazette* attacked the entire Southern jury system. One more piece of criticism—particularly from a graduate of the "elevating atmosphere of Harvard"—was too much for the *Daily.* The Decatur newspaper suggested that White "take a flying leap to Hell—or else remain in Kansas, which amounts to practically the same. . . ." Northerners such as White should toss aside their copies of "Uncle Tom's Cabin and visit Alabama for a deal of first-hand information regarding negroes and whites in general and the case of the Scottsboro babies, muling and puking in their mother's arms in particular." Bitterly the Decatur *Daily* attacked its Northern critics for their statements which were "as revolting as those issued by Samuel Leibowitz, the political belled buzzard of Harlem, in his nobler moments." [137]

[135] An exception might be the Birmingham *Age-Herald,* which analyzed the argument that Negroes were deprived of their rights when all members of the race were systematically excluded from jury service. "Theoretically, legally and morally that principle seems to the *Age-Herald* to be sound. . . ." Significantly, however, the *Herald* called on the state to continue the cases. Birmingham *Age-Herald,* April 6, 1935.

[136] Montgomery *Advertiser,* April 3, 1935.

[137] Decatur *Daily,* April 19, 1935.

On April 30, Leibowitz wrote a long letter to Governor Graves reviewing the case. He emphasized Mrs. Price's background as a "veteran harlot and jail bird." And Leibowitz declared, every "impartial observer at the trial in Decatur . . . came away with the feeling that the conviction of these boys on the evidence presented . . . was a mockery of justice." Pulling out all the stops, the New York lawyer appealed to Graves' anti-communism. Subversive elements were using the case to raise "huge sums of money with which to carry on political propaganda avowedly seeking to tear down our form of government. . . ." Leibowitz noted that "to spend more huge sums of money in the prosecution of nine trials in view of the evidence already so many times adduced is hardly commensurate with good judgment." The former ILD lawyer urged Graves to use his prestige to have the case *nol pros*-ed But, if this were inexpedient, Leibowitz asked for an impartial fact-finding committee composed of such men as Bishop McDowell and the heads of several of the state's colleges and universities. "I, for one, would be ready to abide by the decision of such a group." [138]

The response was a deadening silence. Graves was politically involved in a struggle over his state legislative program, and he had no intention of needlessly antagonizing his supporters by making an unpopular decision in the case. Thomas Knight, Jr., was closer to the sentiment of the people of Alabama when he declared: "Approximately ninety jurors have been found saying the defendants were guilty of the offense with which they are charged and for which the penalty is death." Even though he was no longer attorney general, Knight disclosed, "I have been retained by the State to prosecute the cases and [I] will prosecute the same to their conclusion." [139]

The majority of Alabamians had adopted the position that a mass electrocution was necessary in order to insure the "social stability of this section," observed John Temple Graves, II. It was

[138] Samuel S. Leibowitz to Bibb Graves, April 30, 1935, in Drawer 108, Alabama Executive Files.

[139] New York *Times*, April 2, 1935, p. 1.

the "inflexible if misguided conviction of many Alabamians . . . that a fresh start be made now in the business of getting the accused men to the electric chair." [140] On May 16, the Alabama Supreme Court quashed the existing indictments against the defendants, but the court made it clear that this was only the first step leading to reindictment and retrial.[141] With public opinion in the state rigidly hostile, with the unyielding Callahan still on the bench, and with the defense itself completely divided, the Scottsboro defendants faced a bleak and unpromising future.

[140] *Ibid.,* April 7, 1935, II, p. 4.
[141] *Ibid.,* May 17, 1935, p. 6; Montgomery *Advertiser,* May 17, 1935.

X

THE DEFEAT OF
DIPLOMACY

THROUGH the spring and summer of 1935 the conflict between the ASC and the ILD remained unresolved. The temporary agreement over representation in the Supreme Court arguments touched off speculation that the two groups might achieve a reconciliation, but the same obstacles to cooperation remained. Repeatedly the International Labor Defense offered to discuss steps toward a "solid front in the fight for the unconditional freedom of the Scottsboro boys." Simultaneously, however, the ILD leadership branded the ASC as an organization "backed by the Uncle Toms and Leibowitz" with a policy of "compromise with the white rulers on the life and freedom of the boys . . . [and] cringing servility to the white ruling class. . . ." The American Scottsboro Committee was similarly opposed to involvement with the ILD. Leibowitz and his supporters were convinced the case was hopeless as long as the Communists played a leading role in the defense.[1]

In the summer of 1935, the impasse was indirectly broken by a

[1] James W. Ford, "The United Front in the Field of Negro Work," *The Communist*, XIV (1935), 166. Beginning November, 1934, the "American Scottsboro-Herndon Action Committee" made a series of proposals for conferences to bring unity to the defense. These proposals were inevitably phrased, however, in a way that made their rejection inevitable. New York *Daily Worker*, November 26, 1934; George E. Haynes to Robert Burns Eleazer, November 18, 1935, in Interracial Commission Papers.

convocation of world Communists meeting in Moscow. An International resolution declared, *"at the present historical stage it is the main and immediate task of the international labor movement to establish the united fighting front of the working class."* The "towering menace of fascism" required new tactics, said the International. The Communist parties throughout the world "must strive to secure joint action with the Social-Democratic Parties, reformist trade unions and other organizations against the class enemies of the proletariat, on the basis of short or long term agreements." Stripped of its verbose qualifications, explanations, and amplifications, the resolution meant that the concept of the "popular front from below" was to be abandoned. Stalin, concerned over the growing strength and stability of Germany under Adolph Hitler, had decided the Soviet Union needed as many allies as possible.[2]

In the United States, the CPUSA made an abrupt about-face. Liberals and Socialists, yesterday's "parasites" and "capitalist lackeys," suddenly found themselves honored members of the "people's front." Throughout the fall of 1935, Communist leaders labored to explain the new Party line. Fervently, Earl Browder insisted that the Communist Party had not changed; the American people had shifted to the left. "Even the N.A.A.C.P.," he said, "has been forced by the new mood among the masses to reorientate itself toward the left, to become more bold in demanding equal rights for the Negroes." [3]

The old "national determination for the Black Belt" slogan was one of the first casualties of the new line. Browder explained, somewhat defensively, that a Negro republic in the Deep South remained the Party's "ultimate aim." But he acknowledged that

---

[2] "The Offensive of Fascism and the Tasks of the Communist International in the Fight for the Unity of the Working Class Against Fascism," *The Communist*, XIV (1935), 928–29. The new course in Soviet policy was unveiled May 2, 1935, when the Soviet Union signed an alliance with France. Seton-Watson, *From Lenin to Khrushchev*, 177.

[3] Earl Russell Browder, "New Steps in the United Front," *The Communist*, XIV (1935), 1105. See also, "Tasks of the Communist International in Connection with the Preparations of the Imperialists for a New World War," *The Communist*, XIV (1935), 940–47.

the Negro masses were "not yet ready to carry through the revolution which would make possible the right to self-determination." The Party, therefore, should cooperate with all "democratic elements" in fighting for "partial economic and political demands." [4]

Other factors made the International Labor Defense receptive to the idea of sharing control of the case. The ILD and, indirectly, the Communist Party had been acutely embarrassed over the bobbled attempt to bribe Victoria Price. This incident added to existing disillusionment. Walter White exaggerated only slightly when he said there was "widespread and apparently irremediable distrust of the Communists, especially of their handling of funds. . . ." Many people believed the Party had raised huge amounts for legal defense and then used these funds for propaganda. Moreover, ILD attorneys knew that the grounds on which to appeal to federal courts were dwindling in number, and mass protest had only stiffened the resolve of white Alabamians to see the boys executed. Failure on the part of the ILD to gain complete freedom would be disastrous for the Party's reputation as a defender of the black masses. And there was one last problem. With the exception of Haywood Patterson, all of the Scottsboro boys had drifted back to Leibowitz. Even Patterson seemed to be wavering in his commitment to the International Labor Defense.[5]

In September of 1935, Robert Minor wrote Walter White and told him the International Labor Defense was vitally interested in a broad coalition of organizations to conduct the defense. For White, it was a refrain heard too many times, and he told Minor bluntly that the NAACP was not interested in the kind of popular front the Communist Party seemed always to have in mind.

[4] Earl Russell Browder, "The United Front—The Key to Our New Tactical Orientation," *The Communist,* XIV (1935), 1119–20. See also Browder's book, *What is Communism?* (New York: Vanguard Press, 1936), 186–87.

[5] Memorandum by Walter White, October 14, 1935, in Scottsboro Legal File 6, NAACP Papers. On a visit, November 14, 1935, George E. Haynes asked Haywood about his attitude toward the ASC. When Patterson insisted he was through with the ILD and wanted only Mr. Leibowitz, Haynes recalled, "I told him frankly that his past conduct made us hesitate to believe or trust him now." Patterson protested and declared that all that was behind him. George E. Haynes to Robert Burns Eleazer, November 18, 1935, in Interracial Commission Papers.

White's answer seemed to end hopes for negotiations. On October 1, however, Minor approached Norman Thomas and asked him to use his influence with the NAACP and other liberal organizations. Minor assured the Socialist Party head that the old "popular front from below" was a thing of the past. In fact, he said, the ILD was willing to withdraw into the background if it could make a graceful exit. White remained skeptical and warned Thomas that "whenever it appeared to them to be advantageous . . . they would indulge in sabotage attacks, lying and other tactics of that sort." Thomas, who had endured many calumnies from the Communists, readily agreed, but he argued that the risks were well worth taking if the Scottsboro boys could be saved. Reluctantly, White agreed to a meeting on October 9.[6]

There were many obstacles to any agreement. The Communists, spurred on by the new Popular Front slogans, welcomed their old enemies with open arms. Roger Baldwin of the ACLU had no compunctions about working with the ILD, and White was willing to restrain his resentment if it would aid the Scottsboro boys. But Haynes and the other members of the American Scottsboro Committee were still smarting from the bitter attacks of the Communists and were in an uncooperative mood.[7]

At the first meeting, representatives from the ILD, the NAACP, the ASC, the ACLU, and the League for Industrial Democracy frankly discussed their views.[8] It was apparent from the outset that the main problem was Samuel Leibowitz. Roger Baldwin polled seventeen members of the ACLU Board of Directors, and they were unanimously opposed to participation in any group which retained Leibowitz as chief counsel for the defense. Their opposition was based on the belief that the boys could never be freed as long as the New York attorney remained active in the de-

[6] Walter White to Robert Minor, September 26, 1935; Memorandum by Walter White, October 14, 1935, in Scottsboro Legal File 6, NAACP Papers.

[7] John Haynes Holmes to Walter White, November 21, 1935, in Scottsboro Legal File 6, NAACP Papers. Holmes was a member of the ASC.

[8] The League for Industrial Democracy was the "activist arm" of the Socialist party.

fense.[9] The NAACP had reached a similar conclusion on the basis of correspondence with prominent Southerners. But Leibowitz had no intention of withdrawing. The boys were behind him, he told Morris Ernst, and he was going to continue to defend them. He added that he would "brook no interference or dictation in the handling of the case." As White put it: "We may form a score of united fronts, but if the defendants stick to Leibowitz and he sticks to his present attitude, the united front would be on the outside looking in with no real authority." And more bickering would "further confuse the public mind, which God knows, is confused enough already." [10]

At least twice, the representatives from the interested groups seemed on the verge of abandoning the whole idea. Each time, Norman Thomas used all his prestige and persuasiveness to forestall a collapse of the talks. During the month of November, Roger Baldwin suggested a number of proposals which were debated, modified, and revised. Painfully the group hammered out an agreement. In early December it broke the deadlock over Leibowitz. If he would agree to remain in the background at the next trial, the ACLU, the NAACP, and the ILD would support him as chief counsel. The bulk of the courtroom work would be handled by a first-rate Southern lawyer. Leibowitz accepted the compromise.[11]

On December 19, 1935, representatives of the NAACP, the ILD, the ACLU, the LID, and the Methodist Federation for Social Service signed an agreement creating a "Scottsboro Defense Committee." Under the pact, the new committee was to be made up of individuals and organizations supporting a joint defense program. The authors of the new organization created an executive committee to be composed of one representative from each of the participating organizations. The executive committee in

[9] Memorandum regarding Conference on Scottsboro Joint Committee, October 9, 1935, in Scottsboro Legal File 6, NAACP Papers.

[10] Memorandum Regarding Meeting on Joint Scottsboro Committee by Walter White, November 18, 1935, in Scottsboro Legal File 6, NAACP Papers.

[11] Draft No. 2 of a Memorandum of Agreement Between Organizations Cooperating in the Scottsboro Committee, November 29, 1935; Walter White to George Haynes Houston, December 12, 1935, in Scottsboro Legal File 6, NAACP Papers.

turn was empowered to select a committee chairman independent of any particular faction. There were also a number of safeguards in the agreement requiring that all members support the program of the full committee. This was clearly aimed at preventing the ILD from continuing a program of "mass protest." At the last minute Haynes refused to sign for the ASC, but there was little his organization could do after Leibowitz accepted the agreement. On Christmas Eve, 1935, the ASC officially disbanded and turned all its files over to the new defense committee. In a terse announcement, the New York *Daily Worker* noted that the American Scottsboro Committee "formed in the fall of 1934 to aid in the defense of the nine Negro boys . . . has voted to disband." Thereafter, said the *Worker,* a new group called the Scottsboro Defense Committee (SDC) would defend the boys.[12]

The SDC's first order of business was the selection of a chairman. Several members hoped that Walter Russell Bowie, rector of Grace Church in New York City, might be persuaded to head the committee. Bowie, however, explained that a heavy load of commitments in New York City made it impossible for him to give the SDC the kind of attention it would need. The committee's second choice, Allan Knight Chalmers, accepted. Chalmers, the thirty-eight-year-old pastor of Broadway Tabernacle Congregational Church, had been interested in the case from the very beginning.[13] By nature a conciliator, he possessed an unusual skill at winning the confidence of all persons, even those ideologically opposed to him. Born in Cleveland, Ohio, Chalmers had received his A.B. degree from Johns Hopkins in 1916. He was convinced that a German victory in Europe would be disastrous for the United States, and he traveled to France in 1916 and enlisted in

[12] Memorandum of Agreement Between Organizations Cooperating in the Scottsboro Defense, December 19, 1935, in Scottsboro Legal File 6, NAACP Papers; American Scottsboro Committee Minutes, December 24, 1935, in Chalmers Collection; New York *Daily Worker,* December 31, 1935.

[13] Walter Russell Bowie to Norman Thomas, December 23, 1935, in Scottsboro Legal File 6, NAACP Papers. In March of 1933, Chalmers wrote Governor Miller and urged him to use his influence to have the trials transferred to Birmingham. Allan Knight Chalmers to Governor Benjamin Meeks Miller, March 22, 1933, in Alabama Scottsboro Files.

the Second French Army. But the bloody nightmare of Verdun changed Chalmers forever. From that time on, he was an unshakeable pacifist. When he returned from Europe in 1919, he abandoned his plans to become a history professor and enrolled in Yale Divinity School. Throughout his life he would be deeply involved in pacifism and civil rights.[14]

The problems facing Chalmers were enough to discourage a less confident person. The entire committee, and particularly Chalmers, believed that the boys could never gain their freedom unless public opinion could be mobilized on their side in Alabama.[15] Since 1931, numerous proposals for an Alabama Scottsboro Committee had been made. In November, 1935, George Haynes had visited Alabama for the American Scottsboro Committee. In Birmingham he met at length with Bishop William G. McDowell to explore the possibility of gathering a local group which could cooperate with and advise the ASC. Although McDowell was pessimistic, he collected enough funds to hire a temporary secretary to travel through the state interviewing persons who might be interested in joining such a committee.[16] More than two dozen lawyers, ministers, educators, and industrial leaders endorsed the idea in principle. Those who were interested in the idea were a "Who's Who" of Alabama moderates, said one Birmingham minister. When they outlined their position in a letter to Haynes, however, they made one thing clear. It was impossible, they argued, "to expect an unprejudiced verdict if Mr. Leibowitz presented the case, because of his ILD connections, his previous failures to sence [*sic*] the psychology of southern juries, [and] his intemperate remarks in the papers about the courts and people where the cases must be tried. . . ." Therefore, they could act only if he would

[14] Vita of Allan Knight Chalmers, Chalmers Collection. Despite his hatred of fascism, Chalmers refused to endorse American participation in World War II.

[15] Roger N. Baldwin to William G. McDowell, January 16, 1936, in Chalmers Collection.

[16] William G. McDowell to Robert Burns Eleazer, January 2, 1936, in Interracial Commission Papers.

withdraw from the case in favor of local counsel. Haynes never replied to the Alabama proposal.[17]

When the SDC's executive committee approached a number of Alabama moderates in December, 1935, even though the new organization promised that Leibowitz would remain in the background, its proposal fell on deaf ears. On January 3, Dr. Henry Morris Edmonds, a Birmingham Presbyterian minister, replied to the committee in a bristling letter. "I should hate to be considered brusque or unmindful of the high intentions of the men who constitute the committee," he said. But the committee members were "so misinformed that they are preparing to add further harm to that already done. . . ." Leibowitz's continued presence in the case under any circumstances was totally and completely unacceptable. If the SDC persisted in its insistence on cooperating with the New York attorney, "our hands are still tied in the matter. . . ." [18]

Between the SDC and moderate Alabamians there was an almost unbridgeable gap of suspicion and misunderstanding. Even liberal Southerners like Will Alexander were extremely skeptical over the ILD's decision to relinquish control of the case. "It looks to me as though the Communists are trying to hand somebody the hot end of the poker . . ." he told George Fort Milton. "They [SDC] have decided to approach the Bible Belt with the kind of appeal we can understand," said Bishop McDowell sarcastically. "Namely, a religious united front declaring Holy War on behalf of oppressed humanity as incarnated in the Scottsboro boys. . . ." The SDC was bound for Alabama, he said, "singing Onward Christian Soldiers with Leibowitz in the van and the ILD bringing up the rear with a sheepish grin on their faces." McDowell saw little hope for cooperation with a Northern committee. Inevitably, there would be a repetition of the earlier trials with predictable verdicts of guilty. And the new SDC, like the ILD before it, would then

[17] Henry Morris Edmonds to Allan Knight Chalmers, January 31, 1936, in Chalmers Collection. On the basis of this episode it is clear that either Haynes did not make clear the intimate connection between Leibowitz and the ASC, or the Alabama leaders did not really expect their proposals to be accepted.

[18] Henry Morris Edmonds to Scottsboro Defense Committee, January 3, 1936, in Chalmers Collection.

sabotage hopes of appeal to the governor by "bombarding him with telegrams and insults," declared McDowell. "God forgive us for a lot of fools!" [19]

By the time the SDC officially organized in late December, time was already running out. On November 13 a Jackson County grand jury of thirteen whites and one Negro returned a new indictment against the nine defendants. Judge Callahan announced that the trials would open in his court on January 20, 1936.[20] With efforts to obtain an Alabama committee temporarily shelved, the SDC went ahead with plans for the January trials. In early December, Leibowitz had written Horton and asked for his advice. Horton, who had accepted a position as attorney for the Tennessee Valley Authority after his defeat in 1934, gave Leibowitz the name of a Huntsville lawyer who might be willing to take the case. The "Scottsboro Judge," as he was called, also urged Leibowitz to avoid any verbal fireworks at the next trial. Instead, he recommended almost complete reliance on the medical evidence to show that intercourse did not even take place on the train.[21]

Although Leibowitz knew there was little hope of success, he decided to try once again for a change of venue. During the first week in January, John A. Hackworth, operator of Huntsville's Hackworth Detective Agency, spent four days in Morgan County interviewing people on their attitudes toward the trial. One individual after another told him frankly that there was no chance of a fair trial. A Southern Railway Company inspector said he had attended both trials in Morgan County and had heard "great bitterness and hostility . . . expressed toward the defendants and their attorneys. . . ." On several occasions, he said, persons in the

[19] Will W. Alexander to George Fort Milton, February 18, 1936; William G. McDowell to Robert Burns Eleazer, January 2, 1936, in Interracial Commission Papers.

[20] Creed Conyers, a Paint Rock Negro farmer, was the fourteenth juror drawn. Under Alabama law, a two-thirds vote was necessary in order to return an indictment. Birmingham *Age-Herald*, November 14, November 15, 1935; Scottsboro *Progressive-Age*, November 14, 1935.

[21] Walter White to George Houston, December 12, 1935, in Scottsboro Legal File 6, NAACP Papers.

street had talked openly of lynching the Scottsboro boys and their New York attorneys. Although people were quite willing to discuss the case with Hackworth, they declined to sign affidavits outlining their attitudes.[22]

On January 4, however, "Captain" R. A. Burleson, one of Morgan County's most prominent farmers, overcame his misgivings and signed a statement for the defense. From the beginning, said Burleson, there was a "considerable amount of intense feeling against the defendants and against their lawyers from New York. . . ." While the anger had subsided somewhat, Burleson declared that there had been a "general crystallization of cold and deliberate sentiment against the defendants. . . ." In fact, said Burleson, he had never talked with anyone who did not believe the defendants were guilty and should be convicted.[23]

On January 6, when the boys were arraigned in Decatur, Osmund Fraenkel flew to Alabama to present the defense motion. Contrary to what everyone had expected, he did not ask for transfer to another Alabama court, but to the nearest federal district court. To Callahan, the request implied that it was impossible to obtain a fair trial in an Alabama state court. In a sharply worded denial, he dismissed Fraenkel's motion as "irrelevant, and . . . I might be permitted to say, improper. . . ." Callahan noted that "there isn't a solitary decision of the Supreme Court of the United States that has held that you can have a case removed . . . unless and until it is shown by a petition that the state has passed some law that infringes these [defendants'] rights. . . ." [24]

When the fourth trial of Haywood Patterson opened January 20, the defense learned that Victoria Price would be unsupported by Orville Gilley. Gilley, Knight's star performer in the previous trial, had been arrested and convicted the week before for assaulting and robbing two women in Tennessee.[25] Even though Knight

[22] *Patterson* v. *State,* 234 Ala. 342, Records and Briefs, pp. 15–16.
[23] *Ibid.*
[24] *Ibid.,* 48–50; Decatur *Daily,* January 6, January 7, January 8, 1936.
[25] John Henry Hammond, Jr., "The Trial of Haywood Patterson," *New Republic,* LXXXVI (1936) , 13–14.

had been elected lieutenant governor he was back at the prosecution table. The defense noted that the Alabama constitution specifically forbade any state official from holding "two offices of profit." Knight readily acknowledged that he had been employed by Governor Graves and the new attorney general, Albert Augustus Carmichael. In fact, Knight said, he had already collected part of his fee. But Callahan refused to order his removal. Knight's action did not make him an "officer of the State of Alabama. He is a mere officer of the court." [26]

As the SDC had promised, Leibowitz took a back seat in the 1936 trial of Haywood Patterson. Clarence Watts, the Huntsville attorney recommended by Judge Horton, had reluctantly agreed to join the new defense staff. A graduate of the University of Alabama law school, Watts was a member of one of the region's "better families." His attitude on race relations was strictly paternalistic. As one staff member of the SDC noted, "outside of his belief in the innocence of the boys he certainly has a point of view that is most objectionable." [27] But the fact that he believed firmly, and was willing to state publicly, that Victoria Price was never raped made him acceptable to the defense. Watts's decision had required a great deal of courage. He was to receive a substantial fee of $5,000 for the first trial and $500 for all subsequent proceedings, but this sum was offset by the loss of several Huntsville clients.[28]

During the tedious first day of jury selection, Watts showed that he did not plan to make a perfunctory appearance for the defense. When the proceedings began, there were twelve Negroes among the one hundred veniremen. Diffidently and with considerable hesitation, the dozen took their places before the bench and swore with the other eighty-eight to render a true verdict. They were

[26] Transcript of Record, pp. 51-52, *Patterson* v. *State*, 234 Ala. 342, Tr. pp. 51–52. There was another defense objection. As Leibowitz noted frankly, if "Governor Bibb Graves should die . . . Knight, as acting governor, would have to pass on any plea for clemency from the boys he helped to condemn." Carleton Beals, "The Scottsboro Puppet Show," *The Nation*, CXLII (1936), 149.

[27] Rose Shapiro to Anna Damon, April 2, 1936, in SDC Administrative File 1, NAACP Papers.

[28] Scottsboro Defense Committee Minutes, January 6, 1936, in Chalmers Collection.

not, however, allowed to enter the jury box during the questioning by defense and state lawyers. When one Negro mistakenly stumbled into the area where the whites were seated, Judge Callahan pointed his finger toward the Negro section and called out sharply: "Here, boy, sit over there!" Few of the Negroes seemed particularly anxious to serve. Seven of the twelve, offering a variety of personal reasons, asked and received permission to waive service. They left the courthouse, as Raymond Daniell noted, "looking anything but regretful." The state rejected the remaining five with peremptory challenges.[29]

Apparently the white veniremen wished to perform their civic duty, for they were unanimously willing to serve. A number of those questioned readily acknowledged that they believed in the inferiority of the Negro race, but Callahan refused to strike them for this cause. As long as they did not allow this belief to interfere with their judgment, he said, they were perfectly acceptable. One salesman even told Watts that he had formed an opinion prejudicial to the defendants as a result of having been present at a previous trial. When Watts challenged for this cause, Callahan overruled him with the remark that it "would take a very dumb man not to get some kind of impression."[30]

On Tuesday morning, January 21, the trial finally got underway as Victoria Price told her story for the eighth time. Because of successful objections from the state, the defense was unable to ask questions about her activities in Chattanooga. Examination by the state and the defense was brief and after less than an hour, Victoria left the witness stand. To replace Orville Gilley, the state had a new witness. Obie Golden, a slender youth with hair carefully slicked back and wearing a new suit bought by the state, was a guard at Kilby State Penitentiary. According to Golden, when he was working in the death house in 1934, Patterson had called out one night: "Captain Golden, come here. I want to tell you something." Golden related how Patterson had said, "I am guilty of

[29] New York *Times,* January 21, 1936, p. 2; Decatur *Daily,* January 21, January 22, 1936.
[30] New York *Times,* January 21, 1936, p. 2.

that crime. Also Clarence Norris and also those other seven up there in Birmingham Jail." Golden failed, however, to link Patterson's confession directly to the charge of rape. Callahan leaned forward and asked the young guard: "Is that all he said?" Golden nodded his head. "Is that all the conversation that occurred between you and him there?" repeated Callahan. "Yes sir," replied Golden. Watts then moved to have the statement excluded because "it is not shown what crime he had reference to. . . ." Callahan admitted that the alleged confession did not directly link Patterson to the charge of rape. But Assistant Attorney General Thomas Seay Lawson corrected this error. "For the purpose of refreshing your recollection," he asked Golden, "didn't he tell you he was guilty of messing with them girls?" Watts objected to Lawson's leading question, but Callahan over-ruled him and Golden declared: "Yes, that comes back. He told me he was guilty of messing with those girls, and Clarence Norris was, and all the rest of the seven." [31]

Leibowitz had left all cross-examination to Watts, but he could not resist the opportunity to question Golden. Leibowitz asked the young guard if he knew the importance of the confession. Golden replied that he did. Leibowitz showed that the state witness did not call the warden; he did not write out the confession, although pencil and paper were on his desk in the cell block; and he waited a year and a half before he even reported the damaging statement by Patterson.[32]

As before, the main problem of the defense was Judge Callahan. He continually interspersed objections of his own to the testimony. Most of all, he made no attempt to conceal from the jury either his disgust with the defense attorneys or his contempt for their contentions in the case. As Horton had suggested, Watts emphasized Dr. Bridges' testimony.[33] Its significance, however, was largely lost upon the jury, for Callahan shut off all questions which

---

[31] *Patterson* v. *State,* 234 Ala. 342, Tr. pp. 63–70.

[32] *Ibid.,* 71–72.

[33] Because of illness, Dr. Bridges could not testify personally and his testimony from the first trial before Callahan was read into the record.

might have explained the presence of the semen which Bridges had described.[34]

Watts, therefore, had to devote most of his effort to showing the unreliability of Victoria Price as a witness for the state. He developed the defense's theory that she had attempted to flee by pointing out contradictions in her account of how she had fallen and supposedly fainted. W. W. Hill, the station master at Paint Rock, and Tom Taylor Rousseau, the young part-time Jackson County deputy, both said they had first seen her standing at least ten cars farther back than the gondola where she claimed she fainted as she got out. Callahan broke in, shaking his head. "That strikes me as enough on that. We are magnifying it looks to me like things, that are not very important." Watts asked, "May I ask just one more question?" Sarcastically, Callahan replied, "Well, all right. When you get through with that one then there will be another. It will be some time before you are through." Leibowitz had remained silent throughout the first day, but he suddenly jumped up and asked for a private conference. Knight, Lawson, Leibowitz, Watts, and the judge retired to a courthouse room. When they returned, Raymond Daniell reported that the judge looked "sizzling mad." After the courtroom was quiet, in a barely audible voice, Watts asked for a mistrial on the grounds that "the attitude of the court and the irritability the court has manifested on the bench . . . [are] materially and substantially affecting our ability to proceed here with the trial." Moreover, added Watts, the constant denigration of the evidence offered by the defense inevitably had prejudiced the defendant's rights. Callahan, apparently incredulous at the charge, insisted, "I must confess that I can't see anything that I have done that's wrong. . . ." He denied the motion.[35]

Shortly after 5 P.M., Watts asked the court for an adjournment for the day, but Callahan insisted that he had to push on. The Huntsville attorney protested. "We have been nine and one-half hours continually in the trial of this case," he declared. Because of

[34] *Patterson* v. *State*, 234 Ala. 342, Tr. pp. 111–12.
[35] *Ibid.*, 76, 78, 81, 84, 86–89; New York *Times*, January 22, 1936, p. 20.

the difficulty of the case and the "tenseness of the situation and the atmosphere," he and his fellow attorneys were exhausted. "We don't feel we can properly continue here working longer and do justice to our client." He added, "Commonplace labor don't work that long, if the court please." But Callahan denied the request. There was "lots of work" yet to be done, he said. He could find nothing unreasonable about going on into the night. Just before nine o'clock, after twelve hours of continuous deliberation, the court finally adjourned.[36]

On the second day of the trials, Lester Carter was on the stand again for the defense, but he was able to tell little about the case. Most of his testimony was devoted to answering Lieutenant Governor Knight's questions about where he had been living in the past year and who had been supporting him. When Leibowitz inquired why he had not been permitted to trace the movements of Victoria Price in similar manner, Judge Callahan threatened to cite him for contempt. "I won't have insinuations that you were denied something that somebody else got," he shouted at Leibowitz.[37]

Early in the afternoon the defense rested its case after Patterson and several of the other Scottsboro boys had testified they never saw any girls on the train. Melvin Hutson, who had replaced Wade Wright as the Morgan County Solicitor, opened the summations for the state. Dropping his cud of tobacco into a spittoon, he combed his hair, smoothed his small black bow tie, and launched into his address. Alternately shouting and speaking in a low intimate voice, he warned the jurors that they would have to go home and face their neighbors. His voice rose to a crescendo, and once he choked back a sob brought on by his own eloquence in lauding the martyrdom of Mrs. Price. "She fights for the rights of the womanhood of Alabama," he shouted. Whether "in overalls or furs" the women of the state were protected from rape, the vilest crime of the human species. He pleaded with the jurors to "protect the sacred secret parts of the female," lest the women of the

[36] *Patterson v. State,* 234 Ala. 342, Tr. pp. 93–94.
[37] *Ibid.,* 116; New York *Times,* January 23, 1936, p. 1.

state, "this glorious state," have "to buckle six-shooters about their middles." Hutson, a devout leader of the Methodist church, concluded with his voice at full volume. "Don't go out and quibble over the evidence," he roared. "Say to yourselves, 'We're tired of this job' and put it behind you. Get it done quick and protect the fair womanhood of this great State." [38]

For the defense Watts spoke in a quiet, confidential tone, never raising his voice throughout his summation. He introduced himself as a "friend and neighbor" from Madison County and argued that the story told by Mrs. Price had been refuted by the state's own witnesses. It had also been "contradicted by the physical facts in the case." He remarked that he could not help wondering why the state had left it for the defense to present medical testimony which was in its hands. Answering Hutson's pleas for the protection of womanhood, he appealed for "protection of the innocent." His face strained by three days of continuous courtroom sessions, he said softly, "It takes courage to do the right thing in the face of public clamor for the wrong thing. . . ." But "when justice is not administered fairly," he concluded, "governments disintegrate and there is no protection for anyone, man or woman, black or white." [39]

Just before 5:30 P.M., the summations ended and after a recess, the jury returned to hear Judge Callahan's charge. It lasted for almost two hours and was virtually a repeat of that he had given in the earlier Patterson trial. He even repeated his statement that there was a strong legal presumption that a white woman, whatever her station in life, would not yield voluntarily to intercourse with a Negro. In addition, Judge Callahan gave lengthy instructions on how the jury might find the defendant guilty of conspiracy. In vain, the defense protested that the new grand jury

[38] Beals, "Scottsboro Puppet Show," 150; Hammond, "Trial of Haywood Patterson," 14; New York *Times*, January 23, 1936, p. 1. Fifteen years later, Hutson's biographer described him as a "deeply religious man," who had "taught Sunday School for more than thirty-five years. . . ." To his "neighbors and associates he is known as a man who patterns his daily life and his conduct towards his fellow-man on the precepts of his church." Owen, *Story of Alabama*, V, 1161–62.

[39] New York *Times*, January 23, 1936, p. 1.

indictment did not charge conspiracy on the part of the defendant. At the request of the defense, Callahan made several supplementary charges to the jury, but he would neither retract his instructions on conspiracy nor would he modify his statement that intercourse between a white woman and a Negro man was necessarily rape.[40]

To the defense lawyers and their supporters, there seemed little doubt of the outcome. Author Carleton Beals, covering the trials for *The Nation,* believed that Judge Callahan's attitude alone was enough to insure a death sentence. Beals acknowledged that the case might be free from reversible errors. "But no one who was not present can realize the inflections of the court and the subtly changed meanings that were put upon words." According to Beals, when charging the jury, "Judge Callahan said that if such and such things were true, in a tone implying they probably were, then the defendant was a 'rapist' and should be convicted." As he said these words, said Beals, "he glared over at the defendant in fury, his lips drawn back in a snarl, and he rolled out the word 'r-r-rapist' in a horrendous tone." The record did not show these inflections, "but continue them hour after hour and day after day in an already prejudiced courtroom, and the sum total weighs upon the minds of the jurors." [41]

All day Thursday, while Haywood Patterson's jury deliberated, the court began the task of selecting a jury to try Clarence Norris. In groups of twelve, Callahan asked those called to raise their hands if they had any "fixed opinion" which could not be changed by the evidence. For the defense there was chilling evidence just how strongly Morgan County citizens wanted to see the defendants convicted. In one group of twelve men, Watts discovered three who had sat on earlier juries convicting Haywood Patterson. Not one of the three had raised his hand. Just as the last juror was accepted, there came word from jury foreman John Burleson that the other jury had reached a verdict.[42]

[40] *Patterson* v. *State,* 234 Ala. 342, Tr. pp. 157–60.
[41] Carleton Beals, "Scottsboro Interview," *The Nation,* CXLII (1936), 179.
[42] New York *Times,* January 24, 1936, p. 1.

As the men filed into the room, Leibowitz whispered to Patterson to prepare him for the sentence that everyone expected. The clerk read the slip of folded paper which Burleson handed him. "We, the jury, find the defendant Haywood Patterson guilty as charged and fix his punishment at seventy-five years in prison." There was a moment of shocked silence in the courtroom. Lieutenant Governor Knight and particularly Solicitor Melvin Hutson were visibly stunned by the jury's decision. The two people who seemed most disappointed by the verdict were Haywood Patterson and Victoria Price. Afterwards, the condemned Negro told newsmen he had assumed it would be the electric chair and he had just as soon it was death. "I'd rather die," he said, "than spend another day in jail for something I didn't do." Victoria Price had been laughing and talking in the courthouse corridors while the crowd waited for the verdict. But afterwards she repeated over and over to anyone who would listen that it "wasn't fair." [43]

Samuel Leibowitz also expressed extreme disappointment over the result and pledged a fight until all of the boys were completely free. Nevertheless, as unjust as the verdict seemed to the defense, it was a victory of sorts. As the Birmingham *Age-Herald* noted, the jury's decision "represents probably the first time in the history of the South that a Negro has been convicted of a charge of rape upon a white woman and has been given less than a death sentence." The *New Republic*'s correspondent in Decatur noted that it was difficult for Northerners to conceive of how a verdict of seventy-five years represented a "victory" for the defense. "But when one realizes that the state in its plea never suggested an alternative for the death penalty . . . and that the Judge broadly hinted as to the necessity of the extreme penalty, the compromise becomes all the more remarkable." [44]

The jury's action was owing almost entirely to the persuasiveness of its foreman, John Burleson. Burleson, thirty-five years of age and a devoted Methodist, had never smoked or chewed tobac-

[43] Decatur *Daily*, January 24, 1936; Hammond, "Trial of Haywood Patterson," 14; New York *Times*, January 24, 1936, p. 1.

[44] Birmingham *Age-Herald*, January 24, 1936; Hammond, "Trial of Haywood Patterson," 14.

co or even tasted liquor. As a top athlete at Gulf Coast Military Academy he had considered professional baseball as a future career. But ultimately he settled down on his family's three thousand acre farm to become one of the county's most prosperous farmers. An avid reader, Burleson subscribed to numerous magazines, including the *Saturday Evening Post, Colliers, Liberty, Time, Country Gentleman* and *National Geographic*. Burleson had become convinced of the defendants' innocence as the trial progressed. He simply did not believe Victoria Price's testimony. But the other eleven jurors told him they could not vote for an acquittal and return to the communities in which they lived. Burleson, fearful that a new trial would lead to Patterson's death, finally persuaded the rest of the jury to accept a compromise. He would acquiesce in a guilty verdict if the other jurors would agree to give Patterson a prison sentence rather than the electric chair. As Burleson later confided to his brother, the case was so flimsy he was confident that— once emotions had subsided—Patterson would be released from prison. While he was not happy with the compromise, his persistence led to a break in the continuous string of death sentences. It may well have marked a turning point in the case.[45]

The following morning, the defense attorneys requested a postponement of the trial of Clarence Norris because of the illness of Dr. Bridges. In Patterson's trial, the state had allowed the doctor to waive an appearance. Knight had consented to an agreement whereby the physician's testimony in the first trial before Callahan was read into the record. Apparently sobered by the seventy-five year sentence given to Patterson, Lieutenant Governor Knight made it clear that he would not do the same for Norris. After a half-day of unsuccessful haggling between state and defense attorneys, Judge Callahan announced an indefinite recess until Dr. Bridges could recover sufficiently to take the witness stand. Late in the afternoon of Friday, January 24, Leibowitz and the other attorneys began returning to their homes, while county and state officers loaded the boys into three cars and began the eighty-mile trip back to the Birmingham Jail.[46]

45 New York *Post*, January 29, 1936; Interview with Colonel Joseph Burleson, U.S.A., retired, Tuscaloosa, Ala., September 27, 1978.
46 Decatur *Daily*, January 24, 1936.

G. F. Anderson operated a small filling station south of Decatur, just inside the Morgan County line. Shortly after 4 P.M. on January 25, he looked up to see a black car careening down the highway from side to side; it finally braked to a halt one hundred yards from his station. Almost as soon as it stopped, the front doors flew open and there was the sharp report of a pistol. Anderson reached the car to find two white men standing by the road with weapons drawn; one had a bleeding slash across the fleshy part of his double chin. In the back seat of the car were three manacled Negroes. Two of them, Clarence Norris and Roy Wright, held their hands over their heads and shouted, "Boss, we haven't got anything on us. You can search us, we haven't got anything at all." The third lay slumped in the seat, a stream of blood pouring from the bullet hole in the side of his head. Ozie Powell was alive, but critically wounded.[47]

For the next two days state officials weighed two different accounts of the tragic incident. According to Norris and Wright, Powell had "found" a pocket knife in his cell the morning they left Decatur and had put it in his pocket. Shortly after the car left Decatur, Morgan County Sheriff J. Street Sandlin and his deputy, Edgar Blalock, began "talking rough," and demanding to know why the boys didn't leave their "communist lawyers" alone. Wright quoted Blalock as saying, "All the lawyers want to do is make a big hurrah, to raise more money for their own benefit. . . . The lawyers will profit a million dollars on you and then drop you." Norris, who sat in the middle of the back seat with one hand manacled to each of the boys, claimed that Ozie "sassed" Deputy Blalock. With the back of his hand, Blalock slapped him across the mouth. Ozie was sitting on the right side of the car with his right hand free, and he quietly reached his hand into his pocket, said Norris. When Blalock was once again facing the road, Powell reached across the seat and slashed the deputy's throat. Sheriff Sandlin, the driver of the car, reached back, pushed Powell back in the seat, and then managed to bring the car to a halt, before

[47] *Ibid.*, January 25, 1936.

jumping out, drawing his gun, and firing into the back of the car.[48]

Sheriff Sandlin, however, insisted there was "not a word of truth" in the charges. According to the sheriff, the attack on Blalock was "all planned" the night before they left Decatur. And Sandlin added ominously, "No negroes did the planning." With the help of outsiders they were going to kill him and Blalock and then flee to safety. "We never had a cross word with any of those negroes, and not a word had been spoken for ten miles . . ." he declared. Sandlin also accused Roy Wright of taking part in the assault and claimed that he had found a knife on him.[49]

Initially Birmingham doctors gave the young Negro only a fifty-fifty chance to recover, but gradually he regained his strength. The neurosurgeon at Hillman Hospital in Birmingham who performed the operation, however, concluded that his patient would have permanent brain damage.[50] In the state investigation that followed, Sheriff Sandlin and Deputy Blalock were completely exonerated. According to the report by Captain Porter Smith of the Alabama State Highway Patrol, the knifing of Deputy Blalock was an "unprovoked attack" made for the purpose of escaping. A delivery boy at the jail had either given or sold the knife to Powell on the morning of the assault. Governor Bibb Graves released a statement to the press commending the officers "for handling a most delicate and deplorable situation in an efficient manner." Sandlin and Blalock "did their full duty and are to be commended." Even before Governor Graves released his statement, Alabama newspapers praised Sandlin and Blalock for their "fine measure of self-control." Their conduct, said the Birmingham *Age-Herald,* "should be an answer to unjust charges that Southern

[48] *Ibid.,* January 27, 1936; Birmingham *Age-Herald,* January 25, 1936.

[49] Decatur *Daily,* January 25, 1936. This accusation was later quietly dropped and no charges were ever made against Wright. Witnesses on the scene reported that only Powell was armed.

[50] Dr. Wilmot S. Littlejohn to Governor Bibb Graves, January 24, 1936, in File Drawer 115, Alabama Executive Files. Half of the bullet lodged one and one-half inches within the brain and destroyed some of Powell's brain tissue.

officers are always quick on the trigger when negroes accused of rape attempt to escape." [51]

Outside the state, skepticism greeted the official description of the incident, and the two boys' conflicting account inflamed these doubts. As the New York *Post* noted, the "shameful" course of the Alabama trials had led many Americans to lose faith in the veracity of the state's officials. If this distrust angered Alabamians, they had no one to blame but themselves, said the *Post.* The New York *Times* noted Alabamians' paranoia over "outsiders" and declared: "It would now seem that among the outside intrusions which Alabama would repel from her borders are the laws of probability and common sense. . . ." After noting that Powell was manacled to another prisoner with his left hand and sitting in the rear of an auto, the *Times* argued that "it strains belief that a handcuffed man could . . . be stopped only by a bullet in the brain. If shooting through the head is a delicate and efficient way of handling him, one can only wonder what [Alabama officials] consider a rough-and-ready situation." [52]

In the week following Powell's assault and wounding, telegrams and letters of protest poured into the governor's office. There was never to be a completely satisfactory explanation for the incident. Olen Montgomery, who described the "turrible comeoff" to Anna Damon, made an observation from his perspective. He explained that he was not in the car and therefore did not know exactly what happened. But, he added in an afterthought, Ozie "hasn't real good sense no way I dont believe." [53]

Whatever the causes of the knifing, the results were unmistakeable. As Dr. Henry Edmonds noted, "The cutting and shooting affray near Cullman has seriously altered the whole aspect of the case." The seventy-five-year sentence for Patterson "showed a new and hopeful attitude on the part of Southern juries in such cases."

---

[51] Montgomery *Advertiser,* January 28, 1936; Birmingham *Age-Herald,* January 23, 1936.

[52] New York *Post,* January 25, 1936; New York *Times,* January 29, 1936, p. 22.

[53] Olen Montgomery to Anna Damon, January 26, 1936, in Scottsboro Administrative File 1, NAACP Papers.

But the Birmingham minister added, "If Patterson were tried today he would get death. There is a new tenseness that bodes ill for
the future trials." Although Dr. Edmonds still had many misgivings concerning the possibility of forming a united North-
South defense group, he agreed to a conference during the early
part of February. Birmingham's Bishop McDowell, who had also
agreed to the conference, at the same time made it clear that Leibowitz and any member of the ILD would be unwelcome in Alabama.[54]

When Chalmers met with a number of Alabamians assembled
by Edmonds and McDowell in Birmingham on February 10, he
learned that the conflict over Leibowitz was only one of many
areas in which the SDC and the moderate Southerners disagreed.
The meeting itself was cordial and friendly, but partly because of
its brevity, few details were worked out. Four days later, in a letter
to Chalmers, Bishop McDowell summarized an agreement which
would be acceptable to his friends. First, the SDC would have to
obtain the complete withdrawal of Samuel Leibowitz and keep
the ILD from making public pronouncements on the case. In return, moderate Alabamians would form a local committee to secure Alabama lawyers. The Southern committee would then agree
to "raise its share of the costs" and to "work to prepare public
opinion for a fair estimate of the facts in the case. . . ." It would be
"desirable" if Knight could be induced to withdraw and if "questions like a change of venue or another trial judge" could be carefully explored at a later time. Finally, said McDowell, "It is not
considered necessary that members of the Alabama Committee
commit themselves to the innocence of the Negroes. . . ." Chalmers' understanding of the tentative agreement, however, differed
on two key points. First and most important—and his entire com-

[54] Henry Edmonds to Allan Knight Chalmers, January 31, 1936; William G.
McDowell to Allan Knight Chalmers, January 31, 1936, in Chalmers Collection. On
a trip into Alabama in early February, George Fort Milton found little that was
hopeful. Phobias had been piled on top of each other, said Milton, and the cutting
incident "re-intensified all of the old feelings, and has made confusion even worse
confounded than before." George Fort Milton to Norman Thomas, in Scottsboro
Legal File 7, NAACP Papers. See also article by John Temple Graves II, in New
York *Times*, February 2, 1936, IV, 11.

mittee was adamant on this point—the SDC would never accept a committee of Alabamians who were not convinced of the innocence of the boys. Second, there could be no compromise such as a plea of guilty on a lesser charge and a long prison sentence.[55]

The result was a stalemate. As McDowell said, not one of the Alabamians was willing to commit himself to the belief that the boys were innocent. "This has nothing to do with racial or sectional prejudice, but comes from a careful study of the case from the beginning . . . not from a sentimental, but from a very practical and personal interest in the doing of justice to people who did not have a fair presentation of their day in court." James Edward Chappell, publisher and editor of the Birmingham *Age-Herald,* argued that a verdict of acquittal would be impossible. Therefore the acceptance of a prison term would be the only practical course to adopt.[56]

While Chalmers was discouraged at the apparent breakdown of negotiations, he was not willing to admit defeat. During his brief visit to Alabama he had already begun evaluating the state's leaders of moderation. At first he had tried to enlist McDowell because of the bishop's prestige and long association with the interracial cause in the state. But Chalmers, always the sure-footed negotiator, soon realized that McDowell was rigid, unbending, and far from being liberal on most issues raised by the Scottsboro Case. Quietly he abandoned his efforts with the bishop and turned more and more to Dr. Henry Edmonds, pastor of Birmingham's Independent Presbyterian Church.

Edmonds, a fifty-eight-year-old Alabama-born minister, had come to Birmingham in 1913 as pastor of the South Highland Presbyterian Church. Two years later he organized and became minister of the Independent Presbyterian Church. During his twenty-one-year pastorate he had served in a number of charitable

[55] William G. McDowell to Allan Knight Chalmers, February 14, 1936; Allan Knight Chalmers to William G. McDowell, February 18, 1936, in Chalmers Collection.

[56] William G. McDowell to Allan Knight Chalmers, February 14, 1936; James E. Chappell to Allan Knight Chalmers, March 24, 1936, in Chalmers Collection. Will Alexander was also doubtful that acquittal was a feasible goal. Will Alexander to George Fort Milton, February 18, 1936, in Interracial Commission Papers.

drives and was known for his interest in race relations. After 1930 he served as chairman of the Alabama Commission on Interracial Cooperation. Although moderate by national standards, Edmonds was clearly within the left wing of Alabama white liberalism. Despite repeated charges of "Communist leanings" he forthrightly fought some of the most glaring evils of Southern society—lynching and the educational deprivation and political disfranchisement of the Negro. He acquiesced in segregation as a necessity for maintaining public order, but he refused to accept the notion that Negroes made up a "permanently backward race." Black "inferiority" was rather a result of the harsh bonds of discrimination, he argued.[57]

Despite his liberalism in Alabama, Dr. Edmonds was far removed from the SDC's position. In late March Chalmers tried to revive cooperation with the Alabama moderates by making a modified proposal to Edmonds. He explained to the Alabama minister that he was under extreme pressure from the ILD to produce positive results. If eminent Alabama counsel was not obtained to cooperate with Watts, "the probability is that Leibowitz may have to come into the case again. . . ." Chalmers added in a conciliatory note that the SDC was considering dropping its demand that the Alabama group be committed to the boys' innocence. The response from Edmonds was indignant and negative. "You said that Leibowitz might retire," he declared. "We feel that he must retire." The fact that the boys intended to stand by him "has no bearing. They couldn't get him if he refused to serve." As for the ILD, Edmonds stated bluntly that no Alabamian would enter the case without ironclad assurances that the Communist group would keep its mouth shut and stay out of the case. "You said your committee has reservations as to whether we should demand of our One Hundred that they be committed to the boys' innocence." Even to consider such an idea was out of the question, said Edmonds. "Indeed we are convinced that it would actually prejudice the case by slapping previous juries in the face and dic-

[57] Owen, *Story of Alabama*, V, 1072; Birmingham *News*, October 9, 1933.

tating a verdict to the forthcoming juries." When Chalmers met with the SDC on March 26, he expressed his frank discouragement over the negotiations with Alabama leaders.[58]

Nevertheless, Chalmers decided to travel to Alabama for one more effort. This time, he set aside two full days for consultation and conversation, not only with Edmonds but with other Alabama leaders. Before this trip, the SDC chairman also managed to do his homework more thoroughly in discovering who were potential supporters.[59] Almost through personal charm alone, Chalmers managed to sway several key Alabamians toward some sort of agreement with the SDC. Edmonds refused to commit himself immediately, but three days after Chalmers returned to New York, the Birmingham minister telegraphed that he would head an Alabama committee to work with the SDC. Chalmers responded with a warm letter. "I think that you have a very good understanding of the peace to my soul that your telegram brought." And to a friend, Chalmers expressed his genuine elation. "The Scottsboro project . . . has turned out with almost unbelievable success. Edmonds is taking the Committee chairmanship and it is actively working." [60]

There were still problems to be worked out. But with the new friendship between Chalmers and Edmonds most obstacles were removed. The Alabama Committee dropped its demand that Leibowitz be fired immediately. In return the SDC agreed to accept the Alabama Committee as "an association of Alabama citizens without organic connection with any other group or

[58] Allan Knight Chalmers to Henry Edmonds, March 17, 1936; Henry Edmonds to Allan Knight Chalmers, March 24, 1936; SDC Minutes, March 26, 1936, in Chalmers Collection.

[59] He was aided immeasurably by Joseph Gelders, a local labor organizer and supporter of popular front politics. Gelders, who had originally been professor of physics at the University of Alabama, drew upon his broad knowledge of Alabama political, religious and civic leaders to advise Chalmers. Joseph Gelders to Morris Shapiro, February 2, 1936, February 5, 1936, in Scottsboro Administrative File 1, NAACP Papers. For general information on Gelders' role in the case see Esther F. Gelders, "Professor, How Could You?" *New Republic*, XCIV (1938) , 96–97.

[60] Henry Edmonds to Allan Knight Chalmers, April 25, 1936; Allan Knight Chalmers to Henry Edmonds, April 29, 1936; Allan Knight Chalmers to William J. Campbell, May 1, 1936, in Chalmers Collection. Campbell was President of Atlanta Theological Seminary Foundation at Vanderbilt University.

organization North or South." The Alabama Committee also reserved the right to express interest in the case in any way it saw fit. And finally, there was to be no commitment to the innocence of the Scottsboro boys. The group's only goal was an unprejudiced trial.[61]

During the month of May, Edmonds' group moved into high gear. Organizing under the name of the "Alabama Scottsboro Fair Trial Committee," the handful of persons at the first meeting on April 28 named Edmonds as chairman and Waights M. Taylor of Birmingham as executive secretary. The Interracial Commission appropriated $37.50 per week plus expenses for Taylor, who immediately began traveling over the state enlisting support. By June 5 over fifty prominent citizens throughout the state had agreed to cooperate with the Alabama Committee. The list included such men as Thomas E. Kilby, a former governor of Alabama; Algernon Blaire, Montgomery building contractor; Dean A. J. Farrar of the University of Alabama Law School; Dr. W. D. Partlow, superintendent of Alabama's state mental hospital; Guy E. Snavely, president of Birmingham-Southern College; George H. Denny, president of the University of Alabama; and more than forty other state leaders, including the editors and publishers of several of the largest newspapers. Secretary Waights Taylor and Edmonds also corresponded with Files Crenshaw, Sr., president of the Alabama Bar Association. They asked if it might be possible to secure outstanding Alabama lawyers who would be willing to take the case as a "patriotic duty" to their state. Although Crenshaw made no definite commitment, he was receptive and agreed to explore the idea with several of his colleagues.[62]

The key to the committee's success, however, was secrecy. As Edmonds noted, it was absolutely necessary to maintain tight security over its activities. A premature disclosure of its efforts

[61] Henry Edmonds to Allan Knight Chalmers, April 29, 1936; Allan Knight Chalmers to Henry Edmonds, May 4, 1936, in Chalmers Collection. Leibowitz's removal remained a goal for the Alabama Committee, but not a precondition for organization.

[62] Henry Edmonds to Robert Burns Eleazer, April 29, 1936; Waights M. Taylor to Allan Knight Chalmers, June 5, 1936, in Chalmers Collection.

could lead to a mobilization of public opinion against the committee. Moreover, efforts to find a lawyer who would be suitable to replace Leibowitz would be extremely embarrassing to the SDC, for the New York lawyer knew little of the elaborate negotiations.[63]

Somehow, Lieutenant Governor Thomas E. Knight, Jr., obtained a copy of the Alabama committee's correspondence with Crenshaw. On June 9 he issued a statement to the press making public the contents of the letters. And afterward, with a sly dig at Leibowitz, he declared, "Apparently Dr. Edmonds and Mr. Chalmers are working in unison on a committee to secure adequate representation for the defendants in the 'Scottsboro' case." To the "best of my recollection," said Knight, the nine boys had been represented by twenty-one lawyers, "part of whom were native Alabamians and the rest of the array of counsel were from the Empire State of New York." The correspondence, which had "emanated from New York," implied that the defendants had not received a fair trial. More than "120 grand and petit jurors have passed upon the guilt of each defendant," noted Knight. And he added: "That should answer any questions about the fairness of the proceedings." After delivering his little bombshell, he "sat back and gleefully waited for the feathers to fly," said Waights Taylor. Knight was confident that public opinion would destroy the nascent Alabama committee.[64]

Initially Knight's strategy seemed to work. Leibowitz knew vaguely of the negotiations with Alabamians, but when he heard that he was to be replaced, the New York lawyer exploded with anger. In unmistakable terms he made it clear to Chalmers that the boys were ultimately his responsibility. They had selected him as their attorney, said Leibowitz, and he had no intention of withdrawing unless he was absolutely certain their interests would be

---

[63] The SDC considered notifying Leibowitz of its effort to replace him with a distinguished Alabama lawyer, but decided to wait for a more opportune time. SDC Minutes, April 30, 1936, in Chalmers Collection.

[64] Montgomery *Advertiser*, June 10, 1936; Waights Taylor to Robert Burns Eleazer, June 12, 1936, in Interracial Commission Papers.

safeguarded. Leibowitz noted that too many Southerners seemed to regard life imprisonment as a suitable "compromise" to the case. He did not. Using all his diplomatic skill, Chalmers managed to calm the angry attorney by assuring him that he would have the right to approve any Alabama counsel. By the time the meeting ended, Leibowitz had even agreed to remain in New York for the next trials if a Southern lawyer of national stature could be found to defend the boys.[65]

In Alabama, the reaction to the lieutenant governor's press release boomeranged. Edmonds was known among his friends as a "fighter," and Knight's "unwarranted and ungentlemanly action" (as Edmonds called it) only strengthened his resolve. Between June 11 and June 15, the Birmingham minister abandoned almost all of his pastoral duties to travel over the state to shore up those who had been intimidated by Knight's announcement. By June 16, he was able to write Chalmers, "We are making very definite and rapid strides in the direction of our goal." There were already rumors that Callahan would be replaced for the next trial because of his poor health. Knight's removal would be more difficult, but "we feel that through a little judicious editorial pressure from newspapers throughout the state some change in the prosecution can be effected." Most important of all, said Edmonds, the Alabama Committee had succeeded in retaining Archibald Hill Carmichael, congressman from Alabama's eighth congressional district. Carmichael, a representative from the northwestern corner of the state, had racial views similar to those of Clarence Watts. But Judge Horton's opinion and the transcripts had convinced the Alabama representative, as they had the Huntsville attorney, that the Scottsboro boys were innocent. Carmichael said he was prepared to fight for their unconditional release.[66]

Within less than two weeks Edmonds' hopes had crumbled. Morris Shapiro, secretary of the Scottsboro Defense Committee,

[65] Allan Knight Chalmers to Henry Edmonds, June 11, 1936, in Chalmers Collection.

[66] Henry Edmonds to Allan Knight Chalmers, June 16, 1936, in Chalmers Collection. For a biographical sketch of Representative Carmichael, see Owen, *Story of Alabama*, IV, 709–10.

learned that Representative Carmichael was indeed willing to serve—for ten thousand dollars for the first trial and an additional five thousand dollars for each subsequent trial. These fees were completely beyond the financial resources of the SDC.[67] And, contrary to the widespread rumors, there was no evidence that either Callahan or Knight was willing to withdraw. On June 30, 1936, Leibowitz wrote Clarence Watts and told him that he could no longer consider remaining in New York during the next trials. "Frankly, I am disappointed at what has been accomplished up to the present by the Alabama Scottsboro Committee," said Leibowitz. "It was my impression that they represented so influential a section of the South that they could properly effect the withdrawal of Lieutenant Governor Knight from the prosecution and likewise be influential in having another judge appointed as trial judge in the cases." Reluctantly, said Leibowitz, he had come to the conclusion that despite the "good intentions of the gentlemen who constitute the Alabama Committee," their net accomplishments had been "exactly zero." Under these circumstances, "I can not help but feel that for me to step out of the picture would constitute a desertion of the Scottsboro boys, and such an act I never have and never will voluntarily commit." [68]

The Alabama Scottsboro Fair Trial Committee remained in existence for another six months, but a lack of funds and an inability to unite on a common policy hampered its effectiveness. Throughout the remainder of 1936, the SDC tried to force some action out of the Alabamians. In early January of 1937, Edmonds finally wrote Chalmers charging the SDC with a breach of faith. "Your attitude is that we have elbowed our way into your councils, promising various things, therefore we must meet requirement after requirement." The situation was "just the reverse," said Edmonds. "You were to keep the Communist group silent; you were going to get Leibowitz out; you were going to furnish the money necessary to pay the Alabama counsel." On virtually every

[67] Morris Shapiro to Allan Knight Chalmers, July 20, 1936, in Chalmers Collection.
[68] Samuel Leibowitz to Clarence Watts, June 30, 1936, in Chalmers Collection.

point, he declared, the SDC had failed to uphold its end of the bargain. Leibowitz remained in the case, the Communists continued their attacks on the state of Alabama, and Carmichael had been rejected simply on the grounds that he was too expensive. Now came further demands that there be a change of venue and Judge Callahan and Lieutenant Governor Knight be removed. "These things are simple enough for us to do, in your estimation, though you have been unable to do them." Edmonds added: "Frankly, our feeling here is that your committee, despite your own feeling, doesn't want us in and is determined that we shan't be in." The SDC was "stringing the Alabama Committee along" and every time the Southerners got to the door, the Northern committee proposed "another impossible test." Edmonds apologized for his brusqueness and assured Chalmers that he remained a personal friend, but there could be no further active cooperation by the Alabama Committee. After this letter, Chalmers continued working with Alabama leaders, but as individuals rather than members of the committee.[69]

The temerity and hesitancy of the Alabama Committee was only one of Chalmers' problems. Beginning in mid-1936, most of the defendants had been placed in what amounted to solitary confinement. Birmingham's Sheriff Hawkins explained that he had isolated the seven boys who were there because "when prisoners of their prominence are allowed to mix with other prisoners there is difficulty." Hawkins' action was not without foundation for the Scottsboro boys had been far from model prisoners. On at least two occasions they had rioted in their cells and destroyed the prison fixtures.[70]

Whatever the justification, the mental outlook of the boys showed a definite deterioration under the strain of the isolation. In August of 1936, Chalmers asked the Alabama Committee if it would use its influence to have the boys returned to their normal

[69] Henry Edmonds to Allan Knight Chalmers, January 14, 1937; Allan Knight Chalmers to Henry Edmonds, January 21, 1937, in Chalmers Collection.

[70] Allan Knight Chalmers to Bibb Graves, December 8, 1936, in Chalmers Collection; Birmingham *Age-Herald*, April 11, 1931, April 28, April 29, 1933.

cells. "Much as we deplore the fact that the boys are being kept in solitary confinement," replied Waights Taylor, "it has been the general contention of our committee all along that our work will be more effective if it is confined primarily to the effort of securing a fair and impartial trial. . . ." Any effort to "pressure" prison officials "might ultimately do the defendants more harm than good." In vain Morris Shapiro argued that no one "could misinterpret the humane motives which would prompt such a request." The Alabama Committee flatly refused to intervene, even privately. Gradually, Chalmers began to suspect that the solitary confinement was deliberate. He wrote an old friend that he could reach no other conclusion than that there was a "deliberate attempt to break them down through isolation, no occupation and no exercise." He added, "It is possible that we may yet free the boys only to discover that they have already been executed as far as practical living is concerned." [71]

On December 8, Chalmers wrote Governor Graves and called his attention to the fact that the boys had no chance to get exercise, or even to get reading material in their cells. He told Graves he had just talked long distance with Edmonds and the Birmingham minister "spoke in the gravest of tones about the marked effect upon one of the boys whom he had just seen." Chalmers argued that extenuating circumstances would not excuse the fact "that such treatment has probably driven several of them already into such mental decline and physical disintegration . . . that they are virtually executed without a fair trial. . . ." With candor Chalmers expressed his fear that their confinement would "break them down physically and mentally so that in desperation they may make a false confession." He was willing to give Graves credit for not intending this, but "the record shows clearly . . . that it is happening, and the record from now on will show whether anything was done to prevent this development from continuing after

[71] SDC Minutes, August 20, 1936; Waights M. Taylor to Morris Shapiro, August 15, 1936; Morris Shapiro to Waights Taylor, August 26, 1936; Allan Knight Chalmers to Reverend Noble Strong Elderkin, December 21, 1936, in Chalmers Collection. Elderkin was pastor of the Akron, Ohio, First Congregational Church.

it was brought officially to your attention." Chalmers concluded with a blunt warning that the SDC would use every possible means to bring this situation to the attention of the public. He regretted the necessity of publicity very much, but "we have become conscious through recent reports that we may already have delayed too long in making an emphatic public protest against a situation which, however anyone may try to justify it, is in practice inhumane." [72]

While Chalmers waited for Governor Graves' reply, there was a new development in the case. During the summer and fall of 1936 the SDC had begun to suspect that the officials of Alabama were in a mood to compromise. Clarence Watts discussed the possibility with Attorney General A. A. Carmichael as early as April.[73] And when Chalmers met briefly with Graves in October the governor suggested that the boys plead guilty to a charge of miscegenation. This was unacceptable to either Chalmers or the other members of the committee, but it was further proof that the state was willing to retreat from its previous demand for the death penalty. The committee authorized Watts to meet with Attorney General Carmichael on October 13. Watts' goal should be to have all charges dropped against Olen Montgomery, Willie Roberson, Eugene Williams, and Roy Wright. The committee would be willing to have the other five boys plead guilty to a face-saving charge of simple assault on the grounds that they be released within a very short time. The negotiations came to an abrupt halt, however, when Carmichael told Watts he would accept nothing less than twenty years for each of the boys on a charge of rape.[74]

---

[72] Allan Knight Chalmers to Governor Bibb Graves, December 8, 1936, in Chalmers Collection. In January, 1937, Dr. George C. Branche of Tuskegee Institute made a psychiatric examination of the boys which confirmed the committee's fears. It was quite apparent, he said, that the "six years of incarceration has had a most unfavorable influence upon the mental and physical life of each of them." George C. Branche to William Jay Schieffelin, January 25, 1937, in Scottsboro Administrative File 2, NAACP Papers.

[73] Memorandum by Roy Wilkins, April 3, 1936, in Scottsboro Legal File 7, NAACP Papers.

[74] Memorandum on Scottsboro Case from Roy Wilkins to Walter White, October 10, 1936, in Scottsboro Legal File 7, NAACP Papers.

On his own initiative Chalmers decided to try to smoke the Alabama leaders from their position. On December 9 he delivered an address to the Federal Council of the Churches of Christ in America. He told his audience that he had "very good assurances from sources close to the prosecution" that Alabama was ready to drop charges against four of the boys. Without listing names, he identified three of them by saying that they were the two youngest and the boy who was partially blind. When reached by newsmen, both Knight and Carmichael flatly denied there was any consideration of compromise. On the contrary, said Knight, the boys would go on trial in January, 1937.[75]

Despite the denial, Attorney General Carmichael and Lieutenant Governor Knight suddenly appeared in New York over the Christmas holidays and asked Leibowitz to drop by their hotel suite. Knight, always an astute politician, had seen clearly a shift in public opinion. Most Alabamians had no desire to see the nine defendants released scot free, but there was little of the emotional hostility toward the boys which had existed from 1931 through 1935. Even the knifing of Deputy Blalock had only temporarily aroused the old antagonisms. As Joseph Gelders observed from Birmingham, the public attitude was still one of hostility, but the raw nerve ends were gone and there was a desire to have the case ended. Most of all, there was a general weariness and apathy toward the entire question of the Scottsboro boys.[76]

When Leibowitz arrived, Knight wasted little time in outlining the purpose of his and Carmichael's visit. The Lieutenant Governor's initial proposal was to let an undisclosed number of the boys go free if Patterson, Norris, and a few others would plead guilty to rape. Leibowitz flatly declined the offer. Such a suggestion was "unthinkable," he said. The boys had told him several times "they would rather die in the chair than admit the commis-

---

[75] New York *Times*, December 10, 1936, p. 17; Allan Knight Chalmers, *They Shall Be Free* (Garden City: Doubleday and Co., 1951) 88–89; New York *Times*, December 10, 1936, p. 17.

[76] Joseph Gelders to Morris Shapiro, in Scottsboro Administrative File 1, NAACP Papers. See Waights Taylor to Robert Burns Eleazer, June 12, 1936, in Interracial Commission Papers.

sion of a crime of which they are innocent." As a counter-proposal he offered to plead the boys to vagrancy or to having a fight with the white boys on the train. This would allow the state to retreat without complete loss of face.[77] Ultimately, at a later meeting in Washington, Leibowitz and Carmichael reached an agreement. Haywood Patterson's appeal would be withdrawn, and Ozie Powell would be tried only for assault on Deputy Blalock. Charlie Weems, Andy Wright, and Clarence Norris would plead guilty to some form of assault and would receive sentences of less than five years. Eventually Haywood Patterson would be released so that his term in prison should not be more than that of Charlie, Andy, or Clarence.[78]

When Leibowitz presented his proposal to the SDC there was immediate opposition. Chalmers was out of town at a conference, but he made his position clear before he left. The SDC "cannot be a party to that agreement," he said. "We have all along defended the boys on the conviction that they were not guilty. . . ." A "plea to an assault charge will mean to the general public that we are admitting their guilt in a sex crime." Leibowitz was also unhappy with the deal, but he argued that the alternative might be death or life imprisonment for the boys. The grounds for appeal to the federal courts were running out, he noted pointedly. Reluctantly, the members of the committee agreed that nothing else seemed feasible. When they went around the table to elicit opinion, Morris Shapiro expressed the dismay of them all. "I say yes to the proposal, but with a very heavy heart, and I feel very badly about it." As its official position, the SDC agreed that while it could not approve the compromise, it would not oppose it.[79]

In a letter to Leibowitz in early February, Attorney General Carmichael told Leibowitz he would present the compromise to Callahan and work out the details. When Carmichael had not

[77] Memorandum of Negotiations between Samuel Leibowitz and Thomas Knight and A. A. Carmichael, July 30, 1937, in Scottsboro Legal File 7, NAACP Papers.
[78] Memorandum of Agreement between Carmichael and Leibowitz, January 22, 1937, in Scottsboro Legal File 7, NAACP Papers.
[79] Allan Knight Chalmers to Morris Shapiro, January 4, 1937; Marion Norris to Allan Knight Chalmers, January 5, 1937, in Chalmers Collection.

written by the end of the month, Leibowitz became concerned and tried calling him. The Alabama attorney general, however, remained "out of town" despite repeated telephone calls. Chalmers used every method possible to try to discover what had happened in the negotiations. Forney Johnston, a prominent Birmingham attorney and the son of a former governor, agreed to discuss the matter with Carmichael. When Johnston finally reached the attorney general, he discovered the cause for the breakdown in communications. When Carmichael's assistant, Thomas "Buster" Lawson, approached Callahan, the Decatur judge angrily informed him that the court would never agree to accept a "fifty-dollar fine for rape." [80] When several Birmingham newspapers tried to pressure Callahan by hinting that compromise was likely in the case, Callahan angrily announced that he was going to call a special session of the Morgan County Court to dispose of the remaining cases.[81]

In spite of Judge Callahan's intransigence, Chalmers remained hopeful. Five days before Judge Callahan announced resumption of the trials in July, Thomas Knight, Jr., suddenly died. Knight was the one figure most closely associated with the prosecution, and with his death the chances for compromise brightened.[82] Moreover, the defense gained a key supporter on June 12 when Grover Cleveland Hall came out editorially for a compromise solution to the case. Hall, who had used the columns of the Montgomery *Advertiser* to pillory the Scottsboro boys and their advocates, said he had reached the conclusion that nothing could be gained by continuing the prosecution. Alabama had been vilified and denounced in every civilized country of the world. The good name of the state was worth far more than the honor of two "hook-

[80] Allan Knight Chalmers to Forney Johnston, February 24, April 21, 1937, in Chalmers Collection; Morris Shapiro, "Behind the Scenes at Scottsboro," *The Nation*, CXLV (1937), 171.

[81] New York *Times*, May 26, 1937, p. 22.

[82] And, as John Temple Graves, II, noted, "However much of a bitter-ender the late Lieutenant Governor may have been about the case at first, he was known to have changed his mind in recent months and to feel that the best possible end to the case for every one would be a sentence of imprisonment with the years already served counted out of the term." New York *Times*, May 23, 1937, IV, p. 7.

wormy Magdalenes." "Nothing can be gained by demanding the final pound of flesh," he said, "and the *Advertiser* has reason to believe, even to know, that it is not the wish of the State to exact the final pound of flesh." He concluded his plea to end the Scottsboro Case by declaring: "Throw this body of death away from Alabama." [83]

Even though the Alabama Supreme Court upheld Patterson's guilty verdict on June 14, the newspapers of Alabama continued to report news that a compromise was in the making. The Birmingham *Post* strongly and publicly supported these efforts, and declared that the evidence overwhelmingly indicated the defendants were not guilty.[84]

Forney Johnston began rounding up influential friends in the state who, in turn, pressured Carmichael to override Callahan and to live up to the bargain with Leibowitz. Five days after Callahan made his announcement of the new trials, however, Johnston learned that Callahan was claiming confidentially that he had not blocked the settlement. "I have no reason to doubt the sincerity of the Attorney General in his statement that he fully concurred in the general basis of a settlement and that the only reason it had not progressed to a definite understanding was Judge Callahan's willingness to approve," said Johnston. But the news from Decatur was a disturbing development. "This worries me as to the possibility that the Attorney General may not be willing to drive through." The main problem, said Johnston, was that the entire negotiations were simply taking too long, people were indiscreet, and many of the participants were getting cold feet.[85]

During the month of June, the defense alternated between hope and despair. Late in 1936, Chalmers had committed himself to a

[83] Montgomery *Advertiser,* June 12, 1937. Hall read a copy of the editorial to Governor Graves and to Attorney General Carmichael. Both approved it in principle. Grover Hall to Forney Johnston, June 11, 1937, in Chalmers Collection. The *Advertiser* editorial was reprinted in at least six Alabama dailies: the Birmingham *Post* and Birmingham *News,* the Selma *Times-Journal,* the Huntsville *Times,* the Dothan *Eagle,* and the Eufala *Tribune.* Montgomery *Advertiser,* June 20, 1937.

[84] New York *Times,* June 15, 1937, p. 13; Montgomery *Advertiser,* June 15, 1937; Birmingham *Post,* June 15, 1937.

[85] Forney Johnston to Joseph H. Nathan, May 28, 1937, in Chalmers Collection.

conference in Europe during July and he had no alternative but to entrust the defense to Morris Shapiro and the other members of the SDC. As the trial date of July 12 approached, Alabama newspapers were filled with rumors of a final settlement. Even when Callahan called a news conference on July 4 and insisted he knew "nothing of any compromise," the newspaper reports claimed an "informal source" had disclosed that the boys would be allowed to plead guilty to a lesser charge with their six years in prison counted toward the sentence. On Saturday, July 3, however, Solicitor Melvin Hutson buttonholed Leibowitz, who was in Decatur on a brief trip before the trial. "You have talked with everyone else down here," snarled Hutson, "but you have not talked with me. I am the boss. We will not give in to less than rape." [86] On July 8, Hutson called a press conference and said, "I know nothing about a proposition to settle these cases on a basis of assault as carried by some of the newspapers." As district solicitor, he declared, he would never consider such a proposition. "These defendants are guilty of rape or nothing. The dignity of the state of Alabama demands that they should be convicted of rape or nothing." [87]

The newspapers continued to carry rumors of a compromise from "authoritative sources," but they seemed less than convincing as the trial approached. Almost desperately, Forney Johnston tried personally to reach Carmichael, only to learn that the Alabama attorney general had left the state "on vacation." Despite efforts by influential members of the bar, editors of Alabama newspapers, and others who sought to reach him, Carmichael remained incommunicado at his vacation retreat.[88] He left the entire confused situation in the hands of his assistant, Thomas Lawson, an unenviable position for young Lawson, who was a candidate for attorney general in the next election. Marion Norris, Chalmers' secretary, reported the bad news to the SDC chairman. Both

[86] Marion Norris to Allan Knight Chalmers, July 20, 1937, in Chalmers Collection.

[87] Decatur *Daily*, July 8, 1937.

[88] Shapiro, "Behind the Scenes," 171.

Shapiro and Johnston were "sick about the whole thing," she said. Shapiro was uncertain whether Carmichael really could not accomplish the compromise, or whether he double-crossed Leibowitz and the SDC. But "he was inclined to give Carmichael the benefit of the doubt, and lay it to Callahan, who was impossible." [89] Wearily, Samuel Leibowitz prepared to defend the Scottsboro boys for the fifth time in five years.

[89] Marion Norris to Allan Knight Chalmers, July 20, 1937, in Chalmers Collection.

XI

THE COMPROMISE
OF 1937

THE trial of Clarence Norris began in a torrid Decatur courtroom on July 12, 1937. There had been many changes since the Jackson County posse removed the Scottsboro boys from an Alabama freight train in 1931. Roy Wright and Eugene Williams, barely in their teens at the time, had grown to manhood in the jails and prisons of Alabama. Along with six of the other boys, they were present in the Decatur courtroom.[1] The death of Thomas Knight, Jr., and the abrupt departure of Attorney General Carmichael left Thomas Lawson in charge of the prosecution staff. Leibowitz was back once more, but as he had done in the Patterson trial of 1936, he left most of the courtroom work to Clarence Watts.

Watts and Leibowitz closely questioned a venire of one hundred men, as they had in earlier cases, only to learn that all of the potential jurors claimed they were completely unprejudiced toward Negroes and were anxious to give the Scottsboro boys a fair trial. When the testimony began on Tuesday, July 15, the state almost raced through its presentation. Dr. Bridges had died in March, 1936, and Lawson made no objection when Leibowitz asked the court's permission to read the doctor's testimony from the previous trial. Since the medical testimony apparently had no effect on

[1] Haywood Patterson remained in Birmingham's county jail awaiting the results of his appeal to the federal courts.

Morgan County juries, the defense adopted a new tactic by calling witnesses to describe the character of Victoria Price. Richard S. Watson, a former Huntsville deputy sheriff, said frankly, "I would not believe her [Mrs. Price] under oath." When Clarence Watts asked Watson about Mrs. Price's reputation, he said it was "bad." Sol Wallace, who still served as a Madison County deputy, agreed with Watson's characterization of the state's chief witness. "She is completely untrustworthy," Wallace declared. "I would not believe anything she said." [2]

Late in the afternoon the defense introduced even stronger evidence against Mrs. Price when it called to the stand Emma Bates, the mother of Ruby Bates. The spectators strained to hear the soft-spoken Mrs. Bates as the whir of the ceiling fans and the cries of babies in the courtroom often muffled her voice. Mrs. Bates described how she had gone to visit her daughter in the Jackson County jail the day after the alleged assault. Mrs. Bates said she was shocked to find Ruby and Victoria sharing a cell with two white boys, Odell and Lindsay Gladwell. Ruby's mother explained that she had immediately demanded that the sheriff remove the boys since her daughter had just turned seventeen while Mrs. Price was "a woman grown." To rebut Mrs. Bates, the state called to the stand C. F. Simons, a Jackson County deputy sheriff. Simons denied that Mrs. Bates had said anything to him about the boys, but he sheepishly admitted under cross-examination that the two boys and two girls shared a common cell.[3]

As Leibowitz had feared, however, the testimony of the defense meant "not a snap" to the twelve jurors. On the following day, two hours and thirty minutes after the jury received the case, it made its decision. In the sweltering courtroom the clerk read the verdict. "We the jury find the defendant guilty and fix his punishment at death." [4]

Allan Knight Chalmers was in Oxford, England. When he received the telegram from Morris Shapiro, he was on his way to

[2] New York *Times,* July 14, 1937, p. 3, July 15, 1937, p. 11; Decatur *Daily,* July 14, 1937.

[3] New York *Times,* July 15, 1937, p. 11.

[4] *Ibid.,* July 16, 1937, p. 1.

attend an ecumenical service at St. Mary's Church. He opened the cable and read the full message, "NORRIS SENTENCED TO DEATH." Chalmers had not felt such an "indescribable loneliness" since the nightmare at Verdun when he had heard a shell splinter chug into the body of one of his friends. That evening, he went through the ecumenical church service in a daze. He wanted to worship, he later recalled, "but I was too desperately wounded." As he came out of the church, he stopped, leaned against a wall and—for the first time in twenty years—wept.[5]

Samuel Leibowitz had heard the death sentence pronounced three earlier times in the cases. Although he was heartsick at the verdict, his face betrayed only weariness and discouragement. Slowly he began rearranging the notes on his table. The trial of Andy Wright was next on the court's agenda, but Clarence Watts arose from his seat and, swaying slightly, told the judge he was too ill to continue. The long hours and the blistering courtroom had been more than he could take, said the Huntsville attorney. Callahan appeared to be reluctant to halt the proceedings, but the assistant attorney general remarked that it was plain to see Mr. Watts was very ill and he would prefer to have a recess. Callahan postponed Weems' trial until the following week. It was not the heat which had debilitated Watts, but the pressure. Initially, the SDC had been pleasantly surprised at the courage and forthrightness of the Huntsville lawyer.[6] But the unrelenting hostility of many of his hometown friends wore him down. And when, in spite of his best efforts, he came face to face with the death penalty for his client, it was more than he could take. As Leibowitz confided to Morris Shapiro, Watts' collapse was not physical, but emotional. He completely "lost his nerve." [7]

Leibowitz was ready to fight on, but Norris' death sentence had

---

[5] Chalmers, *They Shall Be Free,* 104–105.

[6] New York *Times,* July 16, 1937, p. 1. Ralph Hammond, writing for the *New Republic* in 1936, declared that Watts had handled the case very skillfully. Many Northerners had feared Watts would make concessions to local prejudice in his handling of the case, but Hammond found him "more straight-forward and uncompromising than Leibowitz had been." Hammond, "Trial of Haywood Patterson," 14.

[7] Marion Norris to Allan Knight Chalmers, July 20, 1937, in Chalmers Collection.

been deeply discouraging. He knew that the defense no longer had a vital federal issue which would sustain an appeal to the United States Supreme Court. And on the basis of past experiences, he expected nothing from the Alabama Supreme Court except a rubber stamp approval of a guilty verdict. When Hutson chatted with newsmen the day before the trials resumed on July 20, however, the Morgan County solicitor remarked that "two of the Negroes whom we regard as the ringleaders of the crime have been convicted." Powell was not "fit mentally or physically to stand trial." That left Charley Weems, Andy Wright, Willie Roberson, Olen Montgomery, and the two juveniles. He added cryptically, "I am anxious to dispose of all these cases as expeditiously as possible so long as the ends of justice are served." When reporters asked Hutson about the meaning of his last remark, he replied with a knowing smile, "One never can tell what may happen." [8]

Further evidence of a willingness to compromise came the following morning when the state announced at the outset of Andy Wright's trial that it would not ask for the death penalty. In exchange, Leibowitz had waived his right to a special venire of sixty-five required by law in capital cases. He agreed to take his chances on the regular panel of thirty-five. As he said later, "It was like being asked to swap a turkey for a horse." [9] Watts had withdrawn from active participation in the case and had gone on an extended vacation. Leibowitz doggedly conducted the cross-examination as though he thought the jury would acquit his client, but he betrayed his weariness and disgust during his summation the following day. After Jackson County's solicitor, H. G. Bailey, had delivered a long impassioned attack on New York City in general and Lester Carter in particular, Leibowitz replied that he was growing weary of listening to attacks on his home state. This extraneous issue was introduced at the close of every trial as a "knockout punch for the defense" delivered by the prosecution. Leibowitz shook his head wearily. "I can't fight this kind of thing.

[8] New York *Times*, July 18, 1937, p. 8; July 19, 1937, p. 34.
[9] Shapiro, "Behind the Scenes," 170–71.

I'm entitled to an acquittal in this case and I ask you men in all seriousness to do what you swore at the outset you would do." The following day, one hour and fifteen minutes after the jury received the case, it returned with a verdict of guilty and a sentence of ninety-nine years.[10]

When the trial of Charley Weems began on Thursday, Leibowitz was fighting mad. Frustrated at his complete inability to break through the wall of prejudice and race hatred, he tore into Mrs. Price during cross-examination. She responded with equal venom, shouting her answers angrily and defiantly. While Leibowitz retained his intellectual control, Mrs. Price soon lost her composure completely and was snared in a maze of contradictions. When Leibowitz began to press her about her testimony regarding the injuries she claimed she suffered, Callahan broke in heatedly. "It is not too late for the court to enforce its orders," he said to Leibowitz. "Your manner is going to lead to trouble . . . and you might as well get ready for it." Leibowitz modulated his voice and changed the subject, but he continued to cross-examine Mrs. Price with gruelling thoroughness. After she became completely confused on several points, Leibowitz asked that the jury be dismissed from the courtroom. The chief defense lawyer turned to Judge Callahan. "I move that the testimony of Victoria Price be stricken from the record on the ground that . . .[it] is so rampant with perjury that the court is constrained—" Callahan, his face red with anger, interrupted Leibowitz. "Motion denied; bring the jurors back into the room." [11] When Victoria Price stepped down from the witness chair, one embarrassed state lawyer confided she was the "sorriest witness I ever saw in a courtroom." [12]

Lawson, as he had in the Wright trial, waived the death penalty for Charley Weems. It was a small consolation for Samuel Leibowitz. When he began his summation to the jury the following morning he took an entirely different tack. Bluntly Leibowitz told

[10] New York *Times,* July 21, 1937, p. 7; July 22, 1937, p. 1.
[11] *Ibid.,* July 23, 1937, p. 3; Decatur *Daily,* July 23, 1937.
[12] Shapiro, "Behind the Scenes," 171.

the jury he had despaired of convincing a white jury that a Negro accused by a white woman might be innocent. In a voice trembling with anger and fatigue he shouted, "I'm sick and tired of this sanctimonious hypocrisy. It isn't Charley Weems on trial in this case, it's a Jew lawyer and New York State put on trial here by the inflammatory remarks of Mr. Bailey." Contemptuously, Leibowitz dismissed the state witnesses as "trained seals" and "performers in a flea circus." Without hedging, he flatly accused Bailey and the officials of Jackson County of suppressing evidence favorable to the defense.[13]

As Leibowitz spoke to the jury, Lawson became so angry at the attacks on his native state he got up and left the courtroom. Callahan walked back and forth behind the bench, his face set in lines of cold fury. But nothing constrained Leibowitz, who was finally expelling from his system all the anger and frustration which had been building for four and a half years. He scornfully dismissed the state's constant reiteration that Negroes received the same justice as whites in an Alabama courtroom. This was so much "poppycock," exclaimed Leibowitz. He had examined more than one thousand prospective jurors from Morgan County, he told the courtroom. And he had not been able to find one member of one venire who would admit prejudice against Negroes or would acknowledge he would treat them any different from white men. Yet, he continued, on the streets of Decatur, white men told him frankly that a Negro under these circumstances did not have a chance in a thousand.[14]

During his final summation, Solicitor Melvin Hutson attacked Leibowitz for jeopardizing the interests of his client. But, as the New York lawyer said, the defense had nothing to lose. If the state had asked for twenty years, the sentence would have been twenty years. If the state had asked for death, the sentence would have been death. The verdict was decided long before he began his remarks. At least the "travesty of justice" should be exposed to the world. Like most good trial lawyers, Samuel Leibowitz had a

[13] New York *Times*, July 24, 1937, p. 30; Decatur *Daily*, July 23, 1937.
[14] *Ibid.*

sizeable ego and the Weems' summation showed just how much the Scottsboro trials had injured his pride. For more than three years the New York attorney had summoned all of his substantial intellectual and forensic talents on the side of the defendants. He had constructed what he felt to be an ironclad case for the defense. More than one person who watched Leibowitz in the Decatur courtroom came away convinced that he had seen a worthy successor to Clarence Darrow. And yet, in the face of the testimony of a convicted prostitute, he had persuaded only one juror to hold out for less than the state demanded.

In the Weems case, the jury deliberated for two hours and twenty-five minutes and then returned with a verdict of guilty. The twelve men fixed the sentence at seventy-five years in the state penitentiary. As soon as Callahan pronounced the sentence on Weems, Sheriff Sandlin brought Ozie Powell into the courtroom. In low whispers, Leibowitz talked with Powell and then brought him before the bench. Lawson announced that the charge of rape had been dropped and Judge Callahan read the indictment of assaulting Deputy Blalock. The judge explained to Ozie that he could plead guilty or not guilty. "Don't plead guilty unless you are guilty," said Leibowitz. "I'm guilty of cutting the deputy," Powell replied, and he entered a plea of guilty. Since the state had agreed to *nol pros* the rape indictment, Hutson told the court he would insist on the maximum penalty for assault, twenty years. In vain, Leibowitz pleaded with the judge to take into consideration the more than six years Powell had already spent in jail. But Callahan replied, if it "had not been that the State had dropped the other charge of rape against him, I would have given him fifteen years. As it is, I will have to sentence him to twenty years in the penitentiary." [15]

It was almost noon on Saturday, and spectators began drifting out of the courtroom. They expected a resumption of the trials the following Monday. Thomas S. Lawson walked before the bench, however, and began speaking in a low voice. Reporters leaned forward and heard the names of the remaining four defend-

[15] New York *Times,* July 25, 1937, p. 1; Decatur *Daily,* July 24, 1937.

ants and then the words: *"nol pros."* The judge nodded in agreement. Even before Lawson had completed his remarks to Callahan, Leibowitz hurriedly walked outside and past Sheriff Sandlin, who was standing on the courthouse lawn. Across the street the chief defense lawyer entered the county jail and handed a court order to one of the jailers. Then Leibowitz motioned to Olen Montgomery, Roy Wright, Willie Roberson, and Eugene Williams. Hesitantly they followed him out through the jailhouse doors and into two waiting cars. As Leibowitz opened the door to get into the front car, Sheriff Sandlin walked over from the courthouse lawn and asked uncertainly, "Why don't you get in there [the courtroom] with your clients, you—" Sandlin's face mirrored his surprise as he realized four of the defendants were in the two cars. Only then did he realize that the Scottsboro trials had ended. As the automobiles roared away from the center of Decatur, Victoria Price silently watched from a second story courthouse window.[16]

Four of the defendants had been released on the same evidence that had convicted four others. As Morris Shapiro observed, the denouement left Alabama in the "anomalous position of providing only 50 per cent protection for the 'flower of Southern womanhood.'" The defensive tone of the prosecution's "explanatory statement" reflected the bizarre finale. The state, read Lawson, was "convinced beyond any question of a doubt . . . that the defendants that have been tried are guilty of raping Mrs. Victoria Price." But, "after careful consideration of all the testimony, every lawyer connected with the prosecution is convinced that the defendants Willie Roberson and Olen Montgomery are not guilty." Lawson pointed out the severe venereal disease of Willie Roberson and the blindness of Olen Montgomery made it unlikely that the two would have taken part. Moreover, the "two men were seen in a box car by a disinterested witness." It was true that Mrs. Price still insisted the two men had raped her, but "we feel that it is a case of mistaken identity." As for Eugene Williams and Roy Wright, a careful investigation had revealed that, "at the time of

16 *Ibid.*

the actual commission of this crime, one of these juveniles was 12 years old and the other one was 13. . . ." In view of the fact that they had been in jail for "six and a half years, the state thinks that the ends of justice would be met at this time by releasing these two juveniles on condition that they leave the State, never to return." [17]

The state's explanation for its action only aroused further opposition. If, as the state now admitted, Olen Montgomery and Willie Roberson were clearly innocent, why were they confined in jail for six long years? "The State would indemnify a farmer . . . for damages he sustained if a State truck ran down and killed his mule," said Leibowitz. But now the state of Alabama had confessed that "for nearly seven years it caged four innocent Negro boys without any evidence against them." Would it not be a small gesture toward justice, said Leibowitz, if state officials furnished "some measure of compensation for the injuries it has inflicted. . . ." Moreover, said Leibowitz, if Victoria Price was "mistaken" in her identification of Willie Roberson and Olen Montgomery, how could any one justify sending four others to death and long prison sentences on her discredited testimony? [18]

The New York *Times* editorially agreed with Leibowitz. Either all were guilty or none was guilty. It was apparent that Alabama had released the four for purely expedient reasons, said the *Times*. The New York newspaper held out the hope that the state would grow calm and "do more complete justice later on." The Richmond *Times-Dispatch* stated bluntly that the dropping of charges against the four "serves as a virtual clincher to the argument that all nine of the Negroes are innocent." Even the Montgomery *Advertiser* hinted that all of the boys should now be released.[19]

Five days after their release, the four Scottsboro boys sat on the

[17] Shapiro, "Behind the Scenes," 170; Decatur *Daily*, July 25, 1937.
[18] New York *Times*, July 26, 1937, p. 32.
[19] *Ibid.*, July 27, 1937, p. 20; Richmond *Times-Dispatch*, July 27, 1937; Montgomery *Advertiser*, July 25, 1937. There was little evidence, however, to indicate that public opinion followed the news media. A Birmingham radio interviewer was unable to find a single passerby on the street who had the slightest doubt all nine were guilty and should have been prosecuted. New York *Times*, August 1, 1937, IV, 7.

stage of the crowded Hippodrome Arena in New York City. They were dressed in new suits and appeared clearly uncomfortable in starched shirts, stiff new shoes, and stylish neckties. Leibowitz, one of the speakers on a crowded program, publicly revealed the story of his 1936 negotiations with Attorney General Carmichael and the late Lieutenant Governor Knight. Leibowitz told the audience of more than five thousand persons that Carmichael and Knight had agreed to accept a plea of assault and battery, but not rape, from four of the boys. They were then to receive a sentence of five years. Leibowitz called on Attorney General Carmichael to see that the terms of the agreement were carried out. "Come forward like a man and a true American citizen who loves liberty and justice and fair dealing, and say to the Governor of Alabama: 'I have given my word that these boys should be given their freedom within two years, and I ask you to honor my promise.' " [20]

In Alabama, Judge Callahan gave an entirely different account of the negotiations. According to the judge, Leibowitz and Lawson reached a "hard and fast agreement" only after Norris' trial and death sentence. Assistant Attorney General Lawson agreed to waive capital punishment in the Wright and Weems cases and to drop the rape charge against Ozie Powell. In return, the defense agreed to appeal only Norris' death sentence. The decision of the state not to press charges against Roberson, Montgomery, Williams, and Roy Wright was reached independently of any negotiations.[21] Publicly the SDC flatly denied that Leibowitz and Lawson had reached any such agreement as described by Judge Callahan. When Allan Knight Chalmers returned from Europe, however, he was unsatisfied with the explanations of Leibowitz. As Chalmers told another member of the SDC, "I still can not make out what he [Leibowitz] did or did not do in Alabama in a deal." Clarence Watts believed that there had been an "understanding" similar to that related by Callahan. In a letter of resignation to the SDC he told Morris Shapiro that both Callahan and Lawson contended that Leibowitz had agreed not to appeal the cases of Andy

[20] New York *Times*, July 30, 1937, p. 8.
[21] *Ibid.*, August 29, 1937, p. 19; Shapiro, "Behind the Scenes," 170.

Wright and Charley Weems. Watts said he accepted "the statement of the court and the contention of the State as correct." [22]
And Thomas Lawson insisted vehemently that Leibowitz was
lying. While carefully skirting the question of whether Leibowitz
and Carmichael had reached a tentative agreement in 1936, Lawson told Grover Hall that the chief defense attorney had come to
terms after the conviction of Norris. "So far as that Goddamned
Leibowitz is concerned I will never make another agreement with
him," said Lawson. "He is a liar and the truth is not in him. He
has lied to me and I will never trust him again under any
circumstances." [23]

In any case the entire dispute over the compromise was soon
academic. On October 26, 1937, without comment, the United
States Supreme Court declined to review the seventy-five year conviction of Haywood Patterson. Defense lawyers knew that the
state's case against Norris, Weems, and Wright was just as strong as
it had been against Patterson. Chalmers acknowledged from his
New York office that the high court's decision "apparently closes
out further legal action in the case of Haywood Patterson." [24]
This did not mean, however, that the SDC was prepared to
acquiesce in the continued imprisonment of the Scottsboro boys.
At the suggestion of Forney Johnston and Grover Hall, Chalmers
decided to appeal directly to Governor Bibb Graves and to ask the
Alabama chief executive to use his pardoning power.

At first glance it would appear that an appeal to Bibb Graves
was a waste of time. As the New York *Times* had observed, Graves
had "venerated and been venerated" by the Alabama Ku Klux
Klan during his first term in office from 1927 to 1931. Graves had
used his influence to defeat an anti-Klan bill in the state legislature and when the Alabama attorney general began an investiga-

[22] Allan Knight Chalmers to Rose Shapiro, August 30, 1937, in Scottsboro
Administrative File 2, NAACP Papers; Clarence Watts to Morris Shapiro, August 31,
1937, in Chalmers Collection. On the other hand, Watts was anxious to terminate
his employment with the SDC, and the dispute over terms of the compromise may
simply have been a convenient excuse.
[23] Grover Hall to Henry Edmonds, December 22, 1937, in Chalmers Collection.
[24] New York *Times*, October 26, 1937, p. 1.

tion of several Klan floggings, Graves threatened to curtail funds
going to the attorney general's office. But there was also another
side to the politician who used the slogan "Keep on Moving on."
During his first term, Graves expanded government services in
many areas: public health, forestry, port facilities, and—most of all
—education. During Graves' second administration beginning in
1934, the Depression curtailed state expenditures, but he continued to work for an expansion of social welfare programs.[25]

On November 11, 1937, Chalmers sent a letter to Graves
through Forney Johnston. Chalmers noted Callahan's insistence
that there was an agreement barring future appeals. "I can assure
you from my stand-point . . . that no such agreement would
possibly be agreed to by our defense committee. If Mr. Leibowitz
made the agreement it was against the express written instruction
of the committee." Regardless of whether an "understanding" was
violated, said Chalmers, "it does not take away from a situation
which all of us have to face." He asked the governor for an opportunity to present the SDC's position in further detail, preferably
at a conference in Montgomery. Johnston and two friends supplemented Chalmers' letter with a petition to the governor, asking
that he use the pardoning power to end the controversy over the
Scottsboro boys. The petition, signed by Johnston, Edmonds, and
the editor of the Birmingham *Post,* argued that it was a "pecu-
liarly opportune time for the Chief Executive of a Southern State
to give consideration to a request for clemency proffered on behalf
of a group of darkies." In the first place, noted the three men,
pressure was growing in the Congress for action on the Wagner-
Costigan "Anti-Lynching Bill." If Graves should free the remaining Scottsboro boys this would dramatize the fact that the
South's opposition to the bill was "not based upon prejudice or indifference to the negro." Secondly, the group pointed to the dis-
reputable character of Victoria Price and observed that Alabama

[25] *Ibid.,* June 15, 1934, p. 20; William E. Gilbert, "Bibb Graves as a Progressive,
1927–1930," *The Alabama Review,* X (1957), 16–17, 28–29; Owen, *Story of Alabama,*
I, 304–305.

was in a vulnerable position now that four of the nine had been released on the same evidence that convicted four others. The three men added: "You would not, of course, make a gesture in this notorious Scottsboro affair for the purpose of strengthening your prestige . . . but there is, after all, a timeliness about all things. . . ." [26]

After reading Chalmers' letter and listening to a personal plea from Forney Johnston, Graves agreed to a conference on December 21, 1937. At the meeting, which was held in Graves' office, Chalmers warned the governor that the national press would continue to criticize the state of Alabama as long as Haywood Patterson, Clarence Norris, Andrew Wright, and Charley Weems remained in prison. The SDC chairman urged the Alabama chief executive to exercise his executive powers and to grant clemency to all the boys still in prison. Grover Hall was also present and he promised the unstinting editorial support of the Montgomery *Advertiser* if the governor should agree to grant pardons. Edmonds, the third member of the group, also approved pardons for the Scottsboro boys, and he told Governor Graves that the editors of the Birmingham newspapers had promised to back him one hundred percent. Graves sat through the presentation without speaking. When the three men had finished, the governor agreed that the position of the state was untenable. Either "all were guilty or all should be freed. . . ." Graves explained that he could take no action so long as the appeals for Norris, Wright, and Weems were still pending in the courts, but when they had been decided he would act "quickly and definitely." He leaned forward and told the three men in a confidential tone, "I cannot make any promise which would look like a deal. I have already stated my feeling that the position of the State is untenable with half out and half in on the same charges and evidence." He said, "My mind is clear on the action required to remedy this impossible position." When the cases came before him he would act promptly. The governor added, "I cannot be any clearer than that, can I?" [27]

The result of the conference was almost too good to be true. Chalmers, who had seen many golden opportunities slip away, remained skeptical. In order to avoid any last minute opposition from Carmichael and Lawson, Hall held a conference with them on December 22. Both men insisted they were completely satisfied with the decision of Graves. They were perfectly willing to support pardon for the Scottsboro boys as long as it did not bargain away the "dignity of the State." At the suggestion of Forney Johnston, Chalmers also wrote Governor Graves offering to withdraw the appeals if the governor would give some concrete assurance they would be unnecessary. As Johnston observed, "I should say that unless he stopped you under these circumstances he would be guilty of the most flagrant bad faith if he then failed to exercise clemency." But the wily Graves had no intention of committing himself in writing. He replied to Chalmers that any activity or statement would be "indelicate" so long as the cases remained in the courts. And Graves urged Chalmers to become more patient since it would be several months before any action could be taken.[28]

Governor Graves' plea for patience did nothing to reassure Chalmers, for the SDC chairman knew that the boys who remained in prison were near the breaking point. Moreover, all of them—particularly Norris and Patterson—feared they had been sold out by the SDC. Bitterly Clarence Norris wrote to Morris Shapiro, "I say you all framed me to the Electric Chair and the others in prison with a lifetime for the freedom of the other four boys." Norris acknowledged that the SDC denied any deal had been made. "Of course I know better. If it had not been the others would be in prison Serving time for something they didnt do."

[27] Memorandum of a conference with Governor Graves held on December 21, 1937, by Edmonds, Hall, and Chalmers, in Chalmers Collection. The memorandum was prepared within minutes after the meeting so that "the record of the conference might be accurate and unquestioned."

[28] Grover Hall to Henry Edmonds, December 22, 1937; Forney Johnston to Allan Knight Chalmers, January 8, 1938; Bibb Graves to Allan Knight Chalmers, May 23, 1938, in Chalmers Collection.

He concluded his letter to Shapiro on a note of bitter resignation. "I have got tired of seeing peoples using me for the good of others. I just soon to be Dead than to be treated like I have been Treated by you all. I Believe all of you all just as much against me as that old lying woman that caused me to suffer near Seven Years." [29] Patterson and Wright, although more restrained in their letters to the SDC, also expressed concern over reports that they had been "traded" for the boys on the outside.[30] Chalmers wrote all of the boys and assured them there had been no "sellout." He explained that he could not give full details of the negotiations because of prison censorship, but he urged them to keep up their courage and he promised good news in the near future.[31]

Throughout the summer of 1938, Chalmers tried to maintain pressure on Governor Graves, but, as usual, Alabama contacts urged "moderation and restraint." When Chalmers complained that the more radical members of the SDC were threatening independent action, Hall warned that any publicity could only "prejudice the cause of the defendants now in the jug. If they know a better 'ole, let them find it." With many misgivings, Chalmers consented to Hall's advice not to pressure the governor.[32]

In mid-June, 1938, the Alabama Supreme Court affirmed the death sentence of Clarence Norris and the prison sentences of Andrew Wright and Charley Weems. As Governor Graves had promised, he commuted Norris' death sentence to life imprisonment.[33] Paradoxically, the commutation of Norris' death sentence

[29] Clarence Norris to Morris Shapiro, January 18, 1938, in Chalmers Collection. As early as October, 1937, Norris had begun to suspect there was a deal. As he sat in his prison cell facing the prospect of death in the electric chair, he became more and more certain he had been betrayed. Clarence Norris to Morris Shapiro, October 27, 1937, in Scottsboro Administrative File 2, NAACP Papers.

[30] Haywood Patterson to Allan Knight Chalmers, March 1, 1938; Andrew Wright to Allan Knight Chalmers, February 23, 1938, in Chalmers Collection.

[31] Allan Knight Chalmers to Clarence Norris, Haywood Patterson, Andrew Wright, Charley Weems, and Ozie Powell, March 4, 1938, in Chalmers Collection. Norris was not reassured and he threatened suicide if something was not done to relieve his mental suffering. Clarence Norris to Allan Knight Chalmers, March 15, 1938, in Chalmers Collection.

[32] Grover Hall to Allan Knight Chalmers, April 2, 1938; Marion Norris to Henry Edmonds, July 6, 1938, in Chalmers Collection.

[33] New York *Times*, June 17, 1938, p. 7; July 6, 1938, p. 1.

alarmed Chalmers. As he asked Edmonds, why had the governor bothered first to commute Norris' sentence to life if he were going to release him? But Grover Hall explained that the governor did not want to appear to be rushing things. The Alabama newsman reasurred Chalmers things were proceeding smoothly, and he once more cautioned against any undue publicity which might disturb the governor's resolve.[34]

Chalmers' sense of urgency was heightened by a fear that the four boys on the outside might trigger some incident that would create a public uproar and thus jeopardize the chances of gaining freedom for the five still in prison. The release of Olen, Willie, Roy, and Eugene came so suddenly that no preparations were made for their future. As Leibowitz admitted the day of their release, they were "problem children." Within hours after arriving in New York, the four boys received more than a dozen commercial offers. Leibowitz emphasized that there would be "no exploitation, no barnstorming, no theatricals of any kind," however, and he went ahead with plans to have the boys placed in various vocational schools. This training would help to "resurrect lives almost crushed out of them by the relentless persecution of the state of Alabama." [35]

But the offers promising easy fortunes proved far more enticing to the boys than the prospect of going to school for two or three years. In this, they were particularly influenced by Thomas S. Harten, a Negro minister from Brooklyn. Harten met the boys shortly after they came to New York, gained their confidence, and then offered himself as their "manager." Harten, who had been involved in several Harlem money-making schemes, soon convinced them that they should break completely with Leibowitz.[36] On August 6, less than two weeks after they had gained their

[34] Marion Norris to Henry Edmonds, July 6, 1938; Grover Hall to Allan Knight Chalmers, July 29, 1938, in Chalmers Collection.

[35] New York *Times*, July 27, 1937, p. 8.

[36] In 1933, the ILD had threatened Harten with legal action after he began raising money, ostensibly for the Scottsboro boys. The Reverend Harten never accounted for any of the funds he collected. William L. Patterson to Thomas S. Harten, April 18, 1933, in ILD Papers.

freedom, the four Scottsboro boys visited Leibowitz in his office and accused him of racketeering at their expense and "making a million." Roy, the group's spokesman, told Leibowitz that he and his friends were tired of other people getting rich and they were going to make money on their own. Without waiting for Leibowitz to reply, they got up and stalked out.[37]

On August 15 Harten, now officially "manager of the Scottsboro boys," announced that his four charges were going on stage. When a New York reporter interviewed Harlem's latest celebrities, he found them sporting canes and dressed in the latest fashion, with their hair slicked to a bright polish. All four made it clear that they liked their new careers and planned to remain in show business. Somewhat nervously, Harten explained that "an idle head is the devil's workshop" and he had arranged the performances in order to keep the boys out of trouble. When the New York *Times* reporter asked Harten if Leibowitz approved the boys' decision, the Brooklyn minister remained silent. But Olen Montgomery, peering from behind his thick-lensed glasses, mumbled that he was free and he planned to be his "own man." The rest of the boys agreed. Despite a last minute plea from the SDC, Roy, Eugene, Olen, and Willie appeared at Harlem's Apollo Theatre on August 20. "Welcome the Scottsboro Boys," declared a handbill. "Appearing IN PERSON as a special added attraction with the novel ALL-GIRL REVIEW . . . a cast of FIFTY FAS-CINATING FEMALES." The Apollo management billed the four youths as "the symbol of a struggle for enlightenment and human brotherhood which will go on and on until it is won!" [38]

The boys soon became disgruntled with their new venture when they discovered there was a "sharecropping system" being used on them. Although they drew a good salary from their engagement, Harten took a substantial cut, and the theater made them pur-

---

[37] As Chalmers' secretary observed, part of the problem was Leibowitz. He was "still treating them like little boys and dictating to them and their parents." While they needed guidance, Leibowitz acted "untactfully and unwisely." Marion Norris to Allan Knight Chalmers, August 6, 1937, in Chalmers Collection.

[38] Morris Shapiro to Roy Wright, Eugene Williams, Olen Montgomery, and Willie Roberson, August 18, 1937; Handbill of Apollo Theatre, in Scottsboro Administrative File 2, NAACP Papers.

chase new suits and accessories at their own expense. At the end of their first week on stage, advance money from the Apollo had to be paid. To their chagrin, they found themselves in debt. As the wife of the SDC's secretary observed, the "millions that they had anticipated making don't seem to be rolling in." [39] Eventually the four straggled back to the Scottsboro Defense Committee for advice and support, but not before a nasty, name-calling episode in which Harten persuaded Olen Montgomery to sign an affidavit publicly accusing the SDC of making a fortune on the case.[40] Chalmers knew that there were always unscrupulous operators like Harten who would resort to anything if a profit were involved. And, although the SDC managed to keep most of its difficulties with the boys out of the press, Chalmers was afraid their problems in adjusting to life on the outside might prejudice Governor Graves against granting a release to the remaining five.

Under Alabama law a three-man board advised the governor on pardon cases. The board, consisting of the attorney general, the state auditor, and the secretary of state only made recommendations; the final decision was up to the governor. In October, 1937, John Temple Graves, II, had remarked that earlier in the Scottsboro Case it would have taken great courage for a politician to free the nine defendants. But "nobody's career is going to be hurt in Alabama now if the remaining Scottsboro Negroes go free," declared the Birmingham newspaper columnist.[41] The Alabama governor did not intend to take any political chances, however, and he asked Grover Hall to round up Alabama newspapers that would support clemency for the remaining defendants. When the pardon board scheduled a hearing on the case for August 16, Graves also passed the word to Forney Johnston that he wanted as many prominent Alabamians present at the meeting as was possible.[42]

[39] Rose Shapiro to Allan Knight Chalmers, August 25, 1937, in Scottsboro Administrative File 2, NAACP Papers.
[40] Memorandum of Marion Norris, January 28, 1938, in Chalmers Collection.
[41] New York *Times,* October 31, 1937, IV, p. 6.
[42] Morris Shapiro to Allan Knight Chalmers, July 27, 1938, in Chalmers Collection.

The board met in the governor's private office and Chalmers was the first speaker. He began by referring to "these boys," but Charles McCall, the state auditor, interrupted and coldly corrected the SDC chairman. The prisoners were "men, not boys," he said. Despite McCall's unconcealed hostility, Chalmers spoke for more than twenty minutes. He deplored the fact that the case got into the wrong hands in the beginning. "Perhaps," he said, "the churches and the people they represented moved too slowly. Perhaps that was why groups interested in the cases turned originally to communistic sources." Chalmers warned that the controversy could become "another Mooney case" and he added: "Unless we work this thing out now there is going to be a repercussion that will not be pleasant. The case will revert to the original hands, who will resume their campaign of agitation." In part, Chalmers' gentle threat was baseless, for the Communists showed little inclination to fight for control of the case. But there was a desire on the part of several members of the SDC board to resume a full-fledged propaganda campaign which would further discredit Alabama and, hopefully, force final action. When Chalmers finished, Forney Johnston and Donald Comer, an Alabama cotton mill owner, urged the board to release the prisoners without regard to their guilt or innocence. The "good name of Alabama" was at stake, they said.[43]

During his trips to Alabama, Morris Shapiro had learned that the secretary of state favored pardon, McCall opposed it, and Carmichael was on the fence. When faced with the necessity of making a public decision, however, the board was unanimous. It recommended a denial of paroles.[44] From Atmore Prison Farm, where he had been transferred in late 1937, Haywood Patterson angrily wrote Chalmers. He had received a telegram from the SDC, he said, and "I was pained to read its contents—for I had not at that time thought about such a thing as another delay." He

[43] Montgomery *Advertiser*, August 17, 1938; New York *Times*, August 17, 1938, p. 38.

[44] Morris Shapiro to Allan Knight Chalmers, July 27, 1938, in Chalmers Collection; Montgomery *Advertiser*, August 18, 1938; New York *Times*, August 18, 1938, p. 3.

continued, "I see it all quite plainly altho it amazes me. . . . I now know that you was the cause of this delay." [45]

Neither Chalmers nor his Alabama contacts had expected the pardon board to make a positive recommendation, but they knew that the unanimous vote of opposition placed further pressure on Governor Graves. Hall hastily called many of his newspaper friends across the state and mobilized editorial support for the governor. Only the Decatur *Daily* attacked the idea of pardoning the remaining Scottsboro boys. Seven major Alabama dailies supported clemency for the prisoners.[46] Despite Hall's continued optimism, the first week of September seemed to last an eternity for the impatient Chalmers as he waited to hear word on the governor's decision. On September 9 Morris Shapiro received an elated, though somewhat cryptic telegram from Grover Hall: "Here's extreme low-down: Powell will join all other stable mates as desired. But advertisement of your notice deemed essential to meet a technicality, after which ripened fruit will fall. I speak as one inspired, after the manner of your friends of the Old Testament." [47] Translated, the telegram meant that Graves had definitely set the date for the pardoning of the remaining Scottsboro boys.

Cautiously optimistic, Chalmers wrote Edmonds. "Naturally no one of us who has been in this for a long time will feel quite secure in any plan until it actually is accomplished." He added that "at the worst, however, it seems that it will only be a matter of a few days delay, and it looks as if our last period of delay is coming to an end." On October 12, Hall wrote in detail to explain that the

[45] Haywood Patterson to Allan Knight Chalmers, August 18, 1938, in Chalmers Collection.

[46] The *Daily* declared that Dr. Chalmers put forth an "amazing case of impudence" in his appearance before the parole board. Decatur *Daily*, August 18, 1938. Those newspapers backing pardon included the Selma *Times-Journal*, August 19, 1938; Anniston *Star*, August 21, 1938; Eufaula *Tribune*, August 19, 1938; Birmingham *Age-Herald*, August 18, 1938; Birmingham *News*, August 19, 1938; Birmingham *Post*, August 19, 1938; and of course, the Montgomery *Advertiser*, August 18, 1938.

[47] Grover Hall to Morris Shapiro, September 9, 1938, in Chalmers Collection. The "advertisement of your notice" referred to the requirement under Alabama law whereby the prisoner (or his sponsors) had to insert a classified advertisement in a daily newspaper announcing his intention to seek parole.

governor had decided against paroling Powell because the knifing of Deputy Blalock was practically unrelated to the rape charge. In the near future, however, he felt certain that something would be done about Powell. Facetiously, Hall explained that he and the other Alabamians had "saved out one defendant so as to insure ourselves that you and Shapiro would have occasion to make numerous other visits to Alabama and thus afford your hook-wormy friends down here the pleasure of seeing you." The date for the release of the four was officially set for October 31 at 11 A.M.[48]

Chalmers made elaborate plans for the boys' release. Eugene Martin, the brother-in-law of Walter White and an Atlanta in-surance executive, arranged to have a seven-passenger limousine and chauffeur waiting in Montgomery. The trip back to Atlanta could be made in a few hours. Waiting there would be the head of the Atlanta School of Social Work. He was to interview the boys and to make suggestions for readjustment in training and voca-tional schools. From there, the four prisoners and Chalmers were to catch a train northward. As the release date approached, Chal-mers completed his last-minute preparations. He made certain the limousine would be waiting, he purchased tickets for himself and for the boys, and he ordered a printed letter asking supporters of the SDC for money to pay off the committee's debt and to support the boys during the six months following their pardon.[49]

On Saturday, October 29, Chalmers was seated in a barber's chair in the University Club in New York when a messenger came in and handed him a telegram from Governor Bibb Graves. The SDC chairman opened it and read: "Please defer Mondays engage-ment until further notice. Am not ready to act. Please acknowl-edge receipt." Chalmers hurriedly telephoned Grover Hall, but the Montgomery publisher was completely bewildered over the governor's action. Hall promised to see Graves as soon as possible.

[48] Allan Knight Chalmers to Henry Edmonds, October 12, 1938; Grover Hall to Allan Knight Chalmers, October 12, 1938, in Chalmers Collection.
[49] Allan Knight Chalmers to Eugene M. Martin, October 24, 1938, in Chalmers Collection. The letter to the SDC supporters was printed and dated November 1, 1938.

Depressed and alarmed over the sudden turn of events, Chalmers cancelled the car from Atlanta and then waited out the long weekend.[50]

Five days later, he received a special delivery letter from Grover Hall. "I had a long and intimate talk with Governor Graves late this afternoon," said Hall. "I found him adamant and passionate in his resolve not to parole the Scottsboro defendants." The governor explained that he had personally interviewed the boys in his office on the twenty-ninth of October and he was "convinced that it would be a wrong against the public and a wrong against their sponsors to release them now." [51]

According to Governor Graves, Norris came into the executive office still in a rage over an earlier quarrel with Patterson. Officials at the Atmore Prison Farm said the dispute centered around a mutual homosexual friend. When the governor questioned Norris about his threats to kill Patterson, the handcuffed prisoner looked Graves in the eye and snarled, "Yes, I'll kill him! I never furgits!" And when guards searched Patterson before ushering him into the governor's office, they found a knife made from a file hidden in the fly of his pants. Graves told Hall that the release of the defendants would be calamitous. "They will humiliate you, Grover, they will humiliate Dr. Chalmers and Mr. Shapiro, they will humiliate Comer and Johnston and all other decent sponsors. They are antisocial, they are bestial, and they are unbelievably stupid and I do not believe they can be rehabilitated in freedom . . ." the governor said.[52]

"If the governor will but withhold his public statement and give you another chance to play Paul before Agrippa, I shall be happy," said Hall. But "in view of his statement to me I am frankly unwilling to challenge him before the people of Alabama on this issue. As for Leibowitz and his leftist group, I commit to you the greatest cartoon that Bruce Bairnsfether ever made, titled,

---

[50] Bibb Graves to Allan Knight Chalmers, October 29, 1938; Memorandum of Allan Knight Chalmers, October 31, 1938, in Chalmers Collection.

[51] Grover Hall to Allan Knight Chalmers, November 1, 1938, in Chalmers Collection.

[52] *Ibid.*

'If you know a better 'ole, find it.' " Hall added that Frank Dixon would become governor on January 16. He "is popular now, but after three months our people probably will want to hang him," said Hall. "I, as his first supporter, would not advise him to pet the body of this dead cat before he puts through his program." [53]

At Chalmers' request, Hall persuaded Graves to postpone announcement of his decision. Reluctantly, the governor also agreed to meet Chalmers on November 10. Despite the bleak outlook, Chalmers tried to convey optimism to his Alabama friends and he outlined the strategy he would take in his meeting with the governor. He would begin by admitting that the boys were "cocky," had caused trouble, and some had even developed homosexual characteristics. But Chalmers said he would also tell Graves there was "no indication of any homosexual characteristics in any of them before their incarceration." And it was "well known that personality maladjustment is almost inevitable in the very nature of prison life." Moreover, said Chalmers, psychiatric reports of the nine had shown that the four already released were least suited for rehabilitation and yet they had caused no serious trouble. And the SDC had made elaborate preparations for the training of Patterson, Norris, Wright, and Weems after their release. In a note to his friends, Chalmers concluded, "I am confident we can win." Frankly, he said, "I hate to contemplate the vials of wrath, the vitriolic bitterness and the restoration to control over the defense by those who believe that it is only by denunciation and violence that justice can be obtained." [54]

When Chalmers went with Grover Hall to the governor's office on November 10, however, he found that his arguments were futile. The governor, said Chalmers, was a "weary, defensive man," adamant in his refusal to release the boys. Afterward, a discouraged Grover Hall acknowledged that the battle was almost lost. But he advised Chalmers to make one more effort and "call out the reserves, including That Man and Eleanor. . . ." The idea

[53] *Ibid.*
[54] Allan Knight Chalmers to Henry Edmonds, Forney Johnston, Grover Hall, and James Chappell, November 5, 1938, in Chalmers Collection.

of asking the President to intervene appealed to Chalmers. He knew that Graves was a devoted partisan of President Roosevelt. And he also knew that the President had been interested in the Scottsboro Case.[55] On November 11, at the request of Chalmers, Walter White met with Mrs. Franklin Roosevelt at the White House. Mrs. Roosevelt agreed to speak to the President and to ask him if he would use his influence in some way that might be helpful. That evening when Mrs. Roosevelt talked with her husband, he offered to invite Graves to visit the summer White House in Warm Springs, Georgia, over the Thanksgiving holidays. There they could talk over the case informally.[56]

When the President extended the invitation, however, Graves declined with the excuse that he had too much work in Montgomery. As Grover Hall observed, Graves "dodged that Man! Otherwise he would have fallen over himself to see the Anti-Christ. . . . He's afraid he might be questioned!" What was worse for the defense, the governor also panicked. On November 14, James E. Chappell, editor of the Birmingham *News*, learned that Graves had decided to announce his decision on the fifteenth. Chappell immediately telegraphed Chalmers the bad news. Forney Johnston wrote that Graves felt himself under "tremendous pressure to act immediately." [57] Grover Hall called the governor and pleaded with him over the telephone, but Graves was adamant in

[55] Grover Hall to Allan Knight Chalmers, November 14, 1938, in Chalmers Collection. Chalmers had no way of knowing just how interested the President was. In 1934, FDR had asked his secretary to obtain a complete memorandum on the case. Randolph Preston, a special assistant to the attorney general, read the trial transcripts and reported to the President that he did not "ever remember to have read a record which is such a mass of contradictions and improbabilities as is the evidence of these two witnesses [Orville Gilley and Victoria Price] upon whose testimony the whole case of the state is found." If the boys were faced with the death sentence, Preston advised that the President intervene as President Woodrow Wilson had done in the Mooney case. Louis McHenry Howe to Attorney General Homer Cummings, June 22, 1934; Memorandum of Randolph Preston, July 3, 1934, in Department of Justice Central Files No. 158260, Sub. 46, Sec. 7.

[56] Allan Knight Chalmers to Forney Johnston, November 11, 1938, in Chalmers Collection.

[57] Grover Hall to Allan Knight Chalmers, November 16, 1938; James E. Chappell to Allan Knight Chalmers, November 14, 1938; Forney Johnston to Allan Knight Chalmers, November 14, 1938, in Chalmers Collection.

his decision. Finally, at 3 o'clock on the morning of November 15, Hall sat down to his typewriter in the darkened offices of the *Advertiser* and composed a last minute appeal to Governor Graves.

Hall began by expressing the warm feeling of friendship he had for the governor. "I believe I could trust your heart as far as I could trust the heart of any other man in public life, even though God in his wisdom advised me not to vote for you upon the three occasions when you ran for king." In short, "I think you are a honey," said Hall; but "as an umpire your close calls are bad, however right your heart may be." The Montgomery newsman expressed his sorrow over the stand of the governor. "You are about to lend your hand to one of the most fateful decisions of your life," said Hall. "You are in a mood to do the wrong thing, in my judgment."

Almost desperately, Hall urged the governor to reconsider his stand:

Who cares whether Norris kills Patterson? I don't. Who cares whether Weems picks fights with all and sundry? I don't. Who cares whether Patterson loves long knives and 'gal men?' I don't. Who cares whether Powell is sullen and impolite? I don't. I don't care if they kill off one another . . . so long as they do it in another state, preferably Ohio or New York. I don't care if they eat one another without benefit of pepper sauce. I do not know whether they are guilty or innocent of the rape of two cut-rate prostitutes. I do not care. What I do care for is a factual structure. The fact is that the character of Alabama and its people is at stake before the world. . . .

Hall concluded by noting that the "Scottsboro 'boys' cannot be half innocent and half guilty. . . ." The worst half were free and "apparently deporting themselves acceptably." Now "go ahead and cuss me and all the rest. I'd like to write 20 pages more, but I am awfully tired and sleepy. I just do not want you to err in the last great days of your administration, and this is my last appeal to you for delay and reconsideration." [58] The letter, delivered by special messenger, was waiting when the governor entered his

[58] Grover Hall to Bibb Graves, November 14, 1938, in Chalmers Collection.

office at 8:30 A.M. But shortly before noon, Graves' press secretary read a brief statement to several reporters. The governor, he said, had decided to deny the pardon applications of the five Scottsboro prisoners.[59]

The issue seemed to be settled. But on December 7, Franklin D. Roosevelt sat down at his desk in the White House and composed a letter to the governor of Alabama. "Dear Bibb," he said, "I am sorry indeed not to have seen you while I was at Warm Springs because I wanted to give you a purely personal, and not in any way official, suggestion." He continued, "You have been such a grand Governor and have done so much for the cause of liberalism in the State of Alabama that I want you to go out of office without the loss of the many friends you have made throughout the nation." Frankly, said the President, there was a "real feeling in very wide circles that you said definitely and positively that you were going to commute the sentences of the remainder of the Scottsboro boys. . . ." Many "warm friends of yours all over the United States relied on what they thought was a definite promise." President Roosevelt added that he did not want to go into the details of the case; he was certain the boys did not have a good record in prison. But he expressed his hope that the boys could be taken "away from the State of Alabama . . . with a guarantee on their part that they would not turn up again. . . !" He concluded, "As I said before, I am writing this only as a very old and warm friend of yours, and I hope you will take it in the spirit it is said." [60]

When Chalmers learned from Mrs. Roosevelt that the President had written, it encouraged the SDC chairman to make one more trip to Alabama to urge Graves to reconsider his decision. On Monday morning, December 12, the governor's secretary ushered Chalmers into Graves' office. As soon as Chalmers began talking, Graves interrupted him. "I can't go through with it. I am finished politically if I do. I know from my colleagues that I'll be finished in Alabama." Chalmers looked at the governor, who seemed tired and frightened. "Governor," said the SDC chairman, "you are

[59] Montgomery *Advertiser*, November 16, 1938.
[60] Franklin Delano Roosevelt to Bibb Graves, December 7, 1938, in FDR Library.

through unless you carry out your original promise to us. You know what affidavits I have on your own stationery. And I have a record of the conversation that we had in this very office with Hall, Edmonds, Johnston, and so on." Graves sat in his chair, sipping his "medicine," as he called it, from a cracked cup. Chalmers continued. "I shall have to publish that record. It is not for me to do as I like with it. It belongs to the [Scottsboro Defense] Committee and they can wipe you out as easily as your political friends." Sadly the governor nodded his head. "What you can do, I do not know," he said. "You will do what it seems necessary for you to do. I, however, know very well what they can do." The interview ended.[61]

For the record, Graves always insisted that he had changed his mind because of his interviews with the Scottsboro boys. But Chalmers suspected this explanation from the very beginning. It was true that Norris was surly in his conversation and Patterson had concealed a knife. But in the jungle of Alabama's prison system during the 1930's, the carrying of weapons was a common practice.[62] Moreover, there was no evidence that either Weems or Wright was anything other than polite and courteous in his interview with the governor. In a letter smuggled out of prison to avoid censorship, Wright said that the governor seemed to be baiting him. According to Andy, Graves asked him, "Didn't you say that all the boys except you and your brother attacked these girls?" When Andy denied it, the governor ordered him out of the room

[61] Chalmers, *They Shall Be Free*, 150.

[62] Patterson's autobiography, written in collaboration with Earl Conrad, is unreliable in many areas. But its account of the appalling state of Alabama prisons during this period is probably accurate in its broad outlines. Patterson, who made numerous enemies at Atmore Prison Farm, carried a knife most of the time. Patterson and Conrad, *Scottsboro Boy*, 84. The deplorable state of Alabama prisons has been documented by a number of writers. For a few examples, see Blake McKelvey, "A Half Century of Southern Penal Exploitation," *Social Forces*, XIII (1934–1935), 112–23; Walter Wilson, "Chain Gangs and Profit," *Harper's Magazine*, CLXVI (1933), 522–33; Malcolm C. Moos, *State Penal Administration in Alabama* (University: University of Alabama Press, 1942); Hilda Jane Zimmerman, "Penal Systems and Penal Reform in the South Since the Civil War" (Ph.D. dissertation, University of North Carolina, 1947), 410–33.

with the remark, "What do you take me to be, a fool?" [63] As Wright said in a letter soon after the interview, "You seem to think that I am the cause of the Governor ruling but I am absolutely not. The Governor just made a fool out of you all." [64]

Norris, who did not have a chance to talk with Wright, also complained that the governor had tried to upset him by insisting that he committed the crime.[65] And even if Norris and Patterson were clearly antisocial and unreliable, Chalmers noted that Wright and Weems were not. Why had they not been released?

James Chappell was closer to the truth when he told Chalmers that the governor had simply got cold feet. Graves had become concerned when he found that his mail was running heavily against the Scottsboro boys. Then, in late September, a threatening mob surrounded the Athens, Alabama, jail holding an accused Negro rapist. The crowd shouted repeatedly, "No more Scottsboro! No more Scottsboro!" On the day that Graves interviewed the Scottsboro boys, former Senator Tom Heflin came into the governor's office prophesying political suicide if Graves should release the boys. Apparently Graves stood up to Heflin, but then an unofficial group of politicians regretfully told the governor he was through politically if he went through with the pardons. This was what had caused Graves to collapse, and this was what he meant when he told Chalmers, "I . . . know very well what they can do." [66]

On Christmas Eve, 1938, Chalmers handed newspaper reporters copies of the correspondence between his committee and the governor. In Montgomery, Graves's only comment was, "I have received the letter along with thousands of other threats and I

<hr />

[63] Apparently the governor had confused Andy with his younger brother. Roy had accused several of the other Scottsboro boys of rape at the first trials, but Andy insisted throughout the case that he never saw any girls. Andrew Wright to Allan Knight Chalmers, December 15, 1938, in Chalmers Collection.

[64] Andrew Wright to Allan Knight Chalmers, December 5, 1938, in Chalmers Collection.

[65] Clarence Norris to Allan Knight Chalmers, December ?, 1938, in Chalmers Collection.

[66] James Chappell to Walter White, November 17, 1938, in Chalmers Collection; Chalmers, *They Shall Be Free*, 146.

have ignored all and shall continue to do so." [67] Graves's explanation failed to satisfy Southerners as well as Northerners. The Tuscaloosa *News*, a long-time foe of the Scottsboro boys, declared that
Graves deserved "an even stronger rebuke than the one which Dr.
Chalmers gave him." And the Richmond *Times-Dispatch* angrily
assailed the Alabama chief executive for "capitulating to the forces
of obscurantism and bigotry which already have dragged this
Scottsboro Case through the courts for over seven years and dis-
graced Alabama and the South in the eyes of the civilized world."
The *Times-Dispatch* noted the governor's statement that Chalmers' letter and press release were a "threat" which he would
continue to ignore. "He can rest assured that the Southern public
isn't that gullible," said the Richmond newspaper.[68]

The entire episode deeply embarrassed the Alabamians who
had worked with Chalmers. Although they remained personally
friendly, Johnston and Hall in particular felt that Chalmers' public attack on Graves was a serious tactical error.[69] Chalmers tried
to explain to his Alabama friends why the release had been necessary. The Scottsboro Defense Committee had allowed him complete freedom, said Chalmers. In return, he promised he would
give them "the complete reasons why I had all these months, been
so confident." And once released to the committee, the account of
Graves' double-cross was also released to the public. Chalmers observed that several of his friends objected to the "moral interpretation" placed on Graves' action. For this, Chalmers said, he had a

[67] New York *Times*, December 25, 1938, p. 18. Graves finally got around to replying to President Roosevelt on December 27. In his letter, Graves declared that there
was "never anything done or said that could directly or indirectly give any one
reason to believe that it was determined what would be the final outcome prior to
the denial." Graves did not know that Chalmers had given the President a complete
brief on the case, including a copy of the memorandum describing the governor's
promise to pardon the boys. Bibb Graves to Franklin Delano Roosevelt, December
27, 1938, in FDR Library.

[68] Tuscaloosa *News*, December 27, 1938; Richmond *Times-Dispatch*, December
24, 1938.

[69] Donald Comer to Allan Knight Chalmers, December 23, 1938; Forney Johnston
to Allan Knight Chalmers, December 28, 1938; James Chappell to Allan Knight
Chalmers, May 8, 1938, in Chalmers Collection. Hall was so embarrassed over the
press release that he temporarily ceased correspondence with Chalmers. Grover Hall
to Allan Knight Chalmers, December 29, 1938.

single comment. "I do not believe it is because I am a minister, and therefore supposedly idealistic, that I feel this way." There was an "essential honor in most men about their word," said Chalmers. And while it was perhaps a tactical error to release the entire record to the public, "for good or ill, I felt I had to say it." [70]

[70] Allan Knight Chalmers to Henry Edmonds, James Chappell, Donald Comer, Grover Hall, Forney Johnston, December 28, 1938, in Chalmers Collection. Only Edmonds was sympathetic. Edmonds wrote Chalmers that he felt from the beginning of Graves' backdown that the entire sordid story had to be aired for the public to hear. "If the results were unfavorable down here, nevertheless the thing had to be done." Henry Edmonds to Allan Knight Chalmers, January 13, 1939, in Chalmers Collection.

XII

FORGOTTEN
HEROES

SCOTTSBORO, one of the top news stories of the 1930's, dropped from the headlines after 1939. Although there was an occasional one-paragraph story, Governor Graves' refusal to pardon the remaining five defendants was the climactic episode in the news media's account of the Scottsboro story. For Allan Knight Chalmers it was the beginning of eleven years of frustration. The governor's disavowal of his earlier promises was a preview of the tragic sequence of negotiation, agreement, and then retraction which would be repeated again and again. As Chalmers sadly learned, freedom for the five Scottsboro prisoners—no longer boys, but men—was in the hands of Alabama officials who were timid, fearful, and sometimes malicious.

The escapades of the four released Scottsboro defendants complicated the delicate negotiations. They eventually renounced their careers in vaudeville and returned to the Scottsboro Defense Committee for help in late 1937. By this time, however, the SDC had expended most of its funds and was preoccupied with freeing the five still in jail. Montgomery, Roberson, Williams, and Leroy Wright received little training or supervision. Eventually Eugene Williams and Willie Roberson became settled in a new life outside prison. Leroy Wright, described in 1937 by an SDC psychiatrist as neurotic and nearly psychotic, made the most satisfactory adjustment. He was soon happily married and had a steady job.[1]

After 1938 the committee's main problem was Olen Montgomery who drifted in and out of jails across the country, usually on charges of public drunkenness or drunk and disorderly. "If he were not a Scottsboro boy," said Chalmers, "he would simply be a somewhat shiftless, not very bright boy who gets in occasional trouble of no importance." But the Alabama authorities were anxious to seize upon any difficulties by the four as proof that the remaining five were incorrigible and irredeemable. That fact "elevates his little difficulties into mountains, and . . . endangers the possibility of freedom for the other boys." [2]

Unskilled, semi-literate, and nearly blind, Montgomery could find only the most menial employment which he quickly abandoned because everywhere he went, "they almost works me to death." Each new job that Roy Wilkins of the NAACP found for him was "just a big dump." The Association gave Olen thirty-five dollars a month allowance to supplement his earnings, but he bitterly complained that this would not even keep him in his "drinking money." [3] In the summer of 1939, Montgomery told Wilkins and Chalmers he had decided to return to Atlanta and live with his mother. Both men had grave misgivings about his plans to return South, but Montgomery insisted this was the only way he could "get straight." He was there only four days before a policeman stopped in front of the house where he stayed, called him out, and demanded to know if he was "one of those G-d D—n Scottsboro niggers?" When Montgomery replied that he was, the policeman drove off with the warning to "be careful," because "they might find you yet." Walter White's brother-in-law, Eugene Mar-

---

[1] Allan Knight Chalmers to Frances Levkoff, January 15, 1940, in Chalmers Collection. Roberson did have one brush with the law. In the summer of 1942 he was present at (and apparently took part in) a midnight brawl at a Harlem night spot. Arrested, tried, and convicted on a charge of disorderly conduct, Roberson denied he had done anything wrong. The "acusation was entirely ficticious and . . . [the] trial was a farce," he said. Willie Roberson to Hester Huntington, July 19, 1942, in ILD Papers.

[2] Allan Knight Chalmers to Eugene M. Martin, October 23, 1942, in Chalmers Collection.

[3] Olen Montgomery to Allan Knight Chalmers, January 22, 1940, in Chalmers Collection.

tin, hastily placed Montgomery on the first train out of the city.[4]

Montgomery returned to Detroit to stay with an aunt and he promised Chalmers to "stay out of trouble." "Dr you can bet your life I will do everything in my power to help those other five boys," he wrote Chalmers. "I wouldn't do anything in this world to hurt the case. . . . And I am more than willing to do my part." Eight months later, in the midst of negotiations with the Alabama authorities, Roy Wilkins learned that Montgomery had been arrested and charged with the rape of a young Negro girl. Through the Detroit NAACP chapter, Wilkins kept the story out of the newspapers and hired one of the city's top criminal lawyers to defend Montgomery. An investigation by the law firm of Roxborough and Taliaferro revealed that Montgomery had been invited into the room of Pauline, alias "Tillie," Faulkner for a drink on the evening of July 26. Shortly before midnight (according to Montgomery), he and Miss Faulkner passed out on her bed. The next thing he knew, the police were taking him to jail with the landlady screaming that he had raped the Faulkner girl. After she recovered from her hangover, Miss Faulkner admitted that she was so drunk she could not recall what happened. Detroit police dropped the charges.[5]

Even after Montgomery got out of jail he remained a vexing problem for Wilkins. Whenever he decided he was ready for a change of scenery, he would demand travel funds from the NAACP. If Wilkins seemed reluctant, Montgomery's inevitable response was: "unless you want a lot of trouble you had better let me go." In Hartford, Connecticut, local NAACP officials got him a job on a local tobacco farm. Within a month he was involved in a dance hall brawl and jailed on a charge of public drunkenness. Although Wilkins insisted that he remain outside the South, Montgomery headed back to Atlanta. He was soon in jail on a drunk and disorderly charge. "I am strongly of the opinion that

[4] Roy Wilkins to Eugene M. Martin, August 17, 1939; Martin to Wilkins, August 21, 1939, in Chalmers Collection.

[5] James J. McClendon to Roy Wilkins, July 27, 1940; McClendon to Thurgood Marshall, July 29, 1940, in Chalmers Collection.

the boy [Montgomery] is a little off," said Eugene Martin. "He is not completely out of his mind, but . . . I think the best proof that he is a little off is the fact that he dares put his feet back here in Georgia. . . ." [6]

In 1943 an ILD official found Montgomery in a Bronx boarding house, completely demoralized, clothed in rags, and recovering from a week-long drunk. "It would be an act of mercy if one would give him a gun to end it all," said Mrs. Francis Levkoff. "He seems to have little to live for." No one was more annoyed with Montgomery than Allan Knight Chalmers. But when he became most angry he thought of the awful loneliness which Montgomery had known since his release from prison. "This city is a stranger," Montgomery had once written from Detroit after spending the night in a slum theatre. If "you haven't got someone to look out for him he is just out." To a discouraged Chalmers, the story of Olen Montgomery was the tragedy of Scottsboro. "I have the feeling that even though we get the rest of them out," he said, "they are probably already too ruined by this experience . . . to adjust . . . to life in this already maladjusted world." Eventually Montgomery receded into obscurity and returned quietly to Monroe, Georgia, the town where he was born. In 1944, in one of his last letters to the ILD officials who had defended him a decade before, he wrote that he was getting along "tolerably well." But, he plaintively added, "nobody doesn't seem to pay much attention to me. . . ." [7]

Despite Chalmers' ability to convey the impression that the four had made a satisfactory adjustment to life outside prison, Alabama officials adamantly opposed freeing the remaining five. As Grover Hall had predicted, Governor Frank Dixon had no intention of petting the "dead cat" of Scottsboro. During the first half of 1939 Chalmers could only wait and hope for better news.

[6] Memorandum by Roy Wilkins on Olen Montgomery, June 10, 1942; Eugene M. Martin to Roy Wilkins, October 19, 1942, in Chalmers Collection.
[7] Frances Levkoff to Allan Knight Chalmers, January 10, 1943; Olen Montgomery to Allan Knight Chalmers, December 2, 1939; Allan Knight Chalmers to Frances Levkoff, January 14, 1943, in Chalmers Collection; Olen Montgomery to ILD Headquarters, June ?, 1944, in ILD Papers.

FRED LEO

Don Wyatt and Raymond Fraley, attorneys for Victoria
Price Street, on their way to the Winchester, Tennessee,
federal courthouse.

FRED LEO

John (Jack) Wheeler, National Broadcasting Company
attorney, and Dan T. Carter returning from a lunch recess
to continue testimony at the Winchester courthouse.

Robert Campbell, National Broadcasting Company
attorney, in the hall of the federal courthouse, Winchester.

Elmer and Ruby Bates Schut at home in Union Gap,
Washington. Mrs. Schut died before her suit against the
National Broadcasting Company came to trial.

Victoria Price Street and her husband Dean Street
outside the federal courthouse at Winchester.

Clarence (Willie) Norris, who in 1977 was apparently the
only survivor among the "Scottsboro boys." Governor
George Wallace signed his pardon.

In August, Hall resumed his correspondence with Chalmers to tell him that the Alabama legislature had created a three-man pardon and parole board which would act on all future requests. Although the board had not yet been appointed, Hall said he was certain it would be "of a calibre that you and I can respect." Hall cautioned Chalmers to be patient for just a little longer, perhaps until early 1940. There had been widespread rumors that the remaining Scottsboro boys would be instantly freed under the new arrangement and the boys would naturally wish to disprove these stories.[8]

In late November, Governor Dixon appointed the pardon board and Hall, despite his earlier decision to "retire from the field," was soon arguing once more for the Scottsboro prisoners. As he told Chalmers, the "sap is flowing again, Yankee!" Hall's initial conference with the new board was an unqualified success. Judge Alex Smith, the chairman, broadly hinted that he and his colleagues were ready to have the case ended once and for all. Half-jokingly, Smith said that if he thought the prisoners could be taken out of Alabama forever, "I'd put half of them in my car and drive them across the border!" The board promised a careful study of the record and it set a public hearing for February 15, 1940. Even when ex-Senator Heflin, the avowed defender of Alabama's "sacred white womanhood," announced that he would testify against pardon for the Scottsboro boys, Hall remained optimistic after Judge Smith confidentially dismissed Heflin as a buffoon. "Why'n the hell don't you fellows do the smart thing and let Heflin appear here alone?" Smith said to Hall. "He wants an audience and a chance to make the first page. Why not disappoint him?" As Hall concluded to Chalmers, "Hold everything. We can't be licked when even members of the board are coaching us!" On February 1 the Montgomery newsman confided to Henry Edmonds that he was confident the battle was won.[9]

[8] Grover Hall to Allan Knight Chalmers, August 24, 1939, in Chalmers Collection.
[9] Grover Hall to Allan Knight Chalmers, November 28, 1939, January 30, 1940; Henry Edmonds to Allan Knight Chalmers, February 1, 1940, in Chalmers Collection.

He was wrong. Three weeks after Heflin had appeared and denounced the Scottsboro boys as "vile despoilers of our precious white women," the board unanimously voted to deny the parole requests of all five prisoners. Defensively, Hall argued for the good intentions of the board. It had "approached the question originally with open minds," but after a thorough study of the record, it concluded that the prisoners were not ready for parole. "With reference to Patterson certainly and possibly one other [Ozie Powell], they seriously doubt if these men can be reclaimed in prison or not." Haywood Patterson insisted, "it seems no matter how good I may be here they always shows the bad side. I may be as good as Christ was here in Atmore [and] they will still say my conduct and attitude is bad." Despite Patterson's disclaimer, there is ample evidence to suggest that both he and Powell were problem prisoners.[10]

The same thing could not be said for the other three. Both Weems and Wright had been in "Class A" during their entire prison sentences. As Wright noted, "I have maintained an excellent record at Kilby." The board, he declared, was "not justified in making a denial." [11]

The board's refusal to grant pardons touched off the first crisis within the Scottsboro Defense Committee. For the second time, hopes for an end to the case had been inflated by the assurances of Alabama officials. For the second time, these hopes had been dashed. As Chalmers told Hall, the SDC saw "this present debacle in the same rank with Graves' going back on his given word."

[10] Montgomery *Advertiser*, February 16, March 9, 1940; Grover Hall to Allan Knight Chalmers, March 8, 1940; Haywood Patterson to Allan Knight Chalmers, March ?, 1940, in Chalmers Collection. The board may also have been influenced by adverse public opinion. David Birmingham, a former official in the Graves administration, declared that it would be a "slap in the face of justice and law if these gorillas should be given a parole." Moreover, such action would "write the death knell to the Parole and Pardon Board. . . ." Montgomery *Advertiser*, February 15, 1940.

[11] Andy Wright to Allan Knight Chalmers, March 18, 1940, in Chalmers Collection. A report issued by prison authorities in 1938 said Weems had given no trouble. Statement of Sentence by Hamp Draper, associate member of the Alabama State Board of Administration, April 7, 1938, in Scottsboro Administrative File 3, NAACP Papers.

Several members of the defense committee clamored for a full-scale program of publicity which would inform the nation of the continued intransigence of Alabama officials. Chalmers was convinced, however, that any mass propaganda campaign would seal the remaining Scottsboro prisoners in their cells for the remainder of their lives. In a long and often emotional meeting of the SDC, he argued for his position. As he later told Hall, "I did win out in the end but by the skin of my teeth." [12]

When Chalmers asked the board to reconsider its decision, he was unceremoniously rebuffed. Mrs. Edwina Mitchell, the board's secretary, wrote Chalmers that he had "lost a proper perspective" in harping on the plight of the Scottsboro prisoners. The Alabama Pardon and Parole Board had spent far too much time considering the five prisoners. There were many men in Alabama prisons who claimed to be innocent, said Mrs. Mitchell, but their trials and convictions did not capture the public's imagination. "They are, however, just as deserving of the consideration of this Board as are your clients, and they are being deprived of that consideration to the extent that we devote more time to these five." She concluded by telling Chalmers that in the future the five would be considered only as individuals. They would never be acted upon as a group. Privately, Mrs. Mitchell told an executive of the *Advertiser* that the board "actively resents the interest Dr. Chalmers takes in the case." [13]

Bitterly, one Alabamian urged Chalmers to stop treating the pardon board so gently. The gloves should be "taken off," said Carroll Kilpatrick, "and the idiots who run the state of Alabama shown up to the people." Kilpatrick, a native of the state and a former editor of the University of Alabama student newspaper, said he was sorry to see the state "humiliated again, but it seems to me it has already humiliated itself beyond repair." But anger was a

[12] Allan Knight Chalmers to Grover Hall, March 19, 1940, in Chalmers Collection.

[13] Mrs. Edwina Mitchell to Allan Knight Chalmers, April 11, 1940; R. F. Hudson to James Chappell, March 17, 1941, in Chalmers Collection.

luxury Chalmers could not afford, and he tried to smooth over relations with the board.[14]

On January 9, 1941, Grover Hall suddenly died. Although James Chappell, editor of the Birmingham *News*, agreed to take Hall's place and to serve as the SDC's unofficial liaison in Alabama, the death of the Montgomery newsman seriously handicapped the efforts of the SDC. As Chappell remarked, Hall "had more influence with Governor Dixon . . . than anybody else, and he probably had more influence on the Board of Pardons and Paroles than any other individual." [15]

In late October of 1941, Chappell wrote that the board had told him confidentially it planned to parole Weems, Norris, and Wright. Patterson and Powell were still considered unsuited for release. Three weeks later, when the time came for a final vote, Judge Smith and Judge Robert M. Hill voted to deny paroles for all five. Mrs. Mitchell dissented. Later she explained to Chappell the reason Smith and Hill changed their minds. A political campaign was approaching in May of 1942. "If we act on so highly controversial a case at this time," they argued, "some candidate may seize upon it as an issue and endeavor to discredit the whole parole and probation system. . . ." [16] Once again, the Scottsboro prisoners had become the victims of Alabama's politics.

Chalmers tried to remain optimistic in the face of the continued setbacks, but he became more and more disheartened during the following year. In November, 1942, James Chappell wrote the SDC chairman to tell him that things had never looked more discouraging. Even men of good will, he said, were "going blind" on the race issue again. The same was true for many of the Southern industrialists who had projected an image of moderation during the 1930's. "It is impossible for liberal southerners to do

---

[14] Carroll Kilpatrick to Morris Shapiro, March 13, 1940; Allan Knight Chalmers to Alabama Pardon and Parole Board, March 26, 1940, in Chalmers Collection.
[15] James Chappell to Allan Knight Chalmers, quoted in Chalmers, *They Shall Be Free*, 193.
[16] James Chappell to Allan Knight Chalmers, October 22, 1941; Chappell to Chalmers, December 26, 1941, in Chalmers Collection.

anything," he said. The Pardon and Parole Board "would not think of touching the Scottsboro case." [17]

On December 17, 1942, Chalmers wrote the five Scottsboro prisoners. His letter was a frank and honest appraisal of the situation. He told them there was little hope for their immediate release because of the tense interracial feeling in the South. Chalmers urged the five to make a good record, even though this was hard when there was little hope for immediate release. He promised he would try again when there seemed any hope. The war, he concluded, had poisoned the minds of Southerners. On Christmas day Andy Wright angrily replied that he could not see what the war had to do with his case. "The way you tell it you all is doing everything in your power for me. Like hell you is, and I no longer wishes to hear those lies . . . any further." [18]

Wright's reaction to the disappointing news was understandable. During the 1930's Alabama's prison system was one of the worst in the nation. The Pardon and Parole Board often talked with Chalmers about the necessity of keeping the men in prison so they could be "rehabilitated." For the most part, however, the state's penal system was a human refuse heap where the inmates were overworked and often brutally mistreated. A few officials tried desperately to institute a rehabilitation program, but limited resources made their efforts seem ineffectual in the face of the gigantic need. Moreover, the low pay, the long hours, and the discouraging conditions meant that the prisons' personnel were often the misfits of society.

Each day within the walls of Kilby was a nightmare, wrote Andy. In a letter smuggled out of the prison, he described the regimen. It was "up in the mornings at 4 o'clock and eat at 4:45 and don't eat dinner until 1:00 p.m., eight hours and fifteen [minutes] and the worse part of it [is] we don't have half enough

[17] James Chappell to Allan Knight Chalmers, November 17, 1942, in Chalmers Collection.

[18] Allan Knight Chalmers to Clarence Norris, Haywood Patterson, Ozie Powell, Charley Weems and Andy Wright, December 17, 1942; Andy Wright to Allan Knight Chalmers, December 25, 1942, in Chalmers Collection. After Andy had a chance to calm down, he apologized to Chalmers.

to eat. . . . ." It was not just the "prison punishment" (whipping with a leather strap) that bothered Andy, but the constant fear. "A colored convict's very best behavior is not good enough for these officials here. Every time they open their mouths it is ['] you black bastard.['] When we think we are doing right we be cursed at and kick around and beat like dogs." [19]

Of the five men, only Patterson psychologically "adjusted" to prison life. He learned to be obsequious with prison officials and "Uncle Tom" (as he put it) with ease. Deprived of normal sexual outlets, he became an aggressive homosexual. When the ILD reduced his allowance he showed considerable initiative by undertaking an extensive letter-writing campaign to organizations he thought might be sympathetic. In this way he occasionally received large amounts of money.[20] Unfortunately, Patterson always overestimated the amount of money he would receive in any one month. Most of his difficulties in the prison—apart from scrapes over homosexual friends—stemmed from the "bank system" which officials openly tolerated. Under this arrangement, prisoners borrowed from loan-sharks within the prison at an interest rate which was often 50 or 100 per cent per week. Thus Haywood got into a fight over a four-dollar loan in August, 1945. He was thrown into Class C for fighting and thus could not receive letters or money. By the time he had worked his way out of Class C two months later, his debt had pyramided to $39.50.[21]

Patterson used every wile he possessed to extract money from Chalmers. The prisoner knew that the SDC chairman wanted him to stay out of trouble. His favorite device was to run up a large

[19] Andy Wright to Mrs. Hester G. Huntington, April 28, 1943, in ILD Papers. Andy begged his friends to send an investigator down to talk with the prisoners. At least "300 convicts will verify my statement," he said. Andy Wright to Allan Knight Chalmers, April 28, 1943, in Chalmers Collection.

[20] Gradually the news of Haywood's letter-writing campaign leaked back to the ILD and the SDC. Louis Colman of the ILD urged all who wrote Patterson to cease sending money. He had "been able to secure considerable . . . sums through a well-organized campaign of letter-writing," said Colman, "and as a result has gotten himself into trouble over and over again in the prison." Louis Colman to Don Jonson, October 9, 1945, in ILD Papers.

[21] Allan Knight Chalmers to Winsor H. Swearingen, October 11, 1945, in Chalmers Collection.

debt with "the bank," and then to insist that the loan had to be paid or there would be "bad trouble." On one occasion, Chalmers sent him forty dollars to pay a large debt. Two months later, Haywood wrote Chalmers, "the money you sent the state minister wasn't given to me nor was my debts paid with it. He gave the money over to the prison authorities in my name. . . ." Of course Haywood had simply drawn five dollars a week from the amount and used it for spending money. As a result, said Patterson, "my debts hasn't been completed yet." He insisted that the entire mixup was the fault of the prison authorities. "I does not have no bad conscience." He demanded more money, "because if I don't soon meet these demands there is likely to be serious trouble." [22]

When all other devices had failed, Patterson always threatened suicide. In a request for money for some "little pleasures," Haywood explained that the Alabama prison officials had been "framing lies on me and disturbing my peace of mind." He had "given up everything, even the hope of an honorable end. . . ." If he should die he said, "I want my sisters to have my body then at least I shall get a decent Burial instead of lying at the Bottom of a no good Alabama grave. Not that it really makes any difference. I just dont like Alabama." [23]

The remaining prisoners suffered psychologically far worse than Patterson. Andy Wright carefully read newspapers which came into the prison. Thoroughly familiar with the developments of his case, he was always perceptive in seeing through the false optimism of his supporters. Unlike most of the others, he reluctantly asked for money and was honest when he explained why he needed funds. Throughout the first eight years of his imprisonment, Wright managed to hold up under the strain. But when he saw four boys released and learned of Graves' doublecross, he began to lose his nerve. "I am trying all that in my power to be brave," he wrote in 1939, "but you understand a person can be brave for a

[22] Haywood Patterson to Allan Knight Chalmers, January 19, 1946, in Chalmers Collection.

[23] Haywood Patterson to Allan Knight Chalmers, June 17, 1945, in Chalmers Collection.

certain length of time and then he is a coward down. That the way it is." [24]

In 1939, Andy developed a "prison psychosis." Although physical examinations by doctors hired by the SDC could reveal nothing organically wrong, Wright constantly complained of sickness. He wrote Chalmers that the trouble was "I have been trying to hold myself up with the expectation that I would be out." But he had begun to lose all hope and "in my present condition I am growing near and near to my grave." When one of his supporters wrote him and urged him to "snap out" of his depression, Andy replied bitterly. "What do you think I am a iron man[?] You all is out there were you can do for yourself and get things done and then have a nerve to write and tell me to cheer up." [25]

The worst of it was the waiting without knowing what was going on. Chalmers and the other members of the SDC were never able to keep the Scottsboro boys informed. The mail to and from the prison was carefully read by officials who might have leaked secret plans to the press. Chalmers, therefore, was only able to talk vaguely of "good news soon" when he felt there was a chance for the boys' release. As the delays of the Pardon and Parole Board stretched on interminably, the patience of the Scottsboro boys snapped. In late 1939, Andy wrote to demand "facts" not promises. "If you all are not going to do or cannot do anything be a man enough to write and tell me and not have me held in suspense. . . . It is enough misery to have the time I have without being put through such agonys." "I wonder what do you all call soon," wrote Clarence Norris, "a month are [sic] two are a year or so. I can't understand what some people call soon." Two months later, in a more bitter mood, Norris declared, "I am tired of serving time in prison for nothing, I would rather be dead and in Hell. . . ." But he added hopelessly, "I realize that I am helpless and cant even do nothing for myself, I am just here depending on you all." [26]

---

[24] Andy Wright to Rose Baron, April 28, 1938, in ILD Papers.

[25] Andy Wright to Allan Knight Chalmers, February 22, 1939, in Chalmers Collection; Andy Wright to Rose Baron, August 2, 1939, in ILD Papers.

[26] Andy Wright to Allan Knight Chalmers, December 25, 1939, in Chalmers

When the prospects for parole brightened in 1943, Chalmers again wrote promising vaguely that they would soon hear "good news." Throughout the summer Andy Wright waited until he could wait no more. "Why cant you tell me something that you means and means to do and why must you continue to write me things that is untrue," he told Chalmers. When the former head of the SDC explained that there had been unforeseen delays and the board was still deliberating, Andy wrote: "Do you realize how long it has been since August. It do not take God in heaven that long to make a decision. . . . I have got tired of waiting. I have lost my health and most of my mind." [27]

The first break finally came on November 17, 1943. After months of patient negotiations, the board of Pardons and Paroles quietly released Weems.[28] And in January the board released Wright, by now age thirty, and Norris, age thirty-two. Despite the earnest pleas of Chalmers, the board refused to allow Norris and Wright to be transferred "up North." Roy Wilkins of the NAACP had obtained a job for them in Cleveland, working at a smelting plant for forty dollars per week. Instead, the board insisted that Andy and Clarence work at a lumber company near Montgomery. The two men, living in a room eight feet by ten feet and sharing a common bed, worked irregular hours for thirteen dollars a week. It was, said Andy, "no difference than prison." When Chalmers asked the board to allow Wright and Norris to go to Cleveland because of the low pay, Mrs. Mitchell coldly replied, "Andy's wages are considerably above the average for an ignorant, untrained negro laborer in this state." As Chalmers had feared, the two men soon despaired and fled northward, leaving the state they hated. Chalmers managed to persuade Wright and Norris to return, but the pardon board—in spite of

Collection; Clarence Norris to Anna Damon, October 3, 1939, in ILD Papers; Clarence Norris to Allan Knight Chalmers, October 30, 1939, in Chalmers Collection.

[27] Andy Wright to Allan Knight Chalmers, September 16, 1943; Chalmers to Wright, September 30, 1943; Wright to Chalmers, November 8, 1943, in Chalmers Collection.

[28] W. P. Shirley to Allan Knight Chalmers, November 17, 1943, in Chalmers Collection. Shirley had temporarily assumed Mrs. Mitchell's duties as secretary of the board.

a promise that it would give them another chance—sent both men back to prison.[29]

When the two were back in prison, Chalmers recalled a letter of distress he had once received from Clarence Norris. It had ended, "So, Doctor, if it's not too absurd, will you help me out?" To Chalmers it all seemed absurd. For years, thousands of dollars and thousands of hours had been spent trying to release nine Negro youths. "No person of responsibility, after the evidence had all been handed in, could take the boys' alleged guilt seriously," said Chalmers. And yet it seemed impossible to illustrate this "already proven fact to the highest courts in the state of Alabama and to the members of the Parole Board of that state." The prisoners themselves had a ready explanation for the "absurdity" of it all. The continued inflexibility of Alabama officials was due to race hatred, said Andrew Wright, "the old traditional cause . . . which we all fully understand." Or as Clarence Norris said in a more bitter mood, "I don't Believe I have a white friend in the world[.] I believe all Races of white peoples hate negroes Especially in the United States." [30]

A discouraged but persistent Chalmers continued his negotiations with the Alabama authorities. Even when the SDC disbanded in 1944, he kept up his efforts with the financial assistance of the NAACP and gradually his patience paid off. In late 1946, the board released Ozie Powell and gave Clarence another parole.[31]

Haywood Patterson was officially described by the Pardon and Parole Board as "sullen, vicious and incorrigible"; there was

[29] Mrs. Edwina Mitchell to Allan Knight Chalmers, February 2, 1944; Allan Knight Chalmers to Ralph W. Riley, September 20, 1944, in Chalmers Collection.

[30] Chalmers, *They Shall Be Free*, 226; Andy Wright to Allan Knight Chalmers, March 18, 1940; Clarence Norris to Allan Knight Chalmers, October 30, 1939, in Chalmers Collection. "I'm . . . being held here because I'm a nigger," said Olen Montgomery in early 1937. "That's why I'm in jail; not nothing I've done." Psychiatric examination of Olen Montgomery by G. C. Branche, M.D., January 10, 1937, in Chalmers Collection.

[31] Allan Knight Chalmers to Nathan K. Christopher, October 11, 1946, in Chalmers Collection. Wright was released for a brief period in 1947, but he had to return to prison when a would-be employer discovered he was a "Scottsboro Boy" and refused to hire him. "Every place I go I be confront with that . . ." said a discouraged Wright. Andrew Wright to Allan Knight Chalmers, February 7, 1947, in Chalmers Collection.

little chance for his release. On a hot summer day in 1948, however, Patterson slipped away from his work gang and fled into the nearby sugar cane fields. For almost a week, he eluded prison dogs and searching airplanes as he made his way first to Atlanta and from there to his sister's home in Detroit. For two years he remained in hiding, assisted by officials of the Civil Rights Congress—the organization which had succeeded the International Labor Defense. When agents of the Federal Bureau of Investigation arrested him, Michigan's Governor G. Mennen Williams refused to sign extradition papers and Alabama authorities announced that they would terminate all efforts to have him returned to the state.[32]

In May, 1950, the Alabama Pardon and Parole Board met and voted unanimously to grant another parole to Andrew Wright. On June 9, 1950, nineteen years and two months after he was taken from a train in Paint Rock, Alabama, Andy Wright walked through the gates of Kilby Prison. Chalmers had arranged for Andy to work as an orderly in an Albany, New York hospital. His parole "pay" amounted to $13.45. One of the reporters who waited outside the gate asked Wright how he felt. "I have no hard feelings toward anyone," he said softly. Someone asked about Mrs. Price. "I'm not mad because the girl lied about me," replied Andy. "If she's still living, I feel sorry for her because I don't guess she sleeps much at night." Without waiting for any further questions, he turned and walked away. The last of the Scottsboro boys was free.[33]

From 1931 to 1937 supporters showered the Scottsboro boys with letters, gifts, and money. It was scant reward for the combined total of more than one hundred years they spent in Alabama's jails and prisons. Once lionized as proletarian heroes, they were forgotten after their release. "I am just like a rabbit in a strange wood and the dogs is after him and no place to hide," wrote Andy Wright. For

[32] Patterson and Conrad, *Scottsboro Boy*, 230–44; New York *Times*, June 28, 1950, p. 14; July 11, 1950, p. 21; July 13, 1950, p. 23.
[33] Montgomery *Advertiser*, June 10, 1950.

nineteen years he had looked to the day when he would be free. Now, without friends or family in Albany, "Freedom don't mean a thing to me."[34] Thirteen months after Wright was released from prison, a middle-aged Albany Negro woman accused him of raping her thirteen-year-old daughter. Defense attorneys later proved that the charge was brought because the woman held a personal grudge against Wright and he was vindicated when he went on trial. It was for Wright, however, one more piece of evidence that the Scottsboro Case had placed a "permanent jinx" on him. "Everywhere I go, it seems like Scottsboro is throwed up in my face," he said. "I don't believe I'll ever live it down."[35]

Wright's younger brother, Roy, met an even more tragic fate in 1959, twenty-two years after his release. When he returned from an extended cruise he discovered his wife at the home of another man. He stabbed her to death, then—filled with remorse—returned to their apartment and took his own life.[36]

In Detroit where he had fled from Alabama, Haywood Patterson talked with journalist Earl Conrad who collaborated on Patterson's "autobiography," *Scottsboro Boy*. On the night of December 18, 1950, Haywood entered a Detroit bar selling copies of the book. Later in the evening the barroom erupted into a brawl and when police arrived they found a twenty-seven-year-old Negro had been stabbed to death. Patterson first denied he was in the bar, then admitted he stabbed the victim, but claimed self-defense. After two mistrials, a Detroit jury convicted him of manslaughter and he received a fifteen- to twenty-year sentence in the Michigan State Prison. Shortly after he began serving his term, prison doctors discovered Patterson was suffering from cancer. He grew steadily weaker through the summer of 1952; on August 24 he died. Haywood Patterson's death earned two brief paragraphs in the New York *Times*.[37]

The remainder of the Scottsboro defendants returned to ob-

---

34 Andy Wright to Allan Knight Chalmers, July ?, 1950, in Chalmers Collection.
35 New York *Times*, July 12, 1951, p. 27; Andy Wright to Allan Knight Chalmers, May, June ?, 1952, in Chalmers Collection.
36 New York *Times*, August 18, 1959, p. 58.
37 Detroit *Free Press*, December 19, 1950, September 26, 1951; Jackson (Michigan) *Citizen-Patriot*, August 25, August 26, 1952.

scurity. One became a hotel bellhop in a midwestern city. Several others, unnoticed by the press, went back to the Southern communities where they were born.

Like the Scottsboro boys, Victoria Price and Ruby Bates were also soon forgotten. In 1938 the Huntsville cotton mill where Mrs. Price worked closed its doors permanently. The former star witness for Alabama stayed in town for six months, then moved north just across the Tennessee border to the rural community of Flintsville. Allan Knight Chalmers heard she was bitter at the way the state had abandoned her and was willing to reverse her testimony. In 1940, an SDC investigator approached Mrs. Price and she readily agreed to retract her accusations—but only for a substantial price. Chalmers refused.[38]

After her dramatic reversal on the witness stand, Ruby Bates briefly toured the country as an ILD speaker. She admitted that the Communist philosophy, slogans, and programs didn't make much sense, but "now I understand that if the people would all work together instead of against each other it would help everybody." Interest in Miss Bates soon passed and despite plaintive requests to the ILD and to Allan Knight Chalmers she was on her own.[39] Officials in the Alabama Attorney General's office insisted she had been set up in a luxurious New York penthouse as a reward for "going red." In fact, after 1934, she went to work in an upstate New York spinning factory. When a medical examination in 1938 revealed a severe case of tuberculosis, she quietly returned to Huntsville to live with her mother. By the 1940's, both women had married and changed their names. According to Scottsboro newspaper editor Fred Bucheit, the two women died in 1961, thirty miles apart from each other.[40]

[38] Reese T. Amis to James Chappell, May 1, 1939; Allan Knight Chalmers to Julian R. Harris, April 25, 1939; Hunt Clement, Jr., to Allan Knight Chalmers, June 12, 1939; Morris Shapiro to Allan Knight Chalmers, June 21, 1940, in Chalmers Collection.

[39] Rose Shapiro to Elizabeth Seeberg, February 11, 1938, in Scottsboro Administration File 3, NAACP Papers; Ruby Bates to Allan Knight Chalmers, October 29, 1937, in Chalmers Collection.

[40] Interview with Scottsboro *Progressive-Sentinel* Editor Fred Bucheit, March 24, 1967.

Stop here!

XIII

WINCHESTER, 1977
THE FINAL TRIAL?

I N the fall of 1968 I wrote an article on the Scottsboro case which appeared in *American Heritage* magazine, circulation 125,000. The following year this book, *Scottsboro: A Tragedy of the American South,* was published by the Louisiana State University Press. While it was hardly a best seller, the original edition went through two printings, and hardcover and paperback sales totaled 25,000 copies during the next seven years. More than 150 book reviews appeared in magazines, journals, and newspapers. Initial publication had prompted news stories recalling the case in the New York *Times,* the Washington *Post,* the Los Angeles *Times,* the Louisville *Courier Journal,* and a half dozen other major metropolitan newspapers.

Although the response was generally favorable, not everyone was pleased with my observations on the Scottsboro case. A handful of white Alabamians sent me rambling letters that alternated between unprintable aspersions upon the circumstances of my birth and demands that I return to northern Alabama to receive my just punishment. William L. Patterson, an aging Communist Party veteran of the 1930s, accused me of joining hands with such degenerate "racists" as William Styron and C. Vann Woodward. My unfortunate geographical and genetic heritage was a mitigating factor, implied the former head of the International Labor Defense (after all, the "South has no monopoly on racism"), but this could not excuse my decision to speak for a ruling class "both desperate and ruthless." These were essentially ideological objections. I had few complaints of errors. Certainly no one raised any questions about the last sentence of the book in which I reported that the two women were dead.[1]

Seven years after the original publication of *Scottsboro*, the National Broadcasting Company telecast a two-hour "docudrama" entitled "Judge Horton and the Scottsboro Boys." It was based, after a fashion, on *Scottsboro*, and in the last twenty-five seconds of the broadcast, a narrator dutifully repeated my statement that the star witnesses in the Scottsboro case were dead. According to the Arthur Neilsen rating company, forty-one million people were watching that television production.

Within three weeks I discovered my report of the death of Victoria Price, like an earlier account of Mark Twain's demise, was greatly exaggerated. Victoria Price was living in a rural Tennessee community under the name of Katherine Queen Victory Street. To add insult to injury I soon found that Ruby Bates was also alive. Her neighbors in the Yakima Valley of Washington state knew her as Lucille Schut.

In the months that followed I learned more about the lives of the two women after the case faded from the headlines. During World War II, Victoria Price had married a Lincoln County farmer (Frank Roland), but they lived together less than three years. In the early 1950s she married for the fourth and last time. Her husband, Walter Dean Street, a local sharecropper, periodically moved from farm to farm in southcentral Tennessee. With the exception of Street and a handful of older residents, neither neighbors nor friends were aware of any connection between the Victoria Price of the 1930s and the woman who called herself Katherine Queen Victory Street.[2]

After the Horton trial Ruby Bates's oldest brother had given her $100 and told her coldly to "go as far away as it would take her." Her sister refused to answer any letters. But when the Communist Party abandoned her in the late 1930s, she wrote a desperate letter

[1] William L. Patterson, "The Lessons of Scottsboro," *Freedomways* 266, 273.
[2] Nashville *Tennessean*, May 9, 1976; Birmingham *News*, May 7, 1976.

to her mother in Huntsville asking for help. Emma Bates told her daughter to return to Huntsville. As one relative later explained apologetically, "It's hard to turn your back on your children regardless of what they've done."[3]

In the next two years, Ruby supported herself with odd jobs, but Huntsville, Alabama, was no place for a former star witness for the Communist Party. In 1940 she left Alabama and traveled twenty-five hundred miles to the rich Yakima Valley of Washington state where she worked for two years as a migrant farm worker. There, she met and married Elmer Schut, a Union Gap, Washington, carpenter in 1942. To her friends, she was known as Lucille. None knew she had been involved in the Scottsboro case. When she returned to Alabama in the early 1960s, where her husband entered a Veterans' Administration hospital, relations with at least some members of her family were still strained. In 1974 Ruby's sister wrote to a cousin assuring her: "You won't be bothered with hearing from Ruby anymore. She's dead."[4]

But Ruby, like Victoria, was very much alive. And, unlike Mark Twain, neither was amused by the report of her demise. Through attorneys, both announced plans for libel and invasion of privacy suits against NBC.

Even before Ruby Bates and Victoria Price resurfaced, I learned from an Alabama newspaperman that Clarence Norris had quietly approached the Alabama Board of Pardons and Paroles seeking a pardon. Norris, apparently the last of the Scottsboro defendants still alive, had jumped parole in 1946 and was technically a fugitive. Encouraged by the response to the television production and supported by the NAACP, Norris had asked Alabama officials for a full and unconditional pardon.

From all over the eastern United States, I heard from other individuals who had been directly or indirectly involved in the case. Hollace Ransdell, an ACLU investigator in the case in 1931, had made one of the earliest (and best) investigations of the original Scottsboro incident. At her home in rural Pennsylvania she dis-

3 Birmingham *News*, May 8, 1976.
4 *Ibid.*; Interview with William Bradford Huie, Hartselle, Alabama, July 26, 1978.

cussed her fact-finding trip to Scottsboro and Huntsville in 1931. She recalled with even greater clarity the horrors of starvation and poverty she had encountered as a young social worker in the rural South of the 1930s. Elias Schwartzbart, a successful New York attorney, described with wry humor his forays into darkest Jackson and Morgan counties as a young lawyer on the Scottsboro defense team. It was Schwartzbart who had examined the Huntsville city records and discovered evidence of the conviction of Victoria Price and L. J. Tiller. And it was Schwartzbart who had taken a photographer and boldly visited the barn of Luther Morris to prove that it was physically impossible for the Jackson County farmer to have witnessed the rape as he testified in Scottsboro.

The son of Jackson County sheriff M. L. Wann had been a teenager at the time of the original arrest. He still remembered the angry men who drove up to the Scottsboro jail on the night of March 25 and shouted threats at the Scottsboro defendants. He described with pride the quiet determination of his father to protect the prisoners under his responsibility. And Leroy and Andrew Wright's sister, in a voice trembling with anger, relived the persecution her mother had suffered in Chattanooga as a "communist" while her two brothers remained in Alabama prisons for a crime she was convinced they never committed. Collectively, their observations and recollections did not alter my understanding of the Scottsboro case. It was one thing, however, to read Clarence Norris' letters from Kilby prison and quite another to sit in my comfortable, book-lined office and hear him describe firsthand the years he spent in Alabama prisons.

It is hardly a revelation to note that more people watch television than read books, particularly a footnote-laden "scholarly" work like *Scottsboro*. Nevertheless, the response to "Judge Horton and the Scottsboro Boys" was a sobering reminder of the pervasive influence which television has in our society. Four and a half decades after the case had begun—twenty-six years after Andrew Wright was released from Alabama's Kilby prison—the Scottsboro case returned to southern politics and to a southern courtroom. Clarence Norris' fight for an unconditional pardon and the lawsuits of Victoria Price and Ruby Bates made it possible for me to take part in the recapitulation of events I had described nearly ten years ago. Like the man being ridden out of town on a rail, I had times when I would just as soon have walked were it not for the honor. But it was a challenge no scholar could reject. It is one thing to have one's sources casually reviewed by an editor or book reviewer. How many historians can boast that they have had their footnotes scrutinized by lawyers on the scent of multi-million-dollar lawsuits?

The following is an account of what may be the final chapter in the Scottsboro case. It is told in the form of a diary and often from a first-person point of view. I emphasize the word *form*, because, even though I kept a loose-leaf diary as the case evolved, I supplemented these recollections with other historical sources and interviews.

Monday, January 13, 1975

I received a telephone call from a New York film producer, Thomas Moore, asking about television film rights for *Scottsboro*. An independent television producer, he had made his initial reputation in the mid-1960s by adapting the comic-book character Batman into a campy hit series. Successful television feature films in the late 1960s and early 1970s revealed another side of Moore: a knack for combining prime-time entertainment and current social issues. In "When the Owl Calls My Name" (1969), a young Episcopal priest (played by Tom Courtnay) came to terms with his terminal illness through the strength of the Canadian Indians he was sent to serve. Two years later Moore, a native Mississippian, celebrated the civil rights movement through the fictional character of a 104-year-old former slave ("The Autobiography of Miss Jane Pittman"). Another Moore film, "Queen of the Stardust Ballroom," captured a nation's growing concern with the social isolation and loneliness of older Americans.

As a teenager growing up in Mississippi, Moore had sold newspapers headlining the Scottsboro case. He admired Judge Horton, and he saw in the case the traditional drama of individual conscience against the tyranny of the mob. I later came to believe that Moore's decision to develop a film celebrating Horton's heroism continued to reflect his unusually sensitive ear for the public mood. In 1971 the story of Jane Pittman garnered the praise of a nation finally at ease with the historical heroism of the civil rights movement. By the mid-1970s a New South seemed to have emerged in the wake of the civil rights movement of the 1960s. Horton's story was an appealing concrete historical link between this new South and the "decent" historical traditions of an older one.

Tuesday, April 15, 1975

I received the first of two telephone conversations from Hollywood script writer John McGreevey. Like Moore, McGreevey said that he was as anxious as possible that the show be "historically accurate." He felt comfortable with the factual material on the trial that was included in my book, but he noted there was little personal material on Horton himself. I managed to find a few items, and I wrote one of Horton's sons for additional information. It was clear, however, that the family had no wish to become involved in a television show completely beyond their control. In the absence of such information, McGreevey improvised fictional scenes describing Horton outside the courtroom. In recapitulating the "historical" aspects of the case, however, McGreevy was much more cautious. Even when he summarized complex courtroom testimony, he tried to use actual courtroom dialogue whenever possible.

Later, I would learn of two exceptions. In the original trial before Judge Horton, Leibowitz had challenged the honesty of Mrs. Price's testimony and concluded by asking if she had "ever heard of any single white women ever being locked up in jail when she is the complaining witness against negroes in the history of the State of Alabama?" Since McGreevey did not have time to recount Leibowitz' questions challenging Mrs. Street's honesty, he inserted the words "for perjury" after the phrase "locked up in jail."[5]

[5] John McGreevey, "Judge Horton and the Scottsboro Boys" (Mimeographed script, November 14, 1975), 66 (copy in possession of author). For the pertinent section of the original testimony, see "Alabama vs. Patterson, April 3–9, 1933, Transcript of Testimony," 160–61.

The second exception was even more substantial. In the third act, in an attempt to represent the tension between Leibowitz and the International Labor Defense, McGreevey created a scene in which ILD attorney Joseph Brodsky urged Leibowitz to treat Victoria gingerly as the "flower of Southern womanhood." The "one thing the defense did establish at Scottsboro," McGreevey had Brodsky say, "was the fact that Victoria was a whore . . . and the jury hated 'em for it." The defense *had* introduced such evidence at Scottsboro in 1931, but Brodsky's statement to Leibowitz was not a matter of historical record.[6]

McGreevey later testified he had no preconceptions concerning the case when he began writing the script. Nevertheless, the decision to concentrate upon the heroic role of Judge Horton inevitably cast Victoria (and, to a lesser extent, Ruby) in an unfavorable light. As Horton made clear on a number of occasions, he regarded Victoria Price as a wanton perjurer who had "knowingly testified falsely in many material aspects of the case." Thus, the production was unbalanced because the evidence was never balanced in the first place. And John McGreevey's script was fair precisely because it accurately summarized evidence which (in Judge Horton's phrase) "greatly preponderates in favor of the defense."[7]

Friday, December 12, 1975

My wife, Jane, our two children, and I visited Monticello, Georgia, where Moore and his production crew were filming "Judge Horton and the Scottsboro Boys." With forty-year-old Fords and Chevys puttering down the streets and extras wandering about in their thread-bare "depression" outfits, the town square and courthouse bore a remarkable resemblance to Decatur, Alabama, in the 1930s. At Moore's insistence, Jane appeared as an extra for one of Arthur Hill's opening scenes. While her film career was brief, consisting of only two seven-second walks across the camera at a distance, she learned the ropes quickly. In the first scene, a camerawise extra

---

6 McGreevey, "Judge Horton and the Scottsboro Boys," 47.

7 "State of Alabama vs. Haywood Patterson; Opinion of Judge James Edwin Horton, Jr., June 22, 1933" (copy in possession of author), 14, 16.

strategically placed herself on the camera side. When the second scene was taken, Jane deftly stepped to the outside.

Afterwards, having heard many of the New York and California cast members' enthusiastic descriptions of the delicious "down home" southern cooking of the local restaurant, we joined them for lunch. With the first taste I had my only misgivings about the authenticity of the film.

Thursday, April 22, 1976

With friends, my wife and I watched the telecast of "Judge Horton and the Scottsboro Boys." There was one unsettling scene in which Horton ordered a reluctant national guard commander to defend the prisoners. (In reality, Captain Joseph Burleson had enthusiastically taken on the responsibility, and he had no misgivings at all about his position.) Nevertheless, I was impressed with the show's accuracy.

Wednesday, May 5, 1976

I received a telephone call from an Alabama newspaper reporter. He had learned, he said, that Birmingham attorney Arthur Hanes planned to file a multimillion-dollar suit on behalf of Ruby Bates against NBC for libel, slander, and invasion of privacy. In addition, he continued, there were rumors that a woman in southeast Tennessee claimed to be Victoria Price, and she was also planning to file a suit. I acknowledged that it was quite possible both were still alive. Defensively I suggested that the lure of a multimillion-dollar judgment made them considerably more accessible than when I tried to learn their whereabouts in the late 1960s.

Monday, July 5, 1976

For the first time, I met with James Simpson and Gusty Yearout, members of the Birmingham law firm representing NBC in the Bates case. Although I acknowledged my lack of legal training, I was perplexed by the Bates/Schut suit. In view of Mrs. Schut's enthusiastic involvement as a voluntary "public figure" in Communist Party causes and activities in the 1930s, it was difficult to

maintain that her privacy had been invaded by reporting information that was a matter of public record. Nor did it seem reasonable
that a jury would sustain a judgment for defamation since the most
offensive portions of the television show (in the view of Mrs.
Bates's attorneys) were based upon her own testimony. The National
Broadcasting Company was thus placed in the anomalous position
of being sued by Ruby Bates/Schut for correctly recounting her
self-incriminating statements.

The key to Hanes's lawsuit seemed to be his belief that the television show was not a documentary and thus was not protected by
the First Amendment to the Constitution. In his view it was a fic-
tionalization loosely based upon the facts, but including numerous
embellishments. Under these circumstances, therefore, NBC had
invaded Mrs. Schut's privacy and was thus subject to suit for
damages. Alabama novelist William Bradford Huie, a long-time
friend of Mrs. Schut, had arranged for Hanes to serve as counsel in
the case, and he was adamant in his insistence that the use of Mrs.
Schut's name required her permission. ("I ought to know," he said
wryly, "I've spent enough money for permission rights and for
lawyers' fees.")[8]

In *Time Inc.* v. *Hill* (1967), however, the Supreme Court had
concluded that dramatized versions of historical events were to be
given the same protection as so-called nonfictional works so long
as the material was not "substantially fictionalized," "exploited for

[8] "Ruby L. Bates Schut v. National Broadcasting Company, Complaint and Prayer
for Injunction," filed in Clerk's Office, Northern District of Alabama, May 7, 1976
(copy in possession of author); Interview with Huie, July 26, 1978. According to
Huie, who had known Mrs. Schut early in the 1960s when she briefly returned to
Alabama, the former star witness in the Scottsboro case was once again prepared
to reverse her story. This time she was to return to her original claim she had been
raped in 1931. Huie has never had any doubts that the two women were assaulted.
"Nine black boys on a train with two white girls? It was the most logical thing in the
world." I don't find it so logical. In any case, I find it difficult to imagine how any
credence could be placed in any of Ruby Bates Schut's accounts of what happened in
1931. In the wake of the television show, one of her relatives who visited her at the
Scottsboro jail recalled: "She told us she had not been raped but that the oldest Negro
did rape Victoria Price and that the others had nothing to do with it." This would
bring to four the number of completely different versions she related. Birmingham
News, May 8, 1976.

the defendants' commercial benefit," and subjected to "material and substantial falsification." Even under these circumstances the court concluded that the plaintiff (in this case, Mrs. Schut) had to show "knowing or reckless falsity." In other words, First Amendment rights seemed to extend even to the so-called "docudramas" like "Judge Horton and the Scottsboro Boys."[9]

Monday, October 25, 1976

Clarence "Willie" Norris, the last survivor of the original nine Scottsboro defendants, was sitting in a Harlem bar when an excited friend burst in with the news that Governor George Wallace had signed a "full and unconditional" pardon restoring his civil rights. Under Alabama law this was tantamount to an acknowledgment that Norris had never committed the crime for which he was convicted.

It was the end of a nightmare that had lasted nearly half a century. First, there had been the arrest, the trials, and Norris' final conviction in 1937. After that came years of uncertainty in Alabama's Kilby prison. Even when he fled north to Cleveland to live with his mother in 1946, he was always conscious of his status as a fugitive. In 1953, seven years after Norris' parole violation, police detectives appeared at his mother's apartment house. Mrs. Norris managed to persuade the police that Clarence was her older son, but the near arrest forced him to leave Cleveland.[10]

From there he went to New York City where he severed all ties with his mother and family. "I figured if I tried to stay in touch with my people they'd run down on 'em," he later recalled. There was no way to contact him later when his mother died. Still, despite occasional problems with drinking ("I have taken on many a

9 *Time Inc.* v. *Hill* (1967), 385 U.S. 374. As Judge Neese pointed out in his decision in Mrs. Street's suit, the Supreme Court has ruled in *Zacchini* v. *Scripps-Howard Broadcasting Company* (1977) that "television entertainment, as well as news reports, is under the blanket of First Amendment protection." "Memorandum Opinion of District Judge C. G. Neese in the United States District Court for the Eastern District of Tennessee in the case of Victoria Price Street v. National Broadcasting Company," filed August 11, 1977, p. 8 (copy in possession of author).

10 Huntsville *Times*, October 17, 18, 1976; New York *Post*, October 26, 1976.

hooker [drink] trying to forget my troubles," Norris later acknowledged), the former Scottsboro defendant married and had two
daughters, established a conventional life, first as a factory worker
in the New York area and finally as a New York City maintenance
worker.[11]

The pardon was a personal triumph for Norris, but it was also a reflection of just how much the South in general, and Alabama in
particular, had changed since the 1930s. NAACP attorneys representing Norris first approached state officials as early as 1969 concerning a pardon for Norris. With Wallace campaigning for the
presidency on a get-tough, anti–civil rights platform, it was not a
propitious time. By the mid-1970s, Alabama politics had under-
gone a political metamorphosis, and few state officials more clearly
reflected this change than the Alabama attorney general, William
(Bill) Baxley.

When NAACP attorney Jimmy Myerson wrote Baxley in 1976,
the Alabama attorney general ordered a review of the Scottsboro
case by members of his staff. On August 5 he dictated a lengthy
letter (supporting the Norris pardon request) to Norman Ussery,
head of the Pardon and Parole Board of the state. When Ussery
insisted that Norris would have to surrender to state authorities
before his pardon could be considered, Baxley again intervened
and reviewed in great detail the evidence presented during the
trials of the 1930s. Victoria Price's testimony was not only uncorroborated, but also contained internal conflicts, argued Baxley,
who flatly concluded: "It is impossible that she was raped as she
alleged." He urged the board to "swiftly grant to Clarence Norris

---

[11] *Ibid.* Although Norris initially insisted that he had no hostility toward Victoria
Price or Ruby Bates ("I have no malice toward anyone"), his anger was apparent in
comments made after he received his pardon. As he told a Washington *Star* reporter,
Alabama owed him "15 years of my life—my best life. Yeah, they owe it to me."
As he said later about Mrs. Street, "I have no sympathy for that woman. None.
She's lying and she knows she's lying." While he had tried to avoid bitterness, "If
I was sitting across from that woman, I don't know what might happen. I just might
go crazy. I know she's lying. And she knows it too." Washington *Star*, January 7,
1977; Atlanta *Journal and Constitution*, July 10, 1977. For Norris' own story see
Clarence Norris with Sybil Washington, *The Last of the Scottsboro Boys: An Auto-
biography* (New York: G. P. Putnam's Sons, 1979).

a full and complete pardon," which would remove from him the "unjust stigma of conviction for a crime that the overwhelming evidence clearly shows he did not commit."[12]

Such an action was quite in keeping with Baxley's tenure as attorney general. He had been elected in 1970 by campaigning as a "people's attorney" attacking strip-miners, polluters, and state agencies such as the Alabama Dairy Commission. Once in office, he had investigated and prosecuted white Alabamians for racial violence against blacks. It was Baxley who ultimately convicted one of the bombers who left four little girls dead in a black Birmingham church in 1963. Alabamians, black and white, often argued over whether Baxley was "sincere" or whether he was simply politically motivated by a desire to gain support from black voters. Their uncertainty obscured the central effect of the changed racial arithmetic of Alabama politics. When Clarence Norris and the Scottsboro "boys" were convicted of raping Victoria Price and Ruby Bates there were fewer than 1,000 registered black voters in the state. Political leaders, acting from patrician or populist traditions, sometimes tried to soften the harsh contours of the state's caste system, but they always risked the devastating political label of "nigger-lovers." The very fact that it might be politically advantageous for Baxley vigorously to defend black political rights was itself a reflection of the quiet revolution that had taken place. Even Governor George Wallace had made his peace with the changing times. It was Wallace who had signed the pardon and, according to insiders, pressured Norman Ussery to expedite the case. While such changes hardly signaled the racial millennium in the state that was the cradle of the Confederacy, the politics of Attorney General Bill Baxley's Alabama was a far cry from that of the late Thomas Knight.

Wednesday, October 27, 1976

Off the record Ruby Bates's attorney had admitted to a Birmingham reporter that the lawsuit was a long shot, but it was even more

---

[12] William J. Baxley to Board of Pardons and Paroles, August 5, 1976; Baxley to Board of Pardons and Paroles, October 25, 1976 (copies in possession of author).

hopeless than he had imagined. In the weeks after she had filed the suit, Ruby Lucille Bates Schut became increasingly ill. On this day she died in a Yakima, Washington, hospital. She was buried in a local cemetery beside her husband who had died one week earlier.[13]

Wednesday, July 6, 1977

Shortly before 9 A.M., Judge Charles Neese of the United States District Court for the Eastern District of Tennessee convened the case of *Victoria Price Street* v. *The National Broadcasting Company*. The new federal courthouse in Winchester with its depressingly antiseptic bus terminal architectural style was a world away from the brass spittoons, ceiling fans, and oiled wood floors of Decatur's courthouse. The bland impersonality of the setting mirrored the general indifference of most local residents. Even though a dozen newspaper reporters were on hand for the trial and local television crews appeared briefly for their thirty seconds of nightly news film, the passions that surrounded the original trials had disappeared. Most of the jurors questioned during the selection process had spent their lives in Tennessee just across the state line from Scottsboro. Only a handful had ever heard of the case. Fayetteville attorney Arthur Simms assisted NBC attorneys in evaluating the jurors' backgrounds.[14]

Technically, the issues as well as the setting had shifted. The essential question of the original trials—however complicated many of the side effects—was always: were Victoria Price and Ruby Bates raped by nine black teenagers aboard an Alabama freight train on March 25, 1931? The July, 1977, trial of *Victoria Price Street* v. *The National Broadcasting Company* involved complex issues of libel, defamation, and invasion of privacy, all to be decided against the shifting constitutional background of the First Amendment to the Constitution. As attorneys for both sides argued in their opening statements, "We are not trying whether Victoria Price was raped in 1931. We are deciding whether she was libeled and de-

13 Atlanta *Constitution,* October 28, 1978.
14 Birmingham *News,* July 6, 1977.

famed in 1976." Despite the best efforts of the attorneys on both sides, however, the case soon returned to that central question. For the jury's perception of Mrs. Street's case was inevitably to be affected by whether they perceived her as a wronged woman, physically assaulted in the 1930s and then slandered in the 1970s, or as a perjurer who had been willing to send nine black teenagers to the electric chair for a crime they had never committed.

After jury selection and brief opening statements by the attorneys in the case, much of the first day was devoted to an oft-interrupted rerun of the television movie. In the darkened courtroom, the four men and two women who made up the civil jury listened intently as Mrs. Street's attorneys repeatedly stopped the video cassette player and complained of inaccuracies in the dramatization. At each break, Mrs. Street's attorneys read from the record of the original trial, often acting out the questions and answers in excited high-pitched voices. Even the juror who had confessed during preselection examination that he slept through most of the original television showing managed to remain awake.[15]

Of Mrs. Street's two lawyers, Raymond Fraley seemed far more emotionally involved in the case. Fraley, the Fayetteville, Tennessee, attorney who had first agreed to represent Mrs. Street, clearly was pleased to have a case of this significance. At one point he even suggested that he would "take bids" from reporters for interviews with Mrs. Street.[16] Eventually, however, he apparently realized that such interviews would not comport with his insistence that Mrs. Street was a private individual who had never sought public attention. Outside the courtroom, the dapper Fraley was the archetypical "good old boy" with a ready smile and a somewhat forced devil-may-care attitude. Once the trial began, his personality seemed to undergo a transformation. Intense and truculent in his cross-examination, he would draw repeated reprimands from Judge Neese.

---

[15] Nashville *Tennessean*, July 7, 1977. "Victoria Price Street v. National Broadcasting Company, July 6–12, 1977; Transcript of Testimony," 212–75 (hereinafter cited as "Street v. NBC, Transcript of Testimony").

[16] Birmingham *News*, May 7, 1976.

His most astute move in the case was to persuade another Fayetteville attorney to join in the litigation. Don Wyatt, a genial man who divided his time between his practice and a successful antique dealership, affected the air of a simple country lawyer. It was an affectation, for his briefs and arguments—particularly on the constitutional issues involved—showed why Fraley had brought him into the case. His courtroom style was quite different from Fraley's. In direct and particularly in cross-examination he probed for weaknesses and contradictions, but he was unfailingly courteous to witnesses for both sides.

For jurors, reporters, and spectators, the first day amounted to an introduction of the issues as well as the participants in the case. The original and amended complaint of Mrs. Street made more than twenty allegations of inaccuracies in the film. Many of these were minor and inconsequential and were apparently designed to discredit the overall accuracy of the film.[17] Once these objections were stripped away, Mrs. Street's lawsuit was reduced to variations on three themes.

First, her attorneys argued, the telecast of "Judge Horton and the Scottsboro Boys," with its recapitulation of these "repulsive, sordid and distasteful events," had caused her to suffer "grave and lasting damage by having her privacy invaded and her peace of mind disturbed. . . ." Secondly, the telecast did "falsely and without foundation make plaintiff out to be guilty of committing perjury. . . ." By dramatizing scenes from a Chattanooga hobo jungle (scenes based upon the testimony of Ruby Bates, Lester Carter, and Dallas Ramsey), the production contradicted her sworn testimony she had spent the night of March 24 with "Callie Brochie." In this connection, Mrs. Street's attorneys complained that the medical testimony of Dr. Bridges as depicted in the film was an "inac-

---

[17] The case against NBC was outlined by Mrs. Street's attorneys in an original and amended complaint. The quotations that follow are from the two documents. See "Complaint of Victoria Price Street v. National Broadcasting Company in the United States District Court for the Eastern District of Tennessee, Winchester Division, filed August 13, 1976" (hereinafter cited as "Complaint of Street v. NBC") and "Motion and Order to Amend Complaint of Victoria Price Street v. National Broadcasting Company, April 6, 1977" (hereinafter cited as "Amended Complaint of Street v. NBC"), (both copies in possession of author).

curate and a false or falacious [sic] interpretation of what he said at the trial." Dr. Bridges had not contradicted Mrs. Street, insisted Fraley and Wyatt, and the implication was that he had thus branded her as a liar. Finally, he objected—most strenuously—to John McGreevey's insertion of the phrase "for perjury" in one of Leibowitz' questions to Victoria Price. This led the viewers to believe that Leibowitz had charged her with being a "perjurer or liar under oath," complained the attorneys, "when this was not said on [at] the trial."

But Mrs. Street was most incensed over the persistent implication that she was "unchaste and perpetually promiscuous. . . ." Or, as her attorneys colorfully put it at one point, "She [Victoria Price] was . . . portrayed . . . as a slattern, mean street woman with sharp, filthy and vituperative tongue—a true Jezebel." They specifically complained of three scenes. In the first, the film had recreated a courtroom scene before Judge Horton in which Leibowitz unsuccessfully sought to introduce court records showing that Victoria Price had been convicted of adultery with L. J. (Jack) Tiller. This was libelous said Mrs. Street's attorneys. In fact, "she knew an L. J. Tillery, not the same as Jack Tiller and she was convicted of nothing. There was another Victoria Price in Huntsville at the same time."

In the second scene, Victoria Price was depicted in a boxcar, seminude with her boyfriend Jack Tiller, Lester Carter, and Ruby Bates. Mrs. Street's attorneys originally overstated their case by arguing that this episode showed the four "in the act of making love and intercourse, with the girls being naked." Had this allegation been literally true, "Judge Horton and the Scottsboro Boys" would undoubtedly have drawn more than 40 million viewers—at least on the second showing. Nevertheless, their description was not totally inaccurate. As the camera faded away, it required little imagination to surmise ensuing events in the box car.

Finally, Mrs. Street's attorneys were most indignant over the dialogue McGreevey had written in which Brodsky warned Leibowitz not to repeat the tactics of the original attorneys at Scottsboro who had "proved" Victoria Price was a "whore."

Thursday, July 7, 1977

Local television and newspaper coverage had aroused the interest of local residents by the second day of the trial. When Judge Neese took his seat in the early morning, the courtroom was almost filled with an audience curious to hear the star witness of the original trials, Victoria Price Street. She was not the same woman who had testified at Scottsboro and Decatur in the 1930s. Heavy set and pale, she had hobbled into the courtroom on Wednesday, her wispy hair tied back with ribbon. Throughout the first day, her head trembled as she sat next to her lawyers in a blue and white dress, occasionally objecting to scenes on the television monitor with a mumbled "Aw, that's a lie." At other times, she wept with bowed head and wiped her face with a crumpled paper towel. She was, as her attorneys described her, an aging "hardworking country woman" in poor health and emotionally distraught.[18]

And that was the emphasis of Fraley's questioning on direct examination. He constantly emphasized her poverty and the fact that she was a "poor, simple country woman," subjected to a "horrifying experience" by a New York television network. Fraley's direct examination was not without problems. At one point Judge Neese reprimanded Fraley for his "gratuitous comments," but her testimony generally supported the complaints raised by her attorney during the preceding day. She seemed particularly incensed over the dramatization of her alleged overnight stay in a hobo jungle. ("I don't even know what a hobo jungle is.")[19]

Cross-examination presented a number of problems for NBC attorney Robert Campbell. While Campbell and his partner, Jack Wheeler, were both native Tennesseans and graduates of the state's law school, they were partners in one of Knoxville's most prestigious law firms, Hodges, Doughty and Carson. In their fashionable three-piece pinstripe suits Campbell and Wheeler made no attempt to conceal the fact that they were highly capable and successful attorneys whose specialty was defending large corporate clients.

18 Birmingham *News*, July 6, 1977; Nashville *Tennessean*, July 7, July 8, 1977.
19 "Street v. NBC, Transcript of Testimony," 297–98.

Here was precisely the image that Fraley and Wyatt wanted to present to the jury: two simple small-town lawyers fighting for the rights of their impoverished client against the representatives of a well-heeled New York corporation. "Six million dollars for a poor country woman. The money to come from a big rich corporation," commented one observer who attended the trials. It was a "natural."[20]

Campbell's questioning minimized his inherent disadvantages as he probed every aspect of Mrs. Street's complaint and skillfully exploited old and new contradictions in her testimony. At the same time he was always gentle and restrained, commenting sympathetically at several points that he knew it had been a long time since the events she described.

Shortly before the trial had begun, Birmingham *News* reporter Andy Kilpatrick had interviewed a juror from the original trials who recalled that Victoria Price had told her story "like a pig a-trotting."[21] If there was anyone in the Winchester courtroom who might have questioned whether this was the same Victoria Price of the 1930s, the first twenty minutes of cross-examination dispelled such doubts. Three decades after she had last testified there was the same fire and anger, the same rough-hewn eloquence of a "wronged woman." "I ain't done nothing but told the truth and nothing but the truth," she exclaimed at one point. "I told it in every trial . . . ; there has been over a thousand pages and everyone of my pages is alike and if I had to do it all over . . . it would be the same thing again. Truth will stand where a lie will fall."[22]

Her insistence that she had always told the truth did not, however, square with her testimony at Winchester. Mrs. Street and her attorneys, for example, had objected to a scene in which the pair of underpants allegedly worn by Mrs. Street during the rape were shown in the television show "intact, when actually the step-ins

---

[20] Will Campbell, "Where to Sit in Scottsboro," *Christianity and Crisis*, XXXVII (August 15, 1977), 190.

[21] Birmingham *News*, July 3, 1977. A second juror interviewed by Kilpatrick said he was not impressed when Ruby Bates told her story before Judge Horton "because she was all dressed up."

[22] "Street v. NBC, Transcript of Testimony," 364.

were torn." When Campbell questioned her about these under-garments, however, Mrs. Street admitted that the step-ins introduced in the 1933 trial were the ones she had worn to the trial on the first day in Decatur. At the request of Attorney General Thomas Knight, Jr., she had removed them in an anteroom and given them to a courthouse matron. Her "main step-ins" had been shown at the Scottsboro trial, she said, [in fact, they were not] but "they wasn't fitten to be shown, tore all to pieces and had lots of blood on them and all that." So she had thrown them in a trash can, she insisted. And that was why she had given Knight the pair she wore to Decatur.

Quite apart from the fact that this made the complaint against the defendants ludicrous, it amounted to a self-indictment for per-jury. For at Winchester, Campbell read into the record testimony that Mrs. Street had given before Judge Horton insisting that the undergarments introduced in the trial were the same ones she wore on the day of the alleged assault.[23]

Equally instructive was the dispute over the scene in the film that introduced the question of her 1931 conviction for adultery with Jack Tiller. During the 1933 trial before Judge Horton, Lei-bowitz had tried to introduce evidence of this and several other convictions. At the time she protested that it was "another" Victoria Price and that L. J. Tiller (sometimes spelled Tillery) was not the same man as her boyfriend, Jack Tiller.

In her 1976 complaint and her testimony in Winchester, she continued to insist that there was "another" Victoria Price, but she changed her story to argue that she had never known Jack Tiller except for the week he served as her "bodyguard." As her attorneys argued in the complaint, "the movie showed that she was convicted with Jack Tiller and knew him when, in fact, she knew an L. J. Tillery, not the same as Jack Tiller." As Campbell questioned her, she created a new story of her relationship with L. J. Tillery, a kindly neighbor who spent his Sundays taking children to church.

---

[23] *Ibid.*, 332ff. Campbell learned of the "undergarment switch" in the deposition he took from Mrs. Street in February of 1977.

"I never knowed Jack Tiller except one week when he was guarding me. I don't know nothing about Jack Tiller."[24]

The problem with this new account was twofold. First, it hardly seemed desirable to emphasize her relationship with L. J. Tiller (or Tillery) since no one denied that he had been convicted of adultery with a "Victoria Price of Huntsville." Moreover, her insistence that she scarcely knew "Jack Tiller" was directly contradicted by her sworn testimony in several of the trials during the 1930s. To anyone familiar with the players in the complex Tiller-Price episode, Mrs. Street's testimony was—to put it in the most charitable light—preposterous. At one point, Mrs. Street insisted "There is three or four Victorias down there [in Huntsville]." The only solace her attorneys could draw from the bewildering exchange was the knowledge that—if *they* were unable to unravel her story well enough to create a consistent response—the jury was unlikely to follow the confusing testimony.

At times Mrs. Street also seemed unable to remember events in her past. Initially she could not recall the names of her first two husbands. (She married Henry Pressley in 1927 and Enos McClendon in 1928.) When Campbell asked her about Pressley she finally recollected the marriage, but she insisted she wasn't with him "but two hours and a half" and she had "never slept with him." She was even hazier in response to questions about her second marriage to Enos McClendon. ("He's the one I couldn't think of.") It may simply have been an embarrassed reluctance to talk about what had been her stormy and unfortunate marital history. Her second hus-

---

[24] Campbell made an interesting observation about Mrs. Street's testimony on this point. When Leibowitz introduced the evidence of her conviction with Jack Tiller without warning, Mrs. Price did not act surprised. Instead, she quickly retorted, "Look [on the conviction sheet] and see if it is not L. J. Tiller [instead of Jack Tiller]." "Amended Complaint of Street v. NBC"; "Street v. NBC, Transcript of Testimony," 336–45. According to the Huntsville city directory for this period, there was only one Tiller (Jack) and one Victoria Price. Interstate's Huntsville, Alabama, *City Directory, 1931* (New Orleans: Interstate Directory Co., 1931), 233, 283. Moreover I knew from a conversation with Elias Schwartzbart (one of the defense attorneys in the 1930s) that the arrest and conviction report had not been found by randomly searching through Huntsville's police court records. Lester Carter had told him the approximate date of Victoria Price's conviction.

band, for example, had "stayed drunk" during much of their eleven-month marriage, which was terminated in 1930 when Mrs. Street shot Mr. McClendon.[25]

But she had no apologies about her forgetfulness. When the soft-spoken Campbell asked her how many times she had testified, she lashed out: "How in the name of God do you think I can keep up with such as that, as many times as I have testified. How in the world do you think I can keep up with that. You must be going loco."

The usually impassive Campbell suppressed a smile and replied solemnly, "I might plead guilty to that."

Campbell's cross-examination probed every aspect of the complaint. Whenever possible he sought to show that many aspects of the show against which she complained were amply borne out by the testimony at various trials. With an almost photographic recollection of all the transcripts that lay on his desk carefully indexed, Campbell drew Mrs. Street into repeated contradictions of her testimony in the 1930s. At several points she flatly denied she had given the testimony that Campbell read from the official transcripts of the trials of the 1930s.[26]

In one particularly revealing segment, Campbell questioned her about the injuries she claimed to have received in the 1930s incident. The exchange is worth quoting in its entirety.

Q. At that time, when you first came to in the grocery store [at Paint Rock], what was your physical condition?

A. Well, they had me druggy and I couldn't tell you. They had put so many shots in me, I don't know, I was crazy nearly.

Q. Were you bleeding?

A. Yes, I was bleeding.

Q. Were you bleeding from being struck on the head?

A. Well, I had been struck on the head and I was bleeding from other parts. I have scars right now where the colored boys

---

[25] "Street v. NBC, Transcript of Testimony," 375–77; "Deposition of Victoria Price Street in the case of Street v. NBC, given February 22, 1977, Fayetteville, Tennessee" (copy in possession of author).

[26] "Street v. NBC, Transcript of Testimony," 372.

put [them] there. There is one right here that the colored boys put on me (indicating) [her chest].

Q. You are indicating you have got a scar on your chest?

A. There it is.

Q. For the record, you are showing scars on your chest, your right cheek and right temple?

A. And on my back. I have scars all over me that they put there.

Q. You have got scars on your back?

A. Got a few.

Q. Is that when they—

A. That is when they throwed me down.

Q. Threw you down?

A. Yes.

Q. Did you have a black eye?

A. Yes, sir. How do you think that great big gash would be there if I hadn't had a black eye?

Q. Were you bleeding from your private parts?

A. Yes sir.[27]

Such testimony, of course, was completely inconsistent with the findings of the examination she had been given by two physicians less than two hours after the alleged rape. It was so contradictory that it undoubtedly raised serious questions about Mrs. Street's credibility. And yet, the unmistakable impression of most court-room observers was her absolute conviction that she had received these massive injuries. Will Campbell's explanation was the most charitable. "I had not the slightest doubt," he said later, that she was "totally convinced that she *had* told the truth." And she had probably been so convinced from the "very day she whispered to her companion as the posse approached that they should say they had been raped."

However inconsistent, contradictory, and improbable her testi-mony, her vehement assertions of wronged innocence and her for-

---

[27] *Ibid.*, 337, 339, 340. Newspaper reporters described her testimony as "confusing" and "belligerent." Nashville *Tennessean*, July 8, 1977; Chattanooga *News-Free Press*, July 8, 1977.

lorn and pathetic appearance were consistent with the tone Fraley
had set in cross-examination. She was, as Fraley had argued, a simple
country woman. Whatever her past, whatever her contradictions in
testimony, she had been exposed to public humiliation and ridicule because of a television show broadcast by a powerful New
York television network. And there were emotional currents that
no one could measure. One local courtroom spectator, for example,
seemed unconcerned about the racial implications of the case, but—
after watching the video tape of the film—he expressed a scornful
resentment over the exaggerated southern accent of the actress who
played Victoria Price. "Those damn yankees," he said. "They think
all Southerners sound like Gomer Pyle."

Friday, July 8, 1977

When Robert Campbell began his defense for NBC late Thursday
afternoon, his strategy was to argue both the law and the facts. With
the jury absent, Campbell made a motion for a dismissal of the
case. Given the facts in the case, he argued, the First Amendment to
the Constitution protected NBC against Mrs. Street's lawsuit.

For example, he argued that Mrs. Street's attorneys had not established adequate grounds for an invasion of privacy suit under
the precedent set in the 1967 *Time Inc.* v. *Hill* decision. That complex case stemmed from a lawsuit brought by James Hill against
Life magazine (Time, Inc.). In 1952 the Hill family had been held
hostage by kidnappers although they were ultimately released un-
harmed. Three years later, a broadway play "reenacted" the incident in an inaccurate fictionalized form and the Hills moved
from their home and changed their names. When *Life* published
a story identifying the Hills and linking them to the play, James
Hill sued on the grounds that his family's privacy had been invaded.
Hill was represented by Richard Nixon in the litigation.

The Supreme Court, however, rejected Hill's claims of invasion
of privacy and, at the same time, established guidelines for such
cases in the future. As long as the plaintiff was involved in a matter
of "public interest" the media could report, even in fictionalized
form, this involvement. Individuals so described could still sue for

invasion of privacy, but they had to establish two conditions before damages could be awarded. First, the plaintiff had to show that the report included "material and substantial falsification." Second, the plaintiff had to establish that the defendant had exhibited "actual malice"; in legal terms, "with knowledge of . . . [the report's] falsity or in reckless disregard of the truth."[28] Campbell was convinced that neither condition could be established. In fact, Fraley and Wyatt had not presented any evidence as to what NBC did or did not do, except to broadcast the Tomorrow Entertainment production.

The complaint of defamation was more substantive, agreed Campbell, but even here, NBC was protected by the guaranties of the First Amendment. In the pivotal *New York Times* v. *Sullivan* case (1964), the Warren Court had attempted to reconcile the traditional common law of libel and the First Amendment right of free speech by declaring that a public official who sued for defamation had to prove with "convincing clarity" that the publication was false and published with "actual malice." Three years later, in *Curtis Publishing Co.* v. *Butts*, the high court concluded that the rules applicable to public officials should also apply to "public figure" plaintiffs. Only by offering such protections to the press could a free and open discussion of important public issues be guaranteed, concluded the court. Somewhat vaguely, Chief Justice Warren defined such public figures as individuals "who were intimately involved in the resolution of important public questions or, by reason of their fame, shape events in areas of concern to society at large."[29]

The Court further strengthened the hand of the press in 1971 in a case involving an accused Philadelphia pornography dealer. George Rosenbloom had sued a Philadelphia radio station because of a broadcast implicating him in the sale of pornographic materials. The Supreme Court sustained the station's parent corporation and concluded that "private" individuals, however indirectly involved in issues involving the public interest, also had to establish

[28] *Time Inc.* v. *Hill* (1967), 385 U.S. 374.
[29] *Curtis Publishing Co.* v. *Butts*, 388 U.S. 130.

actual malice on the part of their detractors in order to win a settlement for defamation. The idea, said the Court, that "certain 'public' figures have voluntarily exposed their entire lives to public inspection, while private individuals have kept theirs carefully shrouded from public view is, at best, a legal fiction."[30]

If this had been the Court's last word on this subject, NBC's defense would have been considerably simplified. In the mid-1970s, however, the "Nixon" Court modified its earlier judgments on First Amendment cases. In *Gertz* v. *Welch* (1974), for example, the Court drew back from its earlier implication that individuals indirectly drawn into issues of public interest had to establish malice on the part of the media if they were to win a libel suit. On the other hand, the Court did strengthen the position of the press in several ways. It refined its definition of public figures to include any individual whether or not he (or she) "voluntarily injects himself or is drawn into a particular public controversy and thereby becomes a public figure for a limited range of issues."[31] As a central participant in one of the most important criminal cases of the twentieth century, argued Campbell, Victoria Price had become a public figure, at least insofar as the circumstances surrounding the Scottsboro case were concerned.

The Supreme Court also barred vague compensatory or punitive damages unless the plaintiff—whether a "public" or a "private" figure—could establish legal malice. Mrs. Street's attorneys had attempted to establish damages by having relatives testify to her poor health. But they introduced no medical evidence, and Campbell was able to establish in his questioning that Mrs. Street had a long history of poor health.

Finally the Court ruled that there could be no financial liability on the part of the media unless the plaintiff in a defamation case established "fault" on the part of the defendant.[32] While Judge

---

30 *Rosenbloom* v. *Metromedia, Inc.*, 403 U.S. 29.

31 *Gertz* v. *Robert Welch, Inc.*, 418 U.S. 323.

32 *Ibid.* Wyatt was much more inclined to emphasize one of the more recent cases on the issue, *Time, Inc.* v. *Mary Alice Firestone* (1976). In the Firestone case, a fragmented court further restricted the scope of the "public figure" concept. It did, however, reaffirm the mandate in the Gertz case that required a showing of fault, limited

Neese appeared to be receptive to Campbell's arguments, he declined to dismiss the case before NBC had presented its case.

The spectators and reporters who attended the trials were not interested in such arcane constitutional issues, and, when scriptwriter John McGreevey took the stand for NBC later in the morning, the factual issues of the Scottsboro case returned to center stage.

McGreevey, the fifty-four-year-old author of the screenplay that
had led to Mrs. Street's lawsuit, had established a reputation as one
of Hollywood's more successful and prolific writers by the time
Thomas Moore approached him in the spring of 1975. A native of
Muncie, Indiana, he graduated from Indiana State University in
the late 1940s and worked for several years as a radio announcer
and writer in radio stations in Indiana and Arizona. After 1953 he
became a full-time free-lance writer, developing his skills as a
screenwriter for "Studio One," Philco, and "Goodyear Playhouse"
during the so-called "golden age" of early television drama. Although he had written screenplays for a number of television mov-
ies, most of his early work had been for such series as "Wagon
Train," "Laredo," and "Ironside." More recently he had written
several scripts for "The Waltons." Trim and graying, with a thin
moustache, McGreevey spoke softly but firmly during his testimony. In direct examination he explained the care he had used in
preparing the script, and he sought to convey to the jury his lack of
bias against Victoria Price.[33]

That was hardly the impression that Mrs. Street's attorneys
wanted the jury to have. For more than three hours Raymond Fraley forced McGreevey to endure a barrage of belligerent and sarcastic questions. McGreevey later acknowledged that the experience
had been useful for a writer, but all in all a rather painful way to
engage in research.

McGreevey's recollection of the facts in the case was surprisingly
precise. And more than once he parried Fraley's accusatory ques-

---

the plaintiff to actual damages, and barred punitive damages in the absence of a
showing of actual malice.

[33] "Street v. NBC, Transcript of Testimony," 437–53.

tions with his careful, soft-spoken replies. When Fraley objected to the use of the term *bums* in the television script to describe Victoria Price and Ruby Bates, McGreevey responded that "to some people's way of thinking if you bum a ride on a train, you are a hobo." And, if there was one thing established, it was that Victoria Price and Ruby Bates had been hoboes on the day of the incident.[34]

But McGreevey was at a disadvantage in the questioning. He was a scriptwriter, not a historian, and he frankly acknowledged that he had made no attempt to duplicate systematically my historical research. While this was standard practice in the television industry, the distinction between researcher and scriptwriter was lost in cross-examination.[35] Thus Fraley was able to question McGreevey regarding sources and individuals he had not consulted. The Fayetteville lawyer even asked McGreevey why he had not interviewed two of the surviving jurors living in north Alabama. When McGreevey explained that he had relied upon my account, Fraley responded with mock astonishment: "You are telling me and this jury it is more important to read a man's book . . . to set an atmosphere when you have live participants you can talk to?"

"It would have been helpful to be able to speak with everybody involved," explained McGreevey, but "the realities in preparing the script led me to use the book." "The realities—," Fraley sarcastically rejoined, "California has telephones doesn't it?"[36]

Fraley was most effective in focusing upon the restaurant scene in which McGreevey had Joseph Brodsky assert that the original attorneys in the case had established at Scottsboro that Victoria Price was "a whore." Belligerently, Fraley asked if the scene was not an "invent." "Did Dan Carter, in his book, ever document the fact, trial transcript or otherwise, that Leibowitz and Brodsky had a conversation in the restaurant and said, 'She is a whore?' " asked

---

[34] *Ibid.*, 518.

[35] It should be noted that Fraley was as unenthusiastic about the researcher as the scriptwriter. At one point he asked McGreevey if he knew that the author of *Scottsboro*, "when he wrote or got started getting information as to the Scottsboro boys . . . was a student." According to courtroom spectators, the word *student* was emphasized with extraordinary disdain.

[36] "Street v. NBC, Transcript of Testimony," 482.

Fraley rhetorically. "No," acknowledged McGreevey. "And that word 'w-h-o-r-e' you invented?" Fraley spelled it out letter by letter. McGreevey did not reply.

John McGreevey had little firsthand experience with the South, although three days at Winchester's Frasserand (pronounced Frazzeran') Motel with meals at the downtown Chuck Wagon restaurant amounted to a cultural introduction to the region. Under the circumstances, NBC's attorneys were not surprised to see Fraley emphasize McGreevey's well-paid status as a writer and his background as a nonsoutherner. In addition to questions about McGreevey's Indiana birth and educational background, Fraley asked him about the large sum paid for his script on the Scottsboro trial ($25,000). Fraley even tried to question the California writer about his annual income.[37]

What was unexpected was the Fayetteville attorney's attempt to introduce issues characterized by their emotional content rather than their relevance to the case. Thus, in probing McGreevey's background, Fraley questioned him about only one of his previous television scripts, a 1976 drama based upon the case of Sergeant Leonard Matlovitch. Matlovitch had informed the Air Force in 1975 that he was a homosexual. When he was given a general rather than an honorable discharge, he had appealed the Air Force decision. The television drama described the Matlovitch case and its repercussions. Fraley brought out in his questioning that Matlovitch was a "proclaimed homosexual" after which the following exchange took place.

Q. Have you talked to Sergeant Matlovitch?

A. Yes I have.

Q. Did you use the transcript [of the hearing] as a source of information?

A. Yes, I did.

Q. But you did talk to this sergeant in the Air Force?

[37] "It is none of our business in this lawsuit how much money he makes," Neese told Fraley. "Just because a person takes a witness stand does not mean you can have carte blanche and ask him anything and everything." Street v. NBC, Transcript of Testimony," 497.

A. I did speak with Sergeant Matlovitch, yes.

Q. Personally?

A. Yes.

Q. You met with him?

A. Yes.[38]

The strategy of Fraley's questioning was made even more explicit in other portions of the cross-examination. After McGreevey had emphasized his reliance upon my book, *Scottsboro*, Fraley asked McGreevey if it were true that I had used "as a major source of information, materials prepared by members of the Communist Party." Still later, when McGreevey characterized Leibowitz as anti-Communist, Fraley demanded to know on what evidence he based such a conclusion. "He worked along with the Communist Party, didn't he?" snapped Fraley.[39]

Campbell had been reluctant to object to Fraley's line of questioning, since it might appear to the jury that the defense had something to hide, but the Leibowitz question was as far as he would allow Fraley to continue without challenging him. "I hesitate, if your Honor please," he interrupted, "but I don't think Judge Leibowitz is on trial here." In raising the issue of Leibowitz' association with the Communist Party, Fraley seemed either unaware of—or unconcerned with—how Judge Neese might respond to this implicit slur on a fellow jurist. For whatever reason, when Neese ruled on Campbell's objection, he gave the Fayetteville attorney a stern lecture.

"As I tried to indicate to Mr. Fraley before, we are not here to decide world political matters," Neese said to the jury. Whether Leibowitz was a "Communist or not," said Judge Neese (and the

---

[38] *Ibid.*, 493–94. Fraley's cross-examination on this point was designed to bring out the fact that McGreevey had interviewed Matlovich and used the transcripts in his Air Force hearing. McGreevey, of course, did not know Mrs. Street was alive and—in the Matlovich case—he did not have a historical study from which he could work.

[39] To make sure the jury did not miss the point, Fraley repeated his question: "Did he [Dan Carter] not use materials that were developed by members of the Communist Party sympathetic with the Scottsboro boys." Fraley's view of American politics may be judged from his next question when he asked McGreevey if the American Civil Liberties Union was not a "branch of the Communist Party?" *Ibid.*, 485–86, 521.

tone of his voice made clear what he thought of this assertion), "he was a distinguished judge." Fixing a steely stare at Fraley, he warned him that his questions did not constitute a proper cross-examination. "We don't want the jury to start trying communism. What we want is for them to try this lawsuit," said Neese. When Fraley responded that he was simply questioning the "accuracy of Mr. McGreevey's research," Judge Neese would have none of it. "By inquiring whether he knows whether Mr. Leibowitz was a Communist or not?" he asked. "That has nothing to do with it."[40]

If the cross-examination of McGreevey was difficult to follow as Fraley shifted from one subject to another, it may have been effective nevertheless. As Andrew Kilpatrick of the Birmingham *News* remarked at the end of McGreevey's day on the stand, "The issues—race, sex, sectionalism, anti-communism, and resentment of outside wealth—although considerably altered since the 1930s have arisen continuously." And no one could predict how members of the jury might respond to these aspects to the case.[41]

Another observer was inclined to give Fraley high marks for effectiveness if not for subtlety. Anthony Badger, a British lecturer in American history at the University of Newcastle, attended the trial, and he commented later: "Fraley not only raised the potentially emotional issues of race and radicalism, he asked John McGreevey questions he could not possibly have answered, thus leaving the jury with the impression he had not adequately researched the facts in the case." Added Badger: "It seemed to me rather shrewd."

Sequestered in the witness room, I knew nothing of the discomfort McGreevey underwent on the stand until I later read the transcripts. But the grim looks of friends outside the courtroom that afternoon were enough to unsettle me throughout the long weekend. I had reviewed the transcript of the original trials line by line and compared them with my book. Apart from the misstatement regarding the death of the two women, I had discovered only one

40 *Ibid.*, 521–22.
41 Birmingham *News*, July 10, 1977.

minor error.[42] Still there was always an element of uncertainty and the lengthiness of McGreevey's testimony, and his obvious weariness as he left the courtroom to catch a plane to Los Angeles left me apprehensive. My uneasiness was not diminished by his farewell of a warm handshake and a solicitous "good luck."

Monday, July 11, 1977

My day on the witness stand did not begin auspiciously. After a sleepless night at the Frasserand, I had ordered a hearty breakfast at the Chuck Wagon restaurant. With the first smell of eggs, bacon, and heavily buttered biscuits I regretted my act of bravado. NBC attorney Jack Wheeler was on hand to soothe my nerves by regaling me with stories of witnesses who reacted to the trauma with symptoms ranging from dyspepsia to hysterical blindness and total amnesia. Fortunately, the waiting was worse than the experience. Once in the witness chair, I answered the first three questions without hesitation (name, address, and occupation).

After a few preliminary questions, Wheeler began to systematically develop three areas of inquiry. Conscious of the persistent implication by Fraley that McGreevey was an outsider with little firsthand experience in the South, Wheeler had me describe my personal and educational background. I had no difficulty in emphasizing my southern birth and education; I did find it difficult to strike a balance between extolling my professional credentials while maintaining an appropriately modest tone. At the same time, I explained to the jury how I had gathered all kinds of materials for my book, and I tried to assure them that my use of Communist Party materials did not mean that I was a card carrying Bolshevik. Finally, I discussed the various disputed segments of the television screenplay and commented upon the factual evidence on which the dialogue was based.

I had been on the witness stand less than twenty minutes before

42 In *Scottsboro* I indicated that Dallas Ramsey had identified Ruby Bates from an enlarged photograph during his direct examination. In fact, he had identified the precise location where he saw her in Chattanooga from an enlarged photograph of the hobo jungle near his home. Then he had identified her by describing her to the jury. See pp. 219–20 herein.

I was reminded of the difference between a courtroom and the historical method. Since Mrs. Street had insisted that the television show overdramatized, even fabricated, the danger of violence at the trial before Horton, Wheeler asked if there was evidence of a "tense or hostile atmosphere." "Certainly," I replied as I described Judge Horton's warning from the bench that any attempt to interfere with the trial would be met with force. "Judge Horton does not issue that kind of admonition from the Bench . . . unless he is concerned about the possible safety of the defendants and their counsel."

Immediately Wyatt objected. "May it please the Court," he interrupted, "we want to object to the conclusion on the part of the witness." On this point, Neese overruled him. "I think the jury will understand that this is a historian talking. . . . He doesn't know. He is just giving his opinion."

With his next objection, Wyatt was more successful. Continuing, Wheeler asked me to comment briefly on the other evidence which led me to conclude there was a danger of violence in Decatur. I began, "In an interview with the solicitor of Jackson County, he said . . ." Immediately, Wyatt was on his feet. "We object to the conversation, your Honor." And this time, Neese sustained his objection, turning to me with an admonition. "You can't tell us what somebody else said. You can say what the source of your information might have been . . . but not what somebody told you."[43]

However gently administered by Judge Neese, the admonition was unnerving. For the next three and a half hours of direct and cross-examination, I would have to evaluate evidence purely on the basis of whether or not it was a part of the record that had been admitted into evidence in the case instead of examining it from the standpoint of reasonableness, consistency with other sources, and bias and motivation on the part of the source. In this case, the interview I had tried to recount was independently described by three newspaper reporters. Jackson County Solicitor H. G. Bailey had much to lose and nothing to gain by acknowledging that his constituents might take the law into their own hands. Under these

43 "Street v. NBC, Transcript of Testimony," 601.

circumstances, on a scale of one to one hundred, I would have rated his statement 99 percent reliable. But I could not repeat a word he said. I could only tell the jury that I based my conclusion upon (among other things) a reading of newspaper interviews granted by Solicitor Bailey.

The problem was even more acute when I began to discuss the character of Victoria Price. During my research I had accumulated an extraordinary body of evidence that established beyond reasonable doubt in my mind that Victoria Price had a questionable reputation. More important was the fact that this material reinforced my misgivings about her veracity in testifying as to the facts in the case. This material ranged from affidavits assembled by the defense in 1931, to reports by Hollace Ransdell of the ACLU; a damning letter by a Huntsville, Alabama, elementary school principal; the testimony of law enforcement officials in later trials; reports by James D. Burton of the Commission on Interracial Cooperation; my interview with Judge Horton; even a letter in the recently opened papers of Alabama's chief prosecutor in the case, Thomas A. Knight.[44] With the exception of the 1931 affidavits and the testimony of two Huntsville law enforcement officials in 1937, however, I could not discuss the contents of these reports, letters, and conversations. Even when I went so far as to describe the individuals Hollace Ransdell interviewed in 1931 (not what they said), Wyatt swiftly objected and Neese sustained the objection. "Were you present?" asked Neese. I acknowledged that I was not.[45]

Fortunately, much of my direct examination was devoted to a comparison of the television scenes with the transcript of the 1933 trial which had been admitted into evidence. I defended the film's brief characterization of Dr. Bridges' testimony before Judge Horton, and I observed that the boxcar scene to which Mrs. Street so

---

44 *Ibid.*, 601–602. In a letter that reflected his condescending attitude toward his chief witness, Knight had described Mrs. Price (and Ruby Bates) as "women of a very low type." He had conceded ("for the purposes of argument") "that they were of more or less easy virtue." Knight to Marcus W. Crenshaw, September 20, 1933, in Thomas K. Knight Papers, Alabama Department of Archives and History, Montgomery.

45 "Street v. NBC, Transcript of Testimony," 605.

vigorously objected was supported by the 1933 testimony of Ruby Bates and Lester Carter. And I pointed out that the fourth person alleged to have taken part in the freight-yard tryst, Jack Tiller, was present at the Decatur courthouse as Mrs. Street's "bodyguard." At any time, the prosecuting attorney could have called him as a witness and delivered a devastating blow to the defense case if he had been willing to corroborate the story of Victoria Price.[46]

My testimony did provide a moment of levity. When Wheeler asked me about that part of the script which stated that the defense attorneys had proved Victoria Price a "whore" at Scottsboro I knew I could not cite off-the-record evidence. I was forced, therefore, to rely heavily upon the transcripts of the original trial. I commented that the original defense attorney bluntly asked Victoria Price if she were a prostitute. In my opinion, I continued, no attorney would ask that "unless he had reason . . ." "May it please the court," Wyatt began his objection, but before he could finish, Judge Neese looked at me and shook his head with a rueful smile. "We don't know the same attorneys," he commented. The courtroom erupted into laughter.[47]

Despite my *faux pas* on this point, I felt reasonably satisfied with the first hour of direct examination. In spite of my apprehensions, I had suffered neither amnesia nor hysterical blindness. I even began to feel at ease on the stand as I recalled names, dates, and specific supporting information. (Too much at ease, said my wife during the lunch break. "Stop leaning back in your chair, and try to look a little more apprehensive.") Jack Wheeler did remind me that Don Wyatt had a few questions he wanted to ask.

While Wyatt's cross-examination lasted more than two hours and left me exhausted, it did not provide the kind of verbal fireworks reporters had expected. In contrast to Fraley, Wyatt was polite, even courtly in his questioning. However strongly he may have felt about the case, he raised his voice only once. For Fraley's emotional and often sarcastic questions, Wyatt substituted a carefully prepared cross-examination with subtly phrased questions—

46 *Ibid.*, 608–14.
47 *Ibid.*, 603–604.

many of them written out on the yellow legal pad he kept before him. He had immersed himself in the transcripts of the Horton trial (and in my book on the case), and he sought with subtle ingenuity to emphasize and reemphasize any differences between the television script, my study of the case, and the transcripts themselves.

He began his cross-examination by challenging my objectivity in the case. It was obvious, he said, that I believed that the Scottsboro boys were innocent. Was this the premise with which I began my research? I insisted I had reached this conviction only after more than a year and a half of research and writing. While I could not relate the specific details of much of the evidence on which I based my conclusion (notably my "hearsay" interview with Judge Horton), I argued that the evidence established "beyond a reasonable doubt" that Mrs. Street was never raped as she testified throughout the 1930s. As I spoke, Mrs. Street sat behind Wyatt sobbing into a crumpled kleenex.

Wyatt's response to my conclusion was one which he repeated on several occasions. "You do realize that these men, all of them, were tried [and found guilty] before a jury of twelve men in Scottsboro and Decatur?" It was my opinion as a "college professor" who had "never tried a case" and was "not a lawyer" against the unanimous conclusion of the more than 100 jurors who had returned guilty verdicts.[48]

The heart of Wyatt's questioning, however, was devoted to a careful examination of the script. Piece by piece, he accumulated the evidence that supported Victoria Price. He asked me about the testimony of Haywood Patterson and Clarence Norris at the original trials when they said they had seen the women raped by others of their number. Despite my resolve to let the facts speak for themselves, I found myself becoming increasingly argumentative, even partisan. Thus, instead of relying upon redirect examination to bring out the fact that Patterson and Norris had later signed affidavits insisting they lied on the stand because they feared for their

48 *Ibid.*, 619–20.

lives, I responded (somewhat truculently) that they so testified in a courtroom surrounded by armed national guardsmen with a mob of ten thousand outside.

When Wyatt asked me if it were not true that Mrs. Price testified she had sexual intercourse only with her husbands, I agreed, but added: "She also testified Jack Tiller was her boyfriend and . . . Tiller was, by her . . . own testimony, a married man at the time."[49]

For the first time in the cross-examination, Wyatt raised his voice. "Mr. Carter," he testily demanded, "will you answer my questions?" "I am trying to, as well as I can," I replied. He looked at me and asked accusingly, "What interest do you have in seeing this case coming back with a verdict for the defendants?" For the first time I became angry; I resented the implication that I would tailor my testimony for financial compensation from the law firm that represented NBC. As far as the verdict was concerned, "I have no financial interest whatsoever," I snapped back. Then Wyatt raised his voice angrily, "I didn't ask you about financial interests. I said what interest." I readily acknowledged that I hoped the jury would sustain my judgment about the facts in the case.

Wyatt was more skillful in highlighting what had always been for me one of the most unsettling aspects of the film: the selection and filming of one version of each disputed scene. In a sense this was inevitable in a ninety-eight-minute telecast if the action was to leave the courtroom. There was not enough time to show each witness' version of events (although John McGreevey considered this approach when he began writing the script). After questioning me about several scenes—the meeting between Horton and Dr. Lynch in the courthouse restroom, the scene in the hobo jungle, the lovemaking episode in the boxcar—Wyatt asked: "So many of these scenes on this film were portrayed as though they actually happened rather [than] as testimony from [the] mouths of witnesses?" He went on, "There is quite a difference between the actual happening and testimony of witnesses. Is that not correct?" Even though I felt that the versions selected by McGreevey were the correct ones, I agreed with Wyatt that there was a difference between the two.[50]

Only twice did I feel that Wyatt misstepped in his questioning. In the first instance, he asked me if I was familiar with a book called *Scottsboro: The Firebrand of Communism*, written by Files Crenshaw, Jr., and Kenneth A. Miller. This 1936 book, which depicted the case as a communist plot to foment revolution in Alabama, is one of the few published books that has concluded that Victoria Price and Ruby Bates were raped as they claimed. I later learned that Fraley had questioned McGreevey about the Crenshaw-Miller book with the clear implication that the scriptwriter was derelict in failing to consult this work on the case. When Wyatt asked me if the book was not "replete with references to the actual record?" I replied: "Yes, to erroneous references to the record." Then, "this cannot be relied upon? But your book can?" he asked with a touch of sarcasm.[51]

I tried to explain how the two Alabama authors had insisted in their preface that they were simply compiling the transcripts so that their readers could make an "unbiased" decision on the guilt or innocence of the Scottsboro defendants. Unfortunately for the truth, the two men had consistently deleted sections of the testimony that contradicted Victoria Price, and they had done so without elision marks or any indication of their omissions. In my opinion, the book was not simply biased, it was intellectually dishonest.[52]

More critical was the issue of the meeting between Judge Horton and Dr. Lynch in which, according to Horton, Lynch said that no

[50] *Ibid.*, 644.
[51] *Ibid.*, 636–37.
[52] *Ibid.*, 665–66. If Wyatt had looked closely at the margins of the Crenshaw-Miller book (my personal copy was used as an exhibit), he would have seen where I had penciled lightly the pages from the original transcript that had been eliminated. One of the more unfortunate aspects of the Crenshaw-Miller book was the fact that it was widely read by white Alabamians in the 1930s who thought they were reading an accurate account of the most important trials in the case. They had no way of knowing that Crenshaw and Miller had stacked the evidence in Victoria Price's favor. Judge Horton's decision, for example, was not included.

rape had taken place. In his cross-examination, Wyatt sought to cast doubts on the authenticity of Horton's account by referring to the judge's age at the time of my interview (he was 88) and by reading the letter Lynch had sent to me denying the meeting. He brought out in his questioning that Lynch's denial, while included in my book, was not a part of the television script.

On redirect examination, Jack Wheeler asked why I accepted Horton's word rather than Lynch's. Wyatt objected but Neese overruled him. "You went into it on cross-examination about why he used the version that was used instead of Dr. Lynch's version."

This was one of the few questions for which I had carefully prepared, and I turned and spoke directly to the jury. Dr. Lynch had refused to see me or even to talk with me on the telephone during the two years I researched the case, I told them. When I sent him a copy of my interview with Judge Horton, he had replied that Horton's account was "absolutely unfounded." But, I went on to say, he qualified this apparently categorical denial in a curious way. He said that no such statements were ever made to Judge Horton *"as far as I can recall"* (emphasis added). I simply found it inconceivable that Dr. Lynch would fail to recall such a critical meeting.[53]

There were other reasons to doubt Lynch's denial, I continued. His letter implied only a peripheral involvement in the case. And yet, in preparing for the trial of Mrs. Street against NBC, I discovered a note Lynch wrote Clarence Watts in the summer of 1937, asking for a *per diem* payment for having attended the 1937 trials as an observer for the defense. The final reason, I concluded, was a "common sense one. Judge Horton . . . had nothing to gain by making up such an account. He was a distinguished man with an extraordinary reputation in his own community. On the other hand . . . the late Dr. Lynch . . . obviously did have reasons to deny it because it reflected upon him."[54]

---

[53] "Street v. NBC, Transcript of Testimony," 685.

[54] *Ibid.* In explaining why I believed Judge Horton, I also pointed out that Lynch had implied in his letter that he would sue me if I published an account of his meeting with Horton. I did so and he never carried through on his threat.

As I stepped down from the witness chair and walked to the back of the courtroom, I passed the row where Victoria Price Street sat beside her husband. On the other side of Mrs. Street were Ed and Don Horton—Judge Horton's sons—along with members of their families. They had come into the courtroom that morning and taken the only seats available on the same row with the Streets.

Their presence seemed all the more appropriate in light of the final stages of the defense argument. Campbell had decided to close out the evidence for NBC by reading Judge Horton's 1933 opinion setting aside the conviction of Haywood Patterson. Shortly after 4 P.M. he began the seventeen-page decision, reading in an unemotional tone without any inflection. I was depressed to see most members of the jury absentmindedly leafing through various defense exhibits. It had been a long day. There was also a restless shuffling of feet and whispering among the spectators. I became concerned that this, one of the most critical summaries of the evidence ever written, would be ignored by a jury fatigued from four days of complex testimony.

As Campbell continued to read the words of the man who had died in 1973, however, the members of the jury began to put away the exhibits, the spectators quietened, and the courtroom became absolutely still. For nearly a week, members of the jury had watched and listened as the two teams of lawyers argued over the case. Through Campbell, they heard for the first time from the man who had been at the center of the case.

The courtroom in 1933 and in 1976 had been filled with arguments over the moral background of Victoria Price, but Horton's words placed that issue in perspective. Quoting from the record of a similar case, he noted that the accusing witness "may be of ill fame for chastity, but she is still under the protection of the law, and not subject to a forced violation of her person for the gratification of the propensities of the man who has strength to overpower her."

Fortunately in this case, noted Horton, there were many areas where her testimony could be corroborated (or disputed) by the physical evidence and the testimony of other witnesses. Mrs. Price had testified as to how "one of the negroes hit her on the side of the head with a pistol causing her head to bleed."During the repeated rapes, Mrs. Price claimed she was "wet on her private parts; that each negro wetted her more and more; that her private parts were bleeding; that the blood was on her clothes; that her coat had semen on it; that when Dr. Bridges and Dr. Lynch examined her they saw her coat and it was all spattered with semen." With more than fifty persons meeting the train at Paint Rock; with the two women, Orville Gilley, and the nine black teenagers taken in charge; with two physicians carefully examining the women "we should expect from all this cloud of witnesses or from the mute but telling physical condition of the women or their clothes some one fact in corroboration of this story."

As Campbell continued to read, I saw that two of the jurors were leaning forward listening intently.

One by one, Horton examined the testimony of state and defense witnesses quoting extensively from the record. The testimony in all important respects contradicted rather than corroborated her story. The only physical evidence to sustain her accusation was the presence of small quantities of nonmotile spermatazoa discovered by Dr. Bridges and Dr. Lynch when they examined her. And, "when we consider as the facts hereafter detailed will show, that this woman had slept side by side with a man the night before in Chattanooga, and had intercourse at Huntsville with [Jack] Tiller on the night before she went to Chattanooga . . . the conclusion becomes clearer and clearer that this woman was not forced into intercourse with all of these negroes upon that train, but that her condition was clearly due to the intercourse that she had had on the nights previous to that time." Moreover, Horton argued, her manner of testifying was "contradictory, often evasive, and time and again she refused to answer pertinent questions." The gravity of the offense demanded "candor and sincerity," said Horton. Instead, the evidence "tends strongly to show that she knowingly testified falsely in many material aspects of the case."

He concluded: "History, sacred and profane and the common experience of mankind teach us that women of the character shown in this case are prone for selfish reasons to make false accusations both of rape and of insult upon the slightest provocation, or even without provocation for ulterior purpose." The law required that the defendant should not be convicted without corroboration where the testimony of the accuser appeared unreliable and improbable. "The testimony of the prosecutrix in this case is not only uncorroborated, but it also bears on its face indications of improbability and is contradicted by other evidence." The evidence "greatly preponderates in favor of the defendant."[55]

When Campbell finished reading Horton's opinion just before 5 p.m. I did not see how the jury—whatever its decision on the issue of defamation—could go into its deliberations placing an ounce of credence in the sworn testimony of Victoria Price Street. The persuasive interlocking logic of the decision itself coupled with the courage that led Horton to fly in the face of overwhelming public opinion from his friends and neighbors made it a devastating document. For the first time I felt genuine pity for the forlorn old woman who sat beside her husband.

Tuesday, July 12, 1977

When Robert Campbell renewed his motion for a dismissal of the case late Monday afternoon after presentation of the evidence was over, Neese surprised the reporters attending the trial by granting Campbell's motion for a dismissal of that portion of the suit involving invasion of privacy. As he later explained, the evidence that Mrs. Street's attorneys presented gave no indication that NBC's personnel were motivated in any way by malice toward their client. "Before she was entitled to recover damages for an invasion of her privacy, she was required by the law to meet the 'malice test' established by *Time, Inc.* v. *Hill* (1967)." But he had refused to dismiss the libel portions of the suit and scheduled the Tuesday morning hearing to discuss the issue in open court with the jury absent.

For nearly an hour, Robert Campbell and Donald Wyatt debated the constitutional issues in the case as Neese challenged their argu-

---

[55] These quotations are from the original copy of Judge Horton's decision, which is appended to the transcript of record of the April, 1933, trial of Haywood Patterson.

ments with a series of probing questions. In a simplified version of his pretrial arguments, Campbell repeated his assertion that Victoria Price was a public figure insofar as the Scottsboro case was concerned. In view of the fact that the plaintiff had failed to establish malice on the part of NBC, argued Campbell, Neese should dismiss the libel charges just as he had done for those involving invasion of privacy. Even if the court rejected the defense contention that Victoria Price Street was a public figure, continued Campbell, the case should be dismissed because her attorneys had failed to establish any specific "fault" or negligence on the part of NBC.[56] (In cases of libel, unlike invasion of privacy, actual malice must be proved by the plaintiff only when the plaintiff is a public figure.)

Wyatt, on the other hand, insisted that Mrs. Street was not a public figure, citing *Time, Inc.* v. *Mary Alice Firestone*, and thus, he argued, she did not have to establish malice on the part of NBC personnel. While he acknowledged that the Supreme Court had established a requirement that fault or negligence be shown in libel cases, he insisted that the jury could infer negligence on the part of NBC simply from the fact that the network had rebroadcast the television show in January of 1977 after Mrs. Street had filed her lawsuit.[57]

Somewhat surprisingly to those who had followed the case, Neese seemed to lean toward Wyatt's contention that Mrs. Street was not a public figure; or rather that she had ceased to be a public figure by the 1970s, whatever her status from 1931 to 1937. He and Campbell sparred over whether or not an individual's involvement in this trial made him (or her) a public figure for the rest of his (or her) life.[58]

---

[56] "Street v. NBC, Transcript of Testimony," 868–82.

[57] *Ibid.*, 882–93. Campbell briefly responded that Mrs. Street's attorneys did not spell out their specific objections to the television show until after the second showing. Wyatt seemed most interested in making sure that the jury, rather than Judge Neese, be given an opportunity to decide the disputed points.

[58] As Neese suggested, "Even though a person can be thrust into the position of a public figure by events, isn't it true that whether a person remains a public figure depends on how public they go." To this Campbell replied with a half smile, "I would respectfully say your Honor is only partially correct." Campbell never tried to argue that Mrs. Street was a public figure for all purposes; only that—in any historical discussion of the Scottsboro case—she would have to be considered a public figure so

On the other hand, Neese seemed unconvinced by Wyatt's insistence that the jury could infer NBC's negligence from the fact that the show had been rebroadcast. As Neese noted, it was Tomorrow Entertainment that had purchased television rights to the story, hired a scriptwriter, produced the film, and then sold it to NBC. Although Mrs. Street's attorneys had spent a great deal of time and effort imputing negligence and inaccuracies to Tomorrow Entertainment, there had been almost no testimony regarding NBC's actions. When Wyatt insisted that the jury should be allowed to decide the question of negligence, Neese interrupted him with a touch of impatience. "Yes, but we can't guess, Mr. Wyatt. There has to be some evidence for them to go on."[59]

Although the participants in the case were not aware at the time, this statement by Neese concisely summarized his view of Mrs. Street's case against NBC. After recess he called the jury back into the courtroom and began speaking informally to them. It was clear from his first sentence that he had decided to grant Campbell's motion for a dismissal. "Ordinarily at this point . . . the lawyers would be reviewing and discussing these facts with you," he began, but he had decided to dismiss the case without allowing it to go to the jury. In colloquial everyday language, Neese explained some of the reasoning he would later outline in his formal opinion in the case.

Under the various rulings handed down by the Supreme Court, said Judge Neese, a person suing a publisher or broadcasting company for libel had to show they were guilty of "fault, 'negligent action,' beyond the mere publication of defamatory material." The problem for Mrs. Street was that her attorneys had spent a great

---

long as the publisher (or broadcaster) did not try to delve into her private life. Ultimately, Neese ruled against Campbell on this point, apparently relying heavily on the decision of Justice William Rehnquist in the Firestone case. In view of the Supreme Court's somewhat confusing decision in this case, Neese may be constitutionally correct, but it virtually destroys the "public figure" defense which journalists (and historians) have traditionally used in describing prominent individuals involved in issues of public importance. If Victoria Price is not a public figure insofar as the Scottsboro case is concerned, then it would seem that the term must be narrowly confined to individuals who have voluntarily sought public attention.

[59] "Street v. NBC, Transcript of Testimony," 893.

deal of time exploring what McGreevey did in preparing the script. "But, Mr. McGreevey was not shown to have been acting for NBC." Similarly, the defense described what "Dr. Carter did and did not do in preparing the book . . . on which Mr. McGreevey based his script." But it was "undisputed by Ms. Street that, apart from his erroneous factual assertion that she had died in 1961, there were no untruths or inaccuracies included in Dr. Carter's book." In any case, "Dr. Carter was not shown to have been acting for NBC. The record is silent as to what NBC did relating to the book Dr. Carter wrote." To find negligence or fault under these circumstances, it would be necessary for the jury to engage in "speculation, conjecture, surmise—'guessing,' " and the courts did not permit a verdict on guesswork.[60]

For the first time in all the trials in which she testified, Victoria Price Street would not have the vindication of a favorable jury verdict. Afterwards a subdued but angry Fraley told reporters he would appeal the verdict. He indicated that he was considering bringing suit against McGreevey.

An equally angry Mrs. Street agreed. "I didn't get justice," she said to anyone who would listen. "I didn't lie in Scottsboro. I didn't lie in Decatur and I ain't lied here. I've told the truth all the way through and I'm a'gonna go on fighting 'til my dying day or 'til justice is done."[61] The last phrase bore an eerie resemblance to Horton's family motto: "Let Justice Be Done."

Thursday, September 24, 1978

As returns from the Alabama gubernatorial runoff came in, it was apparent that Alabama Attorney General William Baxley had lost his bid to become the state's next governor. Fob James, a self-made millionaire and former Republican had used a slick media campaign and thousands of volunteers to build a victory. During

[60] Judge Neese informally outlined his reasons for dismissing the suit in a brief statement to the jury. This is contained in the transcript of testimony, pp. 896–900. Most of these quotations are from the "Memorandum Opinion of District Judge C. G. Neese in the United States District Court for the Eastern District of Tennessee; Victoria Price Street v. National Broadcasting Company, Filed August 11, 1977."

[61] Birmingham *Post-Herald*, July 13, 1977; Birmingham *News*, July 12, 1977.

the campaign James, a former Auburn University football star, told voters "he would run the state like he did the sporting goods business that started in a basement and expanded to several plants." His supporters—middle- and upper-income suburbanites and voters from George Wallace's strongholds in South Alabama—easily defeated Baxley's coalition of industrial city voters, ADC supporters, labor unions, and blacks. While the Baxley-James vote reflected a continuing racial split within the state, it was hardly analogous to the campaigns of the 1960s and early 1970s. Both candidates had openly courted Alabama's black voters with an enthusiasm that would have been politically suicidal as late as 1970.

Since the first trials in Scottsboro—particularly since the 1940s—the collapse of the old cotton-plantation rural economy, the rise of the urban and suburban South, the growth of federal and state bureaucracies, the increasing mobility of Alabama's rural population, and the pervasive sounds and images of radio and television have destroyed the physical and intellectual environment that made the Scottsboro case so chillingly representative of southern race relations. Racism and parochialism remain and isolated communities still exist where the Scottsboro case might be duplicated, but the rural and small-town island community that existed in the 1930s—whether in Birmingham or Opelika—has drastically shrunk. The South of the 1980s will not be changed for the better in every way, but it will have changed.

When the voters of Alabama refused to support William Baxley for governor, they were neither repudiating nor endorsing their past. They were simply ignoring it. In that sense, the three decades after 1945 are as important a watershed in southern history as the Civil War and emancipation.[62]

[62] Atlanta *Constitution*, September 25, 26, 1978; Montgomery *Advertiser*, September 25, 26, 1978. If some things change, however, others remain the same. On October 13, an all-white jury in Cullman, Alabama, convicted a twenty-six-year-old mentally retarded black man for the alleged rape of a Decatur railway clerk. Although Tommy Lee Hines had an IQ of only thirty-nine, the presiding judge in the case admitted into evidence his "confession" which had been given to Decatur police. The trial itself had taken place in an atmosphere of racial tension and hostility with the Ku Klux Klan and the Southern Christian Leadership Conference holding marches, countermarches, rallies, and counterrallies. Hines's two black attorneys are appealing

If the last chapter in the Scottsboro case reflects some of the changes that have overtaken the South, it is also a sobering reminder of the ambiguities of history. When I wrote about the events of the 1930s in the late 1960s, the fundamental issue seemed clear. Scottsboro was a classic example of the most brutal and frightening form of racial control in modern southern history. The outcome of the case seemed even more depressing in view of the background of Victoria Price.

A decade later, however, the discussion of Victoria Price Street's background seemed out of place, however legitimate in the context of the lawsuit. As an angry feminist remarked to me shortly before the trial, "What right have you to even bring up the accusation that she was a prostitute. That has nothing to do with whether she was raped." I understood her point. I also remembered the appeal of Haywood Patterson when one of his lawyers tried to persuade the Alabama Supreme Court that the jury should have known about Victoria Price's acts of sexual intercourse on the nights preceding the alleged rape. It was essential, argued Clarence Watts, that the jury understand that she was attempting to divert attention from "her own unlawful acts, her transgressions, her wickedness." At this point an Alabama justice interrupted and angrily reproached Watts: "In other words, you were trying to try Victoria Price and not the niggers."[63]

That same feeling of uncertainty about the issues is reflected in my response to Victoria Price Street. I am convinced beyond a reasonable doubt that she was never raped. I am convinced to a moral certainty that, as Judge Horton put it, she "knowingly testified falsely in many material aspects of the case." I have read the prison letters of the Scottsboro defendants and talked to a bitter Clarence Norris. I cannot forget the suffering she needlessly inflicted upon nine black teenagers.

As I watched her hobble from the courtroom, however, I was struck by my ambivalence toward this woman. During the 1930s she

---

the case. Atlanta *Journal*, October 1–15, 1978; Atlanta *Constitution*, October 2–14, 1978; Birmingham *News*, October 1–15, 1978.

[63] Joseph Gelders to Allan Knight Chalmers, May 28, 1937, in Chalmers Collection.

had struggled to survive on two to three dollars a week as a cotton mill worker. In the midst of this collapsing economy she had lived by her wits and (according to her accusers) the use of the only collateral she possessed, her body. Whether true or not, the accusation seems irrelevant. Far more damning is the fact that, in Judge Horton's phrase, she "knowingly testified falsely in many material aspects of the case." But if she had lied about the rape, she had done so because she lived in a setting which encouraged and rewarded this monstrous lie.

There are certainly villains in the Scottsboro case, men like Thomas Knight, Jr., who manipulated the fears and hatreds of his fellow Alabamians, knowing full well the shoddy nature of the case he so relentlessly prosecuted. But even there it is difficult to single out Knight. For his cynical tactics were made possible by the silent acquiescence of dozens of other business, religious, and political leaders. Nor was he the only individual—North or South—who exploited the case for personal and ideological reasons, however lofty.

Will Campbell, director of the committee of southern churchmen attended the last day of the trials in Winchester. When he walked into the courtroom, he started to take a seat near Victoria Street, but he hesitated, he said, recalling the "nine captured, caged, tortured, broken, battered and destroyed human beings" sent to prison on the questionable testimony of this woman. He had taken a seat at the back of the courtroom. But Campbell, a remarkable man who has combined a commitment to civil rights with a concern for the southern white dispossessed, could not leave without a word. After Neese dismissed the case and adjourned the court, Campbell went up to Mrs. Street and, in the time-honored way of southerners, greeted her: "How you feeling." Mrs. Street, mistaking the personal concern for political support, launched into an angry defense of her testimony over the years. Campbell said a few words and then hurried away. As he left, he said, he felt depressed that he had not known where to sit in the courtroom, a little confused "and a little sad for Victoria Price, for the Scottsboro boys, and for us all."[64]

[64] Campbell, "Where to Sit in Scottsboro," 191.

ESSAY ON AUTHORITIES

No attempt has been made to discuss every source consulted or cited. For a list of all works used, see the author's "The Scottsboro Case, 1931–1950" (Ph.D. Dissertation, University of North Carolina, 1967), 548–70.

MANUSCRIPTS AND PRIMARY DOCUMENTS

Of all the manuscript collections used in my research, the papers of the National Association for the Advancement of Colored People were most useful. Even when the NAACP withdrew from the Scottsboro Case in 1932, Walter White and Roy Wilkins obtained and filed valuable material. Located in the Library of Congress Manuscripts Division, the association's material is most voluminous for the years 1931, 1935, and 1936. The Southern Commission on Interracial Cooperation was only peripherally involved in the case, but the organization kept in close touch with developments. Correspondence relating to the Scottsboro Case has been separated from the main collection at Atlanta University's Trevor Arnett Library. The Papers of the Association of Southern Women for the Prevention of Lynching, also at Trevor Arnett Library, contained numerous items, but they generally were not as helpful as the Interracial Commission files.

A portion of the correspondence of the International Labor Defense was deposited in the Schomburg Collection of the New York Public Library. This material is uncatalogued, rapidly deteriorating, and sketchy for long periods, but it offers some insight into the operation of an affiliate of the Communist Party. Moreover, it is a corrective to the strongly anti-ILD bias of other surviving manuscripts. The ILD papers are most complete for the years from 1931 to 1935.

The official records of Alabama Governors Benjamin Miller and Bibb Graves offer a totally different perspective. Located in the Alabama Department of Archives and History, their files contain official and confidential letters and reports by Alabama officials. More than fifteen thousand letters, telegrams, postcards, and petitions supporting the Scottsboro boys were sent to state officials during the 1930's. These have been collected and filed chronologically by the Alabama Department of Archives.

There is a similar file of "protest" mail in the archives of the United States Justice Department. In addition to the four thousand letters and telegrams appealing to the U.S. Attorney General to intervene in the case, there are reports from U.S. embassies on the reaction overseas and a Justice Department memorandum prepared at the confidential request of President Roosevelt.

The Allan Knight Chalmers Collection has extensive correspondence on the case beginning in 1936 when Chalmers became chairman of the Scottsboro Defense Committee. The collection contains the official SDC correspondence and the personal papers of Chalmers after the organization folded. All of the material is catalogued in the new Boston University Library.

There were fifty-five items on the Scottsboro Case in the Franklin Delano Roosevelt Library: letters, petitions, and telegrams to President Roosevelt, as well as correspondence between the President and Governor Graves.

The most important and lengthy primary materials used in my research were the transcripts of the first seven trials that took place from 1931 to 1936. In chronological order, the Transcripts of Record used were: *Patterson* v. *Alabama,* 287 U.S. 45 (1932), *Powell* v. *Alabama,* 287 U.S. 45 (1932), *Weems* v. *Alabama,* 287 U.S. 45 (1932), Testimony on Motion to Quash the Indictments and Transcript of Testimony, *Patterson* v. *Alabama* (1933) [Typescript in Cornell University Law Library], *Norris* v. *Alabama,* 294 U.S. 587 (1934), *Patterson* v. *Alabama,* 294 U.S. 599 (1934), and *Patterson* v. *State,* 234 Ala. 342 (1937). Defense attorneys did not appeal the last four convictions in 1937. As a result, the court clerk never prepared official transcripts. In these cases, local newspapers were cited. Judge Horton brilliantly summarized the evidence presented by the state in his 1933 decision, reprinted by the Scottsboro Defense Committee as *The Scottsboro Case: Opinion of Judge James E. Horton* (New York, n.p., 1936). The United States Supreme Court rendered two important decisions in *Powell* v. *Alabama,* 287 U.S. 56 and *Norris* v. *Alabama,* 294 U.S. 599 which reversed the Alabama Supreme Court's findings in *Powell* v. *State,* 224 Ala. 553; *Norris* v. *State,* 229 Ala. 234; and *Patterson* v. *State* 229 Ala. 273.

The manuscripts and primary documents have been supplemented by correspondence with the Reverend Allan Knight Chalmers; Judge Samuel Leibowitz; former Judge James Edwin Horton, Jr.; William L. Patterson, former Executive Secretary of the ILD; and Marvin H. Lynch, M.D., of Scottsboro, Alabama. Interviews were also conducted with Judge Horton, Fred J. Bucheit, editor of the Scottsboro *Sentinel-Age,* and Muriel Rukeyser of New York, who attended the April, 1933, trials.

NEWSPAPERS AND PERIODICALS

Newspapers and periodicals constituted an important source of information. In addition to the New York *Times,* six Alabama dailies were examined for the years 1931 to 1937. The Montgomery *Advertiser,* the Birmingham *Age-Herald,* the Birmingham *News,* the Birmingham *Post,* the Decatur *Daily,* and the Huntsville *Times* published extensive accounts of the case. The *Daily,* the *Times,* and the *Advertiser* emphasized a strongly Southern viewpoint; the three Birmingham newspapers were more moderate in their coverage. Just across the Tennessee border, the Chattanooga *Daily Times* reported behind the scenes legal maneuvers from 1931 to 1933. Two weeklies in Scottsboro, the *Jackson County Sentinel* and the *Progressive Age,* excoriated the Scottsboro defendants and assorted outsiders while strongly defending the good name of Alabama.

Reaction outside the South was divided between the NAACP and the ILD. From 1931 to 1935, the NAACP defended the Scottsboro boys while it attacked both the white South and the Communist Party. The association presented its views in the pages of the *Crisis* and received support from two of the largest Negro weeklies, the Norfolk *Journal and Guide,* and the Pittsburgh *Courier.* The Baltimore *Afro-American,* the Chicago *Defender,* and other Negro newspapers vacillated between the NAACP and the ILD. The *New Republic,* the *Nation,* the *Christian Century,* and most liberal periodicals backed the NAACP. In addition, these magazines published perceptive articles on the case throughout the 1930's.

The Interracial Labor Defense argued the radical viewpoint in the pages of the New York *Daily Worker.* Along with the *New Masses* and the party's Marxist journal, the *Communist,* the *Daily Worker* reported news of the Alabama "lynch verdict" and charged that the NAACP and other liberals were working with the Alabama authorities. Despite their undeniable bias, the press of the Communist Party and its affiliates contained a great deal of information about the role of the Party in the case.

GENERAL STUDIES AND FIRSTHAND ACCOUNTS

Among the first overall accounts were two books written by native Alabamians. The interpretation of both works is evident in their titles: *Scottsboro: The Firebrand of Communism* by Files Crenshaw and Kenneth A. Miller (Montgomery: Brown Printing Company, 1936) and J. Glenn Jordan's *The Unpublished Inside Story of the Infamous Scottsboro Case* (Huntsville: White Printing Company, 1932). Although written within weeks after the first trials and convictions, Hollace Ransdell's unpublished account, "Report on the Scottsboro, Alabama Case" (New York: American Civil Liberties Union, 1931 [Mimeographed]), is far more accurate in its findings. Another perceptive contemporary acount was by Arthur Garfield Hays in *Trial By Prejudice* (New York: Covici, Friede Publishers, 1933), a study of five trial convictions in which race or class prejudice played a crucial role. Quentin Reynolds discussed the Scottsboro Case at considerable length in his biography of Samuel Leibowitz, *Courtroom* (New York: Farrar, Straus and Cudahy, 1950).

George Brown Tindall's *The Emergence of the New South, 1913–1945* (Baton Rouge: Louisiana State University Press, 1967) is one of the few attempts to place the case in the broad context of Southern race relations. Historians have generally been more concerned with the role of the Communist Party. Walter Francis White, Executive Secretary of the NAACP during the 1930's, argued the case against the

ILD and the Communist Party in "The Negro and the Communists," *Harper's Magazine,* CLXIV (December, 1931), 62–72. White's attacks were accepted by Wilson Record in *Race and Radicalism: The NAACP and the Communist Party in Conflict* (Ithaca: Cornell University Press, 1965) and by William A. Nolan in *Communism Versus the Negro* (Chicago: Henry Regnery Company, 1951). In a brief discussion of the case, Irving Howe and Lewis Coser harshly treated the Communist Party's role in *The American Communist Party: A Critical History* (Boston: Beacon Press, 1957). Although he did not have access to the NAACP or ILD papers, Hugh Thomas Murray, Jr., gives a far more balanced account of the role of the Party in "The Scottsboro Rape Case and the Communist Party" (M.A. thesis, Tulane University, 1963). Thomas summarized his main conclusions in an article, "The NAACP versus the Communist Party: The Scottsboro Rape Case, 1931–1932," *Phylon,* XXVIII (1967), 276–87.

There are two firsthand accounts of the case. Haywood Patterson told his story to Earl Conrad in *Scottsboro Boy* (Garden City: Doubleday and Company, 1950). While it is helpful on several points, *Scottsboro Boy* is factually unreliable and highly colored by Conrad's anti-NAACP and pro-ILD bias. Following the release of the last of the nine defendants, Allan Knight Chalmers modestly described his role in *They Shall Be Free* (Garden City: Doubleday and Company, 1951).

The best firsthand accounts are by the defendants themselves in letters to their friends and sponsors. There are four hundred letters altogether in the NAACP Papers, the ILD files, and the Allan Knight Chalmers Collection. Usually brief and painfully written on prison tablets, they give a perspective to the case which cannot be obtained from other sources.

INDEX